Cultural Education—Cultural Sustainability

. . . a fine introduction to the complexities of "Cultural Education." Each of the culture groups presented provides extended information and understanding of the collisions and conundrums it must address in order to make its way toward defining, maintaining, and sustaining its cultural voice. This book serves a broad international community of scholars and school professionals.

Herve Varenne, Teachers College, Columbia University

. . . contributes significantly to current conversations on multicultural education . . . . and promises to add substantively to the terrain by giving space to the voices of various ethnic and cultural groups that are not commonly heard. This is both laudable and educative.

Maenette Benham, Michigan State University

This volume is a path-breaking contribution to the study of the efforts of diaspora, indigenous, and minority groups, broadly defined, to use education (formal and informal) to sustain cultural continuity while grappling with the influences and demands of wider globalizing, nationalizing, or other homogenizing and assimilatory forces. Particular attention is given to groups that use educational elements other than second-language teaching alone in programs to sustain their particular cultural traditions. The focus of the book on cultural sustainability changes the nature of questions posed in multicultural education from those that address the opening of boundaries to issues of preserving boundaries in an open yet sustainable way.

As forced and elective immigration trends are changing the composition of societies and the educational systems within them—bringing a rich diversity of cultural experience to the teaching/learning process—diaspora, indigenous, and minority groups are looking more and more for ways to sustain their cultures in the context of wider socio-political influences. This volume is a first opportunity to consider critically multicultural efforts in dialog with educational options that are culturally particularistic but at the same time tolerant.

Academics will find this an excellent reference book. Practitioners will draw inspiration in learning of others' efforts to sustain cultures and will engage in critical reflection on their own work *vis-à-vis* that of others. Teachers will realize they do not stand alone in their educational efforts and will uncover new strategies and methodologies through which to approach their work.

Zvi Bekerman teaches anthropology of education at the School of Education and the Melton Center for Jewish Education, Hebrew University of Jerusalem. His main interests are in the study of cultural, ethnic and national identity, including identity processes and negotiation during intercultural encounters and in formal/informal learning contexts.

Ezra Kopelowitz is CEO of Research Success Technologies, Israel, and a sociologist specializing in the intersection of technology, knowledge management, and organizational development for non-profits, with a particular interest in the Jewish world and Jewish Education.

Cultural Education— Cultural Sustainability

Minority, Diaspora, Indigenous, and Ethno-Religious Groups in Multicultural Societies

Edited by
Zvi Bekerman and
Ezra Kopelowitz

Routledge
Taylor & Francis Group

NEW YORK AND LONDON

First published 2008
by Routledge
270 Madison Ave, New York, NY 10016

Simultaneously published in the UK
by Routledge
2 Park Square, Milton Park, Abingdon, Oxon OX14 4RN

Routledge is an imprint of the Taylor & Francis Group, an informa business

© 2008 Taylor & Francis

Typeset in Minion and Trade Gothic by
Florence Production Ltd, Stoodleigh, Devon
Printed and bound in the United States of America on acid-free paper by
Edwards Brothers

Library of Congress Cataloging in Publication Data
Cultural education—cultural sustainability: minority, diaspora,
   indigenous and ethno-religious groups in multicultural societies /
   edited by Zvi Bekerman and Ezra Kopelowitz.
      p. cm.
      Includes bibliographical references and index.
   1. Minorities—Education—Cross-cultural studies.   2. Multicultural
   education—Cross-cultural studies.   I. Bekerman, Zvi.   II. Kopelowitz, Ezra.
   LC3719.C84 2008
   371.829—dc22   2007025393

ISBN10: 0–8058–5724–9 (hbk)
ISBN10: 0–203–93836–4 (ebk)

ISBN13: 978–0–8058–5724–5 (hbk)
ISBN13: 978–0–203–93836–2 (ebk)

Contents

religious groups

Preface
Cultural Education—Cultural Sustainability: Towards an Honest Dialog With and Between Communities of Particular Practice

ZVI BEKERMAN AND EZRA KOPELOWITZ

What do groups such as African-Americans, Amish, Armenians, Asian-Americans, Basques, Chaldian Catholics, Coptic Orthodox, Hawaiians, Jews, Koreans, Native Americans, Mongols, Muslims, Tibetans, and Ugyurs have in common? We invite you to grapple with this question as you read through the case studies on these groups in this book.

At the most basic level, and this is the focus of this book, all these minority groups are attempting to pass on their particular ways of life to the next generation. We call this attempt to transmit culture "cultural sustainability." Is it possible to transmit particular life ways from generation to generation in contemporary society? If so, what are the ingredients for success, what are the obstacles that lead to failure?

Our focus is on the educational dimension. What do attempts to educate for cultural sustainability look like in different cultural, diaspora, ethnic, and minority groups? What are the institutions that a minority group needs to have in place? What are the cultural tools—symbols, rituals, ceremonies— they use? What types of teaching practices need to take place? What types of relationships between community institutions and the state contribute to the project of cultural sustainability? What is the impact of different patterns of immigration? All these questions and many others are raised through the comparative framework offered in this book. By comparing the diversity of experiences, it is our hope that readers will find inspiration to learn from the experience of others and to start thinking about the variables that contribute either to the success or failure of the cultural sustainability project.

There are no simple solutions to the challenge of cultural sustainability and, indeed, it is the goal of this book to reveal the complexity of the idea of "cultural sustainability." The possibilities and limitations of cultural sustainability are tied into the living experience of cultural groups living in radically different cultural, social, and political contexts, all attempting to transmit their culture in an often-hostile world.

By presenting the experiences of such a wide variety of groups within a single book, we are offering a pioneering and, hence, extremely exciting project for those who are interested in a comparative understanding of multiculturalism, education, cultural studies, ethnicity, religion, and diasporas. We expect our readers to include academics, activists, educators, public policy makers, and philanthropists, among others, who are personally involved in the struggle of particular cultural, ethnic, and religious groups for cultural sustainability.

For the academic reader (sociologists, anthropologists, political scientists, social psychologists, and others), this book provides a unique source for referencing and conceptualizing the variety of ways ethnic, cultural, and religious groups are working to achieve cultural sustainability. We also expect the book to appeal to activists, educators, and others who belong to minority groups or who are involved in intercultural, cross-cultural, and multicultural education at various levels of policy and practice. Through the prism that this book provides, educators and others will realize they do not stand alone in their efforts and will uncover new strategies and methodologies through which to approach their work. We also assume that religious or sectarian academic institutions (i.e. the various Catholic and Jewish institutions of higher education, as well as those of other groups) and certain educational tracks within educational departments in regular academic institutions will adopt this volume as part of their reading lists when dealing with issues related to multicultural education, socio-historical cultural perspectives in education, and comparative attempts to understand the experience of particular groups *vis-à-vis* others.

Lastly, we aim this book at policy makers, philanthropists, and leaders who represent the host/majority society and/or communal ethnic/religious diaspora, indigenous, and minority groups. We hope that lay leaders will draw inspiration in learning of other efforts to sustain culture and, hence, stimulate new initiatives and engage in critical reflection of their own work in this area.

Acknowledgments

The need to acknowledge those who stand behind an initiative and offer critical support goes undisputed. What might be discussed is the place these acknowledgments have. We choose to place them at the beginning knowing well that, without their support, the initiative in its totality and its end product, this volume, would not be possible. We want to express our deep sense of appreciation to the Melton Center at the Hebrew University in Jerusalem for their substantive support throughout all stages of the initiative, which allowed the scholars in this volume to come together and discuss their perspectives on the multiple and complex issues which burden educational efforts of diaspora, minority, and indigenous groups. A word of thanks is also much in place for Naomi Silverman who, from the start, sensed the importance of the issues raised in our book proposal and to the anonymous reviewers whose strong words of support allowed LEA to take a final decision to publish the volume. Last but not least Julia Schlam, an outstanding student in the Melton Center at Hebrew University, took upon herself a leading task in the coordination of this project in its totality, starting with the conference and concluding with the publication of this volume. Coordination is undoubtedly one of Julia's strengths, but we mostly benefited from her critical and insightful mind, which throughout challenged and bettered our work.

Introduction

ZVI BEKERMAN AND EZRA KOPELOWITZ

Background and Vision

The initiative, of which this book is a part, grows out of a sense of frustration from our many years of involvement in the field of Jewish education, a rather peripheral area of research, but one we are deeply committed to. The frustration comes from our perception that research on Jewish education is a field that lives an almost solipsistic life, compartmentalized both from general research in education and from research done by other ethnic and minority groups struggling to sustain a sense of cultural integrity and belonging in contemporary society.

The lack of contact between researchers of Jewish education and their contemporaries is part of a larger problem faced by ethnic, minority, and indigenous groups. As Caesar knew well, creating divisions among ones' opponents is vital to the strategy of a conqueror. The universality to which liberal Western cultural hegemony strives in general and to which postmodern sensitivities preach in particular lead those inside and outside of academia who are attempting to promote cultural sustainability to look inwards, each to their own ethnic experience, accepting the liberal claim that they are "particular" or "unique" and it is the public sphere of liberal society that is "universal." The analytical result is a failure to recognize that the sum total of "particular" experiences has a universal quality and, indeed, is intertwined into the very fabric of public life in all but the most authoritarian of societies. The practical result is dichotomization and division and the complete failure of academia to produce meaningful tools and resources for those whose common goal is the use of education for the purpose of cultural sustainability.

We hope, through comparative study of particular group experiences, to change the frames of analysis scholars use in their work on issues of multiculturalism. When concepts such as "mainstream" or "liberal society" are portrayed as standing in a zero-sum relationship with the attempts of minority and other groups to sustain their particular cultures, we come up against a fiction that must be dismantled. The fiction is the universal/particular dichotomy. We will see in this book that the life ways pushed forward by these "particularistic" groups are often highly integrated within Western and liberal society, but are always, at the same time, distinct counter-cultures that offer resources to their members to empower them in the attempt to live rich and full human lives.

We do see in some of the case studies presented in this book, especially in the chapters dealing with minority groups in China, a zero-sum relationship between the universal demands of a particular public sphere and the needs of a minority cultural group. However, for our purposes, these cases highlight the different experiences of minority groups in the contemporary West, where people who are members of culturally distinct groups live in a dynamic relationship with other groups and have social memberships in many groups, all of which are fluently juggled in the course of everyday life.

Contemporary theories of multicultural society and education offer a poor start for understanding the dynamic, flowing, and complex experience of cultural sustainability as it is actually lived. If we are to succeed in the study of cultural education and sustainability, we must change the academic starting point—to move beyond the particular/universal distinction to an expanded vision that incorporates the complexity of lived experience.

To achieve an expanded vision we tie our intellectual fate in the area of Jewish education to the fate of our partners from other groups who are also devoted to the idea of cultural education–cultural sustainability. We can only succeed together by joining with others in an ambitious comparative project to redefine the analytic frames of reference from which we all ultimately feed. To understand cultural sustainability and to nurture it, we must use comparative study to redefine our understanding of society, the terms of social membership, and the place of particular cultural groups. This book is the first and very preliminary attempt to push forward this larger project.

A Community of Scholars

The core agenda of the cultural education–cultural sustainability project is to bring together scholars involved in the study of educational efforts invested in by diaspora, indigenous, and minority groups. The goal is to discuss the complexities these minority groups endure and the strategies they develop while searching for ways to sustain a sense of community and belonging.

We are familiar with research that focuses on the dilemmas encountered by minorities of various sorts in "general education" and we also know of work in our specific area of interest—Jewish education. In addition, there is the irregular dialogue sustained within some groups (e.g. Jews, Basques, and Armenians), but we know of no systematic effort to encourage research and dialogue between groups on the specific issues mentioned above.

One area that has received the attention of researchers is the large literature on issues related to bilingualism and its contribution to the understanding of educational cognitive and emotional challenges confronting minorities. Yet, in spite of the importance of the subject, a focus on bilingualism is too narrow a frame for understanding the toolkit available to minorities in their struggle for survival. The tools of cultural sustainability include, to name a few, sacred texts, social organizations, traditional arts, etc. While, on the one hand, theories of bilingualism have much to say about linguistic variation, on the other hand there is silence regarding the larger topic of cultural variation in contemporary society.

"Cultural Education–Cultural Sustainability"

With hesitation, we titled our call for papers "cultural education–cultural sustainability." We say "hesitation" because the word "culture" might lead readers to be suspicious of our intentions. "Culture" is a term that often reifies the subject under discussion, turning humans into dopes that simply act out culture, without offering active consent. We also fear interpretations that our initiative is neoconservative—a call to close boundaries and retreat into imaginary secure borders while denying recognition to otherness. Clearly those are not our aims.

The possibility of viewing cultural education–cultural sustainability as neoconservative can only come from a starting point that accepts a view of the world dominated by Western paradigms built on binary categories such as liberal/conservative, liberal/communitarian, public/private, minority/majority, insider/outsider, citizen/foreigner, and loyalty/disloyalty. By accepting binary categories "minority culture" becomes "a category" that stands out against that which is universal, in a binary and negating relationship.

We situate ourselves on a different dimension. The "universal" is a fiction: public spheres are composed of the ongoing relations between many particular groups. Our call is for a multidisciplinary effort to seriously consider the study of formal and informal education within multiple social/political/historical/economic contexts within which minority groups try to sustain spheres of trust. By spheres of trust we mean the social and cultural capital members of a group create between themselves and between the group and wider society. How do relations of trust play out and determine the human experience? These relations are complex and, except for extreme circumstances, cannot be reduced to binary in/out membership categories. Without these complex spheres of trust, particular cultures of any type cannot survive.

We offer an understanding of a multicultural world that does not assume the majority/minority relationship, in which the role of the minority is to assimilate to the public sphere imposed by the majority. While many scholars agree with this assertion, the fact is that the literature tends to place the burden of proof on those groups that seek to maintain cultural sustainability within a larger public sphere. Relatively little attention is given to the reciprocal, dialogical nature of the relationship between individuals, groups, and institutions that make up the larger social experience.

Members of minority, ethnic, and indigenous groups continually engage multiple others and, in so doing, they construct personal narratives that weave elements of their narrower and broader cultural identities in an ongoing process. The result is often confident and accepting individuals, who are agents of cultural groups seeking survival, but at the same time embody the negation of the idea that culture and identity are fixed and primordial. The need to push forward this complex understanding of cultural sustainability for the study of multicultural education is a key element of our initiative.

The Problems of "Multiculturalism"

Our issues with the multicultural literature are twofold. The first is with the dominant interpretation of the "multicultural" concept, which ironically reinforces the homogenizing categories of Western tradition that multi-culturalists wish to change. Our second belief is with those who are "post-structuralists," who offer a conception of multiculturalism that is, we believe, out of touch with reality.

The prevailing interpretation of the "multicultural" concept focuses on a dominant public sphere to which minority, ethnic, and indigenous groups supposedly need to accommodate. We wish to shift the nature of questions posed by multicultural discourse from a discussion of opening boundaries, to preserving boundaries in an open, yet sustainable fashion. The shift is from one of cultural accommodation to educational efforts at cultural sustainability by these same groups.

We believe that this initiative, if sustained through time and approached in a critical manner, will be liberating in that it changes the way we engage topics touching on "identity" and "culture"—terms that continually bring with them the danger of reification. If successful, we will appreciate the hegemonic nature of over idealized, reified categories of belonging that liberal and conservative Western ideologies use to shape legal and political structures and which then lead to understandings of the identity/culture of minority groups that are not sustainable in the open society. In the world view we are pushing for, the social is stronger than the ideological. Instead of distinct groups who stand against an equally well-defined public sphere, we view the world through the prism of complex spheres of trust. We see collaboration between people, who create a dynamic tapestry that weaves diverse cultural elements together as life is lived. This vision of "flowing culture" stands in direct contrast to "the culture of a minority group" whose strong boundaries are similar to the policed borders of states.

Our second issue *vis-à-vis* the multicultural literature is with those who represent the polar opposite to the problem discussed above. Here we are referring to a postmodernist and poststructuralist interpretation of culture, which we agree with in principle but, as it currently stands, does not provide tools for dealing with the realities of living in the context of Western hegemonies.

Postmodernists may be theoretically "right" in so far as they may provide a good description of the empirical world. The postmodernist description argues against categorizing identity, but rather to approach the experience of life as it is lived. Postmodernists argue that people belong to many groups at the same time, living in a culturally fragmented and flowing life experience, which cannot easily be tied into a single grand narrative that binds the individual into a single and static identity.

However, the theoretical description is weaker than the powerful "reality" of the hegemony that postmodernism seeks to critique. This "reality" significantly affects lives and sets limits on where minority groups live, whom they can marry, and what educational and employment opportunities are available to them. Thus, acknowledging "reality," i.e. working within a positivist perspective, though epistemologically wrong, might be the best way to start.

Allowing for the recognition that identity and culture in the context of everyday life holds positivist qualities, in so far as members of minority, ethnic, and indigenous groups perceive their particular group as a "reality," might soothe the suspicion that relatively postmodern arguments may raise in those groups we want to benefit with our work. This does not mean we support instilling in learners modernist and positivist perspectives, but it does mean acknowledging that, for the theorists involved in poststructuralist theoretical discourse, cultural hybridity and mestizo identity might not be the best place to start our work when trying to understand a complex world where ethnic/religious minorities have a sense that their survival is in danger.

The Challenge of Mapping and the Chapters of this Book

To reach recognition of the world view we propose above, we needed a place from where to start. The working conference that took place in December 2004 at the Hebrew University in Jerusalem provided an opportunity to begin mapping the complex set of issues before us. The conference also served to build a sense of common purpose and enthusiasm among a community of scholars, which we hope you will feel as you read this book.

Much of the discussion at the working conference focused on mapping issues, as has much of our thought in trying to organize the chapters of the book. What does the study of one particular group have to contribute to those interested in the efforts of another group to work for cultural sustainability? While each article specifies issues that the author considers of essential importance for the study of his/her group, our challenge is to create a framework for comparison. On one hand, the goals of this book are modest, in that we intend to leave comparative conclusions at this early stage of our cultural education–cultural sustainability project to our readers: however, the layout of the chapters, nevertheless, are organized to promote the cultural education–cultural sustainability agenda.

The complexity of cultural education–cultural sustainability does not make organizing a volume on the topic an easy challenge. A focus on cultural sustainability allows for no easy cause and effect relationships or simple generalizations, nor does it offer a clear course of action for remedying obstacles faced by ethnic, cultural, and minority groups. The chapters in this volume share in the attempt to grapple with multiple levels of analysis and accept the challenge of complexity and abandon the illusion of proposing fast solutions. All acknowledge the intricacies of individual and group activity and the intermittent nature of meaning making. In a way they all suggest that uncovering complexity is a goal unto itself, leaving us humbled in the face of the multifaceted "realities" encountered during the attempt at cultural sustainability.

Despite this word of caution, we do feel that there is a clear and common theme that serves as a universal experience for groups attempting cultural sustainability. In one way or another, this theme appears in all the chapters in this book—namely, the power of cultural hegemonies promoted by dominant groups and their impact on the minority experience. A defining characteristic of hegemony is the "seen but unnoticed" nature of the particularistic claims of the dominant culture upon minority groups. Hegemonic claims have a powerful impact on the life ways of all who live in a given society, yet they go unnoticed and appear to all as a universal and natural part of the world. The minority group is thus left labeled as being "different," "ethnic," "outsiders," or simply "particularistic." For minority groups to succeed at cultural sustainability they must engage the majority culture in dialogue—in which social membership is not understood and enacted in dichotomous terms of insider/outsider and majority/minority, but is constructed according to an alternative, more dynamic logic. What is the alternative, which makes cultural education–cultural sustainability a possibility? We leave it for each chapter to elaborate the answer to this question and for the reader to piece together in his or her own mind and in the course of the many conversations and publications we hope this book will spark.

PART I

The State as a Determining Factor for Cultural Sustainability

The rise of the centralized state is a key part of the modern experience. The power of the modern state is located in the ability to reach all individuals within its realm very quickly in order to demand compliance to policies promulgated by state institutions. Yet, next to the power of the state to demand compliance is the possibility that the same legal and political framework can offer "citizenship rights," which we will see below are critical to understanding how a minority group might sustain its culture.

On one hand the centralized state is suspicious of minority groups—where do the members of a minority group fall *vis-à-vis* the demand for obedience to the rule of law pushed forward by the state and the universal system of education that most modern states use as a primary tool for socializing citizens to the moral regime it deems correct? Yet, on the other hand, that one legal system is applied to all individuals living within a state's jurisdiction holds out the possibility of protection to minorities and the promotion of rights to a life that might otherwise be impossible.

The manner in which the dialectic between the individual bound by the obligations of citizenship and the right of the same citizen to promote the culture of his or her minority group plays out differently from country to country. Section I offers six case studies, each elaborating on the interaction between states and citizens who belong to minority groups. The common theme, which we elaborate on at the end of this introduction, is the split personality of the modern state—on one hand suspicious of minorities, while on the other hand providing a framework that, for a variety of reasons, protects and enables minority existence.

We encourage you to consider the tension between majority and minority that appears in each chapter. Allowing for the difference in power, members of both share responsibility in the dialogue and both need to consider continually the issues that are part and parcel of living in a multicultural society. The manner in which this majority/minority relationship plays out is very much determined by the nature of the state and its approach to minority rights in a given country.

The first three chapters focus on the Muslim and Jewish experience in England and the Netherlands, and the Jewish minority group in Israel, while Chapters 4–6 focus on minority groups in China. The difference between the first three chapters and the Chinese case studies is that the former portray majority/minority relations in democratic contexts, while the latter focus on the authoritarian Chinese state. Yet, despite the obvious differences between democratic and authoritarian regimes we will see that the hegemonic power of the state is a universal variable that shapes the minority experience—the question is how does the hegemonic power of the state actually play out and what is the impact on the effort of minority educators to create cultural sustainability?

The Impact of the State on Cultural Education–Cultural Sustainability in Democratic Contexts

Each author offers a different angle on issues central to thinking about cultural education–cultural sustainability in democratic contexts. Geoffrey Walford shows the possibilities for minority groups when citizenship rights enable the establishment of schools dedicated to cultural sustainability. In contrast, Chen Bram depicts the hegemonic side of state power that operates through the creation of bureaucratic categories for handling the education of minority groups. Through the bureaucratic process the state reduces the extent to which the cultural autonomy described by Walford can actually play out.

The tension between the processes of cultural autonomy described by Walford and cultural homogenization described by Bram illuminate a central dilemma that anyone concerned with cultural education–cultural sustainability must tackle. Marie Parker-Jenkins addresses this dilemma by weighing in on the side of the liberal state. She asks what is the extent of the obligations that the state should impose on "faith-based schools" in order to ensure the sustainability of common public norms that bind all citizens to a common public sphere.

Geoffrey Walford illuminates the processes by which distinct cultural groups are able to promote semi-autonomous educational communities through a comparison of the development of Moslem schools in England and The Netherlands. Walford examines the effect of state funding policies within the context of immigration patterns over the last 50 years. The Muslim minorities have very different cultural backgrounds in the two countries, with most of the Dutch coming from Morocco and Turkey and most of the English originally coming from Pakistan, Bangladesh, and India. The paper shows how these different cultural backgrounds have influenced the nature of Muslim schooling in these two countries and the diversity of different Muslim schools within each country.

In Chapter 1 Walford ties together the macro-variables of national context and the cultural traditions of the Muslim immigrants through the concept of "communities of practice." Within the community of practice we are able to examine the development and practices needed to create the cultural space necessary for minority groups to sustain themselves within a school environment.

The concept of "communities of practice" enables us to see that individuals do not fashion identity in a vacuum, but within a trajectory as they move within and between communities. Schools constitute and are constituted within the web of multiple-communal memberships. The result is a sophisticated understanding of the interaction of the state, national origins of immigrant groups, and the place of educational institutions within minority communal life, all of which enables an understanding of the role schools play in reproduction of educational and social inequalities and their capacity to help or hinder social and political integration.

In Chapter 2 Chen Bram reverses the equation stated by Walford. While Walford shows the positive side of multicultural practices, Bram demonstrates, in the Israeli context, how the same multicultural policies often lead to disempowerment and misrecognition of socio-cultural diversity and the needs of immigrant populations.

Bram tells a classic story of unintentional outcomes by analyzing bureaucratic "categories" as used by representatives of the Israeli state for dealing with immigrant groups. Bram illustrates the processes of recognition, non-recognition, and misrecognition and their importance to cultural sustainability and multicultural policy.

The case study focuses on the relationship of state bureaucracies in Israel to ethno-cultural immigrant groups originating from the former Soviet Union in general and Caucasian Jews in particular. In order to "absorb" the immigrants the state creates bureaucratic categories by which to organize social services but, in so doing, the Israeli state also sets the terms of discourse between majority and minority with clear implications for the provision of citizenship rights and the possibility of Caucasian Jews achieving cultural sustainability in the Israeli context.

Finally, in Chapter 3 Marie Parker-Jenkins compares the development of Jewish and Muslim schools in Britain. In direct contrast to Bram and, indeed, to most authors in this volume, Parker Jenkins does not regard the state as a suspicious actor. Rather, Parker-Jenkins embraces a classic liberal doctrine that views the state as a positive actor in society, in so far as it creates universal norms to which all citizens should abide. She then poses questions as to whether more should be asked of faith-based schools, especially those funded by the state, regarding the monitoring of legal limits on the curriculum so as to ensure accordance with the values and principles of human rights and democracy.

The Impact of the State on Cultural Education—Cultural Sustainability in an Authoritarian Context

While Walford, Bram, and Parker-Jenkins's chapters focus on democratic contexts, the next three chapters provide a stark comparison, focusing on the meaning of "multiculturalism" and cultural sustainability in the context of the Chinese authoritarian state. Each chapter considers challenges confronting minorities in China today. We learn from the three case studies that the relationship between the majority Han culture and minority groups is complex and filled with ambiguities. Certain groups have managed to create the institutional and cultural infrastructure required for cultural sustainability, while others find themselves under sustained attack from the Chinese state.

Jing Lin provides a macro-overview of the state of higher education among Chinese minority groups and the complex relations of globalization, education, and cultural identity. The chapter focuses on the complex relations between the Chinese state and minority groups as seen through policies of assimilation, preferential treatment, and control. The chapter also explores critical efforts at sustaining minority cultures, such as the creation of minority higher education institutions, bilingual education, and the current strategy of the Chinese Government for promoting multiculturalism within an authoritarian framework.

Bing Wang's chapter focuses on one Mongol high school in China and evaluates the implementation of Chinese multicultural education policy *vis-à-vis* the experience of this particular school. The study shows that current Chinese policy towards ethnic groups, while guaranteeing a variety of cultural freedoms and rights, is plagued by contradictions that are leading to the assimilation of Mongol culture. Wang suggests that Mongol cultural sustainability depends on structural reforms, including further decentralization and greater autonomy for minority education institutions.

In comparison to the Mongol experience, in which a degree of cultural autonomy is permitted by the Chinese state, a more draconian picture is painted by Seonaigh MacPherson and Gulbahar Beckett in their study of the threats Mandarin Chinese language and culture pose to the Uygur and Tibetan languages and cultures. In particular they examine the injustice of Chinese rule over the region and the imposition of educational policies and practices as *de facto* assimilation. They finally describe the struggles of the Tibetans and Uygurs in sustaining their communal identity and illustrate the complex effects of educational modernization and its possible role in the rise of fundamentalism and even cessation.

A Spectrum that Runs from More to Less Cultural Autonomy—But an Autonomy that is Never Complete

The six chapters in this section, when taken together, enable us to learn how the dialectic between the cultural autonomy that is vital for cultural sustainability and the hegemonic and homogenizing power of the state plays out. We are offered a view of a spectrum of minority educational experiences that ranges from more to less cultural autonomy.

On one hand it is clear that, in the contemporary democratic contexts described by Walford and Bram, the state encourages its citizens to promote the sustainability of their particular cultures through multicultural policy. In Walford's case study we learn that state policies can enable the critical amount of cultural autonomy needed for cultural education–cultural sustainability at the level of the local community. Yet from Bram's chapter we learn that these same multicultural policies bring with them the weight and power of bureaucratization. In order for the state to extend the right of cultural sustainability it must create categories by which to fund and implement its policies. At the moment of bureaucratization, the right of individual citizens to shape the educational space necessary for cultural sustainability is necessarily limited.

Thus, on one hand, limits on cultural autonomy are part and parcel of living within a democracy—this is the point that Parker-Jenkins addresses in her chapter. Yet, on the other hand, if we do not focus on the positive side of the equation, namely the communities of practice of the type Walford describes and how they might navigate the impediments and dangers put in place by the state, then we will remain unable to promote coherent policies capable of leading to vital forms of cultural education–cultural sustainability.

A primary difference between authoritarian and democratic contexts is that state power and the demands of the majority group to assimilate are closer to the surface of everyday life and more easily seen. Yet even within the Chinese context we learn that there are some circumstances in which minority groups can fashion a degree of autonomy. In Sheena Choi's chapter on Korean exceptionalism in the next section of this book, we will even see that, in the case of Koreans under Chinese rule, a great deal of cultural autonomy is granted by the state. However, in the case studies addressed by the chapters in this section we learn that the autonomy granted by the Chinese state is relatively limited. The result is to weaken the cultural group—too much centralization of state power and not enough autonomy for the minority group to create a viable counter-culture needed for cultural education–cultural sustainability.

CHAPTER 1

Muslim Schools in England and The Netherlands: Sustaining Cultural Continuity

GEOFFREY WALFORD

Introduction

The last decade or more has seen the development of new schools in both England and The Netherlands designed for children from families of minority faiths. In England there are now more than eighty Muslim schools, as well as schools for Sikhs, Seventh Day Adventists, Hindus, and Greek Orthodox Christians, mainly serving the children of first- or second-generation immigrants. However, in contrast to the long-standing state funding of Church of England, Roman Catholic, and Jewish schools, most of these newer schools serving religious minorities are fee-paying private schools.

In The Netherlands there has been a similar widening of the diversity of schools, again mainly responding to the needs of children of immigrants. There are now thirty-four Muslim schools, as well as a smaller number of schools serving Hindus, Sikhs, and Buddhists. In contrast to England, practically all of these schools are fully funded by the state on a level at least equivalent to other Dutch schools.

This chapter reports some of the findings from a four-year Spencer Foundation-funded comparative research project into state policy on separate schools for religious minorities in England and The Netherlands. This wider project focuses on two religious groups, evangelical Christians and Muslims, but the focus here will be on Muslim schools where, in both countries, there has been a recent growth in the number of such schools. Apart from the investigation of documents, the research has involved interviews with national policy makers and representatives and with head teachers and teachers from a sample of schools. Short periods have also been spent in ethnographic observation within these schools when issues of curriculum and culture were discussed and observed.

Historical Background

The present cannot be understood apart from the past. In Europe the present educational systems of each country are the product of centuries of political and economic struggle and compromise. I have described some of this history for England and The Netherlands in some detail elsewhere (Walford, 2001a), but it is necessary to give an outline here to begin to understand the ways in which these schools have formed.

The key 1944 Education Act for England and Wales built upon an existing understanding between the religious providers of schools and the state. To make it possible to provide secondary schooling for all children it was seen as necessary to include as many as possible of the pre-existing secondary schools that had been founded by the Church of England or the Roman Catholic Church within the state-maintained sector. While some religious schools remained as full private schools, the majority entered into arrangements with the state in one of three categories—voluntary controlled, voluntary aided, or special agreement. The main distinction between the three was the degree of control that the board of governors maintained over the school and the size of the financial contribution expected from the churches in return for this remaining control. Thus, while these schools retained their religious denominational character, they became an integral part of the state-maintained local authority system. The 1944 Education Act also gave the churches the opportunity of building new secondary schools and the Roman Catholics took this up vigorously (O'Keeffe, 1986).

By 2000 about 35 percent of primary and 16 percent of secondary state-maintained schools in England and Wales were still religious schools (Lankshear, 2001). The bulk of such schools were Church of England or Roman Catholic, but there were also some Jewish schools and a very few schools of other Christian origins. What is of note here is that, while it was theoretically possible for the state to support schools of any faiths, in practice until 1998 it was only the established Christian denominations and Jewish schools that obtained funding. Until that date there were no state-funded schools for children of the various new immigrant minority religions.

During the 1950s and 1960s, in order to deal with labour shortages in unskilled jobs, the British Government actively encouraged immigration from Jamaica and the Caribbean and from Pakistan and India. While much of this immigration was originally men only and expected to be temporary, many stayed and eventually brought their wives and families. Immigrant children from these families first started to enter British schools in significant numbers in the 1960s. While there are obviously no direct linkages between the country of origin, ethnicity, and religious adherence, many of the immigrants from Pakistan and Bangladesh were Muslims, while many from the Punjab were Sikhs and most from the rest of India were Hindu. However, the situation is complex, with Muslims in Britain having significant numbers from eight different countries of origin—Pakistan, Bangladesh, India, Kenya, Malaysia, Egypt, Libya, and Morocco—as well as many from the various countries of the Middle East (Parker-Jenkins, 1995). There is now a range of Muslim communities based not only on their country of origin, but also on the various groups within Islam. People from each of these groups tended to settle in particular urban areas within such cities as Birmingham, Blackburn, Bradford, Coventry, Dewsbury, Leicester, London, and Manchester. It is estimated that, by the mid-1990s, there were about 1 million Muslims in England, with about 75 percent having origins in the Indian subcontinent (Peach and Glebe, 1995; Vertovec, 2002) and about 400,000 children of Muslim parents of school age in England (Sarwar, 1994). Most religious minority children are now, of course, second- or third-generation immigrants and the vast majority are in state-funded schools under the governance of local education authorities or, ironically, the Church of England or the Roman Catholic Church.

During the 1980s there was widely perceived to be an increase in secularism within most state-maintained schools—including those voluntary schools owned by the churches. This perception of growing secularism led to concern among various religious minority parents—in particular Muslim parents who believed that their children were likely to be influenced away from their Islamic belief and practices. While it was theoretically possible for local education authorities to support Islamic schools financially, none chose to do so. As a result, in the late 1980s various groups of parents and mosques established small private Muslim schools for their children. While there is considerable diversity between these private Muslim schools, the majority are small schools of less than 100 students with low funding and poor facilities. One major exception to this is a large London school with over 1,000 students originally established for the children of Saudi Arabian diplomats (Dooley, 1991).

Following a long campaign (Walford, 1995a,b) by a variety of religious and other groups, the 1993 Education Act made it possible for groups of potential independent sponsors to apply to the secretary of state for education to start their own state-funded schools, which have the aim of fostering, for example, Muslim, Buddhist, or evangelical Christian beliefs or which wish to promote particular educational philosophies. In particular, existing faith-based private schools could apply to become re-established within the state-maintained sector. In the end only fourteen schools in England (and one in Wales) successfully entered the state system under these new regulations (Walford, 2000) and it was only under a Labour government that one Seventh Day

Adventist school and two Muslim schools were granted state funding. The School Standards and Framework Act of 1998 imposed slightly greater local government control on these schools and they have become part of a redefined voluntary-aided sector. That act allowed for the creation of new voluntary-aided religious schools and three further Muslim schools, two Sikh schools, and one Greek Orthodox school have more recently become state funded.

While state support has been slow in coming in England, the position in The Netherlands was seen as very different. The Dutch system presented several features that made the establishment of new religious schools easier. The most significant of these features are that, since 1917, state and private schools have been financed by the state on an equal basis, about two-thirds of all primary and secondary pupils are taught within private schools, and within the system there is a wide diversity of different types of school.

This diversity of state-funded schools in The Netherlands was the result of geographical, political, and social circumstances very different from those in England. The Netherlands has few natural boundaries on the east and south and linguistic, religious, cultural, and political frontiers have not coincided since the late sixteenth century. Since their division in 1839, Belgium has been relatively homogeneous religiously, but divided linguistically and The Netherlands relatively homogeneous linguistically, but divided religiously (Andeweg and Irwin, 1993). The basic cleavage between Roman Catholic and Protestant became more complex during the nineteenth century as divisions within the Dutch Reformed Church occurred and groups of orthodox Calvinist Protestants broke away from the theologically liberal Dutch Reformed Church to form their own re-reformed (Gereformeerde) churches. These three religious groups eventually became associated with political parties and, with the addition of a further party that developed from the socialist workers' movement and another based upon the relatively affluent Liberals (who held power until universal suffrage), until very recently still formed the basis of the five main political parties in The Netherlands. Funding religious schools on an equal basis to state-provided schools was one of the two major issues in the nineteenth century in The Netherlands and was only finally resolved in the new 1917 Constitution when a Catholic–Calvinist majority coalition led to the "Pacification," which introduced social reform, universal suffrage, and the right to state funding for religious schools on the same basis as the state-provided schools.

The result is a diversity of schools where the state-provided schools do not identify with a particular religion or outlook on life and are open to children of all religions and beliefs or none. Some of these state-run schools base their teaching on special educational ideas such as the Montessori, Jena Plan, Dalton, and Freinet schools, but all are open to everyone who applies—up to the physical limit of the school. Alongside these state-provided schools are many more so-called private schools that have full funding and their buildings provided by the state. Most private schools are Roman Catholic or Protestant, but there are also Jewish, Muslim, Hindu, Humanist, and Steiner schools, as well as some non-denominational schools. There are also further Montessori, Jena Plan, Dalton, and Freinet schools in this private but state-funded sector.

Within the last 25 years, more than 700,000 immigrants and refugees from Islamic countries have settled in The Netherlands, constituting about 4.5 percent of the total population. The two main groups are from Turkey (300,000) and Morocco (252,000) (Sunier and Van Kuijeren, 2002). As in England, these groups have tended to live in the large cities—Amsterdam, Rotterdam, The Hague, and Utrecht—and the first of several Islamic primary schools opened in 1988. It has been shown elsewhere (Walford, 2001b) that starting these schools for religious minorities was not as straightforward as the legislation might suggest. Several of the Muslim schools had difficulty in persuading their local municipalities of the merits of their cases and the events of September 11, 2001 and subsequent international events have led to further suspicion.

It is worth noting that, in both England and The Netherlands, the vast majority of children of Muslim parents attend "ordinary" state-funded schools. In England these may be community schools or those run by the Church of England or the Roman Catholic Church, while in The Netherlands they may be the municipal schools or any one of a range of schools run by the Protestant or Catholic Churches. Most parents do not want their children in separate schools organized specifically for children of their own particular religious beliefs.

It is only a minority of parents who wish their children to attend separate Muslim schools—and, even here, there is often a desire to use other schools if only they are perceived to be more willing to accommodate to particular Muslim religious needs. The desirability of separate schools for religious minorities is widely questioned, even among the relevant believers. And it is certainly widely questioned by many outside those faith communities.

Identity and Communities of Practice

At a general level, these Muslim schools have clearly been established because Muslim parents have become disenchanted with the existing schools to which they have access. There are several facets to this disenchantment. Some parents believed that there was considerable racism in existing schools both between students and coming from teachers in terms of their expectations (especially in terms of academic ability) of students from minority backgrounds. Many parents also wished for schools with a stricter disciplinary structure. In England, a particular issue was that of single-sex education for their female children, especially after puberty. But a common feature for most of those involved in Muslim schools in both countries was that no existing local school was felt an appropriate place for their children's Muslim identity to be nurtured. The concept of identity is, of course, one that is open to great controversy (e.g. Hermans, 2000) but, in this mainly empirical paper, I wish to introduce some elements of a model of identity that has been developed by Etienne Wenger in association with Jean Lave (Lave and Wenger, 1991; Wenger, 1998) in order to understand the nature of these schools.

The theory presented in Wenger's (1998) own book is multilayered and complex (indeed, its detailed exposition takes the whole book!) and he used ethnographic work within a medical insurance claims office to illustrate the various implications of the model. Insurance claims offices may seem some distance from Muslim schools, but I hope to show that elements of his model provide an explanatory structure for our understanding of the development of these Muslim schools and their ongoing practices. I emphasize that I am only taking elements of the full theory here and, indeed, I am stretching some of his precise definitions. But the project is worthwhile because of the insights that can be gained.

For Wenger (1998), there are profound connections between identity and practice. He used the concept of identity to focus on the person without assuming the individual self as a point of departure:

> Building an identity consists of negotiating the meanings of our experience of membership in social communities. [The concept] avoids a simplistic individual–social dichotomy without doing away with the distinction. The resulting perspective is neither individualistic nor abstractly institutional or social. It does justice to the lived experience of identity while recognising its social character—it is the social, the cultural, the historical with a human face.
>
> (Wenger, 1998, p. 145)

He argued that developing a practice requires the formation of a community whose members can engage with one another and, thus, acknowledge each other as participants. Thus, practice entails the negotiation of ways of being a person in each particular context. This dynamic relationship between practice and identity can be conceptualised, Wenger (1998) argued, in terms of five characterizations: (1) identity as negotiated experience, (2) identity as community membership, (3) identity as a learning trajectory, (4) identity as a nexus of multi-membership, and (5) identity as a relation between the local and the global.

1. Wenger (1998) argued that identity is built through the *negotiated experiences* of participation and reification that are the essence of communities of practice. Within any communities of practice, whether they be medical claims insurance offices or Dutch first schools, there are certain practices that are engaged in and the experiences

of participation and what each community pays attention to reifies participants as participants. Claims officers gradually move from level four to level eight, children move from year one (or preschool) to seven, and teachers move from newly appointed to well established. Through participation in particular events and rituals we become what we are. An identity, then, is a layering of events of participation and reification by which our experience and its social interpretation inform each other. As we encounter our effects on the world and develop our relations with others, these layers build upon each other to produce our identity as a very complex interweaving of participative experience and reificative projections. Bringing the two together through the negotiation of meaning, we construct who we are (Wenger, 1998, p. 151).

2. Practice defines a community through three dimensions: mutual engagement, investment in joint enterprise, and a shared repertoire. We become a *community member* not just through reified markers of membership, but through the forms of competence that it entails. When we are with a community of practice of which we are a full member, we can handle ourselves competently; we are in familiar territory. We experience competence and we are experienced as competent. Through mutuality of engagement we develop certain expectations about how to interact, how to treat other people, and how to work together. We "invest ourselves in an enterprise and the forms of accountability through which we are able to contribute to that enterprise make us look at the world in certain ways" (Wenger, 1998, p. 152). We come to understand, interpret, and use the repertoire of that practice.

3. If identity arises out of an interplay of participation and reification, it is not an "object," but a constant becoming—a *learning trajectory.* Identity is not some core of being that already exists, nor something that is acquired once and for all: our identity is constantly renegotiated through the course of our lives. Identity has a crucial temporal dimension and the work of identity is ongoing but, because it is constructed in social contexts, this temporality of identity is more complex than a linear notion of time. Moreover, there is not just one trajectory: identities are defined with respect to the interaction of multiple convergent and divergent trajectories.

4. We all belong to many communities of practice. Some of these will have been in the past, while some are current; of some we will be full members and with others we will be only peripherally involved. We thus experience *multi-membership* of various communities of practice. The membership of one community of practice is only part of our identity. Medical insurance claims processors do not form their identities entirely at work, neither do teachers or children form their identities entirely at school. They belong to various communities of practice, but their

identities are not something that can be turned off or on. Elements of identity from one community of practice spill into other communities of practice: "Our various forms of participation delineate pieces of a puzzle we put together rather than sharp boundaries between disconnected parts of ourselves. An identity is thus more than a single trajectory; instead, it should be viewed as a nexus of multi-memberships" (Wenger, 1998, p. 159). However, for a nexus of multi-memberships to be more that just a fragmented identity, being one person requires some work to reconcile our different forms of membership. Different practices can make different demands that are difficult to combine into a coherent single identity.

5. The final aspect of the work of any community of practice is to create a picture of a broader context in which its practices are located. The relationships between the *local and the global* are an important part of any identity, for the practices of the local community must make sense within a global context. We come together in communities of practice not only to engage in some enterprise, but also to figure out how our engagement fits in the broader scheme of things: "Identity in practice is therefore always an interplay between the local and the global" (Wenger, 1998, p. 162).

Exploring Identity and Communities of Practice in Muslim Schools

Having provided a skeletal outline of Wenger's (1998) framework, I now wish to use it to illuminate certain aspects of the development and practice of Muslim schooling in England and The Netherlands.

First, the parents involved in the establishment of these schools were fundamentally concerned with potential *multi-membership* of different communities of practice. For their children the major communities of practice were the mosque, the home, and the school. They saw a broad coherence between the practices of the mosque and practices in their homes but, with the increased secularization of local schools, they saw a growing disjuncture between the communities of practice into which their children were being introduced in the mosque and home and that of the school. For these particular parents, the essence of a Muslim identity is that it structures practices throughout the whole of life. These parents desire that their children should develop a Muslim identity that is coherent and not one that might be regarded as a "nexus of multi-memberships," which might be contradictory. They feared that the lack of coherence would lead to a fractured identity. In the end, the decision about whether to adopt an identity which embraced Islam was entirely that of the child, but these parents believed that it was necessary to try to ensure that the communities of practice into which they were introduced were positive in an Islamic sense.

In many cases this Muslim identity is also linked to an ethnic identity such that most of the Muslim schools in The Netherlands are actually concerned with building a Turkish or Moroccan identity as well as a religious one. Commonly, there will be Turkish or Moroccan artefacts within the schools and language courses will be a part of the curriculum.

This desire for coherence implied what might be considered by many non-Muslims as an excessive emphasis on protection of the child. This is particularly true for post-puberty girls in England where the most common particular interpretation of Islam that is held is one that stresses separation of the sexes and "modesty" for girls. Interaction between young men and young women is strictly controlled and the young women are restricted in their activities beyond school time. They are also required to keep their bodies covered with a shalwar-quamis and to cover their heads with a chandor or headscarf. Separate Muslim schools allow this to be as firmly policed as it is in the home. This aspect is particularly evident in some English schools in areas where immigration was from particular poor areas of Pakistan.

This element of multi-membership was also important for the Muslim teachers at the schools. Somewhat unexpectedly, in both The Netherlands and England, far from all of the teachers in these schools are themselves Muslim—simply because there are not many Muslim teachers in either country. However, in both cases the situation is improving quite rapidly and, for those teachers who were Muslim, the schools enable them to act out their Islamic beliefs without any inhibition or fear. For these teachers the schools give greater coherence between their homes, mosques, and work and enable them to form a more coherent identity across the various communities of practice of which they are members. In their previous schools these teachers had sometimes been the sole Muslim teacher or had been one of a small group. In separate schools it is accepted that God and religious belief can be talked about in lessons other than religious studies and that, while academic success is of great importance, it is not the only or even main purpose of what teachers are trying to do in school. These teachers do not just teach Islam, they live an Islamic life within the school.

Second, the growth of this new group of schools has only been possible due to the relationship between *local and global* identities. Being one of the world's major religions, Islam is a major force for globalization as well as its strengthening being a reaction against it. An essential part of the faith is the equality of all Muslims before God and the belief that Muslims should help their fellow Muslims where they can. In this way, nationality is less important than religion. Muslims see themselves as being part of a worldwide and increasingly geographically spread Umma (Daun *et al.*, 2004). This interdependence and support from the wider community is not just theoretical. Some of the private Muslim schools in England have received financial support from Muslim organizations in such countries as Saudi Arabia and one of the schools that became state-maintained received similar financial help with its need to provide a proportion of the money required to build a new school (which was necessary before the school could become state maintained).

At the same time, those Muslims involved with these schools had a local identity, which was an ethnic origin identity as well as religious. In both The Netherlands and England, it is illegal for schools to select or exclude based upon ethnicity, but they may do so based on religious belief (of the parents). However, in practice, many of the Muslim schools in The Netherlands have substantial majorities of children with either Turkish or Moroccan origins. In effect, they are ethnically homogeneous schools. Part of this is due to neighbourhood effects, as most cities have areas that are more Turkish or more Moroccan in origin, but it is also the result of parental choice where more than one Muslim school is easily accessible. This inevitably means that, not only is a Muslim identity developed and supported by the schools, but also that a Turkish or Moroccan identity is encouraged. Thus, the appropriate language will be taught as well as the history and social norms of the country or origin.

An emphasis on ethnic identity is also to be found in some of the English Muslim schools, but this is less marked as different from other schools as the English Muslim schools are usually less ethnically homogeneous.

Third, the idea of *community membership* helps to clarify what makes these schools different from some others. In a community of practice we develop certain expectations about how people treat each other and how to work together.

Membership of these communities is rarely chosen lightly. The schools sometimes draw from families linked to several mosques and who are geographically widespread. In each of the schools some children travel many miles each day to get to the school. Both parents and children make sacrifices to be at the school and they do so because they wish to be part of a community of practice where there are shared assumptions about the nature of God, the world, and humanity. These schools teach the Koran as literally true and a guide for all of life. They instruct the students in the ritual aspects of the religion and in the five pillars of Islam and expect appropriate conformity to these as appropriate. They believe in the sinful nature of any sexual activity outside marriage and completely condemn any homosexual activity. Such views are in sharp conflict with the practices accepted by many other schools and other communities of practice.

Community membership also allows the negotiation of a repertoire. Each school has its history of practice in the artefacts, actions, and language of the community. They draw upon that history, but also build upon it. Teachers are in a powerful position to build and develop this repertoire of practice. Most have come to the schools having taught elsewhere before, so come trying to deal with the question of how a Muslim school should differ from other schools where there have been Muslim teachers. In these schools there is still considerable discussion on this basic question. There is negotiation about the curriculum and about textbooks and how they should be modified. In various schools several books had words cut out or deleted with a felt-tip pen because the content was not deemed appropriate. This included references to "magic" in the Oxford Reading Tree in an English school and to such things as drugs and sex in a document on "being healthy." Books to be read were carefully selected such that they offered good models for the children to follow. But different schools adopted slightly different criteria as a result of negotiation. As the schools expand over their first few years of existence, new teachers are employed, each with a different set of personal experiences and histories of what it is to be a Muslim teacher. The school's community of practice will modify their activities, but the activities of the community of practice will also change.

Fourth, through such a process of constant *negotiated experience* where teachers, children, parents, and governors each participate in the school community, a community of practice develops. Daily, weekly, and annual rituals or practices will develop: class prayer with children at the beginning and end of the day, informal lunches where teachers share food and drink together, yearly celebrations for the major religious events, and yearly festivals to celebrate the school. The Koran and national ethnic identity are central to these schools and this is evident in artefacts around the schools. Many of the classrooms in these schools have Koranic texts on the wall and calligraphy is well practised. One of the schools I visited in The Netherlands had a large mural depicting immigrants coming from their original country to The Netherlands and establishing themselves there. The festivals that will be celebrated by each school will be both religious and those related to the country of origin, such that Moroccan or Turkish festivals will be celebrated in different Dutch Muslim schools. Silences can also be important. In many Muslim countries there is a prohibition on depicting images of people. Decoration is usually by way of ornate patterns and designs rather than portraits. The schools differed in the extent to which they allowed students to draw, paint, or sculpt images of people—some prohibiting it altogether while one primary school in The Netherlands had an extensive mural of children playing painted on the fencing all round its own playground. An unhappy compromise had been agreed in one English school whose year one and two classroom had a row of named drawings of the children drawn by themselves stuck to the windows. When I asked about them, it was pointed out to me that each drawing was of a person with a red scarf round its neck. The scarf indicated that the head and the body were not actually attached—although the children themselves probably did not realize it, these were thus children's drawings of themselves dead!

These practices, alongside the minute-by-minute practices of how teachers treat children and how children treat each other, build to become an answer to what makes the school a Muslim school. They give an identity to the school and allow those involved to develop their own identities with a greater coherence between their lives inside and outside of the school.

Fifth, the idea of an identity as a *learning trajectory* is well illustrated by these schools. Wenger (1998) argued for the importance of recognizing the temporal dimension of identity. Identities are continually negotiated and the idea of trajectory places our engagement in practice in this temporal context. Each specific situation that is dealt with is simultaneously part of a history of certain practices and part of a process of becoming a certain person. In short, children and teachers follow learning trajectories—not fixed paths that can be foreseen or charted in advance, but a continuous motion where people make choices about the sort of person they wish to become. This aspect of personal choice is central to Islam and is also to be found in Wenger's (1998) use of the identity concept. It is recognized that, for some children, the school will only provide a peripheral trajectory, which will never lead to full participation in the Muslim community of practice of which the school is a part. For others, while the school's community must essentially foster an outbound trajectory as the children grow and leave the school, it is hoped that they will be prepared for that wider world by deciding to become part of that wider Muslim community of practice. A trajectory provides a context "in which to determine what, among all the things that are potentially significant, actually becomes significant learning . . . It is a way of sorting out what matters and what does not, what contributes to our identity and what remains marginal" (Wenger, 1998, p. 155).

Within these schools the governing body and the teachers attempt to provide a coherent community of practice which will be more in alignment with those found in the childrens' homes and mosques. By doing so they hope that children will enter into that community of practice and accept those practices as their own. In short, they hope to provide a school that will stimulate children to decide to have Islam at the heart of their identity.

Conclusion and Speculations

In this chapter I have outlined some of the changes that have recently occurred in the English and Dutch education systems and shown how some Muslims have reacted to a perceived growth in secularization. I have shown how elements drawn from Wenger's (1998) model of communities of practice and his concept of identity can provide an explanatory structure for our understanding of the development of separate Muslim schools and their ongoing practices. It has been shown that Wenger's (1998) five characterizations of identity as negotiated experience, community membership, learning trajectory, a nexus of multi-membership, and a relation between the local and the global have helped in the understanding of the relationship between practice and identity.

While it is not the subject of this chapter, it is worth noting that elements of the same model might also be used to develop and explore questions about the desirability of such schools and the effects that they might have on pupils who attend them and the wider society. For example, in contrast to these Muslims, many non-Muslims may well believe that it is actually beneficial for children to have multi-membership of differing communities of practice such that they recognize the diversity of practices that are evident within the wider society. Where a family teaches the literal truth of its faith, condemns homosexuality, and tries to pass on a belief that any sexual activity outside marriage is sinful, some would argue that it is the state's duty to ensure that children experience alternative viewpoints. Where these Muslims see the development of a coherent Muslim identity as the most positive possible outcome for their children, others might argue that the attempt to develop such an identity is a form of social control exercised by the group on its children and that children need to engage in negotiated experiences with a wider range of members of the wider society. It contrast, it could also be argued that the state's attempts to ensure that children experience alternative viewpoints is another kind of social control exercised by the state.

Similar arguments surround the fact that many of these Muslim schools in both England and The Netherlands are concerned with ethnic identity as well as religious identity. In The Netherlands, in particular, most Muslim schools are practically mono-ethnic, with the majority serving children with either Moroccan or Turkish origins. While the national demands of the curriculum go some way to ensure that all Dutch children have a somewhat similar academic experience, there remain doubts and questions about the lack of social mixing. It is a strange situation where the law in both England and The Netherlands bans discrimination and segregation on the basis of ethnicity, yet the practice of supporting religious schools almost automatically leads to such discrimination and segregation by choice.

These debates can also be seen in terms of the balance that needs to be maintained between local and global identities. There may be a fear that "the local" may become too narrow and exclusive for the wider society to tolerate. Alternatively, "the global" might be seen as problematic. An important example of this can be seen in a recent Dutch case. Within The Netherlands separate Muslim schools have frequently been the subject of criticism and concern. Reporters have frequently sought out possible financial and other links with Turkey and Morocco and have suggested that undemocratic national groups influence some schools. In early 2001, the concern was so great that the Dutch Government's Internal Intelligence Agency launched an enquiry. The events of September 11, 2001 did nothing to lessen tension, so the report (*The Democratic Order and Islamic Education:*

Foreign Interface and Anti-integration Tendencies) was eagerly awaited when it was finally published in February 2002 (Minisrerie van Binnenlandse Zaken en Koninkrijksrelaties, 2002).

According to the report, up to ten of the schools could have some indirect links to militant Islamic organizations. Some of these have obtained some funding and had school board members with some links to what it called an intolerant Islamic foundation in Saudi Arabia (the private charity al-Waqf al-Islami) and a society that is said to be controlled by Libyan intelligence (the World Islamic Call Society). Not unexpectedly, there were also Turkish links, but they included links to the Turkish Government's Directorate of General Religious Affairs or Diyanet. The report stated that "This interference is . . . not welcome . . . It has become evident that the objectives of the World Islamic Call Society, the al-Waqf al-Islami foundation and the Diyanet are damaging to the Dutch democratic order" (Minisrerie van Binnenlandse Zaken en Koninkrijksrelaties, 2002, p. 7). It also reported that people with "a radical Islamic signature" who "sympathise or even maintain contact with radical political Islamic organizations such as the Egyptian Muslim Brotherhood and the Palestinian Hamas" (Minisrerie van Binnenlandse Zaken en Koninkrijksrelaties, 2002, p. 9) dominate the boards of some of these schools.

The importance of these findings should not be overstated. The links were not strong and it is questionable whether such links should or even could be prohibited in a democratic society. Further, it is not clear what direct impact any of the members of the school board had on the day-to-day running of the schools. The links were personal ones rather than institutional. However, the report was widely discussed in the media and an investigative television programme was able to raise the temperature further. The result was that the Board of the Organization for Islamic School Boards, the umbrella organization for these schools, felt forced to resign saying that it had failed in the performance of some of its duties.

This chapter has dealt with the historical processes by which Muslim schools developed in England and The Netherlands and the current practices within those schools. It has shown how elements of Wenger's (1998) model of communities of practice help in the understanding of these practices. That elements from Wenger's (1998) model might also be used to highlight questions about the desirability of such schools and the effects that they might have on pupils who attend them and the wider society is further evidence of the model's utility in examining identity and the nature of communities of practice. That task, however, remains to be done by others.

Acknowledgments

The research reported was made possible by a grant from the Spencer Foundation for which I am most grateful. I am indebted to the staff of the three schools for their warm generosity and help with this research. The data presented, the statements made, and the views expressed are solely the responsibility of the author. This chapter draws on some of my previous publications (Walford, 2001c, 2002, 2003) and was written in 2004.

Resources and Tools for Educators

Questions

1. In any particular country with minority faith-based as well as secular schools, what is the balance between freedom and choice and social cohesion?
2. In any particular country with minority faith-based as well as secular schools, to what extent should the extra costs of faith-based schools be funded by the state?
3. What are the equity implications of including or excluding faith-based schools from state funding?
4. If minority-faith parents who send their children to private faith schools because there are no state religious schools argue that they should not have to "pay twice" for schooling, both through taxes and fees, why should non- minority-faith parents pay any taxes for schooling?
5. Do children need to be able to negotiate multiple identities?
6. In what ways do and should families and schools differ in the ways they foster children's identities?

For Further Reading

On Muslim Schools

Daun, H. & Walford, G. (Eds.) (2004). *Educational strategies among Muslims in the context of globalization. Some national case studies.* Leiden: Brill.

This edited collection presents case studies of Muslim schooling in England as well as several other European countries. It also includes studies of predominantly Muslim countries such as Morocco, Pakistan, Afghanistan, and Iran.

Parker-Jenkins, M., Hartas, D., & Irving, B. (2004). *In good faith: Schools, religion and public funding.* Aldershot: Ashgate.

This book covers the debate about faith-based schools in England, paying particular attention to Muslim schools and evangelical Christian schools.

Walford, G. (2000). *Policy and politics in education: Sponsored grant-maintained schools and religious diversity.* Aldershot: Ashgate.

This book describes the political processes that led to the acceptance of Muslim and other minority religious schools within the state sector of education in England.

Walford, G. (2003). Separate schools for religious minorities in England and The Netherlands: Using a framework for the comparison and evaluation of policy. *Research Papers in Education, 18*(3), 281–299.

This article uses a framework for the comparison of school systems that include religious schools within them. It compares Dutch and English systems in terms of (1) freedom of choice, (2) productive efficiency, (3) equity, and (4) social cohesion.

On Communities of Practice

Lave, J. & Wenger, E. (1991). *Situated learning: Legitimate peripheral participation.* Cambridge: Cambridge University Press.

Wenger, E. (1998). *Communities of practice: Learning, meaning, and identity.* Cambridge: Cambridge University Press.

Based initially on studies of workplace learning, Lave and Wenger developed their concepts of "situated learning," "legitimate peripheral participation," and "communities of practice" in these two books.

Barton, D. & Tusting, K. (Eds.) (2005). *Beyond communities of practice.* Cambridge: Cambridge University Press.

This edited collection takes further the idea of "communities of practice" developed by Lave and Wenger.

Suggestions for Educators

1. Divide the group into two: one group should take a view that schools for religious minorities should be financed by the state and the other should take a view against this. Then debate.
2. The group should discuss the extent to which their identities differ in different situations—for example, within the family, schools, and with peers.

References

Andeweg, R. B. & Irwin, G. A. (1993). *Dutch Government and politics.* London: Macmillan.
Daun, H., Arjmand, R., & Walford, G. (2004). Muslims and education in a global context. In H. Daun & G. Walford (Eds.), *Educational strategies among Muslims in the context of globalization. Some national case studies.* Leiden: Boston, Brill, pp. 5–36.
Dooley, P. (1991). Muslim private schools. In G. Walford (Ed.), *Private schooling: Tradition, change and diversity.* London: Paul Chapman, pp. 98–114.

Hermans, C. A. M. (2000). Analysing the dialogic construction of identity of religiously affiliated schools in a multicultural society. *International Journal of Education and Religion, 1*(1), 135–165.

Lankshear, D. W. (2001). The religious identity of schools in England—a regional analysis. Paper given at the Education and Ethos Network Conference, Nijmegen, The Netherlands.

Lave, J. & Wenger, E. (1991). *Situated learning: Legitimate peripheral participation.* Cambridge: Cambridge University Press.

Minisrerie van Binnenlandse Zaken en Koninkrijksrelaties (2002). *De democratische rechtsorde en Islamitisch onderwijs.* The Hague: Minisrerie van Binnenlandse Zaken en Koninkrijksrelaties.

O'Keeffe, B. (1986). *Faith, culture and the dual system.* London: Falmer.

Parker-Jenkins, M. (1995). *Children of Islam.* Stoke-on-Trent: Trentham Books.

Peach, C. & Glebe, G. (1995). Muslim minorities in Western Europe. *Ethnic and Racial Studies, 18*(1), 26–45.

Sarwar, G. (1994). *British Muslims and schools.* London: Muslim Education Trust.

Sunier, T. & Van Kuijeren, M. (2002). Islam in The Netherlands. In Y. Y. Haddad (Ed.), *Muslims in the west: From sojourners to citizens.* Oxford: Oxford University Press, pp. 144–157.

Vertovec, S. (2002). Islamophobia and Muslim recognition in Britain. In Y. Y. Haddad (Ed.), *Muslims in the west: From sojourners to citizens.* Oxford: Oxford University Press, pp. 19–35.

Walford, G. (1995a). Faith-based grant-maintained schools: Selective international policy borrowing from The Netherlands. *Journal of Education Policy, 10*(3), 245–257.

Walford, G. (1995b). The Christian schools campaign—a successful educational pressure group? *British Educational Research Journal, 21*(4), 451–464.

Walford, G. (2000). *Policy, politics and education—sponsored grant-maintained schools and religious diversity.* Aldershot: Ashgate.

Walford, G. (2001a). Funding for religious schools in England and The Netherlands: Can the piper call the tune? *Research Papers in Education, 16*(4), 359–380.

Walford, G. (2001b). Evangelical Christian schools in England and The Netherlands. *Oxford Review of Education, 27*(4), 529–541.

Walford, G. (2001c). Building identity through communities of practice: Evangelical Christian schools in The Netherlands. *International Journal of Education and Religion, 2*(2), 126–143.

Walford, G. (2002). Classification and framing of the curriculum in evangelical Christian and Muslim schools in England and The Netherlands. *Educational Studies, 28*(4), 403–419.

Walford, G. (2003). Separate schools for religious minorities in England and The Netherlands: Using a framework for the comparison and evaluation of policy. *Research Papers in Education, 18*(3), 281–299.

Wenger, E. (1998). *Communities of practice: Learning, meaning, and identity.* Cambridge: Cambridge University Press.

CHAPTER 2

The Catch 22 of Categorization: Soviet Jews, Caucasus Jews, and Dilemmas of Multiculturalism in Israel

CHEN BRAM

Foreword

In his article "The Politics of Recognition" Taylor (1992) argued that ". . . our identity is partly shaped by recognition or its absence . . . non-recognition or misrecognition can inflect harm, can be a form of oppression, imprisoning someone in a false, distorted, and reduced mode of living" (p. 25). But what exactly is misrecognition and non-recognition at the level of groups and how does this process develop?

In this chapter I examine the relationships between state bureaucracies and policy in Israel to ethno-cultural groups from the former Soviet Union. This case serves as a prism to learn about the dilemmas of multiculturalism and multicultural policy in Israel. Examining the developments of policy and its relation to ethno-cultural immigrant groups originating from the former Soviet Union allows an anthropological and sociological understanding of the processes of recognition, non-recognition, and misrecognition and their importance to multicultural policy and intergroup relations and the implications of those policies on immigrants' ability to realize citizenship rights, accessibility to social services, and—especially—rights to recognition and the possibility of sustaining cultural identity.

While the majority of the 1.2 million immigrants who have migrated to Israel from the former Soviet Union since the 1970s are Ashkenazi Russian Jews,[1] about 15–25 percent belong to other groups, each one with very different cultural backgrounds—such as Georgian Jews, Bukharian Jews, and Caucasian

Jews, who are the focus of my discussion here. During the last decade the majority of Caucasian Jews, roughly 65,000 people, migrated to Israel, joining the 15,000 who migrated in the 1970s. Others have migrated to Moscow, the U.S. and other destinations. In their historic places of origin only a small minority of the population has remained. Immigration has brought dramatic changes to this age-old community, which has raised questions about the group's integration into their new environment in Israel and about the future of the group's culture and language.

Caucasian Jews are also known as mountain Jews and, recently, as *Kavkazim* in Israel. Their own name is "Juhur" (Juhur'hu in plural) meaning, simply, "Jews." Caucasian Jews are highly diverse and, from the perspective of the local Israeli culture, appear as a relatively unknown, "vague" group, combining some characteristics and influences that are considered to be "oriental" and others that are considered as "Russian" (their original geographic location symbolizes this). These characteristics allow us to examine the connection between questions of social and cultural classifications (especially in policy) and conceptualization of the composition of the society and, especially, the constitution of "ethnic" labels and categories in research and public discourse. Using ethnographic material, this work documents the complicated process by which the newcomers are "identified" and slotted into neatly bounded "ethnic categories" for the purpose of integrating them into the larger social and political culture and state systems and in the educational system in particular.

Methodology

This study is based on long-term anthropological research, with a multidimensional approach, which examines policy, group relations, and everyday interactions. Such an approach allows connecting questions regarding classifications (especially in policy) to conceptualizations of the "ethnic" and of the cultural social field (in research and in public discourse). It combines data from fieldwork among Caucasian Jews and among policy makers and social services in various localities. Observations particularly took place at meetings and events that involved contact between Caucasian Jews, as well as other former Soviet Union groups and agents from different social services[2] and/or policy makers. Data were collected through field observations and interviews—at the state level and in several municipalities.[3] Many documents were collected concerning projected programs or those that were in various stages of being carried out. In addition, some data relates to my own experience as an applied/engaged anthropologist who was involved in some of these processes during the 1990s.[4] Other types of observations took place at local gatherings, cultural events, and meetings between activists and representatives of local services: attention was also given to the contacts between Caucasian

Jews and other members of local communities, including contacts with other immigrants of "Russian/ Soviet" background. Interviews were carried out with activists within the Caucasian community and with policy setters. These were open-ended, in-depth interviews. The methodology attempted to combine a study of policy and its realization at the "macro"-level (although focusing on policies towards a specific community) and an anthropological study of social interactions and community experiences that related to and were influenced by these policies. This involves an attempt to structure the observations according to the logic of a chain of interaction, which could follow issues as they were considered at macro-levels and "meso"-levels and how they impacted on the local scene.[5] In the following, however, I am concentrating on some findings and conclusions from this data at the "macro"-level in regard to the relation between social policy and the process of categorization in the multicultural context.

Caucasian Jews' Situation After Immigration

Overall, movement to Israel has involved downward mobility for Caucasian Jews and a push to the margins of Israeli society. They have moved from a situation of a "normal distribution" within the economic structure of their original society to being very low on the socio-economic ladder. They have not been able to capitalize on resources that they owned in the Caucasus, where most of them had employment and many benefited from participation in the grey economy. In Israel, the group suffers from high unemployment and low-paying jobs and this includes many people who have high school and academic educations. Group members complain that their origin is an obstacle to their efforts to find employment. Similar dilemmas can be seen in the educational system and in other social arenas. Justifiably, they view their situation not only as a consequence of migration, but also as the result of a marginalization process. In recent years efforts have been made by governmental agencies to relate to the employment problems, but the lack of such efforts for this population in their first years in Israel has already influenced their situation.

The combination of dilemmas due to immigration and the processes that derive from marginalization can also be seen in relation to Caucasian Jewish families and community organizations and their interaction with the wider society. Although there was—and there is—an overall desire to integrate into Israeli society, there is also a reluctance to abandon existing values having to do with the norms and structure of family life. These values continue to exist even though concrete arrangements concerning nuclear and extended families have changed. The marginalization process and negative labeling of Caucasian Jews by others (see below) contribute to this situation.

Educators and bureaucrats see this reluctance to change as the immigrants being "closed" to Israeli society, while at the same time group members state that their frustration stems from the feeling that their culture and identity are not recognized. Hence, the situation of Caucasian Jews following their immigration is highly connected to the policy and reaction towards them. This dynamic is described below in order to give the reader an overall understanding of the dilemmas that this group faces.

The Development of Public Policy Towards the Immigrants

It is possible to identify three stages in the way the cultural identities of immigrants from the former Soviet Union were perceived and the resulting social policy from the 1990s through to the present: stage one, where all immigrants from the former Soviet Union were treated as "Russians," stage 2, where there was a perception which stressed a binary distinction between European Russians and "Asians," and stage 3, where there was some recognition of certain subgroups, which led to the formulation of policies specifically designed for these groups and special treatment in education, employment, etc. These developments and policies have raised dilemmas and paradoxes, as will be shown below.

Until the mid-1990s policy makers tended to regard the ex-Soviet immigration *en bloc*, disregarding cultural differences. In a broader context, policy makers distinguished between two main groups of immigrants: those who came from the Commonwealth of Independent States and the "beta Israel" (colloquially "the Russians" and "the Ethiopians").[6] This tendency also reflected the approach of Israeli social research, which usually saw all former Soviet Union immigrants as "Russians" and ignored Caucasian Jews and other distinct ethno-cultural communities among Soviet Jews.[7]

The simplified distinction in the first years of the 1990s policy between "Ethiopians" and "Russians" (seeing former Soviet Union immigrants as one group) had numerous practical implications. One of them was the inability of both policy makers and scholars to foresee the emergence of social problems within certain groups. A good example of this failure is the question of housing and the distribution of the populace. The structure of the family and the community, in addition to prevailing socio-economic elements, brought about a situation in which the Caucasian Jew immigrants were concentrated in fifteen towns in the peripheral parts of Israel, where the situation was already difficult in terms of social and employment conditions.[8] This process, however, was influenced not only by the characteristics of the immigrants, but also by the government's housing planning policy, which supported building new neighborhoods in many peripheral towns, assuming that these would be populated by both Russian immigrants and the local population. The immigrants and the neighboring veteran Israelis refer to some of these quarters using the term "ghettoes." Insufficient involvement of the immigrants in the general social sphere and lack of opportunities for them to do so provoked the escalation in the ongoing process of stigmatization during the first, crucial years of absorption.

Dery (1994, p. 20) noted that Israel's "direct-absorption policy" left the dilemmas of absorption to the local authorities and municipalities, but the latter were not given any real power or sufficient resources. Dery (1994) quoted a director of the Department of Education in a city in central Israel, who said that "there is a feeling that the Ministry of Education took advantage of the public atmosphere of 'a mission' regarding the absorption of new immigrants, and threw a very heavy ball to the local municipalities instead of handling it herself" (p. 21). If this was the case in a central city regarding immigration, the situation in small peripheral towns was much worse. Social services and schooling systems, that serve large, culturally diverse populations of new-comers, did not get enough government support in funds and in guidance in order to implement a sound policy. The arrival of large groups of immigrants from areas such as the Caucasus and Central Asia, together with large groups of Jewish immigrants from rural areas in Ethiopia, were understood mainly as a burden in these towns. But while the dilemmas of Ethiopian Jews were at least recognized among policy makers and there were some attempts to cope with them, the smaller groups from the former Soviet Union (two of them each comprising the size of the Ethiopian immigrants) were neglected. The existence of the former Soviet Union groups and their specific dilemmas had no visibility in the first, crucial years after their arrival. In addition, local leaders and educators were themselves from groups that experienced problems during the mass immigrations of North African and Middle-Eastern Jews in the 1950s and felt that they themselves had finally begun to make it. The result was a situation that did not make a very good starting point for the interaction with the new immigrant groups.

The neglect of cultural diversity therefore came as an additional factor to the already existing problems of interaction between the local establishment and immigrants—especially in the Israeli periphery. But the central question here is not social planning and the failure to take cultural diversity into account, but the dire consequences for the immigrants from smaller ethno-cultural communities. The situation when big groups with unanswered needs settled in weak towns and neighborhoods created a problematic situation.

The following pages focus on local social services and the education system. These, of course, were not the only factors influencing the situation of the Caucasian Jews, but they did provide a substantial contribution to the marginalization of Caucasian Jews.

Ignoring Diversity in a Comparative and Theoretical Perspective

An *en bloc* perception of immigrants, which ignores the identity and needs of different ethno-cultural groups, is not unique. It is an example of a situation in which exiting schemas for categorization in the new society lump different immigrant groups together. Another prominent example of this "lumping process"[9] is the situation of Kurdish, Alevi, and Circassian immigrants who are categorized as "Turks" in Germany (White, 1997) and other European countries. A similar problematic is raised by the "Pan-Indian" question in Canada, where in the past Sikhs, for example, were not recognized as a community unto themselves, contributing to their marginality (Dusenberry, 1997). Although each case has its own characteristics, in most cases this problematic derives not only from the situation of immigration itself, but also from two other dimensions relevant to the way ethno-cultural identities are perceived by official agents. One is the difficulty of dealing with the social complexity of bureaucracy in general and state social agents in particular. Sometimes the tendency to create wider categories of cultural groups can be explained by the "need" to simplify the work of public agencies, although in the long run this strategy can cause bigger dilemmas. Moreover, when there is a need to create categories (in policy, as well as in quantitative research) the problem is often a one-to-one parallel between these wider official categories and the way identities are perceived during interaction between agents of the state (i.e. social services employees, educators, etc.) and the immigrants. In such interactions, non-recognition and misrecognition can become a form of oppression.

But the logic of bureaucracy is only part of the story. A second major dimension that influences the way immigrants and minorities are perceived is the logic of hegemony and control, which in the European Western context is influenced by the heritage of colonialist discourse. Non-recognizing and, more often, misrecognizing "non-European" people and attributing to them general common characteristics is a feature well known from colonialist and particularly orientalist discourse (Said, 1978) that can be seen both in common reactions towards immigrants and also in the reaction of a majority from a "European" background towards the "indigenous" population in immigrant societies such as the U.S. or in former "empires" such as Russia.[10] In the case of immigrants, there is also a tendency, influenced by nationalist discourse, to merge "state" and cultural identity together. Hence, if a person comes from India he or she is simply "Indian" and if he or she comes from Russia or the former Soviet Union he or she is "Russian" or "ex-Soviet." The result of such an approach is not only non-recognition of specific cultural identities, but also a replication of power structures. In many cases people who belonged to a minority group in their original location continue to be dependent on other immigrants from the majority group in their original location while negotiating with different agents in the new surrounding. This is evident in the case of Caucasian Jews, where non-recognition and misrecognition actually replicated power structures and orientalist discourses from the former Soviet Union to Israel.

The Binary Approach: From Non-Recognition to Misrecognition

Scholars paid attention to the ambivalent attitude of veteran Israelis towards Russian Jewish immigrants. On one hand, there was sympathy to immigration. On the other hand, there was fear of the influence of immigration on their communities and fear of competition from newcomers (Lewin *et al.*, 1997). Yet the research ignored questions of the relation towards immigrants from minority former Soviet Union ethno-cultural groups. While officially all immigrants were treated as "Russians," a binary approach emerged at the local level, especially among employees of the social services and educators. This approach or perception manifested itself in a distinction between European Russians and "those coming from the Asiatic parts of the Commonwealth of Independent States."

This distinction became dominant at the "local" level and contributed to negative labeling of Caucasian Jews: not only was their own culture and tradition ignored, in this scheme they were labeled as "non-modern," "uneducated," and even cultureless, depending on the "level" of the orientalistic approach among those who met the immigrants and provided services to them.

Caucasian Jews moved from being one of many ethnic groups in the Caucasus to one of a dichotomous characterization in Israel. In the development towns where many Caucasian Jews reside, the officials in charge of "absorbing" them were often old-timer "Mizrahi" Jews, usually from North Africa. They were responsible for the implementation of social policy and the provision of social rights to the immigrants. In addition, many social agencies started to employ Russian Ashkenazi immigrants—and in many cases they took over administrative responsibility. One process at work is the emergence of a hierarchy in which North Africans look down upon Caucasian Jews, adopting the stance of the Russian "Ashkenazi" immigrants towards the Caucasian newcomers. In a way, this replicates the stance of veteran Israeli Ashkenazi towards the North Africans in the 1950s.

The process of identifying and stigmatizing Caucasian Jews is evident in various ways beyond the simple negative labeling of an immigrant ethnic group. One was the great variation and lack of clarity in the names that were applied to the group—such as "mountain Jews," "Tats" (a name used by Soviet ethnic policy), and others. These also emerged from the very situation of immigration: while policymakers and, in many cases, also researchers discussed the "immigration" of these "groups." In actuality, the "groups" were formed and re-formed during the immigration process. Only after a long and usually conflict-ridden process did they come to constitute a stable "ethnic" or "ethno-cultural" group in their new surroundings. This is evident in the case of Caucasian Jews, who had some shared identity based on a common language (Juhuri or Judeo-Tat), culture, and historical experience, but at the same time came from remote communities with different dialects and surroundings in the very heterogeneous Caucasus region. This situation also affected their possibilities of negotiating with the state and usually weakened them, as can also be seen in other examples (Dusenberry, 1997).

Moreover, in many cases, the question was not only inner diversity among people who after all shared some kind of common cultural identity, but the existence of different ethno-cultural groups among immigrants and the tendency of the host society to see them as similar or identical. This brings us to a second important element in the process of identifying and categorizing Caucasian Jews. Even when social workers and policy makers started to realize that not all the immigrants were "Russians" they confused and misrecognized the different groups originating from the former Soviet Union: Caucasian Jews, Bukharian (Central Asian) Jews, and Georgian Jews. All those groups, as stated above, were conceived as similar in the "binary" model. This pattern also brought about the emergence of new ethnic categorizations in the Israeli context, such as "White Russians"—used by social services personnel to describe Ashkenazi Russian immigrants, in contrast to the smaller ethno-cultural groups, who, according to this perception, are "non-white," e.g. Asians, traditional, etc.

Thus, while negative stereotypes had an impact at the individual and community/municipality level, the situation of ethnic "lack of clarity" or "confusion" became a systemic element in the state bureaucratic response to the needs and rights of the groups. This situation was a barrier to the development of a culturally oriented policy in education and social services. It also had a severe impact on questions of cultural sustainability: while state agencies were usually supportive of the need to provide resources to some folklore activities for each group, they were blind to their needs in regard to broader questions of cultural sustainability in the realms of languages, art, and research. This also limited the possibility of relating to the culture and history of these groups in curricula and developing cultural-oriented educational programs.

The binary model also affected the discourse having to do with the question of continuity and how to grapple with change in the new surroundings and limited the possibility of cultural and social dialogue between the immigrants and host society. While this seems to be a typical situation in many cases of immigration, its impact in the case of Israel should be understood with regard to an ideology that stressed the connections between different Jews and the idea of a "homecoming immigration."[11] In this context, the dissonance between ideology and praxis contributed to the frustration of the immigrants.

Implications of Non-recognition and Misrecognition in Educational Spheres

Education was one sphere where the results from this setting became salient. Teachers and educators who met the immigrant's children did not have any knowledge about their culture and background. Meanwhile, findings from my fieldwork showed that the educators' approach towards these pupils was ambivalent and even negative. A similar dynamic already existed regarding the small group of Caucasian Jew immigrants who came in the 1970s.[12] Asked to check the reasons for reports on failure and under-achievement of immigrant children from the Caucasus, Lieblich *et al.* (1986), using both intelligence and socio-metric examinations, found that the children had normal intelligence, but the approach of teachers and class mates towards them was problematic and full of negative stigmas.[13] The experience of the 1970s encounter, however, did not counter the neglect when tens of thousands immigrants from the Caucasus (together with other groups) came in the 1990s.

In comparison to Caucasian Jews who came in the 1970s, the 1990s immigrants from the Caucasus were a more heterogeneous group. Many of them came from cities and cultural centers in the Caucasus, with diverse professions and educational backgrounds. The dynamic of their interaction with the Israeli educational system, however, at least until the mid-1990s, was similar to the one experienced by their kinsmen who had arrived in the 1970s. A survey in 1998 found that the percentage of dropouts among Caucasian Jewish immigrant young people (in the survey) was 25 percent, compared to 4 percent in the overall Jewish population and much higher then among other immigrant groups.[14]

Difficulties in education and other spheres of life were an experience shared by other group of immigrants and not only by Caucasian Jews (and other minority groups among former Soviet Union immigrants). However, the neglect and non-recognition of their very existence placed groups like Caucasian Jews at a severe disadvantage compared to groups who were targeted by social policy, such as Russian Jews and Ethiopian Jews—each with its own specific needs. This was manifested in, for example, the distribution of funds, the planning and implementation of social policy, the methods used in training manpower for social and educational services, the designing of projects, and drawing workers for the services from the vast pool of immigrant communities. In addition, this neglect had particular consequences on issues of integration, ethnic relations, and the negative stigmas that were attributed to these groups.

The Development of "Special Care Policy" towards Caucasian Jews and its Implications

While the binary approach remains dominant, some recognition of specific groups and diversity among former Soviet Union immigrants has started to develop. From 1997 onwards, Caucasian Jews and, later, Central Asian (Bukharian) Jews, became the target of a "special policy" that was supposed to address their needs in the realms of education, employment, and social services, as well as in the cultural sphere. These developments involved combining resources from different government ministries and non-governmental sources. However, the findings show that this policy shift influenced the distribution of funds and solved salient social problems, but was less influential in the more basic level of acknowledging social and cultural needs and giving place and voice to members of the groups in the shaping of policy towards them. In other words, the implementation of this policy did not place enough emphasis on the empowerment of the groups that were its target.

The emerging approach, which appears to imply some recognition of diversity, arose on an *ad hoc* basis and did not come from or lead to basic rethinking about multiculturalism in Israeli society. It often grew out of a bureaucratic milieu that had decided earlier that Ethiopian Jews needed special treatment. In many cases it replicated policies that were previously directed towards Ethiopian Jews, a group with completely different characteristics.

The ethnic/cognitive and policy dynamics discussed above are intimately related to new organizational forms that have emerged within and in relation to bureaucracies that "deal with" Jews from the Caucasus and other groups of former Soviet Union immigrants. The motivation to solve social problems led to the adoption of a number of organizational tactics. One organizational development is the emergence of new bureaucratic structures. Examples are special units dealing with Caucasian Jews, Bukharian Jews, and Ethiopian Jews.

Problems arising within the context of Ethiopian immigration resulted in dilemmas leading to the justification of special treatment and it may be asked whether "special treatment" has become a bureaucratic catchword that ostensibly calls for a specific understanding of each group while actually bunching various groups together. Each of the groups mentioned above differs from the others in several basic respects. For example, in each group community organization and leadership patterns differ radically from one another, religious consciousness and its expression take completely different forms, and the family structure and values vary. Moreover, while each group aspires to become "Israeli" in one way or another, each has its own language, traditions, and group history. This variety has limited place in the implementation of an emerging policy towards these groups.

A second development involves the selection of personnel from different immigrant groups to serve as "bridging agents" or "mediators" between bureaucracy and, in particular, local education systems and the groups. In some ways this has increased access to resources and social rights, but for the most part these mediating agents have very limited power. The general trend is for them to rapidly become representatives of "the establishment." For the most part, they occupy temporary positions and are not employed as permanent staff. On the other hand, almost no effort was made to locate people from these groups who worked as teachers and educators prior to their migration and to integrate them into the educational institutions. The result is a very limited place for the immigrants' "voice" in the contacts between them and representatives of the state.

These trends point to movement in different directions. It may be said that there are more bureaucratic bodies today than in the past that adopt some sort of piecemeal multicultural discourse and this leads to a degree of power sharing with their clientele. However, overall, the data indicate that "special treatment" has resulted mostly in the centralized transmission of resources and less power sharing. Moreover, the implication of a "special treatment" policy signaled a shift in attitude from a discourse of "non-recognition" to "misrecognition."

Caucasian Jews as a "Special" Category: Cultural and Educational Implications

Not surprisingly, evidence from my fieldwork shows that the development of a "special care" policy went hand in hand with the stigmatization and negative stereotyping of Caucasian Jews. The implementation of a "special care" policy strengthened the image of Caucasian Jews as a primitive group among workers in the social services. This approach built on the binary perception that stresses a modern–traditional dichotomy. The so-called "Asians" or "traditional immigrants" are viewed as an obstacle to modernization and acculturation to Israeli society. Social change during the immigration process is understood as a necessity to be mediated—and actually imposed—by external social agents and not deriving from dialogue between cultures and generations. In such a framework the immigrants are therefore "objects" for policy and not subjects for dialogue. In this kind of atmosphere, these agents perceive the culture and native language of Caucasian Jews as a burden and not as an important source and meaningful heritage for the community that needs further study and support. Of course, officially policy makers do state their acknowledgement of the culture and cultural identity of the immigrants, but the meaning of this recognition is often concentrated at the "folkloric" level, giving some symbolic attention to music, folk tales, and funding folk dance groups, but usually this is done without attention to what the cultural expressions actually represent.

This approach towards so-called "traditional" cultures is rooted in a modernist framework. At its best, the "multicultural" discourse that influenced Israel in the 1990s added to it an assumption that expressions of culture should get a place as part of respect to the past and a component of "symbolic identity." In this approach the group "culture" is understood as a static set of codes that should be understood in order to communicate with the community and introduce "social change" and modernization as part of their "absorption." But in this approach Caucasian Jews' "culture," whether it manifests in "folklore," in patterns of interaction inside the family, or in other areas of life, is not usually seen as meaningful and relevant for the questions the group faces in Israel.

More than anywhere else, misrecognition creates a gap between the school on one side and family and community values on the other side. While social service employees and educators often describe this community as "closed," in fact, this actually represents an attempt to preserve basic values and tradition in a hostile environment.

After all that has been said above of the negative aspects of public policy towards Caucasian Jews, it is also necessary to point out important achievements. As already mentioned, public policies have brought more accessibility to state services and social rights. In the educational sphere, achievements are especially evident in an "informal education" project (which means, in this context, projects that operate outside the "obligatory" schooling system, usually in community centers), which is reaching many Caucasian Jews pupils in different localities.[15] In comparison to school-based policies, this project has succeeded in creating a different atmosphere. The Caucasian Jews have staff positions (although again only in temporary positions) with greater ability to influence the character of the project. At the same time, different educational methods were used and, in particular, the prevailing attitude among the educational staff is that participants are able to succeed just like any other pupil. The Caucasian Jews' cultural identity was not considered a barrier to success.

The informal educational setting and methodology enabled dialogue between educators and Caucasian Jewish pupils and parents, with a positive influence on the latter's self-confidence, including a feeling that Caucasian Jews' identity and traditions are not under attack. This led to greater achievements at school and a reduction in the dropout rates among Caucasian Jews (14 percent compared to 25 percent in 1997). That said, the dropout rate among Caucasian Jews is still much higher than for other sectors.[16] Follow-up findings show that this success was limited to an influence on some of the program's participants, while other dilemmas remained unsolved.[17] Finally, findings from my fieldwork and interviews also show that, while this project was an important success regarding educational achievement, at the same time it contributed to the process of seeing Caucasian Jews' culture as a burden or as that which remained in the past. While Caucasian Jews got recognition in this project as another group in Israeli society at the social level, this had no equivalent at the cultural level. Of course, the inclusion of Caucasian Jewish staff gave some place to this culture *de facto*, but both their low position and limited power in the project setting and their organizational "socialization," while working, did not give much place to Caucasian Jews' culture, history, and language as a resource and value unto itself.

Above all, while some success was achieved in projects that focused on Caucasian Jews (and other groups) in informal education, this did not have a strong influence on the school system itself and, hence, their overall influence remains limited and depends on the continuation of special budgeting. At the same time, basic dilemmas regarding group relations, the attitude towards cultural diversity in social services, and educational institutions remain problematic.

Recognition, Cultural Identity, and the Sociolinguistic Policy

The dilemmas of the meaning of official recognition in the distinctiveness of the community are echoed in the linguistic and socio-linguistic sphere and, more generally, in regard to cultures that are associated with specific languages. In general, so far no official recognition of Juhuri, Caucasian Jews' language, has been given. Some recognition, although in different and not always sufficient degrees, has been given by official agencies of the state to Russian and to Amharic (spoken by the majority in Ethiopian Jews immigrants). This also had an effect on the recognition of the cultures that these languages signify. Symbolic although small support is given to cultural activities in other languages, especially to activities in Yiddish and in Ladino/Judeo-Espaniol (Judezmo). The case of Russian and Ethiopian is an example of some recognition of the importance of language that derives from a multicultural approach towards immigrant groups, assuming that these languages are still used and important to the everyday life of these immigrants. This is a bit different from the later case: recognition of the importance of Yiddish and Ladino signified their importance as "Jewish languages" to the cultural heritage of their speakers—and for Israeli society in general. Paradoxically, recognition of Caucasian Jews' language could have been derived from both logics. On the one hand it is both a language still spoken and important to thousands of immigrants and supporting some arenas of public communication in this language is relevant to the everyday experience of the immigrants. The governmental decision on "special policy towards Caucasian Jews" (April 29, 1997) recommended broadcasting a radio program for Caucasian Jews that would give information on different programs and projects for them. Such a radio program was not implemented—maybe because, for this functionalist goal, information in the Russian media was enough. But this functionalist approach to the need to recognize immigrants' languages did not take into account the emotional, symbolic, and communal significance of the language for its speakers—the significance of which exists even if most of the Caucasian Jews speak Russian.

Besides the question of significance to the group itself, there is also a question of its cultural meaning to society at large in the context of Jewish immigration to Israel. Juhuri of Caucasian Jews, as well as Judeo-Tadjic of Bukharian Jews from Central Asia, are clear examples of "Jewish languages" such as Yiddish and Ladino. Their speakers, however, do not have enough political power to demand that policies that treat Jewish languages as part of the "national cultural heritage" include their language and culture as well.

During their interaction with the new surroundings, Caucasian Jews learn to think about the language as something that belongs not only to the past, but also to a completely different and even inferior cultural sphere (Bram, 2000). Hence, pointing out the role of the language, its importance, and its place as one of the "Jewish languages" does not seem a priority to many Caucasian Jews. These processes create a contradiction between the important place the language still has in the "inner space" of Caucasian Jews' life (expressing feelings, family relations, etc.) and its non-presence in the public sphere. In the long run, an accelerated decline of the language and culture of Caucasian Jews seems certain.[18]

Homecoming Immigration and Recognition of Cultural Identity

These dilemmas of recognition and acknowledgment of cultural identity and the specific features of cultural sustainability in the case of Caucasian Jews should be understood in the specific context of Jewish immigration to Israel. Among other immigrants, labor immigration for example, a distance between the "inner space" of the community and public sphere is common, although not desirable. In the case of Jewish immigrants to Israel, the distance between inner and public space is a source of frustration due to the rhetoric of "coming home" and belonging to the nation and the alienation and marginalization experienced by the immigrants.

Most Caucasian Jews see their immigration to Israel as a "homecoming" that derives from their Jewish identity. They want recognition for their culture in the context of the broader society and not simply the right to practice their culture as a distinct group. They see their future as integrating into Israeli Jewish society, but at the same time they want a place for their own culture and traditions. The reality is that Caucasian Jews feel stigmatized.

The above situation is exacerbated by the comparison Caucasian Jews make between the situation in Israel and their former situation in the Soviet Union. Their understanding is that, in the Soviet Union, there was political manipulation of their ethnic status, but that they enjoyed recognition and esteem from those who were in their immediate social environment. In Israel, they enjoy basic political and religious freedom but suffer from a lack of recognition and low esteem on the part of other Israelis with whom they are in immediate contact. The difficulties they and their children experience in the Israeli educational system stand as the one of the most powerful examples of this gap.

There is also an additional gap between the declarations of public officials and the realities of their practices. In contrast to the "melting pot" ideology, which characterized social and educational policy in Israel in its first few decades, policy makers officially declare that the current approach is to embrace diversity and the need for recognition. The findings of this study, however, show that in many cases the declarations remain at the theoretical or a declarative level. The realization of special policies for Caucasian Jews suggests that current "multicultural" practices are to a large degree a repetition of the practices of marginalization, disempowerment, and misrecognition that characterized Israeli social policy towards immigrants from Asia and North Africa in the 1950s and 1960s.

A comparison to the Asian and North African immigrant experience helps place the current Caucasian Jews' experience in a broader socio-historical context. Since the 1980s there has been more awareness in Israel of the need to recognize the national culture and curricula of different Jewish traditions—especially for those who came from Asia and Africa and suffered from non-recognition and misrecognition during the first few decades of the Israeli state. The anthropologist Dominguez (1989, pp. 96–123), who documented parts of this process in her fieldwork, pointed to the frequent use of the word "heritage" in this context. She suggested that the difference between "heritage" and "culture" refers to a hierarchy between "folklore" and "culture" and also signals that this "heritage" is a remnant of the past, not a culture relevant to contemporary Israeli life.

Dominguez (1989) asked "Might the current emphasis on adding the heritage of oriental Jews to schoolbooks and radio programs not perhaps be a way to appease the non-dominant sector of the population without affecting the long-standing interests of the dominant group?" (p. 122). Israeli social scientists offer different perspectives regarding the extent to which this is still the case at the beginning of the twenty-first century; however, one clear difference is that, following developments in the 1980s and 1990s, the cultural traditions of Jews from the Middle East and North Africa have become, to a bigger or lesser degree, an important part of Israeli culture. Even if there are areas where this process is still slow, at least there is a wide public agreement that legitimates this direction.

However, at the same time the common understanding of Israeli culture is still based on binary oppositions and the "place" that the so-called "oriental" cultures obtain does not necessarily mean that there is recognition of the cultural identities of Caucasian Jews and other immigrant groups. Here, again, "the catch 22 of categorization" has its influence—although this discussion shows that the dilemma goes beyond formal policy to the overall categories in which a society understands itself.

Conclusions

This case study has focused on the interaction between categorization and the development of public policy. For some groups, especially immigrants, issues of recognition, accessibility to various resources, and even basic visibility start with the question of whether they appear as a "category" in the eyes of policy makers or, more generally, are identified as "a group" within the discursive map created by the dominant ethnic political culture and state institutions.

Effective and just policy requires understanding of the cultural background and ethnic distinctions that compose any society—including internal distinctions within immigrant groups. The importance of this understanding is especially salient while dealing with the interaction between the staff of educational institutions and immigrant families.

We have seen that policy makers do not make distinctions between cultural groups using clear categories and boundaries that reflect the immigrants' reality. Rather the official categories are a product of complicated social and cultural processes, which produce different and competing understandings that began with ignoring ethno-cultural minority groups among the mass immigration wave from former Soviet Union to their formal recognition at the end of the 1990s.

Recognition by the state is very important for ethno-cultural groups, since the state is the major agent for education, social services, and even resources for cultural sustainability. Practically, however, "identification" as "a group" deserving special acknowledgement is not always beneficial. Although policy has an impact on access to social services and on educational achievements, these achievements are limited and are not accompanied by an empowerment of the immigrants themselves. There exists a tension between "special policies" towards ethno-cultural groups as a manifestation of the multicultural approach and the actual implementation of those policies as a means for socio-cultural control by state bureaucracy. The result is that such "multicultural" practices often lead to disempowerment and misrecognition of socio-cultural diversity and the resulting needs of members of the immigrant populations. Moreover, such policies can constitute mechanisms of dependence and control that turn the immigrants into objects for special treatment rather than making them partners in a dialogue. The difficulties involved with applying "multicultural" policies should not mean that we put aside the importance of recognition. It calls, however, for further development of a "theory of praxis"—and a further understanding of the meaning of recognition in different contexts and societies.

Acknowledgments

This paper is partially based on research supported by the Minerva Foundation for human rights, the Hebrew University, and by the Ben-Zvi Institute, Jerusalem. It is also partially based on data collected in the framework of research supported by a grant from the Israel Science Foundation (# 907/02). I would like to thank Professor H. Goldberg for supporting and contributing to the research, Dr Ezra Kopelowitz and Dr Zvi Bekerman for their remarks and assistance, and the participants of the cultural education–cultural sustainability workshop for their remarks.

Resources and Tools for Educators

Questions

1. What are the ethnic/cultural/national/religious categories that people use to label groups in your immediate socio-political environment? In your opinion, do these categories account for the variety and heterogeneity that you experience in your interactions with members of these groups?
2. Whose interests are served by the above-mentioned ethnic/cultural/national/religious categorizations? Can you elaborate some of the benefits and disadvantages that result from the use of these categories in matters of public policy?
3. The case study described in the chapter demonstrates a tension between the complexity of cultural identity and the limits of the categories used to identify ethno-cultural groups for practical purposes (i.e. implementation of policy). What are some similar examples of this tension in your immediate environment?

For Further Reading

Eriksen, T. H. (1993). *Ethnicity & nationalism. Anthropological perspectives.* London, Chicago, Illinois: Pluto Press.

This book reviews anthropological approaches to questions of ethnicity that also shed light on questions of cultural identity.

Cohen, R. (1978). Ethnicity: Problems and focus in anthropology. *Annual Review of Anthropology, 7,* 379–403.

This paper focuses on central dilemmas in the study of ethnic identity.

McDermott, R. & Varenne, H. (1995). Culture as disability. *Anthropology and Education Quarterly, 26,* 324–348.

The authors offer a challenging approach to the meaning of cultural identity in educational contexts.

Baubock, R. & Rundell, J. (1998). *Blurred Boundaries, Ethnicity, Citizenship.* Aldershot: Ashgate.

This book discusses issues of current migration and of crossing and blurring of boundaries in international migration.

Suggestions for Educators

Suggest a group discussion on some of the following themes.

1. What is culture? How should we conceptualize it? Hold a critical discussion of the definitions that people suggest (are these definitions essentializing culture or flexible) and then consider the policy implications of adopting any of the definitions offered. While thinking generally about "culture" can you identify cases where there is a tendency to locate group identities/cultures in simple binary schemes (such as traditional/modern)? Try to think of approaches to culture and group identity that can help overcome this tendency.

2. In what contexts would the use of ethnic/cultural categorizations enable minorities greater access to valuable societal resources and/or to support their efforts towards cultural sustainability? Discuss possible contradictions and tensions in efforts to use cultural categories to empower minorities. Finally, in what cases do you see ethnic and cultural differences used in such a way that they become a means of control and a tool for sanctifying social hierarchies? Is it possible to use these differences as a basis for creating dialogue between different identities?

Suggest the following activity.

1. Ask participants in the groups to offer their own descriptions/definitions of the three main ethnic/cultural categories in their immediate socio-political environment. Ask participants to share their descriptions and discuss them.

2. Ask participants to identify members of the groups they described and check their descriptions against the way these members perceive their own groups.

3. Compare the description gathered from the group representatives to the ones produced by the group and consider the source for the identified differences in the descriptions rendered.

Notes

1. "Russian Ashkenazi Jews" is itself a heterogeneous category, which includes Jews from other Slavic areas and from Baltica (see, for example, Gitelman, 2003; Fialkova, 2005). Still, while these differences do have social importance, the commonalities inside this category are salient and the boundaries with the minority ethno-cultural groups are vivid.

2. These also include public non-governmental agencies supported by the government and/or by Jewish organizations who often were the agents who implemented policies towards immigrants.

3. Caucasian Jews are concentrated in about fifteen towns in Israel. I visited most of these communities. Data were particularly collected in seven municipalities.

4. These include both work with the group and an attempt to influence from a standpoint of an engaged anthropologist and in some periods working as an applied anthropologist and advisor to different agents, such as the Ministry of Absorption. This study involves an attempt to re-examine these experiences from a researcher's point of view.

5. A key element of this methodology was to follow community activists in a variety of settings at these different levels.
6. A third category was immigrants from the U.S. and Western Europe (immigrants from developed states in policy terminology) whose numbers where small and were not considered a "target group" for policy.
7. This approach was dominant even though information on these groups was available in the work of Israeli historians and linguists (e.g. Zand, 1991; Altshuler, 1990). This is an example of the lack of a diachronic approach in the social sciences and the need for cooperation between researchers in the social sciences and humanities regarding questions of immigration and cultural sustainability. Moreover, for the most part, research to help in understanding group differences follows the piecemeal emergence of policies rather than being utilized as a basis for formulating such policies. In this manner, this situation regarding former Soviet Union immigrants in the 1990s repeated what was common during the 1950s and 1960s in the treatment of social research and policy on the mass migration from North African and Middle Eastern countries.
8. Ethnic boundaries are also reflected in this process. For example, while Caucasian Jews were concentrated mainly in the southern and northern parts of Israel, immigrants from Central Asia gathered in fringe neighborhoods and in some development towns in the central region.
9. Political struggle after the Gulf War gave more visibility to the Kurdish population as a distinct group from Turks in Germany.
10. On the other hand, in some instances the reaction towards the question of diversity in such a context can take the opposite form, when the state creates or strengthens boundaries and stresses their different group identity in a logic of "divide and rule." Anthropologists were part of this colonial history, since in many cases they gave the "ratio" for such divisions (see, for example, Cohen (1978) for a discussion of the case of the Nuer and Dinka in East Africa).
11. On "homecoming immigration" see, for example, Lomsky Feder and Rappaport (2001).
12. For further discussion of the 1970s immigration of Caucasian Jews see Altshuler (1990, pp. 516–522) and Bram (1999, pp. 21–28).
13. Such methods would probably be considered as not being "politically correct" nowadays and, indeed, raise many dilemmas, but in this case proved quite effective.
14. See Ellenbogen-Frankovitz and Noam (1998, p. 45). The dropout percentage combines both those who do not study at all (10 percent) and those who attend "alternative frameworks" (15 percent).
15. According to Ellenbogen-Frankovitz et al. (2004, p. 34). This project, "*Pele*" was the main support project that operated throughout Israel. In the localities where it operated, 35 percent of Caucasian Jews pupils participated.
16. Among them 6 percent who were not studying at all and 8 percent who attended alternative frameworks (Ellenbogen-Frankovitz et al., 2004, p. vi).
17. The "follow-up study" of Ellenbogen-Frankovitz et al. (2004) contains rich information on the educational situation of Caucasian Jewish young people. However, since this "follow-up" was carried out seven years after the first research (Ellenbogen-Frankovitz and Noam, 1998) there was limited possibility for "follow-up" on the original population. The findings also raise a question regarding the extent to which changes among the Caucasian Jews' success were the result of policy and projects or a natural result of the years that past.
18. For a detailed description of linguistic policy in this case and for the rule of Caucasian Jews' linguistic situation in the Caucasus and in Israel, see Bram (2000).

References

Altshuler, M. (1990). *The Jews of the Eastern Caucasus.* Jerusalem: Ben Zvi Institute and The Institute of Contemporary Jewry, The Hebrew University.

Bram, C. (1999). *From the Caucasus to Israel: The immigration of the mountain Jews—anthropological perspective on the communities in the Caucasus and issues in their integration into Israel.* Jerusalem: JDC-Brookdale Institute (in Hebrew).

Bram, C. (2000). Human dignity and cultural identity. In A. Hareven & C. Bram (Eds.), *Human dignity or humiliation—reality and directions for change* (pp. 58–75). Jerusalem: Hakibutz Hameo'had and Van-Leer Institute (in Hebrew).

Cohen, R. (1978). Ethnicity: Problems and focus in anthropology. *Annual Review of Anthropology, 7,* 379–403.

Dery, D. (with Schwarz-Milner, B.) (1994). *Who governs local government?* Tel-Aviv: Israeli Institute for Democracy, Hidekel Print (in Hebrew).

Domingnez, Virginia, R. (1989) People as subject, people as object: *Selfhood and peoplehood in contemporary Israel.* Madison: University of Wisconsin Press.

Dusenberry, V. A. (1997). The poetics and politics of recognition: diaspora Sikhs in pluralist polities. *American Ethnologist, 24*(4), 738–762.

Ellenbogen-Frankovitz, S. & Noam, G. (1998). *The absorption of immigrant children and youth from the Caucasus.* Jerusalem: JDC-Brookdale Institute (in Hebrew).

Ellenbogen-Frankovitz, S., Konstantinov, V., & Levy, D. (2004). *The absorption of youth from the Caucasus: findings from a follow-up study.* Jerusalem: JDC-Brookdale Institute (in Hebrew).

Fialkova, L. (2005). Byelorussian and Ukrainian languages in Israel: Preliminary remarks. *Jews and Slavs, 15*, 252–264. Special issue: Judeo-Bulgarika, Judeo-Russica et Palaeoslavica. Jerusalem-Sofia.

Gitelman, Z. (2003). The meaning of Jewishness in Russia and Ukraine. In B. R. Eliezer, G. Yosef, & R. Yaakov (Eds.), *Contemporary Jewish: Convergence and divergence* (pp. 194–215). Leiden: Brill.

Lewin, E., Noah, M. G., & Barham, R. (1997). Yes to immigration, but what about the immigrants? Local attitudes to immigrant absorption. In E. Lewin M. G. Noah, Ro'i. Yaacov, & P. Ritterband (Eds.), *Russian Jews on three continents—emigration and resettlement* (pp. 364–388). London: Frank Cass.

Lieblich, A., Ben, S. N., & Raz, N. (1986). Learning and adaptation problems of children from the Caucasus Mountains in Israel. In T. R. Horowitz (Ed.), *Between two worlds: Children from the Soviet Union in Israel* (pp. 203–218). Lanham, MD: University Press of America.

Lomsky Feder, E. & Rappaport, T. (2001). Homecoming, immigration, and the national ethos: Russian Jewish homecomers reading Zionism. *Anthropological Quarterly, 74*(1), 1–14.

Said, E. (1978) *Orientalism.* New York: Pantheon.

Taylor, C. (1992) The politics of recognition. *Multiculturalism and "The politics of recognition":* an essay by Amy Gutmann et al. (pp. 25–73). Princeton, NJ: Princeton University Press.

White, B. J. (1997). Turks in the new Germany. *American Anthropologist, 99*, 754–769.

Zand, M. (1985, 1986). The literature of the mountain Jews of the Caucasus. *Soviet Jewish Affairs, 15*(2), 3–21. (Part I), 16 (1), 35–51 (Part II).

Zand, M. (1991). Notes on the culture of the non Ashkenazi Jewish communities under Soviet rule. In Y. Ro'i and A. Becker (Eds.), *Jewish Culture and Identity in the Soviety Union* (pp. 378–441). New York: New YorkUniversity Press.

CHAPTER 3

Achieving Cultural Sustainability?: The Phenomenon of Jewish and Muslim Schools in England and Wales

MARIE PARKER-JENKINS

Introduction

There have been over 100 Jewish schools founded in Britain since the late seventeenth century, thirty-two of which operate full-time with government funding. Likewise, there are over 100 Muslim schools in the country, which have been established during the last 20 years, five of which receive financial support. While the two religious groups have different cultural and historic roots, they are similar in that they both represent minority groups seeking to sustain their own cultural heritage in the face of assimilationist trends. Both groups demonstrate the efforts of minority diaspora communities at maintaining their socio-historical heritage through educational efforts, that is the establishment of schools operating in the context of a non-Jewish and non-Islamic state. In so doing, both communities also operate in a self-imposed form of segregation, creating a type of cultural enclave locally based, while engaging with the wider community on their own terms. This is in an effort to offset what they see as cultural dilution and the production of hegemonic homogenizing forces caused by government policy on multiculturalism.

This chapter explores these themes, beginning with an historical perspective of the development of schooling and then the phenomenon of Jewish and Muslim schools in England and Wales. This can be seen within the context of immigration and settlement patterns, the diaspora of people to the West, particularly in the post-1960 era, and the introduction of new languages and cultures. Broader philosophical concerns also lead us to look at the allegation that faith-based schools are intent on a cultural sustainability, which can lead to social conflict rather than social harmony. This is particularly apposite in the light of continuing troubles in Northern Ireland, the September 11, 2001 terrorist attacks, and civil disturbances in the Middle East. Furthermore, worries over segregation of children are reviewed in the chapter and, in particular, the claims of "ghettoised" education that promotes religion in a way that goes beyond cultural sustainability to that of "propagandizing" and "fundamentalism." These issues lie at the heart of contemporary debates concerning the wisdom of the state in expanding and financially supporting faith-based schooling: the hostility shown towards religious communities by some sectors of the wider community and the need for accountability to ensure all schools are respecting cultural diversity

Historical Context

Educational provision in Britain was established on denominational lines dating back to the Middle Ages and faith-based groups have continued to perpetuate this tradition (see Rowe, 1992). By the nineteenth century, major social and economic upheaval due to the direct consequences of the Industrial Revolution called for social policy enactment (Wood, 1960). The government at this time was, however, somewhat ambivalent about its role in the provision of educational services (Curtis and Boultwood, 1966). Prior to 1850 what provision there was for educating the "poorer classes" (Wardle, 1976) was by virtue of the charity schools founded by such organizations as the British and Foreign School Society of 1810 and the national schools established in 1811. The origins of popular education in this country are ensconced in these charity schools, which were formed as a direct consequence of the eighteenth and nineteenth centuries' "Age of Philanthropy." Throughout Britain the clergy initiated schooling as a means of carving out their evangelical crusade. While the government began subsidizing education to a limited degree in the form of treasury grants in 1833, it did not assume the role of instigator for educational provision, and universal free schooling was not implemented until the following century (Armitage, 1964). Instead, different faith groups were instrumental in promoting education with a strong inculcation of religious values (Wolffe, 1994) and they began a tradition in denominational schooling with government funding which has continued to the present day, for example those based on Judaism.

Jewish Schools

The Jewish education system can be traced back to the mid-seventeenth century, when day school education was established along with synagogues. This followed the readmission of Jews into England in 1656 (Romain, 1985) and the establishment of Jewish day schools, notably the Creechurch Lane

"Talmud Torah School" in 1657 (Black, 1998). The importance of education within the Jewish tradition goes back much further, however: "when Jacob and his family journeyed to Egypt, his son Judah was sent on ahead to establish a house of training" (Genesis 46: 28). The establishment of Jewish schools such as the "Jews Free School" in 1732 helped to support the need of an educated workforce (Black, 1998). Simultaneously, the Christian Sunday School Movement opened schools close to the early Jewish settlements. Accordingly, within some Jewish communities, "there was great concern that these children would be at risk of losing their Jewish heritage and identity, through compulsory study of Christianity and the New Testament" (Miller, 2001, p. 502).

Such was the perceived threat of missionary zeal by Anglicans that, by 1850, Jewish schools were established in all areas across the country where there were Jewish communities. Financial support was not automatic, however, as the government of the day was not persuaded that "the religious requirements of the Jewish schools closely matched their own" and so state funding was withheld, as it had been initially withheld from Catholic schools (Miller, 2001, pp. 508–509).

Changes were brought about by the work of a pressure group under the leadership of Sir Moses Montefiore. In 1853, the Manchester Jews' School received state funding, putting the Jewish schools on an equal basis for the first time with other denominational schools (Miller, 2001).

A wave of immigration from the 1880s to the First World War resulted in large numbers of Jews arriving from Eastern Europe. This contributed to an increase in the community to around 100,000 Jews living in England, which carried with it obvious implications for the education system (Miller, 2001). The influx helped sustain pupil numbers in the Jewish voluntary schools and in some cases caused an increase (see also Gartner, 1960; Black, 1998). However, the balance increasingly shifted away from attendance at Jewish voluntary schools to the board schools. For example, in 1880, nearly 60 percent of Jewish school-age children were in Jewish schools (Black, 1998), but by 1911 there was less than 25 percent (Miller, 2001). Assimilation rather than integration became more prevalent:

> Judaism became something that happened at home—maybe through the marking of the Sabbath and major festivals . . . as well as keeping the Jewish dietary laws, and the supplementary schools were increasingly expected to provide a Jewish education which had decreasing connection to the lives that the pupils were in practice leading outside the Synagogue classes.
>
> (Miller, 2001, p. 505)

The reason for this demise in Jewish schools was due in part to the ideology and process of integration, which was seized upon by many Jews and other immigrants as a way out of poverty. As such:

acceptance of the Jewish children into an Anglicised way of life meant far more than learning how to speak English. It also included teaching the young people to adapt to English usage in speech and in manner, in culture and in principles, in such a way as to enable them to integrate successfully into the wider English community.

(Miller, 2001, p. 503)

The system of "supplementary" education has existed alongside day schools and different ethnic groups have used this approach as a way of maintaining their own cultural heritage (see, for example, Hall *et al.*, 2002). For Jewish children, this tended to take the form of classes three or four times a week with lessons in Hebrew, Yiddish, and Jewish knowledge. Statistically, 360 centers were established by 1942, accommodating 10,500 pupils, and this number was augmented by the progressive Jewish movements, which coordinated a separate system for over 2,000 children (Miller, 2001). The Reform Synagogues for Great Britain, the Masorti, and the Union of Liberal and Progressive Synagogues are generally known by the umbrella term "progressive movements," as opposed to orthodox or ultra orthodox (Miller and Shire, 2002). As such it would be more correct to talk about different Jewish communities that provide support for the development of a range of Jewish faith-based schools. Due to immigration there is also now a rich cultural heritage from different European communities, most notably the Ashkenazi (European Jews) and the Sephardi (Middle Eastern Jews).

Research has demonstrated the importance of these influences on families, whether from orthodox or progressive communities, in interpreting the process of nurture in the Jewish tradition (Jackson, 1979; Diamant and Cooper, 1991). As with many faiths there are differences in interpretation and adherence to religious texts and communities can loosely be placed on a spectrum from what can be called "orthodox" to "liberal." (For more on this theme see Borowitz (1985) and Gillman (1993).) Where individuals and communities position themselves on this spectrum is governed in part by a test of adherence to the "halacha" or the rules. In terms of schools, therefore, the question "what is a Jew?" is as important a question as "what is a Jewish school?" Once you establish the former, you people the institution accordingly (see Marmur, 1994).

Support for more Jewish schools came from the Jewish Educational Trust. The chief rabbi of the United Synagogue, Lord Jakobovits, spearheaded this in 1971, with the aim of raising the profile of Jewish education within its own community (Sacks, 1994). Numbers have increased in recent times and statistically it is calculated that there are now over 250 supplementary and day schools altogether (Schmool and Cohen, 1998), ninety of which provide full-time education (*Times Educational Supplement*, 2003) and thirty-two are in receipt of voluntary-aided funding (Department for Education and Skills,

2004). In their study of Jewish institutions, Schmool and Cohen (2000, p. 21) reported there were nine reform day schools, seven Zionist day schools, twenty-four strictly orthodox day schools and seventy mainstream orthodox day schools. Miller and Shire (2002) gave the number of primary day schools supported by reform, liberal and Masorti movements as three, which accounts for 5 percent of Jewish children in day schools and there are, in addition, nine nursery schools supported by these groups. In 2000, the number of children aged 4–19 years receiving full-time Jewish education had increased to 22,650, representing 55 percent of the total number of Jewish children in the UK (Rocker, 2000). However, these schools differ considerably in their engagement with other religious communities and other faith-based schools. Short (2003) conducted a study of the way Jewish schools approach cultural diversity. He found that, at primary level, particularly among those schools established by the progressive rather than the orthodox communities, there was a willingness to engage with other religious communities and other faith-based schools. Conversely, at secondary level he reported that only one out of the five schools in the study incorporated multicultural education and the teaching of other faiths with any degree of seriousness. This illustrates the concern that cultural sustainability prevents integration or mutual understanding.

There has also been a growing conviction by Jewish communal and educational leaders that the continuity of Jewish cultural life is dependent on the perpetuation of intensive Jewish education (Schmool and Cohen, 1998; Miller, 2001). Full-time Jewish education is seen as having the advantage of "thickening" (Alexander, 1995) or intensifying links with Judaism. As such, enculturation into Judaism and the possibilities for "thick" Judaism to occur are vastly increased and children may leave primary and secondary school with "a strong sense and secure understanding of who they are in Jewish terms and how they relate to both the Jewish and secular worlds" (Miller, 2001, p. 507). There is scope within the curriculum in full-time Jewish schooling for the teaching of Hebrew, the centrality of Jewish texts, life cycle, festivals and Shabbat, prayer values, and knowledge of Israel. One governing principle is that pupils are raised to contribute at the highest level to British life in general and to Jewish life in particular (Miller, 2001).

The "secular" curriculum in Jewish schools tends to reflect that of the British National Curriculum and some part of the day is concerned with Jewish heritage. There are also cross-over points or overlapping issues, but basically the aim is to provide a Jewish education and this is reflected in the choice of curriculum such as non-contact sports and single-sex instruction for sports and sex education according to the principles of "sneeut" or modesty. Along with other schools, Jewish institutions are open to scrutiny and accountability: assessment is from inside in the form of a "pikuach" inspection conducted through the Jewish community and in keeping with the Education Act (1988) governing religious as opposed to secular inspection.

In the post-1950s era there has been further migration, this time from Asia and Africa in particular. Next we look at the growth of Muslim schools emerging from these communities, that is those established in the last 20 years, which mainly serve the children of first- or second-generation immigrants and which have also been involved in sustaining cultural heritage.

Muslim Schools

There has been little research conducted on the private sector of education and religious schooling in Britain, and Walford (2001) noted that "none has examined Muslim schools as a specific group" (p. 9). There is also the difficulty here of providing an adequate historical lens given the relatively recent immigration of Muslim groups. As such, in this discussion I draw on my own research in this field and that of small, individual studies which have explored Muslim schooling (Parker-Jenkins, 1990, 1991, 1995, 2002; Osler and Hussain, 1995; Parker-Jenkins and Haw, 1996; Hewer, 2001; Parker-Jenkins *et al.*, 2002, 2004; Walford, 2002).

The history of Muslim schooling in Britain has been associated with the struggle for parity with other faith schools, along the lines of that afforded to Anglican, Catholic, and Jewish institutions. As Hewer (2001) noted, there have been Muslims in Britain for centuries, but issues of accommodation within the educational system did not arise until the post-1950s migration period. In addition, the obstacles Muslim communities have faced have been magnified because their supporters are predominantly representative of minority ethnic groups and this wave of immigration raises "complex issues of colour, race and religion" (Hewer, 2001, p. 515).

Muslims are the largest religious minority in Britain, followed by Jews, Hindus, and Sikhs (Weller, 1997). Today, the "official" number of Muslims in Britain is given as just over 1.5 million based on the 2001 census returns (Weller, 2003). Among this number there are variations based not only on national grounds but also on sectarian differences. The general public is probably aware of the Sunni and Shiite sects among adherents to Islam, especially since recent events in the Middle East, but this oversimplifies the Muslim communities since there are other major sectarian divisions (Joly, 1989; Robinson, 1988; Lewis, 1994).

Sarwar (1994) calculated that around 500,000 of the Muslims in Britain are children of compulsory school age and this figure is likely to increase. The Association of Muslim Schools suggests a figure of around 350,000 pupils who are predominantly of Pakistani, Bangladeshi, Indian, and Somali backgrounds (Idris Sears of the Association of Muslim Schools, September 23, 2003).

There are implications in terms of educational policy at the local and national levels and, Hewer (2001) noted that "the Muslim population of

Britain will at least double before it reaches demographic stability" (p. 516) (see also Ballard and Kalra, 1994).

The ideal environment to promote the Muslim identity and faith is believed by some to be within a separate school system, a view shared by other faith-based groups. Islam is not simply a world religion but is also regarded as an all-embracing way of life, requiring submission to God or Allah and adherence to religious principles that lead to harmony and happiness in the hereafter or afterlife (Ashraf, 1993). Education begins in the home before formal education at school and parents see their role in this matter as a duty and a privilege to ensure their children develop an Islamic consciousness (Haneef, 1979). There is also a focus on preserving the tenets of Islam within the context of the "ummah" or community, rather than as an independent nuclear or single unit.

In all aspects of life, Muslims are provided with guidance through religious texts and community interpretation of the Holy Scriptures (Sara, 1992). It is from the Koran that the words "Muslim" and "Islam" are used and five basic duties are practised by Muslims, known as "the five pillars of Islam" (Sarwar, 1992). In many matters of life Muslims describe things as being "halal," which means permissible or "haram," which means forbidden (Sarwar, 1994). This distinction is used with regard to food, behaviour, and social activities and helps shape an Islamic consciousness in the young. For supporters of Muslim schools, the curriculum, both formal and hidden, should ideally reflect an Islamic orientation (Anwar, 1982; Hulmes, 1989; Modood et al., 1997) and it is argued that the rights and duties of Muslim children are supported best within these schools (Haneef, 1979).

Generally, the curriculum has been defined as a transmission of "culture" (Lawton, 1980). Within Muslim schools there is a desire to emphasize an Islamic culture and see this embedded in the teaching and ethos of the school (Parker-Jenkins, 1995). Furthermore, education is seen as a driving force in Muslim communities, amply supported by Islamic texts such as "No gift among all the gifts of a father to his child is better than education" (The Haddith, sayings of the Prophet). As such, the "refracting" of all knowledge and skills acquired in secular subjects takes place through the "optics" of the Islamic religion.

For some people the term "Islamic school" better describes institutions that develop a school along the lines of Koranic scriptures. Within such schools there are no areas of the curriculum that are essentially "secular" subjects, as every area of study should be taught from an Islamic perspective. There is therefore an underlying, distinctive epistemology: "the relation of all created beings and things is given and immutable" (Hewer, 2002, p. 522). In addition, modesty in attire forms an important part of the dress code, as we saw in the development of some Jewish schools and, although provision has been made for this in community schools, there are still cases of Muslim girls being prevented from wearing the hijab or head covering (*Times Educational*

Supplement, 2002a). (See also www.muhajabah.com/islamicblog/veiled4alla hphp.) Objection by schools to the wearing of the hijab has also taken place in France and Germany because it is seen as a political as well as a religious symbol (*Times Educational Supplement*, 2002b).

It is calculated that full-time Muslim schools, both independent and state funded, provide education for around 1 percent of an approximate population of 300,000–500,000 Muslim pupils in Britain (Berliner, 1993; Sarwar, 1994; Association of Muslim Schools, 2003). Varying in number from approximately five to 1,800 on their rolls, Muslim schools coincide with the establishment of Muslim communities around the country, such as the London, Leicester, and Dewsbury areas. Relying on community support, they are seldom purpose built and instead operate above a mosque or in disused schools, invariably connected to one or more mosques based on sectarian divisions, as mentioned earlier. They are also established in homes and similar buildings by concerned parents and community leaders (Hewer, 2001). In some areas of Manchester, for example, parents are also opting for all-Muslim nurseries because they wish to reinforce their children's sense of religious identity (Holmes *et al.*, 2002).

The first independent Muslim school was established in 1979 (Dooley, 1991) and, presently, there are over 100 in Britain, which serve the needs of children whose parents are financially able and willing to pay (Association of Muslim Schools, 2004). The Association of Muslim Schools, which was formed in 1992 to provide coordination and advocacy for these institutions, cites the present number as over 130 which includes two each in Scotland and Wales. All are Sunni, with the exception of one Shia school, which reflects the fact that only 10 percent of the Muslim communities in Britain are Shia (Association of Muslim Schools, 2004). They include a collection of single-sex schools for girls and boys at both the primary and secondary levels and there are also boarding schools and seminaries (Midgeley, 1989; Rafferty, 1991; Association of Muslim Schools, 2004). The thorny issue in granting state aid to Muslim schools has been that, unlike previous denominations, this new group has been perceived as predominantly a "visible minority." Furthermore, these schools have been criticized as potentially creating education ghettos and developing a situation in which diversity is unhealthy, as argued in the aftermath of the Oldham riots and the terrorist attacks of September 11, 2001 in America (*Times Educational Supplement*, 2002c). They have, however, received royal endorsement: during a visit to the Islamia School, Prince Charles paid a similar tribute, saying "I really do believe that the Islamia school is an important model. You are ambassadors for a much-misunderstood faith. You have much to tell people in a secular society like ours" (*British Muslims Monthly Survey*, 2000, p. 1).

The decision to provide state funding for this group of schools now serves as a milestone, as Muslims in Britain have seen their previous applications rejected in the context of increasing "Islamophobia" (Dialogue, 1997; Runnymede Trust, 1997) and fear of "fundamentalism" (Yuval-Davis, 1992).

Statistically, there are now five Muslim schools that are state funded, under the voluntary-aided category, along with approximately 5,000 Anglican, 2,000 Catholic, thirty-two Jewish, two Sikh, one Greek Orthodox, and one Seventh Day Adventist schools (Valley, 1995), which fall under the voluntary-aided and voluntary-controlled headings (Department for Education and Skills, 2003). It would be wrong to assume, however, that support for and against separate Muslim schools falls entirely along ethnic lines because, as in other religious groups, there are wide differences of opinion on this issue.

So far we have looked at Jewish and Muslim schools, their commitment to community, and cultural and religious continuity. It is this shared concern of achieving cultural sustainability that forms the basis of the next section.

Achieving Cultural Sustainability?

From the discussion so far we can see that what both Jewish and Muslim schools have in common is a commitment to community and a strong sense of religious values and traditions. Their shared concerns of community and cultural sustainability are evident in the way they have sought to establish their educational institutions and to foster a particular ethos at home and school. Here we look more closely at the meaning of "community" and "culture" and the significance of these concepts for Jewish and Muslim schools. We also look at the allegation that these schools infringe children's rights via indoctrination and propagandizing and that they foster divisiveness within society as a whole. This leads to consideration of the need for updated and refined theoretical models to articulate adequately the overlapping issues of religious/ethnic identity and the constructed, emergent, and strategic nature of ethnicity today.

Community and Culture

The significance of "community" in the lives of individuals and families, and the impact of culture in shaping values have been themes permeating our discussion so far. Ideologies of assimilation and integration in Britain are seen to reduce and undermine cultural heritage within communities and dilute cultural identity. The importance of strong relationships between teachers, parents, and pupils in securing educational gains is well documented (Bastiani, 1989; Wolfendale, 1992). However, it is important to recognize that "culture" is also likely to impact on the effectiveness of strategies employed to achieve this (Bhatti, 1999).

Taylor *et al.* (2002) stated that the concept of "community" conjures particular images, such as a subcultural community that is sharing values of the wider society but in addition maintaining possession of its own cultural identity. Communities are also important for providing an alternative and empowering space outside the national public sphere (Bourdieu, 1985), for dissent and the mobilizing of social movements (Gilroy, 1993). Sociologists have provided many explanations of "community," but the variety of definitions normally consist of three themes: a social system or set of relations, a fixed locality, and the quality of relationships or "spirit" of a community (Newby, 1980). This would be true of both Jewish and Muslim schools established in Britain. A further aspect of the creation of a strong or cohesive community is the involvement of particular organizations such as the mosque or synagogue in terms of providing a focal point for group cohesiveness. Importantly, noted Werbner (2002), "ethnic and religious movements resemble other new social movements ... in fostering alternative identities and lifestyles which are submerged in the invisible spaces diasporic groups create for themselves" (p. 16). Occasionally, communities mobilize on a large scale as, for example, that of British Muslims in response to the Rushdie affair. In this instance there may be an invigorating and renewing sense of identity within the community as a result of political activity.

By culture we mean "a system of beliefs and practices in terms of which a group of human beings understand, regulate and instruct their individual and collective lives" (Parekh, 2000, p. 34). For some groups, such as Jews and Muslims, many of these beliefs and practices are influenced by their religious affiliation. Religion is commonly interpreted by the United Nations' declaration as being broad in scope rather than the narrowness of historical interpretation and it incorporates freedom of "thought and conscience." The word "faith," which has been used throughout our discussion, is often used by religious groups themselves and refers to a way of life rather than a hierarchical structure. (We should note, however, that it is a Western term and is less commonly used, for example, in Eastern religions.) Faith, identity, and culture are inter-related with subtle layers of meaning and different groups maintain "cultural heritage" differently. Individuals may feel that in some way they are involved in a "trade-off," whereby they are expected to choose parts of religion and not change what they are but change what they do at certain times. This has direct implications for children at school, for example and is a reason why some families opt for faith-based education. There is perceived to be a difficulty at times of secular educationalists understanding religious educationalists and vice versa, in some cases challenging whether there is any place for religion in school. But this is to oversimplify the situation: there are secular teachers of religion and the place of religious education in the school timetable is not contested or undermined in all community schools. Further, despite the differences between religious and secular teachers, there tends to be a shared consensus on the critical place of moral values in the educational process and, understandably, those responsible for community schools in Britain and elsewhere are offended by the assumption that this may be absent in their schools.

Indoctrination and Propagandizing

In school, children have the right to receive education in matters of religion or belief that is in conformity with the wishes of their parents (The European Convention on Human Rights and Fundamental Freedoms). The child should also have access to education that protects against intolerance and encourages a respect for the beliefs of others (for more on this theme see British Humanist Association, 2002). The United Nations Convention on the Rights of the Child stipulates that there must be respect for the child's right to freedom of thought, conscience, and religion as the child gets older. Schools in particular are the place where differences in religion and values come into play. Very importantly, schools have assumed a major responsibility for inculcating ideas of citizenship, which may conflict with the expectations of parents. Accordingly, "for the immigrants and ethnic minorities, the school is a threat at the very same time as it is a necessity" (Nielsen, 1995, p. 8). It is this perceived subversion of core values in society in general and in schools specifically that can be the source of tension.

Some of the accusations aimed at Muslim schools, however, have been that they are engaged in "propagandizing" and "indoctrination" or imbuing with one opinion only and teaching "fundamentalism," not as a return to spiritual guidance but in a derogative manner as oppressive of women and as a racist doctrine. Muslim schools counter that, in the climate of Islamophobia, indoctrination is taking place in some community schools. Muslim schools are also accused of failing to deliver a balanced perspective in teaching citizenship (*Times Educational Supplement*, 2005). This is a key point on which Jewish and Muslim schools are perceived differently within a British context, for while there is evidence of anti-Semitism and fears of attacks on Jewish schools (*Times Educational Supplement*, 2003), allegations of fundamentalism are less commonly made of Jewish schools, nor are they seen as a threat to social harmony in the way that Muslim schools are purported to be by some elements of the media and political establishment. In short, the expansion of Muslim schools has been perceived as inimical to the welfare of society in general, yet these institutions claim they are misunderstood and that they are carrying out their legal right to perpetuate their cultural heritage and identity.

Theoretical Paradigms

It is not always clear whether religion or ethnicity is the dominant characteristic affecting people's understanding of themselves and their personal sense of identity. With particular reference to Muslim communities, it was found in a study into religious discrimination in Britain that they "suffer from colour, racial, ethnic and religious discrimination" because "racists cannot analyse between race and religion" (Weller, 2001, p. 13). Minority ethnic communities and their faith-based schools do not fit easily into current theoretical paradigms, particularly as they relate to the construction of identity. There is a need for theoretical and methodological innovation to articulate clearly differing accounts of the issues regarding equal opportunity within a multicultural setting. Researching into diversity and disadvantage for the Policy Studies Institute, Modood *et al.* (1997) found in their survey that most of the second generation South Asians, for example, were uncomfortable with the idea of "British" being anything more than "a legal title": in particular, they felt that "the majority of white people did not accept them because of their race or cultural background" (p. 331).

Also of relevance to this discussion on the theorizing of multiculturalism is the work of Gilroy (1993). He challenged general assumptions underpinning anti-racist policy and examined shifting notions of race, nation, and power and the failure of the British Government on both sides of the political spectrum to articulate anti-racism in a manner that is inclusive. Echoing Giroux's view (1992) that there are no fixed boundaries, Gilroy (1993) maintained that "the culture which defines the groups we know as races, is never fixed, finished or final. It is fluid, it is actively and continually made and re-made" (p. 80). In challenging existing paradigms on identity, therefore, we need to be aware of broader and more dynamic concepts of culture and ethnicity for, as Modood (1989) argued,

> [N]either Muslims nor other religious–ethnic minorities will be understood unless current race philosophies are re-evaluated. The beginning of that understanding is the appreciation of the centrality of religion to the Muslim, and perhaps also to the Sikh and Hindu, psyche: that it is of far more importance and central to self-definition than 'race' or than can be allowed for by the black-white view of the world.
>
> (p. 284)

Or, in terms of equitable treatment, cultural heritage is encouraged "rather than contemptuously expected to whither away" (Modood *et al.*, 1997, p. 358). This is part of the *raison d'être* of both Jewish and Muslim schools in their pursuit of cultural continuity. There is clearly a potential tension here and Modood *et al.* (1997) concluded that change can only come about "through finding and cultivating points of common ground between dominant and subordinate cultures as well as new syntheses and hybridities" (p. 358). The important thing, they maintained, is that the burden of change or the costs of not changing should not be placed on one party only.

The issue of faith-based schools intent on sustaining cultural heritage falls into the category of shifting social and cultural contexts within which religious and ethnic minority individuals and communities operate. Theoretically, we can draw on the perspectives of race, culture, and difference (Donald and Rattansi, 1992), "the politics of difference" (Young, 1990), and on what Modood (1992) referred to as the difficulties of being accepted by the majority group and having limited access to public resources. To add to the complexity of the situation, under the Race Relations Act (2002) it is not illegal to discriminate on the basis of religion *per se*, yet there are overlapping factors of identity that are inclusive of religious, cultural, political, and personal factors. Modood *et al.* (1997) suggested that "There seem to be various forms of prejudice and discrimination which use cultural difference to vilify or marginalize or demand cultural assimilation from groups who also suffer colour racism" (p. 353).

Significantly, communities choose to select a number of ways to respond to racism and xenophobia and, in some cases, noted Werbner (2002), they may "naturalise their multiple identities, vesting them with current value in Britain" (p. 14). For others there is an ongoing struggle to maintain cultural identity despite discrimination in the wider society, as we have seen in the case of Jewish and Muslim school communities. Further, "cultural xenophobia" and "the experience of alien citizenship" (Werbner, 2002, p. 14) mean that individuals in some communities may feel disaffected and marginalized, which we have seen manifested in racist riots, such as in northern towns in England in 2001 (*Guardian*, 2001). In Britain and elsewhere there was a belief that, under the umbrella of "multiculturalism," social inclusion would prevail. This is part of what we now see as a naïve belief in political ideology, which has not been successful in addressing inequality and highlighting the interface between race, ethnicity, and religion in which cultural identity is a perceived cause of disadvantage and is being challenged by minority groups in a variety of ways, such as through children's education. As such, we need to revise some basic categories through which inter-racial, interethnic, and inter-religious relations have been conceptualized so far in order to conceive better ways of uniting the protection of minority identity through education with successful integration of minority people into mainstream social life. We need also to see ethnicity as something which is constructed, dynamic, and, on occasions, strategic rather than simply a "given."

Finally, there is also the issue of minority racism against other minorities and situations such as in Canada, where schools or educators propagate hatred, violating domestic human rights law. This raises the difficult issue of the potential conflicts between multiculturalism, human rights, equality, and peace. On the one hand minority religious and cultural groups need protections to safeguard identities and equal rights to identity and community and, on the other, they can foster divisiveness and antagonism if they in turn ignore attention to multicultural issues in the classroom.

The Way Forward

There are a number of steps countries could take to ensure a balanced and fair accommodation of cultural sustainability.

1. Develop alternative theoretical models to guide practice and more broadly defined and inclusive of issues of identity, racism, acculturation, and assimilation.
2. Update and refine law that reflects the reality and complexity of community identity to avoid having a black/white polarized version of the world or the privileging of certain groups. Where the law protects religious identity, such as for Jews and Sikhs, this could be extended to other faith-based groups, such as Muslims to ensure equal treatment before the law.
3. Recognize that, despite the best efforts of community schools, some groups who define themselves on religious/ethnic grounds will wish to sustain cultural identity both within and beyond their own community.
4. Distribute public funds fairly to school communities, but also ensure a level of accountability for schools to have a balanced curriculum, encourage outreach to other groups, and ensure that they themselves are required to refrain from fostering racism rather than respect for cultural diversity.

Conclusion

The tradition of establishing faith-based schools has been taken up by Jewish and Muslim groups in Britain in order to create their own institutions as a vehicle for cultural continuity in the face of perceived homogenizing and hegemonic forces. The *raison d'être* of these schools is to sustain minority cultural identity. This is through mechanisms of identity formation and reproduction, which are felt to have no place in mainstream educational institutions. As such, these faith-based schools are felt indispensable by both Jewish and Muslim groups in order to respect minority identities. Rather less attention, however, has been given to the negative effects from separate, faith-based schooling, especially in terms of their auto- or self-segregation and the fact that they constitute a serious challenge to the "ideology" of multi-culturalism as it is functioning in Britain. To this extent, we should pose questions as to whether more should be asked of these schools, especially those funded by the state. More specifically, in terms of implications for policy and practice, state funding could be tied more closely to the monitoring of legal limits on the curriculum and teaching to ensure that they accord with the overall values and principles of human rights, democracy, mutual respect, and the rule of law. This exists in some of these schools already, but needs to be made more explicit with legal underpinning to prevent recalcitrance by governments who are too eager to solicit and appease the "ethnic voter" and too reluctant to engage adequately in what education should mean for all children.

Resources and Tools for Educators

Questions

1. How do faith-based schools relate to different religious schools and to non-religious schools?
2. How are the rights of the child, as opposed to those of the parents, accommodated in faith-based schools, particularly with regard to access to knowledge of different religious and cultural groups?
3. What pedagogical choices do Muslim and Jewish teachers need to make to help their pupils experience and interact with a plural society?

Further Resources

Useful websites and resource centres for educationalists include 1001 Inventions, which is a website providing accessible knowledge of the Islamic contribution to such things as calligraphy, science, technology, and medicine and Liberty and Human Rights Information.

Resources and publications on Jewish education are available at The Leo Baeck Centre College for Jewish Education, 80 East End Road, Finchley, London N3 2SY, U.K.

Suggestions for Educators

1. Introduce a policy of "twinning" schools so staff and other members of a school community can communicate with those outside of their religious/cultural context.
2. Provide meaningful opportunities for pupils to correspond with pupils of a school different from their own in terms of culture or religion, using e-mail and other aspects of technology.
3. Develop a curriculum on "citizenship" that demonstrates the multiple senses of identity an individual can assume based on local, regional, international, and global factors.

Bibliography

Alexander, H. (1995). *Jewish education and the search for authenticity: A study of Jewish identity.* Los Angeles: University of Judaism.

Anwar, M. (1982). *Young Muslims in a multicultural society: Their needs and policy implications.* Leicester: The Islamia Foundation.

Archer, L. (2001). Muslim brothers, black boys, traditional Asians: British Muslim young men's construction of 'race', religion and masculinity. *Feminism and Psychology, 11*(1), 79–105.

Armitage, W. H. G. (1964). *Four hundred years of education.* London: Cambridge University Press.

Ashraf, A. S. (1993). The role of Muslim youth in a multi-religious society. *Muslim Educational Quarterly, 11*(2), 3–13.

Association of Muslim Schools. (2003). *Muslim schools in Britain.* Birmingham: Association of Muslim Schools.

Association of Muslim Schools in Britain (2004). AMS, 5 Bishopsgate Street, Edgbaston, Birmingham B15 1ET.

Ballard, R. & Kalra, V. S. (1994). *The ethnic dimension of the 1991 census: A preliminary report.* Manchester: Manchester University Press.

Barrell, G. & Partington, J. (1970). *Teachers and the law* (6th edn). London: Methuen.

Bastiani, J. (1989). *Working with parents: A whole school approach.* Windsor: NFER-Nelson.

Berliner, W. (1993). Muslims stand their ground. *Education Guardian,* 23 March, pp. 6–7.

Bhatti, G. (1999). *Asian children at home and at school.* London: Routledge.

Black, J. (1998). *JFS: The history of the Jews' Free School. London since 1732.* London: Tymsder Publishers.

Borowitz, E. (1985). *Explaining reform Judaism.* New York: Behrman House.

Bourdieu, P. (1985). The social space and the genesis of groups. *Theory and Society, 14,* 723–744.

Bradney, A. (1993). *Fractured identities: Changing patterns of inequality,* Cambridge: Polity Press.

British Humanist Association. (2002). *A better way forward.* London: British Humanist Association.

British Muslims Monthly Survey. (2000). Prince Charles visits Isalmia. *British Muslims Monthly Survey, 8*(5), 1–2.

Curtis, S. J. & Boultwood, M. E. (1966). *An introductory history of education since 1800* (4th edn). London: University Tutorial Press.

Department for Education and Skills. (2003). *Aiming high: Raising the achievement of minority ethnic pupils.* London: Department for Education and Skills.

Dialogue. (1997). The challenge of Islamophobia, November. London: Public Affairs Committee for Shi'a Muslims, Stone Hall, Chevening Road, London NW6 6TN.

Diamant, A. & Cooper, H. (1991). *Living a Jewish life.* New York: HarperCollins.

Donald, J. and Rattansi, A.(Eds.) (1992). *Race, culture and difference.* London: Sage.

Dooley, P. (1991). Muslim private schools. In G. Walford (Ed.), *Tradition, change and diversity.* London: Paul Chapman.

Gartner, L. (1960). *The Jewish immigrant in England 1870–1914.* London: Wayne State University Press.

Giddens, A. (1995). *Politics, sociology and social theory: Encounters with classical and contemporary social thought.* Cambridge: Polity Press.

Giddens, A. (2001). *Sociology* (4th edn). Cambridge: Polity Press.

Gillman, N. (1993). *Conservative Judaism.* New York: Behrman Press.

Gilroy, P. (1987). *There ain't no Black in the Union Jack.* London: Hutchinson.

Gilroy, P. (1993) *The Black Atlantic: Modernity and double consciousness.* London: Verso.

Giroux, H. A. (1992) *Border Crossings.* New York: Routledge.

Guardian (2001). Mean streets divided. *Guardian,* 12 December, p. 5.

Hall, S., Ozerk, K., Zulfiqar, M., & Tan, J. (2002). This is our school: Provision, purpose and pedagogy of supplementary schools in Leeds and Oslo. *British Educational Research Journal, 28*(3), 399–418.

Haneef, S. (1979). *What everyone should know about Islam and Muslims.* Lahore: Kazi Publications.

Hewer, C. (2001). Schools for Muslims. *Oxford Review of Education, 27*(4), 515–528.

Holmes, R., Jones, L., & McCreery, E. (2002). *The phenomenon of Muslim-only nurseries: Why are parents choosing them?* Paper presented at the Faith Schools: Consensus or Conflict Conference, Institute of Education, University of London.

Hulmes, E. (1989). *Education and cultural diversity.* London: Longman.

Jackson, R. (1979). *Religious education and an interpretive approach.* London: Hodder and Stroughton.

Joly, D. (1989). *Muslims in Europe, ethnic minorities and education in Britain: Interaction between the Muslim community and Birmingham schools.* Research Paper No. 41. Birmingham: Centre for the Study of Islam and Christian-Muslim Relations.

Lawton, D. (1980). *The politics of the school curriculum.* London: Routledge and Kegan Paul.

Lewis, P. (1994). *Islamic Britain: Religion, politics and identity among British Muslims.* London: I B Tauris.

Marmur, D. (1994). *On being a Jew.* Toronto: Holy Blossom.

Midgeley, S. (1989). Muslims turn to separate schools to preserve Islamic faith. *Independent*, 20 January, p. 9.

Miller, H. (2001). Meeting the challenges: The Jewish schooling phenomenon in the UK. *Oxford Review of Education*, 27(4), 501–513.

Miller, H. & Shire, M. J. (2002). *Jewish schools—A value added contribution to faith based education.* London: Leo Baeck Centre–College for Jewish Education.

Moodod, T. (1989). Religious anger and minority rights. *Political Quarterly*, July, pp. 280–284.

Modood, T., Berthoud, R., Lakey, J., Nazoo, J., Smith, P. *et al.* (1997). *Ethnic minorities in Britain: Diversity and disadvantage.* London: Policy Studies Institute.

Moodod, T. (1992). *Not easy being British: Culture and citizenship.* Stoke-on-Trent: Trentham Books.

National Union of Teachers. (1984). *Religious education in a multifaith society: A discussion paper.* London: National Union of Teachers.

Newby, H. (1980). *Rural Sociology.* London: Sage Publications.

Nielsen, J. S. (1995). *Muslims in Europe.* Edinburgh: Edinburgh University Press.

Osler, A. & Hussain, Z. (1995). Parental choice and schooling: Some factors influencing Muslim mothers' decisions about the education of their daughters. *Cambridge Journal of Education*, 25(3), 327–347.

Parekh, B. (2000). *Rethinking multiculturalism: Cultural diversity and political theory.* Basingstoke: Macmillan Press.

Parker-Jenkins, M. (1990). Accommodating Muslim needs. *Canadian School Executive*, 10(5), 13–19.

Parker-Jenkins, M. (1991). Muslim matters: An exploration of the educational needs of Muslim children. *New Community: Journal of Research and Policy of Ethnic Relations*, July, 569–582.

Parker-Jenkins, M. (1995). *Children of Islam.* Stoke-on-Trent: Trentham Books.

Parker-Jenkins, M. (2002). Equal access to state funding: The case of Muslim schools. *Race, Ethnicity and Education*, 5(3), 273–289.

Parker-Jenkins, M. & Haw, K. (1996) Equality within Islam, not without it: The perspectives of Muslim girls. *Muslim Educational Quarterly*, 3, 17–34.

Parker-Jenkins, M., Hartas, D. & Irving, B. (2002). Choice and opportunity: Supporting Muslim girls; Career aspirations. In H. Jawad & T. Benn (Eds.), *Muslim women in the UK and beyond: Experiences and images.* Leiden-Boston: Brill.

Parker-Jenkins, M., Hartas, D. & Irving, B. (2004). *In good faith: Schools, religion and public funding.* Aldershot: Ashgate.

Rafferty, F. (1991). Muslim boarding schools planned. *Times Educational Supplement*, 6 December, p. 5.

Robinson, F. (1988). *Varieties of South Asian Islam.* Research paper 8. Centre for Ethnic Relations, Warwick: Warwick University.

Rocker, S. (2000). Jewish schools on an unstoppable roll. *Jewish Chronicle*, 15 December.

Romain, J. (1985). *The Jews of England.* London: Michael Goulston Educational Foundation.

Rowe, J. (1992). The citizenship as a moral agent—The development of a continuous and progressive conflict-based citizenship curriculum. *Curriculum*, 13(3), 23–36.

Runnymede Trust. (1997) *Islamophobia: A challenge for us all.* London: Runnymede Trust.

Sacks, J. (1994). *Will we have Jewish grandchildren?* London: Valentine Mitchell.

Sarwar, G. (1992). *Islam beliefs and teachings* (4th edn). London: London Muslim Educational Trust.

Sarwar, G. (1994). *British Muslims and schools.* London: London Muslim Educational Trust.

Schmool, M. & Cohen, F. (1998). *A profile of British Jewry: Patterns and trends at the turn of the century.* London: Board of Deputies of British Jews.

Short, G. (2003). Faith schools and social cohesion: Opening up the debate. *British Journal of Religious Education*, 25(2), 129–141.

Taylor, P., Richarson, J., Yeo, A., Marsh, I., Trobe, K. *et al.* (2002). *Sociology in focus.* Ormskirk, Lancashire: Causeway Press.

Times Educational Supplement. (2001a). Faith bid sparks commons rebellion. *Times Educational Supplement*, 8 February, p. 6.

Times Educational Supplement. (2001b). Schools accused of racial segregation. *Times Educational Supplement*, 22 June, p. 3.

Times Educational Supplement. (2001c). Is greater diversity healthy? *Times Educational Supplement*, 3 August, p. 13.

Times Educational Supplement. (2002a). Muslim scarf banned. *Times Educational Supplement*, 19 July, p. 12.

Times Educational Supplement. (2002b). Dark ages ban on Muslim scarf. *Times Educational Supplement*, 13 December, p. 10.

Times Educational Supplement. (2002c). Faith bid sparks commons rebellion. *Times Educational Supplement*, 8 February, p. 6.

Times Educational Supplement. (2003). Jewish schools fearful of attacks. *Times Educational Supplement*, 1 August, p. 3.

Times Educational Supplement. (2005). Fair play in regulating faith sector. *Times Educational Supplement*, 28 January, p. 21.

Valley, C. A. (1995). Managing change in the Seventh Day Adventist Church: An interpretive study of the establishment of the John Loughborough School. Unpublished MBA dissertation, Nottingham University.

Walford, G. (2001). Funding for religious schooling in England and The Netherlands: Can the piper call the tune? *Research Papers in Education, 16*(4), 359–380.

Wardle, D. (1976). *English popular education 1780–1975* (2nd edn). London: Cambridge University Press.

Weller, P. (1997). *Religions in the UK: A multifaith directory*. Derby: Derby University/Multi-Faith Centre.

Weller, P. (2001). Identity politics and the future(s) of religion in the UK: The case of the religion questions in the 2001 census. *Journal of Contemporary Religion, 19*(1), 3–21.

Werbner, P. (2002). *The migrant process: Capital, gifts and offerings among Manchester Muslims*. Oxford: Berg Publishers.

Wolfendale, S. (1992). *Empowering parents and teachers*. London: Cassell.

Wolffe, J. (1994). *The growth of religious diversity: Britain from 1945*. Newcastle: Open University Press.

Wood, A. (1960). *Nineteenth century Britain*. London: Longmans.

Young, I. (1990). *Justice and the politics of difference*. Princeton: Princeton University Press.

Yuval-Davis, N. (1992). Fundamentalism, multiculturalism and women in Britain. In J. Donald & A. Rattansi (Eds.), *Race, culture and difference*. London: Sage Publications.

CHAPTER 4

Education and Cultural Sustainability for the Minority People in China: Challenges in the Era of Economic Reform and Globalization

JING LIN

Forgoing ideological dogmatism for economic pragmatism and pushing for modernization through education and the development of science and technology, China has registered double-digit growth in gross domestic product (GDP) for nearly two decades since the policy of economic reform and opening to the world was adopted in 1978. As the country's burgeoning economy is merging with the trend of globalization, the country is also culturally, socially, and politically engaging in global interactions. In the era of rapid domestic and international transformation, minority cultures are meeting majority culture (in China, the Han culture) and global culture more intensively and extensively than ever. In this process what will happen to minority cultures that are less advantaged? How can Chinese minorities sustain their distinct cultures while interacting with the mainstream culture and the global trend? In what ways are minority educational institutions trying to deal with the challenges of globalization?

In this chapter we will examine the complex relations of globalization, education, cultural identity, and sustainability of ethnic minorities in China. Will Chinese minority groups be able to continue and sustain their culture in this era of rapid globalization and economic development? The chapter will explore this question and situate the discussion on China's history of minority dependency and the government's policy of assimilation, preferential treatment, and control. The paper will examine efforts for sustaining minority cultures, such as the creation of minority languages, bilingual education, and the current strategy of the Chinese Government for "the Great West Development."

At the level of primary and secondary education, we will examine minority cultural sustainability in the context of low economic development, poverty, and low access to education. In higher education we will examine the potential consequences of minority universities that are eagerly joining the majority universities to model after "world class universities." We will ponder on this question: what kind of policies and laws are needed to provide sustainable support for minority education? In a word, education for cultural sustainability for the minority groups is carrying more urgency than ever and this chapter will present China as such an example.

Globalization, Minority Culture, and Multiculturalism

Globalization

We are entering the era of globalization. Globalization is characterized by the breaking down of borders in economic activities and cultural exchanges and interactions. Internet technology has opened up great possibilities for people to learn about different cultures. Individuals and groups have migrated to different places and "the ever increasing flows of individuals from myriad backgrounds provide a number of aesthetic, cognitive, social, and marketplace opportunities. The ability to code-switch—to move fluidly between languages and cultures—has obvious social advantages" (Suarez-Orozco, 2004, p. 174).

"Globalization" can mean the following:

1. The formation of a *global village*—closer contact between different parts of the world, with increasing possibilities of personal exchange, mutual understanding, and friendship between "world citizens" and the creation of a *global civilization.*
2. Economic globalization—"free trade" and increasing relations among members of an industry in different parts of the world (globalization of an industry), with a corresponding erosion of *national sovereignty* in the economic sphere. The International Monetary Fund defined globalization as "the growing economic interdependence of countries worldwide through increasing volume and variety of cross-border transactions in goods and services, freer international capital flows, and more rapid and widespread diffusion of technology" (http://en.wikipedia.org/wiki/Globalization).

Marginson (1999) summed up six characteristics of globalization: finance and trade, communications and information technologies, the international movement of people, the formation of global societies, linguistic, cultural and ideological convergence, and, finally, the world system of signs and images.

Globalization has stirred up great urges for countries to develop their economy. Many once isolated regions are becoming targets for "development." The opportunity of connecting local culture with global culture is also greater in that local cultures will be enriched in the plural cultural environment, while indigenous cultures will maintain their distinct characteristics.

Multiculturalism

Globalization requires theories to give us guidelines in the interaction of cultures, especially the interaction between the mainstream culture and marginalized culture. Multiculturalism is a helpful framework for policy makers and educators alike, as it posits the equality of different cultures and celebrates cultural diversity. Multiculturalism is furthermore a value system, which seeks to empower the disadvantaged and bring the marginalized people from the periphery back to the center. The historically excluded and silenced people would have a voice in politics, culture, and economy. Multiculturalism is ultimately about sharing power and recognition and expanding the human community for inclusion (Banks, 1993, 1995; Ghosh, 1996).

Historically and in contemporary societies, not all cultures have enjoyed equal status. Minority cultures, due to historical reasons, have suffered deculturalization (Spring, 1997), colonial assimilation, and the majority's oppression. Due to the lack of economic development in minority regions, they often face the possibility of extinction in the overwhelming influence of the majority culture. Along with their political and cultural oppression, minority economy has been rendered very dependent on the support of the majority, which results in a dependent mentality (Lin, 1993). Minority languages may be developed and bilingual education promoted locally, but their values and usage could be vastly diminished in the dominant influence of the majority language (Lin, 1997).

Globalization and Multiculturalism in China

In China, globalization has been witnessed by China's opening the door to the world to attract foreign investment, which now flows into China in an amount of more than US$1 billion a week: it has been characterized by exchanges of students and scholars, by which more than 800,000 Chinese students and visiting scholars have been sent to study or visit abroad. It is also featured by the adoption of Western management systems in private and public institutions and by emphasis on accountability, rationality, and standardization. Privatization of state-owned enterprises have spilled over to the education system which now has 1.6 million students or more than 10 percent of the university students studying in private higher learning institutions. China becoming a member of the World Trade Organization dramatically symbolizes the country joining the global community. Today, China has become the world's factory: it is estimated that, in 2015, China's GDP will reach U.S.$3 trillion and per capita income will reach $3,000. The fast development has caused people to wonder if the twenty-first century is going to be "the China Century" (*Newsweek*, 2005).

In this dynamic process, local culture is being connected with global culture and languages, habits, values, and even eating habits are greatly transformed. Such changes were powerfully illustrated in Watson's (1997) study of McDonald's in East Asia. In all, as Kang (1998) remarked, "Chinese culture today is moving on a truly universalizing, or globalizing, course. Global capitalism has infiltrated China's cultural landscape not only with its commercial mass culture products, but also with its academic, intellectual products, namely, contemporary Western 'theory'" (p. 178).

While Chinese mainstream culture is connecting with the global culture, the notion of multiculturalism has not been given much attention by the government and scholars. Instead, ethnic nationalism calling for the revival of the Chinese culture and civilization to fulfill a dream of a strong country has been on the rise (S. Zhao, 2004). This lack of attention to multiculturalism has directly reflected on the policies towards the minorities and impacted on the education for the ethnic minorities in China.

In this chapter, we would like to argue that multiculturalism will contribute to China's development and globalization, for it gives the government a powerful framework for addressing social, economic, political, and educational inequalities. In education, multiculturalism would shed light on how school culture can be made relevant to the children and how teachers can make learning a positive experience for minority students (Ladson-Billings, 1992). Minority higher learning institutions would have a powerful framework for repositioning themselves in global cultural interaction. Finally, a multicultural perspective would enable leaders to see that, while the integration of minorities into the developing economy is important, it should not be at the cost of losing local culture and political participation. Overall, multiculturalism as a movement requires deep commitment to an expansive community and a deep conviction that all human beings are equal, which are preconditions for true equality among all people (Greene, 1993; Lin, 2005).

China's Minorities

China has fifty-five minority groups. According to the census of 2000, they comprised 8.4 percent of the population or 106.4 million people, yet they reside in more than 50 percent of China's land. While they coinhabit with the Han majority people, mainly they live in mountainous areas, plateaus, grasslands, and regions where China borders other countries. In the year 2000, the total number of minority primary and secondary schools was 112,000 and students studying in schools reached 19.49 million. Teachers were numbered at 950,000.

Many minority groups in China have a very long history. They have rich and splendid cultural traditions and arts. Some of them have written languages, while others have oral history passed down in songs and stories. Since 1949, the Chinese Government's policy towards the minorities has been characterized by assimilation, control, preferential treatment, and autonomy. In the 1950s provinces with a significant ratio of minority population were named "minority nationality autonomous regions," indicating they would have greater autonomy than other provinces, which would enable the minority people to self-administer their affairs. In the cultural arena, written languages were created for minority groups, Han teachers were sent to teach in minority communities, and minority research institutes were established to study minority culture, language, and customs. During the 1960s and 1970s, especially during the tumultuous years of the Cultural Revolution (1966–1976), like other parts of China, chaos characterized the government and life of minority people, and policies towards the minority people focused on control and assimilation more than anything else.

Since the early 1980s, along with the great shift of policy from political dogmatism to a relaxation of control in society, the government has implemented preferential policies in minority regions to improve its relationship with the minority peoples. For example, quotas are set to promote government officials from the minority groups and minorities are given preferences in terms of admission to universities. While a Han family can have only one child, a minority family can have two children or more. However, these policies are always implemented with the understanding that the minority regions and provinces must always comply with the centralized control of the government. Indeed, local minority government officials have little autonomy in policy making and implementation.

As we have previously mentioned, China's economy has registered close to 10 percent annual growth for more than two decades and in some years the GDP increase was as high as 20 percent, turning China into a fast developing country. However, in the government's strategic plan for economic development, eastern coast and southern China, where the Han majority people concentrate, have been the government's priority in terms of investment and policy preferences, while minority regions largely have been neglected and economic growth in these regions has been much slower. It was not until the year 2000 that the scheme of "Great West Development" was put forward, which aimed to bring regions mainly resided in by the minorities into the major trend of economic development. Since then, attempts aiming at the integration of the minority economy into the national economy have been massive and largely successful. The natural resources of the minority areas are used as national resources more than ever, sometimes to the displeasure of the local people. Commodities made in cities such as Shanghai are more than ever available in the minority areas (Mackerras, 2004).

Despite improvement in people's life overall, vast areas of minority regions are still beset by poverty. Many families could not afford to send their children to school. A telling contrast is that, while first-year enrollment in primary schools has reached 98 percent in most Han-dominant regions, the ratio for minority regions hovers around 50–70 percent. Access to quality primary and secondary education for the minorities and the direction minority higher education is to take would have a direct impact on the sustainability and development of minority culture.

Cultural Sustainability through Primary and Secondary Education

Cultural education and cultural sustainability are inherently connected to educational access, the quality of education, school finance, local economic development, and government polices. What is the overall situation of minority primary and secondary education in China? Since 1986 nine-year compulsory education has been implemented in the country and access to primary education has reached as high as 99 percent for boys and 98 percent for girls. However, for many minority groups having access to primary education is still very difficult: poverty continues to prevent many children, especially girls, from obtaining primary and secondary education.

Education for Minority Girls

Many minority groups live in remote mountainous areas. A large number of people are still living at subsistence level. Thus, going to school is a luxury to many of them. For the Yao people in Guangxi, for example, the tuition fee of 300–500 yuan a year is a huge sum, as their per capital income ranges between 200 and 500 yuan a year. Every year in the province, thousands of girls apply for support from the government and other donors. Many girls are forced to drop out of school due to their family's financial difficulties. These students started in first grade, started to drop out in third grade, and, while several made it to junior high school, only one to two students finished senior high school. A research project found that in the pre-1990s, 90 percent of the students in a Yao community were enrolled in school, yet in 2004 less than 40 percent entered secondary school and continued their study. The Yao people feel it a great waste of money to spend a large slice of their income in educating their children while there is no longer any guarantee of university graduates finding jobs and the large number of layoffs in urban cities convince them that working and living in cities through climbing the ladder of education is no longer a promise for a good life (Huang, 2004).

In another county in Guangxi, the dropout problem has been very gloomy. In a village (Xiang) in 1985 the first grade had 683 students, of whom 272 were girls, but by 1991 when they graduated from primary school only

50 students remained and five of them were girls (Zhou, 2004). The author pointed out that, as teachers' pay was very low, low morale permeated the teaching force. There is, furthermore, a great lack of teachers teaching in subject areas such as English, music, physical education, arts, and vocational education.

Distance has been a factor leading to the low attendance of minority students. A survey in four western provinces revealed that, of the 5,065 students between the ages of 7 and 15 years, 488 of them or 9.6 percent had a walk of 31–59 minutes to school, while 575 students or 11.4 percent had a walk of more than one hour to go to school. The two groups made up 21 percent of all students.

Local governments have provided funding for allowing some students a room and board in school, yet the number of students who can benefit from this convenience is limited. For students living in hard-to-reach areas, teaching points have been set up, where teachers come to teach for one day and go on to the next teaching point the following day. Students would only learn the basics in reading and counting. Furthermore, many minority groups have a tradition of early marriage and, thus, parents believe that education would not make any difference to their daughters—after all they would become members of another family at age 14–15 years.

Bilingual Education

Minority cultural sustainability has been linked with bilingual education in primary and secondary schools. However, persistent difficulties and dilemmas are hampering the efforts of offering bilingual education to minority children.

Mandarin is the most common language in China. Although many minority groups speak Mandarin, some groups function only in their own language. Take Yunnan province as an example. The province has twenty-five minority groups and the minority population stands at 14.13 million, comprising approximately one-third of the province's 42.41 million people. The minorities live on 70 percent of the province's land. Of the twenty-five minority groups, only three use Mandarin, whereas the rest form into three groups: (1) they use their own language as the main communication tool—7 million people fall into this category; (2) they use both Mandarin and their own language or another language; and (3) they have lost their own language and use only Mandarin. The province of Guangxi, where one-third of the population are minorities, has a similar situation.

However, most minority schools use only Mandarin to teach. Although some students have learned Mandarin in their environment, many do not know the language at all. Students have great difficulty learning the subject content and the Mandarin language at the same time when they enter the first grade. As time goes on, their interest in learning drops and dropout ensues. Not knowing Mandarin is one major cause leading to student dropout.

Cultural relevance is essential to retain students in schools and increase their interest and motivation in learning. A common phenomenon among minority primary and secondary schools is that students feel isolated, have difficulty in understanding their teachers, and find it difficult to identify with the culture in the curriculum. The national curriculum talks about highways, museums, and other countries, while local songs, stories, medicinal knowledge, customs, people, economy, and geography are not included in the curriculum.

Yearning to be connected with one's own culture does not mean that minority students do not want to learn the majority culture. In fact, they wish to be able to master both Chinese and their own language, to benefit from the advantage of both cultures. In a survey of 394 students studying in two Tibetan schools and one general school in Gansu, of whom 57.6 percent of the students were Tibetans and 42.4 percent of the students were Han, Tibetan students expressed a strong desire to learn in both Tibetan and Mandarin. The researcher asked one question: what language do you wish the teachers to use in teaching? It emerged that 30.2 percent of the Tibetan students wished to be taught in Tibetan and the reason they gave was that they were Tibetan, Tibetan was their mother language, and they had strong feelings for their own language. However, 60.1 percent of the Tibetan students wanted to be taught in both Chinese and Tibetan, their reason being that knowing both languages was conducive to learning and that knowing both cultures would lead to other opportunities in the future. Overall, 72 percent of the students believed they should master both languages, whereas only 4.2 percent believed it was enough to just learn Tibetan (Wang et al., 1996).

Cultural Bias in the Curriculum

The national curriculum for minority students has the following characteristics.

1. A lot of focus is placed on the mainstream culture and there is a lack of attention to the minority culture. Hence, there is a gap between students' family life and community experience (Wang, 1996). Currently, the language and history textbooks are the national unified textbooks designed by the Ministry of Education. The school curriculum mainly contains the experience, culture, history, and viewpoints of the Han majority and the rich and splendid cultures of the minority people are largely ignored.
2. There is a lack of teaching about multicultural belief. The notions of civilization, history, development, and prosperity, are still largely viewed from the Han majority perspective. This problem has resulted in a lack of respect for the minority cultures and indifference to local cultural differences.

3. There is furthermore a lack of teaching materials for minority students, and readings materials outside of school in their own language are sorely lacking. Bilingual education courses have been mainly used to help primary school students understand the national unified curriculum (Lin, 1997). The examples cited in the national unified textbooks (the Han majority's great poets and those who study hard and contribute greatly to the society) can in fact be replaced by examples relevant to the minority students (Chen, 2004).

Han scholars often express deep concern and worries in examining the educational situation of the minority people. However, when it comes to analyzing the causes for the minorities' low level of education, Han-centric mentality is obvious. For example, the close-knit relationship characterizing some minority groups, enabling them to survive in harsh environments by providing support to each other, is seen as a negative factor against them becoming open-minded and competitive in the new economy. The attitude of minority students for peace and harmony is seen as a disadvantage to learning well in a competitive higher education context. Minority customs, arts, traditions, and behaviors are often not studied with the intention of gaining a profound understanding of minority people's universe view, world view, and epistemology; rather they are lumped together as "primitive" or viewed as "exotic" or "romantic." The rise of tourism turning it into the main engine for economic growth in minority regions is an illustration of this mentality.

Cultural Sustainability and Higher Education Reform

One challenge of minority cultural sustainability is to define the position and location of minority cultures with regard to the majority culture. This is especially so in the domain of higher education. Currently, in every minority province, there is a comprehensive university, a teacher training institute, and a cadre training school at the provincial capital, whereas at prefecture and county levels two to three teacher training institutes exist to prepare teachers for primary and secondary schools. At the national level, there are regional minority universities and, in Beijing, the Central Minority Nationality University.

Following the Soviet model, from the 1950s to the mid-1990s Chinese universities focused on undergraduate students and each university was highly specialized. To "globalize" Chinese universities an amalgamation began, which saw the combination of several specialized universities into a major university offering comprehensive fields of studies. Since 1998, there has been an ongoing campaign for a group of universities to become "world class universities." The models in the mind of policy makers and educators are Harvard and

Stanford, as these universities are considered to represent "world standards" in their academic and research capabilities and in their personnel management. Aligning themselves with "first class" universities, Chinese universities have moved from emphasizing undergraduate education to graduate education and from emphasizing teaching to focusing on research. Programs are combined or reshuffled to reflect trendy areas of research. Teaching in English, adopting foreign textbooks, and promotion of faculty through involving outside scholars, including international experts, are among some of the changes. As major universities in the country are "connecting with the global track," should minority higher learning institutions in the country follow suit? How do they reposition themselves? What are their advantages and disadvantages?

Historically, minority universities are only for minorities in China. They are ranked behind most public universities in social prestige and quality and their focuses have been mainly teacher training and training of government officials for minority regions. The drive towards becoming comprehensive "world class" universities has also forced minority universities to contemplate a shift from a teaching and training focus to become research oriented and to start focusing on graduate education. To become a part of the mainstream, they are contemplating whether they should significantly boost their enrollment of Han majority students in order to be considered a prestigious institution. What will they lose and what will they gain? Can they take this opportunity to reposition themselves so that they maintain the best from their own culture and take advantage of what the majority Han culture and global culture have to offer?

One obvious change in culture in universities in China, including minority universities, is that research and graduate education are becoming the most important indicators for measuring the reputation of a university. Funding agencies by both the government and overseas donors, including foreign foundations such as the Ford foundation, are providing research funding through competition. Simultaneously, there is a significant increase in graduate students. Before 2000, Chinese universities admitted less than 50,000 graduate students annually; however, this figure reached 270,000 in 2003 and 300,000 in 2004.

In this context, minority nationality universities realize that, if they do not undertake similar reforms as the Han majority universities do, they will lose the historical opportunity to exert their place in higher education. The Central Minority Nationality University and minority universities at regional, provincial, and local levels have sought ways of enhancing their cultural sustainability through realigning their strengths in the competition with other institutions.

In order to be accepted as a "research university" and on the road to being a "first class" university, the first measure the top minority universities have adopted is to increase graduate studies in all aspects of minority culture, economy, and society. They have actively rearranged their programs and applied to the Ministry of Education for new programs. In this process, they attempt to establish the subject of ethnology as a plural, independent, and vast field of study. Currently, those master's and doctoral programs already approved by the State Counsel Degree Committee for minority universities include ethnology, ethnic sociology, ethnic anthropology, Marxist ethnic theory and policy, Chinese ethnic minority economy, Chinese ethnic minority language, and those fields related to minority history, arts, education, customs, religion, legal matters, physical education, ethics, tourism, theatre, fashions, etc. Of these subject areas, ethnic economic study is given special attention. The Central National Minority University has a center that receives major funding from the government and sets up different subcenters around the country training graduate students for the economic development of minority regions (Song, 2004). These new courses aim to build minority studies into a professional field, expanding the study of minority culture and upgrading the field not only to be practice oriented but also with a strong focus on research. Meanwhile, the university has also opened new programs on informational technology, environmental science, law, and finance. They allow the major minority universities to move along with other major universities in China to meet the demand of globalization.

The challenges for building "first class programs," producing "first class research," and "giving the society and students first class service" include identifying the direction of a university's programs, forming a strong force of faculty and staff, linking theory with practical needs, and balancing "generality" with the "particularity" of the minority ethnic studies. How to maintain the traditional special focus of these universities while meeting new challenges? Regardless of the overall trend, minority university administrators and scholars believe it is especially critical to link research with the actual problems in the economic and social development of minority nationality regions (Song, 2004), so that they are still the backbone institutions training educated personnel for the minority regions.

Program changes are not enough, for student learning needs to be improved simultaneously. A survey of 267 students from the Central National Minority University revealed that many minority students are having difficulty in learning. Furthermore, compared with Han students, they experienced greater economic difficulties and had more worries about employment. Misunderstanding and discrimination were also their major worries (Chang, 2004). These issues pose tremendous challenges for minority universities to catch up with Han universities and become "world class." One needs to note that the Central National Minority University is considered the best minority university in the country and the students are considered the best minority students selected from the whole country. Another study carried out in the same institution points to low self-esteem and a poor foundation in academic background as major obstacles for the students. Cultural difference is further another factor. For example, the minority students, affected by their culture and religions, are characterized as sincere, kind, frank, and joyful but unwilling to compete. They see active participation in discussion as self-promotion and disrespectful. They do not wish to counter others in debates and discussions (Sun, 2004). Hence, the promotion of a seminar-style classroom, which is typical in graduate programs in research universities, presents a difficulty to them.

In their aspirations to become first class universities, minority nationality universities realize that they cannot be the same as the majority universities and that they need to play a critical and positive role in the development of minority economy, culture, politics, and education, regardless of any changes they make to their institutions. The reality of the minority people should be the basis of any reform. As J. Zhao (2004) noted:

> The overall goal and tasks of minority higher education are to train talents and quickly alleviate the poverty and backwardness in minority regions; it is to provide talents and service to help realize the equality, unity, mutual development and prosperity of all the nationalities in the country.
>
> (p. 19)

Thoughts and Conclusion

Obviously, in order for minority cultures to be sustained and appreciated, multiculturalism is needed to facilitate the minority cultural repositioning, which is urgently needed in the current national and global context.

In primary and secondary education a truly multicultural perspective needs to be adopted before real changes can take place. While the minority people need to be open to cultures from the outside, it is equally crucial for the dominant group (Han people) and the world to understand the value and develop an appreciation of the minority culture. For example, many minority peoples maintain that nature has a soul and that humans should not exploit nature, rather, they need to form a mutually dependent relationship with all that exists in nature. Many minority groups do not see the purpose of life as accumulating material wealth, rather, they value simplicity and harmony more than anything else. These values and perspectives are very much needed in today's society and should be learned and preserved by all cultural groups. Hence, in discussing cultural understanding and talking about learning between a majority group and a minority group and between developed regions (countries) and developing regions (countries), it is to be kept in mind this process has to be mutual. There exists great wisdom among indigenous cultures as to how to maintain human survival. It would be a great tragedy if this wisdom was wiped out or forgotten in the fulfillment of short-term goals for "economic development."

The problems in minority primary and secondary education highlight to us that education for the minorities must be a simultaneous process of fighting discrimination, biases, and exclusion, and nurturing cultivating respect, appreciation, and inclusion. A plural and respectful mentality for all and an open mind to learn from all people must simultaneously happen with attempts in curriculum changes and teaching reform.

It is also clear that learning for minority students must not be conceived to be only within the wall of schools. Traditional forms of education among most minority groups have always involved the whole village. It is time to consider involving whole communities, for example elderly people and learned people in the local area are to impart knowledge and minority culture to children. This will provide continuity of life and education and enhance relevance to students. Furthermore, flexible forms of schooling are needed, such as evening schools that allow children and adults to learn together and share knowledge of their culture. Parents are to be consulted as to what values they wish their children to develop and what skills students should learn. Teachers who come from the Han group also need to become well versed in minority cultures and languages. They need to learn the local language and ways of expression and use them in the classroom to close the distance between the students' life and the school learning. A knowledgeable teacher would be able to cut across cultural differences and bridge the language gap, hence enhancing students' learning.

The "Great Han" mentality must be challenged in order to appreciate and see the need for sustaining and developing the splendid minority cultures, many of which are rich in genesis, stories, songs, poems, and scientific know-how that have been accumulated over thousands of years. In other words, education for minority cultural sustainability must be accompanied by efforts to de-center majority culture in order to create room for minority cultures to survive and prosper. This requires deep contemplation of the value of all human beings as equal to each other and also a deep understanding of the value and wisdom of the minority cultures that have been created by generations of people. Without this new mentality, it will be difficult for minority cultures to sustain when they encounter with the majority culture and global culture, which are imbued with Han-centric and Eurocentric biases. A highly qualified teacher should know the minority group's language, know their history and culture, and know Chinese as well.

In higher education it is critical that, while making changes, minority higher learning institutions maintain their cultural uniqueness and insist on serving the needs of minority people. They also need to take advantage of the current trends of higher education transformation and build areas such as ethnic sociology, minority religions, and minority economy into solid research fields and programs of study. A vision is needed that these subjects are not only for the minority people, but are for all universities eventually. The mandate and history of minority higher learning institutions require that if they want to turn to research, the research is always to be rooted in serving the needs of the minority people for their social and economic development and cultural sustainability. It is here that they maintain their identity and from here they expand by learning from other cultures. In all, it is critical for the minority universities to realize that they will never be "first class" by losing their cultural characteristics and their identity.

The promotion of multiculturalism will give people a different world view and a lens to appreciate the wisdom and beauty of minority people's culture. This should also guide the change in direction of minority primary, secondary, and higher education. Ultimately it is deep respect originating from realizing we are different yet we are also profoundly similar that will help us all break down the walls of discrimination and prejudice and sustain marginalized cultures as valuable and beautiful.

Resources and Tools for Educators

Questions

1. How to maintain cultural diversity and dynamics through the integration of multiculturalism into policy making and the curriculum? One further question needs to be explored. How can minority groups develop self-efficacy to take proactive actions to sustain and promote their culture?

2. In a related question, how can we improve the quality of education in minority primary and secondary schools through enhancing the relevance of the curriculum and the language of education? How is cultural sustainability related to cultural relevance in school?

3. How can minority universities maintain their strength while meeting the challenges from the pursuit of global excellence? How can they resist pressures to serve the majority rather than the minority whom they have an obligation to serve?

For Further Reading

Mette, H. H. (2001). *Lesson in being Chinese: Minority education and ethnic identity in southwest China.* Seattle: University of Washington Press.

This is a critical as well as a comprehensive study of minority education and ethnic identity in a southwest province in China: Yunnan province. The author pointedly argues that the idea of cultural inefficiency is embedded in the education of minority children. The data were the results of fieldwork the author carried out from 1994 to 1996. The book is most impressive in revealing overt and subtle forms of discrimination.

Spring, J. (2004). *Deculturalization and the struggle for equality* (4th edn). McGraw-Hill Companies Inc.

This book provides a powerful analysis of the history of discrimination of minorities in the U.S. from a cultural perspective. The history of deculturalization of African-Americans, Latinos, Native Americans and Asian-Americans is presented and analyzed critically.

Ladson-Billings, G. (1994). *The dreamkeepers: Successful teachers of African American children.* San Francisco: Jossey-Bass.

This book focuses on African-Americans, but it also bears wide implications. It argues that schools should provide culturally relevant teaching to the minorities and that school learning should connect with the community in terms of its aspirations, needs, and cultural traditions and wisdoms.

Suggestions for Educators

1. Encourage the preparation and publication of reading materials to minority children in their own language;
2. Implement polices that enhance the simultaneous development of economy and culture, that truly establish the equality of minority people with the majority: it is crucial for minorities to have voices, to get heard, and they should be key participants in formulating policies that help with the development of minority education.
3. Integrate stories and the history of the minority people into the teaching process and involve local leaders and elderly people in order to share their knowledge.
4. Give priority to enhancing minority students' self-esteem and ability to learn. Help them develop self-efficacy to take actions and be active agents in changing their situation and that of their community.

References

Banks, J. A. and Banks, C. A. (Eds.) (1993). Multicultural education: Characteristics and goals. In *Multicultural education* (pp. 3–31). Boston, MA: Allyn and Bacon.

Banks, J. A. (1995). The historical reconstruction of knowledge about race: Implications for transformative teaching. *Educational Researcher, 24*(2), 15–25.

Chang, Y. (2004). Events in life affecting the psychological adaptability of ethnic minority university students: An investigation and study of universities and colleges in Beijing. *Journal of Research on Education for Ethnic Minorities, 15*(2), 26–32.

Chen, Y. (2004). A tentative study of offering school-based multicultural courses in ethnic minority regions. *Journal of Research on Education for Ethnic Minorities, 15*(1), 11–15.

Ghosh, R. (1996). *Redefining multicultural education*. Toronto, Canada: Harcourt Brace & Company.
Greene, M. (1993). The passions of pluralism: Multiculturalism and the expanding community. *Educational Researcher*, 22, January–February, 13–18.
Huang, Z.-Y. (2004). An analysis of national character education in ethnic education: An investigation of education of the Yao nationality students in some cities and counties of Guangxi province. *Journal of Research on Education for Ethnic Minorities*, 15(2), 20–25.
Kang, L. (1998) Is there an alternative to (capitalist) globalization? The debate about modernity in China. In F. Jameson & M. Masao (Eds.), *The cultures of globalization* (pp. 164–188). Durham: Duke.
Ladson-Billings, G. (1992). Culturally relevant teaching: The key to making multicultural education work. In C. A. Grant (Ed.), *Research and multicultural education: From the margins to the mainstream* (pp. 106–121). London: Falmer.
Lin, J. (1993). Ethnic relationship and minority education in Guangxi, China: A case study. *Canadian and International Education*, 22(1), 5–21.
Lin, J. (1997). Policies and politics of bilingual education in China. *Journal of Multilingual Multicultural Development*, 18(3), 193–205.
Lin, J. (2005). *Love, peace and wisdom in education: Vision for the 21st century*. Lanham, MD: Scarecrow.
Mackerras, C. (2004). China's minorities and national integration. In L. H. Liew & S. Wang (Eds.), *Nationalism, democracy and national integration in China* (pp. 147–169). London: Routledge Curzon.
Marginson, S. (1999). After globalization: Emerging politics of education. *Journal of Education Policy*, 14(1), 19–31.
Newsweek. (2005). *Newsweek*, May 9. "China's century" is the title of the special issue on China. Detailed information can be accessed on www.prnewswire.com/cgi-bin/stories.pl?ACCT=104&STORY=/www/story/05-01-2005/0003526814&EDATE=.
Song, C. (2004). The goals and trend of the future development of Chinese minority ethnic economic studies. *Journal of Research on Education for Ethnic Minorities*, 15(2), 5–8.
Spring, J. (1997). *Deculturalization and the struggle for equality* (2nd edn). Boston, MA: McGraw-Hill.
Suarez-Orozco, C. (2004). Formulating identity in a globalized world. In M. Suarez-Orozco & D. Qin-Hillard (Eds.), *Globalization: Culture and education in the new millennium* (pp. 173–202). Berkeley, CA: University of California Press.
Sun, Y. (2004). Characteristics of intellectual quality of ethnic minority university students. *Journal of Research on Education for Ethnic Minorities*, 15(2), 33–37.
Wang, M., Xin, Q., & Li, Y. (1999). Research on bilingual background and bilingual learning of Tibetan children. *Journal of Research on Education for Ethnic Minorities*, (3), 16–20.
Wang, X. (1996). On the gap in cultural background in minority education. [Lun shaoshu minzu jiaoyu wenhua Beijing minzu chayixing.] *Minority Education Research* 3, 13–18.
Watson, J. L. (Ed.). (1997). *Golden arches east: McDonald's in East Asia*. San Francisco, CA: Stanford University Press.
Zhao, J. (2004). Reflections on development of ethnic higher education under conditions of market economy. *Journal of Research on Education for Ethnic Minorities*, 15(1), 16–20.
Zhao, S. (2004). *A nation-state by construction: Dynamics of modern Chinese Nationalism*. Stanford University Press.
Zhou, X. (2004). Reflection on the reform and development of Guangxi minority education. In Q. Naichang & Q. Xian'an (Eds. in chief), *Essays from the first international seminar on Zhuang ethnic study* (pp. 565–574). Nanning: Guangxi Ethnic Minority Publishing House.

CHAPTER 5

Cultural Sustainability: An Ethnographic Case Study of a Mongol High School in China

BING WANG

Introduction to the Research Question

China's fifty-five ethnic minorities count for 91.2 million people or 8 percent of the population. Their population is increasing faster than that of the ethnic majority, the Han people, as a result of the relaxed birth policy.[1] This small portion of the population has occupied a crucial place on the government agenda for three reasons—rich resources, large areas, and national defense (Dreyer, 1993; He and Liu, 1995).

The present Chinese Government attaches great importance to minority policies. However, in the past minority policies were characterized by vacillation. When Deng Xiao Ping came to power in 1978, the central government launched the modernization program and took steps to re-establish rapport with ethnic minorities and adopted a new multicultural policy. The new policy principles include ethnic equality and unity, cultural maintenance, anti-discrimination, and regional autonomy.

However, if these multicultural policies are put into the wider context or related to other official ideologies some contradictions emerge, for example the cultural maintenance principle may conflict with the national curriculum. These contradictions may affect the implementation of the policy and result in ethnic hegemony.

Considering the official multicultural education policy to endorse cultural diversity and the practical contradictions, it is interesting to look at how the policy is translated into practice. This research intends to evaluate a Mongol high school in a city in the Inner Mongolian Autonomous Region (or Inner

Mongolia) to see how the multicultural education policy is implemented at the school level and how to better teach and maintain Mongol culture.

Demographic Change and Mongol Education

Inner Mongolia is situated in the North and Northeast of China, bordering on Russia and the State of Mongolia (also called "Outer Mongolia"). Inner Mongolia claims an area of 1,183,000 km² or 12.3 percent of the total area of China and a population of about 21.5 million (1990 census). The population consists of forty-nine ethnic groups, including 17.3 million Han, 3.38 million Mongols, and 0.78 million people of other ethnic minorities (whose percentages of the total population are 80.6, 15.7, and 3.7 percent, respectively). Chinese and Mongolian are the common languages in the region (Wulan, 1994).

The Mongols are well known mainly because Genghis Khan (1162–1227) established the most extensive empire in history. Mongols conquered China and established the Yuan Dynasty (1271–1368) (Jagchid and Hyer, 1979).

The following years during the Ming Dynasty did not see major events in the north frontier until the rise of another nomadic tribe to the northeast—the Manchu (now living in diaspora across China), who conquered both China and Mongolia and set up the Qing empire (1644–1911).

The most far-reaching historical event in the modern history of Inner Mongolia has been Han resettlement in this region. The following tables show the waves of Han migration into this area. It is worth noting that, in just two years (1958–1960), the Han–Mongol ratio increased from 6:1 to 10:1 (Table 5.1) (Harrell, 1995). It was only after the end of the Cultural Revolution (1976) that the migration lost momentum, but it has never stopped.

However, the decreased Han population percentage after the Cultural Revolution should not conceal the fact that the total population in Inner Mongolia has been consistently on the increase (Table 5.2).

Throughout the several historical periods, Mongol education has experienced continuous development, growth, and change. The achievements made in each period are built on the basis of those in the previous periods. Modern

TABLE 5.1 Han–Mongol ratio in Inner Mongolia in five selected years

Year	Ratio
1900	1:1
1928	4:1
1958	6:1
1960	10:1
1968	12:1

Source: Heberer (1989, p. 65).

Mongol education emerged during the late Qing period. In the late nineteenth century, as a result of the efforts of some progressive Mongol princes, the first group of modern Mongol schools came into being and made a great contribution to the education of Mongol people (Hu, 1994).

Throughout the Republican period (1911–1931), Mongol education continued to develop and grow. A notable development was the appearance of a modern primary school system. Meanwhile, secondary schools also appeared and diversified, such as regular schools, normal schools, and technical schools.

During the Japanese occupation (1931–1945), primary schools increased while the secondary school system took shape and then further diversified with various disciplines. Some colleges were also set up. During the Republican and the Japanese periods, the public educational system emerged and grew, while private schools and village-run schools also played an important part in educating Mongol people.

Under the present government (since 1949) large numbers of Mongol experts and technical workers have been trained for the initial industrialization of the country and for the present modernization program. Vigorous development in Mongol education has occurred during this period, most evident in the increased number of schools and students at all levels, diversification of education, and heritage language programs. Now, Inner Mongolia has fully developed educational systems at all three levels.

In addition to the continuity in development and growth, Mongol education has gone through a process of change from a basically private system, through dual private and public systems, to a purely public system. The 1984 Autonomy Law designates public boarding schools as the desired school type for ethnic schools. This implies that no individuals are allowed to run private ethnic schools.

This section has provided the historical background, against which the new policy in ethnic education is understood. What is the ethnic education policy of the local educational authorities? How do students and teachers from

TABLE 5.2 Minorities and the Han population in Inner Mongolia (1947–1990)

Year	Total population (millions)	Minorities (% of total)	Han (% of total)
1947	N/A	25.0	75.0
1958	8.2	14.6	85.4
1959	9.7	13.4	86.6
1969	13.0	7.7	92.3
1976	8.6	4.7	95.3
1990	21.5	19.4	80.6

Sources: Heberer (1989, p. 94) and Lai (1995, p. 94).

various ethnic and cultural backgrounds think about present-day Mongol education? What specific measure should be taken to enhance Mongol cultural education? These questions will be the focus of discussions in this chapter.

Theoretical Considerations

Ethnic Hegemony in Education

It is argued that, as opportunity expands and the occupational structure grows broader with modernization, groups will compete and oppress each other in the struggle for wealth, power, and privilege. The powerful groups exclude the weak ones from the expanded wealth, power, and privilege that come with modernization (Hraba and Hoiberg, 1983; Lenski, 1984). The likely result is inequality because the majority and the minority groups have unequal access to opportunity. Modernity is equated with the growing power of the core and the increasing powerlessness of the periphery and the power of the core to manipulate and shape ethnic groups (Susan, 1995; Forbes, 1997). Education plays a crucial role in ethnic hegemony.

Each pluralist society has its dominant ethnic group that controls power and the access to social rewards and economic resources. Part of this control is exercised through education and, in particular, through the curriculum. It has often been argued that the notion of culture embedded in the curriculum and embodied in examinations and certificates plays a key role in buttressing the existing social order (Modgil et al., 1986; Foster, 1990).

Schools and other educational agencies employ the curriculum as their main strategy for ordering the selection of knowledge for which they are responsible. Among the many aspects of the curriculum the knowledge selection process is crucial. It entails "the gatekeepers of knowledge" of various kinds coming to value-based decisions about the type of society that the educational system serves (De Pass, 1988). In a culturally pluralist society the way is open for knowledge managers to control the life chances of children from ethnic groups through the educational system. This is a form of ethnic hegemony.

The curriculum includes both the explicit and "hidden" curricula. The values and beliefs prevalent in society impinge on the ways teachers perceive their roles and on their attitudes towards students from different cultural backgrounds. Foster (1990) analyzed the effect of teacher and staff attitudes on students. Teachers and staff may have negative views and low expectations of minority students that in turn may reduce their self-esteem and motivation.

Life Styles Versus Life Chances

The distinction between life chances and life styles is at the heart of cultural education and sustainability. Life chances are associated with control over knowledge (power). It is life chances or the chances of the relevant skills, powers, and talents of individuals being discovered, developed, and employed in social competition for a better life. But often educational programs and models of society that stress life styles obscure this distinction. Bullivant (1981) noted that:

> This is easy to do, as they appeal to the vision of society that stresses its "niceness" and one-big-happy-family "holism," rather than the competitive nastiness of the real world. This is far less romantic, but much more pertinent for education.
>
> (p. 233)

Multicultural education programs in many cases may be limited to a certain level of cultural maintenance to enhance ethnic students' life styles, which refer to their knowledge of their traditional culture, customs, and ways of living, but may not lead to an increased chance for up-mobility in society. Multicultural education, in various confused forms, may appear to give ethnic groups what they want in education. In reality this form of multicultural education gives them little that will enhance life chances. That is why Holly (1974) cynically said "Knowledge is power" (p. 56).

Additive Approach and Perspective Change

Banks (1994) advanced four models for ethnic studies as a process of curriculum reform to enhance ethnic students' self-worth and self-pride.

1. Model A (mainstream centric): using mainstream perspectives to view concepts, issues, themes, and events.[2]
2. Model B (ethnic additive): using mainstream perspectives, aided by ethnic perspectives.
3. Model C: (multi-ethnic): using multiple ethnic perspectives; mainstream perspectives being only one of them.
4. Model D: (global): using multinational perspectives (Banks, 1994, p. 203).

Many multicultural programs use Model B, i.e. the additive approach, which may not effectively transform students' points of view. The major perspective change in teaching happens between Models B and C. In Models A and B the mainstream perspectives are used to view events, concepts, etc., while in the other two models at the higher levels the mainstream perspective is only one of several equally valid perspectives.

The significance of using this model lies in Banks's (1994) statement "I am suggesting that curricular reform proceed directly from Model A to Model C, the Multiethnic Model" (p. 203). This indicates a need to effect perspective change in instruction. The curriculum should help students view and interpret events, situations, and conflict from diverse ethnic and cultural perspectives and points of view.

Criteria For Evaluating Policy Implementation

Banks (1994, p. 92) advanced eight criteria for multicultural school, which can be used as a yardstick for the evaluation of how multicultural a school is. This research uses four selected criteria in the evaluation of the policy implementation in the Mongol school as explained in the following.

1. Criteria 1: *general school atmosphere.* Ethnic and cultural diversity should permeate the total school atmosphere. Slogans, notices, posters, and announcements should not reflect only the dominant culture, but instead should reflect cultural diversity.
2. Criteria 2: *local policy statement and monitoring.* The local educational authorities should have a multicultural policy statement that clearly sanctions and supports diversity and the policy should be monitored on a continuing basis.
3. Criteria 3: *staff attitudes and expectations.* The staff members should have positive attitudes and expectations towards diverse students, since they may greatly impinge on students' motivation and achievements.
4. Criteria 4: *transformational curriculum.* Teaching materials present diverse ethnic and cultural perspectives on events, concepts, and issues. Ethnic contributions and heroes should be included in the textbooks and selected from multiple perspectives.

Research Methods

This chapter is based on a qualitative, ethnographic case study of a Mongol high school in a major city in Inner Mongolia. The following tables based on school documents provide the general information of the ethnic composition of the students (Table 5.3) and teachers (Table 5.4). The figures show that the school is ethnically, culturally, and linguistically diverse and, therefore, the provision of multicultural education is crucial to meet the diverse students' needs.

The school is divided into junior high (sixteen classes) and senior high (nine classes), both of which provide Mongolian instruction and Chinese instruction for students to choose from in their starting years. In 1996, 491 students were in Mongolian instruction, while 141 students were in Chinese instruction (Mongol High School in Deer City, 1995–1997).

Observation

The observation included the general school environment, interactions among students and teachers, and school documents (based on Banks's (1994) criterion 1).

TABLE 5.3 Students in the Mongol high school 1997–1998

Total	Mongol	Han	Others
810	509.0	287.0	14.0
100%	62.8%	35.5%	1.7%

Source: Mongol High School in Deer City (1995–1997).

TABLE 5.4 Teachers and staff 1997–1998

	Total	%	Teachers		Adminis-trators	Staff	Workers	Others
			Junior	Senior				
Numbers	166	100.0	45	30	18	22	19	32
Mongols	90	54.2	29	16	12	8	1	24

Source: Mongol High School in Deer City (1995–1997).

Interview

The interview questions were designed on the basis of Banks's (1994) criteria 2 and 3 for local policy and staff attitudes. They were also intended to probe into specific measures to be taken to improve the present situation. These questions were open-ended in order to have more flexibility in probing. The questions were as follows.

1. Do the local educational authorities have a policy statement that supports cultural diversity at school? How is the policy implementation monitored and evaluated?
2. What is your opinion on Mongol culture and how do you predict the future of Mongolian language and culture?
3. What are your expectations for Mongol students' academic achievements?
4. What steps should be taken to enhance the Mongol cultural education and better maintain Mongol culture?

Altogether, 26 subjects from various ethnic and cultural backgrounds were interviewed, including ten teachers, six students, seven administrators, two retired teachers, and an official in charge of local ethnic education.

Textbook Evaluation

This research evaluated three history books as currently used, based on Banks's (1994) criterion 4, to see how ethnic content was included. The two textbooks and a teacher's guide are *China's Modern and Contemporary History* (Wang and Li, 1996) (senior grade one), *China's History* (Wang and Li, 1997) (junior grade two), and *A Guide for Reviewing China's History* (Haidian District Teacher Training School, 1984) (the teacher's guide).

In this research, the four selected criteria are used in the evaluation of the policy implementation in the Mongol high school and data analysis to see how the implementation process falls short of the policy requirements. In the data analysis, special attention is paid to several issues: if and how ethnic hegemony is exercised in the process, especially in knowledge selection, if and how Mongol students' life styles and life chances are compatible or not, and if and how the instruction is transformational. Eventually, suggestion will be made to improve the present situation.

Findings and Discussions

General School Atmosphere

The general atmosphere of the Mongol high school gives some expression of ethnic and cultural diversity but it is far from "permeating" the total school atmosphere as required by Banks's (1994) criterion 1. When the cultural diversity is closely examined, it is noticed to have two features.

First, apart from the Mongolian language used in instruction, cultural diversity is basically reflected only at the macro-level, i.e. at the most conspicuous places and on the most important occasions. For example, the highest part of the school buildings is the Mongol-style dome, larger posters are bilingual, the New Year Gala Night program is very multicultural and colorful, the most typical Mongol painting is on the wall of the main building, and people wear colorful costumes during visits of guests. This kind of cultural diversity betrays a certain artificial effort to impress. However, at the micro-level, i.e. in daily, routine work, cultural diversity is not so noticeable. For example, ordinary notices, bulletins, and decorations in the classrooms, school archives, student dormitories, etc., do not impress one as bilingual or multicultural.

The second feature is Mongolian in form but Chinese in content, e.g. the Mongolian slogans, posters, textbooks, newspapers, etc., do not reflect Mongol culture. The student reading room was observed to see how many newspapers were subscribed to and in what languages. It was found that the school subscribed to nine newspapers altogether, with eight of them being Chinese and only one being Mongolian. It was further noticed that the only Mongolian newspaper available, *Mongolian Daily*, carried very similar articles to those in *Chinese People's Daily*.

All in all, effort towards multicultural education, at best, does not go beyond the so-called "additive approach" and is characterized by tokenism.

Local Policy Statement and Monitoring

The basic education policy is formulated at the national level, but the provincial or regional authorities have obtained substantial power in policy making since the mid-1980s. The Inner Mongolia regional government has further delegated some educational power to the municipal authorities since 1986.

The observation of official documents revealed that, in 1993, the Inner Mongolia Education Ministry issued the new policy document governing ethnic education in the region the *Inner Mongolia Ethnic Education Working Regulations*. This document includes a clear statement that supports cultural diversity in ethnic schools and conveys the authority's commitment to equal educational opportunity for all students from various ethnic and cultural groups. The regional policy document clearly states that China is a culturally diverse country and the ethnic and cultural characteristics of all groups should be respected. It specifies the special preferential treatment in various aspects to ethnic students, heritage language, bilingual, and cultural maintenance programs (Wang and Ma, 1997). One objective of Mongol education is that students, by the time of their graduation from junior or senior high, should "master both Mongolian and Chinese" or "master one language and understand the other" (Wulan, 1994, p.11).

At the city level, the municipal education board is responsible for making specific decisions on the specific amount of additional funding and specific forms of preferential treatment for ethnic education in the city. At present, the preferential treatment for Mongol education can be classified into three types.

The first type is additional educational funding. The Mongol high school now gets 200,000 yuan more than a regular school for new equipment each year. Minority students attending ethnic schools are all provided with special bursaries for boarding. The second is related to admission to institutes of higher learning. The number of Mongol students (both Mongolian and Chinese instructed) who are admitted into post-secondary institutions each year must be higher in proportion than their relative population in the region.

The third is the use of Mongol language in examinations. Mongolian-instructed students may choose to write their examination papers in the Mongolian language both in entrance examinations and examinations for employment.

In short, local government does have a clearly stated policy for supporting cultural diversity. However, good policy, if not effectively monitored, may just do lip service to ethnic students (De Pass, 1988).

An effective monitoring system may include classroom visitations, examination of standardized test scores disaggregated by ethnic groups, and examination of the percentage of minority students who are dropouts and who are classified as exceptional or retarded (Banks, 1994).

The interview and observation revealed that there existed some monitoring schemes in the school. Sometimes, the municipal education board sent inspectors to the school, but their inspections were limited to hearing briefings given by the school chief administrators. The school must submit a year-end summary report on how and to what extent it has done its job towards the educational objectives in the previous year. Once in a while, the school's chief administrators and the department heads observed randomly selected classes. The school's Archive No.5 included a document entitled *General Statistics Report*, which kept a quantitative record of important figures by ethnic groups.

However, these monitoring programs are more inconsistent than systematic and continuing. In response to the question "How often and when do the inspectors come to school?" most interviewees answered "Heaven knows." In addition, though the school leaders sometimes observed classes without notice, the school had not yet developed a systematic method for evaluation. The dean of the school talked about the difficulties in the evaluation of teaching outcomes: "We inspect the classrooms to see how teachers teach and students learn, and how teachers mark students' assignments. We observe in classrooms and make routine evaluation of teachers' work, which is important to motivate teachers in their work."

A problem with the evaluation in the school is its focus on individual teachers, rather than, as multicultural education requires, on the school as a unit (Banks, 1994). Often the purpose of the evaluation is limited to teacher motivation, instead of all program components. In such cases, the feedback derived from the inspection is likely to be inadequate and does not inform new steps to improve the programs towards the policy goals.

Staff Attitudes and Expectations

Staff attitudes and expectations impinge heavily on students' academic performances. The interview data indicated that the multicultural policy is intended to enhance ethnic students' cultural identities, but in reality impedes their life chances. Opting into Mongolian instruction means limited opportunity in further learning and employment.

If not admitted into university, most Mongol-speaking students went back home upon graduation to do physical labor. During the 1980s and 1990s, only about six students each year got university admission on average, compared with an annual 80 percent admission rate for two other regular schools in the same city in the same period (Mongol High School in Deer City, 1996).

Most Han and Mongol teachers pointed to the unfairness in Mongol education, such as the unavailability of Mongolian instruction in universities, lack of Mongolian teaching materials, and the unicultural national curriculum and entrance examinations. This case study tends to confirm the previous research finding that this problem for Mongolian-speaking students has exacerbated with the development of the market economy.

Currently, there are only three universities that offer Mongolian instruction—the Inner Mongolia University, the Inner Mongolia Teachers' University, and the Central University of Nationalities in Beijing. The principal said that "From the bottom of their hearts, most students want to go to study in other large cities. But once they choose Mongolian language, their wings are clipped."

Moreover, Mongol students find their choice of future compromised by a preferential policy—they can use Mongolian language in place of English in entrance examinations. But nearly all universities require a foreign language for admission. The school did not offer an English course until 1997. Since then, the students have been learning three languages—Mongolian, Chinese, and English. But the teacher of English in the Mongolian instruction section said "The Mongolian-instructed students have a heavy load learning three languages. Besides, we do not have English textbooks in Mongolian and we have to use English textbooks in Chinese."

Little opportunity for the future is inexorably related to student motivation and performance. But the major factor that affects them is, as some Mongol teachers believed, the nationally unified curriculum and examinations, which are unfair for minority students.

All textbooks used in Mongolian instruction are exactly the same as those for Chinese instruction. Both the texts and the illustrations are identical except for the language. The following are grievances aired by some history teachers in the Mongolian instruction: "Our textbooks include too little minority history and the entrance exams exclude it" and "History is too tough. The students are not interested at all. Some terms in the textbooks even we teachers do not know. Sometimes, I have to speak Chinese in class for clear understanding."

The interviews and observations indicate a general consensus that the Mongolian language is facing a dim future. All the participants agreed that the situation was becoming tougher and tougher with the growing market economy. The present situation in language learning is that Chinese-speaking students are trying to learn English to study in other areas like Beijing and Shanghai, while Mongolian-speaking students, after graduation from primary schools, are trying to choose Chinese instruction to have a broader choice for the future. When interviewed about the future of the Mongolian language, the former principal expressed his pessimistic view: "It is tough. Especially with the modernization process, not only Mongols in China, other ethnic groups in other countries face the same problem. It is hard to preserve our language."

All Mongolian-speaking participants believed that the main problem for the Mongolian language was the dwindling linguistic environment. A pastoral student said that gold had been found in her home area and a large tract of grassland was being turned into gold mines while herders were becoming gold miners. She believed that preservation of the Mongolian language depended on preservation of the Mongolian ecological environment and life style. Some Mongolian teachers living in the city said that their children used to be able to speak Mongolian, but now they could only understand it for lack of a linguistic environment outside home. They said "We can not force them to speak Mongolian and we also have to consider their future."

Speaking the Mongolian language and increased life chances are evidently incompatible.

The interview questions also probed into staff attitudes towards the Mongol culture because they must be embedded in the hidden curriculum and affect student performance.

One point of view held in common is that the Mongol culture is backward and unity with the Han for mutual prosperity is the only way to ensure a successful future for Mongols. "Advancedness" and "backwardness" are important concepts in understanding ethnic relations in China in the modernization period. These concepts can be seen as a new version of the ancient Chinese ethos about "civilization" and "barbarianism." This view was held by most Mongols and the Han alike. Some Mongol interviewees said:

> The fifty-six ethnic groups are not the same. The Han are the most developed, but Mongols are backward. Inner Mongolia is an under-developed area, with few qualified scientists, even fewer in economics. We Mongols are definitely backward and must learn from the Han.

These low opinions of Mongol culture, held in common, must insinuate into the school's hidden curriculum and negatively affect all the Mongol students.

Textbook Evaluation

The evaluation of the two history textbooks and the supporting material focused on the inclusion of ethnic heroes and contributions, which is perceived to be important in transforming students' perspectives (Banks, 1994).

Textbook evaluation shows that what Mongol students learn at school contradicts the Mongol history learned at home. The first example is Genghis Khan (1162–1227). Though Genghis Khan is a Mongol hero included in the history textbooks, his image is different from what Mongols cherish in their hearts. The Mongols claim themselves proudly to be "the descendant of Genghis Khan." Genghis Khan is recognized in the Chinese history textbook mainly because his grandson Kublai Khan ruled the Yuan Dynasty (1271–1368). Mongols talk about Genghis Khan with pride and admiration, but their feelings hardly find expression in Chinese history books.

The second example is Gada Meilin (1893–1931), a Mongol hero who defended Mongol land against Han immigration. He led a Mongol uprising against the Chinese warlords but was defeated and killed. This Mongol hero, however, is not mentioned in the history books at all.

The third example is Prince De (Demchugdongrub), who was the Mongol nationalist leader in the 1930s. Supported by the Japanese army he established the Mongolian Autonomous Government in 1939. Consequently, the Chinese treat him as a traitor. For many Mongols, he is still a hero, but like Gada Meilin he is excluded from history books.

However, the textbooks do include a Mongol as a hero of "the Chinese nation." That Mongol is described as one of the eight patriotic generals who laid down their lives heroically during the Opium War. The perspective from which Mongol heroes are selected is evident from the fact that only Mongols who contribute to the Chinese nation are recognized.

The two history books cover China's history of 4,000 years and include the achievements made during each period in various fields. In terms of contributions, inventions, and achievements, nearly all names included as great men and women are Han.

Only in a couple of cases are ethnic minorities' contributions briefly mentioned, such as a beautiful folklore of an ethnic group in the fourth century and the contribution made by the Li people in textile techniques in the Yuan Dynasty (Haidian District Teacher Training School, 1984). Other ethnic contributions are not recognized.

Even in chapters about the Mongol-ruled Yuan Dynasty (1271–1368) Mongol contributions are not mentioned. Conversely, what is included is the Mongol emperor's willingness to assimilate to the Han culture (Haidian District Teacher Training School, 1984, pp. 71–73).

The principal of the Mongol high school also perceived the problems with national curriculum used in ethnic schools. He criticized the curriculum:

> The teaching content of an ethnic school should reflect the local ethnic characteristics, such as ethnic history and the origin and evolution of ethnic culture. The textbooks we are using now offer little in these areas. In ethnic education, the young people should have some basic ideas about their own ethnic history, cultural origin and development. The teachers also have few materials available in these areas.

The textbook evaluation indicated that ethnic heroes and contributions are included but selected from the Chinese Han point or view, a typical "additive approach," which is likely to enhance stereotyping and unable to transform students' perspectives.

Conclusions and Suggestions

It can be concluded that current Chinese policy towards ethnic groups guarantees a variety of cultural freedoms and rights, which can be viewed as progress towards multicultural goals. But due to various contradictions in many ways with the broader social context, the policy is distorted in the implementation process and results in ethnic hegemony, most evident in the curricular matters.

It is evident that the new policy should be further supported by structural reform, such as further decentralization and higher autonomy in ethnic education. Only when the Mongols have full rights to decide on their own education matters can many problems discussed above be effectively solved, such as the general school atmosphere, staff attitudes, teaching materials, and so on.

The research finds that Mongol students are instructed in the Mongol language, but what they learn is mainly Han culture, while the Mongol language serves as the medium for indoctrination. Therefore, a distinction must be made between "life styles" and "life chances" in all forms of cultural education. In the Mongol case study, learning the Mongol language is a barrier to further study or employment. An important finding of the research is that many problems revealed in the interviews and observations can be attributed to excessive central control. So, the national curriculum and unified examinations in a multicultural society should not apply.

It is found that one reason for policy distortion in the implementation process may be that there is not a proper monitoring system, which should be systematic, consistent, on a continuous basis, and with a focus on the school as a unit, instead of, as the interview data show, on individual teachers. Therefore, such a monitoring system should be in place in the Mongol case.

The role of ethnic heroes and role models in the socialization of ethnic students can never be overestimated. This research finds Mongol heroes are either excluded or selected and evaluated from the Han Chinese perspective. Since the knowledge selection process is vital in multicultural education, it is suggested that curricular decisions should be made based on a democratic process. Though abolishing the national curriculum will alleviate the problem, involvement of ethnic cultural experts on textbook development is strongly recommended.

This study finds that persuading the Mongols to accept the Han cultural superiority legitimized the dominant control. It is argued that it is only with the help of the Han that the Mongols can change their state of "backwardness" to achieve common prosperity. Though anti-discrimination is one of the policy principles, it is not emphasized in the Mongol high school and discrimination against Mongol culture and students exists among both the Han and the Mongols. Cultural education must be accompanied by anti-racist education. Change of the overt curriculum is far from enough.

Resources and Tools for Educators

Question

1. In multicultural education many programs emphasize the "life style" of ethnic students' with a focus on the maintenance of ethnic cultures and languages. The problem is that these programs often channel ethnic students into dead-end jobs in the job market, for example the jobs in an ethnic enclave. Consequently, ethnic students' "life chances" in the larger society are undermined. In your opinion, how should we strike a balance between students' life style and life chance?

For Further Reading

Banks, J. A. (1994). *Introduction to multicultural education*. Boston: Allyn & Bacon.

Banks explains the basic concepts, assumptions, theories, and models of multicultural education. The book also includes a brief history of the development of multicultural education and summarizes the four levels of ethnic content integration current in multicultural policy in the U.S.

Jagchid, S. & Hyer, P. (1979). *Mongolia's culture and society*. England: Westview Press.

This is a rare English book dealing with the topic of Mongolian culture in a comprehensive way. It includes an analysis of Mongol history, religion, literature, and art, as well as customs. The discussion on every topic is comprehensive and thorough. More important is that the book is written from the Mongolian point of view and the reader may sense the emotions of the authors in the description of their own culture.

Lai, D. C. (1995). *Land of Genghis Khan: The rise and fall of nation-states in China's northern frontiers*. Victoria: University of Victoria.

The author describes the brief history of the Mongols from Genghis Khan's time to the 1990s in simple English and with the help of maps and illustrations. It is a very good book for beginners who want to learn about Mongolian history and people. The book uses adequate statistics in the description of demographic change in Mongolia in modern times.

Sleeter, C. E. & Grant, C. A. (2003). *Making choices for multicultural education: Five approaches to race, class, and gender*. New York: John Wiley and Sons, Inc.

The authors offer the educational community a way of thinking about race, language, culture, class, gender, and disability in teaching. The book focuses on several forms of difference that also define unequal access to power in the U.S. The differences discussed include race, language, social class, gender, disability, and sexual orientation. In the last chapter the authors advocate their approach to multicultural education, that is "education that is multicultural and social reconstructionist."

Suggestions for Educators

Since it takes a long time to compile new, high-quality textbooks, creative teachers may use existing textbooks that are ethno-centric with the goal of enhancing cultural diversity. The following are three ways for teachers to teach using this type of textbook.

1. Knowledge construction and deconstruction. Teachers can help students become aware that textbooks are based on particular perspectives and that knowledge is not the sole domain of experts or government sanctioned authorities: rather, knowledge can be constructed by students themselves. Textbooks should be used as one source of knowledge alongside primary information collected by students. In teaching, a teacher may ask the question "from whose perspective is the specific knowledge constructed?". Students should be helped to approach specific historical events from multiple perspectives.

2. Using interdisciplinary themes. Teacher teams may select empowering themes that bridge disciplines. For example, in the study of discrimination, students can use reading skills to learn the history of discrimination and math skills to calculate and demonstrate income inequalities. Teachers can work in teams to share planning and read samples of students' work in other classes.

3. Enhancing creative thinking. Teachers can help students to study the texts for what they are—a particular point of view and history, literature, and language. One good way is to analyze and compare two or more texts on the same issue. Teachers and students can bring in current news reports from multiple perspectives and compare them with the texts. After acquiring critical thinking skills, students can analyze these textbook presentations. Using texts as foils to encourage critical thinking demystifies the textbooks. Students interact actively with books rather than read and repeat the ideas of others.

Notes

1. China enforced the One-Child Family Law in 1979. But it has not applied this law to ethnic minorities, who may have two children in urban areas, while in rural and pastoral areas some may have three or even four, children.
2. One classical example for this model is to teach Indian students in American history class that Columbus "discovered" America.
3. The total population decreased because of territorial change between 1969 and 1981, when large areas in Inner Mongolia were carved out to other provinces against Russian invasion (Lai, 1995).

References

(An asterisk at the end of some items indicates Chinese language sources.)

Banks, J. A. (1994). *Introduction to multicultural education*. Boston: Allyn & Bacon.

Bullivant, B. M. (1981). *The pluralist dilemma in education: Six case studies*. London: George Allen & Unwin.

De Pass, C. M. (1988). From periphery to periphery: Employment equality for visible minorities in Canada. Unpublished doctoral dissertation, University of Calgary, Calgary.

Dreyer, J. T. (1993). *China's political system: Modernization and tradition*. New York: Paragon House.

Forbes, H. D. (1997). *Ethnic conflict: Commerce, culture and contact hypothesis*. New Haven: Yale University Press.

Foster, P. (1990). *Policy and practice in multicultural and anti-racist education: A case study of a multiethnic comprehensive school*. London: Routledge.

Haidian District Teacher Training School (Ed.) (1984). *A guide for teaching China's history*. Beijing: Geometric Publishing House.*

Harrell, S. (Ed.) (1995). *Cultural encounters on China's ethnic frontiers*. Seattle: University of Washington Press.

He, B. & Liu, S. D. (1995). On the policy of ethnic education. *Ethnic Education Research*, (1), 3–8.*

Heberer, T. (1989). *China and its national minorities: Autonomy or assimilation?* London: M. E. Sharpe.

Holly, D. (Ed.) (1974). *Education or domination? A critical look at educational problems today*. London: Arrow Books.

Hraba, J. & Hoiberg, E. (1983). Ideational origins of modern theories of ethnicity: Individual freedom and organisational growth. *Sociological Quarterly*, 24(3), 381–391.

Hu, C. M. (1994). Mongol school education under the Manchurian Traitor Government. *Ethnic Education Research*, (1), 70–75.*

Jagchid, S. & Hyer, P. (1979). *Mongolia's culture and society*. London: Westview Press.

Lai, D. C. (1995). *Land of Genghis Khan: The rise and fall of nation-states in China's northern frontiers*. Victoria: University of Victoria.

Lenski, G. E. (1984). *Power and privilege: A theory of social stratification*. Raleigh: The University of North Carolina Press.

Modgil, S., Verma, G., Malick, K., & Modgil, C. (Eds.) (1986) *Multicultural education: The interminable debate*. Philadelphia: The Falmer Press.

Mongol High School in Deer City (1996). *A profile of the Mongol high school in Deer City*. (Available from The Mongol High School in Deer City in Inner Mongolia).*

Mongol High School in Deer City (1995–1997). *General statistics reports* (Report No. Compulsory Education Archive A5). Inner Mongolia: The Mongol High School in Deer City.*

Susan, O. (1995). Ethnic minorities and industrial change in Europe and North America. [Review of the dynamics of ethnic competition and conflict]. *Journal of American Ethnic History*, 14(4), 58–59.

Wang, H. Z. & Li, L. G. (Eds.) (1996). *China's modern and contemporary history: The textbook for history for senior high schools (book one)*. Beijing: People's Education Press.*

Wang, H. Z. & Li, L. G. (Eds.) (1997). *China's history: The textbook for junior high schools (book four)*. Beijing: People's Education Press.*

Wang, N. & Ma, J. H. (1997). On the development of special ethnic education policy and its implementation. *China's ethnic education*, (5), 34–35.*

Wulan, T. (Ed.) (1994). *Introduction to ethnic education in Inner Mongolia*. Huhot: Inner Mongolia Cultural Publisher.*

CHAPTER 6

The Hidden Curriculum of Assimilation in Modern Chinese Education: Fuelling Indigenous Tibetan and Uygur Cessation Movements

SEONAIGH MACPHERSON AND GULBAHAR BECKETT

> The supposedly "neutral" ideas called "modernization" and "globalization" carry with them a scorn for linguistic and cultural variation.
>
> Emilia Ferreiro (2003, p. 74)

Background

The People's Republic of China (P.R.C.) is a highly multicultural state with fifty-six "nationalities" with distinctive cultures and languages. Even the Han majority (91 percent) is culturally diverse, with at least eight distinctive language groups (Gladney, 2003, p. 11.) This notwithstanding, many scholars and media perceive and represent China as a monolithic (that is monolingual and monocultural) state. Although the 8–9 percent minority share of the population may seem inconsequential, these indigenous and minority groups lay historical claim to as much as 60 percent of the existing territories of the P.R.C., much of that being in the western and northern regions of Tibet and Xinjiang (Uygur territory). Furthermore, of the fifty-five non-Han "minorities," the Tibetans and Uygurs are two of the most populous indigenous groups, who are also behind the most significant independence and self-determination movements.

Like most modern multicultural states, the P.R.C.'s program of educational modernization has an implicit, hidden curriculum of assimilation, in spite of showcasing explicit policies and documents purporting to support diversity.

The Chinese constitution, as Wang (Chapter 5) reiterates, tacitly supports the maintenance of minority languages and cultures. Article 4 of the constitution states "All nationalities in the People's Republic of China are equal," which is upheld through the promotion of three key principles of multiculturalism: "... [t]he state protects the lawful rights and interests of the minority nationalities and upholds and develops a relationship of equality, unity and mutual assistance among all of China's nationalities" (International Campaign for Tibet, 2001, pp. 41–42). These three principles of "equality, unity, and mutual assistance" are the cornerstone of the P.R.C.'s official multicultural policy. On analysis, they indicate the privileging of principles of multicultural assimilation, such as equity over diversity and national unity over ethnic identification. This intention continues to drive the P.R.C.'s educational and social policies.

Accordingly, despite a policy of official multiculturalism, China continues to treat the languages and cultures of minorities as deficits. Education is a key institution to redress these "deficits," either in the guise of modern Marxist education or global scientific and technological education. For example, Chinese educators and researchers represent Tibetans' purported high illiteracy levels, in excess of 70 percent and the highest by far in China (Lamontagne, 1999, p. 145), as pathologies of their traditional culture arising from their resistance to "progress." During a public presentation in Canada, a leading Chinese curriculum specialist was asked about the conspicuous exclusion of new curricular reforms in Tibet. He blamed the indigenous culture: "The people who live there are backwards, superstitious, and do not believe in science." This conflicts with evidence from the diaspora communities, where Tibetans, even monks, embrace the study of science (e.g. Dalai Lama, 2003; Jinpa, 2003). Tibetan literacy problems are more likely linked to the lack of schools and trained teachers in the region, combined with low school attendance levels given the use of Chinese as the language of instruction (Postiglione, 1999; Upton, 1999).

This chapter offers a theoretical reflection on the hidden curriculum of assimilation in modern secular education through the particular case of the P.R.C.'s educational reforms and their impact on the Tibetan and Uygur peoples. We assume a critical stance towards the polarization between modernity and traditions in education. On the one hand we acknowledge that the P.R.C. has made significant efforts to include previously disenfranchised peoples in its educational reforms. These people include poor, women, and minority peoples in Tibet and Xinjiang. For example, one of the authors, Dr. Beckett, a Uygur woman from Xinjiang, speculates that she might have been a shepherdess herding sheep in Xinjiang rather than a university professor were it not for modern educational reforms in the P.R.C. On the other hand, while we acknowledge that certain people are discriminated against and excluded from traditional forms of religious-based, apprenticeship, or private education (e.g. women, minorities, castes, or classes), so too are indigenous peoples like the Tibetans and Uygurs discriminated against directly or indirectly in modern, secular education by being asked to adopt unfamiliar and at times hostile languages, cultural practices, and world views. Recognizing the challenge of this paradoxical position, we argue for creative, local alternatives to the curriculum and education that can simultaneously serve the need for cultural and linguistic continuity alongside access to enhanced modern economic, technological, and social opportunities. Accordingly, we see the need to move beyond conservative and liberal approaches to multicultural education in the P.R.C. and position our discussion within critical multiculturalism.

Theoretical Context

The Discursive Construction of State Schooling as a Civilizing Project

Just as indigenous cultures are represented as ideologically deficient in the P.R.C., the dominant Han are represented as agents of civilization. Like many modern colonizers, the Han legitimate their control by conceiving of themselves as uniquely burdened with a civilizing mission to help indigenous peoples progress and overcome cultural and linguistic deficits through education (Hansen, 1999, pp. 3–4). Harrell (1995) pointed to the educational metaphor of "peripheral peoples as children" (p. 13) as a hegemonic construct underlying the Chinese civilizing mythology. As early as 1957, Zhou Enlai proclaimed "Without mutual assistance, especially assistance from the Han People, the minority peoples will find it difficult to make significant progress on their own" (International Campaign for Tibet, 2001, pp. 48–49). Such beliefs and rhetoric persist in many Han Chinese, who often refer to Tibet as a burden to the nation, harkening back to the *noblesse oblige* of European colonialism.

Such deeply embedded ethnic arrogance and colonial paternalism arise from a unique combination of Han chauvinism and Marxist modernity. Han chauvinism arises from an historical belief in Han racial and cultural superiority, which even Mao repeatedly identified as a potential threat to national unity (International Campaign for Tibet, 2001). This ethnic arrogance is reinforced in the Marxist theory of progress by legitimating the subjugation of minorities to Han dominance in the name of "progress." According to Harrell (1995), the P.R.C. is the latest in a legacy of "civilizing projects" in the region:

> A civilizing project . . . is a kind of interaction between peoples, in which one group, the civilizing center, interacts with other groups (the peripheral peoples) in terms of a particular kind of inequality.

In this interaction, the inequality between the civilizing center and the peripheral peoples has its ideological basis in the center's claim to a superior degree of civilization, along with a commitment to raise the peripheral peoples' civilization to the level of the center, or at least closer to that level.

(p. 4)

Contemporary Chinese (P.R.C.) multicultural policies and discourse are a hybrid of Marxism and Confucianism. Confucianism distinguished civilizations in a hierarchy according to morality and modes of life, which not surprisingly positioned Han agriculturalists in a superior position to the herders of the steppes (Tibetan, Mongolian, and Uygur) (Crossley, 1990, in Harrell, 1995). In this respect, Tibetans and Uygurs have long stood as "primitive" subalterns reinforcing the Han sense of ethnic and cultural superiority. The civilizing mythology of Confucianism viewed such superiority as a consequence of upbringing and environment rather than race, which rendered the borderland peoples redeemable through moral education and a more civilized (e.g. agricultural) mode of life. The Han Chinese Governments shouldered this mission as a "gift" to the minority and indigenous peoples, disregarding the upheaval their tactics imposed on affected families and communities. Indicative of this is the P.R.C.'s current practice of sending Tibetan and Uygur children to boarding schools in China proper. In this practice the P.R.C. is acting like the state-sponsored Christian residential missionary schools of the 1930s–1950s in Canada, which disrupted an entire generation of indigenous people in what is now considered to be a flagrant abuse of education for assimilation purposes.

THE TROUBLING "GIFT" OF EDUCATION

As Bourdieu (1991) suggested, power and domination are seldom exercised through brute, overt force: instead, they are sublimated and expressed indirectly and covertly as symbolic power and symbolic violence. In his anthropological studies of gift exchanges in the Kabyle society, Bourdieu (1991) recognized these exchanges as much more than the reciprocal structures described by Levi-Strauss. The exchange of gifts was an interactive mechanism through which power was exercised and disguised. In non-modern contexts, symbolic power and violence are exercised through interpersonal relations rather than institutions, whereby the giver exercises power and domination through creating indebtedness in the recipient. In modern contexts, institutions of the state assume greater responsibility for exchanges of symbolic domination. As Thompson describes in his introduction to Bourdieu's (1991) work:

By giving a gift—especially a generous one that cannot be met by a counter-gift of comparable quality—the giver creates a lasting obligation and binds the recipient in a relation of personal indebtedness. Giving is also a way of possessing: it is a way of binding another while shrouding the bond in a gesture of generosity.

(p. 23)

In the case of the P.R.C., the "gift" of development and, in particular, educational development is used to legitimate the central Han-dominated government's control of occupied regions. This discursive legitimization persists in spite of the fact that the "gift" is resisted or outright rejected by many Tibetans and increasingly by Uygurs as well. In their study of Tibetan families, Postiglione et al. (2006) found that many parents persisted in rejecting state-sponsored schooling even when they were offered enticements (bribes) or punishments (hefty fines). In a related study, Postiglione et al. (2004) examined Tibetan rural primary and secondary boarding schools throughout the P.R.C., concluding that representations of the Tibetan culture were restricted to material manifestations in the schools' architecture, art, and artifacts rather than in cultural practices and curricular contents of the classroom and textbooks or in the language of instruction. They concluded that students were forced to choose between "segregation or impact integration," that is between remaining unschooled or compromising the cultural continuity of their families and communities.

Lamontagne (1999) compared Tibetans with other nationalities to demonstrate that Tibetans show some of the lowest "educated population" (e.g. literacy) levels in both Qinghai Province (27.30 percent compared to 54 percent overall) and nationally (26.47 percent compared to 70 percent overall) (p. 148). Of the eighteen minorities of Qinghai Province constituting 42 percent of the province, only the Salars (26.41 percent) have lower educated population levels than the Tibetans. Furthermore, these low rates of educational development (e.g. literacy) have changed little in the last decade, in spite of the fact that this region (e.g. Amdo) was once renowned as a stronghold of Tibetan language and literacy education.[1] Although it is difficult to infer what motivates these low literacy levels, when these statistics are considered alongside the previous evidence of the state's attempts to entice families and children into state-sponsored schools, it is plausible to conclude that the apparently low literacy and education levels of Tibetans are at least in part a reflection of free choice, not just a lack of educational access. Tibetans may be actively rejecting or passively resisting the P.R.C.'s educational modernization and Mandarin literacy programs because of a perceived or actual threat to their cultural continuity (Postiglione, 1997). This suggestion is corroborated by interviews conducted with recent Tibetan refugees in India (Tibetan Centre for Human Rights and Democracy, 1997; MacPherson, 2005).

Furthermore, in Tibet and Xinjiang the exclusion of indigenously trained teachers (e.g. monks, nuns, and imams), local languages, and local subjects or contents from publicly-funded education has further distanced the people from accessing the benefits of development in the region. On the other hand state-recognized teaching credentials are restricted to those who progress through the Han- and Mandarin-dominated secular state school system. In this respect, just as global economic systems set in motion overt forms of inequity and domination through literal indebtedness, modern educational development fossilized inequity and domination through symbolic indebtedness and domination.

Curriculum as Cultural Practice

Every formal curriculum embodies the culture of its inception. To understand how this might be the case, it is important to define what we mean by *culture*. Cultures are not located in ideas, histories, texts, or great works so much as the network of social and cultural practices that give rise to these cultural expressions. In this respect, we can say that curriculum is a cultural practice (Kanu, 2006) because the culture and associated cultural practices are reproduced in its contents, subject areas (disciplines), classroom texts, methods, language of instruction, literacy practices, pedagogical relations, and "classroom" organization. These activities in turn reproduce the same cultural practices and social relations in students that constituted the culture that gave rise to them. In this respect, curricula reproduce cultural practices displaced across both space and time.

At the same time, when a curriculum moves sufficiently across cultural, temporal, and spatial boundaries, it can become an *inter*cultural practice. For example, if a curriculum is rooted in another culture and set of cultural practices distant from one's own, then to engage that curriculum entails some degree of acculturation. Such a curriculum becomes an *inter*cultural practice with assimilative (subtractive) or sustainable (additive) multilingual, multicultural outcomes. Since the colonial period and, accelerating now in the global period, a particular variant of modern, secular curriculum is disseminating around the world. Yet, all too often the cultural biases of modern education are obscured. Instead, modern, secular education is represented as if it were culturally neutral: a blank curricular framework to fill with whatever cultural contents seem appropriate.

Communities depend on multiple institutions to sustain themselves across generations, including the family, religion, and formal education. With respect to formal education, broadly construed, at least six types of cultural knowledge depend on some formal education for transmission and continuity: religion, literacy, medicine, cosmology, arts, and music. Of these, religion, literacy, medicine, and cosmology rely significantly on formal education, whereas the transmission of crafts and music may depend less on formal, literate education and more on apprenticeship learning processes. The key thesis of this is that these five areas of "traditional" cultural knowledge are precisely those subject areas and contents marginalized within modern curricula and, hence, most threatened by processes of modernization and globalization. The local language shift and loss that accompanies such curricular changes further undermines the sustainability of these local cultural knowledges and practices by creating linguistic, epistemic, and cultural gaps. In this way, changes in education and curriculum can have a dramatic effect on the sustainability of small non-dominant cultures.

Two Specific Cases: Uygur and Tibetan

In this section, we introduce the Uygurs and Tibetans as specific cases. We discuss their "traditional" curriculum by separating out two broad domains of curricular contents marginalized in modern, standardized curricula: (1) literacy and religion and (2) crafts, medicine, astrology, and folk music and dance. We do so to illustrate how these peoples enjoyed unique civilizations, languages and cultures, and educational systems that could have continued to serve them well.

Literacy and Religion

UYGURS

The Uygurs (alternatively spelled *Uighurs and Uigurs*) number about 8 million (Columbia Encyclopedia, wwwbartleby.com/65/ui/Uigurs. html, retrieved May 29, 2003), predominantly in the northwestern P.R.C. province of Xinjiang. They constitute 47 percent of the province's population (Xinjiang Nianjian, 1996, cited in Mawkanuli, 2001). Before Chinese colonization, Uygurs had their own independent empires and civilizations, which included the First Turkic Qaghanat Kingdom (the Hun between the third century B.C. and fourth century A.D.) and the Tabgach (Toba, fourth to sixth centuries) and Kok Turk (552–744) Empires. At various stages of historical development, the Uygurs established a number of states including Gaochan (fourth to seventh centuries), the Second Turkic Qaghanat Kingdom, the Manichean State (745–840), the Ganzhou Uighur Kingdom (a Buddhist state between the ninth and eleventh centuries in what is today Gansu Province), the Karakhanid Uighur Kingdom (tenth to twelfth centuries), the Turpan Idikut Kingdom (ninth to fourteenth centuries), and East Turkistan (between 1944 and 1949) (Issiyev, 1991).

The origin of the people has been in debate among scholars and politicians. Most Uygurs believe they are of Turkic origin: however, recent archaeological evidence suggests Uygurs' origins can be traced back to Celtic Saxons who migrated to the region between 18 and 300 B.C. (Mair, 2004). Contemporary Uygurs speak a Turkic language called Uygur and use a modified version of Arabic script that is phonographic (i.e. alphabetic), unlike the logographic Mandarin script (i.e. characters). The Uygur language and scripts were widespread and used not only by Uygurs themselves, but also by other Turkic peoples such as Kazaks, Uzbeks, and Tatars as well as by the Mongols and the Manchus in the early stage of their rule in China (Issiyev, 1991). The official P.R.C. state policies and rhetoric refer to Uygurs as a minority nationality and the Uygur language as a minority language. The Uygur people, however, think of themselves as indigenous people and their language as an indigenous language—one of the native languages of Xinjiang. The Chinese population transfer policy and practice caused the language to become a minority language.

Most Uygurs are secular: in fact some Uyghur intellectuals are fiercely anti-religious (e.g. currently anti-Islamic). According to Rudelson (2002), some intellectuals in Urumqi (the capital city of Xinjiang) advocate blowing up all of Xinjiang's mosques, as they believe doing so would divert Uyghur wealth from mosques to secular schools. Nevertheless, various religions such as Shamanism, Manicheism, Buddhism, Christianity, and Islam have been part of Uygur people's lives throughout their history (Issiyev, 1991). Today, the dominant religion of the Uygur peoples is Islam, which is practiced for the most part by rural Uygurs as an expression of cultural and ethnic identity. Religious identifications also serve as a symbol of solidarity with other minority nationalities and/or indigenous peoples such as the Huis, Kazaks, Uzbeks, and Kirghizs in their fight for democracy and equality (see Gladney, 1996).

TIBETANS

The traditional territories of Tibet span the present-day Tibetan Autonomous Region (TAR), as well as much of Sichuan, Qinghai, and small sections of the Yunnan and Gansu provinces. Most of the 4–5 million Tibetans live outside the TAR in the other four provinces, which are home to 2.5–3 million Tibetan native speakers (Bass, 1998). Like Uygurs, Tibetans enjoyed independent empires and civilizations prior to Chinese colonization. The Tibetan language is part of the Tibetan–Burmese subgroup of the Sino-Tibetan language family (Stites, 1999) with a phonographic script based on Sanskrit, unlike the logographic Mandarin script. The Tibetan script, literature, and traditional (monastic) curriculum were developed primarily to represent, instil, and propagate Indian rather than Chinese (Ch'an) Buddhism.

Tibetans continue to be devoted, even fiercely devoted, to Buddhism (what is commonly referred to as "Tibetan Buddhism"). Indeed, Buddhism is so entangled in the Tibetan identity that some young people become monks and nuns to support Tibetan nationalism and independence, not merely as a gesture of religious aspiration. There are four dominant schools of Tibetan Buddhism: the most common is the Gelugpa or "yellow hat" school. This school has a strong monastic orientation with three large monastic universities (Ganden, Sera, and Drepung) and two advance Tantric colleges (Gyume and Gyuto). It is rooted in the great Indian Buddhist monastic universities of the fifth to eleventh centuries, such as Nalanda and includes an elaborate formal Buddhist philosophy and debate curriculum that can take 20 years to complete (MacPherson, 2000, 2001a). This school is associated with the traditional government of Tibet under the Dalai Lamas, who is also Nyingma ("old" school): the remaining two are the Sakya and Kargyu schools, in addition to various smaller orders or movements. During the Cultural Revolution, the monastic traditions came under brutal attack, with most of their buildings destroyed and the monks and nuns killed or forced into lay life. Since then the monastic life style and education system for both men and women has enjoyed a significant revival, in spite of tight restrictions on recruitment by the P.R.C. Government (Mackerras, 1999).

At the same time, it is important not to overstate the ethnic and religious homogeneity of Tibet or the one-to-one relationship between Tibetan ethnicity and the Tibetan Buddhist religion. In fact, there are non-ethnic Tibetans who practice Tibetan Buddhism: the Tu, Yugur, Monba, Prmi, Nosuo, and part of the Xibe of Xinjiang all adhere to Tibetan Buddhism (Mackerras, 1999). Furthermore, there are non-Buddhist Tibetans, including the 6,000 Hui Islamic community in Lhasa (Gladney, 2003). Like the Uygurs, some secular Tibetan intellectuals—the offspring of modern, secular Chinese education—have become refreshingly vocal advocates for the strengthening of the Tibetan secular culture and literatures inside and outside of Tibet. Yet, they do not critique Tibetan Buddhism so much as the orthodoxy of the more conservative elements of the society—monastic and lay. Another more complicated component of Tibet's present-day diversity is the presence of increasing numbers of Han Chinese. Since 1949, the P.R.C. has resettled Han and other minorities in the Tibetan territories, which has left the Tibetans a minority in their own lands, a condition they share with many indigenous peoples around the globe.

Crafts, Medicine, Astrology, and Folk Music and Dance

UYGURS

Uygurs have a strong expertise in craftsmanship. Some Uygur crafts that still exist include metal processing (e.g. blacksmiths, jewellery, and utensils), carpet and rug production, embroidery (e.g. clothes, curtains, and bed sets), ceramics production (e.g. utensils, tiles, toys, and lamps), painting (e.g. furniture and wall painting of houses, mosques, medreses, and mausoleums), wood carving (e.g. furniture, utensils, and toys), musical instrument making (e.g. duttars, rawaps, daps, and sattars), leather processing, and silk making. Uygur medicine has over 2,700 years of history. According to Issiyev (1991), during the Sung Dynasty (906–960), Uygurs introduced numerous medicinal herbs and medical techniques to the Chinese. It is believed that the Uygurs introduced over 100 herbs into the Chinese medicine recorded in Li Shizhen (1518–1593).

Many Western scholars who have studied Uygur medical documents claim Uygurs introduced medical instruments and techniques to Chinese medicine. They argue that acupuncture originated in Central Asia and that it was the Uygurs who perfected the method (see Issiyev, 1991).

Uygurs are well known for their folk and modern dances and music. Some popular folk dances include the *Sanam, Dolan, Sama, Xadiyana*, and *Nazirkom*. The basis for Uygur music is called 12 Mukam, which many Uygurs proudly refer to as the root of all music. Uygur dances and music are mostly upbeat and believed to be expressions of diligence, bravery, openness, and optimism. These dances and songs are not only performed by professionals in theatres, but also performed by non-professional adults and children at family parties and just casual family gathering. Uygur dances and music are also enjoyed by other nationalities such as Kazaks, Uzbeks, and the Han in the Xijiang region and China proper.

TIBETANS

Tibetans too have a long and rich tradition of folk arts and crafts, many of which were tied to the practice of Buddhism. These included statue making, thangka painting, tailoring (appliqué), woodcarving, woodwork and carpentry, metalwork, and silk screen printing. In exile, the Norbulingka Institute near Dharamsala, India, is a centre for the practice of these various traditional arts and crafts (www.tibet.org/norling). Norbulingka also includes a more academic, seven-year program in the Academy of Tibetan Culture, which includes studies of Tibetan philosophy, poetry, history, and medical theory, alongside English, world history, art history, geography, democracy, politics, Buddhist history and art, and history. This institute gives some indication of how Tibetans view the folk arts and more academic aspects of their culture as interrelated and combines them if given the opportunity. In addition, monks and nuns specialize in religious arts such as butter sculptures, tsok sculpting, and various ritual arts, including sand mandalas, sacred music, and sacred dancing used in Tantric Buddhist initiations.

Tibetan medicine dates back to the eighth century and continues to be very popular among Tibetans (Norberg-Hodge, 1991; MacPherson, 2003). Today, it is practiced alongside allopathic (Western) medicine. So central is Tibetan medicine to the Tibetan culture and identity that the constitution of the exile government entrenches the right to choose it as an alternative form of medicine. It requires at least seven years of formal education to qualify as a Tibetan doctor. Tibetan astrology is studied alongside Tibetan medicine. As in India, traditional astrology is popular and routinely consulted by many Tibetans planning special events, in spite of being excluded from modern curricula.

Tibetan folk music and performing arts include dancing, singing, music, opera, and poetry (song writing). Because Tibet was and continues to be a strongly oral culture, oral "songs" and poetry assumed a unique role in the society (Jackson, 1996). As an oral and more recently written genre, these "songs" disseminated news and expressed dissent in a socially legitimate form. Thus, it is not surprising that poetry and songs became elevated to a central role in the Tibetan protest movement (MacPherson, 2001b). There are several Tibetan musical instruments that require extensive training to master: one resembles a banjo and the other a violin. In exile, the Tibetan Institute of Performing Arts in Dharamsala is the centre for Tibetan performance art education (www.tibetanarts.org, accessed on August 4, 2004).

Standard, Modern Curricula in the P.R.C.

As pointed out earlier, modern education in Xinjiang and Tibet has exposed many locals to Chinese education and culture and perhaps thereby to other cultures of the world: however, it has also marginalized or excluded the aforementioned cultural contents from public education. The basic educational syllabus in the P.R.C. covers reading, writing, basic mathematics, science, history, geography, civics, physical education, music, and drawing (Bastid-Bruguiere, 2001). Added to the exclusion of traditional knowledge areas is the troubling exclusion of Tibetan and Uygur contents from the modern, secular subject areas, such as indigenous language and literature, histories, texts, and heroes. Meanwhile, indigenous cultural knowledge (e.g. religion, medicine, cosmology, folk arts, and music) continues to be restricted to religious, non-formal, or private education, which further drives the Tibetans and Uygurs to opt out of the public, secular system (Postiglione, 2000). These modern, secular subject areas and contents are not only standard in programs across China, but also in other developing and developed world contexts.

Yet, education in Tibet and Xinjiang is not only neglectful of local languages, histories, and cultural identities: in many cases it is actively antagonistic and explicitly intended to generate ideological domination and overt assimilation. Communist propaganda infuses the explicit intentions of much state schooling in the region. Curricula continue to teach principles of communism as "moral education" and the local culture and religion as depraved. For example, for most Tibetans, His Holiness the Dalai Lama is loved and respected, yet any overt display of support for him, including possession of photographs, is perceived by the state as unpatriotic, unlawful, and immoral. In published research, a pilot Tibetan middle school program was determined to be successful first and foremost on ideological grounds, because the students adopted Han culture—in combined Confucian (*ren*) and Marxist (socialism and collectivism) terms—and avoided overt displays of indigenous religious or cultural loyalties ("opposing the separatist activities of the Dalai clique") (Chinese Education & Society, 1997, accessed on-line):

The pilot classes all stressed moral education, put "educating the person" (*jiao shu yu ren*) in first place, assigned constant and unflagging attention to education in patriotism, socialism, and collectivism, and especially to education directed at upholding the motherland's unity and opposing the separatist activities of the Dalai clique. In the past six years, no cases of behavior detrimental to national solidarity or of law-breaking or moral depravity were discovered among students in the pilot classes; 129 of them became Communist Youth League members on the eve of their graduation from senior middle school.

Resisting Assimilation: Tibetan and Uygur Responses

Both overt and covert threats of assimilation posed by educational modernization in the P.R.C. have led the Tibetans and Uygurs to assume one of at least five positions *vis-à-vis* education: (1) outright abandonment of native languages and cultures for pragmatic ends (Tournadre, 2003), (2) outright rejection of modern, secular education in favor of traditional options, (3) social and cultural alienation, (4) creative, hybrid (modern/ traditional) religious, non-formal, or private educational institutions, and/or (5) the outright rejection of the P.R.C. state through participation in independence or self-determination movements (MacPherson, 2005).

UYGURS

The general response of the Uygurs to the fear of Sinocization and assimilation has been to assert their unique cultural and linguistic identity by showcasing contemporary artwork and artifacts and images of historical cultural heroes like Mahmud Kashkiri and Yusup Khas Hajib in public places such as restaurants (Rudelson, 1997; Baranovitch, 2003). Other efforts to sustain Uygur cultures and identities include the production and distribution of films, songs, and music through CD-ROMs (Rudelson, 1997; Smith, 2000; Baranovitch, 2003) and the Internet (e.g. www.meshrep.com; www.uygur world.com), both within and outside Xinjiang. Diaspora efforts include the organization of cultural events and establishing Uygur language schools to teach the Uygur language and culture (see www.meshrep.com, accessed on December 28, 2004).

At the same time, the fear of assimilation has fuelled anti-Chinese sentiment and has resulted in some Uygurs turning to religion in an attempt to distance themselves from anything Chinese. Increasing number of young intellectuals, including university professors, research scientists, and graduate students, who are usually anti-religious, are attending mosques both within and outside Xinjiang. We hear more and more Uygurs referring to themselves as Uygurs from Eastern Turkistan rather than Chinese from China. Some express resistance by refusing to speak Mandarin Chinese, the language they were schooled in. The Islamic revival among Uygurs, perhaps not unlike the Buddhist revival in Tibet, can be interpreted both as a sign of resistance and as a ticket out of China (Alles, 2003).

As with Tibetans, another reaction to the perceived assimilation trends are separatist riots like the one that transpired in the Ili region in February 1997, which resulted in severe crackdowns and even tighter control from the Chinese Government (Baranovitch, 2003). These crackdowns and controls resulted in more refugees streaming into the diaspora communities of Montreal, Washington (D.C.), and Munich. Such displacement seems to be creating even more anti-Chinese resentment. This is a phenomenon that did not exist when Chinese policies towards its minorities were friendlier (e.g. the 1980s), when the government encouraged schooling in the Uygur language and promoted the Uygur culture. During this period (e.g. the 1980s) religion was tolerated both in Xinjiang and Tibet (Bass, 1998; Rudelson, 2004).

TIBETANS

Tibetans are highly motivated to resist Sinocization and assimilation, which may help to explain their purported illiteracy rates in excess of 70 percent. Some have pointed out, however, that these "illiteracy rates" are based on literacy in Mandarin Chinese, which masks their participation in locally administered Tibetan literacy and education programs. Above basic primary level, most education in the region is conducted in Mandarin Chinese. As Postiglione et al. (2004) pointed out, official gestures to include Tibetan culture in the life of the school are extra-curricular and superficial at best: "The school architecture, sculptures, photographs, wall paintings and so forth provide representations of Tibetan culture, albeit selectively and interpreted by the state in terms of the ideological themes of national unity, patriotism, revolutionary traditions, civilised behaviour and love of Tibet" (accessed on-line). Added to this concern is the tendency for successful Tibetan students to be sent to boarding schools in Han-dominated urban areas like Chengdu or Beijing, where they come under the influence of more assimilation pressures. Finally, given the institutionalized ethno-centric state schooling (Tibetan Centre for Human Rights and Democracy, 1997), public education is viewed as antagonistic to the Tibetan people and communities. As the Tibetan exile community's Tibetan Centre for Human Rights and Democracy (1997) document concludes "Education's purpose is not only to teach a child reading, writing, calculation and some abstract academic knowledge, it should also enable the child to understand his or her cultural heritage so that this child can grow up to be a responsible member of his or her cultural group" (p. 45), which does not take place through the modern Chinese public education.

Tibetan attempts to resist Sinocization and assimilation have generated a plethora of grassroots and religious educational alternatives. One popular option is to send children into exile to the Tibetan-administered boarding schools (Tibetan children's villages) in India and Nepal. Another option is to rely on private, local schools sponsored by the local community or foreign donors. Sometimes the diaspora is involved in promoting and funding these private village schools, as are charitable organizations such as Trace Foundation, the Red Cross, and Cultural Survival. In this respect, the educational modernization agenda in the P.R.C. has backfired, driving increasing numbers of Tibetans into educational institutions beyond the immediate control of the state. While there are select, Tibetan-initiated attempts to legitimate indigenous knowledge in some programs, these tend to be marginalized from the formal academic curriculum.

Conclusion

In conclusion, the prescribed centralized curriculum in China has exacerbated assimilation threats for Tibetans and Uygurs. The problems associated with this curriculum include the lack of local, culturally relevant contents, the use of Mandarin Chinese as the language of instruction (Beckett and MacPherson, 2005), and reliance on Chinese boarding schools to educate Tibetans and Uygurs. The standard modern curriculum, even for basic education, reflects the imposition of modern rather than local norms. The exclusion of the Uygur and Tibetan languages, literacy practices, religion, medicine, cosmology, and folks arts, music, and dances conveys the mistaken impression to students that their familial and community cultures are irrelevant. As such, the curriculum is not preparing students for a modern context so much as generating a particular Han Chinese (Marxist) variant of it.

Accordingly, we see the pressing need to develop a strong critical perspective in scholarship on China's multicultural policies and practices. The three prevailing philosophical positions that inform multicultural policies and practices around the globe can be described as conservative, liberal, and critical. The conservative approach presumes the superiority of modern Eurocentric (and, by extension, Han) thought and education and objects to multiculturalism as socially divisive. The liberal position acknowledges diversity only superficially, while focusing on a common, universal human "race." Kubota (2004) referred to this as "political correctness with little substance" (p. 31). An alternative form of liberal multiculturalism is what Kincheloe and Steinberg (1997) called "pluralist multiculturalism," in which cultural differences tend to be trivialized (as dances or food), exoticized, and essentialized as ends in themselves. This often involves a list of how "they" differ from "us." With conservative and liberal approaches to multiculturalism, systemic problems of racism, power inequities, and privilege are erased by the presumption of superiority and the superficial rhetoric of equality, diversity, and political correctness. Conservative and liberal approaches to multiculturalism tend to dominate constitutional, policy, and educational research on multiculturalism in the P.R.C.

Critical multiculturalism makes explicit hidden or masked structures, discourses, and relations of inequity that discriminate against one group and enhance the privileges of another. As Brookfield (2000) suggested, criticizing ideology is central to the critical enterprise and involves "the attempt to unearth and challenge dominant ideology and the power relations this ideology justifies" (p. 38). When coupled with post-structuralism, with its emphasis on the discursive, constructed nature of social relations and structures (McLaren, 1994; Chapman, 2004), critical multiculturalism becomes an intellectual enterprise aimed at deconstructing and reconstructing language to generate a more equitable world. As Chapman (2004) suggested:

> Discourses are linguistic and social structures. They enshrine the following: what knowledge, theories, and concepts are acceptable among groups of people; who in that group accrues power from using that knowledge; what is supposedly normal and what is not; what is supposedly true and what is not; and who to exclude and include. Discourses signify who can speak and who cannot, who can be understood and who cannot.
>
> (p. 97)

The Tibetan and Uygur cultures are strong and the peoples fierce, with historical struggles dating back millennia with their lowland Han neighbors. This has made them very pragmatic, adaptable, and willing to participate in modern education and the opportunities availed by the P.R.C., while nonetheless developing creative ways to resist. At the same time, this does not mitigate the tragedy and injustice of being forced to choose between the false dichotomy of modernization and participation in "traditional" or local cultures and societies. Whereas in diaspora context they are learning to reinvent their traditions in a modern context with relevance to people outside of their ethnicity (e.g. the popularity of Tibetan Buddhism), in Tibet and Xinjiang they tend to fall into one of three paths: (1) outright rejection of all formal education, (b) embracing of religious education that can have "fundamentalist" extremes, or (3) embracing the Han Chinese version of secular modernity that constructs their cultures and people as inferior. This is a terrible and unnecessary choice to ask people to make.

According to Postiglione (2000), increasing numbers of Uygur and Tibetan children are dropping out of school because of the linguistic and cultural discrepancies between their homes and schools. Many working people have and are losing their jobs while new graduates are unable to find employment, thus displacing people physically, socially, economically, and psychologically. This displacement and insecurity further fuels the sense of the need to move towards the linguistic and cultural norms of the dominant group. Yet, this is countered by the deep and historically engrained fears of Han Chinese domination in the region, which encourage both the Uygur and Tibetan peoples to respond by only increasing their efforts to hold on to their language and culture through art, songs, music, and religion, both within and outside China. If this means pursuing private or non-formal education and revoking the privileges of state schooling, many seem ready to make such sacrifices. This only further aggravates and exacerbates the economic, political, and social inequity between the indigenous peoples and the state, thereby fuelling political unrest. Consider the following two testimonials by Tibetans students who finally left Tibet for exile in India (Tibetan Centre for Human Rights and Democracy, 1997): "In our Tibetan book, all the stories were about Mao and his great doings. There was nothing about Tibet, the Dalai Lama or our history" and "In our Tibetan language book it said that 'our capital is Beijing.' Once I crossed out Beijing and wrote Lhasa. When the teacher read this he beat me severely" (p. 47).

Recognizing the injustice of the P.R.C. rule over the region and the imposition of educational policies and practices as *de facto* assimilation, the Uygurs and Tibetans have sustained self-determination movements that range from outright cessation movements through to calls for "human rights" as enhanced local controls over culture, education, and language. These struggles of the Tibetans and Uygurs illustrate the complex effects of educational modernization and its possible role in the rise of fundamentalism and even cessationism. The manner in which curricula are developed and implemented can have a profound effect on the peace and perceived justice of development. When education is responsive to the needs of local peoples and offers a viable path both to local participation and global access, then it can and should promote global understanding. When forcibly imposed, making students choose between assimilation (i.e. betrayal of the local community) and economic or educational opportunities (in the broader nation state or global context), then it can backfire and lead understandably to resistance.

Resources and Tools for Educators

Questions

1. The article deals with marginalized cultures in China. What are some examples from your own country or region?
2. How would you identify the culture of your family or local community? How much of that or those culture(s) are represented in the formal curriculum of schools? What type of cultural knowledge or activities are represented or not represented?
3. Choose a marginalized culture or community with which you are familiar. What forms of knowledge and types of activities are most

important to that culture or community? How well are those knowledges or activities reflected in their local formal school curricula?

For Further Reading

Postiglione, G. A. (2000). National minority regions: Studying school discontinuation. In J. Liu, H. A. Ross, & D. P. Kelly (Eds.), *The ethnographic eye: An interpretative study of education in China* (pp. 51–71). New York: Falmer Press.

This is the best resource concerning cultural and language issues facing minority, indigenous, or other "nationalities" within the P.R.C.

Beckett, G. H. & MacPherson, S. (2005). Researching the impact of English on minority and indigenous languages in non-"Western" contexts. (A response to Nunan, 2003). *TESOL Quarterly, 39*(2), 299–308.

This resource is helpful for those readers intending to do research outside of typical "Western" contexts. The article cautions researchers when representing findings that over-generalize and distort the true diversity and variation of local minority and indigenous communities. The case concerns an article written about the dramatic increase in English as a foreign language education in the Asia-Pacific region, including mainland China. The authors argue their position with reference to the Tibetans and Uygur indigenous "nationalities."

Kanu, Y. (2006). *Curriculum as cultural practice: Postcolonial imaginations.* Toronto, ON: University of Toronto Press.

This forthcoming edited collection offers a broad perspective on post-colonial issues in education from various perspectives across various contexts (Central America, Inuit, and Canadian immigrants) and disciplinary fields (English as a foreign language, language arts, social studies, and mathematics).

Diaspora, Indigenous and Minority Education: An International Journal. Mahwah, NJ: Lawrence Erlbaum & Associates.

This new academic journal publishes research and program studies from around the world that offer insights into initiatives to sustain marginalized or oppressed communities and cultures through education. It arose out of the cultural education–cultural sustainability network and can be accessed for subscriptions through www.leaonline.com.

Suggestions for Educators

1. Discuss the following. What recommendations would you make *vis-à-vis* curricular and educational development to enable it to become more

responsive to the needs of marginalized students and communities? b) What is the place and relative role of formal (e.g. public and institutional) education and non-formal (e.g. community, after-school, or religious) education in cultural education?

2. Group items within the following list of topics or cultural activities into clusters of three to four topics and give each cluster an appropriate category: European or North American history, pottery appreciation, family history/family tree, aboriginal (herbal) medicine, first nations' legends, studying poetry, playing the harmonica, studying songs, playing the flute, the *Oxford English Dictionary*, quilt making, Western (allopathic) medicine, writing poetry, essay writing, folk dancing, the Ten Commandments, the Bible, ballet, *Gulliver's Travels* (a fantasy), the UN Declaration of Human Rights, baseball, "reading" animal tracks, the art of Picasso, the Koran, writing lyrics, making pottery. Compare your categories to the subject areas *and* topics/activities included in your local school curricula (e.g. elementary or secondary). Make a check mark next to each topic you believe is covered and an X next to those you believe are *not* covered in the curricula. Discuss the following. In your opinion, which of the various topics *should be* included in the curricula and which should *not* be included and why? What impact does the subject area or discipline have on the topic, for example if the first nations' legends are discussed in social studies versus language arts? What else do you notice about the types of knowledge and activities that are included and/or excluded in formal curricula?

Note

1. There is an important shortcoming in this data, which is the slippage between the terms educational development and its operational indicator in the percentage of the literate population. The problem is that literacy indicators appear to be restricted to literacy in Mandarin. This operational definition excludes the educational development of monolingual or late bilingual people who end up literate in their native language (e.g. Tibetan) but not in Mandarin. Tibetan-focused literacy programs are often sponsored through local, religious, or privately-sponsored institutions and their curricula emphasize indigenous linguistic and cultural development. This reliability problem poses an interpretive challenge not unlike that arising from immigrant literacy level data in North America based on English language tests.

References

Alles, E. (2003). Muslim religious education in China. *China Perspectives, 45,* 21–29.

Baranovitch, N. (2003). From the Margins to the center: The Uyghur challenge in Beijing. *The China Quarterly, 175,* 726–750.

Bass, C. (1998). *Education in Tibet: Policy and practices since 1950.* London: Zed Books in association with Tibetan Information Network.

Bastid-Bruguiere, M. (2001). Educational diversity in China. *China Perspectives, 36,* 17–26.

Beckett, G. H. & MacPherson, S. (2005). Researching the impact of English on minority and indigenous languages in non-"Western" contexts. *TESOL Quarterly, 39*(2).

Bourdieu, P. (1991). *Language & symbolic power.* Cambridge, MA: Harvard University Press.

Brookfield, S. D. (2000). The concept of critically reflective practice. In A. L. Wilson & E. R. Hayes (Eds.), *Handbook of adult and continuing education*. San Francisco: Jossey-Bass.

Chapman, V. L. (2004). Using critical personal narratives: A post-structural perspective on practice. *Promoting Critical Practice in Adult Education*, (102), 95–103.

Chinese Education & Society. (1997). Summary of pilot project work in middle-school Tibetan-language instruction. *Chinese Education & Society, 30*(4). Accessed online on December 15, 2004.

Crossley, P. K. (1990). Ming ethnology. A paper presented to the China Colloquium of the University of Washington. In S. Harrell (Ed.), *Cultural encounters on China's ethnic frontiers*. Seattle & London: University of Washington Press.

Dalai Lama, His Holiness the XIVth. (2003). Understanding and transforming the mind. In B. A. Wallace (Ed.), *Buddhism and science* (pp. 91–106). New York: Columbia University Press.

Ferreiro, E. (2003). *Past and present of the verbs to read and to write: Essays on literacy* (Trans. Mark Fried). Toronto, ON: Groundwood Books/Douglas & McIntyre.

Gladney, D. C. (1996). *Muslim Chinese: Ethnic nationalism in the People's Republic*. Cambridge, MA: Harvard University Press.

Gladney, D. C. (2003). *Ethnic identity in China: The making of a Muslim minority nationality*. Belmont, CA: Wadsworth/Thomson.

Hansen, M. H. (1999). *Lessons in being Chinese: Minority education and ethnic identity in Southwest China*. Seattle & London: University of Washington Press.

Harrell, S. (Ed.) (1995). *Cultural encounters on China's ethnic frontiers*. Seattle & London: University of Washington Press.

International Campaign for Tibet. (2001). *Jampa: The story of racism in Tibet. Prepared for the United Nations World Conference Against Racism, Durban, South Africa, September 2001*. Washington, DC & Amsterdam: International Campaign for Tibet.

Issiyev, K. (1991). Uighur script. *Eastern Turkistan Information, 1*(2), 1–7.

Jackson, R. R. (1996). "Poetry" in Tibet: *Glu, mGur, sNyan ngag* and "songs of experience." In J. I. Cabezon & R. R. Jackson (Eds.), *Tibetan literature: Studies in genre* (pp. 368–392). Ithaca, NY: Snow Lion Publications.

Jinpa, T. (2003). Science as an ally or a rival philosophy? Tibetan Buddhist thinkers' engagement with modern science. In B. A. Wallace (Ed.), *Buddhism and science* (pp. 71–85). New York: Columbia University Press.

Kanu, Y. (Ed.) (in press). *Curriculum as cultural practice: Post-colonial imaginations*. Toronto, ON: University of Toronto Press.

Kincheloe, J. L. & Steinberg, S. R. (1997). *Changing multiculturalism*. Buckingham, UK: Open University Press.

Kubota, R. (2004). Critical multiculturalism and second language education. In B. Norton & K. Toohey (Eds.), *Critical pedagogies and language learning* (pp. 30–52). New York & Cambridge, UK: Cambridge University Press.

Lamontagne, J. (1999). National minority education in China: A nationwide survey across counties. In G. A. Postiglione (Ed.), *China's national minority education: Culture, schooling, and development* (pp. 133–171). New York & London: Falmer Press.

McLaren, P. (1994). Critical pedagogy, political agency, and the pragmatics of justice: The case of Lyotard. *Educational Theory, 44*(3), 319–340.

MacPherson, S. (2000). A path of learning: Indo-Tibetan Buddhism as education. Unpublished dissertation with the Centre for the Study of Curriculum & Instruction, University of British Columbia.

MacPherson, S. (2001a). An alternative enlightenment praxis: Tibetan Buddhist monastic education. *International Journal of Curriculum & Instruction, 3*(1), 97–114.

MacPherson, S. (2001b). A genre to remember: Tibetan popular poetry & song as remembrance. *Language and Literacy: A Canadian Educational e-Journal, 3*(2), 23pp.

MacPherson, S. (2003). TESOL for biolinguistic sustainability: The ecology of English as a *lingua mundi*. *TESL Canada, 20*(2), 1–22.

MacPherson, S. (2005). Negotiating language contact and identity change in developing Tibetan/English bilingualism. *TESOL Quarterly, 39*(4), 585–607.

Mackerras, C. (1999). Religion and the education of China's minorities. In G. A. Postiglione (Ed.), *China's national minority education: Culture, schooling, and development* (pp. 23–54). New York & London: Falmer Press.

Mair, V. (2004). *The mummy people: A documentary*. WCET-TV. March 27, 2004. Alexandria, VA: Public Broadcasting Service.

Mawkanuli, T. (2001). The Jungar Tuvas: Language and national identity in PRC. *Central Asian Survey, 20*(4), 497–517.

Norberg-Hodge, H. (1991). *Ancient futures: Learning from Ladakh*. San Francisco: Sierra Club Books.

Nunan, D. (2003). The impact of English as a global language on education policies and practices in the Asia-Pacific region. *TESOL Quarterly, 37*(4), 589–613.

Postiglione, G. A. (1997). The schooling of Tibetans (I) & (II). *Chinese Education and Society, 30*(4&5), 3–102.

Postiglione, G. A. (1999). Introduction: State schooling and ethnicity in China. In G. A. Postiglione (Ed.), *China's national minority education: Culture, schooling, and development* (pp. 3–19). New York & London: Falmer Press.

Postiglione, G. A. (2000). National minority regions: Studying school discontinuation. In J. Liu, H. A. Ross, & D. P. Kelly (Eds.), *The ethnographic eye: An interpretative study of education in China* (pp. 51–71). New York: Falmer Press.

Postiglione, G. A., Zhiyong, Z., & Jiao, B. (2004). From ethnic segregation to impact integration: state schooling and identity construction for rural Tibetans. *Asian Ethnicity, 15*(2), 195–217.

Postiglione, G. A., Jiao, B., & Gyatso, S. (2006). Household perspectives on school attendance in rural Tibet, *Educational Review, 58*(3), 317–337.

Rudelson, J. (1997). *Oasis identities: Uyghur nationalism along China's silk road*. New York: Columbia University Press.

Rudelson, J. (2002). *Xinjiang's Uyghirs in the ensuing US–China partnership*. Washington, DC: Congressional-Executive Commission on China, Uyghur Panel.

Rudelson, J. (2004). Cross-border and transnational influences on Xinjiang Uyghur nationalism. *Caucasus and Central Asian News, 5*, 3–7.

Smith, J. (2000). Four generations of Uighurs: The shift towards ethno-political ideologies among Xinjiang's youth. *Inner Asia, 2*, 195–224.

Stites, R. (1999). Writing cultural boundaries: National minority language policy, literacy planning, and bilingual education. In G. A. Postiglione (Ed.), *China's national minority education: Culture, schooling, and development* (pp. 95–130). New York & London: Falmer Press.

Tibetan Centre for Human Rights and Democracy. (1997). *The next generation: The state of education in Tibet today*. Dharamsala: Tibetan Centre for Human Rights and Democracy.

Tournadre, N. (2003). The dynamics of Tibetan–Chinese bilingualism: The current situation and future prospects. *China Perspectives, 45*, 30–36.

Upton, J. (1999). The development of modern school-based Tibetan language education in the PRC. In G. A. Postiglione (Ed.), *China's national minority education: Culture, schooling, and development* (pp. 281–339). New York & London: Falmer Press.

Communal Infrastructure and Cultural Sustainability in Different National Contexts

In the previous section we focused on the importance of policies promulgated by the state for the possibility of cultural education–cultural sustainability. Educational institutions are embedded within national environments of which the state is a key actor. However, no less important is the web of communal institutions within which schools and other educational institutions are embedded. Communal networks filter the influence of the state, each institution creating environments for living everyday life that at once accord with the law and cultural norms of a given country and at the same time enable the autonomous (counter-cultural) space necessary for sustaining the group's particular culture.

From the sociological perspective, individuals belong to a cultural group to the extent that they spend time in the institutions associated with that group. These institutions range from the home, to the school, house of worship, community center, welfare associations, and more. As the individual moves from one to the other in the course of daily life, so he or she builds a sense of concrete connection to fellow members of the cultural group, which in turn anchors the symbolic connection to the larger cultural group the world over.

Cultural education–cultural sustainability is dependent on the robustness of the communal network of institutions. The chapters in this section enable us to understand how institutions contribute to the creation of a vibrant cultural community capable of enabling its members to interact with the wider society in a manner that also enables cultural sustainability. The case studies cover minority and diaspora communities as diverse as the Basques, Koreans in China, Coptic Orthodox and Chaldean Catholic communities in Australia, and Armenians in Bulgaria. Each case study provides a rich description of the communal institutions these groups have created and the challenges they confront.

Gloria Totoricagüena shifts the focus away from schools to the informal educational practices of the Basque Community Center. Totoricagüena describes the place of the community center *vis-à-vis* a variety of other strategies used by diaspora Basque communities to maintain their ethnic identity. She shows how, in the age of globalization and cyber space, a diaspora can be held together or re-created in the mind through cultural maintenance and shared imagination that is routed within communal institutions like the community center.

A key insight into cultural education–cultural sustainability provided by Totoricagüena is her argument that the diasporic community is an excellent example of multiculturalism in practice. Cultural sustainability in an open society requires the ability of an individual to move between multiple cultural contexts, yet at the same time not lose the cultural attachments that tie him or her to the minority group. Successful communal institutions will foment environments that are both pluralistic and able to serve as a vital cultural resource. Totoricagüena argues that the transnational diasporic identity is one of multiple identities: multiple cultures coexist in an individual's identity which in turn is reflected in his or her use of communal institutions.

Totoricagüena's research covers Basque cultural centers in forty-three communities in six countries using quantitative data and qualitative observations. Respondents' attitudes towards traditional Basque identity maintenance and Basque center educational activities are analyzed. The research findings show that respondents who profess a strong sense of Basque identity also embrace multiple identities, presenting them as non-threatening and actually enriching for themselves and the community. This ability is part of the folk knowledge individuals adapt to their particular diaspora context and is not necessarily the consequence of a systematic pedagogic or didactic curriculum or project.

Totoricagüena is reinforcing the argument that communal institutions should actively work to reinforce "informal" or "folk" knowledge and not only think of the transmission of culture in terms of "formal education." The argument raises questions regarding the possibilities and potential of translating lived experience into curricular goals, which often, by the mere fact of becoming intentional, lose their power.

The remaining three chapters in this section move our focus from a particular type of communal institution to a macro-analysis of the development of communal infrastructure in three national contexts. Sheena Choi's chapter focuses on "Korean exceptionalism" in China. Given the rather depressing account of the Mongol, Uygur, and Tibetan experiences in the first section, the extent of Korean exceptionalism is all the more apparent. Ethnic Koreans have achieved one of the highest levels of educational attainment and standard of living and the lowest illiteracy rate and lowest birth rate of any Chinese ethnic minority group, including the Han Chinese. In exploring cultural education–cultural sustainability in the context of ethnic Koreans in China, Choi explains Korean "exceptionalism" by showing how historical context, political economy, cultural heritage, and social dynamics enable the creation of an exceptional communal and educational infrastructure and, hence, the ability to sustain Korean culture among expatriates living in Manchuria. Moreover, the accomplishments of the ethnic Koreans in China result in confidence in their culture and pride in their ethnic identity—a primary ingredient for cultural sustainability.

Richard Rymarz and Marian de Souza examine the attempt of two small Christian communities, Coptic Orthodox and Chaldean Catholic, to pass on their religious and cultural heritage in contemporary Australia. Like the Korean case study, Rymarz and de Souza paint an optimistic picture of how the two groups created the communal infrastructure for a "community of believers" that is confident of its ability to survive in the pluralist Australian environment. The distinctive aspect of the Rymarz and de Souza chapter vis-à-vis others in the book is the importance of the church as a dominant communal institution that interacts with and shapes the relationships between other communal institutions.

The qualitative research effort, conducted among Copts who had a strong association with the Coptic Orthodox Church, explores some of the reasons why the Coptic Orthodox tradition is able to maintain such a prominent part in the lives of its followers. The study shows that, as with many immigrant groups, the church serves as a focus for the whole community. The paper suggests that the Copts display a number of characteristics that will continue to make them a resilient community able to maintain both its cultural and religious identity. The size of their community is large enough to benefit from the current Federal government's policy towards the education of minority groups. The Coptic community has also managed to retain a high level of commitment and identification with religious ideals and beliefs. Finally, Copts have retained a strong identity through their participation in a number of practices that serve as very effective markers between them and the wider culture.

In comparison to the optimism of Choi and Rymarz and de Souza chapters, Mari Firkatian describes a more ambiguous experience for the Armenian community in Bulgaria. The Armenian diaspora has persisted in many foreign environments by depending not only on its church as a beacon of identity but on a large selection of social, civic, and charitable organizations, including institutions dedicated to dance, theatre, athletic, charitable, political, and youth-oriented activity. Through the rich weave of communal institutions, Armenians have traditionally created a core sense of community.

Firkatian's chapter describes the devastating impact of the policies of the communist regime and the difficulties involved in the attempt to rebuild or sustain communal and educational institutions in the post-communist era. Thus, while the Bulgarian Government has no incentive to lure Armenians away from their ethnicity as they are a well-integrated minority and part of the national fabric, their fate is nonetheless the same as many other ethnic minorities of the former Soviet bloc countries. Lack of governmental financial support, a product of the general weakness of the economy, plus the weakened state of the communities infrastructure resulting from Soviet era policies prevents the community from securely re-establishing its traditional institutional networks. The result is that, despite the desire to maintain their culture, the pressures and time demands of modern life drive Armenians to make choices that pull them further away from a vibrant communal life.

In summary, from the four chapters in this section we learn about the importance of communal institutional networks for enabling a vital experience of minority culture in everyday life. Communal institutions literally provide the space within which cultural education–cultural sustainability occurs. The key issues raised in the chapters revolve around Totoricagüena's focus on the informal cultural practices that are enabled in Basque community centers. These informal practices are essential to the cultural toolkit that individuals draw on and they are not easily transmitted through formal educational programs. The other three chapters pick up on this note—all assume that vitality of informal group culture that Totoricagüena describes and take it upon themselves to show us the extent to which combinations of different communal institutions can anchor and secure group culture through both the informal and formal educational dimensions of everyday life. In the case of Koreans in China and Copts and Chaldean Christians in Australia we learn of the strength and stability of these communal networks and the manner in which the relationship between minority groups and the wider society, as well as dynamics within the minority groups, enables community. In the case of Armenians in Bulgaria we see the opposite phenomena—namely, how the policies of the state can negatively impact on internal communal dynamics.

CHAPTER 7

Agents of Socialization: The Educational Agenda of Basque Centers in Basque Transnational Communities

GLORIA TOTORICAGUENA

Introduction

Basques have migrated from their Spanish–French Pyrenees homeland for more than a millennium. They participated in the Roman colonization of Iberia, whaling expeditions in the Atlantic, commercial networks throughout southern Spain and northern Europe, and in the Spanish colonization of the Americas and the Philippines. Basques suffered political and economic exile during and after the French Revolution, the First and Second Carlist Wars of the 1800s in Spain, and throughout the Spanish Civil War of 1936–1939 and subsequent four decades of the Francisco Franco dictatorship. Regardless of the circumstances and destinations, over the centuries millions of Basques living in foreign host societies have maintained ties to their ancestral homeland, language, customs, traditions, and ethnic identity. These links range from emotional and psychological to educational and commercial and today they orient nearly 200 Basque diaspora organizations in twenty-one states around the globe.

The diaspora experience, in general, problematizes Western modernity's linear account of time and space and the deployment of rhetoric such as integration, assimilation, and inclusion. Those who live a diasporic and transnational identity occupy the multidimensional, asymmetrical, and flexible world system to which they contribute. Their goals are often the opposite of assimilation and inclusion in a new society, though acceptance and respect for their identity are desired. Diaspora populations display multiple and partial allegiances and belongings to nation states, ethnicity, and to various cultures and societies. It is a complex reconfiguration of meaning and power and of education and participation in one's community. While the era of modernity demanded state and nation state building, loyalty from citizens, and conformity and obedience to a uniform state culture identity, today's post-modernity or the age of globalization allows for multiple affiliations and associations including diasporic allegiances.

In this chapter, I will utilize quantitative data I collected during 1996–1999 from forty-three Basque communities using anonymous written questionnaires. The numbers of respondents reflect the size of their communities and include individuals from Argentina (269), Australia (102), Belgium (twenty-four), Peru (fourteen), the U.S. (310), and Uruguay (113). The communities represent the most disparate examples of the Basque diaspora, from oldest to most recent migration, largest to smallest Basque diaspora populations, and geographically furthest and nearest to the homeland. By investigating the attitudes, opinions, and values of these immigrants and later generations, I am able to compare aggregate answers by geography, gender, generation, and so on using cross-tabulations. Questionnaire respondents were randomly selected from the Basque center membership lists while controlling for variables of gender and generation of immigrant. Their responses are only generalizable to the Basque center populations, which are the focus of this analysis. The high response rate to the questionnaire of 87 percent is partly attributed to detailed preparation and to this being one of the first quantitative academic sociological surveys of the Basque diaspora. In addition to the conceptual and nominal evidence gathered, qualitative data collected during 1996–2004 adds information from in-depth personal interviews with over 350 self-defining Basques living in the same countries. The interviewees were also members (or the spouses, parents, or children of members) of Basque organizations. The open-ended interviews provided needed explanatory information and insight, which augmented the specific queries asked in the questionnaires and expressed valuable attitudes toward the Basque organizations and their ethnicity maintenance activities (Totoricagüena, 2004b).

These survey research results demonstrate the self-identification of diaspora Basques with various categories of identity. With a low of 3 percent of respondents in the U.S. and a high of 28 percent in Uruguay defining themselves as only host country (i.e. "Uruguayan" without a hyphenation), almost three-quarters of diaspora Basque respondents described themselves as a combination of either Basque–host country (Basque–Argentine) or host country–Basque (Argentine–Basque), and others simply defined themselves as "Basque" with no hyphen. Regardless of their self-labeling, each maintained their Basque identity away from their homeland. This article aims to describe and explain why and how Basque immigrants and their descendants manifest a trans-national identity through Basque center educational activities and will emphasize that the goals of today's multiculturalism should reflect the reality of multiple identities as non-threatening and actually enriching for the individual and the community. Although multicultural identities are being manifest and promoted in the diaspora communities, there is no systematic pedagogical or didactic curriculum or project. The existing success remains a result of haphazard or virtually non-existent planning.

Why have Basque individuals living abroad educated themselves and their descendants with a goal of maintaining "Basqueness?" I argue it is a result of the framework of diasporic ethnic identity, which serves dual purposes with positive social status: individual and communal. Tajfel's social identity theory is especially useful in attempting to explain how Basques are able to construct individual separation and uniqueness by highlighting differences with non-Basques and simultaneously able to experience a feeling of belonging and group consciousness by pertaining to the ethnic community and part of the "us" as opposed to the "them." In this volume, Plamen Makariev also discusses the importance of Taylor's (1994) argumentation that a culture's positive self-image is of decisive importance to self-respect and self-confidence. Richard Rymarz and Marian De Souza discuss Coptic Christians in Australia and the relationship between the unique status, strong sense of being special, and their resilience (see Chapter 9). These values are evident objectives in the informal curriculum and educational programs of the Basque centers as well.

Maintenance of Basque Ethnic Identity in Diaspora Communities

Unlike many other group memberships, ethnicity is generally oriented towards the past, the history and origin of family, group, and nation. However, diasporic ethnic identity and diasporic imagination combine the past with one's present and future selves (Totoricagüena, 2004a, p. xvii). Transnational Basques practice their "Basqueness" in order to maintain their identity and knowledge for the future and their educational activities tend to be aimed at their youth.

Social Identity Theory

A comprehensive sociological conception of ethnic identity maintenance comes from Tajfel's (1978, 1981, 1982; Tajfel and Turner, 1979) "social identity theory," which concerns the perceptions individuals have of themselves in comparison to their perception of others in society. The comparison becomes increasingly salient as people contrast themselves with others while looking for positive distinctiveness and, more specifically, comparing one's group to other groups in a hierarchical manner.

Tajfel believed (1978) that individuals naturally have an upward directional drive and, if one is able to compare oneself favorably to others in society because of one's ethnicity, it follows that this person will maintain the ethnic identity and keep that particular group affiliation in order to augment a comparative social status. When investigating the prestige given to Basque immigrants in Argentina, Uruguay, Peru, Australia, the U.S., and, increasingly, in Belgium, it is possible to determine that this is indeed a significant factor related to Basque identity maintenance. My data demonstrate that, from 59 percent in Belgium to the high of 90 percent of respondents in the U.S., these Basques perceive themselves to have a positive social status in their host country and believe that it is important to perpetuate that recognition. Although they do not blatantly state that this is *the* determining factor in why they maintain their Basqueness, they do tend to mention in interviews—and agree in questionnaires—that activities at the centers should remind children of the "responsibility to maintain a good reputation in the community." Table 7.1 represents the percentages of respondents who agreed or strongly agreed that the reputation of Basques was related to their own reasons for identifying with their Basqueness.

The positive association between "Basque" and "honest" and "hard-working" is equivalent to social praise and the participants reported the pride experienced when telling new acquaintances they are Basque. Though individual respondents remarked that the centers and parents should share these attitudes with their children, they were also cautious about public displays or statements regarding these perceptions because they could be portrayed as arrogance.

TABLE 7.1 Relationship between the perception of Basques' social status and maintenance of ethnic identity (%)

	U.S.	Peru	Australia	Uruguay	Argentina	Belgium
I preserve my Basque identity because I am proud of the reputation of Basques as honest and hardworking people	90	85	81	72	71	59

Total respondents = 832.

Transnationalism and Globalization

Neither globalization nor transnationalism is a new phenomenon and both have positively affected relationships among Basques around the world. I utilize "globalization" to refer to the development of transnational social, political, and economic networks of interaction and exchange. Contemporary effects of technology have accelerated and strengthened these webs. The concept of transnational identity matches well with the goals of multiculturalism and has been aptly defined as:

The ability to add identities rather than being forced to substitute one for another; multiple identities and "cross-pressures" to enhance rather than inhibit one's options; to anchor one's uniqueness in the complex constellation of communities to which one chooses to make a commitment; the opportunity to be different people in different settings . . . each individual is, in effect, a community of the communities individually accepted or chosen.

(Elkins, 1997, p. 150)

Theories of multicultural education promote the societal and individual benefits to preserving ethnic differences and the Basque centers worldwide are unknowingly promoting this vision of multicultural education through informal pedagogical structures such as dance groups, choirs, sports competitions, and Basque summer camps for adolescents. Multicultural experiences teach individuals the skills necessary to cross ethnic and cultural boundaries and to respect and understand others who are different from themselves and the Basque center activities provide these exact opportunities.

The effects of globalization on transnationalism and diasporas "disrupt the spatial-temporal units of analysis" (Lavie and Swedenburg, 1996, p. 14). Basques are physically connected to the host countries where they currently live and emotionally and psychologically connected to ancestral homelands. This is the transnational identity nourished in the Basque diasporic communities' activities and projects. New telecommunications technologies foment transnational ties with increasing speed and the frequency of communication and contact among the diaspora communities—and between the diaspora and the Basque Country—I argue, will continue to increase. For example, in April 2005, Basques around the world gathered at their centers to watch Basque parliamentary election results live on Euskal Telebista (Basque Television) satellite cable, while others participated in elections debate chat rooms on the Internet. These interactions were unthinkable just ten years ago during the 1994 elections. The very idea of open dual citizenship and participation in elections where one has no residency tend to stretch ideas of multiculturalism to other realms, which often causes alarm for politicians and citizens of host and home countries.

Minority communities can be held together and re-created through shared experiences, such as ethno-genesis—a process whereby immigrants practice a transfigured cultural identity creating a sort of hybrid culture or synthesis of the ancestral culture and that of the new host environment. This provides a link from the homeland to the new country for recent emigrants and ties from the new society to the homeland for the latter generations. Researchers of culture have generally assumed that direct and continuous contact between groups of different cultures leads to a decrease in the differences among them and/or an appreciation of each other's identity. That may be a goal of public multicultural education, but in the Basque centers the objectives are the opposite: specifically to maintain the Basque identity and preserve Basque cultural traditions. Rather than defining multiculturalism as a society with plural mono-cultural groups, in the Basque centers, one finds communities with multicultural identities: a combination of host society and homeland.

Each of the countries in this study, exempting Peru, has a demonstrated growth in the establishment of institutions, which includes members of all ages with various activities for differing interests. Since the beginning of the transition to democracy in Spain in 1978, new Basque centers have sprouted in Argentina (48), the U.S. (15), Uruguay (6), Belgium (1), and Australia (1). This is not a result of new emigration out of the Basque Country. If the number of organizations is growing and in several of the existing institutions the membership lists are increasing, I would argue that we are experiencing the opposite of the assimilationist effect and that perhaps globalization residues are facilitating avenues for reconstructing and maintaining transnational and multicultural ethnic identity. Transnational individuals are simultaneously both homeland and host country multicultural subjects. Many are perfectly assimilated in their host country cultures and societies and also are perfectly assimilated in their ethnic communities where they maintain and practice another identity. Education in the Basque cultural centers of the diaspora is neither for preventing assimilation, facilitating integration, promoting social change, or social segregation. Programs simply forward the goals of offering personal enrichment through multidimensional identity construction and reconstruction. The ethnicity maintenance activities in the Basque diasporic communities follow sociological and psychological arguments of belonging, self-fulfilment, and positive social status in one's daily life.

Maintaining Cultural Identity in the Basque Transnational Space

Regardless of their local diversity Basque immigrants have united to form Basque institutions with similar goals of maintaining their traditions and ethnic identity, fomenting the music, dance, poetry, cuisine, history, sports, language, and religious practices of their ancestors' homeland. These are not reproductions of the homeland religious or cultural institutions or networks as seen in several other diaspora communities, but are immigrant-specific organizations, which have evolved into associations for ethnicity education and maintenance.

Throughout Argentina and the U.S., Basque-owned boarding houses and their employees served as surrogate homes and families where Basques could stay short term while traveling to town for doctor visits or in the off-season of agriculture or livestock raising. In Argentina, the U.S., and, on a smaller scale, in Uruguay and Australia these Basque "hotels" served as information centers for news from *Euskal Herria*, unofficial matchmaking centers for young bachelors, "home away from home," and networking for employment (Totoricagüena, 2004a). The significance of the facilities emanates from chain migration, which fomented continued interaction with contemporary information and attitudes directly from the homeland for inter-Basque–community relations (homeland to diaspora) as well as intra-Basque–community relations. Eventually, the established immigrants no longer needed temporary room and board or an informal employment agency: they needed a place to socialize, to communicate with others in their own language, and a place to practice their own traditions and culture. The institutions of the boarding house or Basque hotel were eventually replaced with the Basque cultural centers.

The original functions of the Basque networks and organizations, as so with other ethnic organizations in other host societies, were to reduce the strain of the newcomer status and alleviate cultural adaptation. The Basque centers provided immigrants with economic and social services along with instant acceptance, friendship, and belonging. The end of continuous Basque immigration has changed the necessary functions of today's organizations to those of marketing Basque cultural identity. Participation in these centers is voluntary and now for psychological, emotional, and social fulfillment rather than economic need. Communications tend to be less the daily member-to-member interaction and have evolved to monthly dinners and social gatherings, for example *mus* card game tournaments, annual festival celebrations, and institutional newsletters. The same organizations that taught host country language courses and found accommodation and employment for recent Basque immigrants are now disseminating genealogical information for Basques to research their heritage, teaching *Euskera*, Basque language, rather than the host country language, collecting travel brochures of the Basque Country, and helping members organize tours to their own homeland. Basque immigrants initially needed the services the organizations provided: however, later generations are optional consumers. The focus has changed from educational activities highlighting the future of the immigrant members, to those retaining the Basque historical past and educating later generation Basques about their own culture and identity.

Programs

Typical Basque center-sponsored activities include members dinners, bingo games, dances, *mus* and *briska* card tournaments, Basque cooking classes, language classes, dancing classes, photography exhibits, celebrations of the Basque Day of the Homeland or *Aberri Eguna*, Saint Agatha, Saint Ignatius, picnics, and Christmas dinners with food and crafts bazaars. Athletes also enjoy golf tournaments and *pala* and *pelota* or handball and racquetball, basketball, and soccer tournaments. There are women's clubs and youth groups who gather for films, lunches, and short excursions. These social activities have an agglutinating effect on the community individuals as they meet and socialize with other Basques, leading to friendships and additional reasons to return to future functions.

The purely educational activities are fewer and include language and cuisine classes and, more recently, Basque Country history courses and seminars. Teachers are almost always volunteers, with no pedagogical training, lesson plans, or learning objectives. One course participant stated that:

> You know, it is one thing to speak Basque, but it is another thing entirely to know how to teach it. I do not mean to complain, but one of the reasons that people do not stay in the class is because it is a waste of time and the "teacher" is not really a teacher.

Another individual in a different country stated a similar attitude:

> I signed up for the history class because I want to learn about my past, but this guy just talks about himself and his own family most of the time. There is no mechanism to get rid of him because he is a volunteer and no one else will teach us. I guess something is better than nothing, but they would have more people participating if this could be properly organized and taught.

In 2007, only a handful of the 200 Basque diaspora organizations reported having a structured educational committee or education chairperson, yet all supported activities that educate their members and communities in regards to Basque themes. In the U.S., where there is a center for Basque studies at the University of Nevada, Reno and English language textbooks exist for a wide variety of Basque themes, not one single order for any textbook has ever been placed by any of the nearly forty Basque organizations in that country. Basque center approaches to cultural sustainability in the U.S. and other countries as well tend to be informal, non-systematic, and non-structured. However, there are a few examples in Argentina and Uruguay of well-organized conferences, seminars, and ongoing courses that do utilize didactic materials supplied by the homeland Basque Government and are taught by certified teachers and university professors, who volunteer their expertise.

Ethnic music is a symbolic mode of affiliation for present day diaspora Basques. The preservation of music and, in particular, choral music is an element of ethnicity maintenance in each of the case studies. Most choral repertoires include pieces with nationalist lyrics and are often filled with patriotic love songs to the homeland. The Basque organizations affirm links to music with formal and informal performances of established Basque choirs, with various genre musicians, by teaching folk songs to children, and with background music at events. The seemingly mundane piped-in music of Basque center bars and restaurants, of religious masses and celebrations and that of festivals for singing and dancing, all contribute to the shared memories and experiences and connectedness of the diaspora Basques. Young people who travel to the homeland return with the latest CDs of Basque folk rock. Homeland performers have become popular enough to travel to Basque festivals in Uruguay, Argentina, Venezuela, Mexico, and the U.S. for successful tours to Basque collectivities. Consequently, when first-time Basque travelers to the Basque Country participate in the fiestas and social scene, they recognize the music and can sing along with the homeland populations and, similarly, when visiting other diaspora communities' Basque festival celebrations, feel like "insiders". Regardless of age, the respondents agreed overwhelmingly that "singing traditional songs in Basque" is of "some," "great," or "very great importance" and geographical location did not seriously affect attitudes, with between 84 percent in Australia and 96 percent in Uruguay and the U.S. each also agreeing to its importance. However, because it is not uncommon for individuals to be able to sing a song in Basque but not understand a single word, this points to the ineffectiveness of the informal and passive education methods adopted in these institutions. Language learning and utilization are diminishing.

In several Basque collectivities there are Basque rock bands with diaspora members singing in *Euskera*. These groups add a fundamental element to the Basque community, enticing young people to learn and practice their Basque language in a social setting. They give Basque language and Basque folk music a high status among the listeners and serve as examples for other young musicians. Teenagers in the dancing crowds can sing along with many of the Basque songs while again not understanding a single word of the *Euskera* they have just vocalized. If they could, they might comprehend the nationalist lyrics and meanings behind them.

Almost every Basque collectivity has initiated a traditional folk dance group. Numbering anywhere from a few adolescents to semi-professional troupes of sixty young adults, these groups have served the purpose of ethnic socialization for the youth and for entertainment at ethnic functions. The larger groups also perform for non-Basque gatherings and educate the host country public regarding Basque culture. *Txistularis* (players of a unique three-holed Basque flute) and accordionists accompany the dancers and often give their own separate performances. Conversations with spectators at musical performances and festivals revealed that, because the *txistu* is a Basque instrument, it was preferred over accordions, guitars, and pianos—not because they enjoyed the sound—as it can be quite shrill—but because they equated Basque functions with Basque music played on Basque instruments, which lend authenticity.

In the U.S., in Boise, Idaho, for example, the *Boise'ko Gazteak* or Youth of Boise combines 170 Basque children between the ages of 4 and 14 years to teach traditional Basque dance and song. Every Tuesday night the Basque center, the adjacent Basque Museum and Cultural Center, and next door *fronton* or handball court are filled with the energy of youth, music, and dance led by seventeen teachers and seven musicians. It is an important part of the construction of ethnic identity for the youth to meet each other as children and make friends at the Basque events. Many of these children continue on to dance with the older group, the Oinkari Basque Dancers, as a result of the friendships they have made and the desire to carry on with Basque dance and music. Most of these youth would never join an ethnic folk dance group because of a specific interest in dance. They join because their parents encourage or require it and/or because, through dance, they often acquire a curiosity regarding Basque language and cultural history and subsequently maintain a connection to the Basque collective.

For adolescents, the summer tours of Basque festivals have proven to be a powerful marker in maintaining interest in Basque culture when witnessing hundreds of others their own age participating in these cultural events. It has become "cool" to be ethnic and the positive social status is reinforced at each Basque event. These educational opportunities are often more significant than any number of hours spent in a classroom with a textbook, certified teacher or not and Basque youth are inculcated with examples of multiculturalism or, at least, biculturalism in practice.

The Basque Museum and Cultural Center in Boise, Idaho, houses an extensive display area used for photography, sculpture, and special collections regarding Basques in the homeland and in the American West. There is also a classroom for *Euskera* lessons and dancing, several offices for researchers, the Juanita Uberuaga Hormaechea Collection of photographs, scrapbooks of newspaper articles and announcements regarding Idaho Basques, and the Joseph V. Eiguren Memorial Library—a small library archive. The Basque Museum and Cultural Center has recently finished the transcription of over 200 oral histories of Basques who immigrated to the area. This is all accomplished with committees of volunteers but users still remain few and are almost exclusively from the academic world. The project has not been developed for educational purposes for the general Basque community, nor have individuals shown much interest in utilizing this resource of information. These examples from Boise, Idaho, are representative of other Basque communities' projects, though Boise's may be higher in numbers.

Manifestations of Traditional Definitions of Basqueness

To traditional Basque nationalists, a significant aspect of Basque identity was the maintenance of the Catholic religion and today this remains prominent for diaspora Basques in these organizations. Males and females tend to agree with the statement "Continuing Catholic beliefs and traditions in our families is of 'great' or 'very great' importance." When summing the responses of the two with the next category, "some importance," 71 percent of females agreed, as did 69 percent of the males. For each gender, 17 percent did not think that religion is of any consequence to Basque culture and identity, nor should it be to the Basque people living in the diaspora or the homeland. The aggregate responses from those that did not believe Catholicism is important to Basque identity sustainability ranged from Belgium's 57 percent to that of only 8 percent in the U.S. Being the most recent emigrants, the Belgian Basques exhibited an attitude closer to that of the homeland population, which is less religious. In the U.S., where Basques often felt discriminated against for their religion, it is still fundamental to their ethnic definition, while in those countries where Catholicism was a state religion, such as Peru, Argentina, and Uruguay, it was not considered to be an essential factor of identity. That opposition and reinforcement of group boundaries may have strengthened U.S. Basques' religious resolve.

There was a steady decline by age category believing in Catholicism's relationship with Basqueness. Overall, 46 percent of the 18–30 year olds did not believe religion to have any importance at all and, excepting any Catholic religious revival in each country, this pattern tended to point to its decline in future definitions as well. In personal interviews some expressed the opinion that they are religious, but they do not connect it to ethnicity: "I am not more Basque because I am Catholic," stated one Basque woman in the U.S. Interestingly, many of the Basque diaspora organizational festivals are feast days of saints and a majority of the important Basque calendar's events uphold the tradition of including a Catholic mass. However, none of the Basque centers around the world reported offering any association activities that were specifically for discussing, studying, or learning about Catholicism or its relationship to Basque culture.

Ancestry has traditionally served as another marker for diaspora Basques, who tend to be more exclusive even though this is self-defeating to their communities. It might seem more rational to be more accepting in the diaspora, to include others who also want to share in the maintenance of Basque culture even if that person is not Basque by descent. The more inter-marrying there is with host country populations, it would seem Basques would want to include those spouses in their group categories. However, the data showed the opposite results when the respondents were asked to give their reactions to the following statement: "A person must have Basque ancestors to be a Basque" (Table 7.2).

These affirmative numbers fortified the argument that diaspora activities and definitions of Basqueness from those who are members of the centers tend towards the traditional and conservative including race or ancestry. Belgium has the most frequent communications with the homeland and most recent migration with a more contemporary civic definition of Basqueness and Basque identity and the lowest segment agreeing. Perhaps to maintain their separate identity and unique status diaspora Basques prefer to utilize ancestry

TABLE 7.2 "A person must have Basque ancestors to be a Basque" (%)

	Agree or strongly agree	No opinion	Disagree or strongly disagree
U.S.	91	2	6
Peru	83	0	17
Australia	73	4	23
Uruguay	69	6	26
Argentina	62	8	29
Belgium	50	4	46

Total respondents = 832.

to keep boundaries of differentiation that cannot be transcended and this also requires no extra effort on one's own part to demonstrate Basqueness or to be included in the group.

Euskera, the Basque language, still has not secured itself as a crucial factor of diaspora identity or even of contemporary homeland Basque identity. In the homeland itself, various areas have long since been Francophone in the north or hispanicized in the south and Basque was outlawed as a means of communication during the Franco dictatorship of 1939–1974. Consequently, many emigrants of the political exile era did not speak the language. Though Basques are extremely proud of their unique language and its complexity, most of these respondents did not consider it a defining factor in categorizing a person as a Basque (Table 7.3).

Only 8 percent of Australian respondents knew no Basque language at all compared to Uruguay's 66 percent and this has affected their opinions that Basques should speak Basque. Obviously, the respondents who did not speak Basque themselves would not want this to be a determining characteristic, as they would eliminate themselves from their own ethnic identity. Although there were no marked differences of opinion between age groups regarding language and identity, there were variances in their abilities with Basque language. Half as many youth as elderly could converse in Basque, which bodes ill for its maintenance. The Argentine, Uruguayan, and U.S. scattered centers offer language courses and currently the Basque Government offers free language courses via the Internet: however, small minorities (approximately 2,300 students worldwide signed up with the Department of Culture during 2004) show interest. Even in a 1995 homeland survey, 35 percent of the respondents in the Basque Country's seven provinces stated they had "no interest in the Basque language," referring to learning or using it.

Though traditional Basque nationalism stressed the importance of the Basque language and the last influential wave of migration was of people with this ideology, language loss is evident by the data in Table 7.4, which illustrate

TABLE 7.3 "To be considered a Basque, a person should speak the Basque language" (%)

	Strongly agree or agree	No opinion	Strongly disagree or disagree	Respondents who speak Basque fluently or with some difficulty
Belgium	13	4	83	42
Peru	8	8	83	23
Uruguay	12	6	83	2
U.S.	15	9	76	46
Argentina	24	8	68	16
Australia	36	13	52	56
Total female	18	9	73	31
Total male	21	8	71	32
18–30 years old	19	8	73	25
31–45 years old	20	6	74	26
46–60 years old	20	7	72	27
61–75 years old	18	12	70	38
76–90 years old	16	14	69	61

Total respondents = 832.

TABLE 7.4 Language knowledge, usage, and literacy by host country and by age category (%)

	"I know only a few "words" or "none"	I only use Basque for special phrases" or, "none"	"I can write only a few words in Basque" or, "none"
Uruguay	94	98	95
Argentina	69	84	68
Peru	54	85	54
U.S.	41	67	58
Belgium	38	71	46
Australia	37	53	56
18–30 years old	65	77	65
31–45 years old	60	77	70
46–60 years old	60	76	70
61–75 years old	50	73	59
76–90 years old	32	63	54

Total respondents = 832.

how few of these Basques were actually able to speak and utilize *Euskera* and how many were illiterate in their ancestral language. The respondents were asked to describe their linguistic abilities and frequency of usage. Overall, only 5 percent used Basque regularly and another 5 percent "use Basque everyday, switching back and forth between languages and using Basque equally with other languages." The Australian and U.S. Basques had the highest frequencies in both categories.

There are Basque language programs at the Basque centers in Argentina, Uruguay, Australia, and the U.S., university language courses in Argentina and the U.S., and *ikastolas* or Basque language schools in Argentina and the U.S. While the students and parents do put forth a tremendous effort, sociolinguistics studies have demonstrated that, without a social or economic reason for learning and using a language, it is not likely to be maintained.

In every case of this research, if there was a physical Basque center building, there was a kitchen. The association of ethnic identity with ethnic food, as was mentioned above, is strong. The centers typically have monthly membership dinners and several special occasion feasts with Basque-style selections ranging from typical peasant home cooking to contemporary Basque nouveau cuisine. As in the homeland, often it is the men who rule these *txokos* or private kitchens, though home cooking tends to remain the domain of the women. Although 91 percent of the total respondents believed that it was of "some," "great," or "very great" importance to "teach and use Basque cuisine and food preparation in our homes," the reality was that a combined average of 63 percent actually did prepare Basque style meals in their homes at least "a few times a month." When combining "everyday," "about once a week," and "a few times a month," there were no significant differences in gender responses, although in personal interviews a few males confessed they did not really know which dishes their wives prepared were Basque style or something else. There were differences in country responses that tended to mirror past and recent migration and specific details of Basque educational and organizational activities. In Peru, a substantial number of men met weekly to create a Basque style meal for each other, demonstrating and maintaining cuisine as a significant factor in their lives and in the activities of the Lima Basque Center. Recent migration to Belgium also shows emigrant and first generation Basques preserving food traditions (Table 7.5).

TABLE 7.5 Responses to "How often do you eat Basque-style food at home?" (%)

	Belgium	Peru	Australia	U.S.	Argentina	Uruguay
At least a few times every month	96	93	75	73	56	33

Total respondents = 832. The response percentages combine "everyday," "weekly," and "a few times a month."

From those born in the Basque Country to the fourth generation or later born in their host countries, when combining the percentages again for eating Basque-style food at home "at least a few times a month," the percentages followed a pattern: born in the Basque Country 89 percent, first generation born in the host country 73 percent, second generation born in the host country 51 percent, third generation born in the host country 31 percent, and fourth or later generation born in the host country 30 percent. Many of the Basque centers in Uruguay, Argentina, and the U.S. have restaurants attached that are open to the general public. Cooking classes are sporadically organized but are well attended. The Basque Government has sponsored diaspora tours for homeland award-winning chefs and the centers and private restaurants in Mexico, Venezuela, and Chile have hired several to infuse the tradition of ethnic cooking. Similar to language knowledge and usage, latter-generation Basques tend not to have ethnic cuisine skills though they do distinguish and attempt to maintain knowledge of Basque food preparation.

The Basque collectivities also promulgate the continuation of Basque sports and athletic events. The same activities are practiced regardless of country: competitions in wood chopping, weight carrying and weight lifting, team tug-of-wars, jai alai, *pelota* handball, and *pala*, similar to racquetball. Though the weight carrying and lifting and wood chopping are for exhibitions during festivals, there are regular games of pelota and pala. International exchanges and tournaments of pelota and pala players for festivals are common and enthusiastically received by the Basque audiences. Teaching and "practicing the Basque sports such as pelota, jai alai, wood chopping, weight carrying and lifting" were also singled out for "some," "great," or "very great" importance to the respondents, from a low of 70 percent in Belgium to a high of 93 percent in Peru, the U.S., and Uruguay where there are numerous public and privately owned frontons or courts, in addition to those at the Basque centers. However, the frontons are often devoid of players. In each country there is a national players' association, whose leaderships are extremely wary of the continuance of these Basque sports. There is much encouragement from the organizations and the crowds, but the physical hardship of handball played by Basque rules of no hand protection whatsoever deters younger players from learning. Experienced players' nerve damage, permanent swelling, and hand surgeries easily convince youngsters to try other athletic entertainment.

Classes for young handball players have been so poorly attended that in more than half of the communities they have been dropped altogether or have become a mandatory segment of the more popular dance lessons. Diaspora Basques have not utilized the homeland's colorful and padded handballs used in their own youth instruction, but instead have insisted on continuing "with the real balls and we teach it the way it always used to be taught." Instead of benefiting from contemporary educational methods and materials, the diaspora instructors maintain an orthodox traditional approach, which in the end is self-defeating. In the new millennium, the sporting demonstrations at Basque festivals in Australia, Canada, the U.S., Mexico, Chile, Argentina, Uruguay, Brazil, and Barcelona and the autumn 2003 grand opening of the new Basque center in Paris all relied on "imported" athletes brought from the Basque Country to give demonstrations of their skills. There was a lack of available local talent, which is again indicative of perhaps a lack of interest related to activities meant to carry on knowledge and interest for Basque sport, but also of poor or a lack of pedagogical strategies to train players.

General interest does exist in Basque history and in the books provided gratis by Basque homeland institutions. Over 88 percent of all respondents believed learning about their history and about other Basques in the diaspora to be of "great" or "very great" importance: however, going to the Basque center, browsing through the sources, and actually checking out and reading a book takes time and energy. In any society, whether one is an immigrant or a native, there are those who are motivated enough to do it and a majority who are not. Basque center personnel responsible for librarian duties mentioned that "the lack of readership can be measured by the layers of dust on these books."

There are a wide variety of additional ethnic activities carried on throughout the organizations from art exhibitions, history and politics lectures, and conferences on literature, to medical research of Basque physiology. However, their typical description would be one of passive participation. Small cadres of leaders in each community tend to be the same persons teaching, organizing, directing, and coordinating all activities (including set-up and clean-up) and passive participants also tend to be the same people repeatedly. Members participate by attending and receiving lectures and information or from viewing exhibits and performances. If "learning" implies a change in behavior or attitude because of new knowledge, then annually, several thousand Basque diasporans actually learn something new as a result of these activities.

Conclusion

In the age of globalization and cyberspace, a diaspora can be held together or re-created in the mind through cultural maintenance and a shared imagination such as is present in these Basque centers. An identification with a diaspora serves to bridge the gap between the local and the global identities (Hall, 1991). The Basques' strong identification with the past and not their inability or lack of desire to assimilate in the present permits their diasporic consciousness and enthusiasm for cultural sustainability and ethnic identity maintenance projects. We have seen a generational decline in the numbers of Basques who are able to reproduce homeland Basqueness, yet an increase in the numbers of Basque diaspora institutions and an increase in their numbers of activities. The activities have also changed drastically in their *raison d'être* and now centers are focusing on providing educational activities concerning the homeland and not the immigrant services focusing on the host society.

Basque ethnics have the best of both worlds because the Basque institutions do not usually make any demands on their members. Manifestation of ethnic identity is completely voluntary for the later-generation Basques who speak their host country language perfectly and have migrated to Christian European host societies where White Catholics fit in easily and have even been a part of the dominant state religion in Latin America. The host society does not tend to categorize and separate these individuals as Basques: rather, Basques in the diaspora tend to separate and identify themselves as Basques. This is a "community without cost" (Waters, 1990, p. 149) and perhaps it would be more accurate to think of Basque diasporic ethnic identity maintenance as optional, with activities ranging widely in intensity from passive symbolic ethnicity to active ethnic fundamentalism.

The Basque centers' educational projects demonstrate underdeveloped pedagogical strategies and the didactic approaches are rudimentary. However, Basque ethnic identity maintenance can be evaluated as successful based on the longevity of at least five generations preserving ties to ethnic language, cuisine, religion, music, dance, sport, leisure activities, and other factors of identity and the historical and contemporary creation and re-creation around the world of Basque centers which foment institutional relationships among homeland and diasporic communities

The age of globalization points to a shift to de-territorialized social identities. The world's economics and politics are generally organized vertically according to states and regions: however, individuals and communities exhibit horizontal, overlapping, permeable, and multiple systems of interactions. This current system creates communities of interest based on shared opinions, ethnicities, religions, and so on. Rather than globalization creating a single homogeneous global culture, multiculturalism and transnationalism currently seem to be the dominating forces and those minority groups that prepare their participants for a chameleon-like existence of "fitting in" here *and* there are indeed positively influencing the overall multiculturalism of their communities.

Resources and Tools for Educators

Questions

1. Why do ethnic groups living away from their ancestral homelands maintain a historic/cultural identity?
2. What are the individual and communitarian aspects to diasporic identity?
3. How do ethnic groups attempt to simultaneously construct uniqueness and group consciousness in their ethnic community populations?

4. How do transnationalism and globalization affect educational endeavors in diasporic communities?

For Further Reading

Braziel, J. E. & Mannur, A. (Eds.) (2003). *Theorizing diaspora: A reader.* Oxford: Blackwell Publishing.

Various authors explain and theorize about diasporic identity, globalism, hybridity, minority discourse, and nostalgia.

Grant, C. A. & Gomez, M. L. (1996). *Making schooling multicultural: Campus and classroom.* Englewood Cliffs, NJ: Prentice Hall.

Nineteen chapters describe and analyze various methods for reconstructing educational systems with a goal of better preparing students for life in a globalized society. The subjects investigated include curriculum building, bilingual education, multicultural approaches to mathematics, science as meaning, art education and visual culture, ethno-centrism, and reflective teaching.

Kennedy, P. & Roudometof, V. (Eds.) (2002). *Communities across borders: New immigrants and transnational cultures. London and New York: Routledge.*

Eleven case studies of different ethnic groups in different host countries address migrant, transnational, and de-territorialized communities as well as globalization–localization interplay, dual loyalty, and boundaries of diaspora identity.

Totoricaguena, G. (2005). *Basque diaspora: Migration and transnational identity.* Reno: Center for Basque Studies.

This introductory university-level textbook includes concepts of political science, sociology, anthropology, and history. The author specifically investigates migration theory, cultural representation, diaspora politics, and ethnic identity maintenance. Ideas for student essays, illustrations, and suggested readings follow each chapter.

Suggestions for Educators

1. Oral history projects. Students can conduct oral histories with family members or friends who are emigrants themselves.
2. Students can map the geographical origins of their classmates and list the first in their family to immigrate.
3. Teachers should connect the classroom to the local community cultural events in order for students to have face-to-face contact with difference.

4. Teacher preparation should include a component of total immersion in a culturally diverse school.
5. Teachers should pay special attention to the social organization of the students and should prearrange and design groups and teams.
6. Teachers could invite community ethnic groups to the classroom for presentations and to give the teacher ideas of general or typical ethnic learning styles.
7. Classes could take a walk through the school's area or neighborhood and give special attention to the different churches, synagogues, and mosques and to the different businesses and names, agencies, and architecture and answer questions about how those differences reflect the different people in their community.
8. School administrators and teachers could invite local ethnic group talent to participate in school plays, musical performances, and language and literature courses.

References

Elkins, D. J. (1997). Globalization, telecommunication, and virtual ethnic communities. *International Political Science Review, 18*(2), 139–152.

Glazer, N. & Moynihan, D. P. (Eds.) (1970). *Beyond the melting pot: The Negroes, Puerto Ricans, Jews, Italians, and Irish of New York City* (2nd edn). Cambridge: The MIT Press.

Glazer, N. & Moynihan, D. P. (Eds.) (1975). *Ethnicity: Theory and experience.* Cambridge: Harvard University Press.

Hall, S. (1991). Old and new identities, old and new ethnicities. In A. D. King (Ed.), *Culture, globalization and the world system: Contemporary conditions for the representation of identity,* pp. 41–68. Basingstoke: Macmillan Education.

Lavie, S. & Swedenburg, T. (Eds.) (1996). *Displacement, diaspora, and geographies of identity.* Durham: Duke University Press.

McKay, J. (1982). An explanatory synthesis of primordial and mobilizationist approaches to ethnic phenomena. *Ethnic and Racial Studies, 5*(4), 395–420.

Makariev, P. (1994). Cultural education and the paradigm of recognition. In A. Gutmann (Ed.), *Multiculturalism. Examining the politics of recognition.* Princeton: Princeton University Press.

Slobin, M. (1994). Music in diaspora: The view from Euro-America. *Diaspora, 3*(3), 243–251.

Tajfel, H. (Ed.) (1978). *Differentiation between social groups: Studies in the social psychology of intergroup relations.* London: Academic Press.

Tajfel, H. (1981). *Human groups and social categories.* Cambridge: Cambridge University Press.

Tajfel, H. (1982). *Social identity and intergroup relations.* Cambridge: Cambridge University Press.

Tajfel, H. (Ed.) (1984). *The social dimension: European development in social psychology* (Vol. 2). Cambridge: Cambridge University Press.

Tajfel, H. & Turner, J. C. (1979). An integrative theory of intergroup conflict. In S. Worchel & W. G. Austin (Eds.), *The social psychology of intergroup relations,* pp. 33–47. Monterey, CA: Brooks-Cole.

Taylor, C. (1994). The politics of recognition. In A. Gutmann (Ed.), *Multiculturalism: Examining the politics of recognition.* Princeton: Princeton University Press.

Tölölyan, K. (1996). Rethinking diaspora(s): Stateless power in the transnational moment. *Diaspora, 5*(1), 3–36.

Totoricagüena, G. (2004a). *Comparing the Basque diaspora: Identity, culture, and politics.* Reno: University of Nevada Press.

Totoricagüena, G. (2004b). *Identity, culture, and politics in the Basque diaspora.* Reno: University of Nevada Press.

Waters, M. C. (1990). *Ethnic options: Choosing identities in America.* Berkeley: University of California Press.

CHAPTER 8

Korean Exceptionalism?: History, Culture, Politics, and Ethnic Relations in Northeast China

SHEENA CHOI

Under what circumstances can an ethnic group balance its integration into a mainstream political unit with preservation of its cultural heritage? Would assertion of cultural and ethnic identity be harmful to unity and solidarity across a population? Is cultural education a basis for cultural sustenance of a group? These are essential questions regarding the limits and possibilities of a modern plural society.

Traditionally, two features profoundly influenced the shape of modern nation states: ethno-centrism and racism that disparaged the merits of minority cultures and modernization theories of nation building that favored uniformity and homogeneity over diversity. The essentialist position contends that the more immigrants and ethnic groups identify with their own group, the less they will identify with the larger society and other groups. This view considers cultural and ethnic identity as zero sum: therefore, policies that "affirm ethnic group identities [necessarily] undermine attempts to affirm larger civic identities" (Kymlicka, 2004, p. xiv). Thus, essentialist-influenced schools were entrusted with the task of assimilating minorities within their territories and newly arriving groups through formal education.

Ethnic relations between the ethnic Korean minority in China and mainstream society depart from the prevailing examples. Ethnic Koreans in northeast China sustain their culture by displaying a robust cultural, linguistic, and ethnic identity they are proud of while also being members of China's political community. This persistence in cultural and ethnic identity is the result of laborious community efforts—formal and informal cultural education and various community-sponsored and community-supported cultural events.

The Uniqueness of Koreans in China

Numerous studies have indicated problematic ethnic relations in China. China endeavors to control and assimilate its minority populations, particularly in western and southern border areas and minorities express resentment and resistance to exploitation and Sinicization (Gladney, 1996a, 1996b, 1998, 2003; Bovingdon, 2002, 2004). However, studies of ethnic Koreans in China demonstrate a unique case of balancing cultural sustenance through formal and informal cultural educations. At the same time, they demonstrate successful integration into China's national polity: While identification of Korean ethnicity is based on Chinese nationality policies that recognized Koreans legally (Chinese *Chaoxienzu* and Korean *Chosunjok*), Koreans' attachment to China's polity is vivacious (Min, 1990; Han and Kwon, 1994; Choi, 2004).[1]

Ethnic Koreans have achieved one of the highest levels of educational attainment and highest standard of living and the lowest illiteracy rate and lowest birth rate of any Chinese ethnic minority group, including the Han Chinese (Han and Kwon, 1994; Lee, 2002; Ma, 2003). Such accomplishments confer a confidence in their culture to ethnic Koreans and pride in their ethnic identity—a primary ingredient for cultural sustenance—and have a positive effect on ethnic relations.

Reflecting this, Gladney (1998) noted that the media presents positive images—civility and modernity—of ethnic Koreans that are on par with Han Chinese. As the "unmarked" mainstream group, Han Chinese are regarded as a representation of civility and modernity, "the cultural and technical vanguard, the manifest destiny of all the minorities," while other minority groups are characterized as primitive, sensual, colorful, exotic, and requiring the paternal guidance of the Han majority (Gladney, 1998, p. 117).[2] The reasonable question then is what has enabled such spectacular success of ethnic Koreans in China while others are besieged? In this chapter, I explore the historical, institutional, and social context of Korean cultural substance and cultural education among ethnic Korean populations in Manchuria, which may shed some light on Korean "exceptionalism."

Theoretical Framework

This chapter presents Korean ethnicity and Korean "exceptionalism" in China as historical and contemporary products of political, social, and cultural relations in northeast Asia where power, hegemony, external colonialism, and cultural economy are intertwined. The Korean "exceptionalism" in China is an example of the multiplicity of identities, interests, and institutions—within the context of exile—in which ideas and cultures are engaged, forms of cultural sustenance are fashioned, and substance of cultural education is negotiated.

National Identity

In his seminal study, Anderson (1983) suggested that national identity is best understood as historically contextualized, a socially constituted and constitutive process of infusing "imagined communities" with the belief that they are somehow naturally linked by common identities. Post-structuralist approaches theorize identity as highly contested, multiple, constructed, and negotiated within and between the power relations of the nation state, rather than naturalized and primodial (Malkki, 1992 in Gladney, 1996). Nationalist ideologies are cultural productions (Befu, 1993) in which inventions of tradition and the narrations of social histories become legitimized (Tonkin et al., 1989; Hobsbawm, 1990). Similarly, "people subscribe to certain identities, under certain highly contextualized moments of social relations ... often regulated by nation-states, and limited to certain lines of stereotypical representation" (Gladney, 1996a).

Culture and Society

Weber (1958) maintained that ideas and interests play a major role in social life. In other words, human beings are motivated to action by ideal and material interests. Ideas also shape politics, much as culture shapes economic and political development (Gerth and Mills, 1958; Harrison and Huntington, 2000; Kihl, 2005). In their recent book *Culture Matters: How Values Shape Human Progress*, Harrison and Huntington (2000) investigated how values fashion human development in a modernizing society. The findings of the study led Harrison and Huntington (2000) to conclude there are causal links between culture, economics, politics, and value changes.

Culture and Politics

Drawing from Thompson et al. (1990), Khil asserts that cultural politics and political culture "broadly describe people who share values, beliefs, and preferences legitimating different ways of life." Cultural politics order political priorities (Latin, 1986, p. 11) and define "the symbolic and material objects which people consider valuable and worth fighting for" (Kihl, 2005, p. 30). Thus, cultural politics involve the contexts in which such conflicts occur, the rules of engagement.

Ethnic relations are ultimately affected by and respond to the historical context and social milieu of each group. Politics take place within the cultural and institutional milieus of groups that have distinctive dispositions. Through political action, groups engage and endeavor to improve their position in a society.

Geographical Concentration and Administrative Autonomy

An overwhelming majority of China's 2 million Koreans are concentrated in the three northeastern provinces of Jilin, Liaoning, and Heilonggiang, which are close to the North Korean border. Approximately 42 percent of them reside in the Yanbian area of Jilin Province. The Chinese Government established the Yanbian Korean Autonomous Prefecture in 1952, which gave institutional support to Koreans' cultural autonomy in the area. While ethnic Koreans constitute about 40 percent of the total population, they maintain control over the local government (Min, 1990). This administrative autonomy enables them to facilitate cultural polices—in particular concerning language and education—that serve as a vital force for cultural sustenance and cultural education of ethnic Koreans in China.

In 1952, the Yanbian Autonomous Prefecture decided to issue all official documents in both Chinese and Korean languages and established a government bureau to translate Chinese documents into Korean (Min, 1990). Further, ethnic schooling has been established for all levels of formal education—primary, secondary, and higher education programs. More than 90 percent of ethnic Korean children in Yanbian Autonomous Prefecture attend Korean ethnic schools, where Korean teachers give instruction in the majority of subjects in the Korean language (Lee, 1986). The textbooks are translated into Korean for Korean students. In addition, Korean literature written in the Korean language by Korean writers is taught in schools. The Korean Autonomous Prefecture also maintains a school that specializes in Korean art, music, and dance. They also support centers that specialize in Korean history, literature, language, economy, art, music, and philosophy at Yanbian University. In addition, numerous popular and professional journals are published in the Korean language, facilitating intellectual and cultural development.

There are also various Korean cultural facilities such as centers for ethnic Koreans and libraries. It is observed that the Koreans in China are more successful in maintaining traditional Koran customs, games, and values than those in South Korea, which experienced radical changes influenced by industrialization, urbanization, and Westernization (Min, 1990). Ethnic Koreans in China also retained traditional Korean culinary customs regardless of their residential setting (Hwang, 1989 in Min, 1990). Korean festivals and cuisines are popular among the Han majority.

Influence of Confucianism in Sino-Korean Cultural Interaction

Throughout the Choson period, Korea participated in the Sinocentric world order where China was positioned as the "middle kingdom" in the transnational Confucian cultural sphere. However, Korean scholars felt they were more faithful to authentic Confucianism than were Chinese scholars. Authentic Confucianism, the basis for east Asian civilization, was considered intellectually and morally superior to its Chinese counterpart (Haboush, 1999, p. 69). Korean orthodoxy, according to Haboush and Deuchler (1999), "received its institutional underpinnings when, in 1610, five Korean scholars were enshrined in the Shrine of Confucius (Munmyo) in Seoul" (p. 3). This act, which was a major assertion of Confucian orthodoxy in itself, had not only "symbolic significance for the history of Korean Confucianism," but also significance in the shaping of the Korean psyche in relation to the middle kingdom (Haboush and Deuchler, 1999, p. 3).

Through attaining an eternal and eminent position within the broader framework of Confucian civilization, Korean Confucians crowned themselves on the same level as their intellectual forbearers of Sung China. At times, Koreans even asserted that they were more faithful guardians of Confucian orthodoxy than were the Ming Chinese. Therefore, to the Koreans, enshrinement was an affirmation of the supremacy of Korean Confucian tradition and the neo-Confucian world (Haboush and Deuchler, 1999, p. 3).

Such pride among Koreans in their intellectual and moral supremacy over the Chinese reached its height when Manchus invaded China (Deuchler, 1999). Koreans viewed the rise of Qing as a "barbarian" usurpation of the center of civilization. Korea, only one-fortieth the size of China, had to accept its subordinate status to Qing China politically and militarily. The status–power disequilibrium with Qing China was a constant source of anxiety to Korean intellectuals throughout the Choson dynasty, which led Koreans to feel that they were "responsible for upholding Confucian civilization in the face of barbarian rule in China" (Deuchler, 1999, p. 92). Drawing from *Sukchong sillok* (King Sukchong's Memorial), Haboush (1999) noted that the Choson court routinely referred to Qing envoys as "barbarian messengers (*hoch'a*)" and King Sukchong referred to the K'ang-hsi Emperor as "that northerner (*pugin*)." While Korea's military weakness necessitated their political subordination to Qing China for its security and survival, Koreans harbored cultural contempt towards the barbaric force of its more powerful neighbor.

The twentieth century saw even greater trepidation in Korea as the state was facing *naeu oehwan*: internal crisis and external calamities. The decline of China and ascendancy of Japan resulted in historic changes in regional power formations that had important consequences for the ways in which Koreans viewed the world and themselves. In Koreans' views, the "middle kingdom" no longer occupied the center of civilization and, thus, was decidedly demoted to the periphery, both globally and regionally. And as peripheral, China was "anything but civilized" (Schmid, 2002, p. 11).

The History of Koreans in Manchuria

About two million ethnic Koreans inhabit the northeast region of China, commonly known in the West as Manchuria. However, the Chinese Government rejects the term Manchuria for geopolitical consideration. This region has been associated with the Puyo, the Koguryo, and the Parhae of the ancient Korean states and various ethnic groups later founded states there (Goh, 2002). More recently, Manchus, the ethnic group who conquered China, established the last imperial dynasty of Qing. The Qing Government set aside Manchuria from the rest of the empire with isolationist policies, considering the area the sacred land where their ancestors originated.

As a result, sparsely populated Manchuria became the focus of hegemonic domination between Japan, Russia, warlords, the Kuomintang, and the Communist Party until Japan won a series of wars and finally took control of the area. Most Koreans in Manchuria are a result of this turbulent history—the loss of Korean independence and the following Japanese colonialism in their homeland plus Japan's intensified expansionism into Manchuria.[3]

Two wars are significant to understanding modern Korean history as well as that of Manchuria and ethnic Koreans in the region. First, Qing's defeat in the Sino-Japanese War (1894–1895) thwarted Russian ambition and brought the Japanese into Manchuria. The following Russo-Japanese War (1904–1905) and the Treaty of Portsmouth were important turning points for Korea and for Koreans in northeast China. Korea became a Japanese protectorate in 1905, with final annexation of Korea in 1910. The annexation lasted until 1945, with Japan's defeat in the Second World War. In Manchuria, Japan obtained the southern tip of Manchuria as war spoils and exercised its political influence in the area until finally setting up Manchuguo (1932–1945), a purportedly independent nation under Japanese imperial auspices.

The Japanese colonial regime was repressive and intrusive in all aspects of Korean life: economic, cultural, and political. Economically, over-taxation burdened the rank and file Korean society. Moreover, the Japanese economic plan caused massive displacement of landless peasants. Culturally, speaking Korean was forbidden and Koreans were forced to change Korean names to Japanese style and to worship the Japanese emperor as the living God. Politically, nationalism and communism were outlawed. The regime drafted young males to send to the front and conscripted young women, termed "comfort women," for abuse by Japanese military forces (Kang, 2001). For Koreans suffering under the colonial yoke, Manchuria became a favorite destination.

Largely, two groups of Koreans migrated to Manchuria: landless peasants and political refugees seeking to escape Japanese detection (Shin, 1980; Lee, 1983). Many of these people also converted to Christianity as a liberating religion. These were very important elements in shaping the character of ethnic Koreans in China.

Korean peasants successfully developed rice cultivation in the northeast and, thus, contributed to regional economic growth. The northeast, with its short frost-free period and cold water, was considered difficult even for dry farming and utterly useless for rice cultivation, so Han Chinese in the region cultivated corn, wheat, soybeans, and sorghum. Koreans brought skills in rice cultivation and succeeded with determination, hard work, and adaptation to the local environment. Rice cultivation is labor-intensive: however, it brings high yields. Success in rice cultivation enhanced the region's economy. Rice cultivation was complementary as it provided rice to Han Chinese and Manchus without competing for farming areas, since Koreans developed the wet marsh areas that had been disregarded by other groups as unsuitable for cultivation.

Success in rice cultivation by Koreans in Manchuria, however, had greater cultural meaning in the traditional east Asian value system. The Confucian hierarchical occupational order dictated scholar/gentry, farmer, artisan, and merchants, in that order. The scholar/gentry class, which was the hereditarily privileged class, was considered to have earned the right to govern commoners through merit—being learned men of self-cultivation. Among the rank of commoners, farmers—especially those engaged in rice cultivation—were seen as sacred, fundamental to civilization, and, therefore, most valued, while artisans were regarded as coarse and merchants as parasitic.

Exiled Korean political refugees, who were better educated, enjoyed prestige among the Korean peasant masses. They contributed to the cultivation of Korean consciousness through education in two significant ways: they sought to eliminate illiteracy and at the same time instil a national spirit and patriotism in the students. Therefore, the establishment of schools became an enlightenment project for future independence. Some of these expatriates created military schools to train soldiers to battle the Japanese colonial forces. These military groups engaged in many significant battles against the Japanese military (Lee, 2002). In spite of Japanese repression of nationalist educational efforts, these political refugees set up an intensive educational infrastructure by time of the communist liberation of the area. By 1910, seventy-two schools had been established by Korean expatriates and by 1926 the number had multiplied to 191 (Lee, 1986; Park, 1988, p. 47; *Joongguk Choson Minjok Maljachi Chongso*, 2001).

The creation of Manchuguo in 1932 further accelerated Korean migration to the area as a way for Japan to secure its stronghold in the region. Japan drafted official plans to utilize displaced Korean peasants, relocating them to Manchuguo. During the organized settlement program, Korean settlements spread throughout the northeast and beyond the traditional settlement areas such as Yanbian and Jilin. This settlement pattern became regionalized in such areas as Choongchungdo, Kyungsangdo, and Chollado. For example, immigrants from Hamkyung province predominantly settled in Yanbian, a majority of Liaoning province settlers were from Pyungan province, and the settlers of the Heilonggiang province were mostly from Hamkyung, Cholla, Kyungsang, and Choongchung provinces. More significantly, such settlement patterns allowed easier replication of Korean traditional life and sustained Korean culture. These geographical patterns of settlement in the region continue to retain these characteristics today. The new railway lines, which were built in the north between 1932 and 1936, further facilitated Korean immigration (Olivier, 1993, p. 35).

The establishment of Manchuguo, however, changed Korean educational and resistance activities in the northeast as Japan began to exercise direct and absolute control in the region. Japan attempted to suppress the anti-Japanese resistance movement among Korean exiles through a newly created village responsibility system in which entire villages were held responsible for any kind of insurrection (Lee, 2002). Accordingly, many of the Korean nationalist schools were compelled to close, forcing anti-Japanese resistance activities underground. Many fighters escaped to China proper to join various Korean independence groups, while others remained and cooperated with the Chinese communists in anti-Japanese resistance efforts. Unlike the previous period, in which anti-Japanese resistance activities stressed Korean independence, the underlying motive now changed to the liberation of China (Goh, 2002; Yang, 2005).

As stated earlier, Koreans in the northeast were in general poor peasants and, outside of Yanbian, the center of Korean communism, they were denied equal rights as compared to the Han Chinese. Even in Yanbian, the majority of Koreans were tenants. In the northern provinces of the northeast, up to 80 percent of all Koreans were poor peasants, very few of whom owned land (Olivier, 1993, p. 56). While Korean communists in the northeast were plagued with internal factionalism, general poverty provided fertile ground for the proselytizing activities of Korean communists. Most of the command-force party officials were Koreans, who then played a key role in the planning and implementation of the uprisings (Olivier, 1993). Their aim was to "overthrow Japanese imperialism, destroy the Guomindang military clique, and complete the Communist revolution in Manchuria" (*Chaoxianzu jianshi*, 1986, pp. 76–78). Specifically, communist slogans such as "confiscate the land from the landlords and redistribute it to poor peasants without making differences between ethnic origins" (*Chaoxianzu jianshi*, 1986, pp. 76–78) were particularly enticing to Korean peasants who longed to till their own land, but who had instead been ceaselessly oppressed by the landlords, the colonial Japanese Government, the Guomindang, and bandits.

Northeast China played a decisive role in the Chinese communist victory and Korean participation was significant and necessary. Koreans participated in the Long March and some of them held high positions in the Communist Party (Scalapino and Lee, 1972). Yet, at the time of Japanese capitulation in the area, the Chinese Communist Party lacked any concrete plans for the region. Soviet troops entered the Yanbian area immediately after the Japanese surrender and the Guomindang resumed control over a portion of the area.

However, the Guomingdang was unable to reoccupy the mountainous regions inhabited by hostile Koreans. Korean peasants, who left the peninsula as economic refugees, were unsympathetic toward the Guomintang, who represented the landlord classes and who also carried a notorious reputation for looting the local population during the occupied period (Olivier, 1993). Disillusioned by the Guomindang, the Koreans turned to the Chinese communists.

On the communist side, the Yan'an experience and the Long March confirmed to Mao Zedong the possibility of a smaller China. China lacked the power to contain its neighbors and the non-Han population desired secession rather than reunification with China (Dreyer, 1976). For the Communist Party, a reduction in territory would mean an erosion of legitimacy. However, the party feared even more that these populations could be mobilized in opposition to Han China if their right to independence and self-determination were ignored (*Dangde minzu zhengce wenxian ziliao xuanbian,* 1981, p. 49).

Thus, it was evident to the Communist Party that a plan would be required, not only to dissolve the antagonism of the non-Han Chinese, but to turn them into allies. In this circumstance, at the sixth plenary session of the sixth central committee of the party in 1938, Mao Zedong declared that the non-Han nationalities would "have the right to administer their own affairs while concurrently uniting with the Han nationality and creating a unified state" (*Dangde minzu zhengce wenxian ziliao xuanbian,* 1981, p. 50). This cast secession as an anti-revolutionary concept, labeling it harmful to the overall interests of the proletarian revolution (Olivier, 1993, p. 44).

Japanese defeat in the Second World War created a power vacuum. In "old, liberated areas" of the Yanbian and other mountainous regions of the northeast, the Communist Revolution was led by ethnic Koreans and was for the most part won before the proclamation of the People's Republic of China (P.R.C.). For example, by the end of 1948, 81 percent of the Communist Party's members in Yanbian were Korean (Olivier, 1993, p. 50).[4] In order to capitalize on the Korean revolutionary potential to consolidate power in the northeast, the Communist Party implemented two policies.

The first policy instituted massive land reform. "At the time of the Communist land redistribution in Yanbian, 85.6 percent of all households were Korean, and 81.7 percent of the total arable land was equally redistributed" (Olivier, 1993, p. 56). The success of land reform increased allegiance of the Korean masses towards the new leadership, which gave the administration the ability to mobilize them. The second policy promised autonomy to Koreans to entice them into China's new political entity. This ethnic policy, markedly different from the Guomindang's assimilation policy that alienated ethnic Koreans, won the Koreans' allegiance to the Communist Party.

Drawing from the revolutionary background of their leaders, the Koreans were successful in the indigenization of party, government, and administrative organs. The distinctive historical development of Korean nationality in the northeast brought about the supremacy of Korean nationality groups in the Yanbian and other autonomous Korean areas. The Korean contribution to the Chinese Communist Party in recovering the northeast was rewarded by the new regime and facilitated Korean integration into China's political entity, while at the same time safeguarding their autonomy.

When the autonomous Korean Yanbian region was created in 1952, Article Four of the regulations for its people's government stipulated the Korean language, along with Chinese, would be adopted. New official translation departments in every city and county were created by this act. Official documents were issued in both Korean and Chinese and Korean delegates at all levels spoke Korean at official party or state meetings. Defendants and plaintiffs also spoke Korean during all court proceedings. Local authorities encouraged Koreans to study Chinese and "officially and repeatedly" praised the Han Chinese who studied Korean (Olivier, 1993, p. 90). The proportion of Korean cadres in the cultural and educational spheres in Yanbian surpassed already high political, administrative, and economic levels (Olivier, 1993).

Simultaneously, the party adapted the concepts of "regional autonomy" and "nativization" when Yanbian became the Korean Autonomous Prefecture (Olivier, 1993). In the newly established Changbai Korean Autonomous County and numerous Korean autonomous townships, Koreans were constitutionally guaranteed representation proportional to their population. On all levels—party, government, and administration—Korean representation in fact exceeded the proportion of their population. These Korean groups and party members contributed to the local Korean peasants' acceptance of the new regime. Thus, by delegation of power to the local Koreans, the Chinese Communist Party secured Korean allegiance to the new socialist regime, facilitating the consolidation and infiltration of the party's control into all levels of the local society (Olivier, 1993).

In economic spheres, too, Koreans were enthusiastic participants in the socialist transformation of China's economy. The specific set of historical circumstances that had turned them into allies of the Chinese Communist Party also "facilitated agricultural cooperativization in the Korean nationality areas, and collectivization proceeded more smoothly than in many Han areas" (Olivier, 1993, p. 80). By 1956, Yanbian was recognized as "a model in wet rice cultivation, and a team of 159 delegates from 13 Chinese provinces visited Yanbian to learn from the experiences of the Koreans" (*Yonbyon chosonjok chach'iju kaehwang,* 1984 in Olivier, 1993, p. 81). Again, the percentage of Korean cadres participating in the nativization of the economy in Yanbian exceeded their share of the total population.

All these achievements were recognized, with Mao Zedong declaring, "Koreans had a culture that was comparable to that of the Han" (Olivier, 1993,

p. 85). While Mao Zedong spoke purely for economic and political reasons, his remark helped the Koreans fight Han dominance and enhanced Korean acceptance of Han-influenced leadership at top levels. In spite of the many problems Korean peasants encountered in the process of collectivization, especially in the areas where population was mixed among Koreans and Han Chinese, Koreans performed well and maintained their faith in the new regime. The Korean achievements were praised and "cited as models in the local as well as national press" throughout China (Olivier, 1993, p. 59). The Koreans' comparative advantage in wet rice cultivation and general economic success, along with the recognized revolutionary credentials of most of their leaders, conferred Korean support to the new order.

Korean War

The era following the Korean War (1950–1953) was a significant juncture in Koreans' relationship to China. The legal status of Koreans living in China had not been addressed, leaving them free to choose whether they would remain in China or return to Korea (Olivier, 1993, p. 57). The Sino-Korean border had remained open since the Japanese capitulation of 1945 and people freely moved across the border. All of this changed with China's participation in the Korean War.

China's entrance into the Korean War in aid to North Korea was doubly important to Koreans in the region because ethnic Koreans in China considered North Korea to be the legitimate successor of the Korean state. They considered joining this struggle to serve their ancestral land and defend their adopted nation in a fight against the reactionary forces of the Guomindang, the South Korean "puppets" and their American imperial "master" (Olivier, 1993, p. 59). In this light, China was viewed as a benevolent supporter who was helping Korea during troubled times.

While the Korean War ended in stalemate, it rallied the Koreans behind the P.R.C. Another important consequence of the war was that it forced China to decide the legal status of its Korean ethnic minority. The granting of citizenship status accelerated the integration of the Korean minority into the P.R.C. and drastically changed the significance of the border between the two countries. What was previously abstract was now concrete (Olivier, 1993).

Conclusion

In exploring cultural sustenance and cultural education of ethnic Koreans in China, Korean "exceptionalism" can be highlighted in three broadly related categories of culture and ideas: identities, interests, and institutions (Hall, 1997). Historical context, political consideration, cultural attributes, and social dynamics operated on institutional arrangements and played vital roles in shaping ethnic identity and relations.

Several factors favorably influenced the Koreans' development. Through historical Korean participation in the Confucian world order, Koreans attained cultural capital that placed them on equal ground with their Han Chinese counterparts. Furthermore, traditional Korean claims of their Confucian orthodoxy's superiority over its Chinese counterpart psychologically favored Korean intellectuals in exile over Chinese. Korean peasants' successful introduction of rice cultivation in Manchuria had economic and cultural significance. Economically, its value was in developing and improving the region's economy. However, culturally, rice cultivation privileged them over Chinese using dry farming. Politically, Korean migration to Manchuria began the time when the Korean homeland began the "decentering of the middle kingdom." This meant a decline in the political influence China traditionally had over Korea. At the same time, Japan's oppression united Koreans and Chinese against a common enemy. The political contribution of Koreans in the communist liberation of Manchuria was rewarded with the promise of an autonomous region. Here, one can see the intersecting interests: Korean peasants' desire for land and freedom from political oppression and the Communist Party's need to consolidate the area. Through these interests, Koreans and the Communist Party forged a partnership in the nation-building process. This allowed Koreans to gain administrative control and exercise policy influences in cultural, education, and economic spheres in Korean autonomous areas. Finally, geographical factors privileged Koreans psychologically. Manchuria physically borders Korea. More importantly, Manchuria was never a part of China's integral territory. Moreover, it is a site of ancient Korean kingdoms.

Korean "exceptionalism" in China represents a complex enmeshing of historical, psychocultural, and geopolitical dynamics in historical moments that influence ethnic relationship. Therefore, study of cultural sustenance and cultural education for ethnic minorities requires a multidimensional approach—an understanding of the nature, form, and content of ethnic engagement.

Though beyond the scope of this study, several contemporary developments influence(d) ethnic relations in the region. In the recent past, persecutions by Han extremists of many Korean nationalists as separatists during the Cultural Revolution tested interethnic trust. As a result of the implementation of a market economy following the Cultural Revolution, Koreans are experiencing a relative decline in their standard of living and the subsequent migration of young people to urban areas or South Korea is shifting ethnic dynamics in the region. Heavy investments in the region by the robust South Korean economy (and number one trade partner) in recent decades will undoubtedly shift and redefine ethnic dynamics and are worthwhile topics for further study.

Acknowledgments

The author expresses special appreciation to the vice chancellor of academic affairs at Indiana University-Purdue University, Fort Wayne, the East Asian Studies Center at Indiana University, Bloomington, and the International Program, Indiana University, Bloomington, for their generous grants for this study. This chapter is largely based on work completed under these grants.

I have benefited greatly from the discussion that followed the conference *Cultural Education, Cultural Sustenance*, held at the Hebrew University, Jerusalem, Israel in December 2004. I am indebted to Zvi Bekerman at the Hebrew University for his assistance in producing the final version of this article.

Resources and Tools for Educators

Questions

1. What are the ideal social and structural conditions that cause members of a society to feel that they "belong?"
2. How does the nation-building process influence social relations between ethnic groups?
3. What are some elements in forging an affirmative social contract between majority and minority populations?

For Further Reading

Anderson, B. (1991). *Imagined communities: Reflections on the origins and spread of nationalism* (2nd edn). Verso.

This is a seminal study of a modernist approach to nationalism. Applying a Marxist world view, he argues that several factors—the reduction of privileged access to particular script languages, the movement to abolish the idea of a monarch's divine rule, as well as the emergence of the printing press under a capitalist system—contributed to the emergence of nationalism and the creation of an [ethnic] imagined community.

Kymlicka, W. & Norman, W. (Eds.) (2000). *Citizenship in diverse societies.* Oxford University Press.

This book discusses political philosophies regarding the rights and status of ethno-cultural minorities in a plural society.

Brysk, A. & Shafir, G. (Eds.) (2004). *People out of place: Globalization, human rights, and the citizenship gap.* Routledge.

Globalization is altering the equilibrium of the modern state—moving from membership-based citizenship towards universal human rights. This book discusses how new human rights are generated. The authors argue that traditional citizenship rights should be extended to all, regardless of citizenship status, as universal human rights for global solidarity over local interest.

Shafir, G. (1998). *The citizenship debates: A reader.* University of Minnesota Press.

In a modern welfare state in a globally mobile era, discourses on citizenship facilitate our understanding of individual rights, political and social tension, and the nation state. This book enlightens the readers with historical origins of citizenship and antecedents followed by critiques from various perspectives: liberal, communitarian, social democratic, nationalist, immigrant and multi-culturalists, feminist, and multiple citizenships.

Suggestions for Educators

The most effective policies can be implemented through dialogue between diverse interest groups. In order for teachers, school administrators, and policy makers to be truly effective, they must be empathetic of others views—understanding history and philosophies of other cultures is an effective way of continuing the dialogue.

Recommended Classroom Activity

Have students identify current issues related to inclusive citizenship—cultural, social, political, and human rights. Have students prepare to debate from opposing view points. Diverse aspects such as historical, political, social, economic, and cultural understanding of relationships between the minority group in consideration and the mainstream society should be basis for the debate. After the debate, the two groups come together and create a workable solution to the issue.

Notes

1. The Chinese term *Minzu* is translated as nationality. However, the concept of nationality in China is closer to that of ethnicity in English.
2. The concept of "unmarked" Han-ness is similar to that of "Whiteness" in the U.S.
3. At the end of the Qing period, there had been migration of destitute Korean and Han peasants into Manchuria despite the official Qing prohibition. Furthermore, Koreans of destroyed Korean dynasties, such as Koguryo and Palhae (Chinese Poihai), were absorbed into various rising dynasties in the region.
4. It is estimated that after 1945, approximately 1 million Koreans returned to Korea (both South and North). Those who chose to stay in China included those who were betrothed politically in the Chinese communist movement and poor peasants who gained land through the communist land reform.

Bibliography

Anderson, B. (1983). *Imagined communities: Reflections on the origin and spread of nationalism*. London: Verso.

Banks, J. A., Cookson, P., Gay, G., Hawley, W. D., Irvine, J. J. et al. (2001). *Diversity within unity: Essential principles for teaching and learning in a multicultural society*. Seattle: Center for Multicultural Education, University of Washington.

Befu, H. (1993). Introduction. In H. Befu (Ed.), *Cultural nationalism in the East Asia: Representation and identity* (pp. 1–5). Berkeley: Institute of East Asian Studies.

Bourdieu, P. & Passeron, J. (1990). *Reproduction in education, society and culture* (2nd edn). London: Sage.

Bovingdon, G. (2001). The history of Xinjiang. *Twentieth Century China, 26*(2), 95–139.

Bovingdon, G. (2002). The not-so-silent minority: Uyghur resistance to Han rule in Xinjiang. *Modern China, 28*(1), 39–78.

Bovingdon, G. (2004a). CCP policies and popular responses in Xinjiang, 1949 to the present. In M. Rossabi (Ed.), *China's management of its minorities*. Seattle: University of Washington Press.

Bovingdon, G. (2004b). *Autonomy in Xinjiang: Han nationalist imperatives and Uyghur discontent*. Honolulu: East-West Center.

Bovingdon, G. (in press). Contested histories. In S. F. Starr (Ed.), *Xinjiang: China's Muslim frontier*. M. E. Sharpe.

Chaoxianzu jianshi. (1986). *Chaoxianzu jianshi* (pp. 252–260). Changchun, PRC: Zhongguo kexueyuan minzu yanjiusuo, Jilin shaoshuminzu shehui lishi diaocha baogao.

Choi, S. (2004). Citizenship, education, and identity: a comparative study of ethnic Chinese in Korea and ethnic Koreans in China. *International Journal of Education Reform, 13*(3), 253–266.

Dangde minzu zhengce wenxian ziliao xuanbian (1981). *Dangde minzu zhengce wenxian ziliao xuanbian*. Beijing, PRC: Zhungguo suhui kexueyuan minzuyuengiuso minzu wontililiun yuengiuso.

Deuchler, M. (1999). Despoilers of the way–insulters of the sages: Controversies over the classics in seventeenth-century Korea In J. K. Haboush & M. Deuchler (Eds.), *Culture and the state in late Choson Korea* (pp. 91–133). Cambridge, London: Harvard University Asia Center.

Doyle, M. (1997). *Ways and war and peace*. New York: Norton.

Dreyer, J. T. (1976). *China's forty millions: Minority nationalities and national integration in the People's Republic of China*. Cambridge: Harvard University Press.

Ellicott, M. (2000). The limits of tartary: Canchuria in imperial and national geographies. *The Journal of Asian Studies, 59*(3), 603–646.

Gerth, H. H. & Mills, W. (Eds.) (1958). *From Max Weber: Essays in sociology*. New York: Basic Books.

Gladney, D. (1996a). Relational alterity: Constructing Dungan (Hua), Uygur, and Kazakh identities across China, Central Asia, and Turkey. *History and Anthropology, 9*(2), 445–477.

Gladney, D. (1996b). *Muslim Chinese: Ethnic nationalism in the People's Republic*. Cambridge: Harvard University Press.

Gladney, D. (1998). Getting rich is not so glorious: Contrasting perspectives on prosperity among Muslims and Han in China. In R. W. Hefner (Ed.), *Market cultures: Precedents and cultures in the Chinese and Southeast Asian economic miracles*. Oxford: Westview Press.

Gladney, D. (2003). *Dislocating China: Muslims, minorities, and other subaltern subjects*. Chicago: University of Chicago Press.

Goh, Y. (2002). *Jungguk Chosonminjoksa Yongu*. Seoul: Hagyonmunhwasa.

Graff, G. (1992). *Beyond the cultural wars: How teaching conflicts can revitalize American education*. New York: Norton.

Haboush, J. (1999). Constructing the center: The ritual controversy and the search for a new identity in seventeenth-century. In J. K. Haboush & M. Deuchler (Eds.), *Culture and the state in late Choson Korea* (pp. 46–90). Cambridge, London: Harvard University Asia Center.

Haboush, J. & Deuchler, M. (1999). Introduction. In J. K. Haboush & M. Deuchler (Eds.), *Culture and the state in late Choson Korea* (pp. 1–14). Cambridge, London: Harvard University Asia Center.

Hall, P. (1997). The role of interests, institutions, and ideas in the comparative political economy of the industrialized nationals. In M. I. Lichback & A. S. Zuckerman (Eds.), *Comparative politics: Rationality, culture, and structure* (pp. 174–207). New York: Cambridge University Press.

Han, S.-B. & Kwon, T.-H. (1994). *Joongguk Yonbyun ui Choson jok: Sahoi kujowa Byunhua* [*Ethnic Koreans in China: Social Structure and Change*]. Seoul: Seoul National University Press.

Harrison, L. & Huntington, S. (Eds.) (2000). *Culture matters: How value shape human progress.* New York: Basic Books.

Ho, P. (1967). *Studies on the population of China, 1368–1953.* Cambridge, MA: Harvard University Press.

Hobsbawm, E. (1990). *Nations and nationalism since 1780: Programme, myth, reality.* Cambridge: Cambridge University Press.

Hwang, Yu-Bok (1989). A comparative study of Koreans in China and the United States. *Modern Praxis,* 9: 44–58.

Joongguk Choson Minjok Baljachi Chongso (1999). *Joongguk Choson Minjok Baljachi Chongso* Beijing, PRC: Minzu Chupanshe.

Joongguk e Uri Minjok: Yonbyon Chosonjok Jachiju Gaehwang. Yanji. (1988). *Joongguk e Uri Minjok: Yonbyon Chosonjok Jachiju Gaehwang. Yanji.* PRC: Yonbyon Inmin Chulpansa.

Joongguk Choson Minjok Kyoyuksaryogip. (2001). *Joongguk Choson Minjok Kyoyuksaryogip.* Yanji, PRC: Yonbyon Kyoyuk Chulpansa.

Kang, H. (2001) *Under the black umbrella: Voices from colonial Korea 1910–1945.* Ithaca: Cornell University Press.

Kihl, Y. (2005). *Transforming Korean politics: Democracy, reform, and culture.* New York: M. E. Sharpe.

Kim, B.-M. (1994). *Chosonjok Munhwa Chongso: Joongguk Chosonjok Munhwa Yon'gu.* Seoul: Mokwon Daehaggyo Chulpanbu.

Kim, D. (2003). *Ichejin goto: Manju e yuksa.* Seoul: Samkwa kum.

Kim, J. *et al.* (1996). *Jungguk Chosonjoksa Yongu I.* Seoul; Yanji: Seoul National University Press: Yanbian University Press.

Kim, Y. *et al.* (1987). *Yanbian shehuizhuyi minzu guanxide xingchenghe fazhan.* Yanji: Yanbian minzu chubanshe.

Kymlicka, W. (2004). Foreword. In J. Banks (Ed.), *Diversity and citizenship education: Global perspectives* (pp. xiii–xviii). San Francisco: Jossey-Bass.

Latin, D. (1986). *Hegemony and culture: Politics and religious change among the Yoruba.* Chicago: University of Chicago Press.

Lee, C.-J. (1986). *China's Korean minority: The Politics of ethnic education.* Boulder: Westview Press.

Lee, C.-S. (1983). *Revolutionary struggle in Manchuria: Chinese communism and Soviet interests, 1922–1945.* Berkeley: University of California Press.

Lee, K. G. (2002). *Gyukdongki ei zhongguk chosonjok.* Seoul: Baeksan sodang.

Li, D. (1998). *Imagining the Nation: Asian American literature and cultural consent.* Stanford: Stanford University Press.

Lu, Y. (1987). *Qingdaihe minguo Shandong Yimin Dongbei Shilue.* Shanghai: Shanghai Shehui kexueyuan chubanshe.

Ma, R. (2003). Zhungguo guozuguingide giegushengchecheng. In *Minzu Wonti Yengiu* (pp. 27–35). Beijing, PRC: Zhungguo renmin dashe chubanshe.

McCormack, G. (1977). *Chang Tso-lin in Northeast China, 1911–1918.* Stanford: Stanford University Press.

Malkki, L. (1992, Feb.). National geographic: The rooting of peoples and the territorialization of national identity among scholars and refugees. *Cultural Anthropology, 7*(1): 24–44.

Marshall, T. H. (1950). Citizenship and social class. In T. H. Marshall & T. Bottomore (Eds.), *Citizenship and social class.* London: Pluto Press.

Min, P. G. (1990). A comparison of the Korean minorities in China and Japan. *International Migration Review, 26*(1), 4–21.

Olivier, B. (1993). *The implementation of China's nationality policy in the northeastern provinces.* San Francisco: Mellen Research University Press.

Park, M. (1987). Chaoxianzu zai Dandong. In *Zhongguo Chaoxianzu lishi yanjiu luncong* (pp. 239–248). Yanji: Yanbian daxue chubanshe.

Park, M. *et al.* (1996). *Jungguk Chosonjoksa Yongu II.* Seoul; Yanji: Seoul daehakkyo chulpanbu; Yanbian daxue chubanshe.

Park, Y.-S. (1988). *Jaeman hanin dongnip woondongsa yongu.* Seoul: Ilchogak.

Pieterse, J. N. (2001). *Development theory: Deconstructions/Reconstructions.* London, Thousand Oaks, New Delhi: Sage Publications.

Postiglione, G. (1994). Representing nationality in China: Refiguring majority/minority identity. *Journal of Asian Studies, 53*(1), 92–123.

Postiglione, G. (1999). *China's national minority education: Culture, schooling and development.* New York: Falmer Press.

Postiglione, G. (in press). *Education, inequality and social change on China.* New York: M.E. Sharpe.

Scalapino, R. & Lee, C.-S. (1972). *Communism in Korea.* Berkeley: University of California Press.

Schmid, A. (2002). *Korea between empires 1895–1919.* New York: Studies of East Asian Institute, Columbia University Press.

Shafir, G. (1998). Introduction: The evolving tradition of citizenship. In G. Shafir (Ed.), *The citizenship debates: A reader.* Minneapolis, London: University of Minnesota Press.

Shin, P. (1980). The Korean colony in Chientao: A study of Japanese imperialism and militant Korean nationalism, 1905–1932. Ph.D. dissertation, University of Washington Press, Seattle.

So, K. (1988). *Hukryonggang Choson Minjok* [*Heilongjiang Chaoxian Minzu*]. Mudengiangshi, PRC: Hungnyonggan Choson Minjok Chulpansa [Heilongjiang Chaoxian Minzu Chubanshe].

Tamanoi, M. (2000). Knowledge, power, and racial classifications: The "Japanese" in "Manchuria." *The Journal of Asian Studies, 59*(2), 248–276.

Thompson, M., Ellis, R., & Wildavsky, A. (1990). *Cultural theory.* Boulder: Westview.

Tonkin, E., McDonald, M., & Chapman, M. (1989). *Introduction. History and ethnicity.* London: Routledge.

Weber, M. (1958). In H. H. Gerth, C. W. Mills, & C. Wright (Eds.), *From Max Weber.* New York: Oxford University Press.

Yang, S. (2005). Introduction. In J. Kim and S. Yang (Eds.), *Hidden treasure: lives of first-generation Korean women in Japan* (pp. xiii–xxvii). Lanham, Boulder, New York, Oxford: Rowman & Littlefield. xiii-xxvii.

Yonbyon Chosonjok chach'iju kaehwang. (1984).

Yoon, B. (2003). *Gando Yoksa e Yongu.* Seoul: Gukhak Jaryowon.

Zhang, T. & Huang, R. (1996). *China's minority populations: Surveys and research* [*Zhongguo Shaoshu Minzu Renkou Diaocha Yanjiu*]. Beijing: Gaodeng Giaoyu.

CHAPTER 9

Born with Gold in Your Mouth: Maintaining Identity in Australian Coptic Orthodox Young Adults

RICHARD RYMARZ AND MARIAN DE SOUZA

Governmental Policy on Minority Education

Leaving aside, for reasons of complexity, a discussion of the education of indigenous communities, the main vehicle for government policy on minority education in Australia is funding for schools and educational institutions. Australia illustrates well the demographic trends of a country with a large and diverse immigrant community, many of whom have strong and distinct cultural and ethnic identities (Khoo and Lucas, 2004). Over the past decade there has been a significant shift in the policy of the federal government in providing funds for ethnic or culturally specific schools. Prior to this all levels of government provided limited funding on the basis of individual community application (Lo Bianco and Wickert, 2001). Support of school initiatives by regional authorities and state governments, is still much harder to obtain (Kalantzis *et al.*, 1989). Prior to 1996, in order to qualify for federal government school funding, any group had to meet a variety of selection criteria (National Board of Employment Education and Training, 1995ab). Perhaps the most strident of these required a community to demonstrate that it could sustain an educational initiative for a number of years prior to receiving federal aid. This made it difficult for small communities to begin a school or cultural education center as the initiative had to be self-funding in the early years. As a result, the majority of groups that established educational institutions were ones with quite long-standing roots in the community and sizable assets, as well as trained and qualified community members. More recent arrivals found this educational policy virtually excluded them from receiving governmental support. With a change in the federal government in the mid-1990s, in 1996 there was a shift in policy designed initially to favor groups who wished to establish schools outside of the major existing educational infrastructure. This shift reflected the government's ideological interest in so-called small government and giving individuals choice over how their children were educated at the expense of the state-sponsored schools system. Most of these funds have gone to groups, such as evangelical Christians, which, while maintaining a distinctive educational philosophy, do not claim to be cultural or ethnically distinctive. However, many of the groups that have taken up the offer of federal support have been groups that are interested in preserving a distinctive cultural and ethnic identity. Coptic Christians, the subject of this chapter, have, for example, established five schools in Australia, with plans for a sixth. The Coptic community is large enough to attract funding and has the social and human resources to sustain schools on an ongoing basis. Since 2005, over thirty schools have been established for the education of cultural or ethnic minorities. The majority of these schools have been Islamic schools, but these can reflect an ethnic bias, with different schools established by different ethnic communities such as Turkish or Lebanese groups.

The current policy of the federal government does favor sizable minority groups. Despite federal funding, a community has to be able to generate enough income and interest to sustain the considerable costs in establishing a school. Some have argued that a more effective strategy would also recognize the need for federal assistance at a more local level which would allow an ethnically or culturally diverse community to establish educational services that meet community needs but are not tied to the establishment of a school or similar institution (Luchtenberg, 2004). Another criticism is that the policy does not distinguish between religious and cultural diversity. The case of Chaldean Christians from Iraq is a case in point. Chaldeans are a very distinct ethnic group who, among other things, preserve their own language, Chaldean, as the language of choice in family and community settings. Chaldeans are also Catholics: albeit Eastern rather than Roman (Latin), they enjoy full communion with other Catholics. Catholic schools are a large, established part of the educational landscape in Australia and Chaldeans as Catholics have the option of going to these schools, but do not feel that their cultural distinctiveness is well catered for. They are also not interested in schools established for Muslims, many of whom are from Iraq. As Chaldeans number less than 20,000 in the whole of the country they do not have sufficient critical mass in any area to establish their own school. Attempts to get funding for educational programs through the church or community groups have not been successful.

Exploring Coptic Identity: This Study

Watson (2002) reported high levels of religious affiliation among Copts in the U.K. In Australia Coptic youth and young adults report high levels of both religious belief and affiliation and identification with the tradition (De Souza and Rymarz, 2003, 2004). Many mainstream Christian churches are struggling to establish and maintain links with young people (Davie, 1994; Reeves, 1996; Beaudoin, 1998; D'Antonio *et al.*, 2001; Bendroth, 2002). This disassociation has also been commented on in a variety of other traditional religious groups (Ebaugh and Chafetz, 2000; Keysar *et al.*, 2000). The Coptic Church, however, appears to provide an example of an ancient tradition that is well integrated into the lives of its followers, both old and young. This chapter will explore some of the reasons why the Coptic orthodox tradition is able to maintain such a prominent part in the lives of its followers. It will draw from data gathered from three sources and follows an ethnographic paradigm: firstly, in-depth interviews with Coptic young adults aged between 24 and 32 years of age, secondly from interviews with Coptic leaders, such as the bishop, priests and community leaders, and, lastly, from extensive notes taken by the researchers during an 18-month period of involvement and observation of the Coptic ministry to young adults. This included participation in activities such as dedicated weekends for young adults, conferences, and special events as well as attendance at weekly meetings of Coptic young adults. Data from these sources will be presented as part of a wider discussion that identifies a number of key factors that underline the resilience of Copts in contemporary Western cultures. This study was conducted among Copts who had a strong association with the Coptic Orthodox Church. As with many immigrant groups, the church serves as a focus for the whole community: it is nonetheless important to note that the data reported here do not claim to be a cross-section of Coptic community. The main conceptual framework in which the discussion of why young adult Copts appear to be successful in maintaining their cultural and religious identity will draw heavily on the so-called rational choice theory of religious afflation as proposed by Stark and Finke (2000). Another conceptual perspective that will be used is a discussion of the importance of maintaining markers of cultural life.

A Brief Historical Overview of the Coptic Orthodox Church

The Coptic Orthodox Church is one of the oldest Christian traditions dating back to the time of the apostles (Young, 1983; Meinardus, 1999). The Copts (the name is derived from the ancient term for the indigenous inhabitants of Egypt) claim St. Mark the evangelist, the first Bishop of Alexandria, as their patron (Frend, 1981; Malaty, 1987). The Copts of Egypt were leading figures in defining orthodox Christian belief against the heterodox teachings of both

Arius and Nestorius and, before this, against the multitude of gnostic sects that were prolific in Alexandria (Kelly, 1989; Roukema 1999). Being defenders of orthodox belief remains an important feature of Coptic orthodox religious identity (Watson, 2002)

The first major split in the Christian Church occurred at the Council of Chalcedon in 451 A.D. when the Copts refused to accept the proposed definition of Christ's human and divine natures (Young, 1991). Following the council, the Byzantine emperor placed a patriarch in charge of the church in Alexandria who supported the Chalcedon definitions. This enraged the Copts who, determined to maintain their own identity, supported a rival patriarch, one who was faithful to their tradition (Chadwick, 1964). In 642 CE Egypt was conquered by Arab Islamic forces. This marked the beginning of political domination of Coptic Christians by Muslims, a situation that continues in Egypt to this day. There are officially 6 million Copts living in Egypt today, although the unofficial figure, which is politically sensitive, is much higher than this (Wakin, 2000). Coptic Orthodox Christianity is an important influence in Ethiopia and, to a lesser extent, in Sudan and Eritrea. There are well over 1 million Copts living in a long-standing diaspora. Coptic Orthodox Christians began to arrive in Australia from Egypt in substantial numbers in the 1960s. At present there are between 50,000 and 60,000 Copts in Australia, largely in Melbourne and Sydney.

Part One. Religion and Coptic Identity

Coptic core beliefs are often expressed in metaphysical terms and young adult Copts are not generally comfortable with an expression of religious belief that minimizes the significance of God acting in their lives. Here they are exemplifying what Stark and Finke (2000) described as an exchange with the gods, a pivotal aspect of rational choice theory. The proposition is that individuals will only subscribe to a religious tradition that makes significant demands on them if they are convinced that their subsequent beliefs and practice will allow them to enter into favorable interactions with the gods. Coptic religious beliefs make demands on believers, but at the same time these beliefs also give them a close connection with the divine through interaction with a powerful and personal God who is interested in them. Religious identity is sustained further by articulated beliefs that have a strongly transcendental dimension, that is they place the individual into a realm where they are able to use metaphysical categories to describe their lives (Bouma, 1992). Here is how one Coptic young adult expressed this notion:

> when dealing with other people, we do things from a more "what's right, what's wrong" perspective or "would this please God or wouldn't it." I wouldn't say that we're better than other people, we're

not, we are all equal, but we struggle to do well and we struggle first of all to please God, to glorify God's name. I haven't seen many other cultures do that.

Central to Coptic religious belief is a strongly monotheistic principle that is at the heart of their refusal to endorse the Chalcedonian decrees. According to rational choice theory a strong monotheism reinforces the idea that the believer is dealing with one all-powerful deity rather than a proliferation of weaker and competing Gods (Stark, 2001). Core religious beliefs, such as monotheism, are kept alive for young Copts by constant but effective reminders of the Coptic position. The following formula, a joint statement issued in May 1973 by the Coptic Pope Shenouda III and Pope Paul VI, is recited and is readily recalled by Coptic young Coptic adults (Bunson, 2002):

We confess that our Lord and God and Saviour and King of us all, Jesus Christ, is perfect God with respect to His divinity, and perfect man with respect to His humanity. In Him His divinity is united with His humanity in a real, perfect union without mingling, without commixtion, without confusion, without alteration, without division, without separation.

The contrast with other Christian groups is something that Copts are aware of and they recognize their steadfastness with the accommodation of others:

I know that the Catholic religion tends to make certain subtle changes as time goes by to accommodate the new era and I think as a direct result of those subtle changes the wall begins to crumble and then you start having all these indifferences and people falling out of that particular religion because something doesn't feel right or something doesn't fit. Whereas with Coptic Orthodox, because it has always been set up the same from the word go and has always kept and maintained its tradition, nothing has changed and we've felt ourselves as the sole foundation and we've constantly built upon that and the walls will not crumble.

As well as contrasting themselves with Catholics, Copts also note differences between their community and other orthodox traditions. The religious identity of many orthodox communities is compromised by *phyletism*, the association of the church with a national group (Clark, 2000). Coptic identity, on the other hand, is not primarily with a national group, but rather with a more nebulous historical association with a land and a people that are no longer a dominant political group. Young Copts typically see themselves as Egyptians, the descendents of the Pharaohs and certainly not as Arabs. They speak Arabic but are aware that this not their ancient language, Coptic, which is now largely restricted to liturgical use. Young adult Copts therefore tend to identify with the religious aspects of being a Copt because these are well articulated rather than political expressions that are associated with nationalist aspirations. When religious factors are a major aspect of cultural identity this makes allegiance more resilient (Douglas, 1982; Smith *et al.*, 2002). According to rational choice theory, a strong sense of religious identity is also associated with high levels of satisfaction with the tradition and this reinforces allegiance (Stark and Finke, 2000). Satisfaction in turn is high when believers sees themselves as part of a divine, supranational community, not one that is basically a political or national body and indistinguishable from a range of other ethnic or cultural agencies.

Another aspect of the religious identity of young adult Copts is that they have a strong affiliation with the religious tradition via existing leadership structures. The gap between claimed and accepted authority is relatively low among Copts when compared to other mainline Christian denominations (D'Antonio *et al.*, 2001). Copts are an episcopal church with a sacramental priesthood and a strong sense of apostolic succession, that is the bishop is seen as a successor of the apostles and sharing their authority. Some of the most revered figures in both the ancient and recent history of the Copts have been bishops. Many young people nominate both the current Pope and his predecessor as the most significant figures in their lives. The monk/bishop also has additional credibility within the Coptic community because of the special place that monks have within the tradition (Angaelos, 1997). The wellspring of Coptic spirituality lies in the leadership provided by the great monasteries (Meinardus, 1977). This is most obvious in Egypt where the monasteries are also a treasure trove of Coptic history and culture. It is significant that, in Australia, one of the first actions of the emerging community was to establish a monastery in rural Victoria.

As in other Eastern and Oriental traditions the bishops of the Coptic Orthodox Church are monks (Ware, 1997). Priests, on the other hand, are drawn from the ranks of the laity. Priests are married men who have been selected for priesthood in an exchange between the bishop and the congregation. Typically, when a community gets large enough, the bishop is approached and asked to consider a member of the community for ordination to the priesthood. Note how this gives the community a strong link to the priest, who is seen as one of the community, but who has, nonetheless, been selected for a special grace. The priest wears highly distinctive clothing and in community functions has a place of honor. This is one way of marking the importance of priesthood. The closeness between the priest and the people can be seen in contrast to other Christian denominations where the role and authority of the clergy is increasingly questioned (Russell, 1980; Cozzens, 2000). In terms of rational choice theory, the religious allegiance of a group is reinforced when the religious leader, in this case the priest, is seen as having close links with the congregation and not one who is distant from the concern of the believer.

A consequence of being a minority is living with the possibility of persecution and this has provided a further strengthening of their religious identity. One of the most common self-descriptors used by Copts is the term "the Church of the Martyrs." The Copts have an almost unmatched record among Christians for being able to withstand persecution and to survive despite their minority status. The Coptic calendar begins in the year 284 CE when the Emperor Diocletian came to power. This marked a ferocious persecution of Christians in Egypt. Coptic history is defined by persecution— by Romans, fellow Christians, and Muslims.

The stigma and sacrifice associated with belonging to a minority group can bring with it an associated increase in commitment and participation (Iannaccone, 1994). The experience of having to suffer for their beliefs and practices is at the heart of Coptic self-understanding. In terms of rational choice theory, however, persecution, even the most extreme form, martyrdom, can act as a significant religious compensator to unify a minority faith (Stark and Bainbridge, 1985). The martyr is one who attests to the ultimate value of the religious tradition by showing that life itself is subordinate to religious demands. This is how one young Copt identified the significance of the experience of martyrdom for him today:

> If you lose your traditions, you lose your background and you change so I guess our Church really stuck at it. I mean that's the whole idea of our Church, we stuck at it from the very start. What we got from St Mark has been passed down, it has never changed . . . our Church is we are full of martyrs. We have plenty and thousands of martyrs even to this day. What happened a couple of years ago in one of the villages in Egypt, Muslims killed 30 Egyptians and they were named martyrs.

Copts are used to doing things their own way and realize that they may have to pay a price for being faithful to their traditions and this makes their religious heritage and not national or ethnic issues their defining feature.

Part Two. A Way into the Tradition: the Cultural Markers of Coptic Life

Perhaps the most significant marker of Coptic cultural life is a conceptual one. In our study young adult Copts readily identified what sets them apart from other groups. They were clear about their beliefs and practices and defining boundaries that are critical in sustaining cultural identity (Berger, 1992; Hogg,

1992). The resilience of Coptic cultural life was partly explained by their unique history, which has set them apart. Copts do not have close affinity with other mainstream Christian groups. There are no *close proximal groups* offering a passage to assimilation into Western societies. Feher (1998) noted that groups that have some cultural similarity often act as vectors for assimilation. She gave the example of the assimilation of Iranian Jews into mainstream American culture at the cost of their cultural identity. This process was assisted by the connection between the Iranian Jews and groups of established American Jewish groups. For Copts such proximal groups do not exist.

The unique status of Coptic Christians gives the young adult members of the community great resilience and a strong sense of what makes them special. As one young adult put it, to be a Copt in Egypt is not easy but you must also recognize that you have been born with *gold in your mouth*—that is you have been given a great treasure that others have to strive for. This attitude is expressed in a number of ways, each of which expresses the confidence that Copts feel in being part of a tradition that stretches back to apostolic times. For example, Copts see the liturgy as the most perfect expression of their faith (Schmemann, 1963). Copts are in church a lot over the Easter period: for example, the devout may spend over 100 hours in formal worship. Being able to participate in the liturgy is, however, a great privilege and not something that should be taken for granted. The Divine Liturgy is a foretaste of heaven, where the believer is part of an action that is seen as uniting heaven and earth. To change the liturgy is unthinkable because it represents the patrimony of the ages. As one young Copt put it:

> How can we change the liturgy that has come to us from St Basil? Think of the shame that would come to us, if we were the ones to change the liturgy that our ancestors have died for.

Strong identity is associated with a series of other behaviors which are that are part of group affiliation (Strommen and Hardel, 2000). A close identification with ancient traditions and customs is a feature of Coptic life. This is nowhere more evident than in the practice of fasting. Among Christian churches the Copts probably have the most extensive fasting regime. All Fridays and Wednesdays are fast days, as well as major fasts that correspond with important events in the liturgical calendar. As well as being a practice that has been a constant feature of Christian life since its very origins, fasting serves as one way of linking the individual with a religious tradition. The Coptic young adults who were interviewed identified fasting as the one practice that marked them as Coptic Christians:

> Prayer and fasting is what our Church has taught us firstly. At least two-thirds of our calendar is involved in fasting so through prayer

and fasting you obtain that spirituality, you obtain that closeness to God, you obtain that perfection or struggle for perfection because no-one's perfect.

Practices like fasting unites them with other Copts and is by its very nature an egalitarian practice. The monks, who have an even more rigorous regime and all Copts are united by taking part in activities like the great Lenten Fast. This is a simple but extremely effective way of building a sense of community and fellowship. It also has other cultural effects, such as sparking a distinctive cuisine that includes both dishes for fasting and non-fasting periods and a number of festivals that mark the end of fast periods. The combined effect of this is to allow Copts a way to express their religious identity that is constant and marks them as distinct from the wider community thereby establishing an important boundary between themselves and others. This is done at no great cost to the individual—as well as giving a sense of identity, fasting is not too onerous or without compensation.

Fasting is perhaps the most important way that Copts mark their religious identity but there are many others. A Coptic home, for example, is full of religious art most notably icons, which are painted in a distinctly Coptic style. Copts also have a unique musical culture that incorporates melodies that originated in the Pharonic era—predating Christianity.

Another cultural marker of Coptic life is the way young adults, especially males, are incorporated into the faith community via formalized roles. The most prominent of these is the position of deacon. Deacons are part of the ordained ministry and play an important role in the liturgical life of the church. Deacons are ordained by the bishop, thereby giving them status and dignity. Other Christian traditions have been somewhat reluctant to embrace the use of a permanent diaconate, despite this being part of the classical understanding of the threefold ministry (Fink, 1990). It is not unusual for a young Coptic male to be a deacon of the Church. There are a number of grades of diaconate to accommodate different levels of maturity and commitment, but all of these give the young Copts a sense that they are part of the church in a clear and absolute way. As well as being deacons, another well-developed pathway that can connect the young Copt to the faith tradition is that of servant of the church. Servants do a range of tasks, such as catechesis and family ministry and this is an especially popular role for young women. The servants provide the Coptic with a great human resource asset but also give young adults an important sense of belonging.

The young adult Copts observed here had a highly significant relationship with their confession father, a priest with whom they shared a deep and enduring relationship. Whereas confession has all but disappeared from the Catholic tradition in Western industrial countries, it remains an important feature of Coptic devotional life (Greeley, 1985). Regular confession ensues that the link between the individual and the tradition is maintained through the sharing of intimate and life-shaping personal details. One example of this is provided from our research data. When asked about marriage, a number of young Coptic males, educated professionals in their mid-twenties, stated that, when it came time to marry, their confession Father would play an important role in the selection of a suitable bride, both in advice about the woman and also in discussion with the woman's confession Father. At the very least such a system makes it much more likely that Copts marry within the tradition, a critical aspect of maintaining religious identity, but also indicates the level of trust that individuals place in their confession Father (Keysar et al., 2000). Here is how another young Copt described the importance of the confession Father in her life: "I have a confession regularly in front of my spiritual advisor and he is probably one of the most significant people in my life."

The experience of Australia is a new one for Copts. Compared to Egypt, Australia is a rich and secular country, where religious persecution—at least in the Coptic understanding of the term—does not exist. Nonetheless, the leaders of the church in Australia have been quick to identify the secularism of the wider Australian society as something that is incompatible with Coptic life and must be resisted. One key strategy has been to facilitate social interaction between members. The Coptic community regularly organizes a variety of activities for young people. These are age specific and separate senior school students, those at university, and those in the workforce. Regular meetings of these groups are held at the local, state, and national levels.

The sexual morality of the Copts is at odds with perceived Western promiscuity. They have not made many of the accommodations to modern life that other Christians leaders have. For example, in the Coptic schools, which are co-educational for practical rather than ideological reasons, students are not permitted to dance or to be alone in the company of a member of the opposite sex. A word that is often used in talks by Coptic leaders on these matters is purity. This is a virtue to be practiced and should be reflected in how the Copt dresses and what entertainment they allow themselves and carries through to adult life, where it is manifested in a desire of community members to socialize with other Copts. As one young adult Copt put it:

> I have lots of friends at work but I mainly go out at night with my Coptic ones. It is just that I feel more comfortable with them. We all know what we can and can't do so I am under no pressure when I am with them. A bad situation will not arise.

An example of a *bad situation* could relate to something like alcohol. Copts are not complete abstainers. This is an important distinction between themselves and Muslims in Egypt. It would, nonetheless, be quite shameful for a Copt to drink to excess.

Say every Friday after work they all go to have a drink. While I might accept some of these things I find myself different from my work mates. I might have an orange juice, I might have a coke. I would never put my Christianity to shame by becoming drunk in front of the rest and doing all sorts of stuff and following their ways.

A strategy that many Copts use to avoid this situation is to socialize with other Copts where the collective group would ensure that any individual would not overstep what is accepted behavior. A critical factor in retaining religious affiliations of youth is the existence of social peer networks (Mercadante 1998; Donelson, 1999). Young adult Copts are able to provide each other with a high level of peer support. The Coptic Orthodox Church in Australia has a large enough presence to be able to sustain a variety of community initiatives, many of which are aimed at young people. They have moved beyond the stage of a small and demographically insignificant population that is compelled to look to the wider society for support and sustenance. When the Coptic leader Pope Shenouda III visited Melbourne in November 2002 it is estimated that over 90 percent of Copts aged between 15 and 35 years attended his meetings. This attraction of young Copts is a manifestation of how Coptic leadership assiduously plans to incorporate young people into their mission. For Copts it is quite a natural thing for the leader of the Church to visit a community and to have a dedicated meeting with young people. In all of this planning, the Copts in Australia have set out to ensure that the needs of young people are addressed. By the 1980s Copts, when they began to develop an institutional presence in the country, education of youth was an important part of this consolidation. As the community has grown significantly over the years schools in major centers, as well as two theological academies, two monasteries, and a retirement hospice now express the institutional strength of the Coptic community. A significant milestone in the history of the Copts in Australia was the appointment of the first local bishop in December 1999. This was recognition of the significance of their presence in Australia by the international Coptic community. The bishop sees his outreach to youth and young adults as a vital part of his ministry:

The bishop has brought us all together and because he has brought us all together, all these events that happen, whether it's a youth meeting or whether it's summer competition, activities, conventions, camps, whatever, it brings all the youth together and that way you are still with your Egyptian culture, you are still with your Egyptian friends . . .

You no longer think you are the minority. You walk in and you think there are so many people here, you don't feel like you're singled out again. You have a whole group of people. It gives you a sense of confidence that what I believe in, I should be proud of. Look at what I'm a part of . . .

Some Issues for the Future

Copts in Australia face a number of issues in the future that are consistent with a religious tradition becoming more enmeshed in a secular Western culture. One important challenge is the role to be played by women in the church and in the wider society, an issue that many immigrants to Western cultures face (Haddad *et al.*, 2003). Some of the women interviewed remarked on the different expectations placed on them when compared to males:

> My brother can come home at 12 or 1 o'clock and that's fine, they (*parents*) go to sleep and are not worried. Me, I get 100 calls . . .
>   I think it depends. I'm probably the most different out of the girls. I don't have a curfew but up until a certain age, I did have a curfew. I have an older brother so it did make life a little easier but I think generally it got to the point where after I finished all my schooling, my parents just must have thought about it and said well, she hasn't done that bad so far. She's turned out ok. She's working. She's educated. I think its time she makes up her own mind and there are differences but then there was a certain time when my parents were very concerned about what the community was going to say.

A very significant issue is how the Copts will cope with the challenges of living in Australia after the initial migrant experience is over and the second generation begins to take an ascendant position. This experience has proved to be a critical factor in determining ethic and religious identity in other faith communities (Steinberg, 1965; Alba, 1985; Chai, 1998). This is an issue that the Copts are aware of, both at a leadership and common level:

> What we have behind us is a treasure—it really is and to think of not having that is quite scary really and the one thing, I speak of myself, I want it to grow stronger with me and my family and my children and so on and so forth and just for the church to grow stronger and His Grace always tells us this one little thing. His Holiness had a meeting, I'm not sure whether in Egypt or here and he said to everyone that the church without you is a Church without a future and one of the youth replied and said. Youth without Church is youth without future and the more you think of it, you think, wow.

Conclusion

The argument set out in this paper suggests that the Copts display a number of characteristics that will continue to make them a resilient community that is able to maintain both its cultural and religious identity. To summarize, these characteristics can be grouped into a number of distinct categories. Firstly, the size of the community means that it is large enough to benefit from the current federal government's policy towards the education of minority groups. The Coptic community is able to establish schools and have considerable community support and expertise to be able to sustain this endeavor. At the moment they are well served by the existing attitude of federal authorities but, even if the policy changes in the future, their schools should be well established enough to survive.

The Coptic community has also managed to retain a high level of commitment and identification with religious ideals and beliefs. Copts seem to model well some of the consequences of retaining beliefs that stress a strong metaphysical element and clearly articulate a relationship between the believer and God. In this sense the Coptic community in Australia illustrates well the *exchange with the God's principle* that is an important part of rational choice theory. A critical aspect of Copts being able to retain their cultural identity is a strong attachment to the church as not just a bastion of cultural values, but also a mediator between the human and divine. Because of this understanding the church is able to demand and receive a lot from the community. This serves as a powerful mechanism for keeping the boundaries between the Coptic community and the wider culture secure.

The third way that Copts have been able to retain a strong identity is to participate in a number of practices that serve as very effective markers between them and the wider culture. These practices also allow members of the community to take part at a very human level in rituals that set them apart from wider society. They give shape and direction to community life without being too onerous or divisive. Perhaps the most important cultural marker is the fundamental practice of fasting. Fasting regulates Coptic life and gives shape to a yearly cycle of events, festivals, and commemorations. It gives members of the community a sense that they are the inheritors of an ancient and revered way of life and also ties them to a living and vibrant faith community.

Whether these characteristics are kept in place for an extended period of time is conjecture, but the history of the Copts to this point suggests that they have a community that is confident of its ability to survive in the pluralist Australian environment in which they are a distinct minority.

Resources and Tools for Educators

Questions

1. How transferable is the Coptic experience to those who work with ethnic or indigenous groups in cultural education. Can the lessons learned by studying this group be used by other groups?
2. The Copts place great emphasis on providing young members with opportunities to express their religious and cultural identity. How does

the group you work with deal with this issue. What are some of the ways that identity expression can be strengthened or extended?

3. Copts are very successful at providing links to the community of memory, that is the historical legacy of the community. How important is this for the group that you are involved with. How can you better present the historical chains that tie your community with that of its antecedents?

For Further Reading

Haddad, Y., Smith, J. & Esposito, J. (2003). *Religion and the Immigration.* Walnut Creek, CA: Altamaria Press.

This is an excellent introductory volume. It covers a range of topics of interest to those who work in cultural education and cultural sustainability. The chapter by Diaz-Stevens is particularly relevant to those who wish to gain an appreciation of the challenges facing immigrant groups trying to sustain religious and cultural identity.

Ebaugh, H. & Chafetz, J. (2003). *Religion and the new immigrants.* New York: AltaMira Press.

Another excellent volume that looks at recent immigration to countries such as the U.S.

Warner, R. & Wittner, J. (1998). *Gatherings in the diaspora: Religious communities and the new immigration.* Philadelphia: Temple University Press.

The chapter by Feher gives an intriguing account of cultural sustainability among Iranian Jews in Los Angeles. This can serve as a case study for the challenges facing many minority groups.

Suggestions for Educators

1. Curriculum audit. If you are working in a school take a copy of your curriculum and note all the places where cultural sustainability is addressed. Note how often this is done: also take into account how these themes are developed in the curriculum. For example, how are sustainability issues covered in junior and senior years? Ask yourself is there an obvious improvement in the sophistication of material presented in later years. If material in not covered sufficiently or not developed take steps to adjust the curriculum to reflect the importance that your community places on cultural education and sustainability.

2. Identify best practice. Make links with other groups that share your interest in cultural education and sustainability. What is it that they do very well and that you can learn from and incorporate into your

programs? These can be formal, as in taught or an informal part of a broader leaning environment. The Copts, for example, run very successful youth outreach programs that are aimed at specific age levels. Can your community use ideas such as this?

3. Working with teachers. How well are the teachers in your schools or educational establishments trained to deal with issues of cultural sustainability and cultural education? Do they know what the school is trying to achieve and the ways in which they can assist with this? If the answers to these questions are negative then some type of ongoing teacher development is in order. This type of teacher development may be especially important for teachers who have no strong connection with the host minority or indigenous group.

References

Alba, R. (1985). *The Italians.* Englewood Cliffs, NJ: Prentice-Hall.

Angaelos, B. (1997). *The altar in the midst of Egypt: A brief introduction to the Coptic Orthodox Church.* Stevenage: Coptic Orthodox Centre.

Beaudoin, T. (1998). *Virtual faith.* San Francisco: Jossey-Bass Publishers.

Bendroth, M. (2002). *Growing up Protestant.* Piscataway NJ: Rutgers University Press.

Berger, P. (1992). *A far glory: The quest for faith in an age of credulity.* New York: Anchor Books.

Bouma, G (1992) *Religion: Meaning, transcendence and community in Australia.* Melbourne: Longman Cheshire.

Bunson, M. (Ed.) (2002). *Catholic almanac.* Indiana: Our Sunday Visitor.

Chadwick, H. (1964). *The early Church.* London: Penguin.

Chai, K. (1998). Competing for the second generation: English language ministry in a Korean protestant church. In R. S. Warner & J. G. Wittner (Eds.), *Gatherings in the diaspora: Religious communities and the new immigration,* 295–333. Philadelphia: Temple University Press.

Clark, V. (2000). *Why angels fall: A journey through Orthodox Europe from Byzantium to Kosovo.* London: Picador.

Cozzens, D. (2000). *The changing face of priesthood.* Collegeville, MN: Liturgical Press.

Davie, G. (1994). *Religion in Britain since 1945.* Oxford: Blackwell.

D'Antonio, W., Davidson, J., Hoge, D., & Wallace, R. (1996). *Laity American and Catholic transforming the Church.* Kansas City: Sheed and Ward.

D'Antonio, W., Davidson, J., Hoge, D., & Meyer, K. (2001). *American Catholics: Gender, generation and commitment.* New York: Alta Mira Press.

De Souza, M. & Rymarz, R. (2003). The perceptions of some Australian Coptic students of the influences on their religious development. *Journal of Beliefs and Values, 24*(1), 67–74.

De Souza, M. & Rymarz, R. (2004). The transmission of a religious heritage to younger members of small ethnic communities in a pluralist society: The perceptions of young Australian Copts. *Australian Religion Studies Review, 17*(2), 39–46.

Donelson, E. (1999). Psychology of religion and adolescents in the United States: Past and present. *Journal of Adolescence, 22,* 187–204.

Douglas, M. (1982). The effects of modernization on religious change in religion and America: spirituality in a secular age. In M. Douglas & S. Tipton (Eds.), *Religion and America: Spiritual life in a secular age* (pp. 25–43). Boston: Beacon Press

Ebaugh, H. & Chafetz, J. (2000). *Religion and the new immigrants.* New York: AltaMira Press.

Feher, S. (1998). From the rivers of Babylon to the valleys of Los Angeles: The exodus and adaptions of Iranian Jews. In R. S. Warner & J. G. Wittner (Eds.), *Gatherings in the diaspora: Religious communities and the new immigration* (pp. 71–97) Philadelphia: Temple University Press.

Finke, P. (Ed.) (1990). *The new dictionary of sacramental worship.* Collegeville, MN: The Liturgical Press.

Frend, W. (1981). *The early Church: From the beginnings to 461.* London: SCM Press.

Greeley, A. (1985). *American Catholics since the council: An unauthorised report.* Chicago: Thomas More Press.

Haddad, Y., Smith, J., & Esposito, J. (2003). *Religion and immigration: Christian, Jewish and Muslim experiences in the United States.* New York: AltaMira Press.

Hogg, M. (1992). *The social psychology of group cohesiveness.* New York: New York University Press.

Iannoccone, L.(1994). Why strict Churches are strong. *American Journal of Sociology,* 99, 1180–1211.

Kalantzis, M., Cope, B., & Slade, D. (1989). *Minority languages and dominant culture: issues of education, assessment, and social equity.* London: Falmer Press.

Kelly, J. (1989). *Early Christian doctrines.* London: A & C Black.

Keysar, A., Kosmin, B., & Scheckner, J. (2000). *The next generation: Jewish children and adolescents.* New York: SUNY Press.

Khoo, S. & Lucas, D. (2004). *Australian census analytic program: Australians' ancestries.* Canberra: Australian Bureau of Statistics.

Luchtenberg, S (Ed.) (2004). *Migration, education, and change.* London: New York: Routledge.

Lo Bianco, J. & Wickert, R (Eds.) (2001). *Australian policy activism in language and literacy.* Melbourne: Language Australia.

Malaty, T. (1987). *Introduction to the Coptic Orthodox Church.* Ottawa: St. Marty's Coptic Orthodox Church.

Meinardus, O. (1977). *Christian Egypt, ancient and modern.* Cairo: American University Press.

Meinardus, O. (1999). *Two thousand years of Coptic Christianity.* Cairo: American University Press.

Mercadante, F (1998) *Growing teen disciples.* Winona, MM: Saint Mary's Publications.

National Board of Employment Education and Training. (1995a). *Resources and accountability: Commonwealth funding scenarios for government primary schools 1996–2000.* Canberra: Australian Govt. Pub. Service.

National Board of Employment Education and Training. (1995b). *Review of the level of commonwealth government recurrent funding to government primary schools: report on the consultations/National Board of Employment, Education and Training.* Canberra: Australian Government Publishing Service.

Reeves, T. (1996). *The empty church: Does organized religion matter anymore?* New York: Simon & Schuster.

Roukema, R. (1999). *Gnosis and faith in early Christianity: An introduction to gnosticism.* Harrisburg, PA: Trinity Press International.

Russell, A. (1980). *The clerical profession.* London: SPCK.

Schmemann, A. (1963). *The historical road of Eastern Orthodoxy.* London: Harvill Press.

Smith, C., Denton, R., Faris, R., & Regnerus, M. (2002). Mapping American adolescents and religious participation. *Journal for the Scientific Study of Religion,* 41(4), 597–612.

Stark, R. (2001). *One true God.* Princeton: Princeton University Press.

Stark, R. & Bainbridge, W. (1985). *The future of religion: Secularization, revival and cult formation.* Los Angles: University of California Press.

Stark, R. & Fink, R. (2000). *Acts of faith: Explaining the human side of religion.* Los Angeles: University of California Press.

Steinberg, S. (1965). Reform Judaism: The origins and evolution of a Church Movement, *Journal for the Scientific Study of Religion,* 24, 117–129.

Strommen, M. & Hardel, R. (2000). *Passing on the faith.* Winona, MM: Saint Mary's Press.

Wakin, E. (2000). *A lonely minority: The modern story of Egypt's Copts.* Lincoln: iUniverse.com.

Ware, T. (1997). *The Orthodox Church.* London: Penguin.

Watson, J. (2002). *Among the Copts.* Brighton: Sussex Academic Press.

Young, F. (1983). *From Nicaea to Chalcedon.* London: SCM Press.

Young, F. (1991). *The making of the Creeds.* Philadelphia: Trinity Press International.

CHAPTER 10

Retaining Ethnic Identity:
The Armenians in Bulgaria

MARI FIRKATIAN

This chapter focuses on the attempts of Armenians living in Bulgaria to sustain their identity in the face of assimilation.[1] The Bulgarian Armenians are like all immigrants, forever insecure under normal circumstances and, as Conover (1998) pointed out, they find it essential to cling to some difference that serves as a distinguishing mark of the exclusive, ethnic group. Buchvarov (1998) brought up the "inherited iconography" of a society, namely a collection of symbols, beliefs, images, and ideas that exert a powerful attractive force for the society's members. These connections cement the society and determine the territory, real and figurative, which excludes non-members. They create a framework for the experience of milieu. The iconographic "map" also influences the group's choices and, thus, its behaviors. It enters a member's consciousness first and then the geographic territory, the modern nation. Émigrés exiled from their native land have lost the actual territory of the nation. What they do have is an opportunity after leaving the homeland to retain and sustain over time the possibility of using religion, language, and other iconographies as a way of perpetuating a milieu and a diasporic social formation. Unlike a physical territory, the cultural realm is intangible and difficult to define, but also potentially adaptable. In today's societies, the process of establishing the bona fides of ethnic identity has given rise to the seeking out and reincorporating of practices and rituals that codified membership, the "how-tos" of belonging to a separate, unique ethnic group (Bakalian, 1993). This is the role of "inherited iconography."

Porter (1975) argued that the "role of ethnic group affiliation in solving problems of personal identity is small since . . . identities and psychic shelters can be found in other forms of association and interest groups which are not based on descent" (p. 301). If this is so then those who choose to cultivate identity do it as an emotional priority. They are the ones who will keep cultural individuation viable. One of my sources pointed to the need to feel "a part of the whole" like "a drop of water in the sea" as her motivation to join an Armenian youth group and, thus, to sustain the ethnos.[2] An opportunity to belong to an in-group that automatically separates the individual from the masses presents a safe haven (Conover, 1998). A need to be a part of the whole is a strong motivator, which leads to extraordinary efforts. There exist a host of identities and affiliations that individuals' cycle through their lives, each with different levels of importance or immediacy.

While Armenians live in Bulgaria they are called on to belong to the Bulgarian polity as citizens with rights and obligations. However, that polity does not address all of their needs for identity within the context of the national Bulgarian community. For diaspora Armenians, ties of ethnic affiliation offer a connection, a feeling of security and kinship, not available by any other channel. Furthermore, they lend meaning to life. The Armenian diaspora has persisted in all sorts of foreign environments by depending not only on its church as a beacon of identity but on a large selection of social, civic, and charitable organizations to nurture its population. The community has traditionally attracted and kept its members with a wide array of group memberships made to order for every age group and every taste. Dance, theatre, athletic, charitable, entertainment, political, and youth-oriented organizations have been the mainstay of community existence. By and with these magnets Armenians have managed to create a core sense of community.

Parsons (1975, p. 65) claimed that "the marks of identity are in a very important sense empty symbols. Symbols empty of elaborate social distinctions" and that is "focused on style of life distinctiveness within the larger framework of . . . social structure." He used the example of co-religionists of different ethnicities that marry and seem to manage to adapt or adopt one ethnicity over another. The sociologists Bakalian (1993) and Gans (1996) relegated ethnicity to a future where it will exist only as a symbolic incarnation of ancestral practices. This seems to be borne out in the case in question since, in the contemporary world, it is easier to maintain "empty symbols" rather than the entire panoply of tradition-bound markers of ethnicity.

That indescribable feeling of belonging to the ethnos has overcome centuries of trials. For the Armenians in Bulgaria, as for many minority populations, the "inherited iconography" clashes with "the empty symbols." While a core of ethnic die-hards cling to the inherited iconography there is, whether pulling closer or pushing away, another sector of the population that prefers the allure of empty symbols. The attraction of empty symbols is obvious in the modern world; however, the fact that the community carries on despite dire warnings of its imminent demise is encouraging. The death of the culture has been greatly exaggerated. It is still vibrant but changing, adapting to new life conditions. The key is in the focus on adaptability and a willingness to embrace change as a valuable commodity rather than insisting on time-honored methods of cultural sustenance.

Methodology

The research for this article included interviews with thirty individuals. I chose the following categories of people: school principals, teachers, priests, cultural and charitable organization leaders, newspaper editors and journalists, and Bulgarian Government appointees to the Ministry of Culture and the Ministry of Education who are responsible for the Armenians or minority issues, as well as the consul of the Republic of Armenia's embassy to Sofia. I selected the above individuals because of their proximity to efforts at cultural education, because some of them were educators or worked with educators, and because, by virtue of their professional positions, they were most likely to present a clear picture of the issues at hand. At the same time, their very proximity to the drive to maintain the ethnos called for other points of view. Therefore, I interviewed individual Armenians and Bulgarians who, by virtue of their profession or involvement with the community, were likely to have representative insights. I interviewed an author of fiction, several historians and an ethnographer, business people, a musician, and a sculptor. Their insights were helpful for forming a more balanced image of the Armenian experience in Bulgaria.

I tape recorded my interviews and took notes while we carried on a conversation.

Armenians and the State

The Armenian community in Bulgaria has venerable roots. They have played an important role in many vital industries and cultural enterprises and have had a key role in social and political activism (Maksoudian, 1997). As a group, their relationship with their hosts has been beneficial and highly advantageous for both parties. It is therefore a surprising thought for most Bulgarians that perhaps the community is assimilating and disappearing as a distinct, ethnic entity (Radunchev, 2001). Furthermore, Bulgarians, when asked about Armenians, almost inevitably brought up the Armenian genocide, marking Armenians by their history (Dekmejian, 1997). The Bulgarian national poet Peio Yavrov wrote a spectacularly moving poem about Armenian refugees fleeing from Turkish atrocities in 1894 about which every Bulgarian schoolchild has some knowledge. These massacres forced the first waves of Armenian refugees out of the Ottoman Empire and into Bulgaria. Thus, we see signs of high awareness among Bulgarians about the Armenian historical experience.

However, recent historical experience from the perspective of Armenians is more complex. Through the Communist period and after the fall of Communism, ordinary Bulgarians have continued to maintain an awareness of the Armenian community as distinct and largely prone to clannishness. Nonetheless, the communist regime severely limited the lines of communication with the homeland and, therefore, sustaining the community was difficult (Maksoudian, 1997). After 1944, an Armenian Fatherland Front organization controlled the fate of the entire community. The organization promised to assure the protection of the rights of the Armenian minority at work, in education, and so on. However, communist ideology did not recognize national identity as a legitimate platform and, therefore, shut down all Armenian cultural, social organizations. The regime erected one umbrella organization, Erevan, so that the Communist Party could control the minority directly. In some sense, the system created symbolic ethnicity for its minority populations: a government-controlled essentialization of the ethnos.

Erevan became the representative organization for all Armenians in the country and took on the role of ideological leader of its constituents. Its activities included molding the Armenian minority to the Communist Party model of good citizenship. Good citizenship required Armenians to abandon any thoughts about an independent Armenian state or, by the 1960s, maintaining an Armenian culture that was separate or different in any way from Soviet Armenian culture. In terms of language study, a community whose language had always been the Western dialect of Armenian, spoken by the vast majority of the subjects of the former Ottoman Empire, was banished and the remaining Armenian schools were forced to teach Eastern Armenian (until language study was terminated). Under communism, access to Armenian literature that was published elsewhere besides Soviet Armenia was restricted and the studying of Western Armenian was termed "bourgeois" and incompatible with "socialist education" and therefore forbidden (Boghosian, 1999).

The change in language of instruction was dramatic since the Western variant is the one spoken by the entire Armenian diaspora while the Eastern variant is spoken mainly in the (formerly) Soviet Armenian Republic. The two are sufficiently far apart to make them almost unintelligible to speakers of one with a speaker of the other. In that one act the communists managed to separate and alienate one generation of Armenian speakers from another.

The communist-sponsored Erevan organization supported a newspaper and a cultural organization, both by the same name. It served as a conduit for communist ideology to the Armenian population, while at the same time it served as its only support for the maintenance of an Armenian identity via classes, lectures, holiday celebrations, and the sponsorship of amateur theatre, choir, and dance groups. With centrally controlled, limited options for an ethnically based community life communism reduced the sustenance of culture or its transference to their children by essentializing culture to formulaic symbols of ethnicity.

The legacy of this odd communist era formation is difficult to assess accurately. The communist government had an agenda to support "folk" customs or a peasant ethnos by glorifying the image of the village or farm community for its own ideological reasons. Today, even though there is no ideological agenda on the part of the Bulgarian Government, the reality is quite different. The transition from being part of the Soviet bloc to independence was difficult. Initially, an impoverished, confused and disoriented Bulgarian Government could do little to support minorities and their organizations. Moreover, younger generations of both Bulgarians and Armenians needed to focus on the day-to-day challenges of survival. Historical memory that is only relative in the context of formal studies in school was not enough to spur an urge to preserve one's ethnos.

A Rift in the Community

The course of cultural education on the Armenian community is ambiguous since they have two processes to counter. One is the above mentioned phenomenon and the other is survival of another sort. An economic crisis, which devastated the newly independent Republic of Armenia during the early 1990s, forced an out-migration of young, able-bodied citizens. Those immigrants who arrived (and continue to arrive) in Bulgaria assimilated rapidly because their goals are to be gainfully employed, assimilate, and acculturate.

The newcomers from Armenia, called *Hiastantsi* (those from Hiastan or Armenia), do not seek to support the efforts of the "native" or Bulgarian-born Armenians to maintain the ethnos. The distinction between the Hiastantsi and the "native" Armenian community is manifested mainly by the rapid assimilation of the newly arrived Hiastantsi while the "natives" remain distinct.[3] The Hiastantsi come to Bulgaria for economic reasons and seek only to assure their own economic survival while the "native" Armenian population, most of whom have already assured their own economic survival, still exhibit energies to invest in ethnic, cultural survival. Since the majority of the "native" population consists of descendants of genocide survivors, their *raison d'être* is much different from the newly arrived. The two groups do not readily cooperate, as they perceive the "others" as not Armenian enough.

This may exemplify twenty-first century migratory realities with a twist particular to the Armenian case. While in other diaspora communities the newly arrived accuse the settled populations of losing their ethnic identity, in Bulgaria the situation is the opposite. The "natives" fight to maintain their ethnicity, against incredible odds, while the Hiastantsi seem to spurn this kind of activity.

The numbers of the newly arrived are impossible to confirm. No reliable data are available to document the possibly thousands of Hiastantsi who began entering the country in droves.[4] Those immigrants continue to enter the country on work visas, which are valid for three years, but remain as illegal workers. Most remain with a hope or belief that they will one day return to Armenia, but in any event their status as not quite legal members of the society has led to an under-representation of the Armenian population in the Bulgarian censuses. The figures of Hiastantsi, from community leaders, teachers, and a representative of the Armenian Republic's embassy in Sofia have ranged from a few thousand to over 10,000. Again, these figures' very elusiveness lends some credence to the theory that assimilation is proceeding apace.[5] If we accept the largest possible estimate of Hiastantsi then their numbers would be equal to the numbers of "native" Armenians counted in the last government census, which found only 10,832 Armenians in the entire country. If they are equal in number then their impact on the community will be considerable. They will either form another locus for Armenian ethnos creation or will eventually intermarry with the "natives" or others and melt into society.

Finally, another force may be at work—the incentive to assimilate and acculturate quickly to the dominant culture. Sociologists have noted the preference for immigrant children of other cultures to speak the language of the dominant culture even when offered an opportunity to study in their mother tongue (Khleif, 1975, p. 398). There are inherent advantages to blending in with the majority population, not the least of which is the obvious advantage of finding employment. The dominant culture by its very prevalence exerts an irrefutable pressure to conform and adapt. Therefore, both parents and children have an incentive to learn the dominant language quickly and to blend into the host culture. It should not be surprising that students enrolled in Bulgarian public schools do not exhibit a vigorous drive to acquire and keep Armenian language proficiency or to practice cultural fluency. It is possible that part of the lack of success for the language program in the public schools, especially the one in Sofia, is because the principal and the entire administrative structure of the institution are Bulgarians and they, inadvertently, represent the dominant culture to the students, a model of the society (Khleif, 1975).

Both groups, "natives" and *Hiastantsi*, are within their rights in their complaints about each other, but the "natives" feel betrayed. In fact, betrayal is the word used by more than one interviewee in this context. I quote one interviewee who is a nationally and internationally known author—"Even if one does not speak one's language, one is obliged not to betray one's culture. One must be cognizant and respectful of one's culture."[6] Alternatively, "We are obligated to honor our parents—for all the sacrifices they have made—by not betraying our ethnos." Others are appalled that Hiastantsi choose to marry out of the cultural group in mixed marriages. This perceived divide is an irritant for both groups and bridging it is essential to the survival of the community.

Bulgaria and the European Union

The Bulgarian Government has improved in its treatment of minorities since 1989.[7] Since Bulgaria seeks admission into the European Union (now stated for 2009), it has been willing to depart from its communist–totalitarian and concurrently narrowly nationalist past. The communists relegated minorities to a deliberately quaint and innocuous corner of the national fabric. Today, officially, the fair and equitable treatment of minorities has proceeded as per the requirements of the Council of Europe's Framework Convention for the Protection of National Minorities. Bulgaria has established the National Council on Ethnic and Demographic Issues: it is a state-cum-public body. According to Article 1, the council is "a body for consultations, cooperation and coordination between government bodies and nongovernmental organizations, designed to formulate and implement national policy on ethnic and demographic issues and migration." In addition, the Ministry of Culture has a separate bureau to deal with minority affairs while the Ministry of Education employs specialists, linguists of each distinctive ethnic group, to coordinate and organize the language education of the minority children in the country. At first glance, the accommodation of the minorities is fair and equitable. However, a tiny pool of resources, from which a share is doled out to each group, complicates the situation.[8]

Schools and Language Acquisition

There are two large public schools in Bulgaria called Armenian that are part of the state educational system. They teach students from grade one through to grade eight. One school, William Saroyan or School Number 76, is in Sofia. The other school is in Plovdiv, the second largest city in the country and is called V. and K. Tiutiundzhian. The concentration of Armenians in Plovdiv is much greater than in Sofia and they tend to live in a more compact community.[9] These schools represent the merest shadows of the vibrant pre-communist era Armenian community. Before 1944 Armenian schools were numerous and well attended (Mesrob-Tankaranian, 2004).

The teaching of Eastern Armenian, this confused linguistic legacy, was the most long-lasting and harmful influence of the communist period. Parents and children could not practice the language at home and eventually those children who studied that version of Armenian could not effectively pass it on to their children. The teachers had a difficult time teaching the language and in the community, outside of the classroom, Eastern Armenian was useless. For some interviewees, that change alone can be held responsible for the substantial weakening and, therefore, assimilation of the Armenian community in Bulgaria (Mitseva, 1999a, 1999b).

Although today Armenian language instruction is back to Western Armenian, the damage is irreversible. With little or no language knowledge from home from which to build, Armenian students are acquiring their mother tongue as a second language. This type of bilingualism is exactly the reverse of what Khleif (1975, p. 392) termed "involuntary bilingualism," since for these Armenian children knowing or learning their own tongue has become the equivalent of say acquiring "voluntary bilingualism" by learning French. Students can study the Armenian language as an elective in public schools in eight Bulgarian cities. From grade one to grade two the students study Armenian three hours per week and from grades three through to grade eight they are taught the language for only four hours per week. Although there are opportunities to insert additional instruction in culture and history, those four hours of instruction do not necessarily constitute actual cultural education.

Community involvement plays a pivotal role in sustaining the culture. The Armenian School Association, which was established in 1996, brings together parents and others in the community whose goal is to focus government and municipal resources on the education of their children in their mother tongue. Its main goals are education and culture, the protection and development of Armenian spiritual treasures and traditions, and passing these on to the young.

The Ministry of Education expert on Armenian language, Zari Tankaranian, is responsible for managing the education of their mother tongue to Armenians. She is responsible for supplying the textbooks and, to a certain degree, coordinating the curriculum of the schools. However, her position is part-time, the resources allocated by the government for her to perform her job are modest at best, and she has no real authority other than her title when it comes to implementing her plans: school directors are the ones who make all the substantive decisions.

The textbooks the public schools use are donated or sold to the Armenians from the Middle Eastern Armenian Communities. They are not so much chosen by as bestowed on the teachers: therefore, an analysis of the textbooks would not serve to illuminate any kind of educational strategy since it is largely a matter of expediency. Furthermore, the teachers are Armenians who choose to take a poorly remunerated position in exchange for the largely immeasurable gains of the satisfaction most teachers seek in their profession. There is no uniform plan for choosing the teachers other than a degree in Armenian language and a desire to teach. Most of the recent graduates of the Armenian language program at Sofia's Kliment Ohrid University applied abroad for positions since they have no teaching opportunities in Bulgaria, as there are not enough positions for graduates in the country.

The Armenian student population of twenty-five in the Sofia school is quite modest. There is a designated room for Armenian language lessons, decorated with historic maps, portraits of famous Armenians, and other memorabilia of Armenian culture. These kinds of dedicated rooms exist in the public schools. The portraits tend to be of historic male figures that made significant contributions to their nation as political leaders, writers, poets, and musicians.

Notable by their presence and somewhat incongruous by their different types of prominence are internationally known notables like Cher, Andre Agassi, and Charles Aznavour. The presence of these kinds of role models suggests a move away from an emphasis on traditional, literary, artistic icons. These new idols are readily recognizable and, therefore, more appealing to young Armenians. They represent the global, transnational nature of the diaspora and may act as cultural cement of the far-flung communities.

Although Sofia has a much larger Armenian community, the main difficulty in attracting students is the lack of a bus to collect the children from their far-flung neighborhoods.[10] According to the Bulgarian principal of the school, Ms. Stefanova, there is a lack of interest in the community to support the school and encourage the children to learn their mother tongue. She faults the Armenians themselves for not participating in the maintenance of their own cultural and educational existence.

Armenian cultural leaders in Sofia and Zari Tankaranian have a different perspective on the problem. They believe that a lack of effort or enthusiasm on the part of the principal to support the Armenian program in her school fully, in addition to the large distances and hectic pace of simple economic survival, are the causes for low attendance at the school. Parents seem to make the choice for their children based on expediency and the desire for them to learn something "useful."

In Plovdiv, at the Tiutiundjian public school, the situation is different (Firkatian, 1994). The Armenian principal of that school, Mrs. Hungikian, is very optimistic and proud of her school's ability to nurture Armenian cultural education as well as language acquisition.[11] The Plovdiv school has the largest number of Armenian children attending in the entire country—350 students. It is located in the historic Armenian neighborhood and located in the same courtyard as the Armenian church. The principal believed that "We do all we can do to create close ties among our students, a singular focus on language learning is not enough to create an Armenian spirit. We create reasons or opportunities for the children to come together beyond the classroom." In addition to programs, special events, and holidays, she also takes her children on school trips throughout the country. Her proudest achievement was that the school choir was invited to Kusadasu, Turkey, in 2003 to perform in a choral festival there with Armenian songs. She maintained that the school serves an additional and critical function by creating friendships and close bonds among Armenian schoolchildren who choose to maintain them long after their schooling is finished. This is cultural education of a sort, since these classmates will continue to see each other at social and cultural events and church services and, ultimately, become candidates for membership in clubs and charitable organizations.

I asked about a mission statement for the school. The following is a synopsis of the key points: to provide a solid education, to make the students into first-rate citizens of Bulgaria with a good national consciousness, to focus on the formation of the individual with a well-developed intellectual preparation for citizenship, and to stimulate the development of the child's own particular talents. This is a public school supported by state funds and so nurturing Armenian cultural education cannot be part of their formal mission. In fact, the flag-raising ceremony on the first day of school is a muted affair. They raise the Bulgarian flag on a flagpole in the schoolyard while the Armenian flag they drape out of a school window.

Elsewhere the figures for children learning Armenian in the public schools are the following: in Burgas there are twenty-eight students, in Varna there are forty to forty-five students, and in other cities the numbers of students range between thirteen and fifteen each. In a very tangible way, the Armenian community in Sofia is lagging behind in its support of language and cultural education for its children. Overall, there are a total of 600 students studying Armenian in the public schools.

Beyond public schools, there exist Saturday or Sunday schools that are solely focused on language acquisition and cultural education. No single "expert" in Sofia dictates their curriculum or the textbooks they use. Because volunteers run them the length of the class hours tends to vary. These schools are literally attached to or at least affiliated with the church or a local Armenian organization. Schools of this type are found in six cities. Attendance at classes is difficult to determine and depends on the willingness of the parents to sacrifice their weekend to a supplemental commitment. For example, the Saturday school in Sofia started out with fifteen children but in about two months the figure dropped to two or three students and the teacher was discouraged. In Burgas there was a dispute over the disposition of the Armenian community properties and the designated room for the Armenian Saturday school was moved around until it was shunted to one small room above a café/bar. These examples represent the inconsistency of parent commitment characteristic of these programs.

The language issue is forming a line of division in the community between those who insist that fluency will make the person a bona fide member and those who maintain that claiming Armenian identity and feeling Armenian are enough. The debate is carried on in diaspora communities the world over and it touches on some basic feelings about identity as well as practical considerations. The dilemmas are at the personal, familial, and communal levels.

The pace and demands of life seem to elicit a selective approach to cultural sustainability. Armenians are aware of the vast array of their inherited iconography, but increasingly must choose among a limited selection dictated by time and energy constraints. Bakalian (1993) asserted that "once a collective consciousness is established and distinctive characteristics of an ethnic group are recognized the group" (p. 41) will persist and I agree. The nature of this kind of self-identification, inherent in this kind of selective ethnicity, is the one that is most adaptable to contemporary life demands. As long as

Armenians feel the pressure of the demands of economic survival to the exclusion of other pressures, say the pressure to maintain a strict coda of ethnic identity, then the lure of symbolic ethnic identity will only intensify. The argument is being made and some cases proven for cultural identification and, hence, literacy being as powerful as linguistic fluency or literacy. Being and feeling Armenian can be maintained without the ability to read and speak the language necessarily. Since identity is a fluid state, changeable ethnic identity is also in a constant state of mutation and re-creation.

Charitable and Cultural Organizations

The cultural preservation of the Armenians in Bulgaria rests heavily with their voluntary, charitable, social, and cultural organizations. There is a great variety and a substantial number of these organizations. If one were to judge the vibrancy and potential for survival of the community based simply on the numbers of such organizations, then the inevitable conclusion is that the community is healthy and well supported. The following is a list of the more significant organizations with a brief description of their activities.

Erevan still exists but with a different agenda: it is now part of the Union of Armenian Cultural–Educational Organizations of Bulgaria, which includes, among other organizations, the Armenian School Association and the Church Board. The Union of Armenian Cultural–Educational Organizations of Bulgaria has twelve branches in the country and its primary goal is to preserve and develop the traditions and cultural heritage of the Armenian society in Bulgaria, to pass this on to the younger generation, and to popularize their culture in society. Erevan has organized and supported a theatre troupe, which puts on plays by Armenian playwrights in Armenian. The organization also sponsors a choir, which has recorded albums and both the choir and theatre troupes have participated in national and international festivals. It has also published books on Armenians and Armenian history.

In 1991 Homenetmen was reborn. It is a youth athletic and scout organization, which teaches sports and organizes camps and various athletic games. Hai Tad is an organization whose main goal is to support the Armenian cause by making the general public aware of the Armenian genocide and its consequences for the Armenians and finally to bring some resolution to this long-standing question. HOM, which was reconstituted in 1991, is the Armenian Relief Society, which is primarily a women's organization that works at supporting the community via cultural and educational activities. Their funds help support needy students with free lunch programs and, in Plovdiv, for example, the funding of a free bus to collect students for school.

Parekordzagan is the Armenian General Benevolent Union, which receives significant funding from its New York headquarters. It has the resources to grant stipends to needy students, organize charity cultural events such as art exhibitions and concerts, and to invite notable Armenians to speak as well as putting on dances annually. It has the most concentrated focus on the younger generation by forming a young professionals group and offering its spacious offices as meeting rooms as well as access to its computers for the younger generation of Armenians. They have about fifty members who meet on a regular basis.

Since 1989 the Armenian General Benevolent Union has organized and hosted the European and, in 2004, the World Armenian Athletic Games. It also subsidized the publication of several art catalogs of Armenian artists and a translation of Armenian language classics.

What is not obvious to the casual observer of this community vitality is the fact that the participants in all of these organizations and the events they sponsor are all overlapping groups. For example, members of Homenetmen mainly populate the Varna dance group, which has approximately forty members. Therefore, the multiplicity of events and offerings is not reflective of the true level of community participation. The opportunities to experience "Armenianess" are wide ranging. People make choices guided by individual and family time constraints. The surface gloss of community vibrancy is not very deep. However, it is possible, according to Bakalian (1993, pp. 428–429), for this "inertia to sustain communal structures and institutional forms . . . for a long time."

One commonly voiced complaint is that the older generation is refusing to relinquish leadership in key organizations to the younger generation. By refusing to give up control and allow the young to infuse their organizations with new ideas and possibly new directions, the older generation is threatening to choke the life that remains in the community.[12]

The Church

Described as "the visible soul of the absent fatherland" the Armenian Apostolic Church has traditionally been the institution charged with the survival of its adherents and in particular the task of instilling some kind of Christian values and ethics (Dekmejian, 1997). Credited with sustaining the spiritual Armenian community as well as its secular incarnation, according to Mitseva (1999a, b), the church even has a role in determining the boundary between that which is "authentic" (Armenian) and that which is "foreign." Through the centuries, the church has had to contend with only a few, sparse threats to its authority and dominance in Armenians' cultural and religious development. The most prominent were the threats proposed by the Council of Chalcedon in the fifth century C.E., the founding of a Catholic order of Armenian monks in the seventeenth century by Mkhitar, and communism with its insistence on atheism. Today, a rise in secularism, along with an unprecedented rise in the pressures of day-to-day economic and cultural survival, is a new and serious threat to the survival of the church. In other words, assimilation today is much more of a threat than it ever was due to all sorts of globally universal circumstances. Some of these are mobility, loss of traditional communal living environments, loss of obvious threats to the physical survival of the population in question, and other twenty-first century factors.

Although the church has had to adapt to secularism, it has yet to give in to one pressure, to conduct services in Bulgarian. Armenian priests will not conduct the service in the dominant language or even in the dominant language and Armenian side by side. As one priest stated, ". . . it will be devastating to us. We will have lost one half of ourselves as Armenians by doing just that."[13] There is a real fear among the clergy that their congregations are melting away but they will not compromise on the language issue.

Since priests are well aware of the number of mixed marriages and the small numbers of faithful in church every Sunday, they are most discouraged about the possibility of maintaining the Armenian ethnos in Bulgaria. The clergy stress the need for knowing and practicing the mother tongue. The church supports the cultural sustainability of its adherents by offering church properties for the use of Saturday schools or social and cultural functions and by doggedly continuing to insist on using Armenian in services.

The priests underscored the need to create and maintain an Armenian household. It is in the home that a child learns about significant events in Armenian history or about their heroes. They hold parents responsible for their children's lack of interest in their heritage. In the end, they hold the women most responsible for this negligence. Work by Anthias (1989) and McClintock (1996) on other ethnic groups with a similar dilemma revealed an analogous accusation. A priest interviewee stated that:

> The mother is the "teacher" of the family, if she is not Armenian then that feeling, sense will be lost. Becoming close to one's culture, roots, loving who you are, that love of one's ethnicity are necessary to remain Armenian but in the future only Armenians in Armenia will be able to maintain that sense.

This presumption does not allow for the exigencies of modern life. Mothers are breadwinners like fathers and their responsibilities stretch their resources to the limit. This explains the propensity to latch on to symbolic ethnicity. Only after all the responsibilities that burden families are met can they choose to pursue cultural sustainability.

The family unit has historically been the main and first support for the maintenance of the ethnos. Family obligations take precedence over all other interpersonal obligations. The family served as the center of social interaction with relatives: the constant contact with others reinforced the ethnos in the minds and hearts of the young. Modern families, even if both parents are

Armenians, have little time to spare for this kind of "education" of their young. Bakalian (1993, p. 418) referred to a "time-famine" culture in the U.S. Under communism life used to be less hurried, whereas the struggle for economic survival now makes time and energy equally precious and scarce. Parents will choose to send their children to a school convenient to home rather than the Armenian school. In addition, the fragmentation of ethnic enclaves in cities further diminishes the passive, traditional ways of maintaining and building cultural identity.

Press

Since 1989 there have been three Armenian newspapers published in Bulgaria: *Erevan, Vahan,* and *Haier.* These publications represent another aspect of cultural sustainability. The editors tend to be firm believers in an individual and community effort to support the ethnos and to see it thrive. When Armenians choose to support ethnic newspapers, a visible icon of the ethnos, they practice cultural sustainability. Since the majority of articles are in Bulgarian then one can be a subscriber to Armenian newspapers and feel like a member of the group without a facility for the language.

Appraisal of the Future

In Bulgaria the fiscal limitations of a financially strapped government have more influence than any overt attempt to mold ethnic minorities to some state model of the ideal citizen. The overwhelming impression is one of material wants driving both the state's agenda and those of individual Armenian families. Families might not send their children to an Armenian school or might choose not to perpetuate the language at home by encouraging their children to learn the language of their host country. While the official Bulgarian Government position is to support minority education rights, the pursuit of economic well being and basic survival are seducers that are more potent. Multicultural education is not an issue for the Armenians since official government policy facilitates language learning in public classrooms. The question is not whether language instruction, curriculum development, choice of teachers, or financial support for the schools is adequate or biased. Bulgarians have no incentive to lure Armenians away from their ethnicity by manipulating multicultural education, since a well-integrated Armenian minority is part of the national fabric and does not pose any sort of threat to the state.

The fate of the Armenian ethnos in Bulgaria is the fate in general of all ethnic minorities of the former Soviet bloc countries. Those communities with the financial resources and a strong organizational network of cultural and educational groups will survive. The Bulgarian Government needs to support minorities not simply with figurehead positions in Sofia but with real power, which translates to financial resources. Furthermore, the educational plan, as it stands now, suffers from a lack of coherence. Several teachers opine that harmonization of the curriculum, textbooks, and training of the language teachers would go a long way towards fixing some disparities. Perhaps a plan that would permit educators from various diaspora communities to share and compare experiences and methods would be immensely beneficial for the Armenian diaspora.

The aforementioned organizations choose to create a link between identity and memory, as Smith (1991) and Eyal (2004) suggested, in order to perpetuate the nation. Organizations that evoke images of identity with dances, theatre performances, language and history classes, educational publications, and similar initiatives help fulfill identity voids and support the sustenance of cultural memory. By continually supplying images, that "inherited iconography," or even prototypes of ethnic identity they manage to keep alive an Armenian identity that is at the very least an image for Armenians to strive for.

The revival of the many cultural, social, and charitable organizations has breathed new life into the community. As they insist collectively on clinging to their institutions, Armenians in Bulgaria will have a strong enough connection to their ethnos to persist and survive as an ethnically distinct group. The community has made an effort to revive these organizations: it now needs to find additional lures to attract more Armenians to participate in community sustainability by dipping into the emotional well of the membership and stimulate adherence to this "inherited iconography."

When a theatre or dance group performs the audience is inundated with the images and symbols of the ethnos. When a newspaper calls for a community debate on the fate of its properties it evokes a host of ideas and beliefs that reinforce identities and compel the individual to feel separate from the masses yet a member of that particular group (Conover, 1998). When young people join a community organization and admit that they do it not only for the culturally enriching aspects but also because they want to meet potential Armenian partners, that act is a codification of membership, as Bakalian (1993) noted. As they perpetuate their unique milieu, the diasporic societies continue to evoke the rituals of membership and this process reinforces the ethnic identity. In addition, although the empty symbols of identity may be the prevailing trend, the individuals, when questioned about their practices, insist that they feel Armenian, are Armenian, and will be Armenian in the future.

The overall assessment for the cultural sustainability of the Armenian community in Bulgaria that came through from the interviews is that it will persist for at least a generation more in its present form. Armenians are not abandoning their "inherited iconography" wholesale: however, they are not perpetuating it wholesale either. They seem to approach the notion of cultural sustainability as one would a buffet table: choosing and taking that which is most appealing and leaving that which is not. This smorgasbord approach may not be the answer to cultural sustainability.

What will keep and perpetuate the culture is rather the attitude of the community's young people who, through their willingness to participate in youth-oriented organizations or any cultural, religious, or educational event, express and act on that indefinable need to be a part of a greater whole. The future of the community rests on the elders' ability to attract and retain the younger generations as active members of their community.

Should the community choose to empower and trust the youth to proceed in a productive direction then it may find its future salvation. If the church can sidestep older authority figures for younger ones this may be the single most effective contribution it can make. It is the only institution with enough respect from both sides of the age divide to affect change. Likewise, young people can devote their energies to community sustenance by picking up where the older organizers left off. As Cohen (1997) indicated, the technological tools (Internet, instant messaging, and virtual communities) of the post-modern age may be the innovations that fill the gaps in the cultural fabric for a time-pressed population. The role of the elders is to model "being Armenian" and reminding the younger generations "to be Armenian."

For the short term, some console themselves with beliefs that articulate the new symbolic forms of ethnicity. They claim that knowing perfect Armenian or reading all the great literature or knowing the dance steps and so on is not necessary for one to be Armenian. One is Armenian if one believes it to be so. This is the prevailing trend in the Armenian diaspora. Flexibility and malleability are the only solutions for those who also seek to meet the challenge of material security and professional aspirations. While the desire to maintain one's culture is extremely compelling, the pressures and time demands of modern life drive Armenians to make choices.

As a diaspora group for centuries, Armenians have managed, in benign and hostile environments, to keep a consciousness that is separate despite the lack of territory and a dearth of political or religious power. Armenians do not wish to lose their "inherited iconography," which has sustained the community thus far. Their icons interlock the membership of the ethnos, preserve their memory, and assure their separate status from those outside the ethnos. Therefore, they continue to support charitable and educational institutions and the distinguishing markers of their distinct community and they survive.

Acknowledgments

I am grateful to all of the individuals who willingly answered my questions in Bulgaria. This research project was made possible by travel funding from Hillyer College of the University of Hartford.

Resources and Tools for Educators

Questions

1. Given the diversity of student levels of preparedness, how can teachers make the classroom experience more effective?
2. How can the language and culture of a minority group be made more accessible to a greater number of students? Could more flexible hours or a more focused approach be more accessible for time-strapped and economically challenged families?

For Further Reading

Books in Western languages on Armenian diaspora education are rare. Additional readings can be gleaned from edited collections of articles or in Armenian journals such as *Armenian Review, Armenian Forum,* and *The Society for Armenian Studies Journal.* The diocese of the Armenian Church of America has a website and publishes a newsletter dedicated to reaching college age students of Armenian descent: language and cultural education are part of the content. To subscribe to the newsletter contact julieh@armenian-diocese. org or log-on to armenianchurch.net.

Activities for Educators

1. Implement teacher educational seminars that will enable teachers throughout a country to come together to coordinate teaching methods. With regular periodic meetings they could support each other in their efforts and share teaching strategies and innovations. In the case study in the chapter, opportunities to communicate with teachers of Armenian language beyond the borders of the country would provide a greater range of teaching options and enhance efforts in Bulgarian classrooms.
2. Create and support a screening process for teacher selection that is uniform and that takes into account experience and teaching ability. Discuss how such a screening process would look and work.
3. Consider how the community can create opportunities for the younger generation to have an equal voice in the governance of cultural organizations. As cultural organizations are the primary venue for the extension of formal education, their role is key to maintaining cultural identity.

Notes

1. According to the last census the Bulgarian Statistical Institute listed only 10,832 Armenians in Bulgaria in 2001. However, the real number may be twice as large.
2. *Zaedno* video-taped interviews with members of a Parekordzagan youth group.

3. Interview with Vartan Akobian, advisor to the Armenian Embassy in Bulgaria July 19, 2004. According to him, about 60 percent of Hiastantsi forget or stop speaking Armenian after they settle in Bulgaria. There is no need to speak the language and so they do not bother: instead they focus on economic survival including a high "mixed marriage" rate with non-Armenians including Turks, Arabs, and Gypsies.
4. Interview with Vartan Akobian July 19, 2004. He believes the highest possible figure for Hiastantsi in Bulgaria today is 12,000. However, in reality the number is probably closer to 8,000–10,000, again according to Akobian. The years 1993–1994 saw the severest economic crisis in the Armenian Republic, which caused the greatest immigration to Bulgaria while 1997–1998 were the years of the greatest out-migration from Bulgaria.
5. The Bulgarian Statistical Institute listed only 10 832 Armenians in Bulgaria in the 2001 census.
6. Interviews with Agop Melkonian and Zari Tankaranian July 23, 2004 and July 8, 2004, respectively.
7. The most notable, non-governmental organization is the International Center for Minority Studies and Intercultural relations, which was founded in 1992. It has become both a watchdog and a real aid organization to the minorities in the Balkans, especially Bulgarian Muslims, Turks, Roma, and, to a lesser extent, the smaller minority groups. For example, with their assistance at one time all three Armenian newspapers received funding.
8. For example, Armenian textbooks that are modern and well designed and the Armenian expert at the Ministry of Education has chosen quality publications. However, her work has been stymied by under-funding. While she has found a source for the textbooks—Aleppo, Syria—she has been allotted enough money to buy the books but not enough for shipping to Bulgaria. Therefore, until she discovers a solution the schools will do with old, worn copies of original textbooks that outlived their usefulness years ago.
9. The Bulgarian Statistical Institute's 2001 census tabulated 3,140 Armenians in Plovdiv and 1,672 in Sofia.
10. The Bulgarian Statistical Institute's 2001 census tabulated 1672 Armenians in Sofia.
11. Interviews with Ms. Stefanova and Mrs. Hungikian June 29, 2004 and July 13, 2004, respectively.
12. Interviews with Hari Nigoghosian and Kevork Sarafian July 13, 2004 and July 31, 2004, respectively.
13. Interview with Der Kevork Hacherian July 14, 2004.

References

Anthias, F. and Yuval-Davis, N. (Eds.) (1989). *Woman-Nation-State*. London: Macmillan.
Bakalian, A. P. (1993). *Armenian-Americans: From being to feeling Armenian*. New Brunswick: Transaction Publishers.
Boghosian, M. (1999). *Armentsite v sofia istoricheski ocherk*. Sofia: Board of Directors of the Armenian Church Surp Astvadzadzin.
Buchvarov, M. (1998). Sblusuk na tsivilizatsiite ili kulturna iknografia v globalizirashtia sviat. In A. Krasteva (Ed.), *Obshtnosti is identichnosti* (pp. 241–261). Sofia: Petekston.
Cohen, R. (1997). *Global diasporas: An introduction*. Seattle: University of Washington Press.
Conover, P. J. and Hicks, B. E. (1998). The psychology of overlapping identities: Ethnic, citizen, nation and beyond. In R. Taras (Ed.), *National identities and ethnic minorities in Eastern Europe* (pp. 11–48). New York: St. Martin's Press.
Dekmejian, R. H. (1997). The Armenian diaspora. In R. G. Hovannisian (Ed.), *The Armenian people* (Vol. II, pp. 413–444). New York: St. Martin's Press.
Eyal, G. (2004). Identity and trauma two forms of the will to memory. *History and Memory*, 16(1), 5–36.
Firkatian, M. A. (1994). The Vartanants and Varvarian school in Plovdiv, Bulgaria 1917–1995. *Journal of the Society for Armenian Studies*, 7, 123–134.
Gans, H. J. (1996). Symbolic ethnicity: The future of ethnic groups and cultures in america. In W. Sollors (Ed.), *Theories of ethnicity* (pp. 425–459). New York: New York University Press.
Khleif, B. B. (1975). E*thnic boundaries, identity, and schooling: A socio-cultural study of Welsh-English relations*. Durham: Department of Sociology and Anthropology University of New Hampshire.
Krasteva, A. (1998). Identichnost i vlast: Komunisticheski i postkomunisticheski diskurs vurhu maltsinstvata. In A. Krasteva (Ed.), *Obshtnosti i identichnosti* (pp. 135–163). Sofia: Petekston.

McClintock, A. (1996). No longer in a future heaven: Nationalism, gender, and race. In G. Eley and R. G. Suny (Eds.), *Becoming national: A reader* (pp. 260–284). New York: Oxford University Press.

Maksoudian, K. (1997). Armenian communities in east Europe. In R. G. Hovannisian (Ed.), *The Armenian people: From ancient to modern times* (Vol. II, pp. 51–79). New York: St. Martin' Press.

Mesrob-Tankaranian, M. K. (2004). *Bulgarahai tbrotsneru badmutiun.* Sofia: Daniela Ubenova.

Mitseva, E. (1999a). Armentsite v bulgaria i tehniat folklor. *Bulgarski folklor,* (1/2), 94–102.

Mitseva, E. (1999b). Literatura i folklor v armenskite uchilishta v bulgaria. In *Literaturata na maltsinstvata* (pp. 146–152). Sofia.

Parsons, T. (1975). Some theoretical considerations on the nature and trends of change of ethnicity. In N. Glazer and D. Moynihan (Ed.), *Ethnicity: Theory and experience* (pp. 53–84). Cambridge: Harvard University Press.

Porter, J. (1975) Ethnic pluralism in Canadian perspective. In N. Glazer and D. Moynihan (Eds.), *Ethnicity: Theory and experience* (pp. 267–304). Cambridge: Harvard University Press.

Radunchev, B. (2001). Kulturata v zashtita na etnichnostta. In *Mnogotsvetie* (pp. 20–33). Sofia: MTsPMKV.

Smith, A. (1991). *National identity.* Harmondsworth: Penguin.

PART III

Formal Educational Institutions and the Battle Against the Hegemony of Liberal Culture

We are moving from a focus on the macro- towards the micro-dimensions of cultural education–cultural sustainability. The first section focused on the role of the state in enabling (or not) minority culture, while the second section introduced the community or, better put, networks of minority institutions, which enable individuals to negotiate the demands of the state and experience a vital sense of culture in everyday life. The chapters in this third section continue our move closer towards the everyday life experience.

Whereas in the second section we looked at the total network of institutions that comprise a minority cultural community, here we will focus exclusively on formal educational institutions. We are interested in the complex relationship that occurs between formal educational institutions, the communities they serve, and the attempt to create counter-cultures capable of entering into a sustainable discourse with liberal society.

The chapters in this section are divided into two subsections. The three chapters, in the first subsection, address issues of formal education and the reconstruction of group culture. The common focus is the attempt to reconstruct minority culture ravaged first by the colonial experience and later the assimilatory policies of the liberal state. The four chapters in the second subsection address the limits and possibilities of schools as counter-cultural agents. As we saw in the previous sections of this book, the ability to create counter-cultural space is essential for cultural education–cultural sustainability. Here the authors examine the role schools play in the attempt to construct a coherent counter-culture capable of providing an alternative to the liberal discourse of contemporary Western society.

When reviewing the chapters readers are encouraged to recall that universal educational systems—mandatory schooling—though considered a "natural" event in the everyday life of contemporary Western society—is a rather recent and ever expanding phenomena. For the most part universal education provides, through the inculcation of basic literacy and numeracy skills, the minimal requirements needed by workers in industrialized societies. The declared goals of universal education are traditionally economic opportunity and participation in the democratic community and these goals continue to feed both educational reform and the core debate about the goals of mass education.

Some theoreticians describe schools as tools which allow for access to participation in a democratic society, while others are more critical, arguing that universal education is a powerful tool at the disposal of the state to colonize the culture and life ways of immigrants, minority groups, and the poor. From the critical perspective, the classic approach to universal education in liberal states provides a cultural ranking system, whereby the state is able to direct resources to those groups closest to the majority culture and encourage others to leave behind their "particularistic" practices and assimilate.

The chapters in this third section enable us to understand interaction between the needs of the liberal state and, at the sme time, the attempt of minority groups to counter the liberal demand for assimilation. Through the comparison of a variety of minority experiences we are able to appreciate different types of challenges to the liberal state and national educational systems and the ability of minority groups to negotiate a sustainable degree of autonomy.

Formal Education and the Reconstruction of Group Culture

George Dei reflects on the devastating situation of Afro-Americans and an educational strategy for cultural reconstruction known as "separation by choice." The goal of the separation by choice strategy is to secure effective and efficient instructional, pedagogic, and communicative means for creating a positive sense of belonging to Afro-American society in North America. Critical of what can be shown for 50 years of integration efforts in America, Dei points at how race and poverty demarcate bodies in terms of their involvement in the schooling process. The "marketization of education," he states, has actually intensified differences in schools to the disadvantage of weaker cultural groups.

In order to avoid issues of race and poverty undermining the success of public school systems, Dei argues that we must concretely and openly confront the challenges posed to educators, learners, policy makers, parents, communities, and organizations. Confronting difference implies a critical approach towards the politics of the school curriculum and a clear focus on the outcomes of school change initiatives. For these initiatives to succeed they must recognize the experiences of different communities of learners, as well as the fact that the powerful discourse favoring a "return to basics" continues to serve as a primary means for promoting the interests of the majority and privileged classes.

Dei offers an alternative for the schooling of Black and racial minority youth in the shape of Black-focused/African-centred schools. The concept promotes education primarily (but not exclusively) for African-Americans. These schools aim at allowing African-American students to reinvent their Africanness in a diasporic context. "Black-focused"/African-centred schools will challenge the conventional educational environment by stressing principles of responsibility, interdependence, respect for elders, transparency, and accountability. The goal is to revitalize community and allow African-Americans to re-enter the larger society from a new position of strength.

The chapters by Gay Garland Reed and Celia Haig-Brown and Kaaren Dannenmann focus on attempts to revitalize indigenous/native knowledge. Reed reviews the case of reindigenization of Hawaiian culture through the *Nā Honua Mauli Ola: Hawai'i Guidelines for Culturally Healthy and Responsive Learning Environments*. His paper reviews various forms of revitalization and reindigenization of culture that have taken place in Hawai'i public schools in the last two decades as a means to informing the global community about the unique instances of cultural revival and sustainability that are unfolding in these islands. At the same time, Reed explores the complexity of these processes and acknowledges some of the difficult issues that educators encounter as they indigenize their curricula and pedagogy.

Reed assumes that the process of reclaiming native voices and revitalization of indigenous cultures is for the better but she carefully notes that, in some instances, a genuine concern for the sustainability of indigenous cultures is missing. Rather, cultural reclamation might have more to do with commercialization and cooption of indigenous knowledge for the profit of individuals in the dominant culture. In her closing arguments Reed joins the argument made in the second section by Gloria Totoricagüena, asking whether indigenous knowledge, which is generally learned in non-formal education settings and tends to be orally transmitted and holistic in nature, can be adapted into formal education settings. Whereas in formal educational settings an emphasis is placed on the culture of print and documentation and knowledge that is discipline based, in the lived experience of everyday life, knowledge is usually an implicit and holistic affair. Reed questions if indigenous knowledge can become part of the "regular" curriculum without being relegated to peripheral status or without losing its spiritual essence.

Haig-Brown and Dannenmann discuss the NamekosipiiwAnishinaapek (a Canadian indigenous first nation) Knowledge Instructors' Program based on a pedagogy of the land approach. The authors argue for reversing deculturalization processes through the introduction of a culturally sensitive curriculum and the strong support for native ways of knowing. The program prepares aboriginal people who have some traditional knowledge to pass that knowledge on to others. It also provides opportunity for the prospective instructors to literally remember their own knowledge by using it in everyday living and interactions with others, opportunities which historical circumstances and changing life styles have often reduced to a minimum. Ultimately, the innovation of the course of study draws on very old pedagogies by never losing sight of the land as the "first teacher" in the attempt to re-create in contemporary contexts participatory community-based education. The authors emphasize that these programs do not argue for a return to the "old ways"; rather, they call for re-creation of indigenous knowledge in contemporary contexts as their inevitable outcome. The reader is left to ponder about the meaning of this call, when considering that the contemporary contexts for "indigenous forms" of knowledge are modern industrialized societies.

The Limits and Possibilities of Schools as Counter-cultural Agents

The first three chapters of this section, discussed above, focus on an explicit attempt to reconstruct weakened minority cultures using formal education as a tool. The next four chapters examine the ongoing use of schools for the purpose of culture sustainability by Amish and Jews. These two cultural groups are often thought of as success stories—hence this subsection asks about the limits and possibilities. We can learn of the possibilities because Amish and Jews have consistently, and in many cases successfully, used formal education over a long period of time to promote cultural sustainability. However, even in these cases we learn of the intense dilemmas faced by minority educators in their attempt to integrate the demands of minority and liberal cultures.

Johnson-Weiner explores Old Order Amish education within the larger symbolic framework that structures everyday Old Order life. The study sheds light on how Old Order schools have become agents of change as well as agents of resistance to change while shaping different educational strategies, tools, and philosophies of education that reinforce community values. While the Old Order schools may not function as models for secular education they seem to serve the needs of the community well. By design these schools are not suited for training artists, nor for training science-oriented individuals, nor for training business executives: by intent, they do not function as institutions for upward mobility in the modern industrial complex. Yet, in keeping their schools small, the Old Orders have made them more responsive to the needs of individual students and families and to the concerns of the group, offering a cultural coherence the large, secular schools lack. Moreover, Old Order private schools, because they are community institutions, provide a context in which the community can negotiate its response to change.

In short, the chapter shows how certain communities might resist unacceptable developments in public education. We also learn of different approaches to secular education from one Amish community to the next, each reflected in the architecture of the school building and the willingness to teach secular topics. From the comparison of the different Amish approaches we also become aware of the active dilemma faced by ethno-religious minority groups as how best to approach secular topics that are at once necessary for economic success and cultural acceptance in the wider liberal public sphere, but at the same time can easily marginalize the curricula which is of core concern to the project of cultural sustainability.

The next three chapters all focus on Jewish schools. Each elaborates a distinct dimension of the relationship between the school and the wider Jewish community, a relationship that occurs within the context of the larger attempt to sustain a coherent Jewish counter-culture in both Israel and the Jewish diaspora. As with the chapter on the Amish we become acutely aware of an intensive ongoing effort to balance the educational goals of cultural sustainability with the need to interface and interact with the broader society.

Eli Gottlieb examines how religious Jews in Israel, who are a minority within the wider secular Jewish population, use schools to foster and preserve culturally distinctive epistemologies. He begins by presenting findings from a comparative study of argumentation and epistemology conducted among Israeli children and adolescents in secular and religious schools. In light of these findings, Gottlieb examines how argumentative discourse—both inside and outside of classrooms—functions as a key venue for cultural education.

The empirical findings and theoretical insights have several important implications for educators concerned with issues of cultural sustainability and cultural education. First, Gottlieb shows that cultural education (sometimes) works. He illustrates his argument by pointing to differences in the epistemic values and argumentative practices of students in religious and secular schools and the effectiveness of these educational institutions as promoters and sustainers of cultural capital. We learn that the religious Jewish community in Israel, though numerically a minority, has managed, in its educational institutions, to create a cultural niche, wherein beliefs, values, and practices different to those of the majority secular community are promoted and sustained.

Secondly, Gottlieb shows that cultural education can be pro-active, not only acting when beliefs, values, and practices are under attack, but also working in a systematic fashion that creates tactically situated roadblocks designed to withstand, counter, and assimilate in a positive fashion future and undefined challenges from the liberal environment. The task facing educators who seek to sustain minority cultural practices is shown to extend beyond the need to gain control of curricula, but, more fundamentally, to contest the hegemonic models of rationality and intellectual maturity that underlie the framing of school-based education in liberal society.

In the next two chapters, Alex Pomson and Zvi Bekerman and Ezra Kopelowitz focus on the growth of liberal Jewish parochial schools in the Jewish diaspora. Over the past two decades liberal Jews the world over have begun turning away from public or state schools and are sending their children to Jewish parochial schools in increasing numbers.

Pomson offers an explanation for the shift among liberal Jews towards parochial education. He reviews conventional sociological accounts of the growth of Jewish day schools in North America and then interrogates the sociological paradigm by drawing on data from two ethnographic studies of liberal Jewish families in Canada and the U.S. Of interest is the fact that the parents have eschewed the free public education on which they were raised in favor of private Jewish all-day schooling. Pomson's qualitative study enables exploration of the reasons why individuals who, according to standard sociological measures, are less and less engaged by Jewish institutions nevertheless opt to educate their children within a private Jewish institutional setting.

Pomson shows that, when liberal Jews select parochial schools for their children, their choice includes a number of considerations. The considerations include the determination of parents' to provide their children with educational advantages made possible by private education and the acceptance by Jews of the mainly Christian idea that parochial school education is a way of joining and building affiliation to a cultural community. Traditional Jewish culture viewed education as part of a broader way of life that involved many institutional affiliations and, most importantly, the children were seen as continuing the life experience of the parents. In the case of the liberal Jew, the decision to send a child to a parochial school represents a break from their own life style and educational experience. Moreover, we see an attempt on the part of the parents to further cultural sustainability by giving over the task for Jewish education to the school.

In this light, we see the significance of the third factor cited by Pomson, namely that the choice of day school education signals the parents' search as adults for lives of (spiritual) meaning. Affiliation with the school and knowledge and practices brought home by the children are seen as contributing to their personal search in a positive manner. Finally, Pomson points to the fact that the drift to parochial schooling among liberal Jews neither means a rejection of an assimilatory ideal nor the embrace of Jewish particularism. Above all, Pomson believes, the embrace of day schools by liberal Jews paradoxically confirms their profound believe in the American "way." "Choosing" a Jewish day school as a means for personal self-affirmation of and affiliation with a cultural community, while at the same time living a full life in the broader society, is a supremely North American way of acting.

While Pomson focuses on the relationship of families to the school, Bekerman and Kopelowitz explore the interaction of teachers and students within the liberal Jewish parochial school. The authors ask if teachers' educational strategies enable a Jewish counter-culture capable of distinguishing itself from the assimilatory forces of liberal society. As was noted above, a primary challenge for the minority school is balancing or integrating the demands of liberal and minority cultures without allowing for the marginalization of the latter. It is this dilemma that Bekerman and Kopelowitz explore through comparative research of the teaching of Jewish studies texts in the classrooms of liberal Jewish schools in English- and Spanish-speaking countries.

Bekerman and Kopelowitz argue that cultural sustainability depends on the connection made between classroom learning and the wider life experience. As with arguments made by other authors in connection with Basque, Hawaiian, African-American and indigenous Native American education, Bekerman and Kopelowitz suggest that when "Jewish studies" becomes a discipline that is confined to formal studies in a classroom it runs the danger of defeating its stated purpose—cultural sustainability.

For Jewish education to succeed, educators need to first and foremost work with their students and others in the community to make in-class learning relevant to the wider life experience. Success depends on developing multiple literacies, enabling individuals to read the world as Jews. Instead of employing teaching strategies that draw sharp distinctions between the "Jewish" and the "secular" dimensions of life, the teacher should instead show that Jewish knowledge and texts are relevant for interpreting life in general.

Despite the wide sample of schools in different countries, Bekerman and Kopelowitz's research show that, without exception, all the classroom teachers reinforce the distinction between Jewish education in the classroom and life as it is actually lived outside of the classroom. While on one hand, when interviewed, the teachers agree that their success is dependent on making Jewish studies relevant to lived life, their teaching practices do the opposite, treating "the secular dimension" as irrelevant to Jewish learning. The authors argue that these seen but unnoticed educational practices challenge the assumption among many Jews that the mere fact of sending a child for a parochial Jewish education is the key for cultural sustainability. In fact, the nature of Jewish education in the liberal Jewish parochial school marginalizes the Jewish content of the schools curriculum to the margins of life as it is lived. It is the secular topics such as mathematics and science, which are a prerequisite for acceptance to university, that are regarded as "really important" for the child's success outside of school.

All in all the chapters in this section offer some hope, but also provide insight into the many challenges liberal society places in front of minority educators. These challenges do not just touch upon the immediate realities and practices of school life, but also point at the need to consider the multiple influences of wider forces that influence the choices which indigenous, minority, and diaspora groups make in the attempt to at once safeguard their particular cultural roots and remain engaged in the life of the wider society.

CHAPTER 11

Race and Minority Schooling in Canada: Dealing with Questions of Equity and Access in Education

GEORGE J. SEFA DEI

Introduction

I begin this chapter with a declaration of my political and academic project. I maintain that education is the satisfaction of social, material, economic, and spiritual needs of the self and a collective. Effective education depends on effective and efficient instructional, pedagogic, and communicative means that positively affect the well being and social existence of a people. In harnessing the human potential, education must not only be relevant to the learner but also equip the learner with critical thinking skills to understand their social world and work to transform current situations. In the struggle for educational change I have always disavowed a politics of the moment or situational politics, one which is constantly shifting, not grounded and only pursued where one finds herself or himself. I believe that we must affirm the cultural and political relevance of a critical collective anti-racist resistant politics so that the minoritized are empowered in their pursuit of the multiple and complex identities' around what I prefer to call "a politics of identity." Such politics must be grounded in some identities that are shared, not because these are the only relevant identities for us to speak about, but, rather, because it is important to pursue a political stance that does not absolve the dominance of responsibility by denying collective histories of colonial oppression. I also share the belief that essentialism pursued politically in the service of the devaluation, negation, and domination of others' experiences ought to be distinguished from essentialism pursed in a politics of resistance to domination. At the same time I must be cautious that the "essential self" does not lead to a re-inscription of the hierarchies one is trying to subvert. This is the challenge. It is in combining this understanding of "strategic essentialism" with an anti-racist politics of identity that I employ the notion of "saliency" and the argument for a recognition of the "severity of issues for certain bodies."

In accepting the invitation to contribute to this important collection I could not help but recall a recent public forum held in Toronto in which I participated: "Making the Grade: Are We Failing Black Youth?" In my remarks at this forum I observed that, as far as I was concerned, the answer to the question "are we failing Black youth?" was simply *yes, yes,* and *yes.* I say this not to target individual teachers unfairly and/or deny the responsibility of parents, communities, and students themselves. I am also not denying nor downplaying the fact that there are individual sites and places in schools where some educators, parents, communities, and students are working hard together to produce success for our students.

The fact of the matter is also that some of our students are doing well. So why did I feel the need to answer this question in the affirmative? To me, when I speak of educational failures, I am alluding to systemic failure and our collective responsibility. For far too long Black/African-Canadian parents and community groups have been complaining about the public school system in Ontario. And yet the more we speak about changes the more things remain the same. As many others have noted (e.g. Fine, 1991), good intentions are not enough. We need concrete action and solutions to systemic educational failure. We have enough educational research telling us about the problems. Yet the response has always been a denial. What we need is a commitment, the political and spiritual will to do the utmost for our students. Sometimes, speaking about the challenges we face in our community and at the same time having to "celebrate" our achievements and survival can be painful. How do you celebrate pain and suffering alongside our achievements and survival? No one should be encouraged to engage in celebratory arrogance. The problem of Black youth in the school system is a wound that fails to heal. So we must probe the silences around what the system is doing to our youth. We cannot simply shy away and commit murder of the memory and the spirit.

In my work in Ontario schools I can recall some notable personal experiences. For example, I remember the student who responded to my question about self-esteem among Black youth: "Sir, we have self-esteem but are struggling to keep it at school." I also recall attending a founders network meeting at a local school in Toronto to meet with individual founders about doing more for our schools to help disadvantaged youth. Walking down the corridor before the meeting started, I can never forget the friendly face of an African-Canadian female student who asked me whether I was a supply teacher for the day. To me it was not a surprise that she asked the question. After all, the many times they see Black teachers in the school is when they come in as replacement teachers. It is like schools can give students their Black history month but not the fundamental question of power and representation, Black and minority teachers.

There are a host of issues that can engage a discussion of how to make schools truly inclusive (see Dei and Razack, 1995). We can focus on the challenges of engaging students and the possibilities of how students can and have been engaged in schools. The field of minority education is vast with many issues still under-investigated and in need of critical theorizing. We have Black and other racial minority students contending with issues about their histories, cultures, languages, identities, and the relevance for education in diasporic contexts. For African youths there is a struggle to identify with the school curriculum, texts, knowledge, and the visual culture of our schools. What can be learned from these problems, conflicts, and resistances in schooling and what can the successes that also abound tell us about cultural education and the struggle for cultural sustainability?

In fact, in exploring the strategies for alternative schooling, Ernst and Statzner (1994) not long ago stressed the "imperative need for redirecting social science research from the often hopeless and stereotypical study of educational failure to the heartening exploration of new and creative ways of meeting the needs of minority teachers, students, and their families" (p. 205). Currently I am involved with my graduate students at the Ontario Institute for Studies in Education of the University of Toronto examining the issue of academic success and how those students account for such students and academic excellence. The study has three major aims and objectives. First, the examination of the personal life stories and educational and work experience of high academic achievers and how these inform our understanding of academic and social success. Second, a focus on the specific strategies adopted in school and out of school by high academic achievers to maintain their social and academic success. Third, the implications of such a body of knowledge for improving minority success in schools. In this work we are interested in exploring such questions as what are the varied conceptions of success/achievement and failure/underachievement? That is, how do students and adults (as subjects) define success and failure? We are also asking about how successful learners explain their academic performance and achievement motivation? What are the structural and institutional factors that contribute to success and what are the particular strategies employed by students to attain academic excellence? The study is paying attention to the implications of social difference for understanding school performance, social mobility, and life chances.

Black and Minority Youth Education: Challenges and Responsibilities

We can honor the success, hard work, and dedication of students, teachers, school administrators, guardians, and parents by ensuring that excellence is accessible and equitable in our school system for all students. For those young people who succeed in schools, their educational achievement is testament to the fact that, once given opportunities and access to education that is responsive to their needs and interests and when provided with the requisite knowledge, tools, and dedication of school staff, then students will learn and succeed. Strong leadership from staff is key to educational success for youth. But in order for individual successes to count and rebound to the wider community, there must be collective responsibility not to gloss over the failures.

There is a good amount of research showing that there is a relation between race and the schooling outcomes of students (Canadian Alliance of Black Educators, 1992; Solomon, 1992; Black Educators Working Group, 1993; Dei *et al.*, 1995, 1997; James, 1995, 1996; Brathwaite and James, 1996; D'Oyley and James, 1998). Power can at times be employed in racist ways to alienate or disengage minority students. The attempt to deny these findings can only constitute part of the problem. There have been some successes (White and Black students) in the school system. But despite these successes the fact still remains that we have students at school having problems in negotiating the power and authority structures in schools. We know that in Toronto Black/African-Canadians, First Nations/Aboriginals, and Portuguese have close to 40 percent dropout rates compared to 30 percent for the general population (Brown, 1993; Pejovic, 1994; Ruck and Wortley, 2002). Students from these groups are enrolled in special education and non-university stream programs in disproportionate numbers. There is a human side to stories that many times statistics do not tell us. Particularly for Black/African students there is a trade-off to school/academic success. There are issues emerging from the impact of education on students' self-identity, collective history, and social esteem. Without a doubt our schools need resources (material, financial, and other logistical support) in order to do their work effectively—i.e. deliver education.

The saliency and visibility of race in the schooling experiences of African-Canadian, aboriginal, and other young people are clear when we listen to narratives of these students as they speak about the differential (negative) treatment according to race. Some educators tend to have low expectations of these students. The problem of a lack of curriculum content and pedagogical approach that many students continually speak about has not been fully addressed. When students speak of the need to have a diverse teaching staff, they are pointing to the fact that race and racial identity are significant to their schooling and learning process. We know that the mere physical presence of different bodies (students) in the school/classroom can mask the problem of student disengagement in soul and mind. Furthermore, we know that, as some students do well in the system, they encounter a high cost to personal and cultural identity for their academic success. Of course, the "home" or the "family" is implicated. Students see guardians, parents, and local communities as sites and sources for political and social action for educational change. And schooling is too important to be left in the hands of teachers alone. As schools take credit for students, educators must equally be willing to accept responsibility for failure. We cannot pathologize families and local communities by denying responsibility anytime we encounter problems in youth education. In order to address many of these issues we must openly and sincerely talk about race. We must acknowledge the existence of systemic racism within all our institutions and our school system is no exception.

There is no disputing that changes are taking place in the educational system of North America. Yet it seems the more things appear to have changed the more they remain the same. Whichever way one looks difference is upon and around us. In the context of Ontario the demographics of our schools and the broader society are fast changing. Let us ponder over some interesting statistics in the Toronto District School Board, Canada's largest school board. We learn that approximately 53 percent of secondary school students have English as their first language, 41 percent of students have a first language other than English, and that students speak over seventy different languages at home. In fact Toronto District School Board elementary schools (grades one to eight) receive 8,000 newcomers each year representing more than 170 countries and 12 percent of the secondary students in the board have been in Canada for three years or less. Overall, Toronto District School Board secondary schools receive approximately 4,000 newcomers every year (Dei, 2004; Toronto District School Board, www.tdsb.on.ca). These schools make one point clear. Our schools are truly diverse. The question is how have we responded to such diversity as a source of our collective strength? The wider society is still struggling with the integration challenges for newcomers. The so-called "immigrants" are contending with issues of social alienation, trying to fit in with a socially devalued identity. Many youths face problems of poverty (racialized and gendered poverty), especially among Somalis and Afghans. Likewise, for some youth and adult learners, homelessness and non-status for refugees, post-traumatic stress (coming from war zones), discrimination in housing and the social service sector all have implications for their schooling and educational success. Political action to address these social problems has been too slow. The denial and silence come in the position of these issues as "special interests" concerns. So beyond the long-standing concerns of the lack of curricular sophistication, minority teachers, and differential treatment by race, there is the sidelining of race and equity work as "special interest:" We have the state's shirking of its responsibility to provide social services to racially minority groups. In the specific case of education, the repeated cutbacks in education to frontline services such as school community advisors, equity departments, programs such as English as a Second Language (ESL), African Heritage, and adult education have meant that community organizations have to step in and fill the gap to make sure that the needs of children from racialized communities are being met. Under former conservative administrations we witnessed cutbacks to "after school programs" such as culture and heritage education, indigenous language education, and community forums and workshops.

For many students in the school system, race and class work together to produce social alienation and disengagement. Race and poverty demarcate bodies in terms of their involvement in the schooling process. The "marketization of education" (Kenway, 1993, 1995) has actually intensified differences in schools with undercurrent tensions and divisions that can and continue to tear the fabric of society. All this is ironic because public schools are the true meeting places of diverse bodies, a place where people hang together for a period hoping to acquire knowledge for self- and collective advancement. In order to avoid race and poverty tearing down the success of our public school system we must concretely and openly confront the challenges posed by difference for us as educators, learners, policy makers, parents, communities, and organizations. Many of our schools, particularly those serving diversified communities, are under-resourced. Some schools need differential resources given the context and make up of their populations. The economics of schooling (e.g. the high cost of going to high school, college, and university) is apparent in the ever-increasing tuition money and the abuse that many bodies have to contend with daily.

As the state shirks its responsibility to educating the youth (e.g. through funding cutbacks and the lack of resources for equity and diversity concerns) many community organizations have sprung from marginalized communities to fill a major void. Black/African-Canadian communities (like other communities) are "communities of differences." The high cost of schooling and ever-increasing tuition money requires strategic responses from founders such as youth organizations (grants, scholarships, and bursaries). Such initiatives are responding to the absence in schools of racial minority and working class bodies by offering assistance in areas of community outreach, designing an effective admissions process to attract a diverse pool (e.g. faculties of education and access initiatives). We have many community groups that are playing a larger role in partnership with post-secondary institutions to develop outreach and funding programs for youth and more mature students who have been under-represented in the academy. The establishment of community resource centers is another case in point. Such resources, including the establishment of recreational facilities in poor, minority neighborhoods and the creation of after school programs (e.g. culture and heritage education, indigenous language education, and community forums and workshops), are all steps in the right direction. Similarly, community educational outlets such as community Saturday schools have been an important source of education for minority youth.

Accounting for Difference

While the reality of our world is about difference and the fact that educational issues cut differently for the diverse members of the school population, the popular refrain and approach is that one size shoe must fit all. It is such philosophy and politics that makes it imperative that we examine and critique the institutional structures for delivering education. There are many segments of our larger community that favor a simplistic approach to individualizing social problems and issues rather than highlighting the systemic barriers to academic success. Rather than ask: how do the structures of teaching, learning, and administration contribute to the problem of youth disengagement from school they are quick to call for individual responsibility and accountability. Adding insult into injury, some dominant discourses in schooling environments continue to stereotype and label Black youth as "slow learners," "students with learning disabilities," or having "attention deficit syndrome." Black students continue to suffer from low teacher expectations of them (Solomon, 1992; Brathwaite and James, 1996; Dei *et al.*, 1997; Skiba and Peterson, 1999; Ruck and Wortley, 2002).

The politics of the school curriculum heralds an outcome-based approach to schooling change that fails to recognize the differential experiences of the learner, what it takes to teach a student, what it means to develop expectations of a teacher and a learner, and the implications of having a limited vision for education. A powerful discourse of a "return to basics" has in the past been a discourse of erasure for privileged interests. The implications of the discourse for teaching about responsibility, community, and citizenry have been unexplored or ignored. Similarly, the official rhetoric of the conservative right, "Standards Matter the Most" ignores the implications of standardization in the midst of difference, diversity, and inequity. For example, how do we compare standards when there are differential allocations of resources for schools? Is it unreasonable to expect that schools with a large number of new Canadians would require additional resources (e.g. funding for additional programs)?

In the midst of having to defend themselves against such discursive onslaughts Black youth today must grapple with the question of youth violence and the subsequent misrepresentation of racialized minority cultures. For example, the pejorative term "Black on Black" violence stereotypes a whole community as violent. Of course, we must all be concerned with youth violence, but not at the expense of stereotyping a whole group. Our definitions of violence must be all encompassing so as to account for the symbolic, psychological, emotional, and epistemic violence. In other words, one would argue it is equally a form of violence given the way the media shapes the image of ethno-racial communities in very limiting ways to the extent of creating divisions and leading to the internationalization of racist stereotypes. The power of such discourses to set boundaries for the racially victimized to operate in cannot be diminished. There is also the question of racialization of Black identities and how such identities are paired with punishment and repulsion. In Ontario discussions regarding racial profiling and testimonies of the Ontario Human Rights Commission and the general perception of Brown/ Asian bodies and those with Muslim identities as "terrorists" point to racist underpinnings.

Ontario schools work with a zero-tolerance policy and the Safe School Act that are leading to suspensions and expulsions of minoritized bodies from school, particularly Black male students. For these youth the policy raises the question of fairness and educational access. For many Black immigrant communities the zero tolerance policy and the suspension and expulsion of students deemed to engage in violent behavior is a very contentious issue. Local communities and parent groups are calling upon schools to revisit these policies and practices and also look at the root causes of school violence while bringing a comprehensive understanding to "violence" (Roman, 2004). It is not difficult to understand why some parents are asking what is the school's responsibility? Is it to act as the police or to educate young people? Many of the students who are expelled or suspended are students of color, especially Black and aboriginal youth and males, who are left to languish during their suspension. Personally, it is an eye-opener to see the school boards spending precious limited funds to hire lawyers in a bid to expel students. Minority parents are at an extreme disadvantage when they have to mount legal challenges to such expulsions. We need to question these types of legal actions against students and their families and the misuse of financial resources (Lawson, 2004).

Race is significant for schooling because the act of going to school and receiving an education is a socially and politically mediated experience for youth. Unfortunately not many want to deal honestly with race and racial issues. Silence is the preferred option. Recent debates on the collection of race-based data on academic performance of students by the Toronto District School Board reflect competing visions of education in Ontario. To what extent will these statistics reinforce negative stereotypes, ignore or address low student performance, or simply blame individual educators? These debates raise the issue of how some students, notably racial minorities, are being denied full opportunities by the public school system. The problem of Black youth disengagement from school is well documented. There is a need for a critical dialog to address some disturbing trends regarding youth disengagement from society. Today's youth need opportunities and hope. By strengthening our impoverished neighborhoods—providing jobs, housing, health care and recreational facilities—we move from a blaming-the-victim mentality to recognizing the reality of larger structural dimensions of youth disengagement. Our school system has an important role to play in providing youth with hope and opportunity.

Difference "Matters"

Some of the educational concerns enunciated above stem from the feeling, making, and "othering" of bodies as "different." Embedded in such interpretations are encounters with racial, class, gender, and sexual hostilities for many students and learners in the educational system. For particular groups the issues are further compounded by the broader questions of history and politics. As noted in Dei (2004), a great deal is spoken about difference in Euro/Canadian schooling contexts and yet it is either conceptualized in the mainstream multicultural discourse of saris, samosas, and steel bands that treats difference as an essence and an exotic add-on to the European norm or it is viewed as a problematic in which sameness and the stress on commonality is the preferred solution. Both intersect with each other to sustain and reproduce dominating social relations of power. In the former, difference is conceptualized in authentic, essentialized, exoticized, culturalist terms, positioned as independent of other social experiences such as race, class, gender, disability, and sexuality (see Brah, 1999, p. 129): thus, it is presented and understood as a form of signification that is removed from political, social, and historical/contemporary struggles and constraints (McLaren, 1997, p. 52). In the latter, where difference is viewed as a site of conflict and contestation the discourse of sameness ignores (and denies) both the racialized asymmetrical power relations in which the politics of difference are inscribed and the implication of social materiality embedded within such relations (see Doyle-Wood, 2004b).

Difference is more than simply a site of individual contestation. In Western social systems and institutionalized contexts and arenas such as educational sites, difference (its conceptualization and the ways in which it is engaged in systemic binary oppositional hierarchical terms) mediates through knowledge production and hegemonic discursive/material practices the asymmetrical relations of power that determine to a great extent the dis/engagement, alienation, well being, and spiritual health and happiness of all our students, including the communities of difference from which they emerge (see Dei and Doyle-Wood, 2005a). As Lorde (1984) observed some time ago, Western European history, for example, has indoctrinated us to perceive:

> human differences in simplistic opposition to each other: dominant/ subordinate, good/bad, up/down, superior/inferior [valid/invalid, legitimate/illegitimate, civilized/uncivilized] with always the psychic impregnation of the most desired and valued coming first followed by the inferiorized.
>
> (p. 114)

Difference must connect with the ways educators engage the school curriculum. We must be mindful of the need to work through the lens of a curriculum as cultural practice so as to acknowledge, engage, and re/position difference and diversity as sources of embodied resistance, agency, and transformative knowledge, thereby challenging the epistemic violence of Western cultural knowledge as it relates to the material exigencies of racialized and marginalized subjects and communities (see Dei and Doyle-Wood, 2005b).

But guardians, parents, community workers, and elders must also recognize and respond to difference and diversity. Parents, guardians, community workers, and elders are equal and willing partners in the provision of education to youth because it is realized that education is too important to be left in the hands of schools alone. By becoming sounding boards as youth deal with the pressures of schooling and social maturation, parents and community elders are playing their roles in enhancing learning. There are other ways of enriching learning outcomes. By developing an ability to use "teachable moments" in their homes parents can assist in their children's learning process. As we begin to define parental involvement broadly to include parents, communities, and elders, these participants become sounding boards, creating conditions to assist youth learning and challenging schools to meet their responsibility to a diverse body politic. Education can make a profound impact on the lives of the learners.

There are significant challenges that must be addressed in order to create healthy sustainable schooling environments for all learners. It requires the different stakeholders in our school system to come together to search for effective ways to address ensuing problems. Teachers and school administrators have a special obligation in recognizing and responding to diversity in schools: however, there are two crucial points that I believe we must be mindful of. The first relates to the necessity of making a distinction between the concept of schooling and that of education. Schooling should not be considered in and of itself education. In point of fact formal institutionalized schooling structures and practices have created a split with education. If we view education as a process that entails variegated options, strategies, and multiple ways of knowing through which students come to know, engage with, and understand their world, then we can see how institutionalized discursive and material schooling practices that insist on a formalized monocultural and homogenizing understanding of the world can inscribe and reproduce in students a sense of disengagement and alienation through the process of negating and down-valuing the embodied knowledges of difference that all students bring to their learning environment. As a consequence, such formal schooling practices run the risk of despiritualizing our youth through the enforcement of normalizing routines that effectively coerce students into amputating their differences. The conceptualization and measure of "success" in the increasing marketization of education that constructs student bodies as mere commodities for the so-called global economy becomes predicated on the degree to which students are willing—or able—to negate their differences physically, emotionally, and psychologically in order to pass for what is, in effect, an enforced culturally explicit construction of normalcy (see Doyle-Wood, 2004a). What we have then, given that all students represent a myriad of difference and, therefore, all students are thus wounded to varying degrees, is in fact the imposition of systemic and institutionalized miseducation.

Two other significant issues about schooling and difference relate to language and culture. Language is crucial for claiming identity, history, and agency. Mother tongue is a treasure of knowledge. Within indigenous teaching each language is treasured, respected, and loved. It is the most valuable heritage that each person inherits from his/her mother, parents, family, and community. There is no such thing as poor or primitive language. All languages are rich, profound, and beautiful. And no language deserves to be banned, proscribed, or prohibited. With the death of a language comes the death of a culture, a community, and a people. For language is intrinsically connected to culture and these two are connected to land and territory. Language also forms a most formidable element of each person's identity. That is why the struggle for the maintenance of language/mother tongue has become a site for larger cultural and political struggles in today's world. Governing authorities and educational systems must see to it that all languages in their society are developed and are provided opportunities to flourish on equal footing with each other. A fair and equitable development and promotion of linguistic human rights is even more essential in this era of economic and cultural globalization. Particularly, in this era of globalization, the relationship between English as the lingua franca of the world and other national, regional, and local languages in all corners of the globe ought to be critically examined (Dei and Asgharzadeh, 2003).

Similarly, culture can be evoked in understanding the cultural politics of schooling. This engagement of culture can include such areas as the use of marginalized cultural expressions in media and their use in education (as languages of instruction and learning). The respect for human rights, dignity, difference, diversity, and freedom cannot be materialized unless it is accompanied with a respect for the diversity of cultures and the politics of claiming and reclaiming such cultures in schooling. As discussed in a later section on alternative visions of schooling, culture viewed as the totality of lived experiences of students has a role to play in fashioning transformative education for Black and racial minority youth.

The Possibilities of Anti-racism Education

The possibilities of anti-racism to bring about educational change rests on how effectively classroom practice can create space for each learner to thrive. We need students to be in safe, healthy, and sustaining environments where they can pursue learning by asking some hard questions of themselves, their teachers, and the schools. For today's educator certain questions are paramount. For example, how do we (as educators and social and community workers) ensure that our institutional settings respond to the needs and concerns of a diverse body politic? How do we ensure that all students and, particularly those who are racialized for punishment, are able to develop a sense of belonging and identification with their schools? How do we ensure that excellence is not simply accessible, but is also equitable. How do we move beyond the bland seductive politics of inclusion and begin to speak concretely of the politics of accountability and transparency?

I would argue that these questions are important because, within the academy, we need to engage both the possibilities and limits, in this historical juncture, of every learner escaping racist ideologies. We also need to challenge the fact that most of our students appear set in their knowledge and thinking because of the school curriculum. The intellectual and political project is to examine the ways racism is travelling today (e.g. through colonial discourses, ways of knowledge production and the validation/legitimation of such knowledges, and the making of the race "experts" and the "'knowers" of the other.) We can only do so and be successful if we are able to bring race back into the center of discourse and challenge the politics of de-racing subjects. In addition, critical education must challenge the propensity of the Western academy to celebrate diversity and yet not respond concretely to difference. This is where anti-racist education and critical practice come in.

Anti-racism has come to mean different things to many people. In fact, the most progressive of politics keep blurring the conceptual distinction between multicultural education and anti-racism. And yet not everything that has passed of late for "anti-racism" is actually about anti-racism. The core of anti-racism resides in concrete action to bring about systemic change. Anti-racism can be defined as a discursive and political practice to address the myriad forms of racism and the intersections with other forms of oppression. Anti-racism addresses the systemic and institutional dimensions of racism as well as drawing attention to more than the overt forms of racist acts lodged in individual actions, practices, and beliefs. Anti-racist practice focuses foremost on systemic racism. Within our institutions and other social settings structural racism revolves around certain ontological, epistemological, and axiological foundations. For example, at the ontological level (i.e. understanding the nature of social reality) our institutions are seen as fair, value free, and objective. In the epistemological realm (i.e. particular ways of knowing about this reality) it is argued that, by working with "merit," "excellence," and a "prism of thinking in hierarchies" we can arrive at the ontological foundation of fairness, objectivity, and value-free society. Axiologically (i.e. disputational contours of what is right and wrong) we insist that treating everybody the same (as in social justice for all) and discounting the qualitative value of justice is the most appropriate thing to do. So equal opportunity and colour blindness are much heralded, despite the fact that these views complicate racism by masking its real material and political ramifications. Anti-racism challenges White power and its rationality for dominance. As noted long ago, Whiteness has become the tacit norm everyone references. Eurocentric knowledge masquerades as "universal knowledge" (see Kincheloe and Steinberg, 1998). In schools and other social settings White power and privilege masquerade as excellence and we often know and claim "excellence" if it looks like us.

Anti-racist education works with the notion of "race," making an important distinction between race and ethnicity and culture. On this score it must be noted that many have found the word "race" or "racial" to be problematic, choosing instead to speak about "ethnicity" or "cultural" differences. This is a soft liberal position. Race and racial differences, however constructed, matter in concrete ways and naming them explicitly is very important in the context of what anti-racism is about. Increasingly, today many are falling on other words like "racialized" to identify social processes around race issues. But it is important in critical anti-racism work to name race for what it is. Such naming is a political act and it shows our seriousness to address the problem. Anti-racism is adamant of speaking about race.

Race, like gender, class, ethnicity, religion, and language, disability is an important social category and part of our identities. As a society we live our fears, hopes, and anxieties in racial terms. Thus, we must confront race and this is what anti-racist practice does. Rather than deny race and racial categories, anti-racism calls for challenging the interpretations put on them. So anti-racists discuss race not to create a problem but to allude to a problem that already exists. As educators we cannot simply overlook the destructive presence and insidious nature of race. Contrary to a common belief that anti-racists are obsessed with race, it seems that, as a society, we rather spend too much time avoiding a discussion of race.

Anti-racist education is also about bringing a complex meaning to race. Race is not a static, bounded, or fixed category. The meaning of race keeps changing in different historical contexts. However, critical anti-racist practice also cautions us to be fully aware that the shifting meaning of race and the experiencing of race as contextual applies more to dominant groups than to those who are racialized as Black. In other words, the "race of Blackness is experienced differently than the race of other non-Whites." Race can also not be understood if decoupled from class, gender, sexuality, language, and religion. While drawing on these connections and intersections of social difference, critical anti-racism highlights the saliency of race, that is to argue that, in a racialized society, race trumps other forms of difference. The notion of "saliency" has three conceptual underpinnings. First, it is an acknowledgment of the situational and contextual variations in intensities of oppression. Second, it is the realization of the relative saliencies of different identities.

Third, it is the recognition of the severity of issues for certain bodies. Such understandings speak to the saliency of skin colour as "race," but also argue that race is more than skin color. In other contexts, culture, religion, language, ethnicity, gender, class, sexuality, and disability have become the basis for racializing groups as "different" and subjecting them to different and unequal treatment.

Anti-racist education works with multiple meanings of social justice. In other words, "social justice for all" is just one model of justice. Similarly, a color-blind approach to our work can be limiting when we see the problem as race rather than the interpretations that we bring to colour. So in critical anti-racist practice we must redefine social justice to appreciate its myriad forms depending on contexts and history and to acknowledge the severity of issues for certain bodies in our communities. In other words, "social justice for all" can be a liberal discourse of pluralism that fails to recognize that certain groups at the bottom of rank order ought to target these groups in as much as they are aimed at providing justice for all. The pursuit of social justice must acknowledge and deal with the fact that our society operates with a ranked racial order/hierarchy.

Anti-racism education also calls for understanding the complexity of oppressions. While all oppressions have certain things in common (e.g. they work within structures, are intended to establish material advantage and disadvantage, and also serve to create a self/other distinction), oppressions are not equal in their consequences. In other words, oppressions differ in their consequences and the burden of oppression is not shared equally. The implications of this for critical anti-racist practice is the knowledge that the collective quest for solidarity in anti-oppression work can mask some under-lying ambivalences and tensions when we fail to broach questions of power and privilege. In order to guide against such tensions paralyzing anti-racist projects, the field practitioner and community worker should not seek to separate the politics of difference from the politics of race. This allows domin-ant bodies to deny an interrogation of White privilege and power.

In our schools and within many of our classrooms today some students have to contend with racist mugging and racist moments that require redress. The everydayness of racism requires that, as educators, we pursue anti-racism vigorously to challenge these disturbing encounters which often times reveal an egregious display of White dominance if not White supremacy. For the classroom practitioner anti-racism insists each learner must be assisted to adopt a stance that advocates identifying, challenging, and changing values, structures, and behaviors that perpetuate systemic racism and other forms of oppression. The entrenched inequities and power imbalance among social groups must be addressed. In the context of schooling, the discourse of mosaic, which cherishes difference and plurality and promotes an image of multiple, thriving, mutually respectful, and appreciative of ethno-cultural communities, must be seen as not enough. We need a critical discourse and political practice that challenges persistent inequities among communities and relations of domination and subordination. While education and sharing and exchange of knowledge are relevant, educators need to put in place a mechanism that redresses injustice and seeks fundamental structural and societal change. The problems of schooling are not simply manifested in intolerance and the lack of goodwill. The problems should be seen as questions of bias, discrimination, hatred, exclusion, and violence. Rather than viewing racial prejudice as individual acts of bigots and a violation of democratic rights, racism must be understood as an integral part of the social structure or social order.

Anti-racism highlights the material and experiential realities of minority peoples in their dealing with the school system. Anti-racism also means learning about the experiences of living with racialized identities and understanding how students' lived experiences, in and out of school, implicate their engagement and disengagement from school. Anti-racism uncovers how race, ethnicity, class, gender, sexuality, physical ability, power, and difference influence and are influenced by schooling processes. Anti-racism is about how the processes of teaching, learning, and administration of education combine to produce schooling success and failures for different bodies. Anti-racism opines that addressing questions of power, equity, and social difference is significant to enhance learning outcomes and the provision of social opportunities for all youth.

As anti-racist educators, we have a unique place in the current climate of school advocacy. This is because of the power of new imaginings that critical anti-racism education offers us. If we believe that the future itself is being hotly contested in the schools, families, neighborhoods, union halls, media outlets, and community forums, then anti-racism has to be part of that struggle. Anti-racist educators have unprecedented opportunities to influence many minds and to share and engage in different (dominant, privileged, subjugated, subordinated, and minority) perspectives. The environments in which we work offer advantages and opportunities depending on our subject positions and politics. We can work with the differential allocation of space and resources to further the cause of youth education. It all comes to a question of whether an anti-racist educator wants to see current challenges as obstacles or as opportunities and openings to make change happen. This is not a simplistic assertion.

The Call for African-centered/Black-focused Schools

In concluding this discussion I would like to revisit the idea of an alternative schooling for Black and racial minority youth as one of many things that can be done to enhance learning for African youth. This is not suggested as a panacea for all the problems of youth schooling but as something worthy of experimenting (as have been the case of such schools in the U.S.) to help promote Black youth education. In November 1992, a multilevel government task force in Ontario, the "African-Canadian Community Working Group," proposed creating one predominantly Black junior high school in each of the six metropolitan Toronto municipalities and a five-year pilot scheme to establish what was termed "Black-focused" schools. The Royal Commission on Learning recommended that "school boards, academic authorities, faculties of education, and representatives of the Black community collaborate to establish demonstration schools" in jurisdictions with large numbers of Black students. The school would have predominantly Black and racial minority teaching staff and be open to students from a range of social backgrounds: racial, ethnic, socio-economic, and "immigrant." Community groups such as the Organization of Parents of Black Children have long supported this idea of "Black-focused" schools, acknowledging that racial solidarity alone will not ensure Black youth success in schools.

An informed debate must address two key interrelated questions. First, what is a "Black-focused" or African-centered school? Second, what would such a school look like? The Black-focused/African-centered school is a concept for the promotion of education primarily (but not exclusively) for Black peoples of African descent. Consequently a Black-focused school is the same as an "African-centered" school. We intend to be inclusive in keeping with the objectives of the school and we see one of the many goals of the school to help Black students reinvent their Africanness in a diasporic context. We use "Black" foremost in the cultural sense to include the diverse ethnicities that make up peoples of African descent. But there is also a political usage of "Black" to include the bonds that all peoples experiencing the European colonial encounter share. Since the Black-focused school works with principles that are not exclusive to Black people of African descent, we must see these principles then as providing the *raison d'être* and the connecting links for a diverse group of learners who identify with the proposed schooling system.

A "Black-focused"/African-centered school challenges the conventional educational environment and stresses the principles of responsibility, interdependence, respect for elders, transparency, and accountability. The school seeks to center the learner in her or his own culture, history, personal location, and spiritual identity. History is defined in this context as the totality of the Black lived experience rather than a reference to simply episodic events. Centering the learner in her or his culture simply means education starts with the learner and then allows each learner to make connections with those around them. As a starting base, the learner's culture, history, and identities can be used to make references and links with other peoples. The school will teach Canadian history and how African, Asian, and aboriginal histories are all central to the construction of such history. All learners will be seen as creators and producers of knowledge about their world and lived experiences. The school will emphasize the contributions of all peoples to world civilization leaving no group on the margins. For example, contributions of Africa, Asian, aboriginal peoples, etc., in the areas of the arts, literature, science, technology, language, economics, and politics are duly emphasized. We believe this allows each learner to see herself or himself and their histories and cultures in the educational process. While these principles are not exclusive to such a school, they do provide a model for holistic, socially integrated schooling that all students may benefit from. It will strive for high academic excellence and will meet provincial standards.

The second question calls for imagining new forms of education. A "Black-focused"/African-centered school is organized around communal principles and non-hierarchical structures. In making the totality of Black lived experience relevant to all parts of the curriculum, the school would foster the social, physical, spiritual, and academic development of the student, making him or her a whole subject. In breaking down the separation between the formal school and the wider community, incorporating the family/home and the workplace, the school offers new and creative ways of thinking about knowledge and then engages students to use this knowledge to make positive social changes. The school, home, families, workplaces, and the wider society all become important sites of teaching and learning.

The idea of a Black-focused school engages with education as an expression of shared community responsibility. The goal and purpose of such a school is to create a more nurturing environment where our youth see themselves surrounded by positive images and where teachers work collectively with students and parents teaching about academic and social success, community belonging, sense of social responsibility, mutual interdependence, respect for oneself and peers, and the wisdom and knowledge of elders, parents, and guardians. It is a school in which parents and elders become teachers and learners and students also become learners and teachers. It is a school that works with the idea that discipline, while necessary for the education of youth, is the joint responsibility of homes, families, communities, and schools and not the criminal justice system. It is a school where discipline is taught rather than simply enforced. The school will teach discipline by developing the learners' sense of self-worth, moral and social fiber, personal esteem, and a sense of purpose in society. The school teaches about alternative ways to practice effective discipline without resorting to suspensions, expulsions, and calling law enforcement into the school. It is a school that educates the youth to care about the wider society and recognize that all rights have matching responsibilities. The establishment of this school will be within the public school system. The idea behind this school is no different than that behind the establishment of faith-based schools, all-girls schools, the French immersion programs and the specialized arts program, or even boy-only literacy classes in the junior grades in response to standardized provincial test results indicating lower achievement levels in reading and writing among this group.

It is important to reiterate that a Black-focused/African-centered school is not a Black school. The Black-focused school is not for everyone. It is also a school that does not exclude anyone. The idea of a Black-focused/African-centered school does not call for pulling every African-Canadian youth from the mainstream public school system. Parents must have the choice and right to determine whether this is the school for their children. Since it is being proposed to address the concerns about African-Canadian youth disengagement from school we should expect a majority of students and teachers to be from African-Canadian and Black backgrounds. Since school is defined by its guiding principles rather than by who goes or teaches there, those who share in these ideals must have a right to be in the school. The school is not a call to Balkanize the public school system. We believe, for groups where there is a demonstrated educational advantage, there are legitimate grounds to consider the establishment of such schools as one of the many things to be done to help address the problem of "educational crisis" in the community.

Some also argue that Black-focused schools represent a reversion to the days of segregation. There is a meaningful difference between "forced segregation" and "separation by choice." Segregationists in the first half of the twentieth century sought to exclude Blacks from meaningful participation in society. By contrast, Black-focused/African-centered schools aim to address an "educational crisis" and help minority youth succeed. The school may hold some possibilities for the learner. Every learner must be informed about the complete history of ideas and events that have shaped and continue to shape human growth and development. The learner must be affirmed in all her/his identities (including racial, class, ethnic, gender, language, and religion) if we are to provide a holistic education. While racial solidarity alone cannot guarantee academic success for our youth, we believe being exposed to the realities of society allows us to prepare the learner to deal with society. This means teaching about race and racism, different knowledges, complexity of our identities, and cultures and histories as part of the school curriculum. The school offers a curriculum that relates directly to the lived experiences of all learners so as to prepare the learner for the world outside the school system. It is a school working with excellence and rigorous provincial standards. As a demonstration school to be set up on an experimental basis, we would expect the lessons learned from such schools to be fed back into the mainstream school system to help enhance learning for all youth. In fact, rather than weakening current efforts by mainstream schools to be inclusive of African-Canadian experiences, a Black-focused/African-centered school enhances them. Mainstream schools, however, must continue to strive to be inclusive. There is no reason why the existence of a Black-focused school should lead to such an "either/or" situation. Above all, a Black-focused/African-centered school can ensure that those youth who either drop out and/or are pushed out of the mainstream school system have a chance at education.

Acknowledgments

I would like to thank Alireza Asgharzadeh of the department of sociology and equity studies at the Ontario Institute for Studies in Education of the University of Toronto for comments and suggestions that have contributed to strengthening this paper.

Resources and Tools for Educators

Questions

1. What is an African-centered school?
2. How is such a school different from the current public school system?
3. What are the principles and objectives of an African-centered school?
4. What do you see as the contradictions and tensions in calling for an African-centered school within the broader context and goals of inclusive schooling and education?

For Further Reading

The following suggested readings widen our understanding of the historical and social conditions under which some of the issues related in the chapter evolve and also point at the relevance of developing culturally sensitive educational strategies and pedagogies.

African Canadian Legal Clinic. (2002). Anti-Black racism in education. In. *A report on the Canadian Government's compliance with the International Convention on the Elimination of All Forms if Racial Discrimination.* Available online: www.aclc.net/antiba_rineducation.htm.

Asante, M. (2003). The Afrocentric idea. In A. Mazama (Ed.), *The Afrocentric Paradigm* (pp. 37–53). Trenton, NJ: Africa World Press.

Brathwaite, K. & James, C. (1996). *Educating African-Canadians.* Toronto: John Lorimer and Co., Publishers.

Dei, G. J. S & Lordan, M. (2006). Language, linguistic discrimination, and polyvocality: Bringing language into discussions of discrimination and racism. In G. Dei and N. Amin (Eds.), *The poetics of anti-racism.* Halifax: Fernwood Books.

Dei, G. J. S., James-Wilson, S., & Zine, J. (2002). *Inclusive schooling: A teacher's companion to 'removing the margins'.* Toronto: Canadian Scholar's Press.

Dodds, P. (2005). Here's one that's working: Shiloh Christian Institute in Brampton is tailored to help young black students, says teacher. *Toronto Star*, September 16, 2005. Available online: http://fcis.oise.utoronto.ca/~ gpieters/ afrocentricschools/acschoolnews28.html.

James, C. E. & Shadd, A. (2001). *Talking about identity: Encounters in race, ethnicity and language.* Toronto: Between the Lines Press.

Ladson Billings, G. (1995). Toward a theory of culturally relevant pedagogy. *American Educational Research Review Journal, 32*(3), 465–491.

Pieters, G. (2003). *Disproportionate impact, the Safe Schools Act and racial profiling in schools.* Available online: Afrocentric Research and Education Portal http://fcis.oise.utoronto.ca/~gpieters/afrocentricschools/schlprofiling. html.

Rich, A. (1979). *"Claiming an education". On lies, secrets and silence.* New York: W. W. Norton & Co.

Shockley, G. (2003). *When culture and education meet: An ethnographic investigation of an Africentric private school in Washington, DC.* Available online at https://drum.umd.edu/dspace/bitstream/1903/332/1/dissertation. pdf.

Shujaa, M. J. (1994). *Too much schooling, too little education: A paradox of Black life in White society.* Trenton, NJ: Africa World Press.

Tatum, B. D. (1992). Talking about race, learning about racism: The application of racial identity development theory in the classroom. *Harvard Educational Review, 62*(1), 1–24.

Zine, J. (2000). Redefining resistance: Toward an Islamic sub-culture in schools. *Race Ethnicity and Education, 3*(3), 293–316.

Zine, J. (2001). Muslim youth in Canadian schools: Education and the politics of religious identity. *Anthropology and Education Quarterly, 32*(4), 399–423.

Zine, J. (2004a). Dealing with September 12: The challenge of anti-Islamaphobia education. *Orbit, 33*(3) 39–41.

Zine, J. (2004b). Gendered Islamophobia: Interrogating the politics of veiling in schools and society. *Gender and Society,* 4–5.

Suggestions for Educators

1. Identify ways of accessing pertinent resources for developing an Afrocentric/African-centered curriculum and suggest baseline standards for using such resources.
2. Identify strategies for implementing an African-centered curriculum and suggest baseline standards for assessing the quality of such a curriculum.

3. Identify ways for determining the instructional effectiveness of an Afrocentric/African-centered curriculum.
4. Identify the relevance and practicality of the Afrocentric/African-centered lessons for youth and parents.

References

Black Educators Working Group. (1993). *Submission to the Ontario Royal Commission on Learning.* Toronto: Black Educators Working Group.

Brah, A. (1999). Difference, diversity and differentiation. In J. Donald & A. Rattansi (Eds.), *Race, culture and difference* (p. 111) London: Sage Publications.

Brathwaite, K. & James, C. (1996). *Educating African-Canadians.* Toronto: John Lorimer and Co., Publishers.

Brown, R. S. (1993). *A follow-up of the grade 9 cohort of 1978 Every Secondary Student Survey participants.* Toronto: Toronto Board of Education. Research Services, Report no. 207.

Brown, M. J. (2004). *In their own voices: African-Canadians in the greater Toronto area share experiences of police profiling. Report commission by the African-Canadian community coalition on racial profiling.* Toronto: African-Canadian Coalition on Racial Profiling.

Canadian Alliance of Black Educators. (1992). *Sharing the challenge, I, II, III: A focus on black high school students.* Toronto: Canadian Alliance of Black Educators.

Dei, G. J. S. (2004). The challenge of promoting inclusive education in Ontario schools. Paper presented at the Mayor's Forum on "Youth and Community Safety," University of Toronto, Scarborough Campus.

Dei, G. & Asgharzadeh, A. (2003) Language, education and development: Case studies from southern contexts. *Language and Education: An International Journal, 17*(6), 421–449.

Dei, G. J. S. & Doyle-Wood, S. (2005a). "Is we who haffi ride di staam": Critical knowledge/multiple knowings: Possibilities, challenges and resistance in curriculum cultural contexts. In Y. Kanu (Ed.), *Curriculum/cultural contexts in curriculum as cultural practice: Post colonial imaginations* (pp. 152–153). Toronto: University of Toronto Press.

Dei, G. J. S & Doyle-Wood, S. (2005b). Knowledge or indigenous knowledge? Multiple knowings, challenges and possibilities in the academy. In J. Kincheloe & R. Horn (Eds.), *Encyclopedia of educational psychology* (pp. 89–107). Westport, CT: Greenwood Publishing.

Dei, G. J. S. & Razack, S. (Eds.) (1995). *Inclusive schooling: An inventory of contemporary practices designed to meet the challenges of a diverse student body.* Toronto: Ministry of Education and Training.

Dei, G., Mazzuca, Jo, McIsaac, E., & Zine, J. (1997). *Reconstructing dropout: Understanding the dynamics of black students disengagement from school.* Toronto: University of Toronto Press.

D'Oyley, V. & James, C. (1998). *Re/visioning: Canadian perspectives on the education of Africans in the late 20th century.* Toronto: Captus Press.

Doyle-Wood, S. (2004a). *Defining difference in Canadian schooling contexts.* In G. J. S. Dei, N. Amin and A. Abdi (Eds.), *Social difference and schooling in Canada—pedagogical challenges.* [forthcoming].

Doyle-Wood S. (2004b). Passing for black? The epistemology of passing: Re-reckoning and old trope in A. Asgharzadeh, E. Lawson, A. Wahab *et al.* (Eds.), *Diasporic ruptures: Transnationalism, globalization and identity discourses.* [forthcoming].

Ernst, G. and Statzner, E. (1994). Alternative visions of schooling. *Anthropology & Education Quarterly* 25(3): 200–207.

Fine, M. (1991). *Framing dropouts: Notes on the politics of an urban public high school.* New York: State University of New York Press.

James, C. (1995). *Seeing ourselves: Exploring race, ethnicity and culture.* Toronto: Thompson Educational Publishing.

James, C. E. (1996). What students are saying about African studies courses in high school. *Our Schools/Our Selves* 47: 130–145.

Kenway, J. (with C. Bigum & L. Fitzclarence) (1993). Marketing education in the postmodern age. *Journal of Education* 8(2): 105–122.

Kenway, J. (1995). The marketisation of education: Mapping the contours of a feminist perspective. Paper presented at the Conference of the British Educational Research Association, Bath.

Kincheloe, J. & Steinberg, S. R. (1998). Addressing the crisis of whiteness: Reconfiguring white identity in a pedagogy of whiteness. In J. L. Kincheloe, S. R. Steinberg, N. M Rodriguez, & R. E. Chennault (Eds.), *White reign: Deploying whiteness in America*. New York: St Martin's Press.

Lawson, E. (2004). Personal communication. Department of Sociology and Equity Studies, Ontario Institute for Studies in Education of the University of Toronto.

Lorde, A. (1984). *Sister outsider: Essays and speeches*. Berkley: The Crossing Press.

McLaren, P. (1997). White terror and oppositional agency: Towards a critical multiculturalism. In D. T. Goldberg (Ed.), *Multiculturalism: A critical reader* (pp. 11–12). Oxford: Blackwell.

Pejovic, Z. (1994). *Boulevard of dreams: Croatians and education in Ontario*. Toronto: Canadian Scholars' Press.

Roman, C. G. (2004). *Schools, neighbourhoods and violence: Crime within the daily routines of youth*. New York: Lexington Books.

Ruck, M. D. & Wortley, S. (2002). Racial and ethnic minority high school perceptions of school disciplinary practices: A look at some Canadian findings. *Journal of Youth and Adolescence, 31*(3), 185–195.

Skiba, R. J. & Peterson, R. (1999). The dark side of zero tolerance: Can punishment lead to safe schools? *Phi Delta Kappan, 80*(5), 372–382.

Solomon, P. (1992). *Black resistance in high school: Forging a separatist culture*. New York: SUNY.

CHAPTER 12

Reversing Deculturalization for Better or for Worse: Teaching Hawaiian Culture in Public Schools

GAY GARLAND REED

Introduction

Indigenous researchers such as Smith (2001) and Thaman (2004) have challenged non-indigenous researchers to interrogate their own means and motives. They raise ethical concerns and questions of cultural appropriateness that should be central to the work of all researchers who move across cultural borders to do their work.

With their concerns in mind, I begin by questioning if I have the right to speak. After 14 years in Hawai'i I am somewhere between a *malahini* (newcomer to the islands) and *kamaina* (oldtimer in Hawai'i). I am a *haole*, a foreigner. My light skin suggests that I carry the heritage of the oppressor rather than the lineage of the oppressed. In Banks's (1998) typology of cross-cultural researchers I aspire to be the external insider, one who might at some point in the future be viewed as an "adopted" insider. For now, the best I can do is position myself as a concerned outsider to Hawaiian culture who understands that my epistemological orientation may preclude me from presenting an authentic picture. As a partial corrective, much of the data for this paper is drawn from interviews and conversations with educational leaders in Hawai'i who are knowledgeable about the policies and programs discussed in this study.

This paper reviews various forms of revitalization and re-indigenization of culture that have taken place in Hawaiian public schools in the last two decades as a means to informing the global community about the unique instances of cultural revival and sustainability that are unfolding in these islands. At the same time, it explores the complexity of these processes and acknowledges some of the difficult issues that educators encounter as they indigenize their curricula and pedagogy.

This research assumes that the process of reclaiming native voices and revitalization of indigenous cultures is for the better. However, it must also be noted that, in some instances, this process does not represent a genuine concern for the sustainability of indigenous cultures. Rather, it has more to do with commercialization and cooption of indigenous knowledge for the profit of individuals in the dominant culture. There is also a question of whether indigenous knowledge, which was traditionally transmitted in non-formal educational settings, can find a comfortable fit with formal education settings. If indigenous knowledge is integrated into formal education, will its essential spiritual dimensions be lost? These questions will be addressed in the final section of this inquiry.

On the one hand this chapter provides a catalogue of various public school programs, curricula, and pedagogical approaches that are reflective of Hawaiian culture, language, and ways of knowing. At the same time the paper raises a variety of issues that cultural practitioners, as well as non-indigenous educators, should keep in mind as they engage with Hawaiian content and work towards culturally relevant practice. Finally, I will argue that the revival of indigenous knowledge is important for providing a perspective on global issues.

In this overview of public sector programs in Hawai'i the term "indigenous knowledge" will be used to refer to a broad range of cultural beliefs and practices imbedded and characteristic of indigenous cultures. Drawing on several definitions of indigenous knowledge, a United Nations Educational, Scientific, and Cultural Organization document summarized the essential elements as the following: (1) locally bound, indigenous to a specific area, (2) culture and context specific, (3) non-formal knowledge, (4) orally transmitted and generally not documented, (5) dynamic and adaptive, (6) holistic in nature, and (7) closely related to survival and subsistence for many people worldwide (www.unesco.org/most/ bpindi.htm).

Hawaiian culture is seen as a unique local expression of indigenous knowledge.

The chapter is divided into five sections: (1) Introduction, (2) Historical Context, (3) Research on Native Hawaiian Education: Culturally Relevant Practice, (4) A Catalogue of Programs and Courses in Hawai'i Public Schools, and (5) Analysis and Conclusions: For Better or for Worse.

Historical Context

Historical documentation of the deculturalization of Hawai'i through the educational system (Ah Nee-Benham and Heck, 1998; Kahumoko, 2000) reveals much the same pattern that took place in New Zealand (Aotearoa),

Canada, Australia, mainland U.S., and other parts of the world where the culture and language of indigenous populations have been systematically eradicated by newcomers (Spring, 2001). In Hawai'i the story begins with early visitors to the islands who came to trade and Christianize. When the missionaries arrived they brought not only their religion, but also their language and culture and, in many cases, their cultural ethno-centrism. Some traditional forms of *hula*, for example, were banned and in 1897 English replaced Hawaiian as the official school language. Ah Nee-Benham and Heck (1998) chronicled the silencing of native voices and the marginalization of Hawaiian identity through education. The Americanization of Hawai'i that took place after the overthrow of Queen Lili'uokalani in 1893 and annexation by the U.S. in 1898 not only silenced native voices, it also marginalized the voices of immigrant groups like the Chinese, Japanese, Koreans, and Portuguese who were brought to the islands to work on the sugar plantations (Tamura, 1994).

The Hawaiian renaissance that began in the 1970s has begun to reverse the course of deculturalization and resulted in a new surge of interest in Hawaiian language and culture and a commitment to the revitalization of Hawaiian identity. Part of this revival is reflected in changes in the curriculum and pedagogy of Hawai'i's public schools. These changes came about partly because of systematic research that revealed disconnections between the home culture of the students and the culture of the schools.

Research on Native Hawaiian Education: Culturally Relevant Practice

Researchers at Kamehameha schools conducted much of the early important research on native Hawaiian students. Studies from the Kamehameha Early Education Program continue to inform current teacher practice. Teacher educators and their pre-service education students read the research as a way of developing culturally relevant practice for Hawai'i's sizable population of Hawaiian and part-Hawaiian students in the state.

Many children of Hawaiian ancestry who attend public schools have never heard Hawaiian spoken. The language that most of these children speak is a non-standard dialect of English known as Hawaiian Creole English or Hawaiian island dialect shared by people of many different ancestries who define themselves as "local."

The customary approach to bridging the linguist and cultural gap between home and school was to change the child and sometimes the home to conform to school expectations. The Kamehameha Early Education Program researchers Jordan *et al.* (1992) suggested a different strategy. After careful observations of successful behaviors in home settings and comparing these with what was expected in traditional classrooms, the researchers found a distinct cultural mismatch that helped to explain the underachievement of Hawaiian children at school. They encouraged modifications in the school context that would enable the children to be successful in school by drawing on abilities that they exhibited in non-school settings (Au and Kawakami, 1994).

Changes in curricula, pedagogy, and policies have been ongoing in the state and the research into culturally responsive teaching continues at Kamehameha schools as well as at the University of Hawai'i. Some of the most recent research has to do with evaluation and assessment (Hale, 2004). Through their Extension Education Division, the Kamehameha schools have made important contributions in the public sector.

A Catalogue of Programs and Courses in Hawai'i Public Schools

This chapter focuses on the public sector. Although the Hawaiian renaissance has flourished in the private sector as well, the two overlap in important ways. As indicated in the previous section, the work of educators and researchers at Kamehameha schools has played an important role in moving the renaissance forward. Although some of their important research is cited in this chapter, the focus of the study is public schools where this research has also had an impact.

The study by Kamehameha Schools Bernice Pauahi Bishop Estate, Office of Program Evaluation and Planning (1993) noted that Hawaiian students are the largest group in the Department of Education (p. 14) and that the Hawaiian student population continues to grow (p. 15). The demographics of the State of Hawai'i are unique in that there is no majority ethnic group. According to the 2000 census no other state in the U.S. has such a high percentage of Native Americans/indigenous people in its population.

Overall, 82 percent of Hawai'i's students attend public schools, 16 percent attend private schools (including Kamehameha schools), and 1.5 percent attend public charter schools (Superintendent's Report, 2004, p. 7). Although they are part of the public system, the charter schools are singled out here because they, along with the immersion schools, have a special role to play in cultural sustainability. The state's 27 charter schools (about half of which are Hawaiian culture focused) account for only 4,834 of the total number of students but their numbers are growing (Haug, 2004). Hawaiian language immersion students are counted in the 82 percent of public school attendees and their unique contributions to the re-indigenization of Hawai'i will be discussed below.

As noted earlier, some scholars of multicultural education have worried that patterns of discrimination and marginalization of indigenous students is partially due to a cultural mismatch between teachers and students (Pang, 2001). As in other parts of the U.S., there is a cultural mismatch between Hawai'i's teachers and students in the public sector, albeit a very different cultural disconnect than that found in mainland schools. Overall, 38 percent of Hawai'i's public school teachers are of Japanese ancestry and 26 percent are Caucasians. The largest groups of students, however, are identified as Hawaiian or part-Hawaiian (26 percent) and the second largest group as Filipino (20 percent). Teachers of these ethnic backgrounds are under-represented at 11 percent and 6 percent, respectively. Part of helping children of Hawaiian ancestry become more successful in school is increasing the number of educators who have the cultural competencies to work successfully with them.

Among the most "Hawaiian-focused" public school initiatives are the Hawaiian language immersion schools and the charter schools that are based on Hawaiian culture. When the Hawai'i state legislature passed legislation that permitted the initial creation of 25 charter schools, teachers and community members who were concerned about cultural sustainability seized the opportunity to create schools based on Hawaiian cultural values. Approximately half of the new charter schools design curricula and programs that are based on Hawaiian values and content. In Hawaiian language immersion schools students learn in a Hawaiian medium environment and English is taught as a foreign language. Specifics of these schools will be explored later.

The public sector courses and programs that we will look at in this section are *Ke Kula Kaiapuni* (Hawaiian language immersion), Hawaiian-focused charter schools, the *Kūpuna* Program, character education programs based on Hawaiian values, traditional ecological knowledge (TEK) in the science curriculum, and the revival of Hawaiian language, *hula*, and Hawaiian music.

Table 12.1 shows the range of courses, programs, and schools that currently exist in the public arena. They are not arranged in any particular order but they do express the variety of opportunities for students in Hawai'i to become knowledgeable about Hawaiian language and culture and develop a sense of place. For each category, the student population, language(s), values, and pedagogy are indicated.

Hawaiian Courses and Content

All public school students in grade four learn about pre-contact Hawai'i, grade seven students have one semester of Hawaiian monarchy, and grade nine students learn about modern Hawaiian history for one semester. Parents, especially those of students who come from outside Hawai'i, sometimes express concern that their children are learning "too much" about Hawaiian culture (P. Wilhelm, personal communication). Educators respond by stressing the importance of everyone learning about the place that they are living in. Wherever children live it is important for them to learn about environmental stewardship and how to foster healthy social relationships. Studying Hawaiian culture is one way to learn these values by attending to a sense of place.

TABLE 12.1 Schools, programs, and content that reflect Native Hawaiian values

Native Hawaiian school, program, or content	Students	Language(s)	Values	Pedagogy
Charter schools (Hawaiian based)	Special populations	Hawaiian and/or English	Hawaiian/ Non-Hawaiian	Hawaiian/ Non-Hawaiian
Character education programs	Some public schools	English with some Hawaiian words	Hawaiian	Hawaiian/ Non-Hawaiian
Hawaiian language immersion schools	Special populations	Hawaiian and ESL	Hawaiian	Hawaiian/ Non-Hawaiian
Kūpuna program	All elementary schoolchildren	English with some Hawaiian words	Hawaiian	Hawaiian/ Non-Hawaiian
Hawaiian history	All public high schoolchildren	English with some Hawaiian words	Non-Hawaiian	Non-Hawaiian
Science programs TEK	Some students	English with some Hawaiian words	Some Hawaiian values	Hawaiian/ Non-Hawaiian
Hawaiian, music and hula	Some students	English and Hawaiian	Some Hawaiian Values	Hawaiian/ Non-Hawaiian

It is general practice for states in the U.S. to teach state history. Hawai'i is no exception to this practice. While all students in public middle and high schools learn about aspects of Hawaiian history in their grade nine classes, educators are including Hawaiian content and pedagogy in other classes as well, such as science. Biology classes, for example, focus on indigenous and endemic flora and fauna and students learn about ecologically sustainable forms of land and water management based on traditional Hawaiian practices.

The science curriculum has been enormously enriched by including an indigenous perspective. This approach to science is part of a larger movement towards integrating TEK and there are as many forms of TEK as there are local knowledge systems. A course description for a course on TEK taught in Alaska, for example, reveals important elements of TEK from a Tlingit perspective:

> Tlingit traditional ecological knowledge (TEK) is the product of generations of learning and experience with the lands, waters, fish, plants, wildlife, and other natural resources of Southeast Alaska. As Sitka elder Herman Kitka Sr. shows, Tlingits were trained from an

early age to be aware of and respect the community of living beings that surrounds them. This meant learning not only how to hunt, fish, gather and process key subsistence foods and other necessities, but also how to understand the behavior and roles of other species in the ecosystem, and how to successfully interact with them in sustainable ways. This knowledge was not gained in a classroom but largely passed down by elders through oral histories, songs, crafts, and practical training.

(Alaska Native Knowledge Network website)

In Hawai'i, the science curriculum is currently being developed for children who attend the Hawaiian language immersion schools and the Hawaiian culture-based charter schools and even some public schools are being introduced to the *Ahupua'a* curriculum. There are a number of different versions of the curriculum designed by teachers of younger as well as older children and young adults. One of these curricula describes the *ahupua'a* in this way:

Traditional Hawaiian culture was tied strongly to the natural landscape. The *Ahupua'a* system embodies the Hawaiians' holistic view of the world that incorporated all things from the ocean (*makai*) to the mountain tops (*mauka*). The *ahupua'a* is a traditional land unit, often a wedge-shaped section of land, that formed an economic and social unit that effectively integrated the uses of resources from dispersed ecological zones.

(*Malama I Ka'aina: Caring for the land and its resources*, http://kauila.k12.hi.us/~ahupuaa/)

The ecological aspects of the curriculum are expressed in this view of the *ahupua'a*:

The *ahupua'a* is also good for the land. Because the system is thought of as a whole, the connections between activities in one area and another will be taken under consideration when any resources from any one area are harvested or developed. Several ecological consequences (erosion, over-exploitation, etc.) are much less likely to occur when the entire ecosystem is cared for as one.

(*Life in early Hawai'i: The ahupua'a*, 1994)

The inclusion of a Hawaiian perspective in science classes is particularly significant because native cultures are often described as "unscientific" and indigenous knowledge systems are often dismissed as less valid than Western scientific classification systems. It is important to point out that ethno-botany, which includes therapeutic and medicinal uses for native plants, is also taught at the University of Hawai'i. The University of Hawai'i also offers a certificate in complementary and alternative medicine, a growing field that is a natural extension for students who have been introduced to native plants and Hawaiian healing practices at an early age.

The Kūpuna Program

One of the most important Hawaiian culture-based experiences for elementary school children in Hawai'i is the *Kūpuna* Program. "It is the *kūpuna* who can convey a sense of continuity in family structure and a knowledge of and pride in the Hawaiian cultural heritage" (Pukui *et al.*, 1972, p. 131). The *kūpuna* or elders visit schools and introduce the children to Hawaiian music, provide an oral history of life in Hawai'i, and explain aspects of Hawaiian cosmology. Such opportunities not only foster a sense of place but they also help to increase the students' exposure to cultural knowledge and promote a positive host culture identity for all children in Hawai'i.

The *Kūpuna* Program resulted from a constitutional mandate in 1978 that required instruction in Hawaiian culture, history, and language. When the State Department of Education was seeking to fulfill this mandate, they turned to the community and Hawaiian elders, the *kūpuna*, responded. Because of their knowledge of Hawaiian culture and practices, the elders became a crucial part of the Hawaiian studies curriculum (Thirugnanam, 1999).

Hale (2004) noted that the outcomes of the *Kūpuna* Program include Hawaiian cultural literacy, Hawaiian cultural desire and pride, cultural resiliency, and educational attainment with a strong Hawaiian ethnic identity. The outcomes are achieved through a variety of means. When *kūpuna* work in the schools, they share knowledge of Hawaiian language, knowledge of 'ohana (family) and ahupua'a (traditional land division), knowledge of elements and resources in the environment, knowledge of historic sites, knowledge of music and dance, and knowledge of folklore. Students are encouraged to learn family stories and values and appreciate native Hawaiian heritage (Hale, 2004).

Ke Kula Kaiapuni (Hawaiian Language Immersion)

The Hawaiian renaissance spurred a surge of interest in Hawaiian language courses in the public schools and at the University of Hawai'i. There was a clear recognition that language is central to culture and that the revival of the Hawaiian culture was dependent upon more people gaining facility in the Hawaiian language. At the same time there was a painful recognition that human linguistic resources were aging and passing away at an alarming rate. The 1986 reversal of the 1896 policy that prohibited the use of the Hawaiian language in public schools has steadily grown into a movement among Native Hawaiians as well as non-Hawaiians to study host culture language and culture (Kahumoko, 2000).

The 1978 constitutional amendment that inspired the *Kūpuna* Program also established Hawaiian, along with English, as an official language of the state but it took almost another decade before the restriction against using Hawaiian in public schools was removed. In 1987 the State Board of Education established a Hawaiian language immersion pilot program for children up to grade two. The legislative mandate that created the program was the result of lobbying by parents and Hawaiian language educators who were dedicated to the preservation and perpetuation of the Hawaiian language and culture (Slaughter, 1997). By 1992 the *Ke Kula Kaiapuni* had expanded to include kindergarten through to grade twelve with one hour of English instruction a day at each grade level beginning in grade five (history of *Ke Kula Kaiapuni*, www.k12.hi.us/~kaiapuni/history.html).

Part of the impetus to create a language immersion program came from the Maori of Aotearoa (New Zealand) who challenged Hawaiians to revive their culture through reviving their language. Since that time individuals from Hawai'i and New Zealand have worked together closely to provide mutual moral and technical support and move the goal of native language acquisition forward. In the early stages of the Hawaiian immersion program, techniques for native language acquisition were borrowed not only from Aotearoa, but also from the Navajos of the southwest U.S. and from the Mohawks of Canada (Bowman, 1989).

The initial language effort began at the pre-school level with the *Pūnana Leo* (language nest) pre-school on the island of Kauai in 1984. At the time it was started, Larry Kimura, a Hawaiian language professor at the University of Hawai'i, estimated that there were only about 1,000 native speakers of Hawaiian remaining in Hawai'i (Bowman, 1989). Some federal funding under the Native Hawaiian Education Act has provided assistance in developing more *Pūnana Leo* throughout the state.

Educators in Hawai'i stress the need for more and better Hawaiian language materials (DOE language and culture specialist. Since no Hawaiian language texts had been printed since the nineteenth century, parents whose children attended immersion schools spent hours creating materials for their children to read. It was a painstaking task. Materials written in Hawaiian from the archives are gradually being translated to English or used as original text. Other important resources, like the forty Hawaiian language newspapers from the 1800s (up to 1940), are making their way onto the web both in the original Hawaiian and in English translation and are serving as source materials for students. Since these materials were originally written in Hawaiian they are more reflective of a Hawaiian world view than the materials translated from English.

The creation of reading materials leads to other dilemmas such as vocabulary. There is a need to create words for things that did not exist at the time that Hawaiian was the only language of the islands. This raises questions of who decides and what process of vocabulary standardization needs to be created. This in turn raises a different sort of concern about the "over-standardization" of Hawaiian language. Is the essential variety of terms and expressions that is characteristic of all languages endangered through a process of linguistic reductionism? Some teacher educators express concerns in this area (K. Krug, personal communication).

Then there is the issue of teacher preparation. Who will teach the children? Finding teachers with both linguistic competence and teacher certification is a continuing challenge for the *Kula Kaiapuni*. The University of Hawai'i is developing teacher preparation programs to address the teacher shortage in immersion and Hawaiian culture-based charter schools but the need is greater than the system can accommodate.

Character Education Programs

Children in public schools who do not attend immersion programs or culture-based schools have access to Hawaiian culture through other programs in their schools. One of these may be through character education.

In 1997 the state Board of Education of Hawai'i adopted a character education policy that stated that character education must be incorporated into the curriculum at each grade level in the public schools (Policy No. 2101). While specific guidelines regarding content and implementation were left up to individual schools and communities, the policy is clear that it was to be a joint effort among parents, community, students, staff, and administrators and improvements in student conduct would be a good indicator of success of the program.

Some public schools adopted character education programs that are based on Native Hawaiian values and use Hawaiian terms to help students build community and develop compassion, and a sense of connectedness. What is particularly remarkable about such programs is that, in some instances, students who are not Native Hawaiians are taught by teachers who are not Native Hawaiians through host culture values.

One example of this sort of model is called *'ohana* (family) management. The four pillars of the program are *Kupa'a*, the goal of working together towards a common goal, *Malama*, a conscious awareness to take care of oneself, others, and objects (including the land), *Kuleana*, knowing your responsibilities as a member of the *'ohana* (family), and *Laulima*, the act of cooperating as an *'ohana*. In one public elementary school, all members of the school community, including the parents, teachers, and students, no matter what their ethnic or cultural background, learned the Hawaiian terminology, the chants, the protocols, and the values of the *'ohana* system. The focus was intrapersonal and interpersonal growth and mindfulness. This school community's choice to adopt a character education program that was based in host culture values is significant and underscores the importance of developing a Hawaiian sense of place.

All of the Department of Education courses and programs discussed in this chapter can look to a remarkable new document that was published by the Native Hawaiian Education Council (2002). *Nā Honua Mauli Ola: Hawai'i Guidelines for Culturally Healthy and Responsive Learning Environments* is based on the Alaska Standards for Culturally Responsive Schools. The Hawai'i guidelines have an important role in strengthening the commitment to revitalizing Hawaiian language and culture. The document has separate sections that speak to five overlapping groups who have a role to play in the education of children: learners, educators, schools and institutions, families, and communities. The College of Hawaiian Language at the Hilo campus of the University of Hawai'i, which offers a master's degree in Hawaiian language, was a partner in the development of the guidelines. The statewide Native Hawaiian Education Council, made up of volunteers from seven island subsidiary councils, Hawaiian organizations, educational institutions, and community groups formally adopted the guidelines in 2002. They are now available to all schools and organizations in the state that are concerned with creating culturally healthy and responsive learning environments. This document is a key for fostering cultural sustainability because it provides a framework for culturally appropriate teaching and learning.

Analysis and Conclusion: For Better or for Worse

This final section of the chapter considers the scope of programs and curricula that are based on Hawaiian language, culture, and ways of knowing. It raises questions concerning the extent to which culture is being sustained, re-invented, or appropriated. It underscores the vital re-emergence of Hawaiian identity, but also wonders who has claim to this identity and the knowledge that underpins it. Finally, it suggests that globalization, a process that is often equated with Westernization and "Macdonaldization" can actually offer opportunities to look more carefully and deeply at indigenous cultures and understand how local knowledge can offer important insights about global sustainability.

One issue that is central to the question of cultural sustainability is about who is making choices about what aspects of the culture are preserved and who has control over how the culture is represented to the larger global community. If the cultural capital of any group is manipulated by people who are not members of that group, there are bound to be problems with representation. It becomes easy to abbreviate complex cultural systems into a stereotype.

In her dissertation "The Hawaiian of Old: Representation of Native Hawaiians in the Elementary Curriculum," Thirugnanam (1999) pointed to the inclusionary efforts by dominant groups that actually mask continuing patterns of marginalization. She was concerned that the *Kūpuna* Program, for example, actually creates a group of "cultural laborers" whose status in the classroom as part-time teachers relegates them to the margin. Thirugnanam (1999) was also concerned that they were exploited by the schools to serve the school's ends rather than respected and valued for the cultural perspective and knowledge that they could share. She also cited work by Smith (1990) that critiqued policies surrounding the representation of the New Zealand Maori culture that are defined and initiated by non-Maoris, placing the control of Maori culture and images in the hands of non-Maoris. Both Thirugnanam (1999) and Smith (1990) argued that policies that determine the content, pedagogy, and representation of native populations should be in their own hands and that determinations by outsiders, however well intentioned, are likely to fail because they are lacking the indigenous perspective and voice.

If indigenous knowledge, as the definition at the beginning of this chapter suggests, is generally learned in non-formal education settings, tends to be orally transmitted, and is holistic in nature, how can it be adapted into a formal education setting where print culture and documentation are valued and knowledge is seen as discipline based rather than holistically constructed? Can indigenous knowledge become part of the "regular" curriculum without being relegated to peripheral status or without losing its spiritual essence? In her work on Native Hawaiian epistemology, Meyer (1998, p. 22) noted that Hawaiian descriptions of intellect, skills acquisition, learning, knowledge, and understanding have a spiritual dimension. How can this defining factor of Native Hawaiian epistemology be reconciled with a secular curriculum? These are the sorts of foundational questions that need to be addressed.

The process of deculturalization has sometimes been intentional and systematic. At other times it has been carried out unintentionally and with the most altruistic motives. The reversal of deculturalization is bound to be a painstaking and contested process, contested by outsiders who have no appreciation of indigenous knowledege systems and contested from within by individuals who support differing perspectives on Hawaiian identity, language, pedagogy, and curricula.

The range of programs and courses discussed in this chapter are indicative of a true revival of Hawaiian language and culture and re-indigenization of the curriculum. However, there is inevitable and appropriate concern among Hawaiian educators about this process. However, the publication *Nā Honua Mauli Ola: Hawai'i Guidelines for Culturally Healthy and Responsive Learning Environments* offers a framework for moving this agenda forward in culturally appropriate and responsive ways. Nevertheless, educators need to be mindful of a whole host of issues that need to be examined in the process of developing, implementing, and evaluating culturally sensitive curricula and pedagogy.

There are many reasons to argue for reversing deculturalization and for reviving cultures and languages that are fighting for existence and recognition in the face of globalization. Some of these are human rights and social justice issues like acknowledging native voices that have been silenced, reviving of ways of knowing that have been lost, and providing the opportunity for children of native heritage to affirm their identities. All of these reasons are valid. But there are other reasons that I would like to consider in the final lines of this chapter. Hawaiian culture and language in particular and indigenous cultures in general provide holistic models of sustainability. Educators need to develop sensibilities and introduce children of all heritages to ways of thinking that provide alternatives to some of the damaging practices that accompany industrialization and globalization.

A colleague tells a story of engaging a group of university students in a clean-up effort. Most of the students had graduated from the public school system but one of them was a graduate of the Hawaiian immersion program. In their clean-up efforts the students came across a praying mantis. Most of the students treated the insect roughly, but the immersion graduate rescued it and treated it with care. He gently placed it on a leaf where it was safe from the other students (M. Maglaya, personal communication). The instructor was struck by the difference in the students' sensibilities. The immersion graduate seemed to have developed a sacred sense of the natural world and an intuitive sense of interspecies connectedness. Cultural sustainability may be intimately linked to global sustainability and global sustainability might very well depend on individuals with the sensibilities embodied in this simple action by the immersion graduate.

Resources and Tools for Educators

Questions

1. Who has the right to teach and who has the right to learn? While institutionalization of traditional cultural knowledge systems increases understanding and appreciation, it also prompts questions about who has the power over what is taught and who has the right to learn. In many indigenous traditions knowledge keepers are designated individuals within the group who decide what knowledge should be shared and with whom they will share it.

2. What rights and responsibilities are attached to knowing? In current times we use knowledge to gain access to certain privileges. We place a value on some types of knowledge and devalue other types of knowledge. We sometimes limit access by patenting plants that have been used for millennia in traditional cultures for healing or nourishment. If we integrate traditional knowledge systems into the dominant curriculum, what issues of access and responsibility need to be considered?

For Further Reading

Kamahameha schools are the repository of the most comprehensive information on the education of Native Hawaiian children. They produced a journal called the *Kamehameha Journal of Early Education* from 1990 to 1995 as well as numerous studies, reports, and culturally responsive educational materials.

Pacific Resources in Education and Learning (www.prel.org). This website has a remarkable array of materials related to education in Hawai'i and the Pacific.

Pacific Regional Initiatives for the Delivery of Basic Education Project at the University of the South Pacific (www.sidsnet.org/pacific/usp/index.php/pride/).

One important example of cultural sustainability is a project called the Pride Project, which is housed at the University of the South Pacific. According to their website:

> The purpose of the project is: To expand opportunities for children and youth to acquire the values, knowledge and skills that will enable them to actively participate in the social, spiritual, economic and cultural development of their communities and to contribute positively to creating sustainable futures.

Suggestions for Educators

1. Creating a knowledge(s) web. Schools are places where particular forms of knowledge are transmitted and generated. To help educators think about the range of knowledge(s) and the many pedagogical approaches for "educating" engage them in an activity in which they create a web or concept map. Divide the larger group into smaller groups of three to five people. Give each group a large piece of paper and markers. Write the concept (KNOWLEDGE(S)) in the center of the paper and have each small group work independently to generate ideas related to this concept. After the small groups have completed their webs or concept maps, have them share them with the larger group. This activity prompts discussions about epistemology, philosophy, education, and pedagogy. It also raises important questions about access and ownership. In my experience using this exercise, I have found that educators are astonished at the range of issues that this exercise generates.

2. Interviews/Conversations. Political correctness has forced us into a form of polite conversation that avoids issues of substance. When I teach

multicultural education classes to pre-service and in-service teachers at the University of Hawai'i, I encourage them to engage in conversations that explore cultural differences and reveal aspects of culture that are often misinterpreted in school settings. For this exercise, I encourage students to interview someone of a culture that they have limited or superficial knowledge about. Insights from these conversations are shared with the class and inevitably the unique individual stories lead to deeper understanding of cultural behavior. More importantly they reveal the within-group differences. Cultural sustainability depends on understanding the complexity and nuances that underlie cultural practices.

References

Ah Nee-Benham, M. K. & Heck, R. H. (1998). *Culture and educational policy in Hawai'i: The silencing of native voices.* Mahwah, NJ: Erlbaum.

Alaska Native Knowledge Network website www.ankn.uaf.edu/, accessed July 2004.

Au, K. H. & Kawakami, A. J. (1994). Cultural congruence in instruction. In E. R. Hollins, J. E. King, & W. C. Hayman (Eds.), *Teaching diverse populations: Formulating a knowledge base* (pp. 5–24). Albany: University of New York Press.

Banks, J. A. (1998). The lives and values of researchers: Implications for educating citizens in a multicultural society. *Educational Researcher*, 27(7), 4–17.

Bowman, S. (1989). 'Language nest' revives Hawaii culture for children. *Los Angeles Times*, 5 October, p. 4 (Part V-A).

Hale, K. (2004). Honoring the host culture on the evaluation process. Unpublished masters paper, University of Hawaii at Mānoa.

Haug, K. (2004). Shallow immersion: Hawaiian schools struggle as students and staff go to charter sites. *Honolulu Star-Bulletin*, 1 August, p. 1.

Jordan, C., Tharp, R. G., & Baird-Vogt, L. (1992). 'Just open the door': Cultural compatibility and classroom rapport. In M. Saravia-Shore & S. F. Arvizu (Eds.), *Cross-cultural literacy: Ethnographies of communication in multiethnic classrooms* (pp. 3–18). New York: Garland.

Kahumoko, W. (2000). The dynamics of cultural politics and language policy in public education: The case of native Hawaiians. Dissertation, University of Hawai'i at Manoa.

Kamehameha Schools Bernice Pauahi Bishop Estate, Office of Program Evaluation and Planning (1993). *Native Hawaiian educational assessment 1993.* Honolulu, HI: Kamehameha Schools Bernice Pauahi Bishop Estate, Media and Publications Department.

Kamehameha Schools Bernice Pauahi Bishop Estate, Office of Program Evaluation and Planning (1994). *Life in early Hawaii: The ahupua'a. Life in early Hawaii: The ahupua'a* (3rd Edition). Honolulu: Kamehameha Press.

Meyer, M. A. (1998). Native Hawaiian epistemology: Sites of empowerment and resistance. *Equity and Excellence in Education*, 31(1), 22–28.

Native Hawaiian Education Council (2002). *Nā Honua Mauli Ola: Hawai'i guidelines for culturally healthy and responsive learning environments.* Hawai'i: University of Hawai'i at Hilo.

Pang, V. O. (2001). *Multicultural education: A caring-centered, reflective approach.* Boston: McGraw Hill.

Pukui, M. K., Haertig, E. E., & Lee, C. A. (1972). *Nānā I ke kumu* [*Look to the source*] (Vol. II). Honolulu, HI: Hui Hanai.

Slaughter, H. B. (1997). Indigenous language immersion in Hawai'i: A case study of *Kula Kaiapuni Hawa'ii*, an effort to save the indigenous language of Hawai'i. In R. K. Johnson & M. Swain (Eds.), *Immersion education: International perspectives* (pp. 105–129). London: Cambridge University Press.

Smith, G. H. (1990). Taha Maori: Pakeha capture. In J. Codd, R. Harker, & R. Nash (Eds.), *Political issues in New Zealand education.* Palmerston North, New Zealand: The Dunmore Press.

Smith, L. T. (1999). *Decolonizing methodologies: Research and indigenous peoples.* London: Zed Books.

Spring, J. (2001). *Deculturalization and the struggle for equality.* New York: McGraw-Hill.

Superintendent's Report (2004). State of Hawaii Department of Education, Systems Accountability Office, http://arch.k12.hi.us/state/superintendent%report/sar2004.html.

Tamura, E. H. (1994). *Americanization, acculturation, and ethnic identity: The Nisei generation in Hawai'i.* Urbana, IL: University of Illinois Press.

Thaman, K. H. (2004). Whose values and what responsibility?: Cultural and cognitive democracy in education. Keynote address, Pacific Circle Consortium Conference, April 21–24, Hong Kong, SAR.

Thirugnanam, J. K. (1999). The Hawaiians of old: Representations of Native Hawaiians in the elementary curriculum. Dissertation, University of Hawaii.

CHAPTER 13

The Land is the First Teacher: The Indigenous Knowledge Instructors' Program

CELIA HAIG-BROWN AND KAAREN DANNENMANN

Let us start with the stories. First the legend of the White Man: Trout Lake is located 20 air miles from Red Lake and its coordinates are 51°51″ N and 90°15″ W . . . The water depth of Trout Lake at its deepest is 150 feet . . . The lake lies within the Precambrian Shield and is classified as oligotrophic.

The true story of Namekosipiink is alive and documented in the oral stories and daily practices of her people, the NamekosipiiwAnishinaapek. It is etched on her rocky shores and sandy beaches, on Pinesiwachiink (the ridge that defines her western shore), on the land surrounding the lake with its swamps, hills, and rivers, and on her islands, reefs, and waters.

Namekosipiink: a lake where every day muskrat, otter, and beaver re-enact the dives of the creation story. It is a lake full of gifts where trout, pike, and pickerel swim the deep cold waters and grow big and strong.

Namekosipiink: a lake where first nations women set their nets and their traps just as their aunts and sisters, recent and distant, have done for generations. When they trap a descendant of that first muskrat, they carefully remove the little hands and put them gently back into the lake in honor of the muskrat's sacrifice for creation. They carefully remove the knee-bones as well and return these to the water. They skin the animal and cure its hide for sale or for use on mitts or moccasins. The meat is roasted and the bones gnawed clean and returned to the water. Every gift that an animal gives us is taken and not wasted.

What you are about to read is a study of a community-based education program, the Indigenous Knowledge Instructors' Program. The program prepares aboriginal people who have some traditional knowledge for passing that knowledge on to others. It also provides opportunity for the prospective instructors to literally remember[1] their own knowledge through using it in everyday living and interactions with others. Historical circumstances and changing life styles have often reduced occasions for such activity. With its central focus on a pedagogy of the land, the program design takes a grounded context seriously and an understanding that land and situatedness refer to much more than a material place as defined by legal documents, geological surveys, or points on a map. Ultimately, the innovation of this course of study draws on very old pedagogies by never losing sight of the land as the first teacher. As these old pedagogies are recreated in contemporary context, they lose nothing of their salience and promise new ways to think about participatory community-based education.

The Land as the First Teacher

In current theory, in early childhood education arising out of schools in Reggio Emilia, Italy, the environment is called "the third teacher."[2] This acknowledgment of the tremendous significance of the space in which teaching and learning take place is a welcome addition to curriculum theorizing. In the Indigenous Knowledge Instructors Program, we claim that the land is the first teacher: the use of "first" gestures to the primacy of groundedness in all our learning relations. These include historical connections, indeed connections from time before memory, among indigenous peoples of an area and the earth, air, and water with which they (all of us) interact as well as current connections whereby all knowledge is (re)-cognized[3] as having foundations in and ties to material reality. Even in the depths of the most modern city, we pay attention to and are affected by weather, diverted and abused streams and rivers break their bounds at inopportune moments, and earthquakes and tsunamis rock our deepest assumptions of permanence.

In the Americas, indigenous peoples have lived for generations in good relation (see Hodgson-Smith (1997) for an explication of this notion) with the land in all its complexity. They have known how to listen to the lessons the land is teaching and how to respond in ways that affirm what they have learned. They have taught these lessons to each other down the generations. The conception of land, in relation to which such learning takes place, goes beyond a simple material understanding to the spiritual where lines between animate and inanimate, animal and human, and spirit and material are consciously and deliberately blurred. Such dualities themselves distort the conceptualizations expressed in indigenous languages that embrace complex interconnections, where verbs are the foundation on which all other syntactical and lexical forms depend and where all the world is in motion. This elaborate notion of land encompasses an understanding of interrelationships and subjectivities beyond the human: for example, a river or lake may rejoice or suffer with the actions of those around it. This seemingly idyllic but ultimately very practical relation to land (and air and water along with all that dwell in, under, and on) has too often been ignored by the current nation states of North America. Capitalism-driven colonization arising with the Industrial Revolution in Europe insisted on importing to the Americas incompatible ways of relating to land and resources as entities somehow separate from other life forms, especially human beings.

Rather than concern for future generations—a traditional, guiding principle in many first nations cultures—instant gratification in the form of bottom line profit has become the agenda for many people who currently occupy the Americas. Kaaren's brother, Okimaawikaapow, paraphrasing Squamish leader Sealth, expressed his worries about this approach:

> Whatever befalls the earth befalls the sons of the earth. If men spit upon the earth, they spit upon themselves. Contaminate your bed and you will suffocate in your own waste . . . If you take this forest, please keep a part of it sacred for our children and please teach them that the ground beneath their feet is the ashes of their grandfathers.
>
> (From a letter written in spring 1998 in Kaaren's possession)

How is it that the agenda of resource-hungry business people prevailed? Why were the original people unable to interrupt the ways of those who came first as guests to their lands and then stayed to take possession? The Huron philosopher Sioui (1992) argued that microbes played a significant role:

> The key idea is that, had it not been for the European advantage created by the diseases that the newcomers imported in spite of themselves, the Native peoples would have had a chance to absorb the ideological and political shock, which would been far less powerful.
>
> (p. 3)

Once the power of European ideology was given this advantage, the intensity of the assault on indigenous cultures increased. Institutionalized schooling was one of the most potent of the weapons in efforts to assimilate and eventually annihilate what were assumed to be vanishing cultures. Deputy Superintendent General of Indian Affairs Duncan Campbell Scott's 1920 statement represents this view: "Our object is to continue until there is not a single Indian in Canada that has not been absorbed into the body politic and there is no Indian question and no Indian department . . ." (Haig-Brown, 1988, p. 32). The persistence and resilience of aboriginal peoples in Canada has proven otherwise. The Indigenous Knowledge Instructors Program is one attempt to acknowledge the historical assumptions and assaults on indigenous knowledge and to contribute to re-establishing its place in contemporary life. As we take seriously what it means to see the land as the first teacher, we work to redress this historic and misguided shift in relations among human beings and all other forms. We work towards a pedagogy of the land where teachings are never merely didactic, but most often expressed in a relation. The tensions of such work are revealed in the following comment on divergent pedagogies in an interaction with one of the program participants and her knowledgeable mother who was raised on the land:

> I don't know what the dynamics are that are different but then when I am with her alone, I can see her memories coming back. She'll look at something and she'll work away towards something that we used to do. And when she shows me, her terminology—she'll speak her language for one thing—and then she talks in terms of "This is the way I saw my grandfather do it" or "This is the way it was shown to me." It is never in terms of "Do it this way," or "Do it that way."
>
> (K. D. review meeting, September 27, 1999, 47/64)[5]

What is Indigenous Knowledge Anyway?

Central to the program described and analysed here is indigenous knowledge. Indigenous knowledge is situated knowledge that arises out of a relation with land, i.e. a very particular place. In our work, we build on the following definitions: "1) born or produced naturally in a land or region; native *to* (the soil, region, etc.). b. Inborn, innate. 2. Native" (adapted from Hughes, 2003, p. 11). Although the term has been used in ever expanding ways as it has become a part of popular academic discourse, for our purposes it is inextricable from the complex relation that people of aboriginal ancestry have had with specific lands as the source of all life and all learning and teaching. It is knowledge that has been refined over the years and down the generations. As Kaaren stated in one interview, "Traditional knowledge is all about relationships" (March 2000). It moves beyond a merely physical relation to a spirituality that draws on those innumerable generations of thinking with and through the relation.

The Program Design

The Indigenous Knowledge Instructors Program is an educational and community-building program designed to provide participants with opportunities for learning, remembering, and using indigenous knowledge in its original context. As one of the program designers commented in a planning meeting, "True knowledge is in the use of it. It is so much more than simply being able to articulate it or analyze it." Indigenous knowledge integrates spiritual, intellectual, emotional, and physical ways of thinking and being. Use of the Anishinaape language (Anishinaapemowin) is a fundamental dimension of the program. The program is very small with no more than five students enrolled per session. Environmental impact is one of the concerns and the other is to ensure that each person has maximum opportunity to interact with the land and the other students and teachers.

Students focus on four interrelated aspects of the program. Participation provides the following opportunities.

1. To learn and relearn indigenous knowledge on the land by remembering and building on existing knowledge and/or new learning from the program.
2. To use indigenous knowledge in work and play with others in a supportive context.
3. To learn and/or strengthen use of Anishinaapemowin.
4. To develop appropriate abilities, skills, and knowledge to pass on indigenous teachings to others who have less knowledge. These may be adults, children, or other family members. The teaching and learning may occur in institutionalized (school) or informal (home or community) contexts.

The program, leading to joint certification by the Assembly of First Nations and York University, is made up of three courses: level 1 comprising indigenous knowledge (in the first summer) and working with indigenous knowledge, a practicum (in the intervening seasons) and level 2 comprising indigenous knowledge (in a second summer). Students may choose one of two options for the program. Those who want to use and develop their own knowledge may opt to come for one or more summers. Those who are interested in becoming teachers of indigenous knowledge and who are seeking certification participate in two consecutive summers and an intervening practicum. Practicum times are negotiable with students on an individual basis.

Four people serve as teachers and facilitators for the courses. One of the original designers and co-author of this chapter Kaaren Dannenmann serves as the site coordinator and the heart of the program. As a student said

> We are lucky to have people like Kaaren who open their doors up for us to be able to see what the whole world's about. Not just making money and not just doing things as fast as you can . . . She puts us right into where she was born and raised and into the things she holds most deep in her heart
>
> (A. H. October 2001, 25/29)

Kaaren is responsible for ensuring that the process and content of the courses in the summer remain true to the original intent of providing space for the enactment of indigenous knowledge as well as all the logistics of the program from recruitment to food delivery. Celia serves as the University of York coordinator in charge of the practicum component and continues to work closely with Kaaren on the details of program planning, review, and revision. The practicum student plans and executes an appropriate activity and Celia assesses its success. During the summer course, two other teachers are present: one is a knowledge keeper who has extensive expertise in and experience with indigenous knowledge, is fluent in the language, and who may be considered an elder,[6] while the other, called the facilitator, is a qualified Ontario public school teacher who leads the daily sharing circles described below. All who participate in the summer course are of first nations ancestry.

What do the courses themselves look like? Indigenous knowledge level 1 consists of ten days of actively living on the land in respectful ways, i.e. ways that reflect the values and methods of the original peoples passed through oral tradition. The indigenous knowledge keeper, the site coordinator, and the facilitator guide students in opportunities to learn, express, and use what they know and to consider the pedagogical implications of what they have been doing. Using Anishnaapemowin as much as possible, students work on the land and waters of Namekosipiink where they engage in traditional pedagogical events. That is, they live and learn through watching and doing and through working with one another to literally remember the knowledge that each holds in relation to this activity and this land or another piece of land with which they are more familiar. They may fish and hunt, working with the catch in ways that indicate full appreciation of traditional approaches such as using all parts of the animal and performing appropriate ceremonies. They clean, prepare, and cook what is caught. They may build traditional structures such as a sweat lodge or a waakinokaan for sleeping.

The planning itself provided a time of remembering knowledge as the teachers debated and discussed various ways of conducting sweats with which they had been involved. The number of rocks, the use of various plants for particular purposes, the wood for the frame and for the ceremony itself, the number of rounds to be made, and the teachings during the ceremony were all points of intense discussion and thought. Other possible activities for the students included gathering traditional local plants and identifying their uses, drum making, basket making, and gathering wild rice. The possibilities are as endless as the landscape and as variable as circumstance. As someone commented in the planning meeting, "If the caribou swim, then that's going to change the curriculum and if they don't swim, you've got to have some alternatives." This comment refers to the occasional occurrence of spotting caribou swimming in the lake during the summer.

Once a day all involved come together in circle work (see, for example, Graveline, 1994) to talk through what they have learned, what they are thinking about this learning, and what they want to try to do next. This teaching may be planned with other people who have less knowledge than they do. They may also strategize about negotiating the limits to teaching indigenous knowledge such as those imposed by people who are threatened by it or those who devalue it as a lesser form of knowledge lacking the currency of Euro-/Amerocentric positivism and its so-called technological "advances." They may strategize about convincing band education authorities to fund such work for their band members, about not worrying particular Christian members of their communities who see the devil's work tied up in traditional language and spiritual practices,[7] and about not being seen to be doing subversive work designed to promote militancy for its own sake.

Following the first ten-day session, during the seasons between the summers students complete a practicum called "Working with Indigenous Knowledge." The student teachers choose a context and develop a set of lesson plans to work with others who have less experience with indigenous knowledge than they do. Their teaching is to be at least 40 hours in an educational context of their choosing. The practicum may be with adults or children in institutionalized school, informal community, or extra-curricular situations. The student teachers may work in the city with aboriginal street people. They may work in a literacy program in a northern community. They may bring aboriginal adolescents to this site for a winter camp of their own. The practicum is graded pass or fail based on a written or oral plan, the delivery of the lessons, and a final report and/or interview regarding the work.

For those interested in certification, their final session, indigenous knowledge level 2, is a continuation of level 1. In a second ten-day session, students have the opportunity to review and discuss what happens to knowledge as it is taken up in different contexts. In this second summer of their program (which may or may not be consecutive), students continue to engage in active living on the land. They work with other students in both level 1 and level 2 to continue to expand on their own knowledge.

The Students

The students we want to attract to the program are indigenous knowledge keepers who want to use and share their knowledge with others. Some plan to work with children, some with adults and some are rurally based and some urban based. The participants are self-identified first nations people who have "some traditional knowledge" and "some fluency with the language." In this case, "the" language is Aniishinaapemowin but there is considerable flexibility in this regard and really any first nations language is fine. Aboriginal people from any nation or community are welcome to apply. Although the program takes place in Anishinaape territory, other knowledges are relevant to the work. We remain very conscious of the sensitivity of the issue of knowing language since many well-intentioned assimilative teachers found it one of the more obvious and, therefore, easily attacked aspects of first nations cultures. At the same time, for this iteration of the program, we do want to work with people who have some experience of working with and living with indigenous knowledge. Following the first course offering, we integrated an interview into the admission process to address this concern.

Everyone who comes to the program comes as a student to continue their learning from the land and to learn from each other. In the Freirian sense, all the teachers are students and all the students are teachers. As Kaaren acknowledged during a planning meeting, "I think the students will understand that; they understand that excellently. It's those of us who have gone through the [school] system that have difficulty believing that we really learn from each other." All expect to build on and use what they know. To date, the participants have included a language teacher from the local high school, a resident of a nearby town, an elder from a southern community, a former assembly line worker changing careers to work in aboriginal counseling, a doctoral student from the Delaware Nation (working as research assistant as well), an elementary teacher, a community activist, and many family members from elders to young children.

What People Say about the Courses

The program ran for three summers from 1999 to 2001 as a pilot with about four students each year. In interviews and in meetings before and after the courses, the people involved reflected on their involvement. Blumer (1969) pointed out in his work on symbolic interactionism that meaning is derived from the social interactions that one has with other people. Such meaning is modified through an interpretive process used by the person in dealing with the things encountered (Blumer, 1969, p. 2). What you read is not "the" reality of the program but rather the impressions people were left with, always already filtered through their histories and current concerns. Within these meanings lie possibilities for further reflection and action related to teaching, using, and remembering indigenous knowledge in this and other contexts.

One student who grew up spending time on the land on a lake relatively close to Namekosipiink talked first of that experience, memories of which flooded back to her as she participated in the course. Her reflections encapsulate a precise fulfillment of the intentions of the program design. In her interview she said:

> I remember the time before I went to school really well because we did so many things. Every spring, we would go out spring trapping.

Everybody would move with their dog teams—because at that time when I was growing up, we didn't have snow machines. So everybody went with their dog teams and put their little canoes on [the sleds] and away we would go to some mouth of a river where it opens earlier. We'd go spring trapping and we would be living in either little cabins or tents in springtime till the ice would go away and then we would come back to the village again.

(M. L. interview March 20, 2000, 2/24)

Referring to the moment when her office decided to send her to the program as "a dream come true," she went on to compare her early life experience to her time in the program. Here was an opportunity to use knowledge that had long been lying dormant:

When I got to the Indigenous Knowledge Instructors Program course at Trout Lake, I just loved it. It just reminded me so much of home and all the things we did there, like setting a net and going canoeing and just learning about different things.

(18/24)

Although this comment does fit with what was hoped for in terms of program design, in a review of the first offering, during a meeting held in the fall of 1997, one person commented, "I thought it went totally not the way we expected." Indeed, there were a few surprises as there have been each time the course has been offered. For example, in the initial iteration, we had not planned on students bringing family members with them. We have since recognized that traditionally age group does not separate students from one another and that this is a most appropriate way for the course to proceed. We remember as the course unfolds. One student gave her thoughts on traditional learning: "The Native way of teaching is so different from in the white society . . . In the Native way, you are just learning right beside the person who is teaching you rather than being told or being taught verbally." She continued, "When I was growing up it was more or less, like you'd go with a person and from what their actions and what they're doing, that's how you learn." The issue of what constituted a qualified student based in the experience of the first year led us to revise the admission procedures to include an interview to determine people's level of expertise with using indigenous knowledge.

At the same time, much of what was anticipated did happen. One student noted, "There was a really strong sense of everybody learning at once." Pointing to the importance of orality in this learning, she went on to say, "Some people clearly knew more than others. When they were talking, you listened extra closely because of the things they wouldn't say outright but that they knew and that would come out when we were talking and in the way they were talking." Students (and teachers) went fishing and hunting. Duck soup and lots of freshly caught fish were part of daily menus. Crispy fried pickerel fins reminded one student of potato chips "only better." People compared modes of preparation and cooking. One person with considerable knowledge said:

> There were parts of the fish that I've never eaten before, like the air sacs. I don't remember how we prepared them. I think it was over the fire. Anyway they were amazingly good. The actual filleting of the fish we all did different ways and that was kind of neat.
>
> (K. D. March 25, 2000, 35/36)

People worked together to use knowledge that for most had been submerged for a long time. Preparing a partridge became the focus of two participants working to externalize common but deeply buried knowledge. When one form of preparation included singeing the partridge which most other participants had not seen done before, one person said of another, "It seemed like it was familiar: when one student was doing that [singeing], it was like this memory came back to the other." This work of remembering together the knowledge which had not been used for a long time is painful work. For years, governments and churches worked in a way that devalued much of this knowledge as Christianizing (creating regular church goers) and civilizing (creating farmers or laborers) nearly always interrupted living on the land especially when it involved movement. As a result of this and the removal of children from their homes to attend institutionalized schooling, only a few people still have the knowledge. One of the participants talked of the impact of residential school on her knowledge of both the language and other aspects of living with her parents:

> You know, all of a sudden, I was losing my language and there were sometimes people laughing at me because of the way I was saying things: I wasn't saying things the proper way. We weren't even allowed to speak our language at school. And certain things, especially life skills was where I had problems . . . . I don't want to use the word "stupid" but my knowledge of life skills was so limited because we never did those things at the school. I remember one time pulling the canoe through the portage and I was so clumsy I almost fell between the rocks. And shooting the rapids, I mean these things were so rusted that I couldn't even do these things.
>
> (M. L. March 20, 2000, 9/24)

For those who have never acquired the knowledge or who have lost it for one reason or another, there is often a sense of failure or coming up short. How can one claim indigeneity and have no connection to using traditional knowledge when "true knowledge is in the use of it?" Although such an essentialist view does not do justice to the complexities of aboriginal people's roles and place in the world today, for those who do choose to take up connections to tradition, the way there is often very difficult. Aggravated by non-aboriginal people's stereotypes of "Indians" as people who innately have such knowledge, the absence or "rustiness" of knowledge referred to above becomes a catch 22. If one has the knowledge and uses it, they may be seen as unsophisticated by non-aboriginal people and treated with disrespect. In reviewing the summer course, one of the students talked of a person who had extensive knowledge who seemed to hesitate to contribute. "At one point, she wouldn't participate and we asked her why. She said because I never went to school. It was like she felt inadequate." Over time, as this person saw the other students' level of interest and desire to learn from her, "It was phenomenal the stories she told when she felt she was being appreciated. She opened up."

When one does not have this knowledge, aboriginal people may be dismissive of attempts to learn and non-aboriginal people rarely have the sensitivity to understand the devastating historical circumstances that have led to this absence. At a recent meeting about a related program for youth, one of the non-aboriginal people reacted in surprise when she realized that aboriginal teenagers based in small northern towns might have as little or even less knowledge of traditions than wealthy city kids of comparable age. Even simple things such as chopping kindling can become the focus of feelings of inadequacy. The course provided opportunities for people to revive these skills always in the context of an epistemology that moves the actions beyond mere skills and embeds them in a value system of respect for all things animate and inanimate in the surrounding context. Reviving old trails becomes an oral history lesson and a reclaiming of traditional place on the land. "We all trekked up the trail and everybody was involved. Everybody did something ... We had different people with different skills and we could accomplish things." Frequently people talked of the importance of working to use every part of an animal and treating a carcass with respect. Traditionally,

> food was basically meat and fat and the people ate most of the carcasses, thus deriving all the nutritional value. The other parts of the carcasses were also used: bones for tools and decoration and craft; hair of moose, deer and caribou for mattresses; sinew for sewing, etc.
>
> (K. Dannenmann, unpublished)

Navigating the lake, through reefs and around the islands, refamiliarized community members with knowledge they had worked with at some point in their lives and returned them to that place as one with their ancestors. With the developing security of this knowledge, the participants prepared to teach others with less knowledge and experience than they had. When asked whether she thought the course had gone well, one participant responded positively:

> There are so many people out there who know really important things that are not considered important by many others. For the sake of the welfare and health of their communities, things need to be done in a different way. Why not do it in a different way that has been done for thousands of years? . . . It's the kind of knowledge that seems to be the only successful one. I think that it's very important to give people space to come together and to validate themselves by knowing that there are other people out there who are thinking and feeling the same way and have the same kinds of hopes and struggles. Then to collectively say how are we going to go about getting the information out there . . . Most people don't know that there is an alternative.
>
> (K. S. January 25, 2001, 22/25)

In the sharing circles, the teacher facilitated discussion of the process of the course itself as well as the implications of doing similar work in different contexts. One student commented:

> The circles were very effective. People participated very well and listened very well and took it very seriously to the point where there was some giving of personal information that really, really made the group cohesive. People didn't necessarily have to work that hard but I felt that it was coming from their hearts and they wanted to do that. It was good, you know.
>
> (D. W. June 26, 2001, 12/39)

He went on to describe the content of the circles: planning the days and "polling everyone to give their ideas about what they wanted to do." He had a specific wish to set a net by himself, which didn't work out during the course, partly due to weather conditions. He actually took the time to return to the site to set the net a few weeks later. Another participant talked of the daily circles where they would pray, have a cleansing ceremony (smudge), and plan the day. These often moved into sharing circles where people talked out their feelings of working with indigenous knowledge—feelings of inadequacy, feelings of pride and accomplishment, and feelings of responsibility. On a couple of occasions, they were used specifically for strategizing the future work of teaching indigenous knowledge. This involved negotiating:

> various kinds of obstacles: some of them are religious; some are administrative; some are ideological. The kinds of things that arise with traditional knowledge being a marginal thing in dominant

society that doesn't really share the perspective. How do you introduce programs and practices like this in a society that doesn't have room for them, doesn't know how to incorporate them, might even be hostile to them?

(L. M. September 7, 2000, 8/27)

In follow-up work, the students addressed these concerns as they developed plans for work in other contexts. In an interview, one student talked through some of the complexities of wanting to work with a group of adolescents who were having trouble with school. Ultimately, he wanted to work with students in:

> setting up some log cabins, getting these kids to help me build them and make a little trapline. Not with a view to trapping animals as such, or making money off them or anything like that, but going back to the land, and re-learning some of this stuff and trying to make them in the end better human beings . . . It would give them a feeling of who they are.

Further to that, he worried about some parents' support for such work, "because they would say, oh yeah, he's doing that because he wants to convert them to Native spirituality . . . . It's the local Church people. They've had two hundred years of missionary work and they're not so willing to go back to witchcraft as they call it." Despite these obstacles he is determined to do this work with people committed to indigenous knowledge. He cited the old people as the inspiration for hope.

> Some of the old teachers said that the young ones will take this [knowledge] and they will either bring it back or it will be gone forever. But if they bring it back, it will be quite open and it will be interesting to see how they interpret it, how different it will be. They will take it and run with it. [This distinction] is based on when I was growing up and what's happening now. Like sweatlodge is an example. The young people want to sweat twice a week. We were lucky to sweat once a year. And nobody knew about it. It was out of sight, in the swamp. So it's interesting how much of a journey the sweatlodge has made—the journey from the swamp to my front lawn.

(D. W. June 26, 2001, 21/39)

This comment is accompanied by lots of laughter, a satisfying kind of laugh.

Another student took a group of first nations students for a very successful winter camp at Namekosipiink. Their learning began before the trip started with plans for what to take and how to get to the site of the camp. With the lake frozen, the three snowmobiles provided partial transportation. The students took turns walking and riding. Once there, they were responsible for making the fire, chopping the water hole and getting water, and cleaning and disposing of wastewater. They skied and snowshoed, set snares (no luck), went ice fishing (successfully), and generally had an immersion in pedagogy of the land in winter. They watched the teacher skin a marten that she had trapped and heard a discussion between two of the teachers (both participants in the Indigenous Knowledge Instructors Program) about different ways to skin it. They saw how the teacher treated the carcass with respect, returning it to the land in a gentle way. Most importantly, when they all came to school the day after the trip, "They were all smiles. They all had a really good time." (M. L. January 2000, 12/12, interviewed by Kaaren). They began a process of working with indigenous knowledge that can be built on when the next occasion arises.

Coming Full Circle

In his work *For An Amerindian Autohistory: An Essay on the Foundations of a Social Ethic* Sioui (1992) outlined Native American values in the Sacred Circle of Life as the basis of his arguments for reconceptualizing history. His words resonate with the underlying principles of the Indigenous Knowledge Instructors Program. He wrote:

> Put simply, the Amerindian genius, acknowledging as it does the universal interdependence of all beings, physical and spiritual, tries by every available means to establish intellectual and emotional contact between them, so as to guarantee them—for they are all "relatives"— abundance, equality, and, therefore, peace. This is the sacred circle of life, which is opposed to the [social] evolutionist conception of the world wherein beings are unequal, and are often negated, jostled, and made obsolete by others who seem adapted to evolution.
>
> (Sioui, 1992, p. xxi, author's addition)

He argued that the future lies in what he called the continuing Americization of the settlers and other immigrants to this continent. Through this process, Amerindian values will assume their rightful place in the everyday consciousness and activity of the people who dwell here.[7] None of this position argues for a return to the "old ways." Rather, the re-creation of indigenous knowledge in contemporary context is the inevitable outcome. What does it mean in the middle of a major city to take seriously notions of all our relatives? Rather than risk accusations of proposing a salvation story, we leave you, the reader, to ponder the deep complexity of such a question we might all learn to ask ourselves. The indigenous people who have been relentlessly asking this question in the face of frightening cultural assault are now seeking out spaces to strengthen, reclaim, and remember the knowledge wherein some answers lie.

One of those spaces is in the small and still fragile community-based program this chapter has presented. It has run for three years with next to no budget. The work has been allowed to proceed due to community members' dedication of their time and money along with creative research funding. And yet the program has already demonstrated its potential to accomplish its primary goals: first nations people have learned, done the painful and painstaking work of remembering, and taught one another aspects of indigenous knowledge in ways that have allowed them to imagine continuing the work. They have identified connections with others that will allow the work to continue. Throughout the time of the program planning and evaluation, meetings with various first nations organizations have produced considerable interest in related offerings and endless possibilities for such work. For example, one administrator of a larger first nations organization brightened at the idea of sending recently qualified professionals to the program. While the latter have acquired the skills and knowledge available in mainstream colleges and universities, in order to contribute respectfully in indigenous contexts, in their own communities in many cases, they need to be able to place that knowledge within traditional epistemologies, values, and world views before it can serve in good ways. The Indigenous Knowledge Instructors Program provides one way to acquire and/or build on such knowledge. The re-creation of traditional knowledge in contemporary contexts and the re-creation of EuroCanadian thought and skills in indigenous contexts are central to the mission of the program and other grounded aboriginal institutions. Seeing clearly the failure of conventional business models to create peace and justice for all community members, interest has been piqued in thinking and working through to a place where one might live in the best of both worlds.

Teachers who recognize the short shrift given aboriginal history, current issues, and the place of aboriginal people in Canada, see the program as a site to strengthen and literally ground their pedagogy. Sioui (1992) reminded us that:

> the way history is dispensed to young children—in the absence of many really suitable pedagogical tools—is one of the underlying reasons for the prejudices that keep people from respecting first themselves (for, as an instrument of power, history has cultivated feelings of guilt in people of certain cultures), and then one another (since dividing is the eternal prerequisite for conquering).
>
> (p. xxi)

First nations people living in cities who want to work with indigenous knowledge see such a program providing what they need to build on the knowledge they have garnered in other contexts. In the winter camp referred to above and in other camps held in Namekosipiink, children of all ages have been drawn into an experience where they have spent time on the land and pondered what it means to be respectful of all that it has to teach. First nations children make connections with their ancestors and their histories and prepare to continue passing knowledge down the generations. Non-aboriginal children come to a deeper understanding of the foundational nations and peoples of Canada and are introduced to the values that can heal the rifts which colonization has brought. The connections the authors have made with other community-based first nations educators working with indigenous knowledge have sparked interest in a broadly based conference where ideas on working with indigenous knowledge at the community level may be shared and thinking in the area furthered. Most practically, recognizing that funding may continue to be an issue, there is the possibility of contributing more directly to Americanization of the world, i.e bringing all people to some understanding of what it means to live respectfully—in a good way—with this land. Somewhere in the future, a very select eco-tourism could provide opportunities for non-indigenous people from other places and other continents to learn more about ways of living in good relation with the lands and waters.

In the final analysis, the Indigenous Knowledge Instructors Program serves as a model of a very old pedagogy speaking to the current context and the future. A pedagogy of the land brings material reality to the fore. Based in indigenous epistemologies, this material reality can never lose sight of its complex spiritual, historic, and futuristic possibilities. We leave you with the words of one of the participants in the Indigenous Knowledge Instructors Program. She was the facilitator of the circles and fairly new to traditional knowledge:

> I have survived the onslaught against my people and our culture. I am a survivor because I have survived the intergenerational effects of the residential school system. As I learn my people's traditional ways, I am learning my role and the sacred responsibility to keep alive and vibrant that culture and science and way of living and pass that on to the next generations. . . . I am finding this search for traditional knowledge to be very healing, physically, mentally, emotionally, and spiritually as well as healing for all my relationships. I want to make a contribution towards the healing of my community and to me this means making available to our children the sacred knowledge and customs of our foreparents.
>
> (K. S. letter June 30, 2003)

The work continues.

Acknowledgments

This research was made possible by two grants from the Social Science and Humanities Research Council of Canada. One was a network grant from The Research Network for New Approaches to Lifelong Learning, directed by Professor David Livingstone of the Ontario Institute for Studies in Education, University of Toronto and the other was my own Standard Research Grant, Protocol in Community Partnerships: Redefining Boundaries of Aboriginal/University Knowledges.

Resources and Tools for Educators

Questions

1. In many North American schools, students as future citizens are socialized into historical amnesia particularly in relation to injustices that have been perpetrated as newer nations imposed themselves on the lands of older ones. This chapter looks at the efforts of one first nation to redress this forgetfulness for themselves and for others as a way to acknowledge and build on indigenous knowledge, epistemology, and ontology. How might you as an educator begin to address similar studied forgetfulness in your own specific context? What are the benefits and detriments of such acknowledgment?

2. Competition between and among knowledges is inescapable as cultures and nations encounter one another and engage in interaction. Although this chapter may appear to be about going back to the "old ways," Urion (1999), like some of the participants in this program, tells us that indigenous knowledge is living knowledge. Is it possible to create a context that allows contesting knowledges to coexist even as they inform one another and are constantly shifting within what Homi Bhabha has called a third space? What would such understanding mean for educators, students, and policy makers thinking about nationhood?

For Further Reading

Battiste, M. & Barman, J. (Eds.) (1995) *First nations education in Canada: The circle unfolds.* Vancouver: University of British Columbia Press.

This collection of articles addresses a number of different issues of relevance to people thinking through education in first nations/aboriginal contexts. From twelve standards of "Indian Education" (Hampton) to an extensive list of resources related to first nations pedagogy (Hodgson-Smith), this text has become something of a classic in Canada with clear implications for work in other contexts.

Castellano, M. B., Davis, L., & Lahache, L. (Eds.) (2000) *Aboriginal education: Fulfilling the promise.* Vancouver: University of British Columbia Press.

Contributors to this book emphasize teaching methods, program developments, and institutional designs that respect aboriginal philosophies and current priorities. From questions of language teaching to educational policy issues and from the place of electronic classrooms to first nations-controlled universities, the chapters indicate the commitment to formal schooling from a range of perspectives to which many first nations people adhere.

Stewart-Harawira, M. (2005). *The new imperial order: Indigenous responses to globalization.* New York: Zed Books.

Chapter 1 entitled "Of Order and Being: Towards an Indigenous Global Ontology" is particularly interesting in its efforts to tack between respecting the specificities of local contexts while naming some commonalities of indigenous ontology. It could be very useful for educators who want to understand some of the current thinking in relation to indigenous knowledge as it is used in this chapter.

Activities for Educators

1. First inform yourself about the aboriginal people of the area in which you are working and the histories of formal schooling of that area. Libraries are a good place to start. Once you have done that, contact aboriginal educational leaders in your locale to see what interest they have in contributing to the ongoing work of schooling. If you are working in an aboriginal community yourself or if you are aboriginal yourself, invite community members whose voices have not been represented in recent schooling initiatives. Invite them to your classroom, staff meeting, or policy meeting as participants and/or resource people or even observers if they prefer. Follow an appropriate respectful protocol during their time with you.

2. Experiment with circle work as the format for your next meeting or class. Use Graveline's (1998) text to inform yourself of the power and process of circle work. Begin every session by acknowledging that this circle work is based loosely on a first nations model drawing on Graveline's (1998) text. You might begin from these considerations: each person who chooses to speak may do so uninterrupted, each person speaks only of their own thoughts on a topic and does not respond directly to the position of anyone else, make the number of rounds of the circle needed for everyone to express all that they have to say, allow people who do not want to speak to pass, choose a facilitator who can work calmly and respectfully with the participants to bring the group

to closure—and perhaps consensus—when the topic is exhausted, and, finally, use this approach with care and caution as it is a powerful one.

Notes

1. This term is an effort to capture the idea that such knowledge must be put back together in the new, current context out of fragments held by individuals and communities who have had their traditional ways attacked as wrong for generations. Residential schools, the reservation system, and outlawing potlatches and gatherings to address land claims are only a few of the manifestations of efforts to assimilate aboriginal people into a European-based life style.
2. There are many websites on Reggio Emilia schools. The following is one of the addresses I used to access some basic information that of course does not begin to do justice to the complexities of the schools developed there. The Cyert Center at Carnegie Mellon University has a website (www.cmu.edu/cyert-centre/) for early education with a section on the Reggio Emilia approach. An excerpt from the information available at The Hundred Languages of Children traveling exhibit is particularly helpful. This site was accessed on January 3, 2004.
3. The hyphen in this word is intended to direct the reader to the root of the word and to emphasize the significance of coming to know again both in old ways and in new ways.
4. For transcripts of interviews and meetings, I have given a page number as well as the total number of pages of the transcript. For example, 2/39 indicates that the quote is taken from the second page of a transcript of thirty-nine pages. This symbol gestures to two things: there is a physical and complete transcript of the interaction in existence and it took place over an extended period of time. Although I use very little of each transcript in a publication, I insist that it is important to transcribe the entire work in order to have access to material which, at first reading, may not seem significant, but, as the analysis proceeds, takes on meaning.
5. The term elder is one that demonstrates respect for the indigenous knowledge that a person, usually an older person, has and is capable of passing along to others. The knowledge may be in the form of oral tradition and/or expertise with language and/or living on the land using knowledge reflective of an indigenous world view. Some people are reluctant to accept such a title feeling that they are not worthy of it.
6. One of the urban participants in the course recounted her plane trip to Red Lake. She began talking with a person beside her who had some familiarity with the Indigenous Knowledge Instructors Program and had serious concerns. She recalled him saying that "the problems with Indians all start when they leave Judeo-Christianity . . . He was quite blatant in his opinion: going back to the traditional ways is simply evil. He used the word evil." She was taken aback by his comments, which she saw as "a wake up call. Whoa, you're in different territory; there are clear oppositions up here. There are black and white boundaries that are painted" (L. M. September 2000, p. 2).
7. It is beyond the scope of this chapter to go into the intricate details of Sioui's (1992) argument (which I highly recommend particularly for teachers in schools, the place where the myths of inferior and disappearing cultures begin). He argued that ever since the "discovery" of America, world society has been engaged in a process of ideological unification that may be simply called "the Americization of the world," whereby the essence of original American thought is being communicated to the other continents. (Sioui, 1992)
    Of course, original American thought in this context refers to indigenous knowledge.

References

Blumer, H. (1969). *Symbolic interactionism: Perspective and method.* Upper Saddle River, NJ: Prentice-Hall Inc.

Graveline, F. J. (1998). *Circle works: Transforming Eurocentric consciousness.* Halifax, NS: Fernwood Publications.

Haig-Brown, C. (1988). *Resistance and renewal: Surviving the Indian residential school.* Vancouver: Tillacum Press.

Hodgson-Smith, K. (1997). Seeking good and right relations: Aboriginal student perspectives on the pedagogy of Joe Duquette High School. Unpublished M.Ed. thesis, University of Saskatchewan.

Hughes, L. (2003). *The no-nonsense guide to indigenous peoples.* London: Verso.

Sioui, G. (1992). *For an Ameridian autohistory: An essay on the foundations of a social ethic.* Montreal: McGill-Queen's University Press.

Sioui, G. (1999). *Huron-Wendat: The heritage of the circle.* Vancouver: University of British Columbia Press.

Stewart-Harawira, M. (2005). *The new imperial order: Indigenous responses to globalization.* New York: Zed Books.

Urion, C. (1999). Recording first nations traditional knowledge. Unpublished manuscript U'Mista Cultural Society (p. 11). Alert Bay, BC, Canada.

CHAPTER 14

Old Order Amish Private Schools: Preparing Children and Preserving Community

KAREN M. JOHNSON-WEINER

Introduction

Popular understanding of Old Order Amish private schools is that they are simple remnants of a pioneer past. In a series of articles for the *Lancaster New Era*, since reprinted as a booklet entitled *Amish One-room Schools: Lessons for the Plain Life*, Klimuska (n.d.: 3) wrote, for example, "In Plain schools, the educational clock stopped 50 years ago. It's as if these schools are outposts, fenced in from the competitive pressures of 20th Century learning, protected from its progress and turmoil". Yet, there is little about Old Order education that is nineteenth century, for the Old Order are twenty-first century peoples, daily confronting modernity and making choices about its relevance in their lives (cf. Kraybill, 2001). In response to organizational changes in the school systems of the majority culture, the Old Order Amish and their Old Order Mennonite cousins have developed private schools that, while generally meeting the standards imposed by the state, realize the educational goals of the particular church community rather than the goals of the dominant society.

The Old Order Amish

Numbering roughly 150,000 in the U.S. and Canada, the Old Order Amish, descendants of sixteenth century Anabaptists, maintain a life style informed by "religiously based conflict with the secular environment" (Redekop, 1989: pp. 322–323). They live agriculturally based lives, though many work in factories or retail businesses. Their homes are interspersed with those of their non-Amish neighbors and they interact daily with the non-Old Order world as they shop, travel, visit doctors, or sightsee.

Nevertheless, Old Order religious ideology defines the church community as "God's realm" and demands its separation from the world. All aspects of Old Order culture, from dress to home decoration to economic activity, are circumscribed by community beliefs about proper Christian behavior and changes in one domain of Old Order life affect norms and activities in all other domains.

Today, what the dominant society refers to monolithically as the "Old Order Amish" is, in fact, a diverse population. While the ultra-conservative Swartzentruber Amish see the world as a corrupting influence and continue to shun even participation in farmers' markets, their much more progressive counterparts in northern Indiana and southern Michigan work side by side with non-Amish laborers in factories that produce mobile homes. In isolated, homogeneous settlements like the one in Somerset, Ohio, Old Order families live without indoor plumbing or ice boxes, while in the large Old Order Amish community of Holmes County, Ohio, families enjoy hot and cold running water, indoor bathrooms, and refrigerators. The most conservative groups pay little attention to the beliefs and actions of their non-Old Order neighbors and carefully regulate interaction with them, but the most progressive work in non-Old Order factories, wait on non-Old Order customers in shops and restaurants, and even socialize with non-Old Order friends and neighbors. The most conservative give little thought to the religious beliefs of their non-Amish neighbors, while the most progressive actively support mission work and many increasingly identify their life style as "Christian" rather than Amish.

Each Amish church community decides for itself how it will be Amish and how it will interact with other Old Order Amish church communities and the outside world. Fearing assimilation or "worldliness" and believing that individuals are inherently weak and susceptible to temptation, the Amish find strength in community behavioral norms and carefully evaluate potential changes in life style.

The Motivation for Private Schools

Establishing their own private schools was a life style change that did not come easily to most Old Order communities. Until the 1950s, the over-whelming majority of Old Order children attended small, often one-room public schools with their non-Old Order peers, and Old Order parents, regardless of the differences between church communities, were willing to let their children be educated in public schools as long as these were local institutions over which the parents had considerable influence.

In the mid-twentieth century, however, as state authorities began to consolidate the local one-room schoolhouses and enforce compulsory attendance beyond grade eight, Old Order parents began to resist, first by refusing to allow their children to be bussed to the larger schools or to attend school past grade eight and then by establishing private schools. The number of Old Order private schools grew as Old Order parents in a number of states were fined or jailed for their refusal to obey new education laws. In 1940, there were only four private Old Order Amish schools, whereas by 1960 there were ninety-seven and in 2003 there were over 1,200 (source: *The Blackboard Bulletin*).

Kraybill (2001) suggested that the Old Orders "intuitively grasped that modern schools would immerse their youth in mainstream culture" and "separate children from their parents, their traditions, and their values" (p. 175). Old Order parents were unwilling to send their children to larger, consolidated schools in which, away from the influence of home and church, they risked becoming assimilated to the dominant society. As Old Order writer and publisher Wagler (1963) put it, "[. . .] the one-room country school with its personal touch gave way to the consolidated elementary and high schools with additional unfavorable elements. During the tender years of childhood, our children were [. . .] to receive their education and instruction in worldly schools from worldly teachers, yet it was expected that they should suffer no harm" (reprinted in Stoll, 1967, p. 66).

Huntington (1994) pointed out that going to school does not necessarily mean the same thing for Amish communities as it does for the dominant society. She noted, "The Amish do not confuse schooling with the larger concept of what the world calls education. Although during most periods in they history they have permitted their children to be schooled by 'outsiders,' they have never permitted their children to be educated by the world" (Huntington, 1994, p. 78). The distinction between schooling and education is an important one. Schooling is book learning, the value of which varies in Old Order communities. Education, on the other hand, is the inculcation of values.

For the Old Orders, the true education upon which the church community depends for its survival takes place in the sharing of labor, the doing of chores, and the enjoyment of fellowship at church, around the dinner table, and even in silo filling. Voicing his opposition to sending children to consolidated schools outside the local community, one Amish leader argued, "With us, our religion is inseparable with a day's work, a night's rest, a meal, or any other practice; therefore, our education can much less be separated from our religious practices" (Kraybill, 2001, p. 174).[1] Or, as a Swartzentruber Amish bishop asserted, "By 14 you've pretty much learned all you need to in school but you can't wait 'til then to start learning what you need to live."

Parents in the dominant society hope that public schools will provide their children with the schooling they need for a well-paid job, prepare them for higher education, or, at least, help them to become good citizens. Old Order parents, on the other hand, hope that their private schools will prepare children for the Old Order world and "to live for others, to use [their] talents in service to God and Man, to live an upright and obedient life, and to prepare for the life to come" (Stoll, 1975, p. 31; cf. Hostetler and Huntington, 1992; Hostetler, 1993; Johnson-Weiner, 2006). Choices about what subjects should be taught, what texts used, how teachers should be selected, and what pedagogy is most effective are made with this broad goal in mind.

Conflict with state authorities has abated in the years since the 1972 Supreme Court decision in *Wisconsin* v. *Yoder et al.* "that enforcement of the State's requirement of compulsory formal education after the eighth grade would gravely endanger if not destroy the free exercise of [. . . Amish] religious beliefs" (Keim, 1975, p. 98). Old Order communities have worked out compromises with the state authorities and have continued to construct private schools in their communities. Nevertheless, since the Supreme Court decision, Old Order schools have become increasingly diverse as Old Order communities, each attempting to preserve itself from what it sees as "worldliness," react differently to pressures from the dominant society and from other Old Order communities.

Old Order Amish Schools: Reflecting the Community's Place in the World

In each Old Order community, family and community life reflect the church community's attempt to put into practice Biblical teachings that proscribe the proper relationships between church members and non-church members and the duty of Christians to each other and to God. All Old Order Amish church communities continue to structure their existence according to their belief in a divine order that divides the world and all in it into good and evil, believer and non-believer. Fathers, mothers, sons, and daughters all have their role in the church community, set down in the Bible, codified in the *Ordnung* or discipline of the church, and put into practice through tradition.

As the challenges (e.g. shorter versus longer growing season, price of land, influx of tourism, and access to markets) faced by each church community differ from those faced by others and as members of a church community disagree over how to confront those challenges, groups evolve different understandings of how to be Old Order. Since the Old Order Amish churches are congregationally based, with no strong, organizing body uniting them and standardizing behavior, each church community makes its own decisions as it negotiates its place in the world. Different communities may be in fellowship with each other—that is, ministers from one community may preach at services in the other and marriage between members of the different communities is permitted—but decisions made by one church community are not binding on another.

At the same time, however, a broad network of family, religious, and commercial relationships bind diverse Old Order settlements to each other in important ways. Even between two groups that do not partake in fellowship with each other, there will likely be ties of family and friendship. As one Old Order woman from central Ohio noted, for example, her own church community did not share ministers with a community only a short distance to the north, but the young people continue to socialize with each other and attend church back and forth. Since one does not join church until one is an adult, it is possible for siblings to join different churches. Thus, first cousins may grow up dressing differently, fellowshipping with different communities, experiencing different levels of technology in their daily lives, interacting very differently with their non-Old Order neighbors, and attending very different Old Order schools.[2]

The impact of population, urbanization, economic change, and religious schism—the variables that have shaped Old Order life across North America—is revealed in the diversity of Old Order schools and approaches to education. Old Order communities interact in different ways with the non-Old Order world that surrounds them and this helps to create different needs and goals.

The most obvious evidence of the different ways in which Old Order Amish church communities define themselves vis-à-vis other church communities and the dominant society is found in the schoolhouses themselves. Built according to church standards, schoolhouses embody the church community's definition what it means to be Old Order and, in their furnishings and decor, reflect the values of the communities that use them.

Schoolhouses reveal, for example, the community's notion of humility, simplicity, and resignation (cf. Kraybill and Bowman, 2001). For the Swartzentruber Amish, this means schools are simple, almost meager affairs. Since the first Swartzentruber Amish families arrived in upstate New York, they have built thirteen schools, all to the same pattern. Roughly 20 feet by 30 feet, these wooden structures lack cellars, electricity, and indoor plumbing and the outside is often unpainted, though it may have metal siding. Inside, there is no paneling: the walls and often the floor are particleboard, painted, as are Swartzentruber Amish homes, in white and battleship grey. A wood stove heats the one-room schools and there is generally a platform on top of the stove upon which children can place their lunches to have them heated up. Often wire is strung from the stovepipe to the wall, both to anchor the stovepipe and to provide a drying rack for wet mittens. The main entry to the building is through the wood shed and there are hooks on each side of the door for coats and shelves for lunch boxes. There are no lamps: the building is lit naturally and a single length of dark cloth that is tied to one side covers each window. There is a blackboard along the front wall, a teacher's desk facing the rows of children's desks, and a long bench or several chairs at the front for recitation. While there is a field in which children can play ball games, there is no playground. In the summer, weeds grow up around the school-house, as the schoolyard once again becomes cattle pasture.

The schools built by the progressive Old Order Amish of northern Indiana present a sharp contrast. One school in Topeka, Indiana, for example, has three classrooms, two on the first floor and one at one end of the basement: the other half of the basement is reserved for game playing and there is a ping-pong table. There is also an apartment for teachers. Outside is a large playground with a swing set, merry-go-round, basketball nets, and teeter-totters. There is indoor plumbing. An Old Order Amish school in nearby LaGrange, Indiana, has a curtain that divides a single large room into two classrooms. There are bookshelves, shades on the windows, and pressurized gas lanterns. The walls are painted white and the floor is hardwood. Beside each teacher's desk is a large table, around which children sit when their class is called to work. Like many other schools in Northern Indiana, this one too has a residence for the teachers as part of the school building. These teachers' quarters offer a compact but cozy room, with patterned linoleum and scatter rugs on the floor and a small kitchen. The building is heated by a wood stove in the cellar and the playground features a merry-go-round and swings.

In between the two extremes of the ultra-conservative Swartzentruber Amish and the progressive Old Order Amish of northern Indiana and southern Michigan are the one-room schools of smaller, more isolated Old Order Amish communities across North America. Most, like Swartzentruber schools, are one room and lack indoor plumbing, but the interiors are often decorated with homemade charts, children's drawings, and maps, and many, like the schools of their more progressive counterparts, have shelves of books for leisure-time reading and extra study.

But there are also more subtle ways in which schools reflect and reinforce church community values. In Swartzentruber and other less progressive church communities, teaching school is hardly a career; teachers are paid little and even a young girl who likes teaching will give it up for marriage. Teachers in these communities have only the eight years of formal education that their church and family consider sufficient and they receive little or no special preparation before they begin teaching. In more progressive communities, however, pay is higher and even young men consider teaching an acceptable occupation. Monthly teachers' meetings provide them an opportunity to meet with more experienced teachers to exchange ideas and experiences.

Variations in school architecture and the status of teachers reflect the different role played by the schools themselves in the church community. In Swartzentruber Amish settlements, the private school is an outside institution, state mandated, and designed to meet specific, limited needs. For example, one Swartzentruber Amish woman, a former teacher, says simply that "You have to go [to school] so you can learn to spell and do arithmetic and to satisfy others." Pressed to elaborate, the teacher acknowledged that the school had broader social goals: "You need to go to school to learn to get along with strangers." Yet, by "strangers" she meant Swartzentruber Amish children and others in Swartzentruber church communities outside of the immediate family. In other words, for the Swartzentruber Amish, the school is where children acquire basic literacy and arithmetic skills and the behaviors appropriate for interacting as a member of a Swartzentruber church community. There is little emphasis on other behavioral outcomes or life outside church boundaries, nor is the school important in the daily life of those not attending. Parents do not visit school or pay much attention to school activities. There are no special school programs for parents and friends at holiday time.

In Swartzentruber schools, change comes slowly, for the community is unwilling to depart from practices that have worked for generations. Indeed, the Swartzentruber Amish have, for the most part, simply continued the same educational practices they followed when their one-room school houses were public, using the same texts their parents and grandparents found useful, including the nineteenth century *McGuffey Readers*, the 1919 *Essentials of English Spelling*, and the *Strayer–Upton Arithmetics Series* from the 1930s. Kept in print by Old Order print shops, these texts shield children from modern events, technological advances, and religious and cultural difference. They offer basic language instruction while providing a vocabulary no longer in everyday use, allowing children to become fluent enough for daily exchanges with English neighbors as they buy and sell goods, but not giving them much knowledge about the non-Amish world (see Johnson-Weiner, 1997, 2006).

Where the Swartzentruber Amish have made curricular or other changes in their schools they have tended to go back in time rather than accepting "modernisms," thereby eliminating features of education not immediately applicable to their way of life. Now, for example, children study German once a week so that they will be able to read the Bible and their hymnbook, the Ausbund,[3] but they no have geography or health, subjects their grandparents routinely studied when they attended public schools.

That the Swartzentruber Amish have made many fewer concessions to the demands of technology and modernity than most of their Old Order counterparts is evident in the physically primitive school buildings and the limited curriculum, which helps to reinforce the isolation of the Swartzentruber community. Children do not need to acquire native fluency in English because their church community, unlike other Old Order groups, will not permit them to work "in town" or to work for hourly wages in non-Amish-owned factories, restaurants, or retail businesses. Consequently, there is little or no discussion of grammar or English pronunciation, nor is there any emphasis on English writing other than on handwriting practice and spelling.

Swartzentruber schools further reinforce the teachings of home and church by ensuring that the family tasks and community events that take place outside of the classroom take precedence over schoolwork. School may be canceled for silo filling or a wedding and parents routinely keep children home to help with pressing chores such as butchering or to help clean the home for church services. Nor is there any place in the curriculum for children to explore or question community beliefs or the relationship between different church communities, reinforcing the belief that the Swartzentruber community is alone in the larger hostile world: one is Swartzentruber or one is not. Finally, Swartzentruber schools teach children that working hard is more important than good scores. The teacher may keep charts recording perfect scores on spelling tests, but she does not display these charts where others can see them, nor is there competition between students to see who can do the best. In these ultra-conservative communities, schools turn inward towards the community, filtering the world through pages of archaic texts that shield children from modern events, technological advances, and religious and cultural difference.

In other Old Order communities, however, the private school has become central to community activities and parents and others visit regularly to watch classroom activities. Visitors are welcomed with special songs and there are holiday programs to which the church community is invited. Mothers regularly treat the schoolchildren to hot lunches or special snacks. Teachers often take children on field trips to local museums or businesses or invite parents in to talk about such diverse topics as "Christmas in other lands" or "Down's syndrome."

In many Old Order communities the school has become a social center and its role in ensuring the survival of the church community is openly recognized. Emphasizing the need to teach self-sufficiency and acknowledging that earning a living will involve being in the world, a teacher from a large Old Order Amish settlement in Ohio says, "We expect our schools to provide a basic education for our children that is essential to our way of living and also to be able to communicate and make a living in the outside world." Moreover, she added, the school is where children should learn "discipline and respect to God and fellow men."

Offering a curriculum much like that in the public school, these schools prepare children for an adult life in which they may work for non-Old Order employers or encounter non-Old Order customers daily in local businesses. At the same time, they allow the community to control children's introduction to the world and to limit and shape the world's influence. One Old Order Amish teacher from Ohio wrote, for example:

> I really don't know any thing about public schools, but I just know we don't want Amish children to go there. I don't know do we have different lessons or not, but I know one thing that we do not want

and that is we don't want the Amish children among the English too much. You see you have many things like radios, phones, etc. that we don't have.

This is echoed in the foreword of *Standards of the Old Order Amish and Old Order Mennonite Parochial and Vocational Schools of Penna* (1969), which asserts:

> Any person even remotely acquainted with the Amish and Old Order Mennonite sect knows that there [sic] way of living differs greatly from others. [...] Tradition to them is a sacred trust, and it is a part of their religion to uphold and adhere to the ideals of their forefathers. [...] To maintain these principles in the future is of vital importance to the Amish. This has been the overriding reason for the establishment of the Amish schools in the United States during the last decade.
>
> (p. 1)

Thus, these Old Order private schools recognize change in the dominant society but control access to it, preparing children for work that may take them outside their communities and bring them face to face with technology and behavior that is unacceptable in their Old Order worlds. Children study a wider range of subjects, including geography, American history, and art, but they do so with texts produced specifically for Old Order schools, such as the reading series developed by the Old Order Amish Pathway Publishing Corporation, which help children acquire the language and other skills they need for employment in non-Old Order businesses, but minimize the influence the world may have by reinforcing the values and behaviors of the Old Order community.

In the most progressive communities, such as those found in northern Indiana and in southern Michigan, many Old Order Amish are redefining what it means to be Old Order Amish in ways that are anathema to members of less progressive church communities. According to a retired Old Order teacher from Michigan:

> The last year or so they allowed phones, you can have them right in the shops, just so they're not so handy. They [the church community] didn't want them [members making phone calls] to keep bothering neighbors. One church had them [phones] in the schoolhouse or in shanties at the end of the lane. Now they can have them right in the shop. I don't know of anybody that has them right in the house, although some have voice mail or answering machines.

Several of these progressive church communities also allow rubber tires on large wagons, such as those used to move the church benches and several of the districts now allow bicycles. If the Amish family is living in a home belonging to someone who is not Old Order, then the family may have electricity. Many of the children now ride bicycles to school and a number of Old Order church members carry cell phones.

Schools in progressive communities reflect these changes, offering a curriculum that prepares children to compete economically with their non-Old Order counterparts on a playing field that may be only marginally, if at all, in the Old Order world. They emphasize standard English pronunciation and grammar and devote considerable classroom time to teaching children to use vocabulary appropriately and to write letters and essays.

Teachers work hard to expose their pupils to a variety of cultures outside the boundaries of their church communities. Moreover, many schools in these progressive communities have adopted texts from non-Amish publishers that emphasize evangelism and mission in these texts, marking an awareness of and outward orientation to the world that is absent in the Swartzentruber and other less progressive Old Order schools.

Religion in Old Order Schools

In a sense, the goal of all Old Order private schools is the same: "to prepare the child for the Amish or Mennonite way of living and the responsibilities of adulthood" (*Standards of the Old Order Amish and Old Order Mennonite Parochial and Vocational Schools of Penna*, 1969, p. 5) so that they might achieve everlasting life (cf. Huntington, 1993). Yet, as church communities modify the boundaries between the church and the world, schools must prepare children to deal with the consequences of community change (cf. Pederson, 2002, especially p. 347). For the most progressive Amish, this has meant turning private schools in church-communities into church schools, ultimately rejecting secular education as they educate children to engage the secular world.

When Old Order communities first withdrew their children from public schools, some called for the new Amish private schools to "train our children to be dynamic witnesses for Christ."[4] Most church communities, however, rejected such an active role for the schools. For the Swartzentruber Amish, for example, allowing a young, female schoolteacher to offer religious instruction would be unthinkable and, unlike teachers in many other communities, Swartzentruber teachers do not even lead children's prayer before lunch. Swartzentruber children learn to read the Bible in German, but they never discuss what they read. In other communities, the teacher, in leading the Lord's Prayer at the beginning of the school day or offering silent prayer before lunch, acts as a substitute parent reinforcing lessons taught at home. Yet, the teacher would not dare usurp the place of the ministers or the parents by teaching or interpreting the Bible for the children. The *Standards of the Old Order Amish and Old Order Mennonite Private and Vocational Schools of Penna* (1969) notes that:

> With the exception of devotion [sic] it is the Amish and Old Order Mennonite theory that the Bible be taught in the home & church however [sic] it is further our aim to teach Religion all day long in our curriculum (lessons) and on the play ground.
>
> In Arithmetic by accuracy (no cheating);
>
> In English by learning to say what we mean.
>
> In History by humanity (kindness-mercy)
>
> In Health by teaching cleanliness and thriftiness.
>
> In Geography by learning to make a [sic] honest living from the soil.
>
> In Music by singing praises to God.
>
> On the school ground by teaching honesty, respect, sincerity, humbleness and yes, the Golden Rule.
>
> Is Religion then continuously mentioned? Seldom, just enough to bring the whole thing to a point now and then (p. 2).

In the most progressive Old Order communities, however, the role of religious instruction is being re-evaluated, for many have come to see in Old Order schools an opportunity not simply for subtle reinforcement of values and social behavior but also for overt religious teaching in the daily curriculum. In these church communities, the schools have become an equal partner with the family and the ministry in the struggle to prepare children to be good members of the Amish church.[5] An Old Order Amish teacher from Michigan asserted, for example, "[. . .] our main goal in having our own schools is to be able to implant more Christian morals into our children, to keep them away from (or being exposed to) the many things which aren't good for body and soul." An Old Order teacher from Indiana went further, arguing that "the purpose of our schools is to teach the basic subjects, then teach them about Jesus Christ, getting along with your fellow man, lead them towards joining church later, accepting Jesus, and then inheriting eternal life. That's what we're after."

As they have come to lead lives very similar to those of their non-Amish neighbors, members of progressive Amish church communities increasingly see the world, not in terms of Old Order Amish and non-Old Order Amish, but as Christian and non-Christian. As a consequence, teachers bring religious instruction actively and overtly into the classroom to reinforce church teaching.

God is the foundation of Old Order education, asserted one Old Order Amish bishop addressing a group of Indiana teachers. "The closer one adheres to God's word and God's principles when administering a system of teaching honor, respect, and discipline, the greater one's probability of success." He noted further that there is "no neutral position with respect to good and evil. [. . .] Without exception, our allegiance is with one or the other, and this is as true within the classroom as anywhere else. The classroom is no exception."[6]

In short, in these settlements, as the Old Order life style grows increasingly similar to that of the non-Old Order world, it is through their identity as Christians that the Old Order distinguish themselves. Public schools are secular and so the Old Order schools have become Christian. As a result, these most progressive communities share a sense that schools have an impact beyond the eight years students attend and that teachers perform work of great importance. As the Amish bishop noted in his address to the teachers, "A teacher's work affects eternity, you can never tell where your influence will end."[7] As one teacher put it:

> Religion is the basis of our schools. In order to preserve it for all generations, [our] forefathers started parochial schools. Without the Amish, Christian religion, there would be no parochial school for the area. What is its role? The church builds on it and schools are a branch of the church. It is the vitality of the school.

Difference and Survival

The sociologist Hostetler (1993) noted "A sectarian movement must establish an ideology different from that of the parent group in order to break off relations with it" (p. 48). All Old Order groups are, in fact, the result of schism and each, in defining itself, has emphasized—and continues to emphasize—its differences from the parent group. All see themselves as separate from the dominant "English" or non-Old Order society, but, in fact, they separate themselves from each other. Together these groups offer a picture of considered resistance to worldliness and modernity, in which modernity need not be entirely rejected but must, rather, be considered for its impact. Old Order communities recognize that a community might need to change and, indeed, that some changes preserve the integrity of the community. The private school is just such a change. Its adoption alters the community's involvement in the education of its children, but, at the same time, reinforces community identity. The dangers of change are, thus, mitigated by consideration of change and recognition of selves as conscious outsiders, different both from the world and from other plain communities. In considering change, then, church communities must constantly define themselves against both the world and other Old Order groups.

How an Old Order community conceives the role of the private school reveals how it has positioned itself in and in opposition to the surrounding society and to other Old Order groups. For the Swartzentruber Amish, the dominant non-Old Order society is, in many respects, useful but irrelevant. Swartzentruber Amish engage in economic exchange with the English or non-Amish, they seek medical help when necessary, and many have personal friends in the English world and they recognize these things as necessary to the survival of the church community. Other Old Order groups, however, often pose a greater threat, for they demonstrate the extent to which a church can "modernize" while still remaining visibly separate from the world. Essential to the survival of the community is commitment to the old ways and the evidence that the world can be a powerful lure is most evident in other Old Order groups who have, in Swartzentruber eyes, abandoned the old ways for worldly ones. There are "always some wanting some more modernisms," commented a Swartzentruber bishop about other Old Order groups in his Ohio neighborhood. "They're all one pack to me." A recent schism in the Swartzentruber community was characterized by one woman in terms of change versus the retention of traditional ways. Her own group, she said, "took a step back when they split," rejecting changes, while the others were "just like kids. The grass is always greener."

Hostetler and Huntington (1992) noted "Much of Amish ritual today consists of maintaining the purity and unity of the church community" (p. 10). For the Swartzentruber Amish the practices of daily life reinforce this purity and unity, for the Swartzentruber Amish have drawn a sharp line between themselves and the world and between themselves and Old Order communities that they deem more worldly, those that, in the words of a Swartzentruber bishop, "want to be Amish but don't know how." Other Old Order groups are certainly as committed to God's path as the Swartzentrubers, but have drawn their boundaries in such a way that they must take the world into greater account. Kraybill (2001) wrote that:

> The Amish view social change as a matter of moving cultural fences—holding to old boundaries and setting new ones. This dynamic process involves negotiating symbolic boundaries in the moral order. . . . Cultural fences mark the lines of separation between the two worlds. Coping with social change involves fortifying old fences as well as moving fences and building new ones.
>
> (p. 297)

For a number of Old Order groups, increasing economic pressures and the decreasing ability of the church community to support itself entirely through farming (cf. Kollmorgen, 1942; Olshan, 1994) have meant that, as Olshan (1994) put it, "the old patterns [. . . are] no longer viable [. . .]" (pp. 145–146) and some Old Order groups have begun to permit greater interaction with the public non-Old Order world. While Swartzentruber church communities, intent on ignoring the world unless it forcibly intrudes, consciously resist moving the fences at all, Old Order communities, engaged more with the world economically and, thus, facing different social pressures for change, in private schools find a means of reinforcing the church boundaries against the pressure for change children will encounter after they graduate, a way to hold off the child's introduction to the world.

Amish Schools and Cultural Diversity

Old Order schools cannot function as models for secular education. As Hostetler and Huntington (1992) noted, Old Order schools are simply not designed to meet the needs of the broader secular society:

> By design, Amish schools are not suited for training artists, musicians, painters, and actors; nor for training science-oriented individuals who would pursue engineering, astronomy, paleontology, chemistry, or space technology; nor for training business executives, corporation managers, or occupations leading to government or military careers. The Amish school, by intent, does not function as an institution for upward mobility in the modern industrial complex.
>
> (p. 109)

Nevertheless, in offering small-scale, community-based instruction that emphasizes individual responsibility and discipline, Old Order schools re-affirm qualities secular educators are once again coming to appreciate. Old Order schools are accountable to a clearly defined, community-based authority. Children know their teachers personally as community and family members and instruction is individualized even as the curriculum is not. Moreover, Old Order children learn to take responsibility for their actions and to behave in a disciplined manner. Thus, Old Order education continues to prepare children successfully for what parents view as an appropriate life style and schools continue to reinforce parental values.

In keeping their schools small, the Old Orders have made them more responsive to the needs of individual students and families and to the concerns of the group, offering a cultural coherence the large, secular schools might lack. Children learn in a secure environment from a teacher who knows them well and whose actions reinforce the lessons, values, and discipline important to becoming successful adults. Even when the teacher comes from a different church community than her students, she understands the culture from which they come and the expectations parents have for their children's success. When there is a conflict between parents or between parents and teacher, they can work out their differences in face-to-face discussions in which all involved understand each other and identify with each other as neighbors, Christians, and Old Order church members.

Moreover, Old Order private schools, because they are community institutions, provide a context in which the community can negotiate its response to change. A teacher in Indiana noted that "When all Amish were farmers [. . .] some parents put more emphasis on the farm knowledge than on the basic studies." "Now imagine," he added:

> Farmer Brown's boy decides to go into construction [. . .] The boy finds building an apartment house has more to do with math and a good reading ability than it does with fixing tractors and baling hay. He decides to put more emphasis on the basic studies for his own son in hopes it will make life easier for him.
>
> At this time a low percent of Amish young men enter agriculture as an occupation. [. . .] Instead they go to the factory and make from 15 to 45 dollars an hour. Many have their own businesses. Now you can easily see the change in view of education. The people's needs are changing. Along with more interests in studies, parents are showing perhaps more support to school now than they have in the past. [. . .] and that results in students with a better education when they graduate.

At the same time, Old Order private schools, by helping the community limit the access young people have to the world outside their Old Order community, enable more conservative communities to resist change. As the Swartzentruber Amish have established their own schools, they have adopted more archaic texts, limited the subjects taught, and limited the role of English.

In short, founded by church communities to resist unacceptable developments in public education, Old Order schools have become agents of change as well as agents of resistance to change. In his study of language shift in the Papua New Guinean village of Gapun, Kulick (1992) noted "villagers' ideas about literacy, the millennium, and Christianity form a framework into which all aspects of the modern world are fitted. One domain in which all these themes coalesce is in the villagers' understanding of schooling" (p. 175). Similarly, in Old Order communities, private schools are defined by particular beliefs about the place and practices of church members within the church community and within the larger society. As the group's understanding of what it means to be Old Order shapes different educational strategies, tools, and philosophies of education, these, in turn, reinforce community values.

Acknowledgments

This work could not have been completed without financial support from the National Endowment for the Humanities (Reference FB-37315-01), the Spencer Foundation (No. 200200164), and the Research and Creative Endeavors Program at SUNY, Potsdam.

Resources and Tools for Educators

Questions

1. School consolidation brings together, in one large school, children from many smaller ones. What effect(s)—positive and negative—could this have on a community?
2. Amish schools do not provide a liberal education, that is an education that would enable children to question their lives and/or the lives of their parents—is this fair to Amish children?
3. What is the role of education in a democratic society?

For Further Reading

Dewalt, M. W. (2006). *Amish education in the United States and Canada*. Lanham, MD: Rowan & Littlefield Education.

This book is a result of Mark Dewalt's ongoing ethnographic work among the Old Order Amish. Dewalt discusses such issues as pedagogy, curriculum, and teacher preparation.

Johnson-Weiner, K. M. (2006). *Train up a Child. Old Order Amish and Mennonite schools*. Baltimore, MD: The Johns Hopkins University Press.

The larger work upon which this article is based, this ethnographic study is the result of the author's fieldwork in nine different Old Order communities in five different states. Johnson-Weiner discusses the history of Old Order schools, the relationship between schools and community, and issues such as curriculum, pedagogy, and textbook selection.

Keim, A. N. (1975). *Compulsory education and the Amish. The right not to be modern*. Boston: Beacon Press.

This is a collection of essays on *Wisconsin* v. *Yoder et al.*, the Supreme Court case in which it was decided that laws compelling the Amish to send their children to school beyond grade eight were unconstitutional. It includes the text of the Supreme Court's decision.

Peters, S. F. (2003). *The Yoder case. Religious freedom, education, and parental rights*. Lawrence, KS: University Press of Kansas.

In this text, Peters revisits *Wisconsin* v. *Yoder et al.* and comments on the meaning of the case for contemporary society. He explores the application of the decision in *Wisconsin* v. *Yoder et al.* to other issues of religious freedom.

In addition to book length works, those interested in Old Order schools should explore *The Blackboard Bulletin*, which is available from the Pathway Publishing Corporation, Rt. 4, Aylmer, Ontario. *The Blackboard Bulletin* is a magazine for Old Order Amish and Old Order Mennonite teachers that appears monthly throughout the school year. Pathway also publishes two other magazines, *Family Life* and *Young Companion*.

Finally, a good website to check out is www.holycrosslivonia.org/amish/amishfaq.htm. This is the website of the National Committee for Amish Religious Freedom (Rev. William C. Lindholm, Chair), 15343 Susanna Circle, Livonia, MI 48154 USA (Tel.: 734–464–3908, email: amish@holycrosslivonia.org). The mission of the committee is to "defend and preserve the religious freedom of the Old Order Amish religion in the United States." The committee acted on behalf of the Amish before the U.S. Supreme Court in Wisconsin v. Yoder *et al.*

Activities for Educators

1. Among the reading books used in different Old Order Amish communities are the *McGuffey Readers*, the *Dick and Jane* series, and the *Pathway Readers*. Only the Pathway books are published by the Amish. See if you can find examples of these different books. What conclusions can you draw about communities based on their choice of text?

2. See if you can find a copy of the U.S. Supreme Court decision in Wisconsin v. Yoder *et al.* Explore the assumptions Chief Justice Warren Burger makes about the Amish.

3. There were one-room schoolhouses in many small rural and semi-rural communities. Maybe there is an old schoolhouse near you. See if you can find a schoolhouse in use over 50 years ago—or pictures of one. How is it different from modern-day schools? What role did it play in the community?

Notes

1. Kraybill (2001) attributed this quote to Aaron E. Beiler.
2. One of the reviewers of an earlier draft of this chapter questioned how Old Order children felt about their own schools, in particular how they felt about the differences between their schools, those of other Old Order communities, and those of the non-Old Order world. I should note that a number of Old Order children still attend public schools. Old Order children attending Old Order schools learn little about the schools in communities with which their own does not partake in fellowship and nothing about public schools except that they have things that are unacceptable in their own communities. Thus, while Old Order children are certainly aware of the world outside their own church communities, they come to understand this world through the lens of the church as realized in their Old Order educations. They are taught to be Old Order. That this education is very successful is evident in the low number of those who leave Old Order life—up to 15 percent of young people in progressive communities but as few as 5 percent in the most conservative (see Hostetler, 1993).
3. First printed in 1564, the *Ausbund* is the oldest Protestant hymnbook in continuous use. In Swartzentruber schools, children are not expected to join in the morning singing until grade three, when they begin to study German and so can be expected to know the script.
4. Hershberger argued "the public schools are better equipped to teach 'the 3 R's' (sic) than the Amish ones . . . [yet] . . . the Amish schools must do more . . . we should train our children to be dynamic witnesses for Christ" (pp. 68–69).

5. Writing in the *Blackboard Bulletin* in January 1961, for example, the editor asserted the need to wage a battle against spiritual decay on three fields, "1. The church, represented by the ministry; 2. The home, represented by the parents; 3. and the church school, represented by Christian teachers" (Wagler, 1963).
6. Remarks presented by an Amish bishop at the Fourth Annual Indiana Amish Parochial Teachers' Class held in Parke County, Indiana, on July 13, 2000.
7. Remarks presented by an Amish bishop at the Fourth Annual Indiana Amish Parochial Teachers' Class held in Parke County, Indiana, on July 13, 2000.

References

Hostetler, J. A. (1993). *Amish society* (4th edn). Baltimore: The Johns Hopkins University Press.

Hostetler, J. A. & Huntington, G. E. (1992). *Amish children. Education in the family, school, and community* (2nd edn). New York: Harcourt Brace Jovanovich College Publishers.

Huntington, G. E. (1994). Persistence and change in Amish education. In D. B. Kraybill & M. A. Olshan (Eds.), *The Amish struggle with modernity* (pp. 77–96). Hanover: University Press of New England.

Johnson-Weiner, K. M. (1997). Reinforcing a separate Amish identity: English instruction and the preservation of culture in old order Amish schools. In J. R. Dow & M. Wolff (Eds.), *Languages and lives. Essays in honor of Werner Enninger* (pp. 67–78). New York: Peter Lang.

Johnson-Weiner, K. M. (2006). *Train up a child: Old Order Amish and Mennonite schools.* Baltimore, MD: The Johns Hopkins University Press.

Keim, A. N. (1975). *Compulsory education and the Amish. The right not to be modern.* Boston: Beacon Press.

Klimuska, E. (n.d.). *Amish one-room schools: Lessons for the plain life.* Lancaster, PA: Lancaster Newspapers, Inc.

Kollmorgen, W. M. (1942). Culture of a contemporary community: The Old Order Amish of Lancaster County, Pennsylvania. *Rural Life Studies*, (4). Washington, DC: US Department of Agriculture.

Kraybill, D. B. (2001). *The riddle of Amish culture* (2nd edn). Baltimore, MD: The Johns Hopkins University Press.

Kraybill, D. B. & Bowman, C. F. (2001). *On the backroad to heaven.* Baltimore, MD: The Johns Hopkins University Press.

Kulick, D. (1992). *Language shift and cultural reproduction. Socialization, self, and syncretism in a Papua New Guinean village.* New York: Cambridge University Press.

Olshan, M. A. (1994). Amish cottage industries as Trojan horse. In D. B. Kraybill & M. A. Olshan (Eds.), *The Amish struggle with modernity* (pp. 133–145). Hanover: University Press of New England.

Pederson, J. M. (2002). She may be Amish now, but she won't be Amish long. Anabaptist women and antimodernism. In K. D. Schmidt, D. Zimmerman Umble, & S. D. Reschly (Eds.), *Strangers at home. Amish and Mennonite women in history* (pp. 339–363). Baltimore: The Johns Hopkins University Press.

Redecop, C. (1989). *Mennonite society.* Baltimore: The Johns Hopkins University Press.

Standards of the Old Order Amish and Old Order Mennonite parochial and vocational schools of Penna. (1969). (revised 1973, 1988, reprinted 2003). Gordonville, PA: Gordonville PA Print Shop.

Stoll, J. (1967). *The challenge of the child. Selections from the* Blackboard Bulletin *1957–1966.* Aylmer, Ontario: Pathway Publishing Corporation.

Stoll, J. (1975). Who shall educate our children? In A. N. Keim (Ed.), *Compulsory education and the Amish. The right not to be modern* (pp. 16–42). Boston: Beacon Press.

Wagler, D. (1963). The need and purpose of church schools. Blackboard Bulletin (January). In J. Stoll (Ed.), *The challenge of the child. Selections from the* Blackboard Bulletin *1957–1966* (pp. 65–67). 1967. Aylmer, Ontario: Pathway Publishing Corporation.

CHAPTER 15

Arguments as Venues for Cultural Education: A Comparison of Epistemic Practices at General and Religious Schools in Israel

ELI GOTTLIEB

It does not take particularly extensive travel, anthropological expertise, or keen ethnographic skills to notice that truths considered incontestable in one community are matters of contention in another. One need merely open a newspaper, switch on a television, or boot up a networked computer. Yet we know remarkably little about how such differences come about or how they are sustained. In this chapter, I examine how schools foster and preserve culturally distinctive epistemologies. I begin by presenting some findings from a comparative study of argumentation and epistemology I conducted among Israeli children and adolescents. In light of these findings, I then examine how argumentative discourse—both inside and outside of classrooms—functions as a key venue for cultural education. I then discuss research frameworks currently being developed to investigate such discourse and identify both promise and risk in these approaches. Finally, I discuss the implications for cultural education of both the empirical findings of my own study and of the theoretical perspectives discussed in the latter sections of the chapter.

The original aim of my study was to compare how children of different ages and backgrounds justify their religious beliefs. In individual interviews, I presented participants with a scenario in which two friends are engaged in an argument: One of them believes in God, the other does not and each is attempting to persuade the other that they are right. The participants were asked which of the two characters they most agreed with and why. They were then asked what someone holding an opposing view might say to show that they are wrong, followed by some general questions about the nature of the dispute, such as whether there really are people who hold the opposing view, whether they might after all be right, and whether it is possible to prove who is right.

The 200 participants in the study were recruited from grades five, eight, and twelve at general and religious public schools in Israel. (The mean ages for each grade were 11 years 1 month, 14 years, and 17 years 6 months, respectively.) Because I shall focus here on differences between these two school populations it is worth describing them in some detail. The public school system in Israel includes a Hebrew sector serving the majority Jewish population and an Arabic sector serving the minority Muslim, Christian, and Druze populations. The Hebrew sector is further subdivided into two main streams. General schools are nominally secular, provide no explicit religious instruction, and are targeted at the majority "non-religious" and "traditional" segments of the Jewish–Israeli population. Religious schools, on the other hand, are targeted specifically at the "religious Zionist" community, which constitutes approximately 20 percent of Israel's Jewish population. Religious schools combine the subjects taught at general schools (using the same textbooks and following the same mandatory national curriculum) with an extensive religious education program. Pupils from religious schools thus differ from pupils at general schools with respect to both their family religious backgrounds and their exposure to organized religious instruction.

Numerically speaking, the religious Zionist community is a minority group within Israeli society. However, in terms of its cultural autonomy and control of national resources, it functions in many ways as a dominant class. For example, although religious schools receive more government funding per student than general schools, their curricula are subject to less governmental intervention and control (for a socio-historical account of how this came to be, see Shamai (2000)). This unusual combination of cultural autonomy and numerical minority makes religious schools in Israel an especially intriguing institutional setting in which to explore issues of cultural sustainability. For, unlike groups that possess more limited resources with which to resist the hegemonic forces of majority culture, the religious Zionist community in Israel has been able, through the religious school system and other political and social institutions, to establish powerful practices of cultural resistance and self-preservation. On the practical level, these practices can serve as instructive examples to other minority groups seeking to preserve their cultural identities in the face of hegemonic and assimilatory forces. On the theoretical level, they can serve as thought-provoking counter-examples to overly deterministic assumptions about the relations between majority and minority cultures that are sometimes implicit in socio-cultural analyses of educational institutions and practices.

Cultural Patterns of Belief–Justification

The present study explored various features of participants' argumentation, including the various kinds of justification they provided for their own beliefs, the counter-arguments they expected opponents to use to refute their beliefs, and the various strategies they used to rebut such counter-arguments. However, I focus here on only justifications and refutations and even more specifically on "creation" arguments, i.e. on justifications and refutations that included some reference to God's creation of the universe or human-kind. Moreover, to avoid confounding school differences in argumentation with differing levels of belief in God, I focus only on the justifications and refutations generated by those participants—67 percent of general pupils and 95 percent of religious pupils—who said they believed in God.

To clarify what I mean by creation arguments, here are a few examples. Aryeh is a fifth grader at a religious school. Having stated that he believes in God, I ask him why. He responds, "There has to be someone who created everything and that's the Holy One, Blessed be He." Aryeh appears to be offering a version, albeit a highly condensed and simplified one, of the cosmological or "first cause" argument. Everything that exists must have been brought into existence somehow and the most plausible somehow, as far as Aryeh is concerned, is a divine act of creation.

Not all creation justifications were like Aryeh's. Many participants offered variants of the teleological argument or "argument from design" rather than the cosmological argument. And in most cases their justifications were much more elaborate. However, the justifications I am considering here all shared with Aryeh's response some kind of appeal to evidence that the world or humankind was divinely created.

Conversely, creation refutations are counter-arguments that participants expected non-believers to use to refute their religious belief. Shlomit is a twelfth grader at a religious school. Having already stated and justified her belief in God, she is asked what a non-believer might say to show that she is wrong. She replies, "She'd probably bring up all the scientific proofs: that the world evolved from an explosion and wasn't created by anyone, or that we started out as apes." Shlomit here sets up a combination of "Big Bang" theory and evolutionary biology as a possible challenge to her earlier attempts to justify her religious belief.

Before comparing the distributions of creation arguments among religious and general pupils, it is important to point out that pupils at both types of school encounter evolutionary biology in the context of Israel's national biology curriculum. Indeed, the same biology textbooks are used in both streams. Pupils at religious schools may therefore be assumed to be just as familiar with evolutionary biology as are their peers at general schools.

Given this context, the observed school differences in argumentation are quite striking. Whereas no significant school differences were observed with respect to creation refutations, pupils at religious schools (71 percent) were more than twice as likely as their peers at general schools (33 percent) to employ creation justifications in support of their religious beliefs χ^2 (1,163) = 23.62, $p < 0.001$, and $\phi = 0.38$.

How may this difference be explained? Religious pupils do not appear to be any less *aware* than general pupils of the challenges posed to creationism by contemporary theories of cosmology and evolution. Indeed, although the trend was not statistically significant, religious pupils (29 percent) generated creation refutations *more* often than general pupils (17 percent). Rather, where general and religious pupils seemed to differ was in their respective evaluations of the *seriousness* of these challenges. Whereas religious pupils tended to treat such challenges as if they could be easily dismissed, general pupils were less sanguine.

To illustrate, consider the following interview excerpts. Tehiyah, is a twelfth grader at a religious school. Like her classmate Shlomit, she too cites contemporary scientific accounts of cosmology and evolution as potential counterarguments to belief in God. However, she is almost incredulous that anyone would take such counter-arguments seriously:

> I don't have a shadow of a doubt, especially as someone who has studied biology, that this whole world must have been created by someone . . . not from monkeys, not from colliding rocks, not from any of those things . . . If secular people would just learn biology, then they wouldn't be able to come out with all that Stephen Hawking nonsense, that it's rocks and all that stuff.

By way of contrast let us now look at what Shirli, a twelfth grader at a general school has to say about these same theories: "To me, personally, it doesn't seem logical that the world could come into existence just like that. Personally, that's what I believe." Where Tehiyah rejects evolutionism out of hand as something that is obviously and objectively false, Shirli seeks to diminish its force by relativizing it: rather than framing the evolutionist challenge to creationism as a zero-sum game, Shirli frames it as a question of personal taste or preference. Specifically, she admits by implication that, while evolutionism seems implausible to her, it may seem plausible to others.

Cultural Epistemologies

These distinctive ways of framing the conflict between evolutionist and creationist accounts of origins were not unique to these two particular participants. Nor were they distributed randomly throughout the sample. Rather, they varied systematically with school. Pupils at religious schools tended to reject evolutionism out of hand as nonsensical and ridiculous, whereas pupils at general schools tended to argue that, "personally," they did not find it convincing.

Thus, what might have seemed at first glance to be a simple group difference in the use of a particular kind of justification turns out, on closer inspection, to be symptomatic of a more comprehensive difference in how individuals from these two communities treat theories of origins. Pupils from religious and general schools not only employ different argumentative strategies, they subscribe to different conceptions of cosmology. Religious pupils subscribe to an objectivist conception of cosmology, in which God's creation of the universe is obvious and incontestable. General pupils subscribe to a subjectivist conception in which beliefs about origins are matters of personal preference.

And this is only the tip of the iceberg. As noted earlier, the participants were required not only to justify their own beliefs and to generate possible counter-arguments, but also to respond to various general questions about the nature of the dispute. I will focus on two questions in particular. Is the question rationally decidable? And is it possible that I am wrong? These questions are of particular interest because traditional psychological accounts of epistemic development have used responses to such questions to distinguish levels of epistemological maturity (see, e.g. Kuhn, 1991; King and Kitchener, 1994).

According to such accounts, people progress through at least three discrete stages or levels of epistemological understanding, each following the other in invariant sequence and constituting a comprehensive transformation of the individual's conception of knowledge. At the realist stage, every question is considered to have a single, correct answer that can be known, at least by experts, with absolute certainty. At the relativist stage, all knowledge claims are considered subjective and idiosyncratic to the tastes and preferences of the individual. And at the rationalist stage, knowledge is seen as something that is constructed tentatively by evaluating the evidence for and against competing beliefs and points of view. Thus, according to these accounts, relativists are distinguished from naïve realists by their insistence that there is no rational procedure for deciding between competing knowledge claims, whereas rationalists are distinguished from realists and relativists by their recognition that knowledge is inherently fallible.

In one respect, the age trends in the present sample were consistent with traditional accounts of epistemic development. The fifth graders (71 percent) tended more than eighth (49 percent) or twelfth graders (29 percent) to consider the question of belief in God to be rationally decidable $\chi^2 (2,163) = 19.43$, $p < 0.001$, and $\phi = 0.34$. However, not only were no significant age differences observed with respect to fallibility, but, even among fifth graders, around half the participants acknowledged that their belief might be mistaken.

Moreover, systematic differences were observed between religious and general pupils. Religious pupils (68 percent) tended to consider their religious belief to be infallible more than general pupils (33 percent) χ^2 (1,163) = 20.08, $p < 0.001$, and $\phi = 0.35$. Similarly, religious pupils (60 percent) tended to consider the question of belief in God to be rationally decidable more than general pupils (39 percent) χ^2 (1,163) = 6.07, $p = 0.010$, and $\phi = 0.20$.

These findings suggest that religious pupils differ from general pupils, not only in their preferred strategies of belief–justification, nor only in their general approaches to theories of cosmology and evolution, but also, at a more fundamental level, in their conception of the basic epistemological character of disputes about belief in God. Religious pupils consider such disputes to be not only rationally decidable, but to be decidable conclusively in their own favor. General pupils, on the other hand, consider such disputes to be unsusceptible in principle to rational resolution and are more willing to countenance the possibility that their own belief might be mistaken.

Epistemologies and Identities

If one were to interpret these school differences according to the hierarchical assumptions of traditional accounts of epistemic development one would be forced to conclude that pupils at religious schools are less mature than their peers at general schools. Indeed, this is precisely how some researchers have interpreted their own recent findings of connections between religious orthodoxy, creationism, and epistemological beliefs (cf. Desimpelaere *et al.*, 1999; Sinatra *et al.*, 2001).

This is certainly one possible interpretation of such connections. But it is not the only possible interpretation. It assumes that subscription to realist, relativist, or rationalist epistemological beliefs is a matter of cognitive maturity alone. However, if there are good reasons that cognitively sophisticated and mature individuals might have for subscribing to epistemological beliefs that psychologists have traditionally viewed as naïve and immature then alternative interpretations must be considered.

I propose that there are such reasons and that, therefore, we need to consider alternative interpretations. Specifically, I propose that people's epistemologies are related to their personal and cultural identities—their senses of who they are as individuals and members of communities—and that their epistemological beliefs may be inextricably intertwined with their beliefs about the kinds of people they are or the kinds of people they want to be. Shlomo, a religious twelfth grader, illustrates this point well. Asked directly whether it is possible that his belief in God might be mistaken, Shlomo replies incredulously, "What are you talking about?! I told you: there's absolutely no chance."

From this response, one might reasonably conclude that Shlomo is a realist. After all, he considers the question of God's existence to have a single, correct answer and claims to know with absolute certainty what this answer is. However, when asked a very similar question later in the same interview, Shlomo quickly dispelled this initial impression (interviewer's probes are italicized):

> *You said that you believe in God wholeheartedly. Would you say that you know for certain? [. . .]* Yes, [I know] for certain. It's stupid when you think about it, because if there's one thing that you can't know for certain then it's this. But I do know for certain because, I'm telling you, if I didn't know it for certain, I'd go crazy. No one can accept [that there isn't a God]. There are some people who simply push it away and don't deal with it. That's easy. You can do that. I can too. But I'm telling you, if I knew, if some omniscient person were to come and tell me that there isn't a God, then I'm telling you, I'd go crazy in one second. I couldn't stand it. Suddenly everything would be in doubt. It would be like the floor opening up beneath my feet. Suddenly you don't know anything. Maybe that's what I think. Perhaps it's only me that thinks that, but I'm comfortable thinking it. It's the only thought that I am prepared to accept on this topic.

Shlomo insisted that it is impossible that his belief in God is mistaken. Yet his confidence is not the product of a dispassionate assessment of the grounds for his belief. It is the product of a conscious act of will. Shlomo admitted implicitly that his belief in God may indeed be mistaken. Yet he refused to consider his belief in God as anything but certain, for to do so would be too much for him to bear. Thus, Shlomo's realism is far from naïve. It rests neither on a simplistic understanding of the epistemic status of religious faith nor on delusions of infallibility but on his beliefs about the kind of person he is and the kinds of belief he can live with and the kinds he cannot.

The connections described thus far between cosmologies, epistemologies, and identities illustrate just how complicated it is to disentangle argumentation practices, epistemological beliefs, and conceptions of self. At the same time, however, they emphasize how important it is for educators to distinguish between these various layers or aspects of thinking and being if they are to promote reflective, scientific ways of looking at the world without trampling over the deeply held beliefs and commitments of those they seek to educate. For unless educators appreciate that epistemological beliefs are not merely cognitive or that commitment to creationism may be the result of something other than scientific ignorance, then they are unlikely to take students' values and commitments into account when teaching subject matter that touches on these issues.

The practical implications of these theoretical insights for educators seeking to enact practices of cultural sustainability will be discussed in more detail in the final section of this chapter. However, to appreciate the extent of the practical challenge, one must recognize the conceptual difficulties that underlie it. These conceptual difficulties are well illustrated by recent attempts to study the relations between epistemology, identity, and cultural practices in classrooms. It is to these attempts, therefore, that I now turn.

Socio-cultural Perspectives on School Epistemology: The Promise and the Risk

Current research programs, informed by socio-cultural perspectives, have sought to unravel the complex knot of relations between identities, epistemologies, and cultural practices by looking carefully at moment-to-moment interactions in classrooms for evidence of different kinds of epistemological work getting done. There is much promise in this approach, but also much risk. For if we focus only on moment-to-moment interactions in classrooms we risk underestimating or ignoring the role of practices that take place over longer periods and in other settings.

To illustrate more concretely both the promise and the risk, let us return to my study of religious argumentation and epistemology. So far I have considered cosmologies, epistemologies, and identities in the abstract. Now let us to turn to the contexts within which they get negotiated and constructed. Specifically, let us ask the following question: What is different in the experiences of religious and general pupils that might account for the differences observed above?

Because this was an interview-based study rather than an observational one, we had to rely on second-hand reports by the participants about the discourse practices in which they engaged, rather than on direct observations. Moreover, explicit questions about these practices were not included in the original interview schedule, so we had to rely on participants' unsystematic comments-in-passing. A key contribution of the socio-cultural research frameworks currently being developed is that studies using them would necessarily generate more direct evidence of discourse practices than I am relying on here. Nonetheless, the picture these unsystematic and fragmentary comments painted of divergent discourse practices is quite striking.

It appears that religious and general pupils engage in theological discourse in very different settings and under very different conditions. In religious schools, pupils experience theological discourse within the context of official classes in which teachers or rabbis set out to prove God's existence and to rebut conclusively any potential counter-arguments. As Hannah, a religious eighth grader, commented, "Every seminar they bring up the whole thing; that God exists, proving to us that God exists." In contrast, pupils in general schools reported no such instances of "official" theological discourse. Instead, when referring to previous occasions on which they had discussed the question of God's existence, they tended to cite informal conversations with peers that ended with the opposing sides agreeing to disagree. The following comment by Ron, a secular twelfth grader, is typical: "To tell you the truth, I had exactly the same argument with my friend. We sometimes go hiking and speak about this kind of stuff. And I didn't succeed. I'm always saying stuff to him and he's always saying stuff to me, but neither of us is ever persuaded."

An especially striking example of school discourse practices serving as a venue for cultural education is provided by the phenomenon of "pre-interview coaching." At two of the participating religious elementary schools, my suspicions of such coaching were aroused after encountering almost identical lines of argumentation in my interviews with pupils from a particular class. These suspicions were later confirmed by pupils' explicit admissions at a later point in the interview that they had indeed been "prepared" for my visit. In one school, pupils had been told a story about Rabbi Akiva (though in one version, Akiva had mutated into Maimonides), who convinces a skeptic (in some versions a Gentile, in others a heretic) by showing him a beautiful painting and telling him that his cat (in almost all versions "Mitzi") had painted it by accident by upsetting a box of paints on a canvas. When the skeptic objects that a cat could not have produced such a magnificent work of art, the rabbi points out the much greater complexity and beauty of the natural world, showing that it too must be the result of design. In the other school, pupils were told a story about an inspector who comes to school and goads the children by insisting that, since he cannot see God, God must not exist. One of the pupils in the story then responds that the inspector must have no intelligence, since he cannot see that either. Although no such instances of explicit coaching were observed in religious high schools, religious pupils often referred in their responses to seminars or classes in which theological questions were dealt with by teachers, rabbis, or counselors in similarly summary fashion (see, e.g. Hannah's comment above).

Taken together, these findings suggest that many of the school differences described above may have their roots in the divergent cultures of theological discourse to which religious and secular pupils are exposed. Specifically, by exposing their pupils to models of theological discourse in which all questions can be answered clearly and conclusively in the affirmative, religious schools appear to foster argumentative practices and epistemic orientations that look (at least superficially) very much like naïve realism. Conversely, by implicitly consigning religious beliefs to the private domain, general schools seem to promote a view of theological matters as questions of personal preference that lie beyond the pale of rational debate.

An analysis of this kind demonstrates the importance of a practice-oriented approach to the study of student epistemologies. If we are to understand more fully the processes by which particular epistemological orientations are fostered or discouraged in different educational settings, we must attempt to observe these processes as they are enacted in practice.

I am not sure if the kinds of practice described above qualify as "micro-practices," as defined by Sherin (2004). They seem to be at about the right grain size in the sense that they could be observed in episodes that last minutes or hours. Yet, the *meaning* of these episodes for the people participating in them derives from their being located within a broader context of *other* practices against which they are fore-grounded. For example, religious pupils may learn to treat evolutionary theory differently from other scientific theories, not—or not only—because of discourse practices in biology class, but because of how issues they encounter in biology class are encountered in different ways and under different circumstances in religion class or their principal's sermons on the weekly portion. Moreover, as in the case of theological discourse among general pupils, the practices in which we are interested may be ones that occur beyond the school walls or that are noticeable only by their absence or by contrast with practices in other institutional settings. None-theless, if defined broadly enough, I am confident that the frameworks such as that of Sherin (2004) could encompass practices of these kinds and durations.

However, I am less confident about their ability to encompass processes spread over wider stretches of space or time. The first such process I will consider is that of individual development. Sherin's (2004) micro-practices framework, like many other recent contributions to the literature on student epistemologies, seeks to introduce greater sensitivity to context in the study of epistemic development. As noted earlier, such development was charac-terized in initial studies as a progression through discrete stages or levels of epistemological understanding, each following the other in invariant sequence and constituting a comprehensive transformation of the individual's con-ception of knowledge (see, e.g. Perry, 1970; Chandler, 1975; Kitchener and King, 1981). In more recent studies, researchers have begun to question the comprehensiveness of these shifts in epistemological understanding and to attend more closely to the variety of contexts within which epistemic judgments are made. Some have sought to show that epistemic development is a somewhat "domain-dependent" process that occurs with respect to some kinds of knowledge claim before others (Kuhn *et al.*, 2000; Hallett *et al.*, 2002). Others have sought to show that epistemological beliefs are multidimensional rather than unitary (e.g. Schommer, 1990, 1993; Elby and Hammer, 2001; Hammer and Elby, 2002). And still others have emphasized the importance of cultural context (e.g. Gottlieb, 2002; Chan and Elliott, 2004).

These studies have shown that traditional models of epistemic development were insufficiently sensitive to context. However, in modifying the assump-tions of these models, we should take care not to throw out the developmental baby with the universalist bathwater. Trajectories of epistemic develop-ment may vary systematically across domains, dimensions, and cultures. But that does not mean that there is no such thing as epistemic development or that in fact there are not reasonably stable age trends. For example, despite the differences between religious and general pupils, a stable trend towards considering the question of belief in God was rationally undecidable was observed over the course of adolescence in both groups.

By focusing on micro-practices, researchers necessarily eliminate from their immediate frame of reference processes of individual development that take place over the course of months and years rather than minutes and hours (see e.g. Krakowski, 2004). For all my own interest in context, I think it would be a mistake to ignore these developmental processes. Just as practices emerge and change over time, so too do people. And just as epistemological beliefs, values, and commitments can exist outside individual heads, so too can they exist inside them. If researchers are to keep individual development on their agenda, then the study of micro-practices must be extended to include these processes. Practically speaking, this means studying micro-practices among a wide range of age groups and following changes in micro-practices of a given group longitudinally.

Yet, processes of individual development are only one kind of long-term process that we need to track if we are to understand the emergence of particular epistemological orientations at particular times and places. There are processes of even longer duration that must be considered.

Just as the meaning of a single statement of epistemological belief cannot be understood without situating that statement within the broader context of practices from which it emerged, so too cannot the moment-to-moment practices within an individual classroom be understood without situating them within the broader network of institutional practices that determine what kinds of activities take place in that classroom. Classrooms are located in school buildings that are built and furnished in particular ways, class schedules are structured according to particular curricular, pedagogic, and bureaucratic principles that are developed over long periods by various local and national stakeholders, teachers are trained in various institutions (each with their own agendas and constitutive practices) to interact with students in particular ways, and so on. If the moment-to-moment conversational practices *within* classrooms play an important part in fostering particular epistemologies and ways of thinking then, by extension, so too do these other processes which take place *outside* classrooms, but which largely determine what happens inside them.

Consider general and religious pupils' divergent approaches to evolutionary theory. Undoubtedly, these are attributable—at least in part—to what happens in general and religious classrooms. But the different kinds of things that happen in general and religious classrooms are attributable in turn to such things as the different ways in which class times and spaces are structured, teachers trained, curricula designed, and so on, at each type of institution.

And if things are not complicated enough already, then we can take this one step further. The institutional practices just considered have been discussed ahistorically. But these larger institutional practices are shaped themselves by longer-term processes of historical change. National priorities change, education systems get reorganized, new curriculum topics or pedagogies emerge, and others become contentious. And beyond the official education system: ethnic tensions build up and subside, new political and religious movements emerge, scientific paradigms shift, and so on.

In the case of how religious and general pupils approach evolutionary theory, the importance of such processes cannot be underestimated. Discussions of theories of origins within Jewish theology, views on the centrality of evolutionary theory to modern biological science, changes in biology curricula and the training of science teachers, and policy changes in the Israeli education system in general and the religious stream in particular: all these have their own histories and each of these histories has left some imprint on the discourse practices in contemporary classrooms.

If moment-to-moment interactions in classrooms are micro-practices, then these latter processes might be thought of as macro-practices. We must indeed examine micro-practices if we are to understand better the different kinds of epistemological work that get done in classroom discourse. However, a focus on micro-processes alone risks blinding us to the importance of macro-processes in shaping such discourse.

My point is not that research frameworks such as Sherin's (2004) micro-practices framework are misguided in any way. On the contrary, I believe they serve as an important corrective to the tendency of researchers to study student epistemologies out of context. My concern is only that the particular slices of context on which the micro-practices framework trains its analytic lens are themselves situated within broader networks of practices that need also to be taken into account. The solution is not to try and encompass everything into one complete and true analytic framework or research design—no research framework can encompass everything. It is, rather, to recognize the inherent partiality of our selected framework and to seek out additional perspectives and analytic tools that can be used to complement it, correct some if its biases, and shrink its blind spots.

An example of the kind of simplification that must be resisted is the infamous tendency to infer causal direction from evidence of association. Researchers using an analytic framework that views epistemological beliefs as emergent properties of communicative micro-practices will tend to interpret data that associate group practices with individual beliefs in terms of the former causing the latter. Conversely, researchers using an analytic framework that views discourse practices as products of the epistemological commitments of the individuals who engage in them will tend to interpret the same data in terms of the latter causing the former. Because it is impossible to translate the processes and connections in which we are interested into rigorously controllable and testable laboratory experiments without fatally distorting them, we do not have any clear-cut method for deciding between these competing interpretations. Moreover, as the examples considered in this chapter suggest, each of the associated elements may be mutually reinforcing. For instance, religious certainty is valued within the orthodox community in Israel, is promoted through various discourse practices in religious schools (such as seminars at which proofs for the existence of God are rehearsed and potential counter-arguments rebutted and ridiculed), and is exhibited in religious pupils' rejection out of hand of evolutionary counter-arguments to the argument from design. Do the seminars cause the certainty or does the certainty cause the seminars? Does the creationism cause the belief in God or does the belief in God cause the creationism? Does Shlomo subscribe to the epistemological beliefs that he does because of the person he is or is he the person he is because of the epistemological beliefs to which he subscribes?

The data we have collected thus far do not provide any clear-cut answer to such questions. Nor is it easy to imagine additional data that would. If anything, the data suggest some kind of co-construction rather than a one-way causality in either direction. As cultural psychologists have argued in a number of other contexts, it may be most helpful to conceive of cultural practices and individual cognition as "making each other up" (Shweder *et al.*, 1998 Rogoff, 2003; Shweder, 2003). Stated as baldly as this, the suggestion may sound a little too pat. But placed in the context of the connections described above between argumentative strategies, cosmologies, identities, and discourse practices it begins to look like a subtle and helpful perspective. At the very least, it serves as a corrective to the tendency to jump to any premature conclusions about causal directionality.

Implications for Cultural Education

The empirical findings and theoretical insights presented above have several important implications for educators concerned with issues of cultural sustainability and cultural education. I begin with the obvious and move on to the less immediately apparent.

First, cultural education (sometimes) works. The differences described in the previous sections between the epistemic values and argumentative practices of religious and general pupils demonstrate the effectiveness of educational institutions as promoters and sustainers of cultural capital. Although numerically a minority, the religious Zionist community in Israel has managed, in its educational institutions, to create a cultural niche, wherein beliefs, values, and practices different to those of the majority secular community are promoted and sustained.

Second, cultural education is reactive. Not merely in the general and tautological sense that groups seek to enact practices of cultural sustainability (i.e. they engage in "cultural education", as opposed to "education") only when they perceive their beliefs, values, and practices to be under attack. But also in the more specific and substantive sense that such education assumes the form of tactically situated roadblocks expressly outfitted to withstand and counter predicted incursions. For example, stories ridiculing evolutionary theory do not get told accidentally. They get told to people at times and in places perceived by interested parties to be in need of protection from the lure of evolutionary theory. In an important sense, when we use the term "cultural education," we really mean "counter-cultural education." This does not mean that educators seeking to sustain minority beliefs, values, and practices can never take the initiative or think strategically. But it does mean that their agenda is determined for the most part by the nature of the hegemonic forces against which they wish to operate. Educators ignore these inherent constraints at their peril: One does not survive a bear hug by treating the bear as if it were a mouse.

Third, a curriculum is only one resource at the disposal of cultural education. Even when uncongenial curricular content is imposed from above by a majority culture using all the legal and bureaucratic forces at its disposal, educators who seek to sustain minority beliefs, values, and practices can create niches where the homogenizing sting of such content is subverted or neutralized. The theological discourse practices at religious schools are a case in point. Due to its inclusion in the national biology curriculum, evolutionary theory is granted some measure of validity within the discourse context of biology textbooks, classes, and homework. But when it comes to theological discourse, such validity is explicitly negated and ridicule takes its place. I refrain here from any judgments about either the desirability or effectiveness of such compartmentalization. I wish only to point out that educators sometimes use discourse practices in one area of school life to subvert or neutralize culturally problematic curricular content in another.

Fourth, the task facing educators who seek to sustain minority cultural practices is not merely to gain control of particular curricular decisions. It is also, more fundamentally, to contest the hegemonic models of rationality and intellectual maturity that underlie the framing of such decisions. As we saw above, traditional models of epistemic development equate subscription to a realist epistemology with cognitive immaturity. Yet, we saw also that realist beliefs are actively promoted in some cultural settings and that, in these settings, epistemological realism may be less an expression of cognitive immaturity than of commitment to the values and practices of one's community. Educators whose curricular decisions rest on uncritical acceptance of traditional models of epistemic development may thus be unwitting accomplices in undermining the values and practices of minority communities. And, conversely, educators who seek to sustain minority beliefs, values, and practices need actively to refute the implicit assumption that such beliefs, values, and practices are irrational or backward.

Fifth, educators who seek to implement practices of cultural sustainability must resist the temptation to imagine that the educational settings in which they work are either infinitely mutable on one hand or deterministically closed to intentional modification on the other. In truth, we know very little about how cultural change is brought about. And this is not simply because we have not yet done enough research. As I have attempted to show in the preceding section, it is because there are great conceptual and methodological obstacles to drawing clear conclusions about the causes and effects of cultural phenomena. Our only recourse is to collaborate in the study of cultural sustainability and at several levels, including the disciplinary, the theoretical, the empirical, and the practical.

At the disciplinary level, collaboration is needed to ensure that the unique contributions of psychological, sociological, geographical, economic, historical, political, religious, and linguistic factors (to name but a few) to cultural change are taken into account and given their due. At the theoretical level, collaboration is needed to ensure that our preferred theoretical frameworks within a given discipline do not blind us to alternative descriptions of the same phenomena or even to the very existence of particular phenomena. For example, within the discipline of psychology, the behaviorist, the neuro-psychologist, the psychoanlyst, the cognitivist, and the developmentalist each look at cultural phenomena through different lenses, each with their own areas of sharp focus and each with their own blind spots. At the empirical level, collaboration is needed to ensure that our focus on particular instances or cases of cultural change does not lead us into parochial over-generalization, which itself may serve as a form of cultural hegemony. Issues of cultural sustainability vary enormously, depending on the particularities of the culture seeking to sustain itself and the challenges with which it is faced. Only by comparing across cases (something this conference allows and encourages us to do) can we hope to become wiser about general features of cultural change as well as the nuances specific to particular socio-historical settings. And finally, at the practical level, collaboration is needed to allow us to learn from the successes and failures of others' attempts to enact practices of cultural sustainability. To twist a famous dictum of Tolstoy, every threatened culture may be threatened in its own unique way. But that does not mean that educators concerned with sustaining particular cultures cannot learn from each other. When hegemonic forces leave us with so few options, the least we can do is to learn as much as we can about the options we have.

Acknowledgments

The data reported in this chapter were collected in course of the author's doctoral research at the Hebrew University of Jerusalem. The research was made possible by grants from the Israel Foundation Trustees, the Golda Meir

Fund, the Mandel Foundation, the Memorial Foundation for Jewish Culture, and the Professor Eliezer Stern Institute for the Study and Advancement of Religious Education at Bar Ilan University. Adam Afterman, Eyal Aviv, Tali Berko, and Yasmin Ron assisted in the construction and testing of the coding scheme. Earlier versions of sections of this chapter were presented, respectively, at the Biennial Meeting of the European Association for Research in Learning and Instruction in Padua, Italy in August 2003 and at the Annual Meeting of the American Educational Research Association in San Diego, U.S. in April 2004. The author thanks the participants in those symposia and in the cultural education–cultural sustainability conference in Jerusalem for their penetrating questions and profound insights.

Resources and Tools for Educators

Questions

Educators seeking to apply insights from this paper to their own institutional setting should ask themselves the following questions.

1. On what assumptions about the nature of knowledge are the forms of argumentation practiced in my classroom (or other educational setting) based?
2. What values and beliefs do these practices reflect and support?
3. Where do these values and beliefs diverge from those of the culture(s) I wish to sustain?
4. What am I doing now and what might I do in the future to close this gap?

For Further Reading

For a comparison of different approaches to the study of epistemological understanding and their relations to educational practices, see the special issue of the journal *Educational Psychologist* (Volume 39, Issue 1) guest edited by Barbara K. Hofer in 2004. For more comprehensive analyses of the relations discussed in this paper between cultural practices, models of maturity, and conceptions of truth, beauty, and justice see Barbara Rogoff's (2003) *The Cultural Nature of Human Development* (Oxford: Oxford University Press) and Richard Shweder's (2004) *Why Do Men Barbecue? Recipes for Cultural Psychology* (Cambridge, MA: Harvard University Press).

Suggestions for Educators

My practical advice to cultural educators is threefold: know your context, create niches, and define your goals in your own terms.

1. Know your context. The above analyses have shown how intimately the educational practices of minority cultures are intertwined with the discourse practices of the majority cultures within which they are embedded and with which they interact. To act effectively, cultural educators must acquire a comprehensive understanding of their particular cultural context. They must become experts in the processes of curriculum development, teacher training, performance assessment, policy formation, and so on through which the majority culture seeks to impose its hegemony on educational practices and be able to identify areas of potential conflict and accommodation with the beliefs, values, and practices of the minority cultures they wish to sustain. For example, those who wish to sustain creationist beliefs in the face of hegemonic forces that promote evolutionism must know where and how within the educational system evolutionist beliefs are promoted and what legal and social constraints there are on the promotion within this system of creationist beliefs. The practices described in this paper indicate how successfully and comprehensively modern orthodox educators in Israel have mapped their context and identified points of educational leverage. In different ways, but with some similar outcomes, so have creationists in the U.S.

2. Create niches. Given the overriding imbalance of power between minority cultures and the majority cultures within which they are embedded, one of the most promising strategies of cultural sustainability is the creation of cultural niches within which this balance of power is temporarily and selectively reversed. While representatives of minority cultures rarely have enough power to change a national curriculum, they often have enough power to create protected spaces and times within their educational institutions wherein the epistemological assumptions of a hegemonic national curriculum can be challenged, relativized, or undermined.

3. Define your goals in your own terms. This chapter has shown how seemingly impartial studies of educational processes or apparently neutral theories in developmental psychology turn out on closer inspection to rest on assumptions about the nature of knowledge, maturity, and cultural identity that are specific to a particular Western, secular world view. By taking for granted the forms of educational discourse that are most prevalent in the majority culture, minority educators constrain themselves artificially and perhaps even undermine their own ultimate goals. What practitioners of cultural education mean by "growth," "understanding," "maturity," "knowledge," "justification," and so on may diverge substantially from the meanings of these terms as used in official documents and the "neutral" educational discourse of the dominant culture. Educators concerned with

cultural sustainability must therefore use such terms warily and, where necessary, reject them in favor of culture-specific terms better equipped to communicate their precise goals. For example, it is a mistake to define educational goals in terms of knowledge, understanding, and awareness if the qualities of mind that the cultural educator wishes really to promote and sustain are faith, commitment, and belonging. Cultural educators should be appropriately skeptical of universalist assumptions about the nature of cognitive maturity and have the courage to define their educational goals in terms of their own—culture-specific—conception of the educated person and the ideal society.

You might now want to turn to your community/staff/students etc. and request them to give their own answers to these rather important issues.

References

Chan, K. W. & Elliott, R. G. (2004). Epistemological beliefs across cultures: Critique and analysis of beliefs structure studies. *Educational Psychology*, 24(2), 123–142.

Chandler, M. J. (1975). Relativism and the problem of epistemological loneliness. *Human Development*, 18(3), 171–180.

Desimpelaere, P., Sulas, F., Duriez, B., & Hutsebaut, D. (1999). Psycho-epistemological styles and religious beliefs. *International Journal for the Psychology of Religion*, 9(2), 125–137.

Elby, A. & Hammer, D. (2001). On the substance of a sophisticated epistemology. *Science Education*, 85(5), 554–567.

Gottlieb, E. (2002). Learning how to believe: The mediation of epistemic development by cultural discourse practices. In P. Bell, R. Stevens, & T. Satwicz (Eds.), *Keeping learning complex: Proceedings of the Fifth International Conference of the Learning Sciences* (pp. 118–124). Mahwah, NJ: Erlbaum.

Hallett, D., Chandler, M. J., & Krettenauer, T. (2002). Disentangling the course of epistemic development: Parsing knowledge by epistemic content. *New Ideas in Psychology*, 20(2/3), 285–307.

Hammer, D. & Elby, A. (2002). On the form of a personal epistemology. In B. K. Hofer & P. R. Pintrich (Eds.), *Personal epistemology: The psychology of beliefs about knowledge and knowing* (pp. 169–191). Mahwah, NJ: Erlbaum.

King, P. M. & Kitchener, K. S. (1994). *Developing reflective judgment.* San Francisco: Jossey-Bass.

Kitchener, K. S. & King, P. M. (1981). Reflective judgment: Concepts of justification and their relationship to age and education. *Journal of Applied Developmental Psychology*, 2, 89–116.

Krakowski, M. (2004). Applying the micro-practices framework to ultra-orthodox Jewish education. Paper presented at the Annual Meeting of American Educational Research Association, San Diego, CA.

Kuhn, D. (1991). *The skills of argument.* Cambridge: Cambridge University Press.

Kuhn, D., Cheney, R., & Weinstock, M. (2000). The development of epistemological understanding. *Cognitive Development*, 15(3), 309–328.

Perry, W. G. (1970). *Forms of intellectual and ethical development in the college years: A scheme.* Troy, MO: Holt, Rinehart and Winston.

Rogoff, B. (2003). *The cultural nature of human development.* New York: Oxford University Press.

Schommer, M. (1990). Effects of beliefs about the nature of knowledge on comprehension. *Journal of Educational Psychology*, 82(3), 498–504.

Schommer, M. (1993). Comparisons of beliefs about the nature of knowledge and learning among post-secondary students. *Research in Higher Education*, 34(3), 355–370.

Shamai, S. (2000). "Cultural shift": The case of Jewish religious education in Israel. *British Journal of Sociology of Education*, 21(3), 401–417.

Sherin, B. L. (2004). Micro-practices and four meanings of "epistemology." Paper presented at the Annual Meeting of American Educational Research Association, San Diego, CA.

Sinatra, G. M., Southerland, S., & McConaughy, F. (2001). Intentions, beliefs, and acceptance of evolutionary theory. Paper presented at the Annual Meeting of American Educational Research Association, Seattle, WA.

Shweder, R. (2003). *Why do men barbecue? Recipes for cultural psychology.* Cambridge, MA: Harvard University Press.

Shweder, R. A., Goodnow, J., Hatano, G., LeVine, R. A., Markus, H., & Miller, P. (1998). The cultural psychology of development. In R. M. Lerner (Ed.), *Handbook of child psychology: Vol. 1. Theoretical models of human development* (5th edn, pp. 865–937). New York: Wiley.

CHAPTER 16

"Dorks with Yarmulkes": An Ethnographic Inquiry into the Surprised Embrace of Parochial Day Schools by Liberal American Jews

ALEX POMSON

For most of the last century, the great majority of liberal Jews in North America, if they chose to provide their children with a formal Jewish education, opted to send them to religious supplementary schools. As Sarna (1998) argued, this educational model provided a satisfactory solution to "the most fundamental problem of Jewish life: how to live in two worlds at once, how to be both American and Jewish, part of the larger society and apart from it" (p. 9). During the day children attended public schools along with their fellow citizens and during evenings and weekends they sat alongside co-religionists in synagogue classrooms so as to be exposed to Jewish culture and tradition.

In recent years, it seems as if there has been a changed assessment of what it means to be Jewish in America. Increasing numbers of liberal Jews have abandoned the public school system and have signed up their children for a parochial model of education in which they study a dual curriculum of Jewish and general studies in an all-day setting separate from non-Jewish students.

In this chapter I try to make sense of the shift or drift among liberal Jews towards parochial education. I review conventional sociological accounts of the growth of Jewish day schools in North America and then interrogate the sociological paradigm employed by drawing on data from two ethnographic studies of liberal Jewish families in Canada and the U.S. who have eschewed free public education in favor of private Jewish all-day schooling. These qualitative studies enable me to explore why individuals who, according to standard sociological measures, are less and less engaged by Jewish institutions nevertheless opt to educate their children within a private Jewish institutional setting. I ask whether, after three or more generations of assimilation into majority North American culture, liberal Jews have made minority cultural survival a priority.

A Sociological Account of Day School Growth

Many scholars view the growth of Jewish all-day schooling as one of the most remarkable social facts of North American Jewish life since the Second World War (Ackerman, 1989; Wertheimer, 1999a). In 1944, there were 39 day schools in the U.S., most of them in New York City. Today, there are almost 700 schools located in 33 states and the District of Columbia (Schick, 2000). As the number of schools has increased, so the proportion of Jewish school-age children enrolled has also risen. It is estimated that in 1962 there were 60,000 pupils in day schools, that by 1982/1983 there were some 104,000 students, representing about 10 percent of the Jewish school-age population, (Della Pergola and Schmelz, 1989), and in 2000 approximately 200,000 students, that is nearly one-quarter of all Jewish school-age children (Schick, 2000).

In Canada, the first day schools opened more recently than in the U.S. and grew more rapidly. In Toronto, the first all-day Jewish schools were launched in 1942, but by 1982 more children attended day schools than went to the city's Jewish supplementary schools (Shoub, 1991). In Montreal, the country's second major Jewish population center, schools grew even more quickly. By 1981, thanks to provincial funding for parochial Jewish schools, two-thirds of all Jewish children attended day schools (Weinfeld and Zelkowitz, 1991). By 1983, at least one day school existed in all ten Canadian cities with a Jewish population of 2,000 or more (Kutnick, 1989).

While the great majority of day school students in both Canada and the U.S. were and still are enrolled in orthodox schools, a noteworthy proportion of total day school growth over the last 15 years can be attributed to the registration of children in non-orthodox schools. Today between one-fifth and one-quarter of the total day school population attends non-orthodox schools that have proliferated both in number and variety. The first non-orthodox day school in North America opened in 1951, some 50 years after the first orthodox day school. Today, there are more than 150 day schools either affiliated with non-orthodox denominations or organized as pluralistic or non-denominational institutions.

The growth of day schools in general and of non-orthodox schools in particular has attracted a great deal of popular comment and an ever-thickening scholarly literature. Some tell this story in romantic terms where the charms of parochial education are seen to have lured the Jewish community after a long-running affair with public schooling (Beinart, 1999). Others employ a more tragic tone, claiming that the day school phenomenon threatens to erode a deep consensus about how Jews educate their children (Shrager, 2002).

Invariably, the growth in the non-orthodox (liberal Jewish) day school population has been attributed to four general causes.

1. The decay of public education. Jewish families have turned their backs on public schools as part of a larger withdrawal of the middle classes from public institutions left to decay by the public policies of conservative governments in many Western countries (Shapiro, 1996). In an era when publicly funded institutions have become increasingly synonymous with the poor and when the public perceives standards in public schools as increasingly inferior to those of private schools, Jewish parents, who often are themselves graduates of public schools, have been reluctant to sacrifice their children to an ideal of public education no matter how strongly felt (Zeldin, 1988). From this perspective, parents have turned to day schools, not so much out of an interest in Jewish education *per se*, but rather because Jewish schools seem to offer a quality of general education superior to that offered by most public schools (Kelman, 1984).

2. Jewish embourgoisement. The decay of the public-school system has coincided with the steady embourgoisement of the Jewish community and the increased capacity of many families to pay for private education. Increasingly, Jewish parents have chosen not between public schools and day schools but between different forms of private education, with the Jewish parochial school as one option (Beinart, 1999). The influence of increased affluence on school choice has been seen most vividly in the creation of "boutique" day schools with small enrollments, catering at great expense to families with particular educational tastes. (According to Schick (2000), 40 percent of U.S. day schools enroll 100 or fewer students and in most instances the geographical location and/or religious orientation of these institutions means they are unlikely to grow much larger.) Diamond (2000) argued that a kind of religious consumerism has resulted in this phenomenon, made possible by an expanding spending power that has also spawned a substantial kosher life style industry. From this perspective, increased disposable income among Jewish families has resulted in day school growth. Some commentators have framed this account of day school growth in broader sociological terms by suggesting that the shift to day schools is not only the product of greater spending power, but a reflection of the socio-economic evolution of the Jewish community which in large part no longer consists of first-generation immigrants (Ackerman,

1989). The two great waves of Jewish immigration to the U.S. occurred at the start of the twentieth century and in the immediate aftermath of the Second World War. For new arrivals at those times, the public school system served as an important vehicle for socialization into the majority society. Today, after two or more generations of deepening assimilation into the majority culture, Jewish parents willingly send their children to separate parochial schools. Either they no longer fear being viewed as outsiders or they have indeed become insiders (Shrager, 2002).

3. The confluence of multiculturalism and the "school choice" movement. Some have argued that the turn to day schools has less to do with changes within Jewish society and culture than with a transformation in the larger socio-political milieu of Western societies that has seen an unexpected confluence in aspects of progressive and conservative educational visions (Shapiro, 1996). Over the last 20 years, there has been an increased receptiveness to the incorporation of multiculturalism in the public domain (Banks and Banks, 1995; Cope and Kalantzis, 2000). This has allowed, with different degrees of integrity and effectiveness, a greater diversity of voices in public schools. It has also legitimized efforts by minority communities to counteract the dissolution of their cultures and identities in the public school system, even if that choice involves withdrawal from the system itself (Miller, 2001). The increased legitimacy of the multicultural project has coincided with the proliferation of calls in right-wing circles for government aid for private schools or at least for the use of public funds to support separate or distinctive schools. This move, generally couched in a rhetoric of school choice, has seen the advance of voucher programs and charter schools in a variety of American states. The coincidence of these trends has reduced concerns among minority ethnic and faith communities about withdrawing from common public schools to create their own separate schools. Within the American Jewish community, it has encouraged some liberal organizations that once advocated for Jewish participation in public education to develop their own networks of non-orthodox day schools. Those who once led opposition to public aid for private religious schools have begun to reassess their stance on the separation of church and state in educational matters (Wertheimer, 1999b).

4. Concerns about Jewish continuity. Within the organized Jewish community, day schools are invariably depicted as the most effective available vehicle for promoting the development of a distinct Jewish identity at a time when rates of Jewish–Gentile intermarriage have risen to unprecedented levels (Jewish Educational Services for North America & United Jewish Communities, 1999). Although until now it has been difficult to determine to what extent this issue is important to families

when choosing schools, there is little doubt that, for parents interested in providing their children with a thick Jewish identity, a polarization of educational options has occurred. Alternatives to day school have withered. Jewish supplementary schools have cut back instructional time from more than ten hours a week to five hours a week or fewer, enabling few such schools to claim that they can provide children with a significant foundation in Jewish literacy. If parents want their children to participate actively in Jewish cultural life or if, minimally, they seek a better than even chance that their child will marry another Jewish person, the day school may be their only option.

Arguments such as these that emphasize the effectiveness of day schools in combating Jewish cultural decline have strongly influenced the creation of new schools, that is the supply rather than the demand side of day school growth (Himmelfarb, 1989). Indeed, in the U.S. a significant proportion of the day schools created during the last ten years have come about as a result of the intervention of activist philanthropic foundations that have identified Jewish day schools as a highly effective means to intensify Jewish awareness and solidarity (Partnership for Excellence in Jewish Education, www.peje.org/about.htm).

Moving from the General to the Particular

As I have suggested elsewhere (Pomson, 2002), the problem with a sociological heuristic like this is that, because it operates at a high level of generality, it cannot predict or explain the choices made by particular individuals in particular communities at particular moments. This account possesses the force of generalizability, but lacks the nuance of the particular in attempting to make sense of the growing appeal of Jewish day schools to liberal Jews.

It is this nuance that I seek by taking up the data from two qualitative studies of parents from across a variety of Jewish denominations whose children are enrolled in day schools in Toronto, Ontario, and in Centreville, a pseudonym for a mid-west American city. The studies have been concerned with the inter-actions between parents and day schools and their influence on one another, but, in this instance, the data make visible the calculations and concerns of liberal parents in the process of choosing an elementary school for their children.

Out of a total sample of sixty families interviewed for the two studies there were eight sets of parents whose children were enrolled at a well-established conservative[1] day school (the Frankel School), ten sets of parents whose children attended a recently established reform Jewish day school (the Baeck Academy), and fourteen sets of parents whose children had recently joined Downtown Jewish Day School (DJDS), a religiously pluralist day school. The data employed in this paper derive then from interviews with thirty-two sets of "parent units" of between 45 minutes and 1.5 hours in length conducted by two local research assistants from a semi-structured interview script.

As might be expected in any qualitative case study of this nature, there are local social, economic, and political factors that make the circumstances in these two cities different from those that might shape school choice in other Jewish communities. For example, the proportion of Jewish children enrolled in Centreville day schools is below the national U.S. average of 20 percent, reflecting the high level of affiliation with area reform congregations generally closer to the universalist norms of classical reform Judaism than is the case in other parts of the country. At the same time, there is a long history among the general population in Centreville of above average enrollment in private schools because of the prominence of European immigrants with a preference for Catholic education. A protracted legal battle over school desegregation climaxing in the 1980s also contributed to a general erosion of confidence in public education in the suburban neighborhoods of Centreville where most Jews live.

In Toronto, in a Jewish community that came of age during the post-Second World War period under the leadership of a generation of Holocaust survivors, there has been, over many decades, a high level of community funding and support for Jewish day schools. In addition, the presence of a sizable, provincially funded, Catholic school system has made it less controversial for Jewish parents to withdraw from public schools even if parochial Jewish schools do not receive a government subsidy. These circumstances have meant that rates of day school enrollment in Toronto have been higher than in almost any other North American city.

The three schools are themselves distinguished not only by their denominational identities, but also by a multitude of particular characteristics. Briefly described, the Frankel School, established more than 20 years ago, is a well-resourced and well-organized institution whose program has an impressive record of enabling students both to "make their mark at prestigious universities" and to take up positions of responsibility within the Jewish community. The Baeck Aacdemy, in contrast, is a fledgling institution struggling to realize an alternative vision of Jewish schooling for which few models exist. It is a school whose development has been powerfully shaped by the creative vision of a small handful of pioneers. DJDS is also a new school attempting to establish a pluralistic and progressive model of day school education that has few parallels in the region. The school is a pioneering institution located in a downtown city neighborhood that was once home to a major concentration of Jews, but today is at some distance from centers of Jewish residence in the city.

In all three instances, then, the schools' appeal can be attributed to quite specific factors in their physical resources, leadership styles, and educational orientation. Nevertheless, despite circumstantial factors such as these, the profile of almost all of the parents in the three schools as liberal-minded Jews who commonly during their own childhoods attended public school, means that this sample provides fertile material for examining why increasing numbers of liberal Jews have been attracted by parochial all-day Jewish schooling. Taken together, the sample makes it possible to examine how parents come to see parochial schooling as *plausible* (that is, a reasonable educational option), *desirable* (preferable to other alternatives whether Jewish or not), or *necessary* (a selection about which they believe they have no choice given their own identities and preferences).

Rational Calculations in School Choice

As indicated above, a prominent element in commentary on the growth of non-orthodox Jewish schools has been the notion that the move to day schools was made possible by a perceived or real decay in public education (Beinart, 1999; Shrager, 2002). In these terms, public schooling constitutes a default option that parents abandon *only* when public education fails to meet their needs or expectations.

Behind such an argument lies a view of school choice as a rational process. This argument begins from a conception of individuals as rational decision makers who act out of self-interest and who choose alternatives that provide the highest benefits based on individual preferences, once they have weighed all of the educational options and alternatives (Ostrom and Ostrom, 1971). According to exponents of this "rational choice" perspective, there are four broad considerations which (all) parents take up when choosing schools: (1) academic and curricular, (2) discipline and safety, (3) religion and social values, and (4) convenience. It is suggested that, when public schools fall short in terms of some or all of these considerations, parents are ready to select alternative public or private schools (Goldring and Shapira, 1993).

Although in our sample few parents took up these four considerations in neat or systematic fashion when weighing up the merits of public or private education, there is evidence of such a calculus behind the way a number of interviewees talked about their choices. For example, one family explained that they switched their children from public school to the Frankel School when they "started noticing that . . . educationally something was missing [in public school] which we couldn't put our finger on at the time, and which we later identified as the Judaics side of the school." Other parents emphasized how much safer it was for their children at the Baeck Academy: "By safe I don't mean locks on the doors . . . It's a safe place emotionally and intellectually. It's remarkably free of negative influences, which is not something that you would expect in many other schools based on the news that I see on TV." At DJDS, a number of parents emphasized how they were attracted by a school where they found values, such as social justice, religious pluralism, and the celebration of personal and social difference, that were absent in the other schools they explored for their children.

In general, it is noticeable that, in Centreville, the great majority of interviewees did not relate to public education as a factor "pushing" them towards the consideration of private or Jewish alternatives. Other than for a minority of families who lived close to Centreville City and talked of choosing between moving to a better school district or staying in the city and sending their children to private school, the interviewees indicated that the (poor) quality of public schools did not make it *necessary* to look at private school alternatives.

In Toronto the dynamic was different and more complicated. A substantial minority of parents expressed grave concerns about the public system, as a result of galloping class sizes, insufficient resources for an increasingly diverse student population, or because of what they perceived as latent anti-Semitism. And yet even those who admitted that the "public schools are scaring the heck out of us" reported that for a long time they hesitated about following a parochial school option: they "went back and forth between public and private."

For many non-orthodox parents in Centreville and Toronto, it seems that the quality of public schools did not make it *necessary* to choose private schools, but that if Jewish day schools were at least as good as public schools they became a *plausible* option. To put it differently, public education provided a frame (a set of reference points) for their choice but not its central cause. This is well demonstrated by the responses of a couple of Baeck parents:

BA4a: The day school academics were the number one thing and the religious content was a bonus.

Inter: For you to choose Baeck?

BA4a: Yes.

BA4b: It had to be at least as good as our public school, which is the best in the state, academically. And we moved to this neighborhood for the schools, which are the best in [the state].

BA4a: And when we moved here Baeck had only been around maybe a year or two and we really had no intention of sending our kid anywhere other than the public school

BA4b: Well I'm a product of public school. [Baeck] wasn't even on our radar. And guess what, I was even hired as a freelance writer to write the brochure for Baeck before they opened. And I'm writing it, and thinking this is going to be a great school and I'll never use it. I mean it was not even a consideration.

BA4a: . . . It wasn't Baeck versus other day school considerations or even other private school considerations.

BA4b: If [our girls] were not at Baeck we would be at public school. If there was not a Reform day school option in Centreville we would be in public school.

BA4a: And if it wasn't an excellent reform day school, if it were just the fact that it were a reform day school it wouldn't have been enough. But the fact that they had an excellent academic side and that we feel they do a great job of instilling the Jewish values. There is a lot of character education that goes on about how they treat others, how they treat the world, how they see their place and those were some of the things that were lacking in the public school . . .

These comments are provocative. They demonstrate that Jewish parents are no longer constrained by the concerns of an earlier generation that to "withdraw our children from public schools and establish schools of our own . . . would be fatal to [Jewish] integration" (Benderley cited by Wertheimer, 1999b, p. 50). At the same time, these comments complicate commonplace notions about the impact of perceptions of public education within the process of day school choice. They prompt the question why do people whose values and experiences make them inclined to support public education (and who occasionally express sharp regret about "abandoning public schools") end up choosing day schools? In the words of one Baeck father, who asked rhetorically about himself, how does an individual who would once have viewed "someone who went to Jewish day school as a dork with a yarmulke" become a day school parent, even when, as his own parents have reminded him, "you have the best public school in the country in your backyard?"

I want to suggest two possible answers to these questions, one that takes up concepts from the developing literature on magnet school choice and another that suggests a move in a less conventional interpretative direction.

The Social Context for School Choice

Smrekar and Goldring (1999), in a study of "magnet school" parents, argued that the most telling critique of a "rational choice" analysis of school selection derives from Coleman's (1990) conceptualization of the social networks within which individuals make decisions. These networks, Coleman (1990) argued, not only influence the quantity and quality of information on which individuals draw in order to make choices (about matters such as where to send their children to school), they also shape the values and commitments that determine how individuals act on this information (that is, how they prioritize considerations and concerns). Of course, this does not mean that people's decisions are socially determined but it does emphasize that so-called individual decisions are made in negotiation with given or inherited social circumstances.

In Centreville, the pervasive impact of such networks was evident from numerous interviews. For example, it was hard to find any Frankel School interviewees who were not intimate with other families that had experienced a Solomon Schechter (conservative day school)-style education either in Centreville or elsewhere in the U.S. This impact is well demonstrated by the case of an intermarried couple who were not themselves affiliated with a conservative congregation and where the husband was "not interested in converting." This couple placed their daughter in Frankel after moving to Centreville from another city where their daughter had been in a public school gifted program. They explained that their daughter "needed the bar higher".

> [In the public school] everything was geared towards pulling people up to the middle. And we had friends in Frankel here, we had friends in Schechter in New York, we had friends in Schechter in Chicago. And it just seemed that in Schechter schools the bar was higher . . . It's more challenging for the kids, and then they throw in this great Jewish education . . . We said, we are not Conservative but we are ready to buy in to that . . . We had all of these friends who are not much more observant than we are, and we met people in the community who belonged to reform synagogues and were happy at Frankel. So that was the decision.

In this case and others, the existence of family and friendship networks improved the quality of information people received about the school (by providing them with insider information), but the networks also possessed a different dimension. They helped people feel a sense of belonging with those already in the school. Parents could see themselves fitting in. They saw families who they looked like or who they would like to look like. Social networks thus made the choice of a particular school *plausible* if not *desirable*.

Indeed, it seems that membership in a familial or friendship network can at some point make choice of a particular school not only *desirable* but *necessary*, that is membership in the network acts as predicate for school choice. While this effect was especially noticeable among orthodox Jews whose membership in one or another synagogue more or less determined their choice of school, other no-less powerful networks exercised influence on the school choices of non-orthodox Jews (people often seen as characteristically individualistic in their Jewish choices). Thus, it became apparent that four families came to the Baeck Academy as a result of their association within a Havura (an informal group for worship, fellowship, and prayer made up of six activist reform families). While none cited membership in the Havura as *the* factor which led them to the school, it is surely no coincidence that these families talk about what they get from the school in similar ways, emphasizing "the joy of Judaism" and Jewish spirituality.

In Toronto, social networks exercised a different and somewhat paradoxical effect. The great majority of DJDS families chose to live downtown because of their enthusiasm for cultural diversity and their disengagement from organized and denominational Jewish life. Nevertheless, they were sometimes made aware of the school and found themselves drawn towards it by acquaintances and friends who shared the same feeling of alienation (even if the sources of their alienation were quite diverse). As intellectual, intermarried, gay, poor, relatively old, or wealthy Jewish parents they were drawn together by what Shields (2000) called a sense of sharing "a community of difference" with other parents.

The Personal Content in School Choice

Running through the presentation of these cases is an emphasis on the social circumstances within which school choice is made and the way these circumstances complicate and constrain individuals' attempts to satisfy their needs and goals. While this (weakly deterministic) interpretative orientation provides a more nuanced view of school choice than is proposed by rational choice theory, I suggest that it may not probe deeply enough into the making of decisions that are freighted with existential significance for the decision maker. School choice, I have suggested elsewhere (Pomson, 2004), is an example of such a decision. For some, there are few personal decisions fraught with greater weight. It expresses and shapes an individual's identity and is grounded, therefore, in an internal conversation or what Jenkins (1996, p. 105) called the "dialectical interplay of processes of internal and external definition." In these processes, people's personal histories (and their reflection on those histories) have a significant bearing on their choices.

Parents demonstrated the multiple ways in which their personal histories have shaped their choice of school for their children.

1. A Frankel parent made clear how her own positive day school experiences at a Schechter school influenced her plans for her children, to the extent that she and her husband bought a house a mile and a half from Frankel even before her children were born, "knowing" that was where they were going to send them to school.
2. A DJDS mother, who reported that the formative Jewish experiences of her childhood had all taken place in informal educational settings, explained that she was looking for a school that was "as much as possible like camp."
3. A parent who, in his words, "came from 27,000 years of Catholic education" and who had converted to Judaism attributed his deep commitment to the Baeck Academy to his determination to give his

own children the kind of solid grounding in religion and spirituality he had received as a child, even if he had subsequently rebelled against it.

4. A Frankel parent argued that, having grown up in a small town in the southern U.S. with few Jewish resources and many encounters with anti-semitism, "How can I live in a city where there is a day school option and not try it?"

5. Another Frankel parent suggested that her husband's determination to help his children avoid the horrible experience he suffered in afternoon Hebrew school led him to support her commitment to a more intensive Jewish educational option. When he learned that his son would not have to go to Hebrew school because Judaic studies was integrated within the dual curriculum at Frankel, it was, his wife said, "like a switch went off."[2]

In many instances people cited significant or transformative adult experiences that prompted them to take day school education seriously or which led them to choose one school rather than another.

1. A DJDS mother became aware, after her father's death, when she had been responsible for arranging all of the mourning rituals, "how much I knew [about Judaism] through living it and through osmosis and everything. I realized that I wanted my daughter to know." She came to the school "driven by [her] fear of her [daughter's] ignorance."

2. A divorced mother who lived in various parts of the world with her non-Jewish ex-husband explained that she "couldn't go back" to the supplementary model of Jewish education she had experienced as a child after sending her children to a small orthodox pre-school in Singapore. "We were in school with Jews from all over the world and that was incredible to me. He had two teachers from Israel and they spent half a day talking in Hebrew and half a day talking in English. And they do Kabbalat Shabbat on Friday. You know the parents could come and participate and we all sang and we were there and it was an incredible feeling to me. And I think at that point I knew for me it would always be about a day school."

3. A DJDS family reflected on the impact of a conversionary experience of a more literal kind. They explained that having chosen to live in a neighborhood where there were few other Jewish families, they lack, as a conversionary family, the cultural resources to provide their children with a "sense of Jewish community." They searched for a school to perform a social function that was lacking in their community and in their home, but, as the mother elaborated, they were also "looking for a place where we would fit in, where I wouldn't feel uncomfortable because I converted, where there were more couples like us."

The most powerful transformative experience and the most influential in leading to a day school choice was that of visiting a school and finding something parents had themselves missed in their own childhoods and perhaps all of their lives until now.

1. Many of the interviewees from Baeck talked in these terms about their first encounter with tephilla (prayer) in the school. One mother reported "We walked into the school, we came in, and we were there for the tail-end of tephillah, and you see these children sitting on the floor talking about their blessings for the day, discussing the meaning of what they were saying. How could you not at that point say I want to do this every morning?" Others point to the significance of discovering a formal Jewish educational institution that communicates what many called "the joy of Judaism" and its spirituality, a Judaism that reminds them more of camp than of Hebrew school.

2. A repeated theme among DJDS parents was of being shocked (sometimes moved to tears) on a first visit to the school and, in particular, to the kindergarten class at finding an environment where "people did not have to fit a mold." For adults who had spent most of their lives resisting conformity and what they perceived as religious coercion, the school felt like "a haven": "It is so accepting of everything, you know, whether it's a mixed marriage, whether it's a gay couple, whether it's poor, whether it's wealthy. You know, artsy, intellectual. Like it really doesn't matter. You want to send your kids for a Jewish education, you want to be part of this community, then, welcome."

The stories gathered here can be conceptualized both within the terms of rational choice theory and within Coleman's (1990) social context critique. In other words, the sudden discovery of "what day schools are really like" can be seen as expressing parents' access to information about the educational philosophy and values of schools that enables them to make a more informed (and therefore more rational) choice. Alternatively, the paths to one school or another can be seen as a consequence of increased integration into the social networks of different "value" communities. I want to suggest, instead, that the fluidity and subjectivity present in these accounts calls for an additional interpretive frame, one that takes better account of the personal–historical context for decisions or, putting it differently, the origins and consequences of decisions within the narrative of parents' lives. This narrative perspective locates school choice within the shifting sands of adult Jewish identity and emphasizes how school choices possess significance and consequence for the lives of adults and not only those of their children.

Parochialism in America

In recent years, the case for viewing Jewish identity as a journey or process involving the invention and reinvention of the self has become increasingly compelling. As Horowitz (2000) explained, this view of Jewish identity emphasizes how:

> Jewishness unfolds and gets shaped by the different experiences and encounters in a person's life. Each new context or life-stage brings with it new possibilities. A person's Jewishness can wax, wane, and change in emphasis. It is responsive to social relationships, historical experiences and personal events.
>
> (p. viii)

This fluid concept of identity highlights the extent to which acts of Jewish identification shape and are shaped by an evolving life story. Choosing to send one's children to a Jewish day school emerges, then, from a particular mix of relationships, experiences, and events, but it need not be seen as a terminal moment in which an adult with a fully formed Jewish identity makes a decision about the Jewish life of another. There is a strong sense in the data quoted above that choosing a school for one's children both clarifies and changes the meaning one attributes to past experiences from one's own life. For many, it is an opportunity to think anew about Judaism and Jewish life and implies a readiness to experiment with untried forms of Jewish engagement. For others it is an act that gives expression to long-established Jewish associations and commitments.

At a historical moment when the educational efficacy of desegregated public schooling has been called into question and when liberal Judaism is more likely to be associated with the language of individual spiritual search than social action and civil rights, liberal Jews—departing from more than a century of normative Jewish behavior—find themselves surprised by what parochial schools have to offer. If in the past parochial schools promised only cultural separatism, today they offer the possibility of socio-economic advancement for children and personal meaning for their parents. Choosing a Jewish day school, it seems, no longer means turning one's back on the world in favor of visible shows of parochialism, that is becoming "a dork in a yarmulke."

When liberal Jews select parochial schools for their children (and it is worth emphasizing that only a minority actually do), their choice gestures to a number of impulses. It gives expression to parents' determination to provide their children with educational advantages (not exactly a new concern for Jewish parents, but one that was less conflicted in the past when public schools promised both civic and personal benefits). It indicates their identification with and membership in an increasingly diversified Jewish community where the Christian backgrounds of Jews-by-choice can often inspire a preference for the community provided by parochial schools, and it signals their search as adults for lives of (spiritual) meaning, a concern that their own parents appear to have quieted.

For all the popular comment it has attracted, the drift to parochial schooling among liberal Jews neither means a rejection of an assimiliationist ideal nor the embrace of Jewish particularism. Above all, it confirms what Cohen and Eisen (2000) called the sovereignty of the self, a determined (though frequently conflicted) individualism, in determining how to construct one's Jewish life. Paradoxically, in these terms, "choosing" a Jewish day school is a supremely North American way of acting.

Resources and Tools for Educators

Questions

1. Does the growth of liberal Jewish day schools in North America imply that liberal Jews have abandoned public education and have made cultural survival a priority?
2. What drives school choice? To what extent is choice driven by rational calculations about academic quality, discipline, safety, social values, convenience, and cost or by social and emotional factors rooted in parents' own lives and personal histories?
3. Are liberal day schools likely to grow further or will they struggle to recruit families with limited Jewish social and cultural capital, particularly as the financial cost of private schooling continues to rise.

For Further Reading

This chapter constitutes a synthesis and comparison of two larger studies, in Centreville and at DJDS. The Centreville study is described in full in the following publication.

Pomson, A. D. M. (2007). Schools for parents? What parents want and what they get from their children's Jewish day schools. In J. Wertheimer (Ed.), *Family matters: Jewish education in an age of choice* (pp. 101–142). Waltham, MA: University Press of New England.

The DJDS study is described in full in the following publication.

Pomson, A. D. M. (in press). Jewish parents at home, at school: Jewish day school as a source of meaning in the lives of adult Jews. In A. D. M. Pomson & R. F. Schnoor. *Back to school: Jewish day school in the lives of adult Jews.* Detroit, ML: Wayne University Press.

The most comprehensive statistical survey of day schools of all denominational varieties in the U.S. is provided in the following publication.

Schick, M. (2005). *A census of Jewish day schools in the United States, 2003–2004.* New York: Avi Chai Foundation.

Suggestions for Educators

The marketing of day schools should not to be tied too closely to rational considerations, such as those embodied in the promotional language of "academic excellence." School leaders must be cognizant of subjective factors that will make their schools more desirable to parents. Marketing and programming should cultivate opportunities for parents to connect their own needs and concerns to their children's schools.

Notes

1. In a denominational Jewish context "Conservative" refers to a non-orthodox movement that integrates a liberal orientation to *Halacha* (Jewish law) with a commitment to "conserve" Jewish tradition.
2. Of course, neither a positive childhood day school experience nor an unpleasant supplementary school one need necessarily or even probably result in an inclination let alone a decision to send one's own children to day school. The data cited here indicate the significance of these childhood experiences as factors in adult decisions, but do not imply a causal influence in any particular direction.

References

Ackerman, W. (1989). Strangers to tradition: Idea and constraint in American Jewish education. In H. S. Himmelfarb & S. Della Pergolla (Eds.), *Jewish education worldwide: Cross-cultural perspectives* (pp. 71–116). Lanham, MD: University Press of America.

Banks, J. A. & Banks, C. M. (Eds.) (1995). *Multicultural education: Theory and education.* New York: Macmillan.

Beinart, P. (1999). The rise of the Jewish school. *Atlantic Monthly*, October, *284*(4), 21–23.

Cohen, S. M. & Eisen, A. M. (2000). *The Jew within: Self, family, and community in America.* Bloomington, IN: Indiana University Press.

Coleman, J. (1990). *Foundations of social theory.* Cambridge, MA: Belknap Press.

Cope, B. & Kalantzis, M. (Eds.) (2000). *Multiliteracies: Literacy learning and the design of social futures.* London: Routledge.

Della Pergola, S. & Schmelz, U. O. (1989). Demography and Jewish education in the diaspora: Trends in Jewish school-age population and school enrollment. In H. S. Himmelfarb & S. Della Pergola (Eds.), *Jewish education worldwide: Cross-cultural perspectives* (pp. 43–68). Lanham, MD: University Press of America.

Diamond, E. (2000). *And I will dwell in their midst: Orthodox Jews in suburbia.* Chapel Hill, NC: University of North Carolina Press.

Goldring, E. & Shapira, R. (1993). Choice, empowerment and involvement: what satisfies parents? *Educational Evaluation and Policy Analysis*, *15*(4), 396–409.

Himmelfarb, H. S. (1989). A cross-cultural view of Jewish education. In H. S. Himmelfarb & S. DellaPergolla (Eds.), *Jewish education worldwide: Cross-cultural perspectives* (pp. 3–41). Lanham, MA: University Press of America.

Horowitz, B. (2000). Connections and journeys: Assessing critical opportunities for enhancing Jewish identity. Report to the Commission on Jewish Identity and Renewal. UJA-Federation of New York.

Jenkins, R. (1996) *Social identity.* London: Routledge.

Jewish Educational Services for North America & United Jewish Communities (1999). *Task force on Jewish day school viability and vitality.* New York: Jewish Educational Services for North America.

Kelman, S. (1984). Why parents send their children to non-orthodox Jewish day schools: A study of motivations and goals. *Studies in Jewish Education, 2,* 289–298.

Kutnick, J. (1989). Jewish education in Canada. In H. S. Himmelfarb & S. Della Pergolla (Eds.), *Jewish education worldwide: Cross-cultural perspectives* (pp. 135–169). Lanham, MA: University Press of America.

Miller, H. (2001). Meeting the challenge: The Jewish schooling phenomenon in the UK. *Oxford Review of Education, 27,* 501–513.

Ostrom, V. & Ostrom, E. (1971). Public choice: A different approach to the study of public administration. *Public Administration Review, 31,* 203–216.

Pomson, A. D. M. (2002). Jewish day school growth in Toronto: Freeing policy and research from the constraints of conventional sociological wisdom. *Canadian Journal of Education, 27*(3), 321–340.

Pomson, A. D. M. (2004). Day school parents and their children's schools. *Contemporary Jewry, 24,* 104–123.

Sarna, J. (1998). American Jewish education in historical perspective. *Journal of Jewish Education, 64*(1/2), 8–21.

Schick, M. (2000). *A census of Jewish day schools in the United States.* New York: Avi Chai Foundation.

Shapiro, S. (1996). A parent's dilemma: Public vs. Jewish education. *Tikkun Magazine, 17*(4), 13–16.

Shields, C. (2000). Learning from difference: Considerations for schools as communities. *Curriculum Inquiry, 30*(3), 275–294.

Shoub, B. (1991). *Day school enrollment.* Toronto: UJA Federation of Greater Toronto Board of Jewish Education.

Shrager, H. (2002). More Jewish day schools open as parents reconsider values. *Wall Street Journal,* May 21.

Smrekar, C. & Goldring, E. (1999). *School choice in urban America.* New York: Teachers College Press.

Weinfeld, M. & Zelkowitz, P. (1991). Reflections on the Jewish polity and Jewish education. In D. Elazar (Ed.), *Authority, power and leadership in the Jewish polity: Cases and issues* (pp. 305–317). New York: University Press of America.

Wertheimer, J. (1999a). Jewish education in the United States: Recent trends and issues. In D. Singer (Ed.), *America Jewish yearbook 1999* (Vol. 99, pp. 3–118). New York: American Jewish Committee.

Wertheimer, J. (1999b). Who's afraid of Jewish schools? *Commentary, 108,* 49–54.

Zeldin, M. (1988). *Cultural dissonance in Jewish education: The case of reform day schools.* Los Angeles: Hebrew Union College, Jewish Institute of Religion.

CHAPTER 17

The Unintended Consequence of Liberal Jewish Schooling: A Comparative Study of the Teaching of Jewish Texts for the Purpose of Cultural Sustainability

ZVI BEKERMAN AND EZRA KOPELOWITZ

The Unconsidered Consequences of a Liberal Jewish Education

Over the past 30 years, liberal Jews, the world over, have begun to enthusiastically tout full-time Jewish schooling as an answer to the increasing threat of assimilation. In this chapter we ask: Is this increasing emphasis on formal education the correct strategy for attaining cultural sustainability?

Within the category of "liberal Jewry" we place a wide range of ideological strategies, ranging from reform, conservative and modern orthodox religious movements to secular ideologies such as Zionism and Jewish socialism. Despite substantial differences, the common liberal Jewish goal is to create schools that enable successful cultural and economic integration into the surrounding society, but at the same time provide the younger generations with a sustainable Jewish identity. In most countries liberal Jews constitute the vast majority of the Jewish population.

On one hand, it seems logical that a greater degree of formal Jewish education will fortify the coming generations of Jews as they enter the wider world and increase the chances of them remaining as identifying Jews. On the other hand, the increased emphasis on schooling has come hand in hand with the weakening of the Jewish family and other informal frameworks as agents of socialization. Often, formal educational efforts are almost solely responsible for the development of a strong sense of Jewish identity and commitment to the Jewish people (for a recent review of the field of Jewish education in the U.S. see Wertheimer (1999)). We also argue that formal education in modern societies serves as a major tool for assimilating minority groups and, as such, an increased emphasis on formal schooling by a Jewish community may have the unintended effect of promoting rather than combating cultural assimilation.

Unfortunately, except for a few scholars (Ackerman, 1969; Fox, 1973; Fox et al., 2003; Bekerman, 2004), the ability of full-time Jewish education to contribute to Jewish cultural sustainability is rarely considered. Moreover, the emphasis on philosophical inquiry in the academic study of Jewish education has meant that systematic empirical study of the contribution of Jewish education to cultural sustainability in the diaspora is lacking. Whenever empirical investigation is conducted, major questions arise as to the effectiveness of a liberal Jewish education.

Without appropriate consideration of the balance between the secular and Jewish goals of the liberal day school and its relation to family and community, it is likely that the schooling experience might not serve the goal of Jewish cultural sustainability. Preliminary exploratory research shows Jewish education has had no influence on moral reasoning when its participants are compared to their peers studying in public schools (Hodin, 1999). Moral and civic values as well as the knowledge and skills needed to function in the modern world have been left first to the public system and, more recently, to the secular studies in the Jewish day school (whose investment in Jewish education is not necessarily higher, in terms of hours, than what was previously offered through supplementary Jewish education—averaging 8–10 hours a week). As to the efficacy of Jewish education in averting the greatest acknowledged threats to the community—a weakened identity and intermarriage—the debate is open and there are as yet no conclusive answers.

While some scholars have suggested that education is partially successful in this area (Cohen, 1995), others doubt its impact and point to the length of roots the family has in America as a primary determining factor in its Jewish involvement (Phillips, 1987). In any case, for whatever the studies are interpreted to show, Schoenfeld (1991) posited that all involved in the Jewish educational enterprise would do well to consider the serious difficulties encountered when trying to determine the relationship between childhood Jewish education and adult identification.

Finally, it is critical to note that the Jewish education debate, but for a few exceptions (Bekerman, 2001; Kopelowitz et al., 2005), does not sufficiently take into account current theorizing that stresses the extreme relevance of factors such as polity, economy, and family in the development of individual identification and communal affiliation (Vygotsky, 1986; Obgu, 1993; Wenger, 1997; Rogoff et al., 2003). Except for a few examples (Shkedi, 1998; Pomson,

2002) does the discourse take note of the relevant bodies of research literature on educational practitioners and practices such as Dewey (1938, 1959), Connelly and Clandinin (1987), Schon (1987), and Eisner (1990), to name a few.

In this chapter, we draw on the results of a qualitative comparative study of teachers in a variety of Jewish day schools in English- and Spanish-speaking communities around the world to examine the contribution of formal Jewish education to Jewish cultural sustainability. The focus here is the use of "Jewish texts" in classrooms, based on in-depth interviews with teachers and video recordings of their interactions with students.

We begin with a discussion of the role that mass educational systems play as a socializing and assimilatory agent in modern, liberal political systems. The liberal ethos focuses on the educational attainment of individuals and their ability to integrate successfully into the capitalist economy. The result is the de-emphasis or even purposeful dismantling of counter-cultural norms that minority groups must realize in order to achieve cultural sustainability.

We then illustrate the assimilatory force of liberalism, through the case study of the teaching of Jewish texts in the classrooms covered by our research. We illustrate the dilemmas faced by teachers, who are attempting to grapple with the conflict between Jewish and liberal educational goals, but often lack strategies and clear goals for resolving the conflict in a manner that successfully promotes "usable Jewish knowledge" for their students. Our closing remarks point at the need to reconceptualize the relationship between culture and identity in the context of formal educational and other Jewish institutions.

The Research Population

The data for the preliminary analysis were derived from twenty-five Jewish studies classes in middle schools (students of ages ranging from 12 to 15 years of age) that were videotaped and from in-depth interviews conducted with fourteen teachers who participated in the sample. The videotapes and the interviews where gathered during the 2001–2002 academic years. Schools were chosen upon availability and through professional contacts in the communities that participated in the research. The Jewish educational institutions from Spanish-speaking countries included three from Argentina, one from Mexico, one from Peru, and two from Uruguay. The Jewish educational institutions from English-speaking countries included one from Australia, one from Canada, one from the U.K., one from South Africa, and three from the U.S. But for the French community the sample included representatives of all major Jewish communities in countries of the Western diaspora. In both cases (English- and Spanish-speaking communities) the sample included large (over 30,000 Jews such as in Buenos Aires and Montreal) and small (under 5,000 Jews as in Peru) communities.

All of the fourteen teachers whose interviews and classes were included in the analysis (four male and ten female) held some type of higher education. Nine held teaching certificates, eleven held additional bachelors and masters' degrees, and two held Ph.D. degrees. When considering that, in the last decades and under the influence of similar efforts in the world of public education, a series of high-profile Jewish community commissions have emphasized the need to professionalize the field of Jewish teaching our sample is not representative of the situation in the field: however, we believe, based on our knowledge of Jewish education, that the views expressed are. The teachers in English-speaking communities had relatively higher academic degrees. The number of years of teaching experience of the participants ranged between 10 and 27 years. The teachers in Spanish-speaking communities were relatively older. Of the teachers who expressed a Jewish denominational affiliation in their interviews, seven were identified as conservative/traditional, three were identified as modern orthodox, and two were identified as traditionalists. (For information on the differences between the various denominations of American Judaism see Lazerwitz et al. (1998) and Kopelowitz (2001, 2005).)

All teachers taught at what are traditionally denominated Jewish day schools, i.e. schools that offer a dual general and Jewish studies curriculum. These schools, which are continuously growing in number, are relatively expensive and, though offering stipends for needy families, for the most part cater to populations with relatively high incomes. The schools in the sample for the most part serve what we define as "liberal Jewish populations." Though two of the schools defined themselves as "modern orthodox" they both were open to a wider not necessarily religiously orthodox population and, even when an orthodox population represented the majority of the student body, these came from "modern" orthodox families. By "modern" orthodox we mean those Jews who stress strict observance of traditional religious ritual, but also view successful integration into the capitalist economy as a positive virtue.

Tuition in the Spanish-speaking communities ranged from $1,500 to 5,000 per year. The tuition in schools in English-speaking communities was relatively higher and ranged between $6,000 and 10,000. The gap between the tuition rates was explained by the relative average of income in each locality. However, for one recently opened school in the U.S., attendance was varied between 200 and 1,000 students (for recent studies on the USA day schools see Wertheimer (1999) and Schick (2000)).

Methodology

All videotaped classes and interviews were transcribed for analysis. Names of schools and teachers were changed in keeping with customary research ethics. The teachers were offered a small subsidy for participating in the research (approximately US$250) and the videotaping was conducted with rather simple video home equipment (of the type available in school video laboratories). The basic instructions given for the videotaping included a request for having the camera placed in the back corner of the class so as to disturb the class activities as little as possible and to have the person handling the camera in place before the class started and staying until all participants had left the classroom at the end of class. The basic idea was to have the camera focused widely over the class trying to get us many students as possible in the frame while centered on the teachers' actions.

Interviews were conducted by phone and lasted for at least 1 hour with a few running for 1.5 hours. A simple tape recorder was used to tape the telephone interviews, which was activated after receiving the explicit agreement of teachers to tape the conversation. The interviews were conducted according to qualitative ethnographic principles: The interviewer remained focused on a number of topics that seemed relevant to the study, but allowed subjects to tell their stories without binding the interview to a fixed agenda of questions. The planned interview schedule included queries regarding the school's goals and purposes, the teacher's objectives, and curriculum-related questions.

All interviews and class periods were audio- or videotaped and fully transcribed. They were then analyzed according to conventional qualitative methods (Mason, 1996; Bekerman and Silverman, 1999). We carefully analyzed the data, looking for patterns and thematic issues of relevance, which were then coded to allow for further analysis. The first codification, prepared independently by the principal researcher and a research assistant, raised multiple categories that were narrowed down for further analysis. A second reading of all the recorded materials allowed us to reduce the categories systematically by combining similar terms and eliminating redundant ones. Thus, we arrived at the identifiable themes from which we created our final coding system (Glassner and Loughlin, 1987). Throughout the process, intercoder reliability checks showed strong agreement between coders and high reliability for the coding scheme.

Liberal Modernity and the Jewish Response

Our focus in the coming pages is the place of the "individual" in Jewish education, with a focus on the teaching practices of our research population. By the concept of the "individual," we mean the "modern citizen," a person who is granted political, economic, and social rights from the state and in return is expected to take upon him- or herself corresponding obligations such as paying taxes, obeying the law, etc. (Dumont, 1986; Herzfeld, 1992). From the Jewish perspective, the phenomenon of individuality became a significant social phenomenon over the course of the late eighteenth through to early twentieth century as European states granted citizenship rights to Jews (Katz,

1993 (1958); Birnbaum and Katznelson, 1995). Previously, Jews were treated by the regime as a corporate group and did not receive their economic, political, or social rights or relieve their obligations directly *vis-à-vis* state institutions. Rather individuals worked *vis-à-vis* the institutions of the corporate Jewish community, which in turn demanded a traditional (ethno-religious) way of life. An individual deviating from communal norms was in danger of excommunication and the loss of basic economic, political, and social rights that could not be found elsewhere (Elazar, 1997).

The emancipation process moved hand in hand with the increasingly successful attempts of European regimes to consolidate their power using large-scale rationalized bureaucracies. Of interest to us is the fact that the rationalizing power of modern bureaucracy rests on the principle of citizenship, in which "individuals" rather than corporate communities are the primary repository of political rights and obligations. By affirming individual rights the modern state simultaneously denies recognition of the right of minority or ethno-religious groups to make claims upon individuals that deviate from traditional cultural and legal norms. The result was the radical weakening of the normative and institutional structure of Jewish (and other groups) communal life.

The modern Jew had one of two options. The reactionary response was to attempt to reconstruct the near total barrier between Jew and non-Jew that had existed prior to modernity. Whereas previously the separation between Jew and non-Jew was imposed from without, after emancipation groups known as ultra-orthodox (*Haredi*) Jews attempted to withdraw to the extent possible from interaction with the surrounding society. In contrast, the vast majority of Jews attempted to separate or compartmentalize the Jewish and non-Jewish areas of everyday life. Depending on the ideological strategy a person chose, institutions such as the home, synagogue, and school were endowed with various degrees of Jewish content, while the economic arena was mostly likely viewed as divorced from considerations of Jewish tradition (Heilman, 1977; Bekerman and Silverman, 1999; Kopelowitz, 2001, 2005).

Jewish Education and the Liberal Condition

Building on the previous discussion, we define "liberal society" as the political–social context in which the individual rather than the group is viewed as the primary social unit around which state and society revolve. "Liberal Jews" are those who accept this reality and attempt to balance the demands of liberal individualism with an attempt to maintain a discernibly Jewish life style.

From the first stages of emancipation through to the third quarter of the twentieth century, liberal Jews tended to distinguish between primary and secondary education provided by the state and the supplementary education provided "after school" by the local synagogue or community. "Secular education" prepared the individual for success in the capitalist economy, while "Jewish education" provided a person with the necessary skills to participate in religious rituals of the home and synagogue (Goldberg, 2003).

Beginning at some point in the 1980s, liberal Jews in many different countries changed course and began to embrace "Jewish day schools" enthusiastically as a means to combat the dangers of assimilation (Alex Pomson's chapter in this volume elaborates on the turn of liberal Jews to Jewish day schools). As opposed to the supplementary school, the Jewish day school provides both a secular and religious education and is attended full time. The liberal Jewish day school attempts to provide for basic literacy in Jewish tradition and culture and a strong secular education, which allows their participants to stay socially mobile and economically successful and secure in their respective societies. In short, borrowing from the title of Podhoretz's (1967) book, liberal Jewish education first and foremost ensures the desire of liberal Jews to "make it" in their respective Western countries and societies: in addition, the school attempts to provide for Jewish cultural sustainability.

Our goal in the coming pages is to look at the way teachers in these liberal Jewish day schools perceive the need for their students to make it in the wider society as "liberal individuals," alongside the attempt to educate for cultural sustainability and their resulting educational strategies.

The Conflicting Goals of the Liberal Jewish Day School

The conflict between the Jewish and liberal mission of the liberal Jewish day school was clear when we asked the teachers about the goals of their school. All of the interviewees defined the goal of their institutions as strengthening a sense of Jewish identity and belonging among the students. Of interest, is the fact that all the teachers also acknowledged, not always with ease, that, while their schools were very serious about their Jewish commitments, they had to be (due to parental demands) even more serious about the commitment to excellence in secular education. The interviewees acknowledged that lacking this commitment (or not succeeding in it) the school might not attract enough students. Most teachers recognized that there was a tension between the declared aims of the school and the community's expectations, a tension they saw reflected in the lack of support, they sensed, that parents offered to the schools' efforts to impart a serious Jewish education to their children. We do need to note that families do want a Jewish education for their children or would not choose a Jewish day school: however, there tends to be a marked disparity between the expectations of teachers and parents. The more orthodox the school and served a modern orthodox community, the less this tension was sensed.

For the most part the teachers seemed to identify with the declared aims of the schools. In this sense when speaking about their own objectives they basically repeated what was stated above. Still we believe that, at times, some tensions became apparent. Such was the case for some Spanish-speaking teachers, who seemed to emphasize their intention to create a strong commitment to Zionism and Israel in their students in spite of their sense that the school had somewhat abandoned these objectives or when English-speaking teachers took issue with the school which, in their view, played a double game, declaring on the one hand their strong commitment to Jewish education, but on the other adapting to the parents' expectations for excellence in general studies. These teachers had a sense of being betrayed by these hidden double standards.

The Conflicting Commitments of the Liberal Jewish Day School

The teachers did not have thought-out strategies for negotiating the tension between the Jewish and secular goals of their schools. For example, in spite of the interviewees being prompted to do so, the general statement that the goal of the school was to strengthen Jewish identity was not followed by any more specific comments on the exact meaning of the term. It became apparent that the teachers held essentialist conceptions of identity. "Jewish identity" was there to be strengthened or shaped, but was a given to which little critical or reflexive attention was paid. As we will see below, the idea that Jewish identity is a given, contributes to classroom practices that reinforce the idea of Jewish versus non-Jewish patterns of learning and knowledge, with little effort made to make the connection between the Jewish dimension of the classroom experience and everyday life.

In the following analysis we focus on the strategies that our subjects employed in their use of "Jewish texts" in their classroom as a window through which to look at this larger question of how Jewish studies were conceptualized and taught by the teachers. By "Jewish text" we mean a canonical document that has iconic status in either the religious tradition or as a symbol of secular Jewish culture. In every videotaped class, we found that texts were utilized to varying degrees. In many cases, the texts were presented in Hebrew with accompanying translation either by the teacher or a student with strong teacher support.

Thus, we can confidently assert that Jewish texts are an essential component of the curriculum and deemed an important tool in the educational attempt to bring students to an understanding of themselves as Jews. The teachers encouraged "Jewish" literacy, which they seemed to define as both an ability to deal with the language of the text and an ability to grapple with its meaning(s).

All of the teachers suggested that Jewish issues became significant for the students primarily when applied to their everyday lives, which are executed, for the most part, in non-Jewish spheres. However, we found that for the most part the teaching methods and the resulting discourse within the classrooms led to the opposite results, namely a strong distinction between Jewish and secular issues.

A Case Study of the Teaching of Jewish Texts—Dimensions of the Connection between "Jewish Studies" and the Secular World

In each of the following three dimensions, we see how the teaching of texts reinforces the distinction between Jewish and secular knowledge.

Dimension One: The Classroom as Distinctive Jewish Space

As a rule, Jewish studies in the classrooms we observed appeared as distinct from secular studies. The classroom was presented to the students as a space in which they could grapple with issues that were distinctly Jewish, possibly emphasizing the fact that outside there was no appropriate space in which to grapple with these issues. Generally, the Jewish world/content was presented to the students as something separate from the secular world. The outside world was allowed to enter the Jewish sphere in as much as it became supportive of issues directly related to or influencing that which was considered Jewish.

Still, within this larger conceptual framework that emphasized the classroom as a distinctive Jewish space, we found that more schools from English-speaking countries (all but two) made an effort to connect Jewish issues to non-Jewish issues. We are still considering if what we are confronting is an issue related not to the amount of connections made but to the type of connection the teachers tried to create. For example, for the most part when the teachers we observed in the Spanish-speaking countries did create connections, it was to immediate social/political issues (i.e. social justice in the local community), while teachers in the English-speaking countries created connections to the realm of values as these contrasted with the consumerist Western culture outside.

Dimension Two: Authority and Discourse

The distinction between Jewish studies and everyday life was created in a teaching style that followed known patterns of formal education in the Western world. The teacher was the center and initiator of class interaction, sustaining relatively impersonal teacher–pupil relations. Recitation was the most frequently encountered form of interactive teaching. Teachers, for the most part, sought predictable ("correct") answers and made use of a high percentage of yes/no questions. Only rarely were questions used to assist students in developing more complete or elaborated ideas.

The instructional discourse differed in both structure and content from the ways adults and children spoke in everyday life outside of school. The central goal of the instructional discourse, as we recorded it, was to give children information stipulated in curricula and feedback about their efforts to learn it, while providing teachers with information about their progress. One of the distinctive characteristics of the instructional discourse, which is also well documented in general education, was the initiation–reply–evaluation sequence. Teacher asks, student replies, and teacher provides evaluation. Another special facet of school-based language revealed in the videos was the emphasis placed on the linguistic forms of students' replies. The teacher judged the replies considered appropriate by using turn-taking rules of classroom discourse.

For the most part, the classes followed this turn-taking pattern of discourse. However, except for the school in Peru, all the schools in Spanish-speaking countries seemed to follow a much stricter formal approach. Even in those classes in which teachers used games as part of the educational process, they were the ones who assigned the groups and set all parameters for the activity thus maintaining their central role and total control over the activities. Except for the schools in the U.K. and South Africa the interactions between the teacher and the students in schools from English-speaking countries seemed relatively more relaxed. The teachers from the U.S., Canada, and Australia established greater equilibrium in the student–teacher relationship than the teachers from the U.K. and South Africa. In addition, the teachers from the U.K. and South Africa encouraged fewer questions and less student input. In the school from the U.K., the teacher more frequently asked the students to read from the text rather than to discuss it. In the school from Canada, the teacher set up a dynamic among the students. He genuinely appeared engaged with the students and interested in what they had to add to the lesson. These teachers' assessments of students' performance seemed to be somewhat relaxed when compared to regular secular/general school activities.

Dimension Three: The Canonical Status of Texts

Texts are for the most part presented as normative and canonical. If this approach is drawn as a continuum, we could, paradoxically, say that the more secular the school, the more likely the texts will be represented as expressing "truth" (i.e. the word of God in the case of Bible texts) and lacking ambiguities of meaning: as schools move towards liberal religious perspectives they presented texts as more open to interpretation. The modern orthodox schools in our sample presented both of these characteristics. In general there seemed to be a divide regarding the handling of text, with schools in Spanish-speaking countries being more "traditionalist–orthodox" in their approach, thus making our continuum become an almost closed circle in which the extremes (Spanish-speaking secular and English-speaking orthodox) almost touched each other.

We found that the teachers in English-speaking countries seemed to invest more effort in creating connections between the text and present life situations.

(We should keep in mind that the classes recorded in English-speaking countries were more subject discipline related than the ones recorded in Spanish-speaking countries where Jewish studies seemed to be approached in much more generic ways—Bible studies as opposed to Israeli culture). A greater effort was made in these schools to relate texts to everyday life situations in which the students might find themselves. In the school from Australia, the teacher made a strong effort to bring the texts to life. He had the students act out a portion of the text and subsequently interpret the implications of the texts. In both the school from Canada and one of the schools from the U.S., the teachers verbally encouraged interpretation of the text.

In summation, the significance of texts cannot be overstated. Every video-taped class utilized texts to convey historical and contemporary messages. Texts were seen as providing a stable foundation from which to grapple with issues of identity, tradition, and culture. The teachers seemed to be strongly working through paradigmatic perspectives which pointed at the possibility of transferring knowledge from texts to the children's minds without enabling the recipient to engage the text critically on his or her own terms.

While all the teachers agreed on the need to make traditional texts relevant to the student's everyday experience outside of the school and to secular issues, unfortunately, but for a few exceptions, the teachers were not able to make explicit what they meant when saying they would like texts to become relevant to their students, nor were they able to articulate strategies through which to achieve this relevance.

For some just the ongoing dealing with the texts made them become relevant to the students, while for others being able to point at the roots of cherished modern values in the old texts is what did the trick. Yet others believed this was achieved by adding some modern/humanistic outlooks to traditional religious ones. One teacher mentioned the need to show how the values expressed in the traditional text could be applicable to present life situations.

In the interviews, we regularly asked the participants the following question: "Given that we mostly live in a world which has outlawed murder and in which murder is considered by most to be a sin, how can the learning of the commandment 'though shall not kill' be relevant to your kids?" We were not sure the question was good but the respondents' reactions gave us the sense that the question raised an issue they thought worthwhile considering. As stated, for the most part, other than honestly recognizing the problem, not much was added to what we mentioned above.

Does the Liberal Jewish Day School Transmit "Relevant" Jewish Knowledge?

The most outstanding feature of this first exploratory effort at a systematic comparative study of liberal Jewish education was the dichotomy between

"Jewish" and "secular" worlds that was expressed and mirrored on multiple levels of analysis.

While the teachers expressed a desire to make Jewish knowledge relevant to everyday life and to secular studies in the school, the reality is that they perpetuated a strong compartmentalization between the in-us (Jewish)/out-them (host society) that is typical of the strategy adopted by liberal Jews since the earliest days of the emancipation process. The dichotomy is not expressive of the normative views of those involved but the outcome of the impossibility, yet, of finding the proper ways to overcome the Jewish/secular distinction. It was expressed in the compartmentalization of general and Jewish studies, in the difficulties of weaving together Jewish traditional views and secular liberal values in ways which prevent the fear of losing cultural 'authenticity', in the reified/essentialized perception of Jewish identity and culture, and in the tacit understanding that, ultimately, for a Jewish school to be successful, it must facilitate the sustainability of the present socio-economical positioning of their constituency in the host society.

The descriptions offered of the classroom climate and structure can be characterized as ones which reflected those documented in general by educational research (Hitchcock and Hughes, 1995; Foley and Edwards, 1997). They can be characterized as being removed from contexts of practical activity and as having as a goal the acquisition of skills that will become the means of later activity. The image of reality transmitted at school was fragmented and oriented by disciplinary tracks directed at gaining academic cognitive knowledge with little emphasis on experiential aspects, again reflecting the basic structures of the modern school. The texts so central in class activity were for the most part presented as normative and canonical and they were seen as able to provide a stable foundation from which to grapple with issues of identity, tradition, and culture. The teachers seemed to be strongly working through paradigmatic perspectives that pointed at the possibility of transferring knowledge from texts to the children's minds. All in all, the teachers seemed to sustain reified perspectives on the meaning of identity and culture.

Jewish studies were presented as distinct from general studies. In other words, the classroom was the students' space in which to grapple with issues that were distinctly Jewish, possibly emphasizing the fact that outside there was no appropriate space in which to grapple with these issues. The outside world was allowed to enter the Jewish sphere in as much as it became supportive of issues directly related to or influencing that which is considered Jewish.

Marginalizing "Jewish Experience"

The problem with perpetuating the compartmentalization between the Jewish and non-Jewish spheres is that it replicates the very conditions that the day school was created to counter. To the extent that "Jewish" is conceptualized as a compartmentalized category for organizing meaning in the learning environment, so the students will continue to receive the message that the Jewish experience is a marginal one and not relevant for life in the wider world of which they are apart.

Taylor (1994) contended that, though a liberal world grants equality and the right of participation, it does not take into account existing cultural differences that impede the realization of equality. More precisely, since the liberal commitment focuses on individuals and not on their specific cultural affiliations and attachments, it does not lend dignity to these cultural groupings, but demeans, marginalizes, and excludes them.

The development of mass education, through schooling, is closely related to the Industrial Revolution and the development of the nation state, both of which are dependent on weakening the cultural authority of corporate groups and dealing directly with the "individual" in order to recruit the masses to their service (Gellner, 1983; Smith, 1998; Bekerman and Silberman, 2003). The "successful" individual has the basic cognitive and behavioral skills to serve the needs of the nation state and its economic structure. Thus, schools are in no way disinterested arenas within which neutral knowledge or skills are transmitted from the minds of specialists to those of passive individuals. In the modern era, schools have served as the primary means by which sovereigns have unified the different local groups inhabiting the areas they were successful in subordinating to their power, under one flag, one language, and one narrative. Thus, the central lynchpin of formal schooling, as it has developed within the modern state, represents a particular paradigmatic perspective that we doubt is beneficial for Jews or any other minority that take seriously the notion of cultural sustainability.

What Can Be Done?

What, then, can be done to overcome the secular/Jewish dichotomy within the macro-constraints (i.e. the need to train students for success in the capitalist economy) faced by the school? Is it possible to create a teaching methodology that dismantles the binary relationship between the Jewish and the secular and replaces it with a learning experience based on integration of the two realms into one? We believe that the answer to this question might be positive, if Jewish education is reconceptualized as a particular case of cultural education. By cultural education we mean the educational efforts invested by minority groups who seek to sustain what they perceive to be their socio-historical heritage, in the face of the homogenizing assimilatory power of a hegemonic global West.

Based on the previous analysis of the interviews, we argue that the presence of three basic ingredients will enable the integration of Jewish and secular dimensions in the educational experience.

1. Dismantling the conception of classroom as "differentiated space." Here we refer to the conception of classroom as distinctive "Jewish" space that serves as a haven from the surrounding world. Instead, the Jewish dimensions of the classroom should serve as a resource from which to build a critical perspective on cardinal social issues facing the student in everyday life.

2. Doing away with the "recitation method" of teaching: Instead of the teacher providing information and the student repeating that information back, a discursive environment within the classroom must promote student responsibility to think independently of the teacher.

3. Finally, the "truth value" of texts must be tackled in a critical fashion: Rather than encourage students to relate uncritically to the "truth" value of canonical texts, students must be encouraged to grapple with the ambiguities of meaning that appear within text.

Viewed in this fashion, Jewish texts are "alternative texts" that spark a critical discussion about the nature of contemporary morality. In the case of "teaching texts," we assume that, without choosing alternative texts and creating a discourse around them that is relevant to everyday life, every "innovative" educational effort will fail. The sources of the texts that are chosen are not important, as long as they stem from a cultural context that is relevant to the participants. The process might be envisioned along lines similar to those described by Freire (1970), who argued that critical education or *concientizacao* entails learning to perceive social, political, and economic contradictions and to take action against the oppressive elements of reality. It is important to note that Freire's (1970) call is not one that points only at the need for cognitive alertness, but also one that points at the primacy of practical activity, namely activity that focuses on immediate "real" events. Freire's (1970) activity is outwardly conducted: it is not constrained by the narrow limits of school (Jewish or other) or their proximal communities, but focuses on the society that surrounds it while adopting a critical gaze and amassing the needed courage to create coalitions for action.

Examples of successful use of text by counter-cultural groups exist. For example, Teitelbaum (1991) described the socialist movement's resistance as reflected in their Sunday afternoon schools in early twentieth-century America. The socialists used the study of texts to offer competing outlooks to those that were accepted as natural in the given historical context and enabled the participants to weigh up, argue their arguments, and examine their situation in a new light. Likewise, Reay and Mirza (1997), in a more recent study, showed Black supplementary schools in the U.K. as not just poor responses to mainstream educational exclusion and poor provision from the side of the hegemonic powers, but as central tools in the creation of oppositional meanings (Mueller, 1986). These counter-cultural meanings decentered the assumptions of mainstream schooling and provided evidence of thriving Black communities.

Educators need to first and foremost work with their students and others in the community to read the world—theirs as well as any other. To do this they are in need of a vocabulary that enables description of the world in counter-cultural terms. Only with a counter-cultural vocabulary is it possible to create a cultural education capable of uncovering and coping with the complexity of living as a liberal Jew in contemporary society.

The ability to speak a counter-cultural vocabulary implies engaging in (1) economic discourse for discussing commodities, supplies, and management, (2) aesthetic discourse for discussing architecture, advertising, and display, (3) political discourse for discussing bodies, policies, planning, and discipline, (4) ethnographic discourse for finding the beauty of the particular responses to all of the above, (5) historical discourse for discussing about change in organization, consumption, and community, and (6) interpretative discourses, which will allow them to articulate understandings of each of the texts that, in concert, create culture, Jewish or other.

In order for texts to serve as a springboard for a vibrant counter-cultural discourse, they cannot stand alone. Rather, the vibrancy of the text comes from its "intertextuality"—its relation to other texts and languages that are read and spoken throughout the life experience. Reading text in this fashion enables counter-culture. The reader learns to read the world and its activities in a manner that allows for alternative pathways of action and meaning. This might not be all that is needed but it is a start, a critical one, without which the rest will not follow.

All in all, the above argument points at the need to enrich educators (students and community leaders) with languages, dialects, and discourses that are necessary for reading the world in a counter-cultural manner. The solution we offer rests on "language in action" as the originating tool for individual and social experience. Indeed we write assuming that it is expression (the act of reading and speaking) that organizes experience and not the other way round. "Self" from this perspective is generated and fashioned in dialog that occurs in social networks that develop their own relatively coherent and recognizable style. While always unfinished, the language resources that are found in particularistic social networks provides the individual the tools to become a member of a particular cultural, ethnic, or religious group (Bekerman, 2005). Knowledge of the uses of language (gesture and verb), the learning of "languaging" (Maturana and Valera, 1987), enables the recognition that we are continually immersed in a discourse with others, while at the same time authoring our worlds (Becker, 1995).

The questions that we are left with after reviewing the data we collected on the teaching of texts in liberal Jewish day schools focus us on the gap between the ideal and the real. As we noted above, the group of teachers interviewed for this work were more educated that the norm—nine hold teaching certificates, eleven holding additional bachelors and masters' degrees and two holding Ph.D. degrees. If this group of educators is not teaching in a manner that promotes the ability of students to speak the language of a counter-culture, then what of the wider experience in the Jewish world? Our conclusion is that Jewish studies classes in day schools are not being used to immerse the student in a form of counter-cultural discourse that is essential to Jewish cultural sustainability. Rather, the encounter with text and language reinforces mainstream liberal categories of private/public, insider/outsider, secular/religious, and non-Jewish/Jewish, which leads to the final conclusion of that which is outside of the Jewish studies classroom as "real" and that which in inside as irrelevant to life as it is lived outside of the classroom.

Acknowledgments

We wish to thank David Gerwin, Celia Haig-Brown, Plamen Makariev, and Gloria Totoricagüena for comments they gave us on this paper. The project on which this paper is based was funded by The Joint Program for Jewish Education.

Resources and Tools for Educators

Questions

1. What is the connection between the rise of national educational systems that are part of modern states and the assimilation of minority groups?
2. When, in the opinion of the authors, does the organization of school curricula by disciplines (i.e. mathematics, science, and Jewish studies) contribute to the assimilatory process?
3. What are the possible benefits and limitations of using formal schooling as a main institutional setting for cultural sustainability?
4. What are the key differences between an approach to education that stresses "knowledge transmission" as opposed to "experiential activity?"
5. What are the implications of these two approaches to education in terms of classroom teaching and how do they appear in terms of interaction between teacher and student?
6. In your opinion, what are the pluses and minuses of each approach for cultural sustainability?
7. What are the basic assumptions about the nature of classroom learning upon which Jewish education is conducted in the educational setting in which we work? How are these assumptions translated into the

relationship between teacher and student and the classroom, the school, and life outside of school?

8. What are the basic assumptions about the nature of Judaism upon which Jewish education is conducted in the educational setting in which we work? How are these assumptions translated into the relationship between teacher and student and the classroom, the school, and life outside of school?

For Further Reading

Verenne, H. & McDermott, R. (1998). *Successful failure: The schools America builds.* Boulder, CO: Westview Press.

A provocative book that combines a compelling discussion on the theoretical assumptions of educational processes with illustrative studies on schooling and education.

Spindler, G. & Hammond, L. (Eds.) (2006). *Innovations in educational ethnography.* Mahwah, NJ: Lawrence Earlbaum Associates.

A wonderful book that provides excellent examples of trends in the ethnography of education, shedding light on educational processes framed by the complex internationalized societies in which we live today.

Wenger, E. (1998). *Communities of practice: learning, meaning, and identity.* Cambridge: Cambridge University Press.

A rather easy way to get acquainted with the complexities involved in revealing the foundations of knowledge production, while engaging in a serious discussion of the meaning of seminal educational concepts such as identity, practice, and culture.

Bekerman, Z. & Silverman, M. (1999). Slaves of tradition—Slaves of freedom: Social constructivist perspectives on the 'culture' of Israeli traditionalists and liberals. *Israel Studies, 4*(2), 90–120.

A challenging and critical study of foundational beliefs within the liberal Jewish tradition as these shape educational thinking.

Kopelowitz, E. (2005). Jewish Identities. In N. de Lange & M. Freud-Kandel (Eds.), *Modern Judaism: An Oxford guide* (pp. 205–215). Oxford: Oxford University Press.

An overview of the major cultural/religious streams among American and Israeli Jews. The article looks at the differences between cultural/religious streams, both in terms of their organization of space and time in everyday life and the impact of national public spheres on the nature of Jewish belonging.

Suggestions for Educators

1. Consider from your personal experience which social settings (school, family, sports club, etc.) that most influence your own sense of ethnic/cultural identity and belonging?

2. Try to identify and discuss the variety of practices/strategies/activities adopted in each of these different settings that you feel support and strengthen ethnic/cultural identification and belonging? What are the similarity and differences between them?

3. Consider which educational assumptions stand behind the practices/strategies/activities you just identified in each of the settings in terms of the interaction between the "nature" of what is learned (i.e. in connection to Jewish belonging), the role of the learner/participant, the role of the teacher/facilitator, and the relation of all of the above to the broader social and communal environment within which the learning is taking place.

4. Discuss with educators, lay leaders, and/or policy makers the pros and cons of creating bicultural integrated schools (such as for example a Japanese-Jewish school in the U.S.).

5. Try to create educational opportunities for educators/parents/policy makers, from a variety of cultural/ethnic backgrounds to meet and discuss their educational aims and their best practices when attempting to achieve their groups cultural sustainability.

6. Use videotaped classroom events dealing with a variety of cultural curricula to identify the practices implemented when trying to teach culturally valuable concepts.

References

Ackerman, W. I. (1969). Jewish education-for what? *American Jewish Year Book*, 70, 1–35.

Becker, A. L. (1995). *Beyond translation: Essays toward a modern philology*. Ann Arbor, MI: The University of Michigan Press.

Bekerman, Z. (2001). Constructivist perspectives on language, identity and culture: Implications for Jewish identity and the education of Jews. *Religious Education*, 96(4), 462–473.

Bekerman, Z. (2004). Successful failure: The building of liberal Jewish education. In J. Bashi, M. B. Peretz & A. Bouganim (Eds.), *Education and Professional Training* (pp. 7–30). Jerusalem: Eliner Library.

Bekerman, Z. (2005). Paradigmatic change: Towards the social and the cultural in Jewish education. In M. Nisan & O. Schremer (Eds.), *Educational deliberations, studies in education dedicated to Shlomo (Seymour) Fox* (pp. 324–342). Jerusalem: Keter.

Bekerman, Z. & Silberman, M. (1999). Slaves of tradition-slaves of freedom: Social constructivist perspectives on the "culture" of Israeli traditionalists and liberals. *Israel Studies*, 4(2), 90–120.

Bekerman, Z. & Silberman, M. (2003). The corruption of culture and education by the nation state. *Journal of Modern Jewish Studies*, 2(1), 19–34.

Birnbaum, P. & Katznelson, I. (Eds.) (1995). *Paths of emancipation: Jews, states, and citizenship*. Princeton: Princeton University Press.

Cohen, S. M. (1995). The impact of varieties of Jewish education upon Jewish identity: An inter generational perspective. *Contemporary Jewry*, 16, 68–96.

Connelly, F. M. & Clandinin, D. J. (1987). On narrative method, biography and narrative unities in the study of teaching. *The Journal of Educational Thought*, 21(3), 13–33.

Dewey, J. (1938). *Art as experience*. New York: Perigee Books.

Dewey, J. (1959). The child and the curriculum. In M. S. Dworkin (Ed.), *Dewey on education* (pp. 91–111). New York: Bureau of Publications, Teachers College, Columbia University.

Dumont, L. (1986). *Essays on individualism: Modern ideology in anthropological perspective*. Chicago: University of Chicago Press.

Eisner, E. W. (1990). Creative curriculum development and practice. *Journal of Curriculum and Supervision*, 6(1), 62–73.

Elazar, D. J. (1997). The Kehillah. In D. J. Elazar (Ed.), *Kinship and consent: The Jewish political tradition and its contemporary uses* (pp. 233–276). New Brunswick, NJ and London: Transaction Publishers.

Foley, M. W. & Edwards, B. (1997). Escape from politics? Social theory and the social capital debate. *American Behavioral Scientist*, 40(5), 550–561.

Fox, S. (1973). Towards a general theory of Jewish education. In D. Sidorsky (Ed.), *The future of the Jewish community in America* (pp. 260–270). New York: Basic Books.

Fox, S., Scheffler, I., & Marom, D. (Eds.) (2003). *Visions of Jewish education*. Cambridge: Cambridge University Press.

Freire, P. (1970). *Pedagogy of the oppressed*. New York: Seabury.

Gellner, E. (1983). *Nations and nationalism*. Oxford: Basic Blackwell.

Glassner, B. & Loughlin, J. (1987). *Drugs in adolescent worlds: Burnouts to strights*. New York: St. Martin's Press.

Goldberg, H. (2003). *Jewish passages: Cycles of Jewish life*. Berkeley: University of California Press.

Heilman, S. C. (1977). Inner and outer identities: Sociological ambivalence among Orthodox Jews. *Jewish Social Studies*, 39, 227–240.

Herzfeld, M. (1992). *The social production of indifference: Exploring the symbolic roots of western bureaucracy*. Chicago: The University of Chicago Press.

Hitchcock, G. & Hughes, D. (1995). *Research and the teacher* (2nd edn). New York: Routledge-Falmer.

Hodin, L. K. (1999). *The impact of Jewish education on the moral reasoning of Jewish high school students: An exploration study*. Washington, DC: American University.

Katz, J. (1993 (1958)). *Tradition and crisis: Jewish society at the end of the Middle Ages*. New York: Schocken Books.

Kopelowitz, E. (2001). Who has the right to change tradition? Changing conceptions of religious authority and their consequences for the Jewish people. In *Studies in contemporary Jewry* (Vol. 17). Oxford: Oxford University Press.

Kopelowitz, E. (2005). Jewish identities. In N. de Lange & M. Freud-Kandel (Eds.), *Modern Judaism: An Oxford guide* (pp. 205–215). Oxford: Oxford University Press.

Kopelowitz, E., Yaffee, M., & Weiss, B. (2005). *How to determine a "successful Jewish education" for secular Jews in Israeli mamlachti schools*. Ramat Gan: Panim for Jewish Renaissance in Israel.

Lazerwitz, B., Winter, J. A., Dashefsky, A., & Tabory, E. (1998). *Jewish choices: American Jewish denominationalism*. Albany: State University of New York Press.

Mason, J. (1996). *Qualitative researching*. London: Sage Publications.

Maturana, U. & Valera, F. (1987). *The tree of knowledge: The biological roots of human understanding*. Boston: New Science Library.

Mueller, D. J. (1986). *Measuring social attitudes*. New York: Teachers College Press.

Obgu, J. U. (1993). Variability in minority school performance: A problem in search of an explanation. In E. Jacob & C. Jordan (Eds.), *Minority education: Anthropological perspectives* (pp. 83–113). Norwood, NJ: Ablex.

Phillips, B. A. (1987). *Re-examining intermarriage: Trends, textures & strategies*. Boston: Wilstein Institute of Jewish Policy Studies.

Podhoretz, N. (1967). *Making it*. New York: Random House.

Pomson, A. (2002). The Rebbe reworked: An inquiry into the persistence of inherited traditions of teaching. *Teaching and Teacher Education*, 18(1), 23–34.

Reay, D. and Mirza, H. S. (1997). Uncovering genealogies of the margins: Black supplementary schooling. *British Journal of Sociology of Education*, 18(4), 477–499.

Rogoff, B., Paradise, R., Arauz, R. M., Correa-Chavez, M., & Angelillo, C. (2003). First hand learning through intent participation. *Annual Review of Psychology, 54*(1), 175–203.

Schick, M. (2000). *A census of Jewish schools in the United States.* New York: Avi Chai Foundation.

Schon, D. A. (1987). *Educating the reflective practitioner.* San Francisco: Jossey-Bass Publishers.

Shkedi, A. (1998). Can the curriculum guide both emancipate and educate teachers? *Curriculum Inquiry, 28*(2), 209–229.

Schoenfeld, S. (1991). Three survey approaches to Jewish identity and their implications for research on Jewish education. Presented at the conference of the Research Network on Jewish Education, Cleveland.

Smith, A. D. (1998). *Nationalism and modernism.* London: Routledge.

Taylor, C. (1994). The politics of recognition. In D. T. Goldberg (Ed.), *Multiculturalism: A critical reader* (pp. 75–106). Oxford: Blackwell.

Teitelbaum, K. (1991). Critical lessons from our past: Curricula of socialist Sunday schools in the US. In M. Y. Apple & L. K. Christian-Smith (Eds.), T*he politics of the text book* (pp. 105–133). New York: Routledge.

Vygotsky, L. S. (1986). *Thought and language* (Trans. A. Kozulin,). Cambridge, MA: MIT Press.

Wenger, B. (1997). The politics of women's ordination: Jewish law, institutional power, and the debate over women in the rabbinate. In J. Wertheimer (Ed.), *Tradition renewed: A history of the Jewish Theological Seminary of American* (Vol. 2, pp. 485–523). New York: The Jewish Theological Seminary of America.

Wertheimer, J. (1999). The rabbi, the synagogue, and the community. In E. Abrams & D. G. Dalin (Eds.), *Secularism, spirituality, and the future of American Jewry* (pp. 47–50). Washington, DC: Ethics and Public Policy Center.

PART IV

Everyday Life and the Medias of Cultural Transmission

In the previous sections we examined the impact of state policy on minority education, the nature of communal institutions, and the place of educational institutions within a community. We now move to the level of everyday life in order to grapple with issues touching on the transmission of culture as it occurs in face-to-face and other forms of intimate interpersonal interaction.

While understanding the impact of concepts such as the "state" and "community" are important for furthering educational efforts to sustain minority, diaspora, and indigenous culture, it is no less important to dive into the everyday realm. How are cultural activities initiated and sustained by group members in the course of life as it is actually experienced on a day-to-day basis? Anthropologists, philosophers, psychologists, and sociologists of education increasingly recognize the need to attend to spheres and sites other than schools, as places where education takes place. These chapters follow in this tradition.

In the previous sections we looked at the challenge for formal educational institutions to make learning relevant and applicable to life outside the school. Several authors also asked if transmission of lived culture is possible when it becomes formalized as a curriculum. The act of formalizing culture and "teaching it" changes the nature of the beast and in some cases might even kill it—turning lived experience into a discipline relevant to classroom learning, examinations, and grades. With this in mind, educators have much to learn by looking at culture as it plays out in everyday contexts. When we view the dynamic nature of group life in everyday contexts the immensity of the challenge facing school-based educators becomes clear.

The three chapters in this fourth section focus on the dynamics of cultural transmission in everyday contexts of the family or conversations that take place in cyberspace or face-to-face interactions. The chapters present some promising theoretical advances in the field and analyze a variety of social, cultural, political, historical, and economic contexts within which non-formal educational strategies support cultural efforts. The authors also probe the nature of cultural knowledge and the practices through which culture is transmitted in everyday life. The theoretical and methodological choices express the authors' intentions to treat cultural learning as something that happens in a variety of places and to think of these places as sites that generate learning in a variety of forms. The message is clear: we need to broaden the meaning of cultural education to encompass lived life outside of educational institutions.

Joi Freed-Garrod describes the power inherent in song and culturally rich conversation. Freed-Garrod draws an ethnographic picture of a group of friends, women who sing together in the context of a Jewish Renewal synagogue in Canada. The rich description of the manner in which song and conversation weave together in the course of their interactions with one another and others enables an appreciation of the dynamic movement between Jewish and non-Jewish elements of culture that, taken together, provide a basis for coherent and sustainable counter-culture.

Freed-Garrod suggests that music is a powerful means for cultural sustainability. Sound and songs have long told the story of the human condition and, she emphasizes, serve as a central medium for oral tradition that is portable and dynamic, enabling communication and memory. Moreover, sound and song enable enduring and compelling narratives that identify and sustain a culture over time and across place.

Musical expression, like other cultural codes, reflects the values and behavioral norms of a given culture. Freed-Garrod theoretically substantiates the importance of music and song for enabling cultural sustainability within a post-modern paradigm that situates lived experience in relational terms. Learning is contextual, she tells us and through music, story, and conversation we remember and shape that which is meaningful to us. In pre-literate societies, the structure for memory construction and meaning making was oral, contemporarily situated, and part of intersubjective conversational dialogues. Despite the radical changes from pre-literate to contemporary society, the use of song, sound, story telling, and conversation continue to be important cognitive tools for cultural transmission.

Music as conversation or story includes both language (words and vocals) and musical sound. Freed-Garrod suggests songs as a dialogical process, subjectively and collaboratively, telling stories of people, events, and feelings through both lyrics (language) and sound (musical elements). We learn that the collaborative process of telling, re-telling, modifying, and creating meaning in real time is central to the transmission of culture. This dynamic process enables past and present to interact with one another in the dialectic of cultural creation, which, as we learn from the chapter, occurs as part of the very act in which culture is sustained.

In her chapter, M. Gail Hickey also focuses on the interaction between women in everyday contexts. Hickey provides an ethnographic account of the attempt by Asian Indian women to retain their culture after immigration to the U.S. Her analysis exemplifies how women employing a variety of means —including child rearing practices, family socialization, informal and formal language and/or religious instruction, formal instruction in ethnic music and/or dance, habits of diet and dress, and communication in the home as well as in public venues such as the workplace—serve as central agents for the transmission and maintenance of traditional cultural or ethnic values. The women attempt on the one hand to maintain traditional values, while on the other hand simultaneously facilitating the transition of themselves and their families into the American Western value system.

Hickey's work underlines the centrality of identity development as it is negotiated in the dynamic space formed by family interactions. Hickey shows why the family is an important site for cultural reproduction. She encourages us to further our understanding of the family's role in reproducing and reinforcing values and behaviors vital in understanding the individual's sense of self, both as a member of an ethnic group and other possibly opposing value structures coming out of simultaneous membership in other social groups.

Finally, Lucia Clark takes us into a quintessentially post-modern realm of everyday life. Clark provides an analysis of the informal cyber-communities that are growing around the websites of Italian ethnic groups. Clark argues that the Internet has become a venue of expression for ethnic language revival with the ability to counter the hegemonic and assimilatory claims of the nation state.

Clark shows how the Internet offers a place where cultural identities can survive and, indeed, thrive. The Internet changes concepts of time and cultural transmission. We have been culturally conditioned to look at our past in order to know ourselves in the present; but the digital past is now and we are spectators and actors forging the future while constantly changing it. Far from becoming the great equalizer, the Internet has indeed acted as a forum for the reaffirmation of long dormant ethnic identities. Websites and chat rooms enable people to exchange ideas in their native language and festivals can be advertised online where they attract people from all over the world. The Virtual Village and the Real Village have become one.

These virtual sites result in multiple outcomes. They facilitate the rediscovery of old traditions, support political cohesion, and also support dissent. The web is but another forum for the extraordinary vitality of cultures, Italian or other. Minority groups can use the Internet to create virtual communities where they can survive and, in so doing, they are managing to defeat globalization with their "dialects" and the wealth of discursive traditions that they bring forth. These communities cut across political borders and reaffirm struggling minority, diaspora, and indigenous groups. Clark's exploration points at the dynamics of the new global society and the possibilities afforded to minority groups by the growth of the European Union.

Taken together the chapters in this section call our attention to the multiple paths that can be traveled outside of formal educational institutions in the search for cultural sustainability. From the perspective of the larger cultural education–cultural sustainability project, we argue that, even though the non-formal dimensions of culture described by the authors are no doubt essential to cultural sustainability, they are nevertheless passed over by many who are concerned with minority, diaspora, and indigenous education. While the importance of the interpersonal and contextual dimensions of culture are essential, they are not easily translated to methods of formal education and for that reason alone should grab a substantial amount of our attention. The opposite currently occurs.

Developing a heightened sense of the importance of lived life makes it a productive sphere for understanding how culture is transmitted without allowing for the invasion by the formal, which can easily change and destroy the adventurous, dynamic, and meaningful character of everyday life. While the challenge is not easy, rediscovering and revitalizing the non-formal might hold a promise for cultural vitality that many formal educational institutions are currently unable to deliver.

CHAPTER 18

Singing the Stories of Diaspora: Jewish Identity in Canada

JOI FREED-GARROD

Introduction

When I sing the Kaddish prayer on Yom Kippur that I composed in memory of my father, I feel his presence and energy in the room. I am aware of two parts of myself—one is singing and the other is listening; the listening part hears, in the intense, attentive silence of the congregation, their collective "voices" joining me in reaching out to those no longer physically embodied here.

(Italicized blocks of narrative are voices of participants in this study, while my personal reflections as participant–researcher are in alternate font.)

Music can be a powerful means of cultural sustainability: sound and songs have long told the story of the human condition. It is a key medium of oral tradition, providing a portable, dynamic medium for communicating and holding in memory enduring and compelling narratives that identify and sustain a culture over time and across place. Musical expression, like other cultural codes, reflects the values and behavioral norms of a given culture. Applying Peirce's semiotics, Martinez (1998) and Bonnycastle (1997) suggest that people interpret those codes, reshaping, modifying, and transforming signs that are meaningful to them. Music is a cultural semiotic: songs and/or instruments are used to transmit spiritual messages[1] and genres and styles are identified through unique cultural attributes such as rhythmic and melodic patterns, harmonies, meters, and keys. Poly-rhythmic drumbeats of African ritual music and African-American work songs, Jewish cantorial melodies in minor keys, or the consonant, thick harmonies of high church choral music are examples of the cultural "signposts" expressed through music that connect us to a given culture's past and join communities of like-minded people with similar experiences, thereby sustaining their cultural identity through shared memory. Many religions use the cultural medium of sacred song to call people to prayer, to communicate important behaviors and norms, and to invite collective engagement at a deep emotional and psychic level through singing/chanting during services or rituals. Jewish traditions are steeped in music: our Sabbath services begin with an introductory set of songs/chants that have a meditative "calling together" or uplifting praise-like quality. The prayer service that follows juxtaposes rhythmic chant and silent sections. Rhythm, silence, and melody, essential, integral parts of music, represent particular stylistic devices that make each culture's music identifiable. As Bowman (2004) noted, "[m]usic and identity (individual and collective, embodied and social) are joined at the hip" (pp. 43 and 45).

Theoretically, the notion of music and song as instruments of cultural sustainability connects to the post-modern paradigm that situates lived experience in relational terms. Learning is contextual. We create and remember that which is meaningful to us (Lave and Wenger, 1991). In pre-literate societies, the structure for memory construction and meaning-making was oral: contemporarily, intersubjective conversational dialogs or story continue to be important cognitive tools. Music as conversation or story includes both language (words and vocals) and musical sound. Songs as a dialogical process, subjectively and collaboratively, tell stories of people, events, and feelings through both the lyrics (language) and sound (musical elements). There is interaction between various participants listening/singing/talking with each other, between performers and the audience, and between the music and singers as performers and/or creators. The collaborative process of telling, retelling, modifying, and creating occurs in a temporal context, linking past and present during the interaction and collaboration.

This study explores the experiences of members of an informal singing group who use music to represent, understand, and transform cultural experience as a means to sustain and transform their Jewish identity as women in the contemporary diaspora context of a congregation aligned with the Jewish Renewal movement.[2]

Research Design

Theoretical Framework

This study is grounded in Bakhtin's (1981) theory of dialogicality, whereby identity is constructed and expressed in a variety of ways including gesture, laughter, song, and speech. In Bakhtin's (1981) dialogical theory, the components include the construction of identity as dialogic and intersubjective, meaning-making as an evolutionary, transitory, and transformational process, views of the world and human understanding that are poly-vocal and poly-logical, a recognition of the tension in everyday human interactions between the official and popular socio-cultural voices, and the notion of "Carnivale" taken from the medieval festival, which afforded people the opportunity to engage in spontaneous, informal, interactive experiences unfettered by hierarchical protocols. For Bakhtin (1981), the often unpredictable, unstructured, and informal public arena provides the background for the organic process whereby people negotiate realities in order to survive and flourish. He proposed that an ontology of *becoming* rather than *being* is more appropriate in real life, as having a monological or hegemonic view of the world is incomplete. Being in the world is an act "of our actual experience ... [looking] ... in two opposite directions—like a two-faced Janus. It looks at the objective entity of a domain of culture and at the ever-repeatable uniqueness of actually lived and experienced life" (1993, pp. 2–3).

In Bakhtin's (1981, 1993) view, dialogically exploring lived experience develops individual and collective identities and the agency that enables the construction of dynamic, shared communities of practice. For the women in this study, singing together became the context for sharing cultural traditions and innovations in a variety of informal and portable times and spaces, many of which represented carnivalesque moments of disrupted routine and release from the official social order which shaped and sustained their individual and collective cultural identity.

Methodology

This qualitative study is a participant–observer ethnography of six women in an informal singing group emerging from a larger cultural religious community. The questions posed center around personal and community identity construction and issues of exclusivity and inclusion within the particularity of this self-selected group of empowered, well-educated, professional women engaged in public life. The "lived experience" (Van Manen, 1990) of these women provides the context for the ethnographic investigation. Validity for the interpretation includes the triangulation of those accountings by various data collection tools and individuals (Maxwell, 1996) in which the researcher looked for patterns and surprises in the intersubjective dialogs and the creative processes within singing activities. Reflexive accounts of personal experience are utilized: the researcher's experiences, observations, and voice, as she takes on the dual role of participant–observer, are considered primary data (Ellis, 1991). The data in this study included stories, songs (original and traditional), informal conversation and oral history, interviews, rehearsal interactions, interpretations of known songs, reflections from performances, and our interpersonal relationships, created by both the participants and the researcher and "retold" by the researcher through her lens.

Ethnographic Profiles

The participant group originally formed in order to honor a member of our congregation for completing his rabbinical studies with a musical "roast." Although we originally thought of ourselves as a temporary *ad hoc* singing group, rehearsing for this event provided a catalyst for our decision to keep meeting. We began to define ourselves within the framework of this singing group, naming ourselves The Madrigals. The conversation, laughter, intellectual stimulation, and emotional support were as important as the joy of music making: the singing group became the structure within which the dialogical processes of cultural transformation, education, and sustenance took place. Individually, we are diverse in background and experience: as a community of practice, our individual identities interact to support, enhance, and instruct each other as we form and reform our communal identity:

Susan is a lawyer and judge. With her deep interest in ritual and extensive liturgical and *halachic* (Jewish legal codes) understanding, she instigates much of our participation and contribution to services and life cycle events. As an experienced amateur musician and Talmudic scholar, she often brings a new interpretation of a text or song for us to explore.

Sue is a medical doctor who has recently achieved her Ph.D. in biomedical ethics. Part of her research took her to Israel, where she has family and friends. Through the years of her studies, her visits there prompted many discussions about contemporary Jewish concerns within the socio-cultural contexts of our collective experiences as diaspora Jews belonging to a particular cultural religious perspective and from our own personal perspectives, which varied depending on the issue raised. She also brought tunes and texts that she learned in Israel to share, prompting us to be messengers of new cultural identity through music for other congregation members. Sharing the very real tensions of the time and space constrictions in her various life contexts —secular day school versus yeshiva for her two children, trying to live an observant life (including taking the Sabbath) when she was "on-call" at work, and contradictory ethical realities encountered on a daily basis—we often rehearsed at her home, which became both the "temple" and "school" for our portable cultural community.

Reva is an anthropologist who works in the prison system with male offenders, mostly First Nations. Among other duties, she facilitates programs to help them build a sense of cultural identity and belonging. She lends a different cultural perspective to our dialogs, helping us see the similarities and make cross-cultural connections in practices and observances. As a long-time singer with an internationally acclaimed community choir, she brings a stability and consistency to our musical awareness and interpretation. She has also been the inspiration for new compositions, often because she senses the time is right for renewing our own or community interest in a part of a ritual or service.

Ruth is a clinical psychologist who works with patients primarily on a one-to-one basis. Her solitary work life has led her to seek out our group for social, musical, and cultural religious reasons. She is the most recent of us to have a death in her close family. Such events make us realize how important it is to have close friends who share cultural traditions and experiences in times of grief and other life cycle events. Our small group has succoured each other with talk, song, tears, hugs, and laughter—all the elements of the dialogic frame that builds relationships and identities.

These four have their roots in the Winnipeg Jewish community, a very old, established, and thriving cultural and religious community. None of us has our roots in Vancouver: as members of our congregation we represent a secondary diaspora community within the larger North American diaspora. And as members of The Madrigals (women taking leadership roles), we are members of yet another diaspora.

Carol Ann is a motivational consultant. Laughter and humor are two of her most effective tools and interpersonal relationships are her forte. She guides us through the messiness of our differences and provides the means to understand attitudes, values, and beliefs of our own and others' socio-cultural perspectives. She loves to perform and is often the one who pushes us to share our creative selves and new learning through music. From Halifax originally, she brings different cultural traditions (along with many different versions of songs we know).

Joi is a university professor and musician. Originally from the U.S. and a family who only celebrated High Holy Days and Passover, she is the least knowledgeable in official texts, although she knows many of the songs and prayers from years of rote repetition as an original member of our congregation. For her, cultural religious learning and sustenance is deeply communicated through music. As the composer in the group, her music often represents a consolidation and extension of our cultural dialog.

Music as Cultural, Intersubjective Dialog

Our cultural identity as individuals has been framed in both secular and sacred contexts. Points of connection for sustaining and educating each of us cross past and present experience in our various life contexts. Through choice, we are an exclusive group. However, the boundaries for this group are flexible and portable: our numbers vary as we invite others to sing with us; purposes vary, from fun to ritual to life cycle events; and place and time vary, based on any number of contextual factors. Through our varied, emergent dialogs our identities evolve within our exclusivity, which supports and enriches us. This in-group provides us with the foundation from which we expand into our larger cultural religious community (an exclusive group in itself). The inter-subjective, public dialogs between these two groups bridge the informal with the formal, providing a framework for inclusion (e.g. sharing our songs and teaching others to sing with us).

Our singing group participates in various poly-vocal dialogs.

1. Jewish tradition. Through singing *nigunim* (vocalized tunes without words) or cantorial prayers, we use music as a means to convey under-standing of official and traditional texts. According to Van Schalkwyk (2002), both words and music are forms of communication that use abstract symbols to transfer meaning: as such, they are essential tools for cultural education. On an individual basis, we reaffirm our identity as Jews through our experiences with these texts, mindful of Bakhtin's (1981) assertion that our perceptions are based in the mirror of others' understandings as well as our own personal ones.

2. The contemporary Jewish Renewal movement. Women's roles are changing: there is a need to negotiate tensions between formal and informal, traditional and contemporary, official and democratic expec-tations and needs, both personal and collective, in regards to cultural identity construction. As our identities transform and *become*, we are agents of change and transgression, crossing and pushing boundaries set for women within traditional Judaism.

3. Local Jewish women's community. Through discussions, song, laughter, tears, and hugs, we explore musical, aesthetic, cultural, political, or personal issues within our small group and in the larger sacred and secular cultural religious communities. As people who define them-selves (in part) as The Madrigals, we solidify ourselves as a particular "community" of informal education and sustenance through music. As we share what we know and invite others to join us in the music/meaning making, the boundaries of exclusivity are expanded and shared cultural identity constructed.

These dialogs are often spontaneous and disorderly. Our voices are heard in the counterpoint of unpredictable rhythm patterns and truncated motifs as we talk over each other, dispute memories, change topics midstream, and deal with interruptions from family members or the telephone, while following various conversational streams.

All six of us are here, which is unusual, because of our busy schedules. We are leading the preparatory service, P'sukei d'Zimrah. We try out several pitches for each song and the accompanying dialog usually goes something like this: "Didn't we start on "D" last time we sang this? How come we're starting now on "C?" "I guess we're getting older and our voices are getting lower!" "No, it's just that we let Sue give us the starting pitch and you know she always starts too low!"

Carol Ann sings a tune that she learned in Halifax as a child, Reva sings her "definitive" version from Winnipeg, and Sue adds a new harmony that she learned on her recent trip to Israel. An anecdote accompanies each person's contribution, calling forth cultural threads that look backwards to traditions as well as forward into innovation. When we are done, our version may be further transformed . . . and if our wider congregation likes it well enough, it may become a new tradition.

History and story are inextricably linked in all cultures as story telling enables people to build, strengthen, reaffirm, and/or renew a sense of place (Waller, 2003, p. 5). Good stories, according to Ellis (2001), involve both the listener and the teller in discourse that stimulates thinking, enriches the ensuing dialog, and creates meaning. In our conversations, cognitive dissonance is part of the creative dialog. We laugh even as we debate and disagree. Musical decisions emerge from dialogs arising out of the democracy of our informality and our memories. Differences of opinion about prayer, tune, or pitch choices are not taken seriously: it is part of the process. The interactive discourse has a flow, a sense of accomplishment and positivity, that I take for granted in this group, yet seems to be missing from some of my other life contexts where any difference is seen as negative or argumentative. I believe this is a cultural component, one that identifies "Jewishness"; intellectual dialogs that challenge thinking are an integral part of Jewish teaching and learning. Our rehearsals reflect this essential aspect of cultural sustainability, which brings traditions forward while simultaneously inviting transformation of those traditions.

Intersubjective Identity Construction

In strict orthodox tradition, cultural transmission is the female's role and responsibility—dialogical practices around rituals, food, life cycle events, etc. are located outside the sacred space of the sanctuary, portable, flexible as to time, interpersonal, and intersubjective. Liturgical study and transmission of official texts are the male's right and responsibility. The Torah (scripture) and Talmud (commentary) are digested, discussed, and argued about primarily within sacred spaces and bounded time, intrapersonal as well as interpersonal/ intersubjective. Women in Jewish Renewal and other egalitarian communities of practice reframe gender, space, and time parameters through relocating, shifting, and democratizing "official" dialogs. The inherent tensions exposed through the disruption of expected patterns of cultural identity exchange can be springboards for identity reaffirmation and/or transformation. One such example is the event of singing the *Sh'ma* described in the following narrative. (The *Sh'ma* is the prayer at the very core of Judaism: traditionally in every service and important ritual, it is part of the official curriculum/texts.)

> *A member of our congregation plays in a Japanese Taiko drumming group that is presenting a concert. He has an idea for a cross-cultural collaboration that would combine singing the Sh'ma with the elemental rhythms of Taiko.*
>
> As we rehearse our song, it amazes me how easily the two different genres blend—"the whole is more than the sum of its parts" seems to be a perfect metaphor for intercultural understanding. I find myself wishing that it would be as easy to accept another culture alongside our own as it is to interweave Jewish and Japanese music together, each individual and separate yet at the same time fitting together and enhancing each other. In this moment of space and time, the past, present, and future seem to come together with the interaction of tradition and innovation. It is a powerful dialog of multiple voices and is a microcosm of Judaism, where, typically, "what is new is old; what is old is new . . . every time we repeat our experience of Judaism we find in it something new" (Sacks, 2000).

> *Our piece begins: as I walk onstage and sing this sacred music, I am transported into it—I feel the song coming out of the core of my body; I have no sense of my physical self, just the sound of the tune and rhythms.*
>
> Both musical and cultural components played equally integral parts as I identified with the musical sound and the sacred prayer. Part of the magic of this experience was the connection I felt to an audience that included others outside my cultural background who did not know that prayer and its meaning. The enduring quality of certain cultural texts was also made clear to me through this experience: although transformed into a contemporary context and informed by unusual accompaniment (the drums and cymbals of Taiko as well as the different rhythm patterns of Japanese music as opposed to Jewish music), this prayer still had currency and power to draw new listeners into it across the boundaries of the normative time and space constraints of religious/cultural expression (e.g. in the synagogue or on a particular day or at a particular time). The Sh'ma is at the heart of the traditional, male, sacred liturgy. As women singing it in a public place integrated with a fundamental aspect of another culture (traditional musical rhythms), including cross-cultural musicians for a multicultural audience, gender, time, and space boundaries shifted and became relocated. We transgressed many traditional cultural boundaries and the value of such

experience may be seen in the cross-cultural, cross-temporal, and cross-contextual poly-vocal dialogs that enrich both individual and collective meaning making.

Singing is a transformational act through which people, often marginalized, have shared cultural experience in many places and times: African-American slaves "sang" their way to freedom with coded songs, ". . . the Estonian people sang themselves into becoming a nation" (Kuutma, 2004, p. 4), and music sustained Jews in the concentration camps as they sang the songs representative of their cultural identity. Music has long been linked with memory and the passing on of significant historical narratives. Rehearsing the individual parts of the song for accuracy, making aesthetic sense of the ways the musical elements interact (interpretation), and singing to share with others are all listening and performative acts: all are interactive and intersubjective (with self and others). Knowledge gained is a process, ever evolving and recursive, acted on by all participants; " knowledge not grounded in perfection but always in the process of becoming . . . especially germane to an ethics of inter-subjectivity, of meeting the other on the other's own terms . . . As a result, the actual musical encounters increasingly become powerful 'transformances' (Schechner, 1988) of inclusion and rejection, of convergence and divergence, euphony and cacophony, familiarity and alienation, mastery and contingency" (Bogdan, 2002, p. 33). Specific to this study, the ideas of the dialogical and of transformance can be intertwined in musical experience, exploration, and expression. Dialogical voices in the context of our particular singing group are formed around our Jewish, cultural life; the transformances are the sharing of our cultural attitudes, values, and beliefs through the medium of song.

Communities of Practice

What is our group for? Laughing, of course . . . eating, complaining . . . singing together with people in shul.

It is because we are who we are and sing what we sing that keeps us connected . . . It is a different outlet for me than any other in my life. I feel good about myself, accepted as I come and honored for what I bring . . . the giggles.

Singing is the way I connect with my Jewish spirituality, singing harmony connects me with other people. Singing harmony with The Madrigals lets my spirit soar.

Cultural sustainability depends on continuance: those of us who are already in the "inner circle" of our culture through one of its prime markers—ritual, life style, diet, music, or language—will remain. At issue is how we can draw in those who are on the periphery, whose day-to-day life worlds differ from their traditional culture and find it somewhat difficult to construct an ongoing identify that is flexible enough to fit in both contexts. Reconceptualization of their identity has been a common feature of diaspora Jews. Throughout two millennia in a wide variety of contexts, Jewish communities have been reframing and reconstructing their practices and culture; their identity and understanding/knowing is constantly emerging and evolving, in a fluid state of "becoming." One of the qualities of becoming is a sense of hopefulness, of possibility—and a sense of hope has always been inherent in Jewishness; it is one of the things that sustains us as a culture. Music is a fundamental and pervasive part of our spiritual community; everyone joins in the singing and chanting (we have no choir or cantor). Services are usually a mix of old, traditional melodies, ones that are becoming "traditional" in our congregation because we have sung them for some time and new ones (always encouraged). In this way, music is a prime agent of inclusion as it has been utilized as an educative tool reaching other congregations beyond ourselves.

> A key factor for our singing group is its informality. Rehearsals are sporadic and the reasons for getting together are fluid; sometimes we have a specific event that we are singing in or leading and other times we meet because one of us says *"I need to schmooze and laugh"* or *"I miss the comfort and safety of being with people who like me and who are like me, who don't say that I'm too loud or impolite because I interrupt."* Even when we are working intensely to reach a goal, our rehearsals do not have a rigid, formal quality. The fact that they always combine talking, eating, and singing was never discussed, yet always implicitly understood, a result, we believe, of the combination of our cultural background, familial roles, and gender as well as some intuition that senses as well as intellect need to be satisfied. We "feed" ourselves and each other—both literally and figuratively—we have feasted on such things as contemporarily elegant lox, bagel, cream cheese and capers brunches, traditional "comfort" food like *cholent*, the rich stew of meat, beans, barley, and vegetables that cooks slowly for hours sending out waves of delicious smells as it simmers, perfect for over the Sabbath when no work (cooking included) is done, endless honey cakes and matzo balls, complete with the mandatory complaints and compliments about *"my Baba's is better,"* etc. Alternately, we feed our minds, hearts, and souls through community connection and making or listening to music, filling and nourishing ourselves and each other by "eating" together.

Making music together and sharing ideas, laughter, pain, all the "stuff of life," has created strong bonds. We have learned, over the years, that there is much needed solace in laughter and song. Bakhtin's (1968) belief that laughter is a crucial aspect of identity construction is illustrated regularly within the kind of carnivalesque model that our informal singing group approximates. Beyond our group, the relationships and experiences that we share have had a positive and enriching ripple effect out to our families and the larger cultural religious community of which we are all still a part, extending the boundaries of our exclusive group to those on the periphery.

In the particular context of this singing group, our responses to the music are integral to the formation of meaning (interpretation of music and text), which impacts on how we view our identity within the cultural context; in addition, members of the larger congregation who participate in singing along with us are also engaging in the act of identity creating. Each time we sing, the heterophony that inherently emerges from groups singing together in unstructured frameworks makes the music and with it the cultural components, works in progress. In addition, each time we sing/hear a song we take it in and simultaneously pass it on—this evolution or triadic set of intersubjective dialogs is both a real representation of and a metaphor for the process of identity building and sustenance of diaspora Judaism.

The dynamic tension between tradition and innovation has kept our ongoing learning constructively and passionately alive. Not only have we learned music, but also The Torah and traditions of observance. We have led Sabbath and High Holy Days services, shared our songs in life cycle events, and participated in city-wide sacred music festivals. We have integrated and infused the distinct yet related customs and living patterns of the secular, non-Jewish parts of our lives with our spiritual/religious observances, largely through the language of music, for ourselves and shared with others outside our religious community.

Through song, we transform traditions and cultural knowledge, keeping them alive and relevant in our own time and place. As agents of change and transgressors of boundaries, we are carrying on the traditions and rituals as Jewish women always have done, outside the formality of the synagogue (for the most part), relocating the sacred into secular contexts (rehearsing for a CD or "roast" to honor achievement or singing favorite songs at a pot luck Sabbath meal), and back again into the sacred setting, albeit transformed (a new tune for a traditional text, a new song honoring a bar/bat mitzvah "coming of age" ceremony, or a memorial marking the passing of a parent). This idea of portability, relocation, and transformation is typical of Judaism in the diaspora. As women, our roles as leaders in cultural transmission are recognized as instrumental; coming together in various informal music making and sharing settings and purposes demonstrates the power of dialogic acts in the creating and sustaining of cultural identity.

Findings and Contributions to the Field

The data collected were interpreted searching for patterns, narrative threads, themes, and surprises. The analyses are collaborative and ongoing, which means that all our perceptions, memories, and interpretations are in flux; over time, further experiences and dialog may change the written text that appears here. At this time, the following insights regarding some of the ways that music can informally educate and sustain cultural identity have emerged from the data.

1. Singing is *living* ritual. "The essence of music lies not in musical works but in taking part in performance, in social action. Music is not so much a noun as a verb, 'to music'. To music is to take part, in any capacity, in a musical performance . . . that means not only to perform but also to listen, to provide material for performance (what we call composing), to prepare for a performance (what we call practicing or rehearsing), or to take part in any activity that can affect the nature of that style of human encounter which is a musical performance" (Small, 1999, pp. 9 and 12). Rituals are markers of identity; identities change and their construction is a live, embodied, continuous process, to which singing is a powerful adjunct.

2. Singing is a powerful way of shaping and expressing individual and community cultural identity. Singing together shapes our relationship to each other and the wider cultural spiritual community. Music/chant/sound are memory aids: traditional Jewish songs bring sacred text and sound from the past into the present. We sing the same songs to our children that our grandparents sang to us, part of our Jewish identities across time; there is a sense of familiarity and place-out-of-time when we hear the same *nigun* in a synagogue in Florence, Italy, that we have sung in our synagogue in Vancouver. Collaborating on the creation of new melodies or chants to prayers makes new meaning as we imbue the music with our contemporary attitudes, values, and beliefs; re-situating 'old' text also serves to clarify and extend our knowledge and understanding about the religious/spiritual content within the language. As a result of the ongoing sharing and re-presenting, through us we propel enduring cultural sounds into the future, perhaps to be heard even by our children's children.

3. Informal settings (within a carnivalesque model) where others are "invited in" to the music making by singing along may be more compelling for sustaining culture than more formal "performance" settings where the listeners are distanced and passive. Sounds and actions of encounters across the full range of emotions, from laughter to tears, between individuals within our group, between "us" and the larger communities, and between our human and musical identities bring hope into our immediate physical space and time, carry the joy and peace of the Sabbath into the work week, and give us tools for solace to ease pain from situations that we cannot change. In terms of cultural

sustainability, the invitation to the wider congregation to join in, either by singing along or actively listening, engages others in identity building, in that the boundaries of exclusivity are blurred or expanded; regarding cultural education, music forms the texts by which we teach and learn those within our community and also enables us to reach out to "others."

4. Women are leaders in the dialog of cultural education between formal, sacred, and informal secular (con)texts. There are tensions between the perceived patriarchical formalities of tradition and the feminine informality associated with innovative contemporary settings which re-form and re-create cultural narratives through conversation, laughter, story telling, and singing. The phrase *"talk among yourselves"* is a Jewish joke that illustrates the belief that conversations shape informal cultural education.

Implications and Conclusion

In this study, intersubjective dialogical processes, including expressive acts of talking, singing, laughing, debating, and co-composing, inform cultural identity for an informal group of women in the Jewish diaspora. Through acts of reproducing, creating, and re-creating cultural texts in the form of music, the dynamic tension between the official dialog of Jewish tradition and the democratic, transformative, female voice emerges in various discourse forms, which become the curriculum of a lively educational process to co-construct cultural meaning. Their shared community of practice is an example of both cultural exclusivity and boundary transgression. In terms of cultural sustainability as well as education, traditional structures, ritual, texts, etc. are fundamental; equally essential are innovative, boundary stretching structures/contexts. While this study investigated the stories of a specific group, an invitation is extended to other communities of practice to join in dialogs that explore and extend lived cultural curriculum for the purpose of educating and sustaining cultural identity.

Resources for Educators

Questions

1. What is the nature of the informal education process in this chapter?
2. What aspects of informal education might be utilized in another context/setting?
3. Intersubjective dialog, as proposed by Bakhtin (1991), requires an openness to the "other" as well as both the capacity to reflect on and mediate one's attitudes, values, and beliefs (cultural biases). To create such an environment what strategies might you use to teach and/or

scaffold your students to develop these capacities and what problems might arise and what action might be taken to move the group forward?

4. What touches you or attracts your engagement to music? What makes music (song, chant, instrumental selection) compelling for you?

5. Regarding your relationship to your cultural heritage do you actively engage in practice, do you know anything about your heritage, and what else do you want to know? How do you sustain and/or educate yourself/your family about your cultural heritage?

For Further Reading

Bresler, L. & Marme/Thompson, C. (Eds.) (2002). *The arts in children's lives: Context, cultures and curriculum.* Dordrecht: Kluwer Academic Publishers.

Conceptions of "self" developing in particular cultural situations are discussed from varying psychological, educational, and arts-focused perspectives in fifteen separate chapters. Essays are grouped into three broad sections: socio-cultural context, learning and development through the eyes of children and adults, and looking at content from various curriculum "types" (Goodlad, 1979). The chapters challenge attitudes and beliefs about children's capabilities and the role of arts in education; provocative insights in the area of arts education in both formal and informal settings are also provided.

Freed Carlin, J. (1998). *Can you think a little louder? A classroom-based ethnography of eight and nine year olds composing with music and language.* Unpublished doctoral thesis, University of British Columbia, Vancouver, Canada.

Within the formal context of school, this inquiry was based in an informal structure where students were invited to express their personal conceptions and understanding of a given prompt through sound (musical compositions). Twenty-four students in a grade three classroom worked in partners to share ideas using oral conversation, peer critique, and a variety of musical and environmental sounds to design a representation of their meaning making and communicate it to others in the form of musical compositions. One of the key findings was that previous socio-cultural experience and understanding was a primary factor influencing choices for sound sources, musical form, and representational sounds.

Jaffurs, S. (2004). The impact of informal music learning practices in the classroom, or how I learned how to teach from a garage band. *International Journal of Music Education, 22*(3), 189–200.

This ethnographic study is an investigation of the environment that students create when making music that is meaningful to them. The significance of the study may be in the discovery of ways to "counter mechanisms of dominance inherent" (Fornas *et al.*, 1995, p. 263) in many formal environments. The author reflects on the lessons of informal music learning practices (from the article abstract).

Knowles, J. & Cole, A. (2002). Transforming research: Possibilities for arts-informed scholarship? In E. O'Sullivan, A. Morrell & M. A. O'Conner (Eds.), *Expanding the boundaries of transformational learning* (pp. 199–228). New York: Palgrave Publishing.

Arts-informed scholarship is explored as an alternative perspective and methodology for social science research, particularly within the educational field. Examples of studies using arts-informed inquiry are included.

Tiedt, P. L. & Tiedt, I. M. (1995). *Multicultural teaching: A handbook of activities, information and resources* (3rd. edn). Boston: Allyn & Bacon.

Covering a huge range of issues about multicultural education in its 409 pages, this book offers both theoretical and practical information for educators across curriculum areas and interpersonal communication skills/student needs. The goal of this book is to provide clear, relevant, and respectful strategies as well as specific lessons for developing multicultural understanding. Included is an excellent (if slightly outdated) categorized listing of books for both adults and children that address specific concepts and content areas. This resource is full of well-constructed and effectively presented material for the multicultural educator.

Suggestions for Educators

1. Create contemporary narratives using the students' own folk idioms (for example, blend traditional stories with contemporary music structures, focusing on significant issues as determined by the teacher and students together).

2. Engage students in project-based inquiry into historical events documented in music/song. Some possible prompts include Shostakovich's politically transgressive instrumental compositions and U.S. slave songs and other coded songs of oppression (e.g. *Follow the Drinking Gourd* (North America), *Dona, Dona, Dona* (Yiddish), and *Beds are Burning* (Australia)).

3. Construct personal geographies; Research and chronicle your own family's cultural history and include artifacts, anecdotes, favorite rituals, songs, 'secret' recipes, etc. (Teachers should have students look for patterns of similarities and differences across cultural backgrounds.)

Notes

1. For details of chant patterns (*nusach*) and explanations of the characteristics of Jewish music, see, among others, the University of Calgary, Alberta, Canada's Special Collections for the Canadian Broadcasting Company radio transcripts of music programs produced by Srul Irving Glick.
2. Jewish Renewal is non- or trans-denominational and not a denomination in itself. Believing that Judaism is an evolving religious civilization, Jewish Renewal embraces a variety of modalities as vehicles to authentic prayer, including dance, song, chant, meditation, and mysticism, as it seeks to carry forward two of the core ideas of Judaism—the perpetual process of renewal and a sense of hope. (The source for this and more information is the ALEPH website: www.aleph.org/renewal.html.)

References

Bakhtin, M. (1968). *Rabalais and his world* (trans. by Helene Iswoldy). Cambridge: MIT Press.
Bakhtin, M. (1981). *The dialogic imagination: Four essays* (Ed. and trans. by M. Holoquist) (pp. 84–258). Austin, TX: University of Texas Press.
Bakhtin, M. (1993). In M. Holquist & V Liapunov (Eds.), *Towards a philosophy of the act* (trans. and notes by V. Liapunov). Austin, TX: Univeristy of Texas Press.
Bogdan, D. (2002). Music performance as embodied listening. In S. Abbey (Ed.), *Ways of knowing in and through the body: Diverse perspectives on embodiment* (pp. 215–218). Proceedings of the CASWE Summer Institute. Welland, Ontario. SOLEIL.
Bonnycastle, D. (1997). *If only I could dance this: Semiotics and instructional design.* www.usaskca/education/coursework/802papers/Bonnycastle/Bonnycastle.HTML, retrieved, 04/30/06.
Bowman, W. (2004). Cognition and the body: Perspectives from music education. In L. Bressler, (Ed.), *Knowing bodies, moving minds* (pp. 29–50). Boston: Kluwer Academic Publishers
Ellis, C. (1991). Sociological introspection and emotional experience. *Symbolic Interaction, 14*(1), 23–50.
Kuutma, K. (1998). Cultural identity, nationalism and changes in singing traditions. Folklore. An electronic journal of folklore, 2, 124–141. Accessed at http://haldjas.folklore.ee/folklore/vol2/ident.htm, pp. 1–16. Retrieved, 04/17/06.
Lave, J. & Wenger, E. (1991). *Situated learning: Legitimate peripheral participation.* Cambridge: Cambridge University Press.
Martinez, J. (1998). A semiotic theory of music: According to a Peircean rationale. Sixth International Conference on Musical Signification. University of Helsinki, December 1–5. Accessed at www.pucsp.br/pos/cos/rism/jlm6ICMS.htm.
Maxwell, J. (1996). *Qualitative research design: An interactive approach.* Thousand Oaks, CA: Sage Press.
Sacks, J. (2000). Lecture: "What is Faith?" September 26. www.chiefrabbi.org/faith/faith.html. Retrieved, 04/30/06.
Small, C. (1999). Musicking—the meanings of performing and listening, a lecture. *Music Education Research, 1*(1), 9–22.
Van Manen, M. (1990). *Researching lived experience.* New York: SUNY Press.
Van Schalkwyk, G. (2002). Music as a metaphor for thesis writing. *The Qualitative Report, 7*(2).
Waller, S. (2003). Storytelling and community visioning: Tools for sustainability. Background paper for state sustainability strategy, Western Australia Department of the Premier and Cabinet. Accessed at: www.sustainability.dpc.wa.gov.au/docs/BGPapers/Waller%20S%20%20Storytelling.pdf. Retrieved, 05/11/04.

CHAPTER 19

New Worlds, Old Values: Cultural Maintenance in Asian Indian Women Immigrants' Narratives

M. GAIL HICKEY

Asian Indians represent one of the most rapidly growing ethnic groups in the U.S. today, totaling more than 1.9 million by the end of the twentieth century. The majority of Asian Indians residing in the U.S. are English language proficient, have a high socio-economic status, are better educated than the general populace, and are well represented among professional career groups (Takaki, 1989; Helweg and Helweg, 1990; Mogelonsky, 1995; Chandras, 1997). In spite of their strong presence in U.S. institutions and economy, little research has focused on the everyday experiences of Asian Indian families in the U.S. (Bhola, 1996; Mehra, 1997). Voices of Asian Indian women, in particular, have been absent from the literature.

Women serve as the guardians or gatekeepers of traditional values and belief structures in nearly every culture (Lessinger, 1995). The recent rapid influx of immigrants places an undue burden upon South Asian women (from India, Pakistan, Sri Lanka, and Bangladesh) to perpetuate an "authentic" South Asian culture for their families, with its Eastern interdependent and patriarchical perspectives, within the individualistic and democratic mainstream culture of the U.S. (Inman *et al.*, 2001). Asian Indian immigrants confirm the cultural power assigned to and assumed by adult women, who accept primary responsibility for the maintenance and transmission of moral values and religious traditions within the family and local ethnic organizations (Rayaprol, 1997).

Knowledge about the everyday lives and cultural traditions of specific immigrant groups can be as valuable to researchers as knowledge about immigration trends and demographics. Hollins (1996) noted that culture is "the essence of who we are and how we exist in the world" (p. 18). Culture is derived from "understandings acquired by people through experience and observation (at times speculation) about how to live together as a community, how to interact with the physical environment, and knowledge or beliefs about their relationships or positions within the universe." Culture teaches children about their families and ethnic groups and shapes children's identities, beliefs, and behaviors (Gollnick and Chinn, 1998). Knowledge and understandings *about* culture—cultural beliefs and practices, cultural interpretations of gender and family roles, and the effects of birth and host culture on identity development—can facilitate interactions between and among members of diverse populations and others, including educators, social workers, and medical personnel.

Theoretical Frameworks

Exploring the degree of discrepancy between the culture of origin and predominant culture in the resettlement country is an accepted model for conducting research on specific immigrant communities (Berry, 1997; Sam, 2000). Social behavior and the related constructs represented by values, belief systems, gender, and familial roles differ significantly between collectivistic cultures of the East, such as the Indian subcontinent and individualistic cultures of the West, such as the U.S. (Triandis, 1990; Berry, 1997).

Birman's (1994) framework for examining the acculturation experience permits researchers to "capture [the] diversity of experiences of acculturation" present in a multicultural host society such as the U.S. (p. 275). Birman (1994) believed the acculturative process occurs in stages: as the individual experiences cultural change over a period of time, he or she may become more or less positively attuned to the host society.

Employment of the oral history technique permits researchers to consider the changes in behaviors and attitudes of individual immigrants that take place over time, as well as the strategies and structures these individuals employ for the maintenance and transmission of ethnic culture. Using these theoretical frameworks, the investigator was able to explore instances of cultural change for individual female immigrants to the U.S. through a developmental psychological perspective, as well as through the perspectives of cultural education–cultural sustainability.

Cultural Education–Cultural Sustainability and Asian Indian Immigrants in the U.S.

Asian Indian culture is strongly influenced by Hindu traditions and value systems. Children and adolescents in India "breathe in the values of Hindu life" (Fenton, 1988, p. 127), learning to be "Indian" through everyday existence.

Asian Indian immigrant families in the U.S., however, must transmit cultural traditions and religious mores in a more explicit fashion (Kurien, 1999). The task of educating children in matters of Asian Indian culture and tradition is performed by women within the household and in local organizational settings such as language classes or training in traditional music and dance (Rayaprol, 1997).

The research on first-generation Hindu immigrants suggests successful acculturation: these persons maintain their own value systems while negotiating with the values and expectations of the host society (Fenton, 1988; Dhruvarajan, 1993). The research also shows that first-generation Asian Indian immigrants experience stressors over value conflicts associated with child-rearing (Hodge, 2004). In response, first-generation Asian Indian immigrants tend to re-create an Indian community within the home environment and insist their children maintain ethnic traditions (Kurien, 2001).

Identity development is negotiated and developed in the dynamic space formed by family interactions (Atkin *et al.*, 2002). The family, then, is an important site of cultural reproduction (Rex, 1991). Understanding the family's role in reproducing and reinforcing values and behaviors is vital to understanding an individual's sense of self, both as a member of an ethnic group and within possibly opposing value structures of out-groups (Ahmad *et al.*, 1998). Family-based education, religious teachings and observances, and community ethnic groups each play a part in cultural maintenance and reproduction (Modood *et al.*, 1994; Atkin *et al.*, 2002). This study examines cultural maintenance strategies employed by Asian Indian families in the U.S. through oral history narratives by Asian Indian women.

Methodology

Twenty women immigrants from the Indian subcontinent[1] residing in the Midwestern U.S. participated in audiotaped oral history interviews as part of a larger study exploring the experiences and perspectives of contemporary U.S. immigrants. The interviewees ranged in age from 18 to 66 years and represented women professionals, office workers, department store employees, housewives, and students. Many interviewees were members of Pan-Indian organizations who learned of the study from acquaintances, while others were identified through a snowball effect. Kurien (1999) reported Pan-Indian associations "most explicitly codify . . . Indian American ethnicity" among U.S. immigrants (p. 649).

The investigator employed a semi-structured, open-ended questionnaire to lend consistency to the interview process. Ogbu's (1991) definition of *immigrant* was used to identify potential oral history informants: immigrant refers not only to those who are actual immigrants, but also to those whose parents were immigrants and who continue to maintain a separate group identity. Just over 50 percent of the interviewees were first-generation immigrants and just under 50 percent were second-generation immigrants. All first-generation interviewees were married, while most second-generation interviewees were unmarried at the time of their interviews. Nearly all first-generation interviewees had received some post-secondary education in the natal culture and had married prior to migration. Major Asian Indian religious groups were represented in the sample, including Hindus, Sikhs, Muslims, Christians, and Parsi Zoroastrians, although the majority of participants were Hindus and Muslims. All major geographic regions of the Indian subcontinent were represented, including the countries of Pakistan, Sri Lanka, and Bangladesh as well as India. Two interviewees retained their Indian citizenship, whereas all others had either acquired U.S. citizenship or were in the process of doing so at the time of their interview.

Drawing upon Minister's (1991) *feminist frame* for interviewing, voluntary women immigrants were interviewed in their own homes or offices and, when requested, in their native language through the use of interpreters (Anderson and Jack, 1991). The interviews were transcribed and, where necessary, translated into English. The transcripts were analyzed for patterns using the constant comparative method (Glaser and Strauss, 1967). Each interviewee reviewed her own transcript for clarity and accuracy.

Possible limitations of the study involved (1) the participation of chiefly Hindu and Muslim Asian Indian immigrants mainly from well-educated middle-class to upper-middle class families in the U.S. and (2) the participation of interviewees who resided within the geographic confines of one state at the time of their interview. Finally, while not all participants belonged to a Pan-Indian organization, the study results may be somewhat skewed towards the families of educated, middle-class professionals who tend to participate in such organizations.

Findings and Discussion

The interviewees' narratives document experiences of relocation, strategies for cultural and/or historical preservation, and identity negotiation while establishing their presence in a new environment. In some instances—particularly for first-generation interviewees—the narratives support findings from earlier studies that suggest Asian Indians in the U.S. actively reproduce the traditional Indian culture of their parents and grandparents (Saran and Eames, 1985; Helweg and Helweg, 1990). In other instances, the narratives show deliberate efforts being expended by interviewees to merge Asian Indian tradition with Western social and/or ideological practices. In nearly all narratives, family expectations and traditional social sanctions on females occupy a central position. Indeed, as Hegde (1998) observes, the costs of Asian Indian women's acculturation experience in the U.S. is "surviving a trapeze act replete with precarious swinging from the demands of one world to another" (p. 35).

Three themes emerged from the data analysis, including (1) differences in gender roles, (2) strategies for the maintenance of ethnic culture, such as the use of native language in the home, diet, clothing, and participation in the Indian American community, and (3) differences in family life, such as perspectives on child-rearing, dating, and arranged marriages, values of importance. In their narratives, Asian Indian women interviewees both attempted to define their position and location as Asian Indians in relation to mainstream U.S. American culture and to communicate the myriad ways in which Asian Indian cultural sustainability in the U.S. depends on the family, ethnic community, religion, and formal education.

Gender Roles

An ancient Indian proverb states "A person has to have sinned in his past life to be born a woman" (Agarwal, 1991). Each interviewee emphasized differences in women's roles between Indian and mainstream U.S. cultures. Sociologists studying immigrant adjustment factors have concluded that gender differences between the U.S. and birth culture may be as great or greater than interethnic differences (Sodowsky and Carey, 1987; Yao, 1989; Barringer *et al.*, 1990). The interviewees appeared to agree, acknowledging that locating oneself as an educated, articulate woman of Eastern philosophical roots in the mainstream Western environment of U.S. society was an ongoing process. Tahira,[2] for example, reflected the interviewees' interest in U.S. women's greater social and decision-making freedoms when she observed "Women [in the U.S.] are very independent; they get to go out and do things on their own. They take their children places. Over there, women don't get to do this." Mehjabeen agreed: "The culture over there is so different from over here. Here, basically, whatever you want to do, you can go and do it . . . you can be more independent."

In India, a woman's behavior is viewed as a reflection of her family's *izzat* or honor at each stage in her life (Mandelbaum, 1988). Community and religious expectations reinforce adherence to accepted standards of behavior for females: thus, while family members may not object individually to a woman's working outside the home, if she takes a job while male family members are able to support her she brings dishonor upon the entire family. Mehjabeen discussed family *izzat* from the perspective of Asian Indian women's roles as wives and mothers: "I think ladies in India want to go out and get into the careers, but I still see them more at home, the caring and nurturing . . . It is a career in itself, running a household, cooking, cleaning, taking care of the kids, the husband. That is a full time job."

Advanced education is among the most-desired characteristics for young Asian Indian brides (Helweg and Helweg, 1990). Once the marriage occurs, however, the new wife may be discouraged from working outside the home. One interviewee told the following story about her cousin in India: "She has a degree in economics. She is very intelligent. If she is allowed to, she will have a job. Over there, it is still not her decision. Her relatives, her husband, will have a lot to say in it."

Asian Indian men usually do not consult their wives when an important family decision must be made. Zohra talked about her husband's decision to leave India and resettle the family in the U.S. Zohra believed Asian Indian women must adhere to specific codes of behavior and that doing so confers *izzat* on everyone concerned: "My husband was the one who made the decision. In India, and in my village, women don't make such decisions."

Women brought up in the more individualistic Western ideals of mainstream American society may chaff at the idea of seclusion engendered by these *purdah* practices (Mandelbaum, 1988). To many interviewees in this study, however, *purdah* allows women measures of security and respect unknown in the U.S. Zohra explained:

Women back home are protected and well taken care of. There is always a man figure who would always help her and take care of her. Before the marriage, the father and brother take care of her. After that, her husband takes care [of her]. Here in America, women are left alone to take care of herself. Even an 18-year-old girl becomes independent and has to pay off her bills and lives on her own.

Zohra and several other interviewees believed women may achieve *izzat* for themselves and their families through constant attention to the *dharma* of wives and mothers (code of appropriate behavior for the different stages of human development). The *izzat* achievements open to a woman mainly involve giving birth to a set of healthy offspring—particularly sons—and rearing them to be dutiful children (Johnson *et al.*, 1999). Even though her children are now adult graduate students, Zohra continued to practice behavior that brings honor or *izzat* to her family: "I prefer to stay home and take care of the household. I think it is important for the mother to take care of the kids. If the mother is not home, who will instil the values and culture? The mother is a very important person in the child's life."

Shahnaz found it difficult to adapt to the Western concept of equality between the sexes. Gender-specific role expectations are particularly strong in Asian Indian culture. Females in Asian Indian families are expected to maintain a subordinate role and refrain from assuming decision-making power or taking on financial responsibilities—including most paid employment (Bhattacharya, 1998). In the U.S., women and men may be employed to do the same jobs and each is expected to fulfill duties consistently. Shahnaz described her confusion over U.S gender role expectations:

Here, woman stands next to man in the factory and works at the machine. I never saw that in Pakistan. Woman here does the same job that man does. [When a] woman in Pakistan has kids, she is in the bed for 40 days, and someone is always taking care of her. Here when the woman has the baby, she's back at work in a few weeks or even days. Men anywhere in the world are hard working, because they have no choice.

Asked which aspects of her birth culture she wants to pass on to her daughter Nida, Shahnaz emphasized the importance of religion and ethnicity, saying "I want her to be proud of who she is. No matter where she lives or where she works, always to be proud of who she is or where she comes from—I want her to be proud of being a Muslim and being a Pakistani." Also in response to this question, Shahnaz again referred to the necessity women's behavior holds toward family honor: "After you get married, you just do things for your husband and your kids. You forget about yourself."

Aside from perceived differences in gender expectations between U.S. and Indian cultures, another important factor begs consideration. In India, boys are valued more than girls (Mandelbaum, 1988; Bumiller, 1990). A common blessing for Asian Indian brides is "May you be the mother of a hundred sons" (Bumiller, 1990). Divia linked the Indian preference for male babies to, among other things, the financial practices surrounding Indian weddings:

[In the U.S.] I've seen the people share the cost of marriage, but in India it's not like that. The parents of the bride bear all the cost of the marriage. That is one of the reasons why girls are not favored. *Still* not. It is expensive to have more girls . . . they were killing the girls because of the marriage problem. It is still going on in villages.

Preference for male infants goes deeper than simple concern for future wedding expenses. In another excerpt, Divia linked male gender preference to belief structures, attitudes, values, and family tradition:

In India, boys are considered to be very lucky. The first baby, you want a boy . . . that's the way everybody feels. If they have an older [boy], he takes care of the parents. You have a boy, you carry on your name to the next generation.

Strategies for Maintenance of Ethnic Culture

A review of the sparse literature concerning U.S. Asian Indian families underscores the importance these families place upon maintaining Indian culture and traditions (Bhola, 1996; Mehra, 1997). Mehra's (1997) interviews with Asian Indians in Chicago documented that, despite decades of residence in the U.S., Asian Indians' commitment to home-based cultural values, such as "belief in marriage as life-long commitment, religious affiliation, preservation of native dress, maintenance of native language and food habits," remains unchanged (p. 11). The interviewees in this study supported Mehra's (1997) finding and revealed specific strategies used by Asian Indian parents to ensure cultural continuity in successive generations.

Nearly all the interviewees discussed the importance of maintaining their native language. India is a nation of diverse languages—the India Constitution recognizes fifteen languages and 700 dialects (Barringer *et al.*, 1990). English is the preferred language of business—most Asian Indians who come to the U.S. speak English fluently. First-generation adults tend to speak English outside the home and their native language or dialect within the home environment (Yao, 1989). Asian Indian children in the U.S. tend to speak English within the home as well as at school. The following excerpts confirm these preferences: "We all speak English. Well, no, I didn't [speak English to my son at home]. I spoke in Tamil, but he always answered in English" (first-generation mother) and "At home . . . my parents will usually speak Malayalam to us, but we speak English right back to them" (second-generation graduate student).

Parents are not deterred from the goal of language maintenance, even when their children show little or no interest in speaking the native language. Many parents send their children to language classes (Bhola, 1996) and families regularly participate in Indian cultural events or organizations.

Parents are especially concerned about maintaining an Indian identity and bringing up their children "in the Indian way" (Saran, 1985; Mehra, 1997). First- and second-generation Asian Indians in the U.S. regularly maintain connections with the extended family in India through letters, telephone calls, visits, and e-mail. Throughout their immigration history in the U.S., Asian Indians have also maintained cultural identity by establishing and supporting Indian cultural organizations within the larger metropolitan areas (Bhola, 1996). Girls from middle-class Asian Indian immigrant families and, in some cases, boys are encouraged by parents to participate in music and dance lessons taught through the local Indian organization. Group participation in ethnic music and dance lessons link the second generation to the classical artistic and religious traditions of India. Lessinger (1995) noted that, as Asian Indian immigrant parents "struggle to retain the high culture they see as one of the finest aspects of their heritage and to incorporate that culture into a new Indian-American identity," they find music and dance lessons "help counterbalance the pervasive influence of American popular culture" on the children (p. 53).

Asian Indians feel they receive more than just psychological gratification in maintaining their Indian identity, yet the sense of community engendered through participation in Indian organizations does provide a much-needed psychological boost (Saran, 1985; Bhola, 1996). Indian organizations and cultural and/or religious events serve as vital cultural conduits for immigrant families in the U.S., often taking the place of the extended family as well as the language/religious group left behind. Beenu described the importance Indian cultural organizations hold for her family and for the local Asian Indian population:

> We have an Indian Association over here, and everybody's a member of that association. That association does some events, like twelve events a year, so everybody, they go there. We have our own community center here, so we go there. And then every weekend one or the other Indian [family], they have the party, so they invite like forty, fifty families.

Shari spoke of the time she and her husband lived in a state without a large Indian population, emphasizing how their need for community was fulfilled through the local Indian organization: "We had only ten or fifteen Indian families there, but we had an Indian association and we got very much involved in that association." Shari recalled her parents' emphasis on maintaining ethnic Indian culture and traditions:

> When we girls were growing up, we were expected to learn some kind of Rabindranath Tagore songs, or dancing. We will participate in dramas and all sorts of things. We used to read [Indian] literature. Our parents put a lot of emphasis that you have to be well versed and knowledgeable [about your culture].

Thus far, this discussion has focused on the ways Asian Indian immigrants to the U.S. create ethnic identity within the private spheres of their homes or in the company of other Indian immigrants who share their regional and language affiliation. Other more public means of maintaining and communicating one's ethnicity were described by the interviewees in this study, including public celebration of ethnic holidays, wearing ethnic dress outside the home, and adherence to ethnic diet preferences.

A favorite holiday celebration described by interviewees was Diwali or the Festival of Lights. Lessinger (1995) believed participation in ethnic festivals is one of the ways Asian Indians in the U.S. make themselves visible and define themselves within the larger society. Festivals such as Diwali celebrate events in India's history or its religious traditions, but these celebrations also had multiple meanings for the Asian Indian interviewees. In India, traditional public celebrations were often "occasions for solidarity across the lines of class and religion" that define the larger Indian subcontinent (Lessinger, 1995, p. 56). The American forms of traditional Indian festivals attract Asian Indian immigrant families representing a wide variety of geographic regions, languages, economic classes, and even religions—yet at the same time these festivals engender a momentary sense of community in the adopted society. Prema talked about the Indic Society in her community and how the individual family celebration of Diwali has changed as a result of being in the U.S.:

> [It's] Pan-Indian. Anyone can join. And it's a multiregional [group]—we have here Bengalis in it. We have Gujratis, we have Punjabis, we have south Indians. We have [people] from every part of India.
>
> When my children were growing up, the Indian Student Association would always have a big Diwali celebration . . . We all went as a family to that. And every other [Asian Indian] family came, too . . . In India [for Diwali] you light small clay lamps all around the house, you decorate, you have sweets, you have people visiting. You have firecrackers, also, and displays of fireworks. It's very joyful. You wear new clothes . . . But over here, it's usually a dinner of lights and some kind of a program that the Indian students would put together.

Thayammal has adapted the Diwali festival to celebrate with students in American school classrooms since coming to the U.S. "I [celebrate Diwali] in the classroom with the kids," she says. "And since I don't have young kids myself—if I have grandchildren [someday], I may take the effort to do that with them."

Dress and diet are two visible ways Asian Indians maintain their ethnic and cultural identity in the U.S. Mehta and Belk (1991) asserted "the appearance of being Indian may be more critical to maintaining a visible identity" than maintenance of caste identity and extended family structure (p. 409). Women, in particular, favor Indian dress over Western-style clothing when participating in Indian cultural events, as seen in this excerpt: "Whenever we go to Indian parties, which is almost every weekend, we always dress in Indian saris . . . All the ladies are decked up in Indian attire, like the saris and the bindis." However, fewer than one-third of the interviewees wore ethnic dress at work. Behroz wore Indian clothing at work as well as on special occasions: "A lot of working places [however] don't like . . . the sari. I don't know a lot of professional Indian females who wear *salwar kameez,* like I do, at work." Prema wore ethnic clothing because "I enjoy it . . . not only as clothing, but as a work of traditional art."

The interviewees preferred Indian food and usually ate Indian-style food at home. Due to the unavailability of either vegetarian and/or authentic Indian-style restaurants and to the kinds of meals normally served in schools and college cafeterias, most families no longer try a to follow a strict Indian diet outside the home. As one interviewee stated, "We follow totally Indian food [at home]. Once in a while, we go out and eat Chinese, Japanese."

Not all Asian Indians are vegetarian and not all who are vegetarian observe a strict diet after coming to the U.S. Some Asian Indians eat fish and some eat chicken. Then there are those who occasionally will eat beef, such as Behroz: "Most of the time, I cook Indian food. We enjoy it; that doesn't mean that we don't enjoy the other. I cook some pasta and steaks and that kind of stuff too, but we enjoy the Indian spices and the Indian cooking."

Three second-generation interviewees discussed their experiences and perspectives on maintaining ethnic culture while interacting with ethnically different peers in social settings. Aliyah, for example, believed there are advantages to bi-culturalism. She said she and her Asian Indian friends have both the advantage of their birth culture combined with ". . . the American touch. I learned a lot of things here, when I go back [to visit] I see how they are, and I feel privileged. You become a little more polished. The schooling is better here. I think you have to adapt to wherever you are."

Nida said she "most definitely" wanted to keep her ethnic culture, especially where behavior toward one's elders is concerned: "I think I would keep the culture in me even if I could go out [date] more. There is more respect [for parents and elders] there. Like here, we are more like friends. [In India] you have to be very formal."

Mehjabeen never wanted to forget her ethnic identity or cultural roots:

> Being in this culture [American], you forget who you are, and you get too wrapped up in society. Sometimes you shouldn't be doing things you are doing. Going [to India] and seeing my family, seeing the girls and all the things that they do, just basically hit home: "Hey, this is something that I should be doing." The sense of family is so strong.
>
> Religion is such an important part of your life, yet it is so easy to go astray. It is so easy to do the wrong thing. It may be right for people here, but it is wrong for us. In India, it is always emphasized: "This is who you are, and this is how you behave."

Differences in Family Life

In India, collectivist cultural values such as respect for elders, self-discipline, and deferred gratification exert strong influences on child-rearing. Most Indian parents teach their children to value educational achievement, respect their elders and authority figures, feel responsibility for other family members, and exhibit self-control. Asian Indian children tend to be more dependent, conforming, and willing to place their family's welfare over their own wishes or individual needs than their non-Indian peers. These values and characteristics generally described expectations in the interviewees' homes as well. Asian Indian parents emphasize most often the virtues of "obedience, politeness, peaceableness" (Mandelbaum, 1988). Differences between values taught at home and in school were mentioned frequently by the interviewees.

Divia found it difficult to adjust to a different perspective of child-rearing after coming to the U.S. She is concerned once her young son starts school, he will lose sight of his Indian values and upbringing:

> I will try to tell [my children] right from wrong, if they listen ... You never know what goes on [outside the home]. Here you can lose control of your kids, because the kids see the parents [as doing] the traditional things, then there's school and college. Things are so different over here.

Shweta was concerned about the dichotomy that occurs when Asian Indian family values and child-rearing preferences conflict with peer expectations: "I understand my children have a hard life here. When they go out there to mingle with their friends and go to school, they are to live in American society ... Then [they] come home to us, where we try to instil them with Indian culture and Indian heritage. It's a confusing life for them."

Zohra was confident of her children's grounding in Indian values and in their abilities to withstand opposing U.S. influences:

> I am very proud of [my children]. Although they have come here at a very young age, they still like the company of Indian friends. They have American friends, but they know the limits they can go. We both have taught them the values. I think these values were instilled [in our children] from back home: Family is very important, and no one can take their place.
>
> Here, the teenager can do what they want. There is no one to hold them back—even the parents don't have a hold on them. They have strong minds and are very independent. Our children follow our rules. They try very hard to please us, even if they don't want to do it.

Many Asian Indian families in the U.S. are very close knit, basing most if not all social activities around the family itself or around the local Indian cultural community. Parents may insist on using native language at home, maintaining ethnic dress and diet within the home setting, and retaining traditional Indian religious practices (Mehra, 1997). These strategies bode well for the health of the family unit: divorces are rare and the proportion of single-parent households is lower for Asian Indians than for any other group (Gardner *et al.*, 1989). Within U.S. society, however, especially for immigrant families with school-aged children, Asian Indian traditions may cause confusion or difficulties for individual family members.

Shweta explained a major developmental difference between Asian Indian and U.S. mainstream child-rearing practices:

In India we don't have what you call a teenage age year. In India up to eighteen years you are still a kid in the house, you always do what your parents want you to do, you listen to them, you respect them. So as far as life goes in India for a teenager and a young man or woman, it's totally different than what they have in life here.

It appears there is no adolescence in Asian Indian society. While Asian Indian families in the U.S. are active socially, their socialization occurs as a family and usually takes place with or among other Asian Indian families. Unlike U.S. teenagers, most teenagers in India avoid unchaperoned circumstances requiring them to interact with persons of the opposite gender. Asian Indian teenagers in the U.S. have similar restrictions on their social lives. Acceptable social activities include family outings, Indian community events, or having friends visit their home under the watchful eye of Asian Indian parents. An Asian Indian tradition strongly supported by the interviewees in this study is the dating taboo: young men and women from many Asian Indian families do not date prior to marriage (Yao, 1989; Mehra, 1997). Mehjabeen elaborated:

Over there, everything revolves around the family. Over here, there is a lot more freedom. Dating is one big difference [between U.S. and Indian culture]. We were not allowed to do it. Sometimes I had a problem with that because a whole group of friends [were] going out to dinner. That was not really a big thing [to them], but that is forbidden in our religion.

Parents are especially concerned when children interact with friends who are not from an Asian Indian family. Aliyah said that, while her relationship with her parents was "pretty cool," they questioned her extensively before she participated in any activity with non-Indian friends:

When I do things with American friends, we usually just stay at my house. I don't go to their house. If we go over to their house, they say, "Well, I don't want to get bored, so let's go out." My parents like it better when people are [at our home], rather than we go out. If I'm with [Indian friends], my parents don't mind so much. The other night I went out with these [Indian friends], and my parents said it was alright to stay out as late as possible.

Another interviewee recalled a similar experience: "The kids who came to play at our house were always Indian. We had a set of Indian friends and a set of American friends. The American friends were for school, and the Indian friends were for everything else."

Nida was very aware of the differences between her U.S. friends' social lives and her own: "My friends' parents are more outgoing. My friends can go out, can have boyfriends . . . and more social life than we do. [My parents] are more strict. I guess they just want to keep the culture in me."

Yao (1989) stated that the "most evident tradition maintained by Indians is the arranged marriage" (p. 300). While changes related to the abolishment of the caste system in India have eased some traditions associated with arranged marriages, most first-generation Asian Indian parents in the U.S. play a major role in spouses selection for their children. Virtually all the interviewees expected their children—particularly their daughters—to have some form of arranged marriage. All preferred potential spouses to be selected from among Asian Indian families of similar socio-economic backgrounds, either in the U.S. or India: most would agree to a match where differences in socio-economic and educational levels existed so long as there was similarity in religion and ethnic background.

Shahnaz came to the U.S. with her brother, who was traveling on a business visa. Her brother's new friend saw Shahnaz and then "asked my brother if he could marry me. Then parents talk, and his parents talk to me on the phone." Her suitor sent his parents a photograph of Shahnaz. "Then his brother in Boston came to meet me. I had finished school . . . so we got married . . . I saw him first time in July, and we got married in August."

Shahnaz was happy with the marriage her family arranged for her and hoped her daugher Nida would honor the tradition. Nida's opportunities for freedom of choice in U.S. culture concerned Shahnaz. The grounding provided by Islamic teachings, however, sustained her:

> Education here is excellent, but I worry about other things . . . Like Nida, and who she is going to marry . . . if we are going to find a nice person for her, or if she is going to find someone. If she finds someone, it doesn't matter from where, as long as he is Muslim and they can pray and follow the religion together.
>
> [Muslim] children living in the U.S. get so confused about religion. There are some American women here who have married Pakistani men; they come to the religious functions, but they think it is just a dinner. They don't realize why they are really here. What will they teach their children? Then the next generation will be more American, and more and more American. But if you believe in Islam, then you can teach your children 100 percent, and they can teach their children and their children.

Umama, a Muslim graduate student, considered how her culture and religious beliefs affected her behavior towards her fiancé in an arranged marriage: "I have never gone out alone with him," Umama related, "But I have talked to him on the phone."

Some form of arranged marriage practices are common for families of Asian Indians in the Midwestern U.S. interviewed for this study. Second-generation interviewees, while deferring to parental wisdom and the expectation of daughterly submission, described marriage plans that involved at least a meeting between potential spouses. Theoretically, either potential partner may refuse to finalize the match after the meeting, but traditionally a child of marriageable age respects the guidance of his or her parents in matters such as choosing a spouse or a career. Sarogini, from Sri Lanka, confirmed:

> Most . . . 80 percent of the marriages are arranged. An older person who knows another family, they come and visit and [say] "There is a young man who would be good enough [for a] match with your daughter." And [your parents] arrange it. On the day of the wedding, you had to go on your knees and worship your parents before you take off to the wedding.

The traditional practice is to allow one's elders to arrange a marriage, especially for daughters, but some couples help the process along a bit through subtle arrangements of their own. Sarogini described how her own wedding took place:

> We were neighborhood sweethearts. We met at a neighborhood funeral. I remember he said "hi" to me. My brother [and he] went to the same medical school. [He] wanted to be my brother's friend so that he can . . . see me. But there, you can't date. There's no dating allowed. No, none at all. So when I used to take my piano lessons, he would come to my piano teacher's just to . . . meet me and stuff like that.
>
> That [went on] for about a year, or two. My parents found out; [people in the neighborhood] let them know something was going on here. So then my parents decided that he had to come visit me at the house . . . we were to be chaperoned. When I finished school [we were married].

Interestingly, some U.S. Asian Indian parents restrict daughters' social lives while permitting sons greater freedom. Ilora wanted her son to "be Americanized . . . in the mainstream." She mentioned "He dated in high school. Actually, he's living with his girlfriend right now. I don't mind that. It's OK with me."

Conclusion

This study analyzed the role of women in cultural education and cultural sustainability in Asian Indian families living in the U.S. through the use of oral history interviews. The findings demonstrate Asian Indian immigrants to the U.S. employ various means of sustaining their ethnic culture within the home and community, including child-rearing practices, family socialization, informal and formal language and/or religious instruction, formal instruction in ethnic music and/or dance, and habits of diet and dress communicated in the home as well as in public venues such as the workplace.

The interviewees stressed the profound cultural differences between U.S. Asian Indian families and their host society: U.S. American culture is derived from Western European ideologies and emphasizes individual competition and personal initiative, while traditional Asian Indian families teach deference and obedience to one's elders and presumed social superiors. Western values are taught and rewarded in mainstream American families as well as through government-sponsored schools, while traditional Asian Indian values are stressed at home and within the ethnic community. Children in Indian families soon learn they are an essential part of the family structure and have well-defined roles, whereas children in American families learn early that they are individuals who must soon fend for themselves.

Asian Indian women, as do women in many cultures worldwide, take on the role of transmission and maintenance of traditional cultural or ethnic values. In the case of Asian Indian women in the U.S., however, these women attempt on the one hand to maintain traditional values, while on the other hand simultaneously facilitating family and individuals' transition into the American Western value system. Complicating this transition are the wide gaps between women's roles in traditional Indian society and in American society. Girls in both India and the U.S. are encouraged to get a good education: in India education defines girls as more suitable marriage partners who will be better able to care for husbands and children, while in the U.S. education helps prepare girls for a career or paid employment outside the home. Girls in India have limited, chaperoned social contact with the opposite sex and may have arranged marriages, whereas girls in the U.S. are expected to socialize with boys and date for several years before selecting a marriage partner on their own. Like girls, women in India have limited contact with the world outside their home and are protected from the rigors of business or financial concerns, while women in the U.S. enjoy greater personal freedoms but must seek paid employment to help support their families.

These findings document some of the cultural education–cultural sustainability strategies employed by Asian Indian families residing in the Midwestern U.S. and illuminate the processes of acculturation and identity negotiation for recent Asian Indian immigrants. Rushdie (1991) suggested that the developing identities of migrants in a new land are established in memories and defined by a sense of otherness. Immigrants experience "unprecedented unions between what they were and where they find themselves" (Rushdie,

1991, p. 124). Such blending of the past and present, together with the "reality of the cultural in-between," has a significant effect on Asian Indian women residing in the U.S. (Hegde, 1998, p. 34).

In general, Asian Indian migrants to the U.S. emphasize that their core ethnic values are essential to their identities and sense of self. While Asian Indian immigrants may integrate quickly into the American social milieu through their facility with English, high levels of education, professional or technical careers, and middle-class to upper-middle class suburban dwellings, at home they continue to stress traditional Indian values and customs and transmit these ethnic traditions to the next generation.

Resources for Educators

Questions

1. In this study, Asian Indian immigrants to the U.S. communicated their concern that Asian Indian families' cultural maintenance–cultural sustainability efforts are hampered by children's American schooling experiences. List some important Asian Indian ethnic values and discuss if/how these values may be contraindicated by common U.S. educational practices.

2. Using the Asian Indian ethnic values listed above as a reference point, consider ways gender socialization practices might differ between India and the U.S. How might these differences affect U.S. Asian Indian families' cultural maintenance–cultural sustainability efforts?

For Further Reading

Ahmad, I. & Szpara, M. Y. (2003). Muslim children in urban America: The New York City schools experience. *Journal of Muslim Minority Affairs, 23*(2), 295–301.

Ahmed, K. (1999). Adolescent development for South Asian American girls. In S. R. Gupta (Ed.), *Emerging voices: South Asian American women redefine self, family, and community* (pp. 37–49). Walnut Creek, CA: Altamira Press.

Das Gupta, M. (1997). 'What is Indian about you?' A gendered, transnational approach to ethnicity. *Gender & Society, 11*(5), 572–596.

Farver, J. M., Narang, S. K., & Bhadha, B. R. (2002). East meets west: Ethnic identity, acculturation, and conflict in Asian Indian families. *Journal of Family Psychology 16*(3), 338–350.

Gibson, M. A. (1988). *Accommodation without assimilation: Sikh immigrants in an American high school.* Ithaca, NY: Cornell University Press.

Patel, N., Power, T. G., & Bhavnagri, N. P. (1996). Socialization values and practices of Indian immigrant parents: Correlates of modernity and acculturation. *Child Development, 67,* 302–313.

Ramachandran, P. (2001). Gender discrimination in school system. *The Hindu,* 18 December, p. 5.

Sekhon, J. (2000). *Modern India.* Boston, MA: McGraw-Hill.

Suggestions for Educators

Teachers, school administrators, counselors, social workers, and others who interact with Asian Indian children and their families should be aware of potential sources of conflict between home and school and should take steps to ease such conflict wherever possible. Tensions between immigrant families' values and school practices might be mediated through thoughtful attention to cultural differences—alternative dress codes, for example or gender-based physical education classes. Standards for parental involvement might be reassessed to incorporate Asian Indian parents' at-home emphases on achievement, high regard for teachers, and culturally based social events.

Consider with your educational staff if such sensibilities have been developed in their immediate educational contexts and suggest ways for their becoming more apparent in shaping educational planning.

Notes

1. The Indian subcontinent has been described as the "cultural India" (Bhola 1996) and includes Pakistan, Bangladesh, Nepal, Tibet, Bhutan, and Sri Lanka as well as the present-day political India.
2. Some names are pseudonyms.

References

Agarwal, P. (1991) *Passage from India: Post-1965 Indian immigrants and their children.* Palos Verdes: Yuvati Publications.

Ahmad, W. I. U., Darr, A., Jones, L., & Nisar, G. (1998). *Deafness and ethnicity: Services, policy and politics.* Bristol: Policy Press.

Anderson, K. & Jack, D. C. (1991). Learning to listen: Interview techniques and analyses. In S. B. Gluck & D. Patai (Eds.), *Women's words: The feminist practice of oral history* (pp. 11–26). New York: Routledge.

Atkin, K., Waqar, I. U., Ahmad, W. I. U., & Jones, L. (2002). Young South Asian deaf people and their families: Negotiating relationships and identities. *Sociology of Health and Illness, 24*(1), 21–45.

Barringer, H. R., Takeuchi, D. T., & Xenos, P. (1990). Education, occupational prestige, and income of Asian Americans. *Sociology of Education, 63*(11), 27–43.

Berry, J. W. (1997). Immigration, acculturation, and adaptation. *Applied Psychology: An International Review, 46,* 5–68.

Bhattacharya, G. (1998). Drug use among Asian Indian adolescents: Identifying protective/risk. *Adolescence, 33*(129), 169–186.

Bhola, H. S. (1996). Asian Indians. In R. M. Taylor Jr & C. A. McBirney (Eds.), *Peopling Indiana: The ethnic experience* (pp. 38–53). Indianapolis, IN: Indiana Historical Society.

Birman, D. (1994). Acculturation and human diversity in a multicultural society. In E. J. Trickett, R. Watts, & D. Birman (Eds.), *Human diversity: Perspectives on people in context* (pp. 261–284). San Francisco: Jossey-Bass.

Bumiller, E. (1990). *'May you be the mother of a hundred sons': A journey among the women of India.* New York: Random.

Chandras, K. V. (1997). Training multiculturally competent counselors to work with Asian Indian Americans. *Counselor Education & Supervision 37*(1), 50–60.

Dhruvarajan, V. (1993). Ethnic cultural retention and transmission among first generation Hindu Asian Indians in a Canadian prairie city. *Journal of Comparative Family Studies, 24*, 63–79.

Fenton, J. (1988). *Transplanting religious traditions, Asian Indians in America.* New York: Praeger.

Gardner, R. W., Robey, B., & Smith, P. C. (1989). *Asian Indians: Growth, change, and diversity* (revised edn). Washington, DC: Population Reference Bureau, Inc.

Glaser, B. & Strauss, A. L. (1967). *The discovery of grounded theory: Strategies for qualitative research.* Chicago, IL: Aldine.

Gollnick, D. M. & Chinn, P. C. (1998). *Multicultural education in a pluralistic society* (5th edn). New York: Macmillan.

Hegde, R. S. (1998). Swinging the trapeze: The negotiation of identity among Asian Indian women in the United States. In D. V. Tanno & A. Gonzalez (Eds.), *Communication and identity across cultures. National Communication Association: International and Intercultural Communication Annual* (Vol. XXI, pp. 34–55). Thousand Oaks, CA: Sage.

Helweg, A. W., & Helweg, U. M. (1990). *An immigrant success story: East Indians in America.* Philadelphia: University of Pennsylvania.

Hodge, D. R. (2004). Working with Hindu clients in a spiritually sensitive manner. *Social Work, 49*(1), 27–38.

Hollins, E. R. (1996). *Culture in school learning: Revealing the deep meaning.* Mahwah, NJ: Lawrence Erlbaum Associates.

Inman, A. G., Ladany, N., Constantine, M. G., & Morano, C. K. (2001). Development and preliminary validation of the cultural values conflict scale for South Asian women. *Journal of Counseling Psychology, 48*(1), 17–27.

Johnson, D. J., Johnson, J. E., & Clark, L. (1999). *Through Indian eyes: A living tradition* (revised edn). New York: A Cite Book.

Kurien, P. (1999). Gendered ethnicity: Creating a Hindu Indian identity in the United States. *American Behavioral Scientist, 42*(4), 648–670.

Kurien, P. (2001). Becoming American by becoming Hindu: Indian Americans take their place at the multicultural table. In R. Stephen Warner and Judith G. Wittner (Eds.), *Gatherings in diaspora: Religious communities and the new immigration* (pp. 37–70). Philadelphia, PA: Temple University Press.

Lessinger, J. (1995). *From the Ganges to the Hudson: Indian immigrants in New York City.* Needham Heights, MA: Allyn & Bacon.

Mandelbaum, D. G. (1988). *Women's seclusion and men's honor: Sex roles in North India, Bangladesh, and Pakistan.* Tucson, AZ: The University of Arizona Press.

Mehra, B. S. (1997). Parents and their cultural model of schooling: Case of Asian Indians. Paper presented at the Annual Meeting of the American Educational Research Association, Chicago, IL.

Mehta, R. & Belk, R. W. (1991). Artifacts, identity, and transition: Favorite possessions of Indian immigrants to the United States. *Journal of Consumer Research, 17*, 398–411.

Minister, K. (1991). A feminist frame for the oral history interview. In S. B. Gluck & D. Patai (Eds.), *Women's words: The feminist practice of oral history* (pp. 27–41). New York: Routledge.

Modood, T., Beishon, S., & Virdee, S. (1994). *Changing ethnic identities.* London: Policy Studies Institute.

Mogelonsky, M. (1995). Asian-Indian Americans. *American Demographics, 17*(8), 32–39.

Ogbu, J. U. (1991). Immigrant and involuntary minorities in comparative perspective. In M. A. Gibson & J. U. Ogbu (Eds.), *Minority status and schooling: A comparative study of immigrant and voluntary minorities* (pp. 3–33). New York: Garland.

Rayaprol, A. (1997). *Negotiating identities: Women in the Indian diaspora.* Delhi: Oxford University Press.

Rex, J. (1991). *Ethnic identity and ethnic mobilisation in Britain.* Warwick: Centre for Research in Ethnic Relations.

Rushdie, S. (1991). *Imaginary homelands.* New York: Penguin.

Sam, D. L. (2000). Psychological adaptation of adolescents with immigrant backgrounds. *Journal of Social Psychology, 140*(1), 5–26.

Saran, P. (1985). *The Asian Indian experience in the United States.* New Delhi, India: Vikas.

Saran, P. & Eames, E. (Eds.) (1985). *The new ethnics: Asian Indians in the United States.* New York: Praeger.

Sodowsky, G. R. & Carey, J. C. (1987). Asian Indian immigrants in America: Factors related to adjustment. *Journal of Multicultural Counseling and Development, 15,* 129–141.

Takaki, R. (1989). *Strangers from a different shore.* Boston, MA: Little, Brown, and Company.

Triandis, H. C. (1990). Cross-cultural studies of individualism and collectivism. In J. J. Berman (Ed.), *Nebraska symposium on motivation 1989: Cross-cultural perspectives* (pp. 41–133). Lincoln: University of Nebraska Press.

Yao, E. L. (1989). Understanding Indian immigrant learners. *Elementary School Guidance and Counseling, 23,* 298–305.

CHAPTER 20

Cyberspace and Ethnic Identities: The Creation of Virtual Communities. The Case of Italy

LUCIA CLARK

The Internet: Not "McDonaldland"

The Internet has proven to be a pivotal event that has changed our lives. It is perhaps of the same magnitude as the discovery of fire or the invention of the wheel. And, logically enough, its definition, even if somewhat glorified, can be found on the Internet itself:

> The Internet has revolutionized the computer and communications world like nothing before. The invention of the telegraph, telephone, radio, and computer set the stage for this unprecedented integration of capabilities. *The Internet is at once a world-wide broadcasting capability, a mechanism for information dissemination, and a medium for collaboration and interaction between individuals and their computers without regard for geographic location.*
>
> (retrieved from Leiner, Internet Society website, www.isoc.org/internet/history/brief.shtml, italics added)

The Internet is therefore the culmination of other technological discoveries that helped create a society without barriers, where communication and interaction are truly instantaneous.

This fact has aroused the worries of many that saw the danger of creating a uniform society patterned on American life style. McLuhan (1967) created the definition of our age: "*the new electronic interdependence creates the world in the image of a global village*" (italics added). The term Global Village came to be understood to mean that the world would become uniform at the expense of marginalized communities left out by the new economic and cultural realities. In this chapter I attempt to address this fear. My findings will bear out that, far from being the great equalizer, the Internet is proving to be a useful tool in the defense and propagation of minority cultures and identities. Indeed, the Internet has made possible the creation of imagined or "virtual" communities where these identities can flourish. The very nature of a minority culture, particularly in a diaspora situation, where a culture is not able to depend on a geographical location, fits into the "virtual" scope of Internet communities.

The nature of the Internet, however, requires a rethinking of the process of culture sustainability. Waters (1995, p. 150) noted that McLuhan's (1967, pp. 66–67) Global Village was perhaps misnamed because a village without circuits of gossip could not possibly function. And, of course, in 1995 the chat rooms and mailing lists, systems of multiple and instantaneous communication, were not yet possible. As technology improved, it became possible, indeed, to interact around the globe, regardless of location. Technological improvements came at a fast pace, creating a state of change so rapid that it was difficult to maintain a balance:

> The struggle is between the old order and the new, between what society is and what is becoming. The Internet is now at this stage of becoming, a period of rapid growth and change. It is still being invented and is characterized by open options, unknown possibilities, confusion, and imperfect technology. Our social structures, cultural assumptions, and legal structures are co-evolving with the Internet.
> (Stefik, 1999, p. 4)

At that point he could not have understood that the Internet, by its very nature, is perpetually in a stage of becoming. But then we could say that this perpetual stage of becoming is the very definition of a vital culture. We will see how the Internet offers a pace where cultural identities can survive and, indeed, thrive in these virtual, ever-"becoming" villages. On the other hand we are caged in a perpetual ever-changing present and we have little control over it. This is contrary to the way we have been culturally conditioned to look at ourselves. Typically, we look at our past in order to know ourselves. But the digital past is now and we are spectators and actors. By the same token the future is being forged and changes constantly.

In his book *Imagined Communities* Anderson (1983) recognized that communities can have a definite entity independently from a geographical location. Indeed, many imagined communities exist *without* a geographical location. Often these communities are defined by religion or the very cultural core of their civilization, as in the case of Judaism or Hellenism. Judaism survived as a cultural and religious entity long before the creation of the state of Israel, when it achieved a political reality. The Internet provides precisely that very reality to other diaspora and minority groups. The creation of a website gives a group a virtual but nevertheless real locality that transcends time and space and it is precisely this transcendence of time and space that is the focal factor of any Internet society.

Imagined Realities in Europe: Europe of Nations or Europe of the People?

Let us focus our analysis on Europe, the arena of one of Anderson's (1983) imagined communities, the European Union (EU). A movement to eliminate economic barriers began shortly after the Second World War and is presently culminating with the creation of a federation of European nations, the ramifications of which are enormously complex given the diversity of the nations that are being admitted. This complexity is reflected by the vote of no confidence given to the EU constitution during the summer of 2005.

According to Treanor in *Europe: Which Europe?* (http://web.inter.nl.net/users/Paul.Treanor/which.europe.html), the present EU is not only a Europe of the nations, rather it is "Europe *for* the nation state" (italics in original). Treanor recognized that another movement was taking shape and represented a serious challenge to the Europe of the nation states, in the form of the Europe of the peoples, the Europe of the ethnic identities. And, in fact, since the creation of the EU we have seen a process of rethinking of what a national identity should be. This has caused the formation of secessionist groups in many parts of Europe, such as the Corsican, the Catalan, and the Basque minority movements, whose borders, a typical problem with minority groups, actually fall both within the Spanish and French nation states. In her chapter Gloria Totoricagüena tells us that Basque websites help reinforce a diaspora identity among the group.

Italy, its Peoples, and Cyberspace

The process of redefining the nature of national identities is not limited to minorities or diaspora groups. Indeed, it has caused a movement towards federalism in Italy, where regional identities have complex and deep roots. Italian scholar Massimo Fini coined the term "L'Europa delle Piccole Patrie," Europe of the small fatherlands, in contrast with the Europa delle Patrie, Europe of the nation states. The "Piccole Patrie" that have been taking political form in Italy since October 2004 with the federalization of Italy's regions reflect Italy's profound ethnic diversity.

By its very position, jutting out from the Alps and slicing the Mediterranean Sea in the middle, Italy has always been a land of transit, and the destination of settlers and invaders. The many languages spoken in the Italian peninsula since prehistoric times documents the diversity of the peoples that have inhabited Italy (see *Languages of Italy*, Viteliu website www.evolpub.com/LCA/VTLhome.html). Well before the foundation of Rome in 753 B.C., Italy was populated by a number of small nations that put up a fierce fight against the emerging power of Rome. During the same period, Greek colonists occupied lands in the south of Italy and Sicily, displacing or assimilating the original populations.

Eventually Rome succeeded in conquering all of Italy. However, Latin never completely replaced the local languages, but became a lingua franca and gave a base of mutual intelligibility to the developing new idioms. But what came to be spoken in the provinces maintained enough of their original languages to create forms of Latin somewhat differentiated from each other. It is from these languages that the Italian "dialects" developed (Clark, 2004).

The fall of the Roman Empire saw the fragmentation of Italy along two fronts: northern Italy, where the pre-Roman city states came back under the form of independent small potentates and remained well in contact with the rest of Europe and Magna Grecia, which remained under the power of Byzantium and, consequently, suffered Saracen and Norman invasions from the ninth to the eleventh centuries. Eventually the former Magna Grecia came under the rule of the Spanish Borbons. Rome regained a strong temporal power of its own with the emerging Catholic Church and remained an insurmountable geographical barrier between the two Italies until 1870.

The Italian Risorgimento, waged from 1848 to 1870 by the Savoy kings of Piedmont in northern Italy, created one political entity from a profoundly diverse population and this entity, the Italian nation, has only existed since 1870. During the Risorgimento political scholar Carlo Cattaneo dedicated his life work to the necessity of a federation of regions in Italy, in order to save the integrity of the regions' identities. The makers of the new Italy ignored him and it was only recently that the importance of his work was recognized and published in book form. The very title, *Stati Uniti d'Italia* (*United States of Italy*), carries a powerful and very specific message: for Italians, the political reality of the Italian nation state is very different from the ethnic reality of its peoples. The Savoy Government chose instead to form a nation state.

The south suffered an economic collapse after the Risorgimento. Naples, capital of the Borbon kingdom of the Due Sicilie, was a strong economic power second only to London. The Savoy closed down many schools and most factories and the south never really recovered. These measures, seen by many as acts of colonialism, created the "problema del Sud," the polarization between north and south, which continues to divide Italy to this day (Moscati, 1960). Furthermore, after the Risorgimento, Florentine Tuscan became the literary and business language of choice. This form of Italian had been developed by the literary academy Accademia della Crusca (www. accademiadellacrusca.it/) and became the official language of the Savoy state, even if the Savoy kings spoke French among themselves. Nevertheless, the official Italian became the only language allowed in schools. The linguistic wealth of the "dialects" became a source of shame and social mobility became limited to those who could afford to stay in school long enough to learn Italian. This aggravated the disenfranchisement of the rural poor, particularly in the south.

The rise of fascism after the chaos left in the aftermath of the First World War dealt an even more serious blow to ethnic identities. To be aware of one's ethnic identity became downright unpatriotic.

A Good Fascist is a Citizen without Ethnic Roots

Like all totalitarian regimes, fascism had no use for the ancient identities that could question its legitimacy. In order to create a faithful fascist citizen, Mussolini continued the work initiated by the Savoy. The marginalization of the poorest classes had already created the new fascist urban class, the *borghesia*, that looked at village life and culture as a primitive and antiquated past. Unfortunately, its rich ethnic cultural patrimony was forgotten in the process. (Montanelli, 1980) Under fascism Italy lost much of its popular music and dances and, only in recent years, as a reaction to the uniformity inherent in the culture of the nation state, has there been an effort to revitalize this patrimony. Logically enough, it is among the classes that had been marginalized by the Savoy and fascism that the folk arts survived. The Tarantella, the dance that most defines Italian folk dance and music, originated in Puglia as the "*Pizzica*," the sting and spread in the entire south as a form of musical therapy against the bite of spiders (De Martino, 1961).

Does the mythical Italian wanted by the Savoy and Mussolini exist? The answer to this question is a qualified yes. The school system has reinforced a sense of patriotism, a love for Italy as the fatherland. The schools teach that Italians are one people under one flag, speaking one language. The ideal Italian language is unaccented, devoid of those idiomatic expressions that have their roots deep into the pre–Roman past. But that Italian is impossible to achieve. Written Italian is precise, grammatically correct, even elegant, but when it is spoken there is enough of local inflections to reveal the individual ethnic identities. To use a very apt metaphor, Italy has to be seen not as a fresco, but as a mosaic, each little "tessera," the stones that form the pictures, representing the very deep roots of these identities. These identities surface in the way Italian is pronounced, which effectively becomes a koine flavored with local inflections.

The EU Paradoxically Redefines Ethnic Identities

When Italy finally saw its entrance into the EU as an immediate possibility, the polarization between north and south surfaced immediately.

Politician Umberto Bossi mobilized other sympathizers in the northern regions and formed the Lega del Nord, an association with an intent to secede from Italy and join the EU as an independent state (www.leganord.org/). The emerging power of the Internet was seen as a new tool of communication and politicians quickly launched their web pages. Since then other web pages have been launched by groups that saw themselves as minorities, such as the Due Sicilie (www.duesicilie.org), the Griko Milumè, the Partitu Sardu, and the Associazione Lingue Padane. What started as a virtual forum to vent old political grievances took the form of a reaffirmation of one's identity, in contrast with the forced identity of the Italian nation state. As the communist bloc collapsed and its former states gained membership to the EU, the Italian websites clamored for the same thing: to gain access to the EU as Sicilians or Padanians, not Italians. Those identities that had been suppressed by the Savoy and Mussolini had to be rediscovered and nurtured and the websites became the instruments of this rebirth. This message was conveyed personally to me during a "mailing list" dialog:

> What is taking place in Sardinia now is more than "risveglio etnico." It is, explicitly, a demand for auto determination and a declaration of sovereignty of the Sardinian Nation. It is not simply a political message, it is the voice of our soul . . . that soul that is our ancestral and historic memory, our identity is one and the same with our language, our culture and our motherland.
>
> (Antonmaria, personal communication, author's translation)

With the "mailing list," a process that allows e-mail messages to reach all the subscribers of a group, Leiner's predictions came true: communication within the sites was truly instantaneous. When voice technology became available, subscribers could meet at determined times and actually talk to each other. The Internet is truly now a place where people can meet in a virtual village square, regardless of where their geographical locality might be. With voice technology and mailing lists, Waters' (1995) requirement for a circuit of gossip, as pointed out earlier in the chapter, has become a reality. Every Friday a group of people log on to a "Paltalk," a chat room dedicated to the speakers of Griko, a form of Italo-Greek spoken in a few villages in southern Italy. It is 3 p.m. in Boston, 12 a.m. in Los Angeles, and 9 p.m. in Italy. At this time the participants of this chat room enter this virtual cafe in cyberspace in order to meet old friends and welcome new ones, to talk about "local affairs." Here "local" has to be taken as out of spatial limits and in multiple temporal places, in the present that has transcended earth's limitations.

Elsewhere in cyberspace a very active group of scholars exchanges opinions daily on the diversity of languages spoken in the Po region, roughly the place that saw the birth of the Lega del Nord. Their intent is not political *per se*: rather, it is a laborious exercise in the codification of the intricacies of their languages. For all of these people the meeting place is an imagined reality, a place of their own making. These are the communities where time and space are transcended and re-created in a virtual reality.

The Virtual City State

The home pages of the websites become, in all senses, the "portals" to the virtual villages, through which one can enter the home town, where one can go, finally, home. The links that connect to the history of the group and of the region, political platforms, cultural events, women's groups, and, being Italy, sports guide the virtual travelers to the discovery of their history and of themselves. Ultimately, the virtual villages answer those questions that the nation state could not answer: "Who, really, am I, what is my purpose in this land?" And the virtual villages, much like their brick and stone counterparts, have a complex and varied life of their own. We can define two main virtual entities.

1. Cultural linguistic entities, the main purpose of which is to preserve or, in many instances, give a fresh structure to a moribund language and culture.
2. Political and secessionist entities, the purpose of which varies from a profound and latent rebellion against the results of the Risorgimento to an active secessionist federalist agenda. There is a third entity, a Greek nationalism, the aim of which is to reclaim the Hellephone regions of southern Italy to the Greek motherland.

Cultural Linguistic Virtual Communities

One of the links in the Lega del Nord connects to the Associazione Lingue Padane (ALP, www.geocities.com/Athens/Thebes/8042/), which covers the area around the Po River, from the Alps in the north to the sweeping curve of the Apennines in the south, roughly near Bologna. Besides meeting online, the members of ALP convene periodically in a geographical locality to discuss all the problems related to maintaining a virtual association. In November 2003 the debate was focused on which name best defined their identity. Here are some choices: Antica Congrega Linguistica Reto Cisalpina, Accademia delle Lingue Reto-Cisalpine, and Associazion Lenguistega Reto-Cisalpina.

The first two choices are historical–geographical, while the third, written in one of the minority languages, uses the language itself to affirm a local identity. The members also have codified a new form of spelling, the "Grafia Verna," from the name of its creator, which better conveys those sounds that do not conform to the Tuscan pronunciation of standard Italian. Far from being purely academic, these activities have found a practical outlet in Bergamo's public schools. In 2003 a young father created a homework assignment book entirely written in Bergamasc using the Grafia Verna. Local schools adopted the book, thus giving this "dialect" new legitimacy and a new audience. (G. Giaáss, personal communication, 2003).

Al Sit Bulgnais

In most minority or diaspora sites the choice of languages includes English, logically enough, given the large number of emigrants that reside in the U.S. One exception is the site dedicated to Bulgnais, the language of Bologna. Al Sit Bulgnais (www.bulgnais.com/) maintains a strict bilingualism, Bulgnais and standard Italian. There are several initiatives to revitalize Bulgnais: meetings, plays, and publications duly advertised and discussed online. These virtual discussions again led to real endeavors: in 2001 a group of people opened the first school in Bulgnais, where students actually earn a diploma in Bulgnais, using long forgotten plays and stories written in Bulgnais before the Risorgimento (D. V. Vitali and R. S. Serra, personal communications, 2002). The founders of the movement devised a Bulgnais spelling method, again to convey those sounds absent from standard Italian. The method is available from the website, from where its "citizens" can download it into their computers. Below is an example of "shortcuts".

F2	F3	F4	F5	F6	F7	F8	F9
â	Ä	å	ê	î	ó	ô	û

For co-founders Daniele Vitali and Roberto Serra language represents a tie with their family and their past. For both of them as well as their students, it was the language used by their grandparents and neglected by their parents, who saw Italian as the key to adequate education and opportunities for their children and Bulgnais as a relict of the past.

Griko Milumè

This reaction was even more pronounced in the southern Italian communities of Greek origins. There are two distinct clusters, in Puglia and Calabria, which have managed to preserve their language, Griko or Grecanico, all through the historical events that have shaped Italy. While being Italian citizens, they are acutely aware of their Greek roots and again the defense of their language is the key to their identity. From 1999 to roughly 2002, their website Griko

Milumè was a virtual symposium of collections of old poems and ballads and debates on the meaning of words and the choice of alphabets, Italian or Greek. As we have seen, eventually Paltalk technology gave them a locality to hold real conversations in Griko. This website became a ready source of information vital to the sustainability of their culture: alerted of the resources offered by the EU charter for the defense of minority languages, they obtained funds to open schools in Griko and for other cultural events.

Gruppo Napulitano

As the use of the web has become more widespread, yet another phenomenon has taken place: the creation of a virtual community composed almost exclusively of diaspora members, from the U.S. to South America. These "virtual citizens" have one thing in common: they are all of Neapolitan descent and know Neapolitan only as a "dialect" spoken by their grandparents. In the fall of 2005 the group began the endeavor to rediscover their language and obtain for that language official recognition. They soon realized that it was not a simple task:

> . . . The response from official institutions, such as the University of Naples and the Naples municipal government, have all been that Neapolitan is not a language . . . most of the university personnel grew up in an Italian-speaking environment where Neapolitan was considered the speech of the lower classes and therefore they are not qualified to teach it in any case.
>
> (e-mail of 9/28/2005)

The codification of the language became an Internet journey into their cultural patrimony: they exchanged websites for written text of the many Neapolitan songs and learning tips:

> I may only advise to read the texts of the songs, the dialect poems and theatre. Unfortunately Neapolitano can only be learned in full immersion, on the spot . . . A good site where you may find interesting links and materials is "Bucksfan University"—School of Languages and Linguistics—Department of Neapolitan.
>
> (e-mail of 9/21/2005)

This e-mail underlines the fact that Italy's linguistic plurality tends to be recognized by foreign institutions and ignored by Italian official ones. Officialdom finally came thanks to Wikipedia, the online encyclopedia. Webmaster Sabine Cretella and Neapolitan moderator Carmine Colacino, literally in answer to a virtual *vox populi*, have created the Neapolitan page: http://nap.wikipedia.org/wiki/Paggena_prencepale.

Political and Secessionist Entities in European Politics

If there is one unifying factor among Italians, it is a political fervor that has surfaced in about fifty political parties in the Italian Government. The Lega del Nord, we remember, was formed as a form of political protest that culminated in the realization of federalism in 2004. This political fervor continues in the regions that have achieved political autonomy, such as Sardinia. The political passion of this island was exemplified in the home page of an early separatist site, posted in 1998, that reflected in its slogan the reaction to the fallacies of the Risorgimento: "Nemos, si no Sardu, poded illiberare sa Sardinia dae su Colonialismu pro nde faghere un'Isola zivile" ("No one except for Sardinian people can free Sardinia from its colonialism and transform it into a civilized island") (retrieved from Partito Sardo, www. psdaz-ichnos.com).

The Lega del Nord

We have seen how the immediate scope of several sites was a desire to secede from the Italian nation state. The message in the 1998 Sardinia site spoke of nothing less than freedom from colonialism. Umberto Bossi wanted a federation of northern regions for its Lega del Nord:

> Our chosen form of Autonomy had to be ethno federalist, i.e. a union of several ethno national entities in a unified political instrument capable of victory. Not isolationism, but a fight against the centralized power of the State!
> (retrieved from Lega del Nord, 1998, www.leganord.org/)

In 1989 Bossi's movement fell neatly in Treanor's "federalism of the people." His ideas shaped the politics of the time and were reflected by other statements posted on the website. In 1996 the site posted a true declaration of Independence of Padania that was introduced as part of a historical sequence after the German Unification of 1990, the independence of the Soviet Republics in 1991, and the 1993 separation of Czechoslovakia (Clark, 2004).

Due Sicilie and the Italo-Greek virtual communities

A site from the south answered the Lega del Nord's challenge by adopting the name of the Borbon kingdom Due Sicilie:

> (Our) purpose is to form a **single political block representing the entire Southern part of the Italian peninsula**, with the aim of realizing the interests of those peoples originally belonging to the Kingdom of the Two Sicilies, later annexed by force to the state of Piedmont.

... We the People of the Two Sicilie legitimately can and must therefore aspire to found again our State in Europe, as we had had it for eight hundred years before the invasion by Piedmont, when we "alone" belonged to a very flourishing State.
(retrieved from Due Sicilie, 1998, www.duesicilie.org)

We have seen how the Risorgimento's conquest left the south largely disenfranchised. This discontent is eloquently expressed in the virtual villages of the Due Sicilie and in a strong sense of ethnic traditions. Their roots, however, are not in Italy but in Greece. These are the lands of Magna Graecia, where the Greek cities built colonies that would expand the culture of Greece into southern Italy. Together in the cultural efforts to preserve Griko, their sites have responded to the challenge of the Lega del Nord. The name of an early site stressed the importance of their Greek heritage and gave a powerful hint: "Per Raggiungere Itaca" ("To go back to Ithaca") (site not available since 2000). The Griki of southern Italy are the children of Odysseus and, like him, must go back to the motherland. The activities of cultural exchange sponsored by subsequent sites have proliferated in the last few years. In 2004 the website Grecia.it offered vacations, fully paid, for fifty Griko-Italian students in the island of Zante and twenty-five or thirty older Griko-Italians in the city of Sparta. Many Greek Nationalists and sympathizers are taking an active part in this effort and increasingly many of the messages in the mailing lists consist of commemoration of Greek historical events and notices of the expansion of Greek cultural activities, including twin cities projects, between Greek cities and Italian cities outside the Magna Grecia area. Often central and northern Italian towns are given, somewhat creatively, Greek origins (see www.grecia.it/portale/index.php, 2005).

We have seen how the European trends towards secessionism have been expressed in the websites. The major dichotomy is from modernism, the Hegelian state, and post-modernism, "le Piccole Patrie", the regions. All groups want a voice and a place on the EU, but it has to be their own voice and their own place, distinct and separate from the voice of the Italian state.

Enotita

Our next inquiry is on the movements that transcend the Europe of the people and long for a return to old ideologies based on religion and ethnicity. Enotita is a site that expounds a return to the Greek Orthodox ideals by forming a federation of Byzantine cities. Again, there is the choice of a "perfect past" against the "flawed present." Their agenda is quite specific:

Enotita is a Neo-Byzantine Nationalist organization that wishes to bring together the different Nationalist movements of our region

together into a common goal for the good of Orthodoxy and the
Aryan Race ... Enotita is an organization that stresses national
and religious pride among all Orthodox people ... Since the time
of the Crusades in 1096 to the present day bombing of Yugoslavia
the Western world has tried to enslave and destroy us for staying true
to the path set before us by Jesus Christ himself and the original
Church ... Christianity was kept divided by the Turk to keep us under
Islamic control. ... We will no longer sit by and watch our people
be destroyed by Pan-Turkism, Greater Albanian Dreams, and Western expansion.

(retrieved from Enotita, 2005,
http://enotitanpride.tripod.com/enotita/, no author given)

I include this site among my Italian discourse because many of the Italo-
Hellenic organizations fiercely defend the theory that the Griki's ancestors
come from the Byzantine period and therefore belong by rights of birth to the
federation. The site's scope is to create a federation of ancient Byzantine cities
on a cultural and racial basis, including cities all over the Mediterranean coasts.
A federation of Byzantine cities would be an Andersonian-imagined reality in
all its aspects. As a political reality, the possibilities raised by such a site would
include a remapping of the Mediterranean. Would such a remapping remain
peaceful? Perhaps. But the Balkan recent history leaves a terrible scenario.

Ever since I began my analysis, the possibility of secession has haunted me.
How far will the "old" identities go? Will the disillusion with the Risorgimento
take a concrete form? Both the Lega del Nord and the Due Sicilie based their
political message on a rejection of the nation state. However, Bossi has joined
the right-wing government of Silvio Berlusconi and federalism has become a
reality. The Griko sites, on the other hand, have attracted a consistent and
increasing interest from the Greek Nationalists. The interactions between
southern Italians and Greece have changed from virtual communications to
very real symposia, paid vacations, and study in Greece. Since 2001 Grecanic
towns in Calabria have introduced modern Greek in middle school, a unique
step in Italy, where Greek is offered only in specialized high schools. Most
teachers have been educated in Greek universities and they explained to me
that, considering Italy's chronic neglect of the area, the hope for the young
people lies with Greece and they can retain their identity only by adopting the
language of their ancestral homeland (S. D., personal communications, 2003,
2004). At a conference in Irakleion in 1999 the Italo-Hellenic organizations
voted for a return to the Greek alphabet and the substitution of non-Greek
words from Grecanico with "proper" Greek words. This makes the language
difficult to read for their current speakers, mostly elderly people with limited
education. Grecanico as it has been transmitted through the centuries will
possibly perish. Will the identity of the people be able to remain? This question
remains unanswered.

The study of modern Greek will put Grecanic young people within the sphere of Greek economic and academic opportunities. In the near future, when these young people will enter the job market, the virtual reality could become real. The pull of the ancestral motherland could mean simply another "brain drain," this time to Greece instead of the U.S. or northern Europe. The invitation "per raggiungere Itaca" has indeed taken concrete form. But will the Greek economy be able to absorb this new wave of migrant workers, albeit "lost children of the motherland?" Or will the message of Enotita result in a Byzantine Federation? Again, the answer is in the future.

Conclusions

Far from becoming the great equalizer, the Internet has indeed acted as a forum for the reaffirmation of long-dormant Italian ethnic identities. Websites and chat rooms keep people exchanging ideas in their languages and festivals can be advertised online where they attract people from all over the world. This is really where the Virtual Village and the Real Village become one and, indeed, I have seen virtual friends become real ones. Virtual meetings resulted in the rediscovery of the rich Neapolitan traditions. They can also divulge messages of secession. In the old days, messages of protest would have been pasted on the walls of our street, where everyone, including the police, could read them. Today freedom of expression allows political views to be printed freely, but it is the web that has given dissent an instantaneous forum. We have already seen how the Lega del Nord, founded on the streets but propagated on the web, has found a political place in the Italian Government. The web also offers a forum to potentially disastrous messages of secession. It remains to be seen if Grecia or Enotita will be able to materialize their ideas in concrete form.

However, the web is but another forum for the extraordinary vitality of Italian cultures. They have maintained their individuality in spite of the many attempts to create uniformity through history. They have used the Internet to create virtual communities where they can survive and, in so doing, they are managing to defeat globalization with their "dialects," that wealth of linguistic traditions that truly defines who we are.

Virtual communities cut across political borders and reaffirm struggling identities. The Italian experiment is an example of ethnic minorities using new technologies to reaffirm and celebrate their right to exist.

For all the voices that were stilled, and all the songs that were silenced. May they be heard again.

Acknowledgments

This paper is a synopsis of a thesis for a master of liberal arts in extension studies obtained from Harvard University in 2004. My thesis is under my full legal name, Lucia Dentice-Clark.

I would like to thank my thesis director and mentor Professor David Maybury-Lewis, who believed in me and allowed me to go into cyberspace to look for ethnic identities.

Resources and Tools for Educators

Questions

1. Is the existence of minority cultures endangered by the globally industrialized, equalizing nation state? If yes, what are the methods used by the nation states that are culturally dangerous for minority groups?
2. How does the digital age contribute to the defense of endangered cultures by providing a virtual forum for dialog, mutual recognition, and the rediscovery of one's heritage?

For Further Reading

For the digital age, to follow up on McLuhan's (1967) analysis on the media and the Global Village, see the Maastricht McLuhan Institute, European Centre for Digital Culture, Knowledge Organisation and Learning Technology (2006, www.mmi.unimaas.nl/). Also see websites with links on digital culture, recent papers, news, and contacts.

Rumford, C. (2002) *The European Union: A political sociology.* Padstow: Blackwell Publishing.

The book addresses the relation between the EU and globalization, the nature of the EU state, and the concept of European society in terms of citizenship, cohesion, intranation migrations, social exclusion, and resulting cultural clashes.

Del Duca, L. F. & Del Duca, P. (n.d.). An Italian federalism?—The state, its institutions and national culture as rule of law guarantor (retrieved from Manatt, www.manatt.com/newsevents.aspx?id=3695&folder=24).

This is a short synopsis on the metamorphosis of the Italian state in the framework of its laws. Italy has affirmed its identity and continuity by "deconstructing itself," regional governments are active in areas formerly reserved for the centralized national government, and all of this functions in the context of the EU.

Tarr, G. A., Williams, R. F., and Marko, J. (Eds.) (2004). *Federalism, subnational constitutions, and minority rights.* Westport: Praeger Publishers.

This is a comparative study of federalism and minority rights. Does regional government protect or endanger the rights of minorities? The answer varies from the prevalent view in the U.S., that federalism has been detrimental to minority rights, to the views in other countries, who see federalism as a crucial tool in safeguarding the rights of ethnic and religious minorities.

Ziblatt, D. (2006). *Structuring the state: The formation of Italy and Germany and the puzzle of federalism.* Princeton: Princeton University Press.

This is a comparative study of the path towards federalism in Germany and Italy. The book traces the history of the "formation by conquest" of the Italian nation state to the present day movement towards federalism, from the Lega del Nord to the government of Berlusconi.

Suggestions for Educators

This is for those who wish to join or to create a mailing list and/or a website (please note that Internet technologies evolve fast and the annotations below reflect the technologies available to this writing, in 2006).

Websites

The easiest way to locate a website of interest is to type the name of the language/group in the search space. For example, the word "Griko" will generate a number of entries, from the history of the language, to websites with links to mailing lists, dictionaries, and chat rooms in Griko, and the inevitable tourism links. There are an increasing number of search engines that offer the possibility to create a website, at little or no cost. With Internet telephone services such as Skype, the educators can organize regularly scheduled conference calls among members at no cost.

Yahoo

The first engine to offer mailing list technology, Yahoo remains the most efficient and easiest to use. One simply types "Yahoo groups" in the search areas of Google or any other engine and is guided towards existing mailing groups or the means to create a new one. The links to minority and official languages have grown steadily, in 2006 totaling 1,706 languages.

Wikipedia

Wikipedia is the first online encyclopedia where, theoretically, anyone can be a contributor. However, there are some firm guidelines to ensure sound scholarship. This writer observed the creation of the Neapolitan language entry, as it is described in this paper. To create a new language entry, the web masters require five native speakers who submit dictionaries and historical backgrounds. Other authors may upload relevant papers on the topic. Contact the web master for guidelines.

Blogs

An easy and popular way to "self-publish" on the web, a blog has a space dedicated to reader comments, even if not quite as far-reaching as a mailing list. Again, type "create a blog" in your search engine and follow directions.

References

Anderson, B. (1983). *Imagined communities*. London: Verso.
Cattaneo, C. (1992). *Stati Uniti d'Italia*. Milano: Sugarco Edizioni.
Clark, L. (2004). Ethnic identities in cyberspace. Masters thesis, Harvard University.
De Martino, E. (1961). *La Terra del Rimorso*. Milano: Il Saggiatore.
Hull, J. (1988). *Polyglot Italy*. Sidney: CIS Educational.
McLuhan, M. (1967). *The medium is the massage*. Corte Madera, CA: Gingkopress.
Montanelli, I. (1957). *Storia di Roma*. Milano: Longanesi.
Montanelli, I. (1980). *L'Italia dell'asse*. Milano: Rizzoli.
Moscati, R. (1960). *La fine del Regno di Napoli*. Napoli: Le Monnier.
Stefik, M. (1999). *The Internet edge*. Cambridge, MA: MIT Press.
Waters, M. (1995). *Globalization*. New York: Routledge.

URLs

European Charter for Regional Minority Languages (2005). www.minelres.lv/coe/crml.htm.
Grecia Salentina (2005). www.geocities.com/enosi_griko/.
Magna Graecia (2005). www.grikamilume.com/magnagraecia2.htm.
Padania (2005). www.lapadania.it/.
Sardigna Natzione (2005). www.sardignanatzione.it/.

PART V

Cultural Education–Cultural Sustainability: The Parameters of Cultural Dialogue in the Context of Hegemony

The power of hegemony is a central theme for any attempt to grapple with the cultural education–cultural sustainability project. The issue of the hegemony topic was especially apparent to the chapters in the first section that examined the impact of state policies on minority groups. The hegemony of the culture of the majority and, in some cases, of the multicultural ideologies of these same groups promote through the state policies, which leave the claims of members of minority communities "unnoticed." The chapter written by Chen Bram in the first section is particularly useful for understanding the problem, through his description of the unintentional consequences of liberal multicultural policies promoted by the Israeli state.

In the first of two chapters in this concluding section Plamen Makariev addresses the challenge of creating dialogue between majority and minority, where currently there is only monologue. Makariev's chapter is followed by our own concluding remarks.

We chose to close the book with Makariev's chapter for he offers a different perspective than the other authors in this book (with the exception of Marie Parker-Jenkins). Makariev approaches the issue of hegemony and its consequences from the perspective of the majority and its needs in the multicultural dialogue. If not carefully approached this issue might be easily construed as a conservative discourse disguised in liberal clothing. However, we strongly believe, coming as we do from a constructivist dialogic perspective, that any solutions to the many problems confronted by minorities in host societies implies the need to sustain a serious two-way dialogue. The need to consider the majority is as important as the needs of minority group. Otherwise it is impossible to move forward in a constructivist fashion—in which each creates and sustains the other in the course of the interactions between them. Calling for cultural recognition implies recognition of all involved.

Makariev's paper discusses a problem of multicultural education, through a case study of art education. Makariev asks whether multiculturalism implies an obligation to appraise positively the artistic "products" of other cultures. For example, if we work within the multicultural paradigm, are we somehow obliged to represent to our students folklore, literature, and contemporary music which is culturally specific to a particular ethnic minority that live in our country? Must we present this minority culture as worthy of praise, appreciation, and admiration, even though we ourselves might not be comfortable with elements of that same culture?

Makariev focuses on the challenge of dialogue between minority and majority cultures, examining the ambiguities evident in two dominant approaches to multiculturalism in current philosophical discussions. Charles Taylor represents one approach, while the other is represented by Lawrence Blum. Makariev argues that recognition by the majority of minorities requires intercultural competence that must be nurtured through educational institutions. If we conceive multicultural education as a form of recognition of the value of cultural (especially minority) identity, the educational goal will not be the portrayal of minority cultures as necessarily possessing admirable features in an absolute sense (although the search for such features is, of course, desirable), but rather to cultivate rational (informed and selective) acceptance of the manifestations of these cultures in public life.

Makariev shows that it is perfectly possible to make interpretations of cultural identity from a liberal point of view that reveal moral reasons for developing multicultural practices and the respect of cultural rights. Makariev rightfully calls our attention to the fact that, even if recognition of minority cultural practices are ethically justified in principle, their concrete forms need to be "tuned" to the respective social and cultural environment for the granting of cultural rights to an ethnic or religious minority. The result is a change in the lives of members of majority and minority groups that might not be welcomed by either.

Balancing out the needs of all involved in the recognition game might be the greatest challenge in an attempt to enable positive forms of cultural heterogeneity in the face of globalizing forces. As a partial solution, Makariev argues for "intercultural competence." In order to respect minority identities in an active way, i.e. to provide "room" for them in the public domain (at the expense of imposing restrictions on ourselves), we must be able to distinguish between these cultures' actual needs and any unjustified claims for rights and privileges that we might encounter. We can achieve intercultural competence by communicating with minority cultures, not (or not so much) with the goal of becoming aware of their merits, but rather to better comprehend the moral meaning of the actions taken by members of the minority in terms of their frames of reference. From this point of recognition an effort then has to be made to grapple with the relation of the particular moral stance *vis-à-vis* universal values capable of enabling constructive interactions between majority and minority. The effort to achieve such an understanding will result in a new moral middle ground that is ever shifting as each side adjusts to the other. This process of mutual translation of moral "languages" is a necessary condition for the legitimization of cultural rights.

CHAPTER 21

Cultural Education and the Paradigm of Recognition

PLAMEN MAKARIEV

The Educational Problem

This chapter discusses a problem of multicultural education that is very much related to matters of art education, namely the question of whether multiculturalism implies an obligation to appraise positively the artistic "products" of other cultures. For example, if we work within the multiculturalist paradigm, are we somehow obliged to represent to our students the folklore, literature, and contemporary music that are culturally specific, let us say, for an ethnic minority within our country, as worthy of praise, appreciation, admiration, etc.? Of course, not in their entirety, but as represented by selected samples, which deserve special attention.

Very often teachers who follow a multiculturalist methodology familiarize their students with folk tales, songs, dances, traditional costumes, religious artifacts, etc., of minority cultures. Should this be carried out as a purely intellectual enterprise—to enhance the competence of the children in dealing with the cultures in question or maybe it should also involve a positive aesthetic, emotional experience?

On the one hand, the latter option is more attractive, because it can contribute more to the fulfillment of the objectives of multicultural education, namely to prepare children for a harmonious coexistence with representatives of other cultures. In order to live together with culturally different people in a peaceful and cooperative way, one needs not only to know about their way of life, but also to have a positive attitude towards them. On the other hand, however, this practice of cultural education entails considerable risks. What if the students, maybe not all of them, but a considerable number, happen not to like the artistic products of the minority culture. What if they find a song primitive, a tale stupid, a traditional costume grotesque, or a religious painting strange and repulsive? After all, they are supposed to judge about the artistic merits of these cultural forms from the point of view of their own cultural standards.[1] And unless there is some happy coincidence, some contingent "rapport" between the two cultures in question, it is quite probable that the perception of the other culture by the students would be to some extent problematic.

What should the teacher do in such a situation? Argue with the children that they have bad taste? Or accuse them of being ethno-centric and prejudiced? Or maybe try to convince them that they should, for the sake of political correctness, pretend in such cases that they appreciate the artistic achievements of the minority culture?

Actually, the multiculturalist conceptualization of cultural diversity involves quite a few trends of positive interpretation, which do not depend on recognizing the value of one or another culture *per se*. In order to "celebrate diversity" we do not need to be fascinated by different cultures. We can appreciate the cultural differences as such, even if we do not try to esteem the "quality" of the cultures that differ.

Some authors claim that the good thing about diversity is that it is a challenge to the inertia of our own cultural life. "Many cultural differences— in foods, dress, music, dance, visual arts, language, and ways of seeing the world—are widely experienced as stimulating and enriching, even by those who are deeply loyal to their own cultures" (Green, 1998, p. 429). Is it necessary that a contrasting experience, resulting from a contact with a different way of life, should be a positive one, in order to provoke a critical reflection on our own culture? I do not see such a necessity.

In a similar vein other authors have written about cultural diversity as a driving force for development. ". . . culture mixing is attractive. It promotes innovation, lets out creative energies and has been a driving force in history" (Lauritzen, 1998, p. 45). Again we can ask, should a cultural encounter, in order to produce original forms of cultural synthesis, be by all means one of affinity and mutual appreciation? There are plenty of examples in history that a lot of productive energy has been released by bitter cultural confrontations (let us think, for instance, about the Reformation in Western European Christianity).

According to other opinions, the communication across cultural "barriers" can be regarded as a means of establishing trust with the "others" (see Arnaut and Arnaut, 1998, p. 53) or as cultivating empathy towards the culturally different people and solidarity with them (see Lauritzen, 1998, pp. 43 and 45). Do trust, empathy, and solidarity presuppose an aesthetic appraisal?

Some scholars consider cultural diversity in more general terms. They write, for example, about ". . . an intellectual and aesthetic stance of *openness* toward divergent cultural experiences" (Hannerz, quoted after Incirlioglu and Tandogan, 1999, p. 60). Or about ". . . the translation of local knowledges and their interconnections of particular cultural groups so as to allow them to be shared by others as a major factor in the continuous process of nation building that . . . strives for unity in and through diversity" (Outlaw, 1998, p. 393).

Openness towards the cultural experiences of the others and readiness to share them (after they have been appropriately "translated") do not, I think, entail necessarily an attitude of appreciation. A plurality of perspectives, cultural flexibility, toleration of ambiguity, etc., are qualities that are immensely valuable for living in a multicultural environment, but they do not require an affinity with any of the other cultures with whom we are interacting.

Of course, the issues of positive appraisal, appreciation, esteem, praise, and honor (see Peters, 1999, p. 34) of other cultures cannot be easily dissociated from the "celebration of diversity." We must not overlook the task of creating positive images of, especially, the minority cultures, in order to overcome the negative stereotypes, which are in many cases hindering intercultural relations (see Liegeois, 1999, p. 146). But how can we effectively struggle with genuine acts of distaste, like the one, described by the two Turkish authors, whose article was cited above? They reproduce the comments of Turkish intellectuals on the negative attitude of many Germans towards the Turkish guest workers, especially concerning the ways that the Turkish immigrants dress: "The colors those women wear. God. Pinks and greens on bright 'tomb green' and yellow. Floral pyjama bottoms under chequered skirts. Awfully ugly. In horribly bad taste" (Incirlioglu and Tandogan, 1999, p. 57).

It seems that there are three opportunities to prevent such judgments. One of them is presented by the authors of the article themselves. They mention a case when a German teacher comments, before Turkish immigrants, about some poems written by Turks living in Germany. Although the poems were obviously of bad quality, the teacher kept saying " 'how nice as if she was talking about the work of lesser people. The poems were good enough for Turks" (Incirlioglu and Tandogan, 1999, p. 59).

So, this opportunity is to apply double standards and pretend that you appreciate things that you actually dislike. This is obviously bad for both sides. Usually the representatives of the culture that is being appraised in such a way are aware of the discrepancy in the other "party's" judgment and, for them, this is an even more offensive attitude than a frank expression of indifference or distaste. And, as far as the active, evaluating side is concerned, the hypocrisy exercised in this respect can be "internalized" and develop from a mere expression of politeness to a style of intercultural behavior in general. Besides, the arrogance towards the "inferior" culture, disguised by apparent political correctness, can remain unchallenged and persist further.

Another option is to make an effort to relativize one's criteria for what is aesthetically acceptable and what is not. This is not an easy task, because these criteria are culturally laden. If we succeed to some extent in such an enterprise, this would mean to cease to take our culture's standards of behavior too seriously and to admit that, from the fact that we do not like something, follows nothing about its value in itself (if there is such a value at all). Such a dissociation of the intercultural relations from the "stuff" of the cultures that interact moves us into the direction of the liberal paradigm in considering cultural issues, which is generally an alternative to multiculturalism.[2] What is at stake in such cases from a liberal point of view is that an unjust treatment of individuals is prevented, i.e. that they are not discriminated against because of their cultural difference. An ethno-centric negative assessment of other cultures' worth is of course a form of discrimination: it is unjust and, from this, follows a moral obligation to overcome our own (and those of our students) inclinations in this direction. However, multicultural education goes further—beyond intercultural tolerance and the mere abstaining from discrimination.

The third opportunity is not to relativize, but to change our cultural standards. To make them more "open," more inclusive. If we happen not to like an artistic "product" of a culture, such an approach would not merely stop us from making a negative conclusion about that culture's value, but would motivate us to work on our own cultural criteria—to try to learn more about that culture, to make an effort to understand it, and, maybe after some time, after a "fusion of horizons" (in the hermeneutical sense) has been achieved, to begin to like it.

From a multiculturalist point of view this option is by all means desirable. What I am asking here, however, is whether we are morally obliged to do all this. The obligation to avoid discrimination is obvious, because to discriminate is to treat someone unjustly. Would it be unjust, also, if we refrain from engaging ourselves with the enterprise to explore other cultures and to adapt ourselves to them for the sake of harmonious coexistence with other racial or ethnic groups or religious communities.

By this I do not mean the much less demanding "obligations" to approach other cultures with an *a priori* positive attitude or to enjoy the contact with them, when tastes happen to coincide. It is enough not to be prejudiced in order to take such a position, i.e. the latter belongs rather to the liberal paradigm. The question is whether we are obliged to do more—to "reconstruct" our identity in order to "adjust" it to our cultural environment. Changes in cultural identity do happen all the time. The influence of the interactions with other cultures, especially the impact of international publicity, such as the so-called McDonaldization or the effects produced by the Hollywood film industry, substantially reshape the mentality of young people. It would be an essentialist simplification if we ignore the fact that cultures interact, overlap, mix, and enrich each other.[3] The point is, however, whether we have a moral obligation to conduct an educational policy in the direction of some kind of "symbiosis" between our culture and other ones that happen to be around.

The Conceptual Setting

One of the important arguments in favor of the claim that appreciating the value of other cultures should be regarded as a moral imperative is the famous thesis of Taylor (1994): "that our identity is partly shaped by recognition or its absence" (p. 25). In his chapter "The Politics of Recognition" Taylor (1994) claimed that individual and group identity are of dialogical nature. Our self-understanding, our ability to define ourselves are linked with our relations with the so called "significant others" (see Taylor, 1994, p. 32). It is impossible to build or maintain a positive self-consciousness and self-understanding, in other words—to achieve the self-confidence and self-respect, which are necessary for a proper human being, if the others do not accord you recognition of your identity. "Due recognition is not just a courtesy we owe people. It is a vital human need" (Taylor, 1994, p. 26).

From this it follows that, in education (as far as the curricula and syllabi, the teacher training, and the overall psychological "climate" at school are concerned), the minority cultures (as a constitutive factor for the respective identities) should neither be ignored nor depreciated, but treated as of equal worth with the mainstream one.

However, a certain ambiguity is present in these considerations. Do we have reasons to recognize the value of minority cultures in themselves as an objective quality of theirs? Or, on the contrary, to recognize their value in a relative sense—as being valuable merely for the communities that are characterized by them. In other words, should we respect the culture of a given community because it is of considerable value as compared with other world cultures or should we respect the right of this community to value its culture highly, whatever its "quality" in comparison with other cultures. In the first case we focus our attention on the contribution of the culture in question to the achievements of mankind in general, while in the second we are interested in the role that this culture plays for the identity and the cultural well-being of the respective community (the first perspective was adopted by Taylor (1994) in his seminal article, while the second was clearly outlined in Blum's (1998) chapter "Recognition, Value and Equality" from the collection *Theorizing Multiculturalism: A Guide to the Current Debate*).

As we have already seen, Taylor's (1994) argumentation in favor of recognition refers to a substantial interdependence between the identity of individuals or groups on the one hand and their culture on the other. The appreciation of one's culture plays a vital role in shaping that person's (or group's) identity, i.e. the claim is that the general public should value a minority culture not for its own sake, but in the name of the respective minority's identity. However, Taylor (1994) maintained that recognition can have the necessary effect only if the minority culture has value in an objective sense. He insisted that, in terms of recognition, we owe to all cultures equal respect (see Taylor, 1994, p. 97) or, in other words, that they should be placed on an equal footing or that we should approach them with a presumption of equal worth (see Taylor, 1994, p. 98).[4]

Taylor (1994) discarded the idea that equal worth be ascribed to minority cultures not because of their objective characteristics, but merely because of respect to the minority groups themselves. He rejected the prospect of declaring a minority culture's creations to be of worth even if we consider it to be of inferior quality. This is hypocritical, patronizing, condescending, etc. (see Taylor 1994, p. 100).

Taylor's (1994) "objectivist" approach to the value of cultures has been criticized in many aspects (see, for example, Blum, 1998, p. 83). The very idea that cultures can be compared with regard to their value entails an element of cultural evolutionism. Besides, it presupposes the rather optimistic assumption that cultures are generally commensurable. And, most importantly, the commitment to find at any cost admirable traits in any culture that one would encounter seems to be too demanding, if we take into account the vast scope of cultural differences.

Of course, we face all these conceptual problems only if we regard the recognition of the value of the other's cultural identity as a moral duty. If we consider this kind of recognition to be merely desirable, we do not have to struggle with conceptual difficulties. Why not seek objective merits in other cultures—not only relying on happy coincidences of attitudes and tastes, but also at the expense of reforming our own identity, i.e. of broadening our understanding of value in both an aesthetic and moral sense. Such a benevolent search would present no confusion, if it proceeds as a more or less spontaneous enterprise, which might succeed in some cases and might fail in other cases. And if it happens to fail, this would not mean that there is something wrong with the identity that we are dealing with or with our own one. However, if recognition is taken as a moral obligation towards the other cultures in principle, it becomes too difficult to exercise it in an objectivist mode. We would demonstrate a lack of understanding of identity's nature, if we insist that one should be able to "tune" herself/himself to all kinds of cultural manifestations, so as to be able to genuinely appreciate them.

The Positive Perspectives

Let us recall once again what was Taylor's (1994) argument in favor of his thesis that we owe recognition to all cultures. Its cornerstone was the claim that a culture's self-image is of decisive importance for the self-respect and self-confidence—in sum, for the identity of the groups and individuals whose culture it is. And people cannot build a positive self-image if they meet the negative attitude of the "significant others."

Can a positive attitude of the "significant others" also take other forms, different from the obligation to seek in any culture "something that deserves our admiration and respect" (Taylor, 1994, p. 72)? Taylor (1994) himself also used formulations, which are not so demanding. One of them is the already mentioned "recognition of equal worth" (Taylor, 1994, p. 64). Such a statement does not necessarily mean an acknowledgment of a culture's inherent value, which is equal to that of all other cultures. It can also mean something quite different: that the merits of cultures are incommensurable. If this is the case, we cannot find out whether any culture is of higher value than any other. In this sense they cannot be of different value. The statement "all cultures should be considered to have equal worth" can mean simply that we refrain from comparing them.

Another formulation is that "we owe equal respect to all cultures." It also can be interpreted in different ways. One of them is that we have to treat them equally, without prejudice, without discrimination, i.e. in a liberal fashion. Another possible interpretation is that we are obliged to respect the right of all people to value their cultures. As Blum (1998, p. 79) showed in his chapter "Recognition, Value and Equality" (already mentioned above), in order to recognize that someone's culture matters to her/him, we do not need to like that particular culture or to find out that it possesses some inherent, objective merits. He insisted that recognition should not concern the absolute value of minority cultures, but the right of minority groups to have distinct cultures. In the situation that he described in order to illustrate his thesis, a Mexican American student, who claims the right to speak Spanish at school ". . . simply wants recognition of the value, importance, and meaningfulness of her Mexican-American cultural identity *to her*" (Blum, 1998, p. 79). If the teachers and the school administration acknowledged such a right of the Mexican-American students, this would not be done because of the world importance of the Spanish language, but because it is the mother tongue of the students in question.

Blum's (1998) criticism against Taylor's (1994) version of recognition is quite convincing. The alternative that he proposed, however, is not so acceptable from a multiculturalist viewpoint, because it reduces recognition to tolerance. As far as education is concerned, this alternative would mean that it is not necessary to develop positive attitudes to other cultures. It should not be an objective of education to motivate the students to study and try to understand and appreciate other cultures. A polite indifference should be enough.

So, the alternative interpretations of recognition as moral duty made by Taylor (1994) and Blum (1998) outline the following dilemma. Should we adopt the obligation to find by all means some inherent, objective valuable traits in any other culture in order to pay the due tribute to the respective community's identity or should we rather manifest our positive attitude towards the other within the limits of recognizing the right of minorities to value their cultures? From my point of view both alternatives are unacceptable. Taylor's (1994) version of recognition is too demanding. To claim that ". . . all human cultures that have animated whole societies over some considerable stretch of time have something important to say to all human beings" (Taylor, 1994, p. 66) is to underestimate the scope of cultural differences. On the other hand, in Blum's (1998) interpretation, recognition seems not to involve an interest in other cultures. It implies only the moral obligation to let the others enjoy their culture, without demonstrating a demeaning attitude towards their way of life.

From a philosophical point of view, the latter understanding of recognition tends towards the liberalist methodology of dealing with intercultural relations. That is to say it is not up to you to decide whether the other's commitment to her/his culture is justified or not (depending on whether you find something objectively valuable in it). You acknowledge one's autonomy and dignity by recognizing her/his right to value her/his culture, whatever its content.

However, within a broader interpretation of this conception one can single out different possible understandings of recognition, among which maybe we can find some that do not contradict so much the multiculturalist intuitions.

An extremely liberalist approach would be to regard the recognition of one's cultural distinctness as but another instance of acknowledging the right of individuals to do whatever they please, as long as they do not affect the interests of the others. Whether someone is fascinated with her/his own culture or with her/his hobby or with her/his house—these are all idiosyncrasies, which should be treated with respect, as long as they are harmless.

It is obvious that such an attitude is much more a demonstration of liberal tolerance than recognition of the value of cultural identity. An attempt to move in the latter direction would be to substantiate the importance of this identity for the individual's well-being by representing culture as a source of meaningful options. One can decide freely and rationally what is a good life for her/him, only if she/he can choose among the possibly richest set of alternatives (see, for example, Dworkin, 1985, p. 232; Raz, 1994). In this sense one's culture may matter to him or her much more than the commonplace details in her/his social environment and that is why one's affinity with a culture should be respected in a different way, in comparison with most of the other preferences that one happens to hold.

A step further in the same direction is the argument that the integrity of one's personality presupposes an unrestricted access to patterns of communication, social relations, traditions, etc., that are combined in a harmonious whole, namely a distinct culture. This does not need to be the individual's culture of origin, but neither should it be necessarily the culture that happens to dominate the society where that individual happens to live (see for example Habermas, 2003).

An even more radical defense of recognition as acknowledgment of the right of people to value their culture is the thesis that a necessary condition for a "meaningful individual choice"[5] is access to a "societal culture." The latter term was defined by Kymlicka as ". . . a culture which provides its members with meaningful ways of life across the full range of human activities, including social, educational, religious, recreational, and economic life, encompassing both public and private spheres" (p. 76). From this it follows that it is a matter of justice not only to respect the right of individuals to have a positive attitude to their culture, but also, in the case of minorities,[6] that society provides them with the conditions necessary for sustaining and developing their distinct way of life.

In sum, these liberal justifications of recognition demonstrate the possibility of ethically grounding the multiculturalist practices without resorting to the extreme Taylorian conception, which represents the positive treatment of other cultures as contingent upon whether they have objective value.[7] This "minimalist" liberal approach to recognition has the big advantage that it relieves multiculturalists from the obligation to seek valuable traits in other cultures. It is, of course, desirable, from a multiculturalist point of view, to approach different cultures with positive expectations, to be open to diversity, and to enjoy as much as possible intercultural contacts. But to declare all this to be a moral duty would be too much, especially if we take into account how cultures diverge in some cases.

On the other hand, however, can the liberal approach to recognition justify and motivate an interest in other cultures? If, together with Taylor (1994), we accept that we owe to their representatives a positive attitude in the form of appreciating their achievements, this obliges us to study and even try to understand them. But what if we simply acknowledge the right of the people to value, sustain, and develop their cultures, whatever they are? Would this be enough as fulfillment of our moral duty in this respect and may we remain indifferent to cultural otherness?

As we have already seen, it is perfectly possible to make interpretations of cultural identity from a liberal point of view, which reveals moral reasons for developing multiculturalist practices and respecting cultural rights in the public domain. However, the realization of these practices and rights presupposes their legitimization—on the level both of policy making and of everyday life. Even if they are ethically justified in principle, their concrete forms need to be "tuned" to the respective social and cultural environment.

The granting of cultural rights to an ethnic or religious minority may bring about changes in the life of the other citizens that are not welcome by them. As far as education is concerned, for example, modifications in the syllabi of subjects like literature and history, aiming at the inclusion of the contributions of a minority to the common cultural and political heritage, might seem like putting national integrity at risk. The studying of minority folklore in art education can be perceived by most of the students and teachers as an unnecessary burden. Bilingual education can be criticized as an obstacle for the integration of minority students into society. The wearing of headscarves by Muslim schoolgirls may look like an Islamist provocation. If the people belonging to the general public cannot assure themselves that the concrete forms of realization of minorities' cultural rights in one or another case are necessary for the sustaining of the respective cultural identities, the legitimacy of these cultural manifestations will be in doubt. This would be the case even if everybody respects in principle the right of the people to value their identity, i.e. if the liberal version of recognition is universally accepted.

So, my thesis here is that this interpretation of recognition implies the necessity of intercultural competence. In order to respect minority identities in an active way, i.e. to provide "room" for them in the public domain (at the expense of imposing restrictions on ourselves), we must be able to distinguish between these cultures' actual needs and any unjustified claims for rights and privileges that we might encounter (for details of the importance of such a demarcation see, for example, Barry (2001, Chapter 8)). This can be achieved by communicating with minority cultures not (or not so much) in order to become aware of their merits, but rather with the aim to comprehend better the moral meaning of the actions of these people in their own value framework, as well as to get a better idea about the relation of this moral setting towards the relevant universal values and towards the moral setting of our own. The mutual translatability of the moral "languages" of the different cultures is a necessary condition for the legitimization of cultural rights.

Such a cognitive realization of the multiculturalist positive interest in other cultures would not undervalue minority identities. It would rather help to draw more clearly a demarcation line between what is desirable and what is a moral obligation in the relations between individuals or communities with different cultural affiliations.

In conclusion, I have tried to show that, if we conceive multicultural education as a form of recognition of the value of cultural (especially minority) identity, its main goal should not be the portrayal of minority cultures as necessarily possessing admirable features in an absolute sense (although the search for such features is, of course, desirable), but rather to cultivate among the students rational (informed, selective) acceptance of the justified manifestations of these cultures in public life.

Resources and Tools for Educators

Questions

1. What should the main features of a multicultural policy be in your immediate setting?
2. What can a majority earn from adopting a multicultural policy?

For Further Reading

Fraser, N. and Honneth, A. (2003). *Redistribution or recognition?: A political-philosophical exchange.* London: Verso.

Most relevant to the subject matter of this paper is the second part of the book, written by A. Honneth, in which he presents his theory of recognition. Honneth explores the possibility of recognizing the value of the other's identity without dealing with culture at all. Especially interesting in this respect is the chapter entitled "Cultural Identity and Conflicts of Recognition", where the author discusses minority claims for cultural rights.

Kymlicka, W. (2001). Western political theory and ethnic relations in Eastern Europe. In W. Kymlicka & M. Opalski (Eds.), *Can liberal pluralism be exported?* (pp. 13–107). Oxford: Oxford University Press.

This is the leading chapter of a collection of articles on ethnic and minority issues in Central and Eastern Europe. Kymlicka offers a well-articulated typology of minorities and, respectively, five models of recognition of minority rights. He elaborates his idea about societal culture as a matter of the rights of national (non-immigrant) minorities, considering also the option of cultural (non-territorial) autonomy.

Carens, J. (2000). *Culture, citizenship and community.* Oxford: Oxford University Press.

This book deals with a "classical" dilemma in contemporary political philosophy—whether to treat cultural differences according to a liberal or to a communitarian methodology. The author's approach is innovative in two aspects. He insists on a contextual approach to this matter and offers an alternative to the liberal interpretation of justice as neutrality with respect to culture, namely justice as evenhandedness. In both respects his book is quite helpful for someone looking for an orientation to the contemporary debate on multiculturalism.

Tomlinson, C. A. (1999). *The differentiated classroom,* Alexandria, VA, ASCD.

The "differentiated classroom" model, which is presented in this book, belongs to a trend in contemporary innovative pedagogy oriented to the adaptation of training activities to the needs of learners. This trend also includes "child-centered" and "student-centered education" as well as, in a larger sense, "child-directed education" and "developmentally appropriate practice." The author discusses methods such as "project-based learning," "case-based learning," "learning contracts," "group investigation," and "interest centers": all of these can be used in multicultural education as means of working with minority cultures within the standard, mainstream curriculum.

Suggestions for Educators

Here I illustrate opportunities to apply philosophical paradigms of dealing with cultural diversity, as discussed in this chapter, to education. I sketch four possible models of studying minority literature in mainstream schools. For the sake of clarity I refer to a hypothetical case of large ethnic, or national or racial minorities (such as, for example, the Roma in Bulgaria or the Hungarians in Romania or the Afro-Americans in the U.S.). I assume that there are considerable numbers of minority students in many schools in any respective country. Educators might wish to discuss the following options in terms of the manner in which they play out in multiple educational settings:

1. A curricular policy, designed strictly in the liberal paradigm, would imply no special treatment of literary works created by individuals who belong to minorities. Such titles could be included in the syllabi of compulsory subjects only on the basis of free competition of their merits with all other achievements of the country's literature cannon as a whole. Texts by minority authors can be a matter of special interest only in student clubs, which function as an extracurricular form of free student initiative.

2. The opposite approach, following the "classical" multiculturalist (Taylorian) strategy requires that texts, which are representative of the minorities' literature, be included into the subject matter of compulsory curriculum. Any minority's culture, including its literary products, ought to be treated as worthy of praise. Diversity ought to be celebrated. If this literature in general (not by one or another work in particular) does not especially impress some students, this should be interpreted by the teacher as an alarming sign of ethno-centrism. Her/His proper reaction in such a case is to make an effort at extending her/his students' cultural horizon, so that they will begin to apprehend the manifestations of other cultures in a more open way.

3. The liberal multiculturalist paradigm, exemplified by the model described by Blum (1998) (more liberal than multiculturalist actually), can be applied to our case by including minority literature into the syllabi of elective subjects. The key assumption here is that students,

who belong to a respective minority, will have one more opportunity to reassure themselves about the merits of their culture—an opportunity of a kind that society owes to these people. This approach differs from the "classical" multiculturalist position in that it does not involve the other students in the "celebration" of this particular form of cultural diversity in an obligatory manner. However, it does not oppose the study of literary works by minority authors within the compulsory curriculum, if they happen to be of a quality commensurable with the best achievements of mainstream literature.

4. The fourth paradigm in this sequence is another liberal multiculturalist one (more distinctly multiculturalist), which justifies the public realization of minority cultures and which needs, as I have argued above, to be complemented by a cognitive approach. The recognition of the other's identity is understood here not as praise of the other culture's value, but as granting to this culture a societal status. Therefore, the appropriate place of the study of minority literature is a compulsory curriculum, however not as aesthetic reflection but rather as inquiry into the life world of the respective community. Of course, this approach does not preclude the treatment of minority literature also on a par with any other literary creations, just as was the case with the liberal and liberal multiculturalist paradigms that were considered above.

Notes

1. The very fact that people tend to appreciate certain cultural traits and not others—the fact that we are not culturally "omnivorous" and that there is some consistency in that selectiveness of ours—speaks in favor of the popular idea of culture as "patterns of learned behavior." It is another issue that it would be a too great essentialization to claim that the real individuals who belong to a given culture do stick, all of them, strictly to its ideal model of behavior. But this does not mean that identity, be it individual or collective, does not entail certain cultural preferences.
2. The trend, called "liberal multiculturalism," will be especially discussed further in this text.
3. A strong, though somewhat provocative argumentation in this direction can be found in Waldron (1995, p. 107).
4. For the sake of accuracy, we should note that Taylor (1994) regarded the presumption of equal worth only as an initial, so to say a priori, attitude that we owe to other cultures. The true understanding of the specific worth of an other culture can be the result only of its actual study and a consequent change in our own cultural standards (a "fusion of horizons") (see Taylor, 1994, p. 67), so that we are able to make adequate judgments about its merits.
5. In the meaning used in the works of Dworkin (1985) and Raz (1994) quoted above.
6. In his book Multicultural Citizenship Kymlicka (1995) considered the right to societal culture as due exclusively to "national," i.e. non-immigrant, minorities.
7. An overview of more theories in the same trend can be found in Kymlicka (1995, pp. 89–90).

References

Arnaut, S. & Arnaut, L. (1998). There are no shortcuts to intercultural learning: It can be fun but it won't be easy. European Journal of Intercultural studies, 9(Suppl.), 53–59.

Barry, B. (2001). Culture and equality. Cambridge: Polity Press.

Blum, L. (1998). Recognition, value and equality. In C. Willet (Ed.), Theorizing multiculturalism. A guide to the current debate (pp. 73–99). Oxford: Blackwell.

Dworkin, R. (1985). *A matter of principle*. Cambridge, MA: Harvard University Press.

Green, J. (1998). Educational multiculturalism. Critical pluralism and deep democracy. In C. Willet (Ed.), *Theorizing multiculturalism. A guide to the current debate* (pp. 422–448). Oxford: Blackwell.

Habermas, J. (2003). Kulturelle Gleichbehandlung—und die Grenzen des postmodernen Liberalismus. *Deutsche Zeitschrift fuer Philosophie, 51*(3), 367–394.

Incirlioglu, E. O. & Tandogan, Z. G. (1999). Cultural diversity, public space, aesthetics and power. *European Journal of Intercultural Studies, 10*(1), 55–62.

Kymlicka, W. (1995). *Multicultural citizenship*. Oxford: Oxford University Press.

Lauritzen, P. (1998). Intercultural learning—one big bluff or a learning strategy for the future? Concepts, objectives and practices of intercultural learning in informal education. *European Journal of Intercultural Studies, 9*(Suppl.), 42–51.

Liegeois, J.-P. (1999). School provision for Roma children: A European perspective. *European Journal of Intercultural studies, 10*(2), 144–151.

Outlaw Jr, L. (1998). "Multiculturalism", citizenship, education, and American liberal democracy. In C. Willet (Ed.), *Theorizing multiculturalism. A guide to the current debate* (pp. 382–389). Oxford: Blackwell.

Peters, B. (1999). *Understanding multiculturalism*, In IIS-Arbeitspapier No. 14/99. Bremen: Universitaet Bremen.

Raz, J. (1994). Multiculturalism: A liberal perspective. In J. Raz (Ed.), *Ethics in the public domain.* (67–79). Oxford: Oxford University Press.

Taylor, C. (1994). The politics of recognition. In A. Gutmann (Ed.), *Multiculturalism. Examining the politics of recognition.* (pp. 25–73). Princeton: Princeton University Press.

Waldron, J. (1995). Minority cultures and the cosmopolitan alternative. In W. Kymlicka (Ed.), *The rights of minority cultures* (pp. 93–119). Oxford: Oxford University Press

CHAPTER 22

Embracing Complexity:
Some Concluding Remarks

ZVI BEKERMAN AND EZRA KOPELOWITZ

We asked in our opening remarks what do groups, such as African-Americans, Amish, Armenians, Basques, Chadian Catholics, Coptic Orthodox, Hawaiians, Jews, Koreans, Native Americans, Mongols, Muslims, Tibetans, and Ugyurs, have in common and we invited the reader to grapple with this question as he or she reads the many chapters in the book. We hope by now you, the reader, have your own answers. At this point, we want to take the opportunity to tell you what we have learned in this long journey, of which the book is a partial culmination.

"To Belong" is a Complex Experience: We Either Embrace that Complexity and Make it our Own or Ignore it at our Peril

Confronting complexity is our first lesson learned. While our approach to the social sciences led us from the beginning to search out and appreciate the complex ways people live their lives, the cultural education–cultural sustainability project has brought us to much deeper realization, namely complexity can either be an enemy or the friend of minority, diaspora, or indigenous groups and the quest to educate for cultural sustainability.

In this book we have taken a breathtaking tour of the complexity of minority belonging—from the dynamic nature of everyday life in which individuals move between multiple affiliation groups, drawing on the resources provided by communal institutions, all of which are shaped by the political, legal, and social systems of the nation state and increasingly global world.

Hegemony Reduces Complexity by turning Minority Belonging into a Neat Category of Thought and Experience

When we ignore complexity, we face the complex nature of minority existence without recognizing the dangers involved. As a result, we default to the educational methodologies given to us by the modern nation state that are in effect the same methods used to assimilate minority groups.

We refer throughout the book to "hegemony." By hegemony we mean a situation in which forces that shape our lives are "unseen, yet present." By failing to address these forces we also fail to harness and shape them to our advantage. Do the organizing frames for cultural education enable the creation of vibrant counter cultures? If we ignore the complex nature of lived experience the answer to this question will be "no!"

Modernity introduced many tools for categorizing and simplifying lived experience—all of which work against the attempt to promote cultural sustainability for minority groups if we fail to address them head on. The tool promoted by the modern state, which is of greatest interest to the authors in this book, is the school. Formal education is built on categorization of knowledge and the compartmentalization of lived experience into disciplines that are antithetical to the non-formal culture that many of the authors in this book point to as vital to cultural sustainability. Non-formal culture refers to the moments of daily life in which memory, ritual, symbol, and ceremony make belonging to a group a meaningful, emotional, and rich human experience.

The attempt of minority educators or well-intentioned employees of Ministries of Education to promote "cultural education" is doomed to fail so long as the disciplinary structure of formal educational institutions remains the backbone of the educational experience. The disciplinary structure of education is hegemonic in that it is taken for granted by educators—unchallenged and, hence, destructive. By structuring knowledge as discipline we simplify reality, thereby taking out the complexity that is a vital part of the lived experience.

When we accept that cultural knowledge is reducible to neat narratives learned in history books or through school-based ceremonies that are divorced from the dynamic contexts of family, community, and the complex realities of everyday life, we are in trouble.

Embracing Complexity: Move One—Education for Cultural Sustainability Rejects the Disciplinization of Knowledge and the Compartmentalization of Academic Discourse

We started the journey from our own experience as scholars looking at our own group. We both found ourselves frustrated by the seemingly solipsistic life Jewish education conducts compartmentalized from general education and from others researching the particularities of other minority, diasporas, and indigenous groups. We also believe that this isolated existence leads to embracing Jewish education as a discipline that can be taught like mathematics and science, replicating the hegemonic conditions that are the source of cultural assimilation.

Indeed, we often hear from our colleagues that Jews share a unique experience that differentiates them from other groups. We are also told that a good Jewish education requires students to absorb large amounts of knowledge that are packaged and transmitted according to the logic of school-based education —in which the ultimate success is found in the standardization of Jewish culture so that it can compete in an examination-based environment with the prestige of mathematics and the sciences.

The larger cultural education–cultural sustainability project of which this book is a part is our attempt to understand and communicate the idea that the compartmentalization of Jewish education as a narrow discipline is part and parcel of a much larger problem that members of all minority groups face. By bringing together under a single scholarly umbrella diverse research traditions dealing with marginalized minorities and education we are able to highlight the common need of all these groups to grapple with the danger of divorcing lived cultural experience from education. We think the effort has been successful, although we feel humbled by the realization of the depth of the complexity of minority life and the difficulty in communicating this experience to our academic colleagues, not to mention those who stand outside of academia.

Embracing Complexity: Move Two—Cultural Sustainability is about Enabling Individuals to Live in an Open Society

In the dialog between our academic colleagues from other minority groups we attempt to embody a greater principle, namely that, because of our differences, we need to communicate with one another. As members of minority groups we continually interact with other members of society and we need to reproduce this type of open-ended communication in our own academic venture.

As academics we all need to grapple with members of our minority diaspora and indigenous groups, inside and outside of academia, who, like ostriches with their heads in the ground, retreat into cultural orthodoxy rather than grapple with the complexity of living life in a pluralistic society. By building the cultural education–cultural sustainability network on the principle of dialog between different groups, we build on the power of pluralism and do not allow it to defeat us.

The modern state gains its life force by creating borders. Everyone within the nation resides within a geographic boundary and we come to think of citizens of a state as a single homogeneous group, somehow different from those who live on the other side of the border. National education systems are primary tools for maintaining borders and sanctifying differences between those who are inside and outside of the nation.

Within the cultural education–cultural sustainability project it has become apparent to us that the state, as a modern political organization, profoundly influences the ways people negotiate the complexity of lived life. Replicating the logic of national education systems and the homogenizing policies of the nation state leads minority educators to turn inwards and spend their creative energies creating boundaries between those who belong to the minority group and those who do not. The result is educational orthodoxies that promote education for cultural sustainability that uses the logic of disciplines and the compartmentalization of knowledge. These same educators, who are charged with the responsibility of transmitting culture, actively work against the complexity required for successful culture practices that are at once meaningful to the life their students live in a pluralistic society and, at the same time, are sustainable from generation to generation.

The members of the minority groups studied in this book all live their lives within pluralistic societies. It seems logical that educators should embrace the complexity of this lived experience and not attempt to promote disciplinary categories to organize knowledge that replicates the assimilatory policies of the modern state.

Embracing Complexity: Move Three—Dialog is a Process Involving both Majority and Minority

While much of the energy of the authors in this book go towards revealing the complexity of living within a minority group, in his chapter Plamen Makariev shows us that, in order to promote cultural education–cultural sustainability, we need not only analyze the interaction of minority with majority, but also majority with minority.

What might be surprising or not is that the case studies discussed in the book do not allow us to point to any of the varied state ideologies as the source of the intolerance of "the majority" towards minority groups. The assimilatory power of modern society has less to do with the intention of the state to assimilate minority groups and more to do with the fact that the greatest power of any hegemony is the one that allows it to go unnoticed. Indeed, the dominant group is, in reality, not a single homogeneous entity, but rather exists as an assumed way of life that requires minority groups to resist actively if they do not wish to assimilate. In this situation the onus is placed on the minority to justify their differences.

The consciousness of all involved is shaped by historical developments that are beyond any one person. This clearly does not exonerate us and, indeed, the only way to counter hegemony is to reveal its power. This is the spirit of philosophers such as Freire and other emancipatory thinkers/educators, who are well aware of the power of hegemony and urge those adversely affected to work towards their own emancipation. We must help emancipate the oppressor of his or her own oppressing conduct. Yet, there is also the approach taken by Makariev, who asks that the rhetoric of multiculturalism, when approaching minority cultures, is taken seriously by members of the majority and that they enter into dialog with them. Instead of trying "to help" or "appreciate" other groups, members of the majority should grapple with the implications of minority culture for their lives and the claims by minorities regarding how everyday life should be lived. Some of those claims will be rejected while others are accepted: so long as it is done through dialog we can begin to speak about cultural education–cultural sustainability. In a situation of dialog it is possible to do away with concepts such as minority versus minority and rather focus on the methods we use for transmitting memory and meaning in ways that enables us to live rich human lives that do not negate the same attempts being made by others.

Embracing Complexity: Move Four—Transmitting Complexity on Macro-, Communal and Everyday Dimensions of Educational Discourse

The move from everyday life, through communal institutions to the state and global society is a fluid movement—each impacts on the other—offering danger and possibility. The success of cultural education–cultural sustainability depends on embracing the emancipatory potential of living in a pluralistic society that builds at once on everyday, communal, national, and global dimensions of life, but at the same time avoiding the dangers.

The chapters in this book help us grapple with the complex relationships of everyday life with more abstract dimensions of social organization, by investigating the potential power of social organizations and the practices they enable. As individuals move through the multiple institutions of communal life they create strategies for integrating their particular cultural traditions with resources for social success available from the broader environment. At the moment of cultural integration we have the secret to promoting cultural sustainability and the challenge for cultural education.

If we look at cultural sustainability in terms of strategies for integrating cultural traditions and other resources offered by the macro-environment then everyday life in a pluralistic society becomes a space of opportunity. On the one hand diaspora, minority, and indigenous groups find, almost everywhere today, increasing challenges to sustaining what they perceive to be their socio-historical heritage. These challenges are only accelerating with globalization. In this respect, transnationalism threatens small communities with potential hegemonic, homogenizing effects that equal or surpass those posed by the assimilatory powers of the nation state.

On the other hand globalization weakens the borders and homogenizing ideology of the nation state and, with that, offers new ways for integrating particular cultures within the everyday life of a pluralistic society. Some of these resources include transnational networks, new communication technologies, and more efficient forms of transportation, which have supported the formation of complex alliances. The cultural education–cultural sustainability network of academics is an example of such an alliance. Between Internet technology and affordable plane fares we were able to share knowledge and devise new forms of academic practices that, if successful, will impact on the imagination of the educators with whom we interact.

Our Motivations

Last but not least, we find ourselves questioning our own means and motivations when choosing to get involved in cultural sustainability projects. Are we involved to better our group's lot in the present world or are we truly committed to pay attention to our own voices and traditions as well as others so as to encourage ourselves to imagine a world in dialogic terms, where our success depends on the ability of others to devise strategies of cultural sustainability.

In order to push forward dialog in the academic context, the challenges facing the cultural education–cultural sustainability network are to enable sustained inquiry into the relations between (1) home and school cultures, (2) educational development, curriculum, and cultural change, (3) culture, ethnicity, and gender in identity construction, and (4) societal attitudes and cultural variation. All of these educational and social processes must be conceptualized in order to embrace the complexity of the strategies individuals use to integrate their minority cultural traditions with the resources available to them from the institutions, communities, and broader societies in which they live.

The challenge is to raise the sophistication of our analysis to enable dialog and, as such, deepen our understanding. The result we expect will be an increasing sophistication in our ability to conceptualize the place of the following processes on cultural education.

1. The impact of politics and economics on educational initiatives to sustain languages and cultures.
2. The formation and consequences of religious/ethnic/national identities in educational contexts.
3. The sustained dialog between majority and minority cultures within a variety of contexts.

4. Cultural and language policies and rights in educational contexts.
5. The relationship between ecological, linguistic, and/or cultural sustainability.
6. Exemplary programs and/or "best practices" in cultural sustainability through education.
7. The potential contribution of indigenous knowledge to educational paradigms and practices.
8. Curricular and/or language of instruction issues and their impact on cultural sustainability.
9. The relationship between home/local linguistic and cultural socialization and schooling.
10. Educational practices and programs that promote cultural sustainability and tolerance.
11. The role of religion and/or ideologies in educational cultural policies.

No one volume or research effort can offer answers to all these complex questions. Still we do hope the chapters in this volume contribute some of the knowledge needed but even more so to engage others in continuing the search. We hope the volume helps further an attempt to address the urgent need to ground multicultural educational theory in practical case studies and research on alternative forms of education to balance the needs of individuals and minority communities with those of other members of society and the needs of nation states.

We have attempted to embody the complexity of this task in the methodology of dialog between an international group of scholars. The complexity of our experience in the cultural education–cultural sustainability framework enables the insights generated by this book and, indeed, we feel, if only for a moment, liberated.

We are committed to developing the work begun in this book further. We invite all readers to join and help in enlarging the network of educators, scholars, and policy makers. The commitment of the authors in this book and others has already produced the publication of a new referred journal entitled *Diaspora, Indigenous, and Minority Education: An International Journal,* which is published by Taylor & Francis. We heartedly encourage you to join its readership and to contribute to its scholarship. By promoting the sharing of research from small, submerged, marginalized, or entrenched communities, this network will offer an avenue for researchers and communities to form constructive alliances.

Lastly, we suggest the way forward is through a combination of ambition and modesty. We find it useful to look for simple principals to guide us through what is a very complex world. Beauty is in minimalism: on one hand to seek clarity, but on the other hand to accept complexity and the need to diagnose the ailments we face continually. There is no single solution for all problems: the work of caring is difficult and takes place by paying attention to the details, but, at the same time, not giving up the attempt to focus on the larger picture.

Contributors

Gulbahar Beckett is affiliated with the College of Education, Criminal Justice, and Human Services at the University of Cincinnati, U.S.A. Her research interests and areas of expertise include language and cultural sustainability, in particular the Uygur efforts and Chinese minority language education policies and practices. Dr. Beckett also conducts research and publishes in the area of critical issues in the globalization of English and educational development, second-language and culture acquisition, and first-language and culture attrition.

Zvi Bekerman teaches anthropology of education at the School of Education and The Melton Center, Hebrew University of Jerusalem. He is also a research fellow at the Truman Institute for the Advancement of Peace, Hebrew University. His main interests are in the study of cultural, ethnic, and national identity, including identity processes and negotiation during intercultural encounters and in formal/informal learning contexts. Since 1999 he has been conducting a long-term ethnographic research project in the integrated/bilingual Palestinian—Jewish schools in Israel. He has published numerous papers in these fields of study and is the editor (with Seonaigh MacPherson) of the refereed journal *Diaspora, Indigenous, ad Minority Education: An International Journal* (LEA, 2007). Among his recently published books is, with Nicholas Burbules and Diana Keller Silverman, an edited volume entitled *Learning in Places: The Informal Education Reader* (Peter Lang, 2006).

Chen Bram is an anthropologist and organizational psychologist and is a research fellow at the Truman Institute, Hebrew University. He has conducted fieldwork in Israel and in the Caucasus among Adyghe (Circassians) and Caucasus Jews (Juhur) and worked with various organizations and projects in the fields of multiculturalism, emigration, conflict resolution, and alternative tourism. His Ph.D. dissertation was about "Ethnic Categories and Multicultural Policy: Caucasus Jews between Europe and Asia" and he teaches in the Department of Sociology and Anthropology at the Hebrew University.

Sheena Choi is an assistant professor at the Indiana University–Purdue University Fort Wayne. She specializes in the East Asian countries of South Korea and China. Her research foci include culture and policy influences in education including school choice and identity formation, civic education, and international education. Her contribution is co-authored with Pamela Lee Gray.

Lucia Clark is affiliated with the Department of Cultural Survival at Harvard University and is the research coordinator for Canada and Europe. Her areas of research include Italian and European linguistic minorities and Rom and Sinti in Italy. More generally she also researches Roma in Europe, native nations in Canada, and native people in Hawai'i. She is particularly interested in the role of the Internet in ethnic identity revival and defense.

Kaaren Dannenmann is an Anishinaapekwe, a resident of Namekosipiink, Canada. She is committed to education for people of all ages and her work focuses on the use and teaching of traditional knowledge while living on the land. She works as a trapper in the area where her mother's family has lived since time before memory. She is the head instructor for Treaty #3 trapper education and is a member of the Treaty #3 Trappers Steering Committee.

Marian de Souza is a lecturer in the School of Education, Australian Catholic University, Aquinas Campus, Ballarat Campus, and has taught at undergraduate and postgraduate levels. Marian is most interested in contemporary understandings of spirituality and its role in the intellectual and emotional well-being of young people and has conducted several funded and unfunded research projects that have examined young people's perceptions and expressions of their own spirituality.

George J. Sefa Dei is professor and chair in the Department of Sociology and Equity Studies, Ontario Institute for Studies in Education of the University of Toronto. His teaching and research interests are in the areas of anti-racism, minority schooling, international development, and anti-colonial thought. His published books include *Anti-racism Education: Theory and*

Practice (Fernwood Publishing, Halifax, 1996), *Hardships and Survival in Rural West Africa*, which was published in both English and French (CODESRIA, 1992), *Schooling and Education in Africa: The Case of Ghana* (Africa World Press, Trenton, NJ, 2004), and *Critical Issues in Anti-racist Research Methodologies*, which he co-edited with Gurpreet Singh Johal (Peter Lang, New York, 2005).

Mari Firkatian is an assistant professor of history at Hillyer College, University of Hartford. Her areas of expertise include Armenians and Eastern European history. Trained as a linguist and a historian, her research interests include minority populations, diplomatic history, and intellectual history.

Joi Freed-Garrod is an assistant professor at the University College of the Cariboo, School of Education, British Colombia and an adjunct faculty member of Lesley University, Graduate School of Arts and Social Sciences, Creative Arts and Learning Division, Massachusetts. Her current research interests include children's creativity in music, imagination in educational curriculum and pedagogy, and the efficacy of teacher education programs. She currently teaches music methods, integrated arts, and core education courses.

Eli Gottlieb is director of the Jerusalem Fellows, an international professional development program for leaders in the field of Jewish education, which is housed at the Mandel Leadership Institute in Jerusalem. His research focuses on the relations between cognition, culture, and identity.

Celia Haig-Brown is a professor in the Faculty of Education at York University in Canada. Her areas of expertise include various cultures of first nations people in Canada. She facilitates research projects pertaining to education and work protocols between aboriginal communities and universities. She focuses on the implications of indigenous knowledge for healing the scars of colonization and for better understanding decolonization processes.

M. Gail Hickey is a professor of education at Indiana University–Purdue University Fort Wayne, Indiana. Her research interests include the use of oral history methodology and narrative inquiry to study the experiences and perspectives of contemporary immigrants to the U.S. In particular, she focuses on Asian Indian immigrants and immigrants from the Indian subcontinent (particularly Hindus and Muslims) and southeast Asian immigrants and refugees (Buddhists and other). Dr. Hickey's research has focused on Asian Indian immigrants in the Midwestern U.S. and the ethnic Burmese refugee community in Indiana.

Karen M. Johnson-Weiner is an associate professor of anthropology at the State University of New York, Potsdam, where she teaches courses in linguistic anthropology and Anabaptist cultures. Her areas of expertise include Old Order Amish, Old Order Mennonite, and other Anabaptist groups. Research interests include language and culture maintenance and shift. Her manuscript "Train up a Child: Old Order Amish and the Old Order Mennonite Schools" (2006, The Johns Hopkins University Press).

Ezra Kopelowitz is a sociologist specializing in the intersection of technology, knowledge management, and organizational development for non-profits, with a particular interest in the Jewish world. His publications focus on areas such as Jewish peoplehood, Israel–diaspora relations, American and Israeli Jewish identity, Jewish education, and the consumption of knowledge in Jewish organizations. Dr. Kopelowitz is founder and chief executive officer of Research Success Technologies, a company providing data management and research solutions for non-profits (www.researchsuccess.com).

Seonaigh MacPherson is from the University of Manitoba, Canada. Her expertise is in second-language education, with a focus on teaching of English as a second language/SESD. Her areas of research include intercultural language education, language contact, Tibetan and Chinese indigenous/minority education, Tibetan Buddhist education, and Canadian indigenous education. She is also interested in the general impact of globalization on language loss and on language, education, and cultural sustainability.

Jing Lin is a professor at the Department of Educational Policy and Leadership at the University of Maryland, College Park. Her area of expertise includes minorities in China and she has done extensive research on Chinese education, culture, and society. Her research interests include globalization and minority cultural sustainability, economic development and minority education, and multicultural education. Jing Lin has authored several books including *The Opening of the Chinese Mind* (1994) and *Social Transformation and Private Education in China* (1999). Her fifth book, *School for Love: Education in the 21st Century*, was published in 2004.

Plamen Makariev is affiliated with the Department of Philosophy at Sofia University, Bulgaria and has expertise in educational strategies and research policy. His areas of interest include the media and intercultural communications.

Marie Parker-Jenkins is a professor of research in education at Derby University. Her research interests are in the field of cultural diversity, in particular overlapping discourses surrounding religion and ethnicity. In the last two years she has conducted research on Anglican, Catholic, Jewish, Muslim, Sikh, and Hindu schools in Britain, which will serve as the basis for her forthcoming book *In Good Faith: Schools, Religion and Public Funding* (2004).

Alex Pomson is a lecturer at the Melton Centre for Jewish Education, Hebrew University. Previously, he was associate professor in the Faculty of Education at York University, Toronto, where he coordinated the Jewish teacher education program. He is presently engaged in a longitudinal study funded by the Social Sciences and Humanities Research Council of Canada entitled Parents and their Children's Schools: An Ethnographic Inquiry into the Purposes and Practices of Jewish Schools. His work has been published in numerous academic journals, including *Teachers College Record, Educational Research,* and the *Journal of Curriculum Studies.*

Gay Garland Reed is an associate professor in the Department of Educational Foundations at the University of Hawai'i at Manoa. She currently teaches courses on multicultural education and the social and cultural contexts of education. Her research focuses on moral/political education in China, Korea, and the U.S., identity construction, culturally appropriate pedagogy, and the intersection between values and culture.

Richard Rymarz is a lecturer at the Australian Catholic University in the School of Religious Education. His expertise includes Eastern Christian groups such as Copts, Chaldeans, and Maronites, Islamic communities from a variety of backgrounds, and ethnic-religious school systems. His research interests include religious and cultural inheritance, the dynamics of family life in small religious communities, and religious education in denominational school settings.

Gloria Totoricagüena is an assistant professor of Basque studies at the University of Nevada, Reno. Her expertise includes Basques in the Basque Country and Basques in the diaspora. Her research interests include Basque diaspora, comparative diasporas, non-state actors in foreign policy, ethnic identity maintenance in transnational communities, and intradiasporic and interdiasporic networks.

Geoffrey Walford is professor of education policy and a fellow of Green College at the University of Oxford. His research foci are the relationships between central government policy and local processes of implementation, choice of schools, religiously based schools, and qualitative research methodology. His recent publications include *Policy, Politics and Education —Sponsored Grant-maintained Schools and Religious Diversity* (Ashgate, 2000) and *Doing Qualitative Educational Research* (Continuum, 2001). He is editor of the *Oxford Review of Education* and editor of the annual volume *Studies in Educational Ethnography.*

Bing Wang is professor at the Liaoning Normal University in Liaoning, China. He specializes in multicultural education, multiculturalism, and ethnic studies. His recent publications include "Cultural Maintenance of

Chinese New Immigrants in Vancouver" (*World Nationalities,* 4, 129–137, 2003), *Cultural Mosaic: Immigration History in Canada* (Beijing: Ethnic Publishing House, 2003), and "Multiethnic State and Multiculturalism" (in J. Peng (Ed.), *Canadian Civilizations* (pp. 138–242). Beijing: Social Sciences Publishing House, 2001).

Index